THE THEORY AND PRACTICE OF CHANGE MANAGEMENT

Fourth edition

JOHN HAYES

palgrave
macmillan

First published 2002
Second edition published 2006
Third edition published 2010

Fourth edition published 2014 by
PALGRAVE MACMILLAN

Palgrave Macmillan in the UK is an imprint of Macmillan Publishers Limited,
registered in England, company number 785998, of Houndmills, Basingstoke,
Hampshire RG21 6XS.

Palgrave Macmillan in the US is a division of St Martin's Press LLC,
175 Fifth Avenue, New York, NY 10010.

Palgrave Macmillan is the global academic imprint of the above companies
and has companies and representatives throughout the world.

Palgrave® and Macmillan® are registered trademarks in the United States,
the United Kingdom, Europe and other countries.

ISBN: 978–1–137–27534–9

This book is printed on paper suitable for recycling and made from fully
managed and sustained forest sources. Logging, pulping and manufacturing
processes are expected to conform to the environmental regulations of the
country of origin.

A catalogue record for this book is available from the British Library.

A catalog record for this book is available from the Library of Congress.

Typeset by Aardvark Editorial Limited, Metfield, Suffolk.

Printed in China

To Mercia

Contents

List of figures and tables

Figures

Tables

List of research reports and change tools

Research reports

Change tools

Preface and acknowledgements

On many academic programmes, change management is positioned as the integrating course because it requires students to reflect on and synthesize the various perspectives on organizational functioning offered by other modules, such as finance, operations management, marketing, organizational behaviour and strategic management.

Studying change management is important because factors such as the availability of credit, technological advances, changing patterns of demand, increasing competitive pressures, changes in the boundaries of organizations, the development of new organizational forms, regulatory reforms and globalization are creating opportunities and threats that organizations need to address if they are to survive and prosper. Managers, at all levels, have to be competent at identifying the need for change. They also have to be able to act in ways that will secure change. Getting it 'wrong' can be costly. It is, therefore, imperative that managers get it 'right', but getting it 'right' is not easy. There is no single 'recipe' that can be applied to all organizations at all times. This book addresses a broad range of issues that will affect the likelihood that change efforts will be successful.

Studying change management will provide you with an opportunity to reflect on what you have learned from other courses and from your work experience, particularly on:

- *sense making:* drawing on different perspectives of organizational functioning
- *ways of knowing:* looking at different sources of data and evaluating evidence
- *shaping behaviours:* examining ways of influencing and coordinating behaviour
- *designing interventions:* considering ways of 'doing' that purposely disrupt the status quo in order to move the organization towards a more effective state.

The Theory and Practice of Change Management does what is says on the cover. It provides a scholarly discussion of change management (the *theory*) and a host of insights into how theory can be applied to improve your *practice* of change management. It aims to help you:

- develop your investigative and diagnostic skills so that you will be more effective in assessing what is going on in organizations
- extend your ability to manage issues arising from internally planned and externally imposed organizational changes
- improve your awareness of how people can facilitate or resist change and extend your ability to manage human resources in the context of change.

Key changes to the fourth edition

Part I presents the process model of change management that provides the conceptual framework for the rest of the book. Chapter 1 is completely new. It introduces four process theories: teleological, dialectical, life cycle and evolutionary. All four view change as a series of interconnected events, decisions and actions, but they differ in terms of the degree to which they present change as a necessary sequence of stages and the extent to which the direction of change is constructed or predetermined. Life cycle and evolutionary theories present change as a predetermined process that unfolds over time in a given direction. Teleological and dialectical theories, on the other hand, view change trajectories as constructed, in the sense that goals, and the steps taken to achieve goals, can be changed at the will of (at least some of) those involved in the process.

Chapter 2 builds on the ideas discussed in Chapter 1 and offers a process model of change based on teleological and dialectical theories. It provides a conceptual framework that those leading change can use to identify the issues they need to address if they are to secure desired outcomes. It argues that when managing change is viewed as a process and events, decisions, actions and reactions are seen to be connected, those leading the change are more likely to be able to take action and intervene in ways that can break inefficient patterns and move the change process in a direction that is more likely to deliver superior outcomes.

The process model presented in Chapter 2 builds on the model that was presented in the third edition. It conceptualizes the management of change as a purposeful, constructed but often contested process that involves attending to a number of core activities. These activities are presented as separate elements of the change process because, although the boundaries between them are not always clear-cut and there can be some backtracking, the decisions and actions associated with each activity tend to dominate at different points in the process. There are, however, some differences between the elements of the model presented in this edition and the one in the third edition: the planning phase has been expanded to include a review of different types of intervention; reviewing change has been combined with implementation; and learning has been introduced as a new element in the model.

These activities (elements of the model) provide the framework for Parts II–VIII:

- Part II: Recognizing the need for change and starting the change process
- Part III: Diagnosing what needs to be changed and formulating a vision of a preferred future state
- Part IV: Leading and managing the people issues
- Part V: Planning how to intervene in order to achieve the desired change
- Part VI: Implementing plans and reviewing progress
- Part VII: Sustaining the change
- Part VIII: Learning.

The importance of leadership and learning from the experience of managing change are two themes that are given more attention in this edition. They are introduced in Part I and developed throughout the book:

- *Leadership:* Chapter 9 on the role of leadership in change management has been rewritten and Part IV has been changed to reflect the importance of leadership.
- *Learning:* At the end of Chapter 2, Figure 2.5 summarizes the seven elements of the process model and presents a list of questions, linked to each element, that those leading a change might find useful to consider. At various points throughout the book, you are invited to reflect on and review these questions and generate your own set of questions that could help you learn from your experience and improve your practice of change management. Chapter 29, on individual and collective learning, provides a more detailed examination of what those leading change can do to learn from their experience and what they can do to help others engage in a process of collective learning.

An overview of other changes

- Two completely new chapters, one on process models of change (Chapter 1) and the other on implementing change (Chapter 25), and a substantially revised chapter on individual and collective learning (Chapter 29), in which the section on individual learning is completely new.
- There are now more case studies than ever, with 62 in total, of which 38 are based outside the UK to reflect the significance of globalization on change management and to appeal to the international readership of the textbook. See the Case study and examples grid on p. xxiv.
- A brand new feature, Managing change in practice, combines interviews with change practitioners from a variety of organizations especially recorded for this edition with questions and exercises in the textbook. See p. xxii for more information.
- Additional cross-referencing to provide a more holistic view of change management.
- A new engaging page design with illustrative, full-colour photographs.
- A new structure based on the revised model of change in Chapter 2, which provides the framework for a number of more detailed changes:
  - Patterns of change (Chapter 1 in the 3rd edition) is now Chapter 3 at the beginning of Part II
  - Modes of intervening (Chapter 13 in the 3rd edition) has been moved and is now Chapter 6, Building change relationships, in Part II on Recognizing the need for change and starting the change process
  - Chapters 5 and 6 in the 3rd edition (Open systems models and alignment and Other diagnostic models) have been combined into a new Chapter 7, Diagnosis
  - The title of Part IV has been changed from Managing the people issues to Leading and managing the people issues. This reflects the greater emphasis given to leading change
  - The introduction to Part IV includes a two-part case study that provides many examples of how people-related issues can affect the success of change projects. The issues identified in this case are explored in the five chapters that make up Part IV
  - Chapters 19–24 in the 3rd edition (different ways of intervening, such as appreciative inquiry and process re-engineering) have been moved to Part V, Planning and preparing for change
  - Chapter 17, Selecting interventions, has also been moved to Part V
  - Merging groups (Chapter 26 in the 3rd edition) has been omitted but much of the content of this chapter can be found in the new chapter on Culture profiling (Chapter 23 in Part V)
  - Part VI, Implementing change and reviewing progress, now focuses on the issues that change managers need to attend to when implementing change. A new Chapter 25 examines implementation in the context of one company acquiring control of another and uses this case to highlight some of the factors that can affect the success of any attempt to implement change
  - Restructuring for strategic gain (Chapter 25 in the 3rd edition) has been omitted but much of the content of this chapter can be found in the new Chapter 25, Implementing change

- Part VIII is new and examines what those leading change can do to learn from their own experience and help others engage in a process of collective learning.

The content of all chapters has also been revised and updated and some content has been moved to different chapters. For example:

- Greiner's model of the five phase of growth, PEST analysis and Strebel's evolutionary cycle of competitive behaviour have been moved from Chapter 6 to Chapter 4
- There are new sections throughout on contemporary topics such as the impact of new technology on the pace of change, CSR and ethics
- There is more emphasis on people issues throughout and on the importance of communicating change.

Pathways

One of the strengths of this book is its wide scope. Not everybody, however, will want to read all 30 chapters. Some may want a quick overview of the 'essentials' of change management and others may want to focus on a particular issue.

The 'essentials'

If you want to use the book to quickly grasp the essentials of change management, you might find it helpful to read the following chapters:

- Chapter 1: Process models of change
- Chapter 2: Leading change: a process perspective
- Chapter 4: Recognizing a need or opportunity for change
- Chapter 7: Diagnosis
- Chapter 9: The role of leadership in change management
- Chapter 10: Power, politics and stakeholder management
- Chapter 11: Communicating change
- Chapter 14: Shaping implementation strategies
- Chapter 15: Developing a change plan
- Chapter 25: Implementing change
- Chapter 27: Making change stick
- Chapter 29: Individual and collective learning.

Recognizing the need for change

If, to start with, you just want to focus on recognizing the need for change, you might find it useful to look at:

- Chapter 1: Process models of change
- Chapter 3: Patterns of change
- Chapter 4: Recognizing a need or opportunity of change.

Diagnosis

Diagnosis is rarely a one-off activity. It is an ongoing endeavour that is often closely intertwined with other activities, such as recognizing a need or opportunity for change, identifying what needs to be changed, and reviewing how successfully change plans have need implemented. Sometimes, these activities can be so closely intertwined that it is difficult to distinguish one from the other. For example, when attempts to implement a change plan fail to deliver the expected outcome, the failure can provide those leading the change with new insights (implementation becomes diagnosis) that inform new plans that are then implemented, and so the sequence continues. A pathway that highlights diagnosis might include:

- Chapter 3: Patterns of change
- Chapter 4: Recognizing a need or opportunity for change
- Chapter 7: Diagnosis
- Chapter 8: Gathering and interpreting information
- Chapter 26: Reviewing and keeping the change on track.

Implementing change

If you want to review the theory and practice that relates to implementation, you might find the following pathway helpful:

- Chapter 2: Leading change: a process perspective
- Chapter 9: The role of leadership in change management
- Chapter 10: Power, politics and stakeholder management
- Chapter 11: Communicating change
- Chapter 14: Shaping implementation strategies
- Chapter 15: Developing a change plan
- Chapter 16: Types of intervention
- Chapters 17–23. These chapters review a number of different approaches to intervening to secure change. Chapters 17 and 18 review interventions that focus on human process problems, Chapters 19 and 20 focus on interventions that address human resource issues, Chapters 21 and 22 focus on technostructural interventions and Chapter 23 considers an intervention that can be used to address either strategic or human process issues
- Chapter 25: Implementing change
- Chapter 26: Reviewing and keeping the change on track.

Other ways to access content relevant to your needs

You might want to start by dipping into chapters that relate to an immediate concern. Use the contents section and the subject index to identify relevant chapters. For example, if you want to read about corporate citizenship and corporate social responsibility, you might find it useful to dip into Chapter 10; if your concern is sustaining change, you might want to start with Chapters 27 and 28; if you want to learn more about mergers or acquisitions, you might want to begin by looking at Chapters 23 and 25; and if you want some ideas about who should lead the change process, you might find it helpful to look at Chapters 5, 9 and 15.

Acknowledgments

A new feature of this edition is the videos of practitioners talking about their experience of managing change. They draw attention to many of the issues that those managing change have to contend with and demonstrate how theory can be applied to the practice of change management. Their contributions bring the subject to life. I would like to give my special thanks to:

Steve Gorton
Colin Ions
Debbie Middleton
Jo North
John Oakland
Paul Simpson
Mick Yates

I am also very grateful for the considered and constructive feedback provided by the review panel at various stages in the publishing process. I would like to thank:

Tina Bass at Coventry University, UK
Tom Calvard at Edinburgh University, UK
Andrew Chan at City University of Hong Kong, Hong Kong
John Clarke at London Metropolitan University, UK
Richard Daft at Vanderbilt University, USA
Svetlana Holt at Woodbury University, USA
Payyazhi Jayashree at the University of Wollongong, Dubai
Dave Lees at the University of Derby, UK
Lorna McCallum at Edinburgh Napier University, UK
Anja Maier at Denmark Technical University, Denmark
Joanne Murphy at Queen's University Belfast, UK
Allan Ramdhony at Edinburgh Napier University, UK
Jonathan Smith at Anglia Ruskin University, UK
Nilakant Venkataraman at the University of Canterbury, New Zealand
Carolyn Ward at the University of Teesside, UK
Celeste Wilderom at the University of Twente, Netherlands

John Hayes
December 2013

Tour of the book and companion website

Exercises

These invite you to articulate and critically examine your own implicit theories of change, drawing on your personal experience, whether that is in a company you have worked for, a club or society you have attended, or in your everyday life. They also often ask you to apply concepts and theories studied in the chapter to this experience

---

☑ *Exercise **24.1** Choice of interventions*

Review some of the change programmes that have be organization and, with reference to the content of this choice of interventions. Are you able to identify oc interventions were used? Give reasons and suggest in been more effective.

If you are a full-time student with little work e research an organization online, such as the NHS in research project and interview members of an organi sity or a local company, to identify the type of inte achieve change, observe whether they were carefully c stances, and assess whether inappropriate interventior

---

Change tools

Change management is most effective when the use of tools and techniques is guided by theory. Throughout the book, a number of carefully selected change tools are presented alongside theory to provide change managers with some ideas about what might be useful in specific circumstances

---

🔧 *Change tool **15.1** The Awakishi diagram*

The Awakishi diagram (Newman, 1995) is a useful tool what needs to be done. Let us assume that the chan plant to achieve cost savings. An individual (or gro about what needs to be done to achieve this goal. The large number of issues requiring attention, which can The most important categories provide the main 'b spine of the skeleton (see Figure 15.1). These could be equipment, inventories and people.

Using these bones as prompts, the other things that identified and prioritized. For example, what needs to which plant to close, which equipment to dispose of, Attention can then be given to what needs to be don plant, dispose of surplus equipment, and manage

---

Research reports

Much of the knowledge about the management of change that is available to managers is practice based. There is, however, a growing body of research evidence that can complement, and in some cases challenge, this craft-based expertise. Throughout the book, there are frequent references to research studies, but occasionally selected studies are presented in research reports. These give a flavour of some of this research-based knowledge, how research is contributing to our knowledge about change management and different research methods that can be used

---

🔍 *Research report **2.1** A test of the validity of Lewin's three-step model*

Ford, M.W and Greer, B.M. (2006) Profiling change: An empirical study of change process patterns, *Journal of Applied Behavioral Science*, 42(4): 420–46.

Theory

This study compared profiles of activity at different stages of a change to investigate the validity of Lewin's three-phase model. Lewin's model implies that activities relating to unfreezing should be observable before activities relating to movement and refreezing. Unfreezing to destabilize the status quo needs to occur first otherwise the organization will be poorly prepared for change. Movement requires at least some old ways of doing things to be discarded in favour of new behaviours. It is only after these new behaviours have been established that refreezing will facilitate the stabilization of the organization at a new equilibrium. Ford and Greer argue that if such a progression or sequence exists, then intensity levels of factors linked to each of the three stages of Lewin's model should change as implementation proceeds. They make two hypotheses:

1 As implementation progresses, ch profiles will display higher levels c 'refreezing' factors.

2 Change process profiles associate degrees of implementation succe higher levels of unfreezing, move refreezing factors than change pr associated with lower degrees of

This second hypothesis relates to th unfreezing-moving-refreezing activi the degree of implementation succe does not suggest that any of the thr dominate, for example although refr in the change process, it is just as in unfreezing, so it follows that implem will be associated with more intense process factors.

Method

After studying conceptualizations o Greer developed a set of change pr could be linked to Lewin's three pha

Examples

These illustrate key points and describe an instance or refer to a pattern of behaviour that demonstrates the relevance and aids the understanding of a concept or theory

Example **18.2** *Using appreciative inquiry at Nutrimen*

Nutrimental Foods is a Brazilian manufacturer that specialized in the production of dehydrated foods that it supplied to federal institutions such as the army, hospitals and schools. After enjoying this privileged position for 26 years, a new government changed its procurement policy and decentralized the purchase of foods. This had a devastating impact on Nutrimental. It had to refocus on supplying the consumer market and downsize from 2,000 to 650 employees to avoid being driven out of business. The CEO, Rodrigo Loures, quickly recognized that something had to be done to revitalize the demoralized workforce and gain a competitive edge in the consumer market. Appreciative inquiry was identified as a possible way forward.

After a successful pilot project, Cooperrider and Barros were invited to lead an appreciative inquiry summit. In preparation for this event, 180 people attended a one-day meeting where they were introduced to appreciative inquiry and given the

opportu
summit
stakehol
coming
about N
share the
and com
opportu
future ge
Follov
main eve
develop
formed t
compan
increase
producti
new mo
this inte

Case studies

A multitude of international case studies invite you to apply theory to a variety of real-life organizational situations. They are situated across a wide range of industries and countries and are all based on actual events, although in some instances, the name and location of the organization have been changed. Each case study includes questions to answer or tasks to complete

Case study **22.1** *Grampian Police*

Members of the public were frustrated because they were finding it difficult to contact Grampian Police. There were over 70 different telephone lines the public could use. Some went to a central switchboard, others directly to various departments or local police stations, many of which were so small that they were not manned on a continuous basis. Consequently, many calls were not answered or were answered by somebody who was not in a position to resolve the caller's problem. Grampian Police responded by creating a new state-of-the-art call centre. Operators could use a geographical information system to identify where a caller was calling from, and could access a crime information system so that they were instantly

Before
think lea
problem
Attent
calling th
found th
firearms
with mar
shotgun:
analysis
of them
associate
licences.
problem

Managing change in practice

These interactive features invite you to watch specially recorded videos in which change practitioners with an impressive range of experience across various organizations discuss their view of key topics in change management. The videos are available on the companion website and link back to questions and exercises in the textbook

Managing change in practice **9.1** *Jo N*

Jo North is the managing director of The consultancy that works with businesses ously, she was deputy managing direct Coast Mainline Company Ltd, commerc of sales and marketing at FirstGroup, UK

In her video, 'Start with the end in m **www.palgrave.com/companion/hayes** what she sees as four key leadership included earlier in Table 9.2. Is one list b the same ground?

Leadership style

Hackman (2002) argues that too much a of leadership style and asserts that leader

Companion website

A comprehensive companion website, **www.palgrave. com/companion/hayes-change-management4**, accompanies the textbook, featuring audiovisual presentations on key topics, video interviews with change practitioners and notes on presentation skills for students. There is also a range of material for lecturers, including PowerPoint lecture slides and case study debriefs

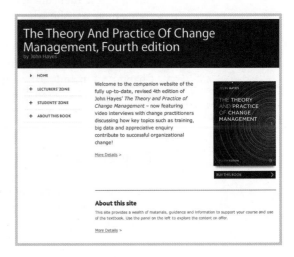

Managing change in practice: video and text feature

A collection of video interviews with experienced change practitioners have been specially recorded for the new edition of *The Theory and Practice of Change Management* and are available on the companion website at **www.palgrave.com/companion/hayes-change-management4**. The practitioners give their views on the importance of key topics in change management, such as motivational coaching to help people navigate transitions, the implications of big data, and using training to deliver culture change. They discuss how these topics work *in practice*, drawing on their experience of working in organizations such as Norwich Union (now Aviva), P&G, The Big Bang Partnership and Oakland Consulting.

Managing change in practice **15.1** *John Oakland: Figure of eight framework to prepare and review plans for change*

John Oakland is chairman of Oakland Consulting plc and Emeritus Professor of Business Excellence and Quality Management at Leeds University Business School.

For over 30 years, he has researched and consulted in all aspects of quality management and business improvement in thousands of organizations. He is also the author of several bestselling books, including *Total Organizational Excellence, Total Quality Management, Oakland on Quality Management, Statistical Process Control* and *Production and Operations Management*. Oakland Consulting, in its original form, was created by Professor Oakland in 1985 and now operates throughout the world, helping organizations in all areas of business improvement.

Visit the book's companion website at **www.palgrave.com/companion/hayes-change-management4** to watch John Oakland talking about how he has used this figure of eight framework in his consulting work with a wide range of organizations.

The Managing change in practice feature appears in selected chapters of the textbook and includes a short biography of the change practitioner in question, summarizing their qualifications and experience. This is followed by a link to the companion website where you can watch them discussing key topics in change management.

The videos are 5–10 minutes long and are often split into sections so you can navigate to the part that interests you most. Some, like John Oakland's video in Chapter 15, include extra figures and diagrams to help you get to grips with the ideas being considered. You can then refer back to the textbook in order to answer the questions or complete the exercises based on what you have seen.

The practitioners

There are eight Managing change in practice features in the book, which link to eight videos on the companion website. The chapters you can find them in and brief descriptions of the practitioners and their videos are given below:

- Chapter 4: Mick Yates from dunnhumby discusses the impact of big data and how it can change the way the enterprise makes decisions, how departments within an organization talk to each other and how the business interacts with its customers.
- Chapter 5: Colin Ions from DLA Piper argues that HR managers can make a strong contribution to change so long as they are on the right agenda and 'get into the mind of the CEO'.
- Chapter 9: Jo North from The Big Bang Partnership Ltd highlights what she sees as four key leadership tasks.
- Chapter 13: Debbie Middleton from Middleton Green Executive Resourcing talks about what happens when people are forced to let go of their current job and move to a different role within the same organization or when they are released from their job and made redundant.
- Chapter 14: Steve Gorton from Enabling Development argues that those managers who are too focused on a top-down approach will be less successful than those who do everything they can to win the hearts and minds of all those involved in or affected by the change.
- Chapter 15: John Oakland from Oakland Consulting talks about how he has used his 'figure of eight' framework in his consulting work with a wide range of organizations.
- Chapter 18: John Hayes (author) provides an overview of appreciative inquiry, expanding on key points in the chapter.
- Chapter 19: Paul Simpson is a freelance HR and OD practitioner. He discusses how training was used to help change the culture of a special metals business and the limitations of using training to deliver this kind of systemic change.

Case studies and examples grid

Chapter	Title	Industry	Location
1, p. 6	Example 1.1 A car importer responds to imposed change	Automobile	Europe, India and East Asia
1, p. 9	Example 1.2 BA cabin crew dispute	Aviation	UK
1, p. 11	Example 1.3 Nokia: sticking with a winning formula for too long	Telecommunications	Worldwide
1, p. 12	Example 1.4 Failure of the FiReControl project	Emergency services	England
1, p. 13	Example 1.5 Unrealistic goals for change at Direct Banking	Banking	The Netherlands, Europe
2, p. 32	Example 2.1 Concrete Flags Ltd	Paving manufacturing	UK
3, p. 52	Example 3.1 Marks & Spencer	Retail	UK, worldwide
3, p. 58	Example 3.2 UK Coal: the simultaneous pursuit of adaption and reorientation	Mining	UK
3, p. 62	Case study 3.1 The BBC	Media	UK
3, p. 63	Case study 3.2 Leicester Royal Infirmary	Healthcare	UK
3, p. 64	Case study 3.3 McDonald's	Service	UK, worldwide
3, p. 65	Case study 3.4 GNER	Rail travel	UK
4, p. 76	Example 4.1 Horizontal misalignments in a large snacks and confectionery manufacturing company	Food manufacturing	UK
4, p. 82	Case study 4.1 The Active Sports Equipment Company	Sports equipment manufacturing	UK
5, p. 90	Case study 5.1 Failure to convince others of the need for change at AT&T	Telephone manufacturing	USA
5, p. 93	Example 5.1 Leading change at Lyons Confectionery	Confectionery manufacturing	UK
6, p. 109	Example 6.1 Using a supportive approach	Manufacturing	USA
6, p. 110	Example 6.2 Using force-field analysis	Auto components manufacturing	Worldwide
6, p. 112	Example 6.3 Using a challenging approach	Education	UK
6, p. 113	Example 6.4 Using an information-gathering approach	Sales	UK
7, p. 122	Case study 7.1 Site Security and Secure Escorts	Security services	Worldwide
8, p. 154	Example 8.1 The effect of being observed	Manufacturing	UK
8, p. 157	Example 8.2 Northern Rock	Financial services	UK
9, p. 171	Example 9.1 Involving staff in developing a new vision for Íslandsbanki	Banking	Iceland
9, p. 173	Example 9.2 Reorganizing the emergency response function in a Dutch police organization	Emergency services	The Netherlands
9, p. 175	Example 9.3 Stephen Elop's burning platform memo	Telecommunications	Worldwide
10, p. 201	Case study 10.1 Merger of two hospitals: stakeholder brainstorm	Healthcare	UK
10, p. 204	Case study 10.2 Merger of two hospitals: stakeholder mapping	Healthcare	UK
10, p. 206	Case study 10.3 Merger of two hospitals: managing stakeholder relationships	Healthcare	UK
11, p. 212	Case study 11.1 Connect2	Advertising	Australia
11, p. 219	Example 11.1 Poor upward communication at HBOS	Banking	UK
11, p. 224	Example 11.2 PCBtec	Electronics	France
11, p. 230	Case study 11.2 Galaxy	Home appliance manufacturing	Germany, Europe, India, China

Chapter	Title	Industry	Location
12, p. 238	Example 12.1 Legal templates	Law firm	UK
12, p. 243	Example 12.2 Actions can speak louder than words	Auto components manufacturing	USA
12, p. 251	Case study 12.1 Managing change at the Douglas refinery	Oil refinery	Ireland
14, p. 279	Case study 14.1 Asda: a winning formula	Retail	UK
14, p. 284	Example 14.1 The implementation of an economic strategy at the BBC	Media	UK
14, p. 285	Example 14.2 The implementation of an OD strategy at the BBC	Media	UK
15, p. 298	Case study 15.1 Planning for change at Bairrada Wines	Wine manufacturing	Portugal
15, p. 305	Example 15.1 Matrix structures	Auto components manufacturing	UK, France and Spain
17, p. 335	Example 17.1 Action research at the Harwood Manufacturing Company	Garment manufacturing	USA
17, p. 337	Example 17.2 Action research at Freedman House	Ex-offenders hostel service	UK
17, p. 341	Example 17.3 Action research at Xerox	Printer manufacturing	USA
18, p. 346	Example 18.1 Médecins Sans Frontières: a positive organization	Charity	Worldwide
18, p. 353	Example 18.2 Using appreciative inquiry at Nutrimental Foods	Food manufacturing	Brazil
18, p. 354	Example 18.3 Using collective inquiry for organization development at Médecins Sans Frontières	Charity	Worldwide
18, p. 355	Example 18.4 Using appreciative inquiry to clarify values at Hammersmith Hospital NHS trust	Healthcare	UK
21, p. 385	Example 21.1 Mapping a GP referral for a routine X-ray at a local hospital	Healthcare	England
21, p. 387	Example 21.2 The claims settlement process	Financial services	USA
22, p. 398	Example 22.1 The Toyota Production System	Automobile manufacturing	Japan, worldwide
22, p. 400	Example 22.2 Lessons learned from a failed attempt to implement lean	Manufacturing	Switzerland
22, p. 404	Case study 22.1 Grampian Police	Emergency services	Scotland
23, p. 410	Example 23.1 BT Cellnet's acquisition of Martin Dawes	Mobile communications	UK
25, p. 437	Case study 25.1 KeyChemicals' acquisition of Eco-Pure: recognizing the opportunity and starting the process	Chemical distribution	Switzerland, Denmark
25, p. 440	Example 25.1 Due diligence for the acquisition of Eco-Pure	Chemical distribution	Switzerland, Denmark
25, p. 441	Example 25.2 Planning the integration of KeyChemicals and Eco-Pure	Chemical distribution	Switzerland, Denmark
25, p. 442	Example 25.3 The implementation plan	Chemical distribution	Switzerland, Denmark
25, p. 446	Example 25.4 Announcing the acquisition to Eco-Pure employees	Chemical distribution	Switzerland, Denmark
25, p. 448	Example 25.5 Managing the integration of the two organizations	Chemical distribution	Switzerland, Denmark
26, p. 457	Example 26.1 Customer care at Maersk Line	Shipping	Denmark, worldwide
28, p. 479	Example 28.1 Asda's roll-out of 'store renewal'	Retail	UK
29, p. 493	Example 29.1 Concrete Flags Ltd	Paving manufacturing	UK
29, p. 501	Example 29.2 Bone density scans	Healthcare	UK
29, p. 505	Example 29.3 Google as a learning organization	Online services	Worldwide
30, p. 502	Case study 30.1 Managing change in the Urology Department of a hospital in England	Healthcare	UK

Publisher's acknowledgements

The author and publisher wish to thank the following for permission to reproduce copyright material:

The Academy of Management for Figure 1.2 'The constitution of an organizational path', Sydow, J., Schreyögg, G. and Koch, J. (2009) Organizational path dependence: Opening the black box, *Academy of Management Review*, 34(4): 689–709; Figure 22.2 'The Toyota Production System house', Liker, J.K. and Morgan, J.M. (2006) The Toyota way in services: The case of lean product development, *Academy of Management Perspectives*, 20(2): 7; Figures 23.1 and 23.2 'Acquired unit's preferred mode of acculturation' and 'Acquiring unit's preferred mode of acculturation', Nahavandi, A. and Malekzadeh, A.R. (1988) Acculturation in mergers and acquisitions, *Academy of Management Review*, 13(1): 83–4; Figure 23.3 'Acculturative model for implementing organizational fit', adapted from Nahavandi, A. and Malekzadeh, A.R. (1988) Acculturation in mergers and acquisitions, *Academy of Management Review*, 13(1): 83–4; Table 23.1 'Suitability of culture matches', Cartwright, S. and Cooper, C.L. (1993) The role of culture compatibility in successful organizational marriage, *Academy of Management Executive*, 7(2): 57–70; Table 28.1 'Implementation climate and innovation/values fit: effects on employees' affective responses and innovation use', Klein, K.L. and Sorra, J.S. (1996) The challenge of innovation implementation, *Academy of Management Review*, 21(4): 1066.

Berrett-Koehler Publishers Inc. for Figure 17.4 'The meeting canoe', Axelrod, R.H., Axelrod, J.B. and Jacobs, R.W. (2004) *You Don't Have to Do it Alone: How to Involve Others to Get Things Done.*

Cengage Learning Inc. for Figure 16.3 'Cummings and Worley's typology of interventions based on focal issues', Cummings, T.G. and Worley C.G. (2001) *Organizational Development and Change* (7th edn) p. 146.

Da Capo Press, a member of Perseus Books Group, for Figure 13.1 'Bridges' model of transition', Bridges, W. (2009) *Managing Transitions: Making the Most of Change*, Reading, MA: Addison Wesley, p. 70.

Elsevier Publishers for Figure 7.5 'The McKinsey 7S model', Waterman, R.H., Peters, T. and Philips, J.R. (1980) Structure is not organization, *Business Horizons*, 23(3): 14; Table 13.1 'The social readjustment rating scale', adapted from Holmes, T. and Rahe, R. (1967) The Social Readjustment Rating Scale, *Journal of Psychosomatic Research*, 11: 215; Figure 23.4 'Harrison's continuum: the degree of constraint different culture types place on individuals', Cartwright S. and Cooper C. (1992) *Mergers and Acquisitions: The Human Factor*, Butterworth-Heinemann.

Emerald Group Publishing for Figure 27.1 'Classes of sustainability at cell level' and Figure 27.2 'Factory-level improvement model', Bateman, N. and David, A. (2002)

Process improvement programmes: A model for assessing sustainability, *International Journal of Operations and Production Management*, 22(5/6): 520.

Harvard Business Review for Figure 4.2 'Internal factors that can trigger discontinuous change', adapted from Greiner, L.E. (1972) Evolution and revolution as organizations grow, *Harvard Business Review*, 50(4): 41.

John Oakland for Figure 15.6 'Oakland's figure of eight framework for successful change', Figure 15.7 'Readiness to change' and Figure 15.8 'Implementing change'.

John Wiley & Sons for Figure 3.4 'Types of organizational change' and Figure 4.3 'The trap of success', adapted from Nadler, D., Shaw, R.B. and Walton, A.E. (1995) *Discontinuous Change: Leading Organizational Transformation*, San Francisco, CA: Jossey-Bass, p. 24 and p. 11; Exercise 7.1 'Raising awareness of your implicit model of organizational functioning', based on Tichy, N.M. and Hornstein, H.A. (1980) Collaborative model building, in E.E. Lawler, D.A. Nadler and C. Cammann (eds) *Organizational Assessment*; Figure 7.4 'Kotter's integrative model of organizational dynamics', Kotter, J.P. (1980) An integrative model of organizational dynamics, in E.E. Lawler, D.A. Nadler and C. Cammann (eds) *Organizational Assessment*, p. 282; Table 7.5 'Examples of element states that do and do not facilitate system adaptation', adapted from Kotter, J.P. (1980) An integrative model of organizational dynamics, in E.E. Lawler, D.A. Nadler and C. Cammann (eds) *Organizational Assessment*, p. 292.

Médecins Sans Frontières for its logo and Florian Lems/MSF for the photograph, both in Chapter 18.

Pearson Education for Figure 4.1 'Stebel's cycle of competitive behaviour', adapted from Strebel, P. (1998) *The Change Pact: Building Commitment to Ongoing Change*, Financial Times/Prentice Hall.

Peter Thompson/Greenpeace for the image of Brent Spar in Chapter 10.

Sage Publications for Figure 7.6 'Weisbord's six-box model', Weisbord, M.R. (1976) Organization diagnosis: Six places to look for trouble with or without a theory, *Group and Organization Management*, 1(4): 432; Figure 7.7 'The Burke-Litwin causal model of organizational performance and change' and Figure 7.8 'The transformational factors', Burke, W.W. and Litwin, G.H. (1992) A causal model of organizational performance and change, *Journal of Management*, 18(3): 523–45.

Taylor and Francis Ltd for Figure 15.2 'Change participants' perceptions of the appeal and likelihood of the change', Dibella, A.J. (2007) Critical perceptions of organisational change, *Journal of Change Management*, 7(3/4): 231–42.

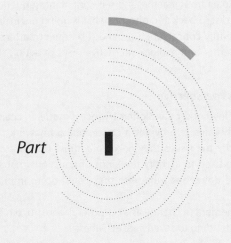

Part **I**

MANAGING CHANGE: A PROCESS PERSPECTIVE

Introduction to Part **I**

Part I introduces the process theories of change that provide the conceptual framework for the discussion of the theory and practice of change management presented in Parts II to VIII.

Chapter **1** *Process models of change*

Chapter 1 introduces four process theories: teleological, dialectical, life cycle and evolutionary. All four view change as a series of interconnected events, decisions and actions, but they differ in terms of the degree to which they present change as a necessary sequence of stages and the extent to which the direction of change is constructed or predetermined.

Life cycle and evolutionary theories present change as a predetermined process that unfolds over time in a prespecified direction. Teleological and dialectical theories, on the other hand, view change trajectories as constructed, in the sense that goals, and the steps taken to achieve goals, can be changed at the will of (at least some of) those involved in the process. However, this may not always be easy to achieve in practice because those involved, especially those leading the change, may fail to recognize some of the dynamics that affect outcomes.

Attention is given to the impact of reactive and self-reinforcing sequences:

- *Reactive sequences:* When change involves different individuals and groups each seeking to pursue their own interests, then, depending on the balance of power, reactive sequences are likely to emerge and one party may challenge another party's attempt to secure a particular outcome. Negative reactions may produce only minor deviations from the intended path or they may be so strong that they may delay, transform or block the change. Those leading change can improve their effectiveness by scanning their environment for threats and anticipating resistance or responding quickly when others fail to support their actions.
- *Self-reinforcing sequences:* When a decision or action produces positive feedback, it reinforces earlier events and this reinforcement induces further movement in the same direction. While self-reinforcing sequences can deliver benefits over the short term, change managers need to be alert to the possibility that they may divert their attention away from alternative ways of responding to situations, narrow their options, and lock them into a path that may deliver suboptimal outcomes over the longer term.

In order to minimize any negative impact from reactive and self-reinforcing sequences, those leading change need to be able to step back and observe what is going on, including their own and others' behaviour, identify critical junctures and subsequent patterns – some of which may be difficult to discern – and explore alternative ways of acting that might deliver superior outcomes.

Chapter **2** *Leading change: a process perspective*

Chapter 2 builds on the ideas discussed in Chapter 1 and offers a process model of change based on teleological and dialectical theories. It provides a conceptual framework that those leading change can use to identify the issues they need to address if they are to secure desired outcomes. It can also be used to identify the kinds of questions that will help them reflect on how well they are doing and what else they could do to improve performance.

The model conceptualizes the management of change as a purposeful, constructed but often contested process that involves attending to seven core activities:

1 recognizing the need for change and starting the change process
2 diagnosing what needs to be changed and formulating a vision of a preferred future state
3 planning how to intervene in order to achieve the desired change
4 implementing plans and reviewing progress
5 sustaining the change
6 leading and managing the people issues
7 learning.

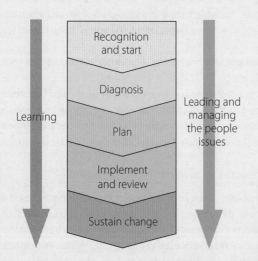

These activities are presented as separate elements of the change process, because the decisions and actions associated with them tend to dominate at different points and there is a logical sequence connecting them. However, in practice, the boundaries are not always clear-cut. For example, the recognition of a need for change is based on an initial diagnosis of the situation, and attempts to implement plans for change that lead to unintended consequences also contribute to an unfolding diagnosis. Also, the sequence of elements specified in the model is not linear. It is often iterative, with some issues (such as diagnosis) being addressed more than once. Some issues can also be addressed simultaneously with others. For example, learning can occur at any or every point in the process and people issues need to be addressed throughout. This said, all the activities, such as diagnosis, planning and implementing, are important and need to be attended to by those leading a change.

When managing change is viewed as a process and events, decisions, actions and reactions are seen to be connected, those leading the change are more likely to be able to take action and intervene in ways that can break inefficient patterns and move the change process in a direction that is more likely to deliver superior outcomes.

The way in which Chapters 1–29 relate to the generic model is illustrated in Figure I.1.

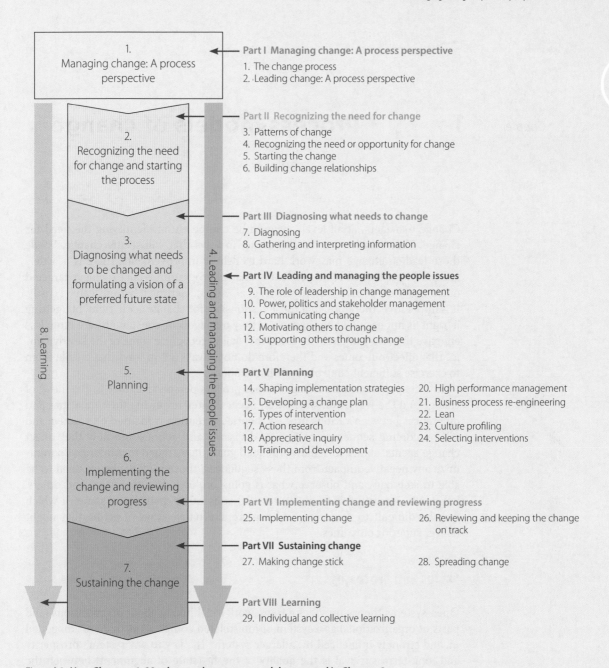

Part I Managing change: A process perspective

1. The change process
2. Leading change: A process perspective

Part II Recognizing the need for change

3. Patterns of change
4. Recognizing the need or opportunity for change
5. Starting the change
6. Building change relationships

Part III Diagnosing what needs to change

7. Diagnosing
8. Gathering and interpreting information

Part IV Leading and managing the people issues

9. The role of leadership in change management
10. Power, politics and stakeholder management
11. Communicating change
12. Motivating others to change
13. Supporting others through change

Part V Planning

14. Shaping implementation strategies
15. Developing a change plan
16. Types of intervention
17. Action research
18. Appreciative inquiry
19. Training and development
20. High performance management
21. Business process re-engineering
22. Lean
23. Culture profiling
24. Selecting interventions

Part VI Implementing change and reviewing progress

25. Implementing change
26. Reviewing and keeping the change on track

Part VII Sustaining change

27. Making change stick
28. Spreading change

Part VIII Learning

29. Individual and collective learning

Figure **I.1** *How Chapters 1–29 relate to the process model presented in Chapter 2*

Chapter **1**

Process models of change

Change managers, at all levels, have to be competent at identifying the need for change. They also have to be able to act in ways that will secure change. While those leading change may work hard to deliver improvements, there is a widely accepted view that up to 60 per cent of change programmes fail to achieve targeted outcomes (Beer et al., 1990; Jørgensen et al., 2008). Getting it 'wrong' can be costly. It is imperative, therefore, that those responsible for change get it 'right', but getting it 'right' is not easy. Change agents, be they managers or consultants, are often less effective than they might be because they fail to recognize some of the key dynamics that affect outcomes and therefore do not always act in ways that enable them to exercise sufficient control over what happens.

This chapter examines change from a process perspective, that is, the 'how' of change and the way a transformation occurs. After reviewing the similarities and differences between various process theories, attention is focused on reactive and self-reinforcing sequences of events, decisions and actions and how they affect change agents' ability to achieve intended goals. It is argued that in order to minimize any negative impact from these sequences, those leading change need to be able to step back and observe what is going on, including their own and others' behaviour, identify critical junctures and subsequent patterns – some of which may be difficult to discern – and explore alternative ways of acting that might deliver superior outcomes.

States and processes

Open systems theory provides a framework for thinking about organizations (and parts of organizations) as a system of interrelated components that are embedded in, and strongly influenced by, a larger system. The key to any system's prosperity and long-term survival is the quality of the fit (state of alignment) between the internal components of that system, for example the alignment between an organization's manufacturing technology and the skill set of the workforce, and between this system and the wider system of which it is a part, for example the alignment between the organization's strategy and the opportunities and threats presented by the external environment. Schneider et al. (2003, p. 125) assert that internal and external alignment promote organizational effectiveness because, when aligned, the various components of a system reinforce rather than disrupt each other, thereby minimizing the loss of system energy (the 'get-up-and-go' of an organization) and resources. Effective leaders are those who set a direction for change and influence others to achieve goals that improve internal and external alignment.

Miles and Snow (1984) argue that instead of thinking about alignment as a state (because perfect alignment is rarely achieved), it is more productive to think of it as a process that involves a quest for the best possible fit between the organization and its environment and between the various internal components of the organization. Barnett and Carroll (1995) elaborate the distinction between states and processes. The state (or content) perspective focuses attention on 'what' it is that needs to be, is being or has been changed. The process perspective, on the other hand, attends to the 'how' of change and focuses on the way a transformation occurs. It draws attention to issues such as the pace of change and the sequence of activities, the way decisions are made and communicated, and the ways in which people respond to the actions of others. Change managers play a key role in this transformation process.

The change process

On the basis of an extensive interdisciplinary review of the literature, Van de Ven and Poole (1995) found over 20 different process theories. Further analysis led them to identify four ideal types – teleological, dialectical, life cycle and evolutionary theories – that provide alternative views of the change process:

- *Teleological theories:* assume that organizations are purposeful and adaptive, and present change as an unfolding cycle of goal formulation, implementation, evaluation and learning. Learning is important because it can lead to the modification of goals or the actions taken to achieve them.
- *Dialectical theories:* focus on conflicting goals between different interest groups and explain stability and change in terms of confrontation and the balance of power between the opposing entities.
- *Life cycle theories:* assume that change is a process that progresses through a necessary sequence of stages that are cumulative, in the sense that each stage contributes a piece to the final outcome, and related – each stage is a necessary precursor for the next.
- *Evolutionary theories:* posit that change proceeds through a continuous cycle of variation, selection and retention. Variations just happen and are not therefore purposeful, but are then selected on the basis of best fit with available resources and environmental demands. Retention is the perpetuation and maintenance of the organizational forms that arise from these variations via forces of inertia and persistence.

A common feature of all four theories is that they view change as involving a number of events, decisions and actions that are connected in some sort of sequence, but they differ in terms of the degree to which they present change as following certain essential stages and the extent to which the direction of change is constructed or predetermined.

The ordering of stages

Some theories place more emphasis on the order of the stages in the change process than others. For example, life cycle theories are more prescriptive about this than teleological theories. Flamholtz (1995) asserts that organizations progress through seven stages of development from new venture to decline and possible revitalization. He argues that at each stage of development, the criteria of organizational effectiveness change. The major concern during the first stage of the organization's life cycle is survival and critical areas for development are markets and products. In the second stage, resources are often stretched and operating systems become overwhelmed, so resource management and the development of operating systems emerge as key tasks. The third stage of the life cycle is the point where more formal management systems, such as planning and management development, are required to ensure the long-term functioning of the business, and so on through the seven stages of the life cycle.

Teleological theories are less prescriptive about the ordering of stages. They present development and change as a repetitive sequence of goal formulation, implementation and evaluation, leading to the modification of an envisioned end state based on what was learned or intended by the people involved (Van de Ven and Sun, 2011, p. 61). While each of these stages is important and there is a logical sequence connecting them, the sequence does not have to, and often does not, unfold in a way that follows the ordered linear sequence presented above. For example, while an initial diagnosis may clarify a problem, it may fail to identify a desired end state, so the process may have to unfold in a tentative way that involves constant testing or some backtracking to earlier stages in order to achieve a valued outcome. Even when a goal can be specified at an early point in the process, it is not uncommon for unanticipated problems or new pressures for change to emerge and require attention even though the current change sequence has not been completed. Example 1.1 illustrates this point.

Example **1.1** *A car importer responds to imposed change*

An importer of value-for-money, low-cost cars had, over several years, built up a network of independent dealers to retail the vehicles to customers with relatively low disposable incomes. It was a successful business.

Early in 2010, the manufacturer alerted the importer to a forthcoming change. In order to counter anticipated competition from even cheaper imported cars from India and China, it had decided to reposition

its brand. It wanted to widen its market to include customers who normally bought more expensive vehicles, such as Ford or Opel. The manufacturer had already announced the launch of a new model that was technically superior to other cars in its range, but the early 2008 announcement made it clear that it intended to follow this up by rebranding and repositioning the entire range.

The importer quickly recognized that this would require a lot of changes to its own business. Many of the retailers who were part of its dealer network had started out selling second-hand cars. Their showrooms tended to be located in premises adjacent to their original petrol retailing or repair shop businesses. They had long-standing relationships with many of their customers who had first come to them to buy second-hand cars and then moved on to purchase models from their range of inexpensive imported cars. An initial diagnosis indicated that the importer would have to encourage many of these dealers to refurbish and modernize their premises and, in some cases, relocate in order to attract the type of customer who would be interested in better quality, more expensive cars. Some dealers also had a relatively unsophisticated approach to selling, indicating a need for training and development. The importer quickly began to formulate a change strategy, but initial approaches to a sample of dealers to test out plans for change met with strong resistance.

This triggered a rethink. The problem was reframed and another diagnostic exercise was undertaken to explore the possibility of replacing some of the existing dealers with dealers who were already selling more upmarket vehicles and who might be interested in either transferring their allegiance or taking on an additional brand and selling the imported cars alongside their existing range. When this strategy was tested, not many distributors of other brands showed much interest in transferring or diluting their allegiance, so this prompted yet a further rethink.

This third way forward involved working with some (maybe a majority) of the existing dealers to help them make the changes required to sell the rebranded cars and, alongside this approach, exploring the possibility of developing a new relationship with an Indian manufacturer of cheap cars. The plan was to establish a related business to import and distribute its vehicles using those dealers who were not prepared to move upmarket. Before plans to pursue this strategy were well advanced, the aftereffects of the credit crunch hit car sales, slowing plans to move the majority of dealers upmarket, and the Indian manufacturer announced a delay in its plans to launch its low-cost vehicles in European markets. These changes called for yet a further rethink of the situation.

Predetermined versus constructed trajectories

Van de Ven and Poole (1995) argue that life cycle and evolutionary theories present change as a predetermined process that unfolds over time in a prespecified direction. This kind of change involves incrementally adapting organizational forms in predictable ways. The process may be prescribed by some inherent code (as in biological evolution) or by the limits imposed by a wider system. Greenwood and Hinings (1996), for example, argue that an organization's institutional context can limit the possibilities for change, especially when the organization is embedded in a wider system that has tightly coupled relationships (see Chapter 3).

Teleological and dialectical theories, on the other hand, view change trajectories as constructed, in the sense that goals, and the steps taken to achieve goals, can be changed at the will of (at least some of) those involved in the process. According to this perspective, the process is not unduly constrained by an inherent code or factors external to the immediate system. Those leading the change have the power to intervene and act in ways that can make a real difference. The strategic choice framework, for example, asserts that one of the key factors determining the effectiveness of an organization is the quality of the strategic choices made by members of the dominant coalition who lead the organization. Teleological and dialectical theories highlight the role of human agency and assert that change agents can act to affect change in ways that will either promote or undermine organizational effectiveness.

The impact of sequence on outcome

Although teleological and dialectical theories suggest that members of a system have considerable freedom to construct change trajectories, and assert that it is possible for them to break away from established routines and intentionally move the system towards redefined goals, this may not always be easy to achieve in practice. The nature of the change sequence, whether reactive or self-reinforcing (see Mahoney, 2000 and the sections below), will affect the extent to which those leading the change will be able to realize this possibility.

A change process involves a number of events, decisions and actions that are connected in a sequence. They are connected in the sense that each event is influenced by earlier events and also helps to shape subsequent events. In the sequence A>B>C>D>E, event B is both a response to event A and a factor that shapes event C, which in turn effects D and so on. The way an earlier event will impact later events depends on how others respond.

Reactive sequences

Dialectical theories focus on the conflicting goals of those involved in a situation. These conflicts give rise to reactive sequences, in which one party challenges another party's attempt to secure a particular change. In reactive sequences, subsequent events challenge rather than reinforce earlier events. This is illustrated in Figure 1.1. A leader implements a decision (A) as the first step along the way to achieving a particular outcome (F). This action leads to responses (events B and C) that reinforce the leader's initial intention, but (in this example) this support is short-lived. The earlier events provoke a reaction from others, maybe because they see little or no benefit in the current direction of change. The outcome of this critical juncture is that the change is pushed in a new direction. But this new direction may not be sustained for long. In this example, it is challenged following event Y.

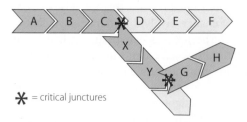

✱ = critical junctures

Figure **1.1** *A reactive sequence*

While those leading a change may attempt to avoid conflict by formulating a vision that accommodates the interests of many constituencies – bosses, peers, subordinates, customers, suppliers, bankers – it may not always be possible to satisfy them all and some may resist the change. This highlights the importance of not only working to set a viable direction for change but also acting in ways that will align all those involved to support it.

In some cases, negative reactions may only lead to minor deviations from the leader's intended path but sometimes the reaction can block or radically transform the change. Mahoney (2000) refers to the possibility of a 'backlash', and Pierson (1998) observes that events can trigger counter-reactions that are powerful enough to move the system in a completely new direction. Example 1.1 provides a good illustration when the car dealers resisted the importer's plans for change. Example 1.2 presents another instance of this at British Airways.

Example **1.2** *BA cabin crew dispute*

British Airways (BA) needed to change in order to compete against the increasing number of low-cost airlines, absorb rising fuel prices and adapt to the global recession.

In October 2009, BA announced changes in staffing levels, pay and conditions in order to cut costs. A number of changes were implemented, including some staff switching to part-time working and others taking voluntary redundancy, but a proposal to reduce the number of cabin crew on long-haul flights from 15 to 14 was fiercely resisted.

Actions and reactions, including strikes, suspensions and dismissals, continued for 18 months. Early on in the dispute, reactions escalated to the point where cabin crew decided on a 12-day strike over the Christmas holiday period. BA responded by taking legal action that prevented the strike from taking place. After two weeks of talks between BA management and Unite (the trade union representing cabin crew), the union decided to reballot members and the result was a vote in favour of strike action, starting with an initial 3-day strike in March 2010. Following the strike, the company withdrew generous travel concessions from those workers who had participated in the industrial action.

Action and reaction continued to escalate the dispute. In May 2010, after failing to reach a compromise with its staff, BA won a court injunction preventing a series of planned strikes. Talks to avert further action broke down when demonstrators stormed the building and the CEO had to be escorted away for his own protection. After more strikes and a bitter war of words, it was reported in the press that BA had suspended 80 cabin crew and sacked a further 13 because of incidents relating to the dispute, including the intimidation of cabin crew who wanted to continue working. Further votes for strike action and legal wrangling to prevent industrial action continued until, in May 2011, the dispute was eventually resolved.

© PHOTODISC/GETTY IMAGES

Self-reinforcing sequences

Self-reinforcing sequences occur when a decision or action produces positive feedback that reinforces earlier events and supports the direction of change. This reinforcement induces further movement in the same direction. While self-reinforcing sequences can deliver benefits over the short term, change managers need to be alert to the possibility that they may draw them into a path that will deliver suboptimal outcomes over the longer term. This will be illustrated with reference to three drivers of self-reinforcing sequences: increasing returns, psychological commitment to past decisions, and cognitive biases.

Increasing returns

An important driver of self-reinforcing sequences is increasing returns, a concept that initially received attention from economists. Pierson (2000) traces early interest to Arthur (1994) and David (1985). They argued that a particular technology that is first to market or widely adopted by early users, for example the QWERTY keyboard and VHS video format, may generate increasing returns and achieve a decisive advantage over competing technologies, such as the Dvorak keyboard and Betamax video format, even though it may not be the most efficient alternative. Arthur (1994) points to four conditions that can promote increasing returns. These conditions are not restricted to the adoption and diffusion of new technologies, but apply to almost every aspect of organizational change:

1 *Set-up costs:* Where these are high, there is an incentive to stick with a chosen option so as to spread costs over a longer run of activity. For example, following the implementation of a new business process, increasing returns from the initial investment (set-up costs) are likely to be achieved if the new arrangements persist over a period of time.
2 *Learning:* Knowledge gained from repetitive use can lead to increased proficiency and continuous improvement. For example, organizational members learn by doing and the more they do, the more proficient they become. This learning provides a powerful incentive to continue down the same path because doing yet more of the same leads to increasing returns from exploiting these acquired competences. Switching to new ways of working might, at least in the short term, lead to diminishing returns while new competences are developed.
3 *Coordination:* The benefits received from a particular activity increase as others adopt the same option. Arthur observed that as more people bought VHS video recorders, video stores found it advantageous to stock VHS rather than Betamax tapes, which, in turn, encouraged more people to buy VHS recorders.
4 *Betting on the right horse:* People recognize that options that fail to win broad acceptance will have drawbacks later on, therefore they are motivated to select the option they think will be adopted by most others. They anticipate that persisting with this choice will generate increasing returns in the future.

Example 1.3 is an illustration of how increasing returns can create a situation where a company sticks with a winning formula too long and fails to respond to new opportunities and threats as they emerge.

This example illustrates the danger of increasing returns, which, in the case of Nokia, had led to too much attention being focused on devices. The company had missed the new big trend and was in danger of being squeezed out of what was fast becoming the most highly profitable segment of the market. Growing profits from

------

● *Example* 1.3 *Nokia: sticking with a winning formula for too long*

Nokia started out as a wood pulp and paper manufacturer in 1865 and evolved into an industrial conglomerate producing rubber boots, cables, generators, military communications equipment, televisions and other consumer electronics. In 1992, the company changed strategy, focusing on telecommunications and beginning to sell off its interests in other sectors. By 1998, this new focus plus the company's early investment in GSM (global system for mobile communication) technologies and second-generation mobile technology (which could carry both voice and data traffic) led to Nokia becoming the world's largest producer of mobile phones. Between 1996 and 2001, turnover increased from €6.5 to €31 billion and the growth in sales and profitability continued until 2008. Economies of scale, competences – especially in hardware design – and widespread consumer confidence all contributed to the company's success. New devices continued to be developed, including Nokia's first touch screen phone, released in 2007, and a phone with a full QWERTY keyboard to compete with BlackBerry devices, released in 2008. Nokia also developed phones with music and social networking capabilities. However, research and development effort was focused on exploiting what Nokia was already good at rather than exploring new opportunities.

By 2011, the company employed 130,000 staff in 120 countries but in February of that year, Stephen Elop, the newly appointed CEO, circulated a memo alerting staff to an unfolding crisis (Constantinescu, 2011). He told them that consumers, while still valuing devices, were increasingly attracted by software and went on to argue that Apple had redefined the smartphone in a way that attracted developers to a closed but powerful ecosystem. It has 'changed the game, and today Apple owns the high end range'. He went on to talk about how the Android operating system had, in just two years, created a platform that attracted application developers, service providers and hardware manufacturers such as Samsung, and how Google had become 'a gravitational force, drawing much of the industry's innovation to its core'.

For almost two decades, hardware had delivered increasing returns and been the source of Nokia's profitability, but Elop argued that:

> The battle of devices has now become a war of ecosystems, where ecosystems include not only the hardware and software of the device, but developers, applications, ecommerce, advertising, search, social applications, location-based services, unified communications and many other things. Our competitors aren't taking our market share with devices; they are taking our market share with an entire ecosystem.

------

hardware and Nokia's dominant position in the mobile phone market had undermined its long-term success. Not long after Elop's memo was circulated, Nokia announced a new strategic direction, which involved a partnership with Microsoft to build a new mobile ecosystem. Nokia also announced that the Windows Phone operating system would be its primary smartphone platform.

Psychological commitment to past decisions

Another self-reinforcing mechanism is psychological commitment to past decisions. While most decision theories posit that individuals are prospectively rational and make decisions in order to maximize future benefit, Staw (1976, 1981) argues that, in practice, decision makers are often motivated by retrospective rationality and the need to justify past decisions. Staw (1976) observed that, when faced with negative outcomes following a decision, leaders may commit additional resources in order to justify the earlier decision and demonstrate the ultimate rationality of their original course of action. But the additional investment may not rescue the situation. Instead, it might lead to further negative consequences, which, in turn, trigger another decision to invest yet more in an attempt to secure a positive outcome. Staw refers to this negative cycle as the 'escalation of commitment' to a chosen course of action.

Two factors appear to encourage this escalation of commitment. The first is change managers' need to demonstrate their own competence and justify an earlier decision. This can take the form of self-justification to protect their own self-image, or justification to others in order to prove to them that an earlier decision was not wrong. The second is a response to a perceived pressure for consistency. Staw (1981) argues that in many organizational settings there is a perception that change managers who are consistent in their actions are better leaders than those who switch from one course of action to another. Consistent change managers who persist with a course of action in the face of early setbacks are often viewed as being courageous, committed and steadfast, whereas those who monitor performance and, if results are not as good as anticipated, are prepared to change course can be seen to be indecisive and less effective.

These forces can encourage change managers to escalate their commitment to past decisions in the hope this commitment will demonstrate that an apparent poor decision was actually a good decision when viewed over the long term. This self-reinforcing mechanism often makes it difficult to change course, even when those leading the change are aware that a series of past decisions have been suboptimal. Example 1.4 illustrates how the escalation of commitment contributed to the loss of £469 million when the FiReControl project failed.

Example **1.4 Failure of the FiReControl project**

The FiReControl project involved replacing the control rooms in 46 local Fire and Rescue Services across England with a network of nine purpose-built regional control centres that were to be linked by a new national computer system. This new interlinked network was designed to enable fire brigades to be directed more easily to the scenes of large emergencies, such as terrorist attacks, industrial accidents, rail crashes or floods, and to improve national resilience. The project was launched in 2004 with a budget of £70 million, but, following a series of delays and difficulties, was terminated in December 2010, with none of the original objectives achieved and a minimum of £469 million being wasted. Eight of the purpose-built centres had been empty for up to three years, at a cost of £4 million a month in maintenance, because the new computer system had not been delivered.

In April 2010, members of Parliament (MPs) on the Communities and Local Government Select Committee were critical of the way the project was being managed but expressed the view that because so much money had already been spent, the project should continue and would eventually reap benefits. The Fire Brigades Union (FBU) disagreed and argued that to continue would involve 'throwing good money after bad'. However,

Shahid Malik, the then fire minister, backed the committee's view that the project should go ahead: 'The government agrees with the select committee that the FiReControl project should continue with renewed vigour.' Not everybody was happy with this recommendation. John McDonnell MP, FBU parliamentary group secretary, said on BBC Radio 4's *Face the Facts* (29 August 2010):

> It is very difficult for senior civil servants, ministers and secretaries of state to admit they have made a mistake … What usually happens is rather than admit a mistake they throw more money at it and try to save the phenomenon.

In September 2011, Margaret Hodge MP, chair of the Public Accounts Committee (PAC), described the FiReControl project as a complete failure. The PAC heard that the department in charge of the project had failed to secure the cooperation of the locally accountable and independent Fire and Rescue Services and had attempted to rush the project without a proper understanding of the costs or risks. When the project was finally cancelled, Matt Wrack, general secretary of the FBU, said: 'We have been sounding the alarm about this project for seven years, often as a lone voice, and this decision shows that we were right.'

Cognitive biases and interpretive frames

A change manager's implicit theory about how things work and selective perceptions about what is important can give rise to cognitive biases and idiosyncratic ways of interpreting events, which can push them to develop and persist with visions and goals for change that may be unfit for purpose. Conger (1990) suggests that while those leading change need to make a realistic assessment of the opportunities and constraints in a situation and be sensitive to the needs and priorities of those who have a stake in the change, this may not happen. Those leading the change can become so committed to a project that they only pay attention to information that supports their own position. Edwards (2001) suggests that leaders have a tendency to classify decisions into categories by comparing immediate decisions with similar past decision scenarios. This encourages them to evaluate outcomes by focusing attention on only those attributes of the immediate situation that are consistent with the selected scenario category. Important but inconsistent information is ignored as they develop a mindset that restricts their attention to (only) those aspects of a situation they perceive to be relevant. Their failure to pay attention to inconsistent or negative feedback creates an illusion that they are acting effectively. This cognitive bias may be reinforced if change managers have a history of past successes, because a successful track record can promote a sense of self-belief and the perception that they are able to exercise sufficient control to achieve desired outcomes (see Chapter 4 for more on the 'trap of success'). Where a change is led by a cohesive leadership team, this self-reinforcing mechanism can be further strengthened if members suppress dissent and impede reality testing by engaging in what Janis (1972) describes as 'groupthink'. Example 1.5 provides an example of cognitive biases at work.

Example 1.5 Unrealistic goals for change at Direct Banking

A successful Dutch-based telephone and internet bank (referred to here as Direct Banking) serves customers across much of Europe. Over the past 14 years, it has developed an organizational culture that values the customer and focuses everybody's attention on delivering exceptional customer service. Staff working in the service centres are not restricted to narrow 'scripts' when talking to customers and are encouraged to develop relationships with them in order to identify and satisfy their needs. Over 85 per cent of Direct Banking's customers have recommended the bank to their friends and family, and the quality of its communication with customers has been a major factor contributing to its success.

Following a 10-year period of rapid growth, costs began to increase and margins were squeezed. A new CEO was appointed to tackle the problem. Soon after taking up his post, he brought in two new managers to replace two existing members of the bank's executive team. One of the displaced managers took early retirement and the other moved into a new role within the bank.

After being in post for just four weeks, the CEO informed the executive team that he wanted to introduce voice automation and routing (VAR). His vision was to drive down costs by using speech recognition-based technology to analyse in-bound calls in order to identify callers, why they are calling and what kind of transaction they required. In those cases where full automation of the transaction was not possible, he argued that partial automation could provide an intermediate solution by collecting routine data (such as account numbers and the service required) and routing the call to a specialized agent who could complete the transaction.

The new CEO was respected for his outstanding past record of using technical innovation to drive down costs and increase margins and, since joining the bank, he made good use of already established internal communication channels to convince others that

▶

radical change was required to restore the bank's profitability. However, some senior managers, who had been involved for over a decade in developing the bank's outstanding reputation for customer service, informed the CEO they were worried that the proposed automation would damage the brand and do little to rescue the situation. They were particularly concerned because the new CEO had no previous experience of running a service-oriented brand. The new CEO listened but was not diverted from his chosen way forward. With the aid of his two new appointees, he managed the internal politics with considerable skill and convinced some of the doubters by suggesting ways in which the new technology could be adapted to increase its appeal to customers.

A project team was established and set to work. At an early stage, the team informed the CEO that the third-party vendor who was to provide the VAR technology felt that the plans to modify the system to address possible customer concerns were too ambitious. This feedback did little to modify the CEO's view and he persisted with his plan to implement VAR. It was not until relatively late in the change process that the CEO's assumptions about customer acceptance were tested. The results from focus groups with customers were so negative that it was obvious that implementing VAR would do serious damage to the brand. It was this belated feedback that eventually forced the CEO to revise his position and abandon the project.

Path dependence

An important feature of many self-reinforcing sequences is that early steps in a particular direction can produce further movement in the same direction and, over time, this process can constrain change leaders' freedom to construct and manage an effective change trajectory. Sydow et al. (2009) refer to this constraining process as 'organizational path dependence'. Path dependence begins with a critical event that triggers a pattern of self-reinforcing practices, which eventually squeeze out alternatives and limit a change manager's scope for action. Sydow et al. (2009) conceptualize path dependence as a three-phase process: preformation, path formation, and lock-in (Figure 1.2).

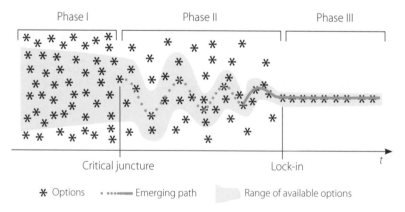

Figure **1.2** *The constitution of an organizational path*
Source: Sydow et al., 2009, p. 692

1 In the *preformation phase*, there are few constraints on change managers' freedom to act other than organizations' established routines and practices. However, during this phase, one or more decisions or actions trigger a self-reinforcing sequence. This point is a critical juncture that marks the start of the

second phase. Collier and Collier (1991) suggest that critical junctures can involve relatively brief periods, in which one particular direction emerges as the way forward, or they can involve an extended period of reorientation.

2 In the *path formation phase*, self-reinforcing sequences lead to the development of a pattern of events, decisions and actions that begins to dominate and divert change managers' attention away from alternative ways forward. While there is still a range of available options, this range narrows and it becomes progressively difficult to change course.

3 The *lock-in phase* is characterized by a further narrowing of options and the process becomes locked into a particular path. Schreyögg and Sydow (2011, p. 325) describe the most precarious feature of this stage as the risk of becoming dysfunctional as leaders lose the capability to adapt to new circumstances or better alternatives. They become locked in to a particular way of functioning. When faced by more efficient alternatives or critical changes in the environment, established processes and practices persist and the system fails to adjust.

Minimizing the impact of reactive and self-reinforcing sequences

Sometimes, those leading a change are less effective than they might be because they fail to recognize some of the dynamics that affect outcomes, and so they do not always act in ways that will enable them to exercise as much control as they could over what happens.

Reactive sequences

When change involves different parties that are each seeking to pursue their own interests, then, depending on the balance of power, reactive sequences are likely to emerge. Often, reactions that are negative (from the point of view of the change agent's intentions) can be quickly detected but this is not always the case, especially when those who are unhappy with the emerging direction of change lack the confidence to voice their concerns, or have insufficient power to challenge events as they unfold. In the short term, those affected by the change may comply with leaders' directions but, at a later juncture, they may develop the confidence or acquire the power to challenge the way the change is being managed.

Change agents can improve their effectiveness by scanning their environment for threats and anticipating resistance, or responding quickly when others fail to support their actions. Mangham (1978), drawing on earlier work by Goffman (1959), discusses how leaders, like actors, can assess their 'audience' prior to a performance. He refers to Goffman's observation that some actors use mirrors so that they can practise and become an object to themselves backstage, before going 'onstage' and becoming an object to others. In a similar way, change managers can anticipate how those affected by a change might react to events. Mangham even suggests that leaders can simulate several stages into a number of alternative futures, a form of mental chess in which various moves and their consequences can be tested. A stakeholder analysis, which draws attention to those who will be affected by or can affect the outcome of a change, assesses how much power they have to determine the course of events, and anticipates their attitude towards an event, can facilitate this testing.

Self-reinforcing sequences

A danger with self-reinforcing sequences, whether they are driven by increasing returns, a psychological commitment to past decisions or cognitive biases, is that they can undermine change managers' flexibility and their ability to adapt to changing circumstances (see the discussion of deep structures in Chapter 3). Schreyögg and Sydow (2011, p. 322) refer to self-reinforcing sequences as entrapping processes that 'often unfold behind the backs of actors and bring about an escalating situation with unexpected results'. Sydow et al. (2009) argue that a minimum condition for breaking out of the path dependency that is often associated with self-reinforcing sequences is the restoration of choice. Change managers need to do whatever they can to maintain an awareness of and the freedom to adopt alternative courses of action.

Complex patterns

Sometimes, change unfolds as a pattern of punctuated equilibrium (see Chapter 3), which involves an alternation between self-reinforcing sequences, during which increasing returns and other forces promote the development of routines that narrow the scope for action, and reactive sequences where negative reactions and a hostile context can trigger discontinuities that push the change in a new direction. These self-reinforcing reactive cycles can be observed over different time periods, such as a few days, months or even years, and in relation to different processes, such as the development of interpersonal relations within a project team, the design of new products and services, and the formulation and implementation of a new business strategy.

Chapter 2 considers what leaders can do to improve the practice of change management and argues that change managers can learn to be more effective if they step back and monitor what is going on – paying particular attention to how others react to what they do and how their decisions impact on immediate and longer term outcomes – and use these observations to guide their behaviour.

Summary

A review of the four process theories of change – teleological, dialectical, life cycle and evolutionary – revealed that they all view change as involving a number of events, decisions and actions that are connected in some sort of sequence, but they differ in terms of the degree to which they present change as following certain essential stages and the extent to which the direction of change is constructed or predetermined:

- *The ordering of stages:* Some theories place more emphasis on the order of the stages than others. For example, life cycle theories assume that change is a process that progresses through a necessary sequence of stages that are cumulative, in the sense that each stage contributes a piece to the final outcome, and related – each stage is a necessary precursor for the next. Teleological theories, on the other hand, are less prescriptive about the ordering of stages.
- *Predetermined versus constructed trajectories:* Life cycle and evolutionary theories present change as a predetermined process that unfolds over time in a prespecified direction. This kind of change involves incrementally adapting organizational forms in predictable ways. Teleological and dialectical theories, on the other hand, view change trajectories as constructed, in the sense that goals, and the steps taken to achieve goals, can be changed at the will of (at least some of) those involved in the process. According to this perspective, the

process is not unduly constrained by an inherent code or factors external to the immediate system.

- *The impact of sequence on outcome:* Although teleological and dialectical theories suggest that members of a system have considerable freedom to construct change trajectories and assert that it is possible for them to break away from established routines and intentionally move the system towards redefined goals, this may not always be easy to achieve in practice. The nature of the change sequence, whether reactive or self-reinforcing, will affect the extent to which those leading the change will be able to realize this possibility.
- *Reactive sequences:* In reactive sequences, subsequent events challenge rather than reinforce earlier events. Negative reactions may produce only minor deviations from the intended path or they may be so strong that they may delay, transform or block the change.
- *Self-reinforcing sequences:* Self-reinforcing sequences involve positive feedback that reinforces earlier events and supports the direction of change. Three drivers of self-reinforcing sequences are increasing returns, a psychological commitment to past decisions, and cognitive biases. An important feature of self-reinforcing sequences is that early steps in a particular direction can produce further movement in the same direction and, over time, can constrain leaders' freedom to construct and manage an effective change trajectory.

It was argued that in order to minimize any negative impact from reactive and self-reinforcing sequences, those leading change need to be able to step back and observe what is going on, including their own and others' behaviour, identify critical junctures and subsequent patterns – some of which may be difficult to discern – and explore alternative ways of acting that might deliver superior outcomes.

Before reading Chapter 2, you might find it useful to think about managing change from the perspective of timing and the sequencing of actions. Exercise 1.1 explores some of the issues and choices that have to be considered when thinking about how best to introduce a change into an organization.

✓ *Exercise* **1.1** *Managing a branch closure programme: an exercise in planning and managing the process of change*

The aim of this activity is to explore the issues and choices involved in developing an overall strategy for large-scale change.

The scenario

A long-established bank is facing strong competition from new entrants into the retail banking market. The new entrants have acquired some high-street branches but specialize in the provision of telephone and internet banking services. Consequently, they have a lower cost base because they do not carry the overheads associated with a large branch network.

The operations board of the traditional bank is busy working on a number of important projects and does not seem to have recognized the potential impact of the new competition on their market share and margins.

You are a member of the operations board and you have given a lot of thought to the problem. You believe that the only viable strategy is to reduce the size of the existing branch network in order to reduce overheads, but to do so in a way that will lead to an increase in net revenue per customer. At this stage, you have not thought through all the details of the strategy. For example, should the branches targeted for closure be city-centre branches occupying expensive properties, but providing services for high net worth customers who the bank would be reluctant to lose, or small rural branches occupying less expensive premises but with fewer customers of high net worth to the bank?

Step 1

You have brainstormed a list of possible actions that could provide the basis for a way forward. These are listed below in Table 1.1.

You are invited to review and revise this list of actions and use your experience to:

- Delete any items that, on reflection, you feel are unimportant or irrelevant.
- Add, in the space provided at the bottom of Table 1.1, any other actions that you feel should be included. You are allowed to add up to four additional actions.
- Think about how the actions might be sequenced from start to finish. For each action, identify whether you think it should occur early or late in the change management process. You can record this view in the space provided on the right-hand side of the table.

Table **1.1** *Possible actions that will inform the strategy taken by the bank*

		Early			Late	
1	Identify key stakeholders who might be affected by the change					
2	Provide a counselling service and retraining for those who are to be displaced					
3	Inform staff how they, personally, will be affected by the closure plan					
5	Identify a project leader and set up a branch closure team					
6	Announce the scope and scale of the closure plan to all staff					
7	Brief key managers about the problem and win their support for the closure plan					
8	Identify which branches are to be closed					
9	Review the success (or otherwise) of the closure programme and disseminate throughout the organization any lessons learned about change management					
10	Identify the information that will be required in order to decide the number and location of branches to be closed in order to achieve targeted benefits					
11	Announce closure plan to existing customers					
12	Train members of the branch closure team in change management skills					
13	Identify (and quantify) benefits sought from closures					
14	Develop a personnel package for displaced staff					
15	Assess effects of the closures on other aspects of the bank's functioning					
16	Plan any training that may be required for staff who are to be reassigned to other work					
17	Hold team meetings to brief staff about the closure plans and indicate when they will be informed about how they (personally) will be affected by the change					
18	Identify what steps could be taken to retain high value customers affected by the closures					
20	Issue newsletter outlining progress towards full implementation					
21	Decide who should be involved in analysing the information relating to whether a closure plan will deliver sufficient benefits to justify the costs involved					
22	Seek views of customers who might be affected by the closures about what issues should be given attention					

▶

23	Seek views of branch staff about the issues that will have to be given attention if the closure plan is to be successfully accomplished					
24	Post-implementation, provide feedback to staff about how the change is affecting performance					
25	Initiate programme to make properties suitable for disposal (e.g. remove vaults)					
26	Celebrate successes and build on them in order to motivate people to continue working to improve the bank's competitive position					
27	Decide on date for first closures					
28	Identify any personal gains or losses that might be perceived by those employees who will be affected by the closures					
29	Specify timetable for implementing the closure plan					
30	Consider what might be done to motivate employees to accept the change					
31	Issue a press release about the closure plan					
32	Monitor progress against timetable and anticipated benefits					
33	Explore the best way of disposing of redundant properties					
34	Identify social banking issues raised by the closures (e.g. what will happen to customers without transport when their local branch closes)					
35	Plan what will happen to displaced staff (redeployment, early retirement, redundancy)					
36	Arrange an awayday for members of the ops board to focus their thinking on emerging threats and opportunities					
38	Reflect on how well the change is progressing and discuss with colleagues what else could be done to ensure the change is successful					
39	Decide who should be involved in identifying which branches are to be closed					

Step 2

Consider your list of action statements and assemble them into a plan.

- Identify the sequence of actions from start to finish, recognizing that some actions may occur in parallel or be repeated.
- Identify relationships between actions in your plan and consider how different actions might be grouped together to form separate steps or distinctive parts of your plan.
- Summarize your plan as a flow diagram. For help with this, visit the companion website at **www.palgrave.com/companion/hayes-change-management4** for a list of the action statements you can drag and drop into a flow diagram. This will enable you to experiment with different ways of sequencing actions, and grouping them into categories that reflect the main steps in your approach to managing the change process.

You might find it useful to compare the change model you developed here to manage the branch closures with the model presented at the end of Chapter 2. As you read the remaining chapters of this book, you might also find it helpful to reflect on how the content of each chapter might influence your approach to managing this kind of change.

References

Arthur, W.B. (1994) *Increasing Returns and Path Dependence in the Economy*. Ann Arbor, MI: University of Michigan Press.

Barnett, W.P. and Carroll, G.R. (1995) Modeling internal organizational change, *Annual Review of Sociology*, 21: 217–36.

Beer, M., Eisenstat, R. and Spector, B. (1990) Why change programs don't produce change, *Harvard Business Review*, 68(6): 158–67.

Collier, R.B. and Collier, D. (1991) *Shaping the Political Arena: Critical Junctures, the Labor Movement, and Regime Dynamics in Latin America*. Princeton, PA: Princeton University Press.

Conger, J.A. (1990) The dark side of leadership, *Organizational Dynamics*, 19(2): 44–5.

David, P. (1985) Clio and the economics of QWERTY, *American Economic Review*, 75(2): 332–7.

Constantinescu, S. (2011) Leaked: Nokia's memo discussing the iPhone, Android, and the need for drastic change, IntoMobile, 8 February, www.intomobile.com/2011/02/08/leaked-nokias-memo-discusses-need-for-drastic-change/.

Edwards, J.C. (2001) Self-fulfilling prophecy and escalating commitment: Fuel for the Waco fire, *Journal of Applied Behavioral Science*, 37(3): 343–60.

Flamholtz, E. (1995) Managing organizational transition: Implications for corporate and human resource management, *European Management Journal*, 13(1): 39–51.

Goffman, E. (1959) *The Presentation of Self in Everyday Life*. New York: Doubleday.

Greenwood, R. and Hinings, C.R. (1996) Understanding radical organizational change: Bringing together the old and the new institutionalism, *Academy of Management Review*, 21(4): 1022–54.

Janis, I.L. (1972) *Victims of Groupthink: A Psychological Study of Foreign Policy Decisions and Fiascos*. Boston, MA: Houghton-Mifflin.

Jørgensen, H.H., Owen, L. and Neus, A. (2008) *Making Change Work*, IBM Global Services, www-935.ibm.com/services/us/gbs/bus/pdf/gbe03100-usen-03-making-change-work.pdf.

Mahoney, J. (2000) Path dependence in historical sociology, *Theory and Society*, 29(4): 507–48.

Mangham, I.L. (1978) *Interactions and Interventions in Organizations*. Chichester: Wiley.

Miles, R.E. and Snow, C.C. (1984) Designing strategic human resource systems, *Organizational Dynamics*, 13(11): 36–52.

Pierson, P. (1998) Not just what, but *when*: Issues of timing and sequence in comparative politics. American Political Science Association meeting, Boston, September.

Pierson, P. (2000) Increasing returns, path dependence, and the study of politics, *American Political Science Review*, 94(2): 51–267.

Schneider, B., Hayes, S.C., Lim, B. et al. (2003) The human side of strategy: Employee experiences of strategic alignment in a service organisation, *Organizational Dynamics*, 32(2): 122–41.

Schreyögg, G. and Sydow, J. (2011) Organizational path dependence: A process view, *Organization Studies*, 32(3): 321–35.

Staw, B.M. (1976) Knee deep in the big muddy: A study of escalating commitment to a chosen course of action, *Organizational Behavior and Human Performance*, 16(1): 27–44.

Staw, B.M. (1981) The escalation of commitment to a course of action, *Academy of Management Review*, 6(4): 577–87.

Sydow, J., Schreyögg, G. and Koch, J. (2009) Organizational path dependence: Opening the black box, *Academy of Management Review*, 34(4): 689–709.

Van de Ven, A.H. and Poole, M.S. (1995) Explaining development and change in organizations, *Academy of Management Review*, 20(5): 510–40.

Van de Ven, A.H. and Sun, K. (2011) Breakdowns in implementing models of organizational change, *Academy of Management Perspectives*, 25(3): 58–74.

2

Leading change: a process perspective

This chapter builds on the ideas discussed in Chapter 1 and presents a process model based on teleological and dialectical theories that conceptualize change as a purposeful, constructed and often contested process. The model provides a conceptual framework that those leading change can use to identify the issues they need to address if they are to secure desired outcomes. The model can also be used to identify the kinds of questions that will help leaders reflect on how well they are doing and what else they could do to improve performance.

The intentional management of change

While leaders who recognize or anticipate shifts in their organization's external environment may be better placed to initiate change, recognition of a need (or opportunity) for change may not be sufficient to ensure that it will happen. Lewin (1951) provided some useful insights into the nature of change that are relevant for those who seek to intentionally change the status quo. He argued that the state of no change does not refer to a situation in which everything is stationary. It involves a condition of 'stable quasi-stationary equilibrium' comparable to that of a river that flows with a given velocity in a given direction. A change in the behaviour of an individual, group or organization can be likened to a change in the river's velocity or direction. For example, members of two groups in the marketing department might engage in competitive and collaborative behaviours when they come together in departmental meetings. The way they relate to each other reflects the current state of stable quasi-stationary equilibrium (the flow, in terms of Lewin's metaphor). The head of marketing might feel that, on balance, there is too much disruptive intergroup competition and insufficient friendly cooperation, and might decide to intervene in order to promote more constructive collaboration. In this example, they want to move the dynamics of the departmental meeting from one state of stable quasi-stationary equilibrium to another.

Lewin argued that any level of behaviour is maintained in a condition of quasi-stationary equilibrium by a force-field comprising a balance of forces pushing for and resisting change. This level of behaviour can be changed by either adding forces for change in the desired direction or by diminishing the opposing or resisting forces (Figure 2.1). Both approaches can result in change but, according to Lewin, the secondary effects associated with each approach will be different. Where change is brought about by increasing the forces pushing for change, this will result in an increase in tension. If this rises beyond a certain level, it may be accompanied by high aggressiveness (especially towards the source of the increased pressure for change), high emotionality and low levels of constructive behaviour and can trigger a reactive sequence (see Chapter 1) that challenges the change agent's intention. On the other hand, where change is brought about by diminishing the forces that oppose or resist change, the secondary effect will be a state of relatively low tension.

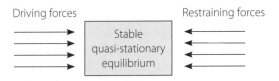

Figure **2.1** *A force-field*

Lewin's field theory led him to advocate an approach to managing change that emphasized the importance of reducing the restraining forces (a pull strategy) in preference to a high pressured approach that only focused on increasing the forces pushing for change (a push strategy). He argued that approaches involving the removal of restraining forces within the individual, group or organization are likely to increase commitment and result in a more permanent change than approaches involving the application of outside pressure for change.

Lewin's three-step process

Lewin suggested that successful change requires a three-step process that involves the stages of unfreezing, moving and refreezing.

Managing change, therefore, involves helping an individual, group or organization:

1 unfreeze or unlock the existing level of behaviour
2 move to a new level
3 refreeze behaviour at this new level.

Unfreezing involves destabilizing the balance of driving and restraining forces. Kotter (1995) argues that the current state of equilibrium can be destabilized by alerting organizational members to the need for change. Creating a vision of a more desirable future state and providing information that creates a sense of urgency can weaken restraining and strengthen driving forces. Such action can motive individuals and groups to let go of current ways of behaving and encourage them to search out more effective alternatives. Schein (1996) also points to how disconfirming people's assessment of the benefits of the current state can motivate learning and change.

Lewin's second phase, movement, is where the balance of driving and restraining forces is modified to shift the equilibrium to a new level. Although these forces can assume many forms, they tend to manifest in terms of behaviours that affect performance (Ford and Greer, 2006). Consequently, movement tends to be achieved by adjusting attitudes and beliefs, and modifying the processes, systems and structures that shape behaviour.

Refreezing involves reinforcing new behaviours in order to maintain new levels of performance and avoid regression. Feedback that signals the effectiveness and consistency of new behaviours and incentives that reward new levels of performance can help embed new practices.

Burnes (2004a, 2004b) has observed a tendency in recent years to play down the significance of Lewin's work for contemporary organizations. For example, Dawson

(2003) and Kantor et al. (1992) argue that the notion of refreezing is not relevant for organizations operating in turbulent environments. They argue that organizations need to be fluid and adaptable and that it would be counterintuitive for them to be frozen into some given way of functioning. Lewin's point, however, is that all too often change is short-lived. After a 'shot in the arm', the change is not sustained and life returns to the way it was before. In his view, it is not enough to think of change in terms of simply *reaching* a new state, for example achieving a short-term improvement in the level of collaboration in the marketing department's meetings. He asserted that permanency, for as long as it is relevant, needs to be an important part of the goal. This state may be brief and involve little more than taking stock before moving on to yet more change. It is, however, important to think in terms of consolidation in order to minimize the danger of slipping back to the way things were before.

Hendry (1996, p. 624) testifies to Lewin's lasting contribution to change management, by noting: 'Scratch any account of creating and managing change and the idea that change is a three-stage process which necessarily begins with a process of unfreezing will not be far below the surface.' However, as Burnes (2004a) has observed, the strength of Lewin's contribution to the theory and practice of organizational change is when this three-step model is viewed as part of an integrated theory that includes field theory, group dynamics (see Chapter 16) and action research (see Chapter 17). Research report 2.1 presents the results of an empirical test of Lewin's theory and the three-step model of change.

Research report 2.1 A test of the validity of Lewin's three-step model

Ford, M.W and Greer, B.M. (2006) Profiling change: An empirical study of change process patterns, *Journal of Applied Behavioral Science*, 42(4): 420–46.

Theory

This study compared profiles of activity at different stages of a change to investigate the validity of Lewin's three-phase model. Lewin's model implies that activities relating to unfreezing should be observable before activities relating to movement and refreezing. Unfreezing to destabilize the status quo needs to occur first otherwise the organization will be poorly prepared for change. Movement requires at least some old ways of doing things to be discarded in favour of new behaviours. It is only after these new behaviours have been established that refreezing will facilitate the stabilization of the organization at a new equilibrium. Ford and Greer argue that if such a progression or sequence exists, then intensity levels of factors linked to each of the three stages of Lewin's model should change as implementation proceeds. They make two hypotheses:

1 As implementation progresses, change process profiles will display higher levels of 'movement' and 'refreezing' factors.

2 Change process profiles associated with higher degrees of implementation success will display higher levels of unfreezing, movement and refreezing factors than change process profiles associated with lower degrees of success.

This second hypothesis relates to the levels of unfreezing-moving-refreezing activity associated with the degree of implementation success. Lewin's theory does not suggest that any of the three phases will dominate, for example although refreezing occurs late in the change process, it is just as important as unfreezing, so it follows that implementation success will be associated with more intense use of all change process factors.

Method

After studying conceptualizations of change, Ford and Greer developed a set of change process factors that could be linked to Lewin's three phases:

1 *Goal setting* was identified as a measure of *unfreezing*, on the grounds that it is an activity that challenges existing expectations and motivates an analysis and assessment of the organization's relationship with its environment. A three-item scale was developed to measure this factor.

2 *Skill development* was identified as a measure of *movement,* on the grounds that moving an organization towards a new and improved state requires behavioural adjustment, and new behaviours require the development and delivery of new skills and competences.

3 *Feedback and management control* were identified as measures of *refreezing,* on the grounds that refreezing requires confirmatory feedback and rewards to reinforce desired behaviours. Consistent with this need for feedback is the development of management control systems that monitor behaviour and keep the change on track.

A measure of implementation success was also developed and data were gathered from a cross-sectional sample of more than 100 managers involved in change implementation.

To test hypothesis 1, the data were split into four groups representing different levels of change implementation. Findings indicated that early in the implementation process, usage of feedback and management control, that is, the refreezing variables, was significantly below that of the other change process variables. As implementation progressed, the usage of refreezing variables increased relative to the other change process variables. Movement activities also increased as implementation progressed, but to a lesser degree.

To test hypothesis 2, the data were split into three groups representing different levels of implementation success. Results indicated a highly significant overall difference across the outcome groups, with higher levels of usage of all process variables – goal setting, skill development, feedback and management control – being associated with implementation success. A particularly interesting finding, pointing to the importance of sustaining change (discussed in Chapter 27), was that when the success of change implementation was low, the use of refreezing activities, such as feedback and management control, was significantly lower than in the change profiles associated with implementation success.

Ford and Greer's findings support the general progression from unfreezing to refreezing as theorized by Lewin. They also found, as implied by Lewin's framework, that organizations that achieve higher levels of implementation employ unfreezing, movement and refreezing activities at a higher level of intensity.

Stages in the process of managing change

Three other process models of change, which can be viewed as elaborations of Lewin's basic model, are briefly reviewed:

1 Lippitt et al. (1958) expanded Lewin's three-stage model. After reviewing descriptions of change in persons, groups, organizations and communities, they felt that the moving phase divided naturally into three substages. These were:
 • The clarification or diagnosis of the client's problem
 • The examination of alternative routes and goals, and the establishment of goals and intentions for action
 • The transformation of intentions into actual change efforts.

They also argued that change managers can only be effective when they develop and maintain an appropriate relationship with those involved in or affected by the change. This led them to introduce two further stages into the helping process, one concerned with the formation and the other with the termination of relationships. Termination has to be managed carefully if the momentum for change is to be maintained.

2 Egan (1996) developed a similar model based on Lewin's three stages of unfreezing, moving and refreezing, but it focuses most attention on the unfreezing and moving phases, with detailed consideration being given to the assessment of the current scenario (diagnosis), the creation of a preferred scenario (visioning), and the design of plans that move the system from the current to the preferred scenario (planning for change). The essential elements of these three stages are:
   - *The current scenario:* assessing problems and opportunities, developing new perspectives, and choosing high-impact problems or opportunities for attention.
   - *The preferred scenario:* developing a range of possible futures, evaluating alternative possibilities to establish a viable agenda for change, and gaining commitment to the new agenda.
   - *Strategies and plans for moving to the preferred scenario:* brainstorming strategies for getting there, choosing the best strategy or best fit package of strategies, and turning these strategies into a viable plan.

3 Beckhard and Harris (1987) present a three-stage model that focuses on defining the present and the future, managing the transition, and maintaining and updating the change. Special consideration is given to some of the issues associated with the moving or transitional stage, including the need for transitional arrangements, such as the appointment of a transition manager and the development of transition plans, and the gaining of commitment from key stakeholders. They also consider the conditions required to maintain the change.

These models highlight the importance of:

- *Developing change relationships:* between change agents and those affected by the change.
- *Diagnosis:* change managers need to give attention to where the organization is now and to what a more desirable (and attainable) state would look like.
- *Strategies and plans:* to move the organization towards the desired state.
- *Implementation:* translating intentions (strategies and plans) into actual change efforts.
- *Maintaining the change:* and holding on to gains.

Key steps in the change process

The model presented in Figure 2.2 builds on and synthesizes these ideas and conceptualizes managing change as a purposeful, constructed and often contested process that involves attending to seven core activities:

1 recognizing the need for change and starting the change process
2 diagnosing what needs to be changed and formulating a vision of a preferred future state
3 planning how to intervene in order to achieve the desired change
4 implementing plans and reviewing progress
5 sustaining the change
6 leading and managing the people issues
7 learning.

As noted in Chapter 1, these activities are presented as separate elements of the change process because the decisions and actions associated with them tend to

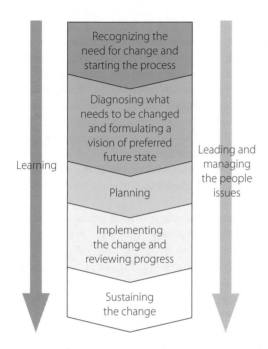

Figure **2.2** *The change process*

dominate at different points and there is a logical sequence connecting them, but in practice the boundaries are not always clear-cut and the sequence can be iterative, in the sense that some activities (such as diagnosis) can be addressed more than once. Also, some issues can be addressed simultaneously with others. For example, learning can occur at any or every point in the process and people issues need to be addressed throughout.

Recognizing the need for change and starting the change process

The start of the process is the recognition that external events, such as the credit crunch, or internal circumstances, such as the retirement of key staff or the development of a new product, require a change to take place. Recognition involves complex processes of perception, interpretation and decision making that, if not managed carefully, can lead to inappropriate outcomes, for example the organization might fail to change when it needs to or it may change when change is not required.

Leaders sometimes fail to recognize the need for change because they pay insufficient attention to what is happening in the wider environment. Even where organizational members are aware of what is going on outside, they may fail to recognize the implications this could have for the organization.

One way of challenging accepted ways of thinking is to involve new people in the formulation of the change agenda. Often, this activity is restricted to senior managers at the top of a department or the organization, but people located at multiple levels in the hierarchy, for example members of the sales team, customer service staff or those who have close contact with suppliers, may be better informed about emerging threats and opportunities.

Starting the change

Following recognition of the need for change, the next step involves translating the need into a desire for change. Leaders often underestimate how hard it can be to drive people out of their comfort zones. Creating a readiness to change involves alerting organizational members to the need for change and motivating them to let go of the status quo. Many factors can make this difficult, including a history of past success and the lack of an immediate crisis. Change managers might respond to this situation in different ways but many factors will affect whether a particular response will be effective. If, for example, the need for change is urgent (maybe because leaders were slow to recognize an emerging threat), there may be insufficient time to involve others or to experiment with alternative solutions. Change managers may feel that their only option is to adopt a more or less directive approach. In some circumstances, this may work but in others it may be resisted and organizational members may react in ways that block the change. However, in different circumstances, for example where those leading the change have recognized the need for change in good time, they may feel able to consider alternative actions including involving others in a preliminary diagnosis in order to create a shared perception of the need for change.

It is also important to decide who will be involved in managing the change. Kotter (1995) argues that unless those who recognize the need for change can put together a strong enough 'guiding coalition' to direct the process, the change initiative is unlikely to get off the ground. He suggests that while this guiding coalition does not have to include all senior managers, it is much more likely to succeed if, in terms of titles, information, experience, reputations and contacts, it is seen to signal a real commitment to change. In terms of background and experience, Clegg (2000) observes that it is often assumed that the lead should be a technical expert rather than the manager who will be responsible for making the change work post-implementation. He challenges this assumption and argues that unless users play a central role in managing the process, implementation may not be as successful as change managers anticipate.

Attention also needs to be given to building effective relationships between change agents and those affected by the change to ensure that there is a sufficient level of trust and understanding between all those involved. Early stages of this relationship building are important because people quickly form impressions about the change agent's competence, ability to help and motives.

This discussion illustrates that, from the perspective of leading change, early events in the process can be particularly important. A failure to identify a need for change or an ill-considered decision or action can set in motion a chain of reactions and counter-reactions and/or self-reinforcing sequences that can accumulate over time to impact the direction of change and produce unintended consequences.

Some questions that might help leaders reflect on how they are managing this stage of the process include:

- Who formulates the agenda for change? Should others be involved?
- Do change managers recognize and listen to informed others?
- Is the need for change translated into a desire for change?
- Is there a guiding coalition with sufficient power to get things done?
- Are the managers who will be responsible for making the change work sufficiently well represented in the guiding coalition?

Diagnosing what needs to be changed

This stage in the process involves:

1 Assessing problems and opportunities, developing new perspectives, and choosing high-impact problems or opportunities for attention.
2 Developing a range of possible futures and evaluating alternative possibilities to establish a viable agenda for change.

Although reviewing the present and identifying the future state may, at first sight, seem to be separate and distinct activities, they are often integrated in practice. These two steps frequently go through several iterations, progressing from broad concepts towards a vision of a more desirable state that is sufficiently concrete and detailed to be implemented. There is some debate about whether the process should start with looking at the present or the future. The argument for starting with the present is to ensure that the change is not conceived as a 'utopian leap' to an unrealistic future that cannot be reached from the current situation. On the other hand, focusing too heavily on the present may limit horizons and lead to the goals for change being too cautious and constrained by current experience.

Reviewing the present state

The present state of the organization can often only be understood in terms of the context of its history, its external environment, and the reactive and self-reinforcing sequences that have contributed to the current situation. The precise objectives for reviewing the present state will depend on the type of change that is being managed. Common reasons are to:

- help identify the required change by diagnosing the cause of a problem, identifying current deficiencies or clarifying opportunities
- establish a baseline so that it is clear what is changing
- help define the future direction.

Data gained from this kind of review can also be used to help assess how organizational members and other stakeholders will react, and to prepare people for change.

Identifying the future state

What is required when identifying the future state depends on the kind of change, for example incremental or transformational, being undertaken and change managers' role in the overall process. If change managers are responsible for initiating the change, their task is likely to involve developing a view or 'vision' of what they (and others involved in the diagnostic process) think the organization ought to look like in the future. If, on the other hand, their role is to implement a vision that is being imposed from elsewhere, their task might be more limited to thinking through and envisioning the likely impact of the change for their part of the organization.

Quality of the vision

The quality of the vision can be affected by those responsible for the diagnosis. They need the knowledge and experience – including knowledge of the local situation – to diagnose all the issues and envision an end state that will be acceptable to all key stakeholders. This is important because a vision of a more desirable future state can provide a focus for attention and action. It can mobilize energy and effort. Locke and Latham (1984) argue that people are motivated to achieve goals to which they are committed and they try harder and are less willing to give up when goals are clear and realistic.

Despite the obvious importance of the vision, those leading the change sometimes have a vested interest in a particular outcome, or they lock on to the first vision they generate, and in so doing lock out the possibility of considering alternatives. The first vision may not be the best, either in terms of the desirability of the envisioned end state or its power to motive those who need to be engaged with the change, for example the flawed vision championed by the new CEO of Direct Banking in Example 1.5.

The way the diagnostic stage is managed can affect whether or not the need for change is translated into a desire for change. Schein (1996) argues that organizational members are more likely to be motivated to let go of the status quo and seek a more desirable state if:

- the diagnostic process disconfirms their view that all is well with the existing state of affairs
- this challenge produces a sufficient level of anxiety to motivate organizational members to search for new possibilities

- the vision of what might be offers sufficient promise to make the effort of changing worthwhile.

Summarizing the essence of these three points, Schein argues that unless the unfreezing process offers a promise of psychological safety, with either some benefit or, at worst, a minimal threat to their wellbeing, any disconfirmation provided by the diagnostic phase will be denied or defended against and those involved will not be motivated to change.

This discussion of how diagnosis can help unfreeze a situation and help create a readiness for change illustrates a point made earlier that the boundaries between the stages presented in Figure 2.2 are not clear-cut. Diagnosis has a role to play in the recognition of problems and opportunities and later in the process, implementation and reviewing change can also contribute to an unfolding diagnosis as new problems and opportunities are identified.

Some questions that might help leaders reflect on how they are managing this stage of the process include:

- Who does the diagnosing: senior managers, consultants or those who will be responsible for making the change work?
- Are leaders willing to accept new data or do they only attend to data that defend the status quo or support their preconceived view?
- Does the diagnosis create a realistic and inspiring vision that will motivate others and help direct the change effort?

Planning and preparing for change

The planning stage is concerned with working out and articulating how the change goals will be achieved. Those leading the change sometimes give insufficient attention to this. When discussing Lewin's contribution to change management, Burnes (2004a) observes that, following unfreezing, change managers need to explore possibilities for movement by reviewing all the driving and restraining forces at work. This further emphasizes the point that, to some extent, diagnosis is embedded in every step of the change process.

Choice of the overall change strategy, whether push, pull or a blend of both, is important because it can have a big impact on the outcome of the change. Consideration also needs to be given to the types of interventions that will be most effective. Chapter 16 presents a typology of interventions and Chapters 17–23 provide a detailed review of selected examples. Attention also needs to be given to the many details that will have to be attended to in order to achieve the desired change. There will be different lead times associated with the various tasks, interdependencies between them and resource and other constraints. Poor decisions at this stage can have implications later on. For example, in those situations where key resources are scarce, an early decision to commit resources to one course of action may limit the possibility of switching direction later because, once committed, the resources might not be reusable for another purpose.

It is possible to engage in more detailed planning when the type of change in question is what is sometimes referred to as a 'blueprint' change. Blueprint changes are those where the end point can be specified in advance. Typical examples of a blueprint change include relocation, computerization of a business process, or the introduction of a new appraisal or grading system. In these circumstances, it is easier to anticipate what needs to be done, and the management of change can be viewed from the perspective of a 'planned change' that involves a predetermined linear process – following step by step the successive stages in the model presented in Figure 2.2.

Often, however, it is not possible to specify the end point in advance of implementation. While a need for change might be recognized, for example because the organization is losing market share or failing to innovate as fast as its competitors, it may be less obvious what needs to be done to improve matters. There may be a broadly defined goal and a direction for change, for example improving competitiveness, but it may not be possible to provide a detailed specification of what this end state will look like or what needs to be done to achieve it. In some situations, it may not even be helpful to think in terms of specific end states, because the rate of change in the operating environment may be such that the precise definition of a desirable end state may be subject to constant revision. In these circumstances, a blueprint approach to change is inappropriate. Planning needs to be viewed as a more open-ended, iterative process that emerges and evolves over time. As plans are implemented, they are tested before further steps are planned.

It is important that change managers do not simply view planning from a technical perspective. Careful attention also needs to be given to people issues. Plans need to address the extent to which people are ready for and accepting of change and whether the process threatens them in any way.

Some questions that might help leaders reflect on how they are managing this stage of the process include:

- Is the change strategy appropriate, for example push, pull or a blend of both?
- Is it clear what needs to be done?
- Is sufficient thought being given to the longer term implications of decisions?
- Is sufficient attention being given to anticipating how people may react to the change?
- Is it clear what kind of intervention would be most effective?

Implementing change and reviewing progress

Whatever has been planned now needs to be implemented and the focus shifts from planning to action. Often, change plans are not implemented as intended because change managers fail to give sufficient attention to managing the people issues. Even though a change manager may see obvious benefits from the change for the organization as a whole, individual organizational members may see little benefit for themselves and this will affect their motivation to support or resist the change. Careful attention needs to be given to communicating the change, motivating individuals and groups to support the change, and managing stakeholder interests.

Attention also needs to be given to reviewing the change and monitoring progress. Buchanan and Storey (1997) argue that change can involve much backtracking. Burke (2002) echoes this view and argues that the change process is often more like a series of loops rather than a straight line, reflecting the reality that things rarely progress as planned, and even when plans are implemented as intended, there are often unanticipated consequences. Change managers frequently report that they constantly have to 'fix things' to keep the change on track. It was noted above (when discussing planning) that, in some circumstances, change involves taking tentative incremental steps in, what it is hoped is, the right direction and, after each step, reviewing the step itself to establish if it worked and if the direction still holds good. Seeking out and attending to feedback is essential if leaders are to monitor whether the change plan is working.

Change managers need to be alert to the possibility that while planned interventions may be being implemented as intended, they may not be producing the anticipated effect. This could be because of factors such as a lack of commitment and motivation on the part of those immediately affected by the change, reward systems that penalize new behaviour, inflexible organizational structures, a lack of political support from those in a position to sabotage the project, or insufficient resources. It could also be that some of the initial benefits that were derived from early steps in the implementation may evaporate as path-dependent behaviours lead to rigidities that narrow the scope for action. Feedback on how the change is progressing can signal a need to think again about the change plan and the way it is being implemented.

All too often, those leading the change fail to deliberately seek out available feedback and only realize that the change is producing unintended consequences when some third party or unplanned happening draws it to their attention. Example 2.1 illustrates this point.

Example **2.1** *Concrete Flags Ltd*

Concrete Flags Ltd adopted a new business strategy, which involved a shift from manufacturing concrete paving stones (flags) for builders merchants, DIY outlets and garden centres to providing end consumers with their 'dream patio' delivered direct to their home on a pallet. This shift required a new approach to marketing and the design and installation of a more automated production technology.

Before the change the company had manufactured a limited range of concrete flags in batches using a basic process that relied on a large input of low skilled labour. While reliable it was costly, because batch production required the company to hold large inventories of

different flags. The new strategy required the company to develop the capability to manufacture a wider range of concrete flags. Taking into account variations in shape, size, colour and texture, the company aimed to manufacture 150 different products on demand. Managers worked with a supplier to design the new automated production system. The plan was to install and test one machine first and then purchase additional equipment as the new marketing strategy generated additional demand.

The equipment was installed on time and appeared to be performing well, but it was not long before managers became aware that production targets were not being

© STOCKSOLUTIONS/ISTOCKPHOTO.COM

met. They identified the problem as wet concrete sticking in the weigh boxes. The supplier acknowledged a minor design fault that was quickly rectified.

It was while they were modifying the equipment that the supplier discovered, and reported to managers at Concrete Flags, that operators had attempted to keep the machine running by hitting the weigh boxes with a large hammer. It appeared that this crude method of moving wet concrete had worked well enough with the old (less sophisticated and more robust) equipment but it had caused damage to the new machine. This feedback alerted managers to an important misalignment between the new equipment and the operators' knowledge and skills. They responded by arranging a number of training sessions, which led to an immediate improvement in the way they operated and maintained the new equipment.

Within a short while, another problem emerged. Achieving the vision of delivering tailor-made patios-on-pallets direct to end users included providing them with a booklet containing laying instructions. Unfortunately, the importance of this booklet had not been explained to the workers, who still defined their role as making concrete paving stones. On investigation, managers found that the workers regarded inserting the booklet before the pallet was shrink-wrapped as an unnecessary complication. It was

just a bit of paper. When supplies ran out, they had continued to dispatch patios-on-pallets without the laying instructions. Managers had been unaware of this problem until customers began to complain that they had not received the promised booklet.

This feedback led managers to appreciate that while they had given a lot of attention to developing a new marketing strategy and designing and installing the new equipment, they had given relatively little attention to how the change would affect the operators. They had not consulted or reassured the workers about the change. Managers had assumed that they would welcome it, but they were wrong. The operators saw it as a 'management ploy to make money', which threatened their job security. Nobody had informed them that the plan was to purchase additional machines and increase production, thereby safeguarding jobs, in order to satisfy the anticipated growth in demand.

Many of the corrective actions required to keep the change on track had been prompted by unsolicited feedback from the suppliers of new equipment and customers. One of the lessons learned by managers at Concrete Flags was that they could have done much more to communicate the change and deliberately seek out feedback that would have made it easier to monitor how the change was being implemented.

Even when change managers recognize the importance of reviewing and monitoring progress, they might still encounter difficulties because the necessary information is unavailable or difficult to use. One reason for this is the fragmentation of the change process. Clegg and Walsh (2004) cite the example of software design, where the typical process involves stages of strategy, feasibility, conceptual design, detailed design, programming, implementation, use, and maintenance. Each of these stages tends to involve different people who often have different goals and priorities. This fragmentation undermines the feedback process. One group may nudge the project in a particular direction and not recognize a need to inform others about this, or may confront and address a problem without recognizing the implications of their actions for end users. Even when they are aware that others may need to know, they may not always identify who should be informed, and those who are informed may not recognize the significance of what they have been told. Clegg and Walsh observe that this lack of continuity and feedback can make it difficult for those involved in the change process to influence and learn from one another. Chapter 29 considers some to the tools that can help facilitate this review process.

Coordination is important. All those who have a leadership role need to promote alignment and communicate with others in ways that will inspire them to work together to support the change. It is not unusual for 'expert' change agents to decide when and where change is required and to define change objectives without taking into account the concerns of stakeholders or recognizing the ways in which they can contribute to or sabotage the change process.

Some questions that might help leaders reflect on how they are managing this stage of the process include:

- Do change managers communicate a compelling vision and set realistic goals?
- Are stakeholders being managed effectively?
- Is uncertainty managed in a way that maintains commitment?
- Do change managers seek feedback in order to eliminate impediments to implementation?
- Is there sufficient coordination between those involved in implementing the change?

Sustaining change

Lewin (1951) argued that change is all too often short-lived. After a 'shot in the arm', life returns to the way it was before. In his view, it is not enough to think of change in terms of simply reaching a new state. Attention needs to be given to sustaining this new state *for as long as it is beneficial to do so*; this caveat is important because there are circumstances where, because of new developments, it may not be beneficial to continue to maintain a change.

The NHS Modernisation Agency (2002, p. 12) defines a sustained change as one where 'new ways of working and improved outcomes become the norm' and where 'the thinking and attitudes behind them are fundamentally altered and the systems surrounding them are transformed in support'. Sustainability can be affected by many factors. One is the way the whole change process is managed from the beginning. Tough top-down (push) strategies are more likely to foster compliance, which can evaporate when the pressure to maintain the change is eased, whereas more involving (pull) strategies can win a higher level of commitment that is more likely to be sustained.

Another factor is how leaders act after initial change goals have been achieved. Just because a change goal has been achieved and is delivering improved outcomes does not mean that it has become the new norm. Kotter (1995) cautions against declaring victory too soon because he believes that this can kill momentum before the thinking and attitudes required to support the new way of working have been embedded. He also argues that leaders should take every opportunity, post-implementation, to show individuals and groups how their efforts are helping to deliver benefits. He calls for relevant, understandable and focused feedback that organizational members can use to direct their efforts at those things that are really making a difference. Several writers (Beckhard and Harris, 1987; Nadler, 1993) argue that tailored feedback mechanisms not only facilitate monitoring and control during the implementation phase of a change, but can also help to sustain change. Change managers can help to develop this kind of feedback by working with operational managers, who will have ongoing responsibility for day-to-day management once the change has been implemented, to design feedback mechanisms they can use for themselves to monitor and manage the situation over the longer term.

Kotter identifies 'churn' as another factor that can undermine change. This is supported by Buchanan et al. (2007a) who, following extensive research in the UK's

National Health Service (NHS), observed that when leaders had moved on, their successors often wanted to pursue their own agenda and gave priority to different issues. In order to minimize the impact of churn, great care needs to be exercised to ensure that the next generation of leaders continues to support the new approach. However, even when leaders remain, turnover can still be a problem if some of the other people who have been involved in the change leave and their knowledge and experience of the new ways of working is lost. Buchanan et al. (2007b) suggest that this problem can be exacerbated when replacements import attitudes and work habits that are incongruent with the change. Proper attention to selection and induction can help in these circumstances.

Some questions that might help leaders reflect on how they are managing this stage of the process include:

- Do change managers pursue a change strategy that wins long-term commitment?
- Do they reinforce changes post-implementation?
- Do they avoid declaring victory too soon?
- Is sufficient attention given to managing the consequences of churn?

Leading and managing the people issues

Those leading change sometimes approach issues when developing and implementing plans for change from a purely technical perspective and give insufficient attention to what some refer to as the 'softer' people issues, such as:

- different goals and priorities
- internal politics and the power of stakeholders to affect outcomes
- the way leaders relate with the intended recipients of change
- communication
- trust
- motivation and commitment
- support for those who will be affected by the change.

The Triumph case in the Introduction to Part IV provides a good example of how issues such as communication, motivation and stakeholder management can affect the success of a change project, in this case the sourcing of components from cost-competitive countries.

The issues presented in Figure 2.2 above, such as recognizing the need for change, diagnosing what needs to be changed, and developing plans for change, are not benign activities. Stakeholders may resist any attempt to even consider the possibility that change might be required, fail to cooperate with managers in the formulation of plans for change, and work hard to block a change that is being implemented. Nadler (1987, 1993) refers to the importance of shaping the political dynamics of change and motivating constructive behaviour, an issue that is addressed in Chapter 10.

Some questions that might help those who are leading the change reflect on how they are managing this aspect of the change process include:

- Do leaders empathize with others and understand how they might react to the possibility of change?
- Do they act in ways that will promote trust and win commitment?
- Do they identify and engage those individuals and groups who can affect the success of the change?

- Are they good communicators?
- Do they empower others to contribute to the change?
- Do they support those who are threatened by the change?

Learning

Effective leaders are those who can learn from their experience and utilize this learning to modify their behaviour in order to improve their performance. Argyris and Schön (1978) distinguish between single-loop and double-loop learning.

Single-loop learning

Single-loop learning (Figure 2.3) occurs when leaders focus their attention on detecting errors and acting on this feedback to modify their and other people's behaviour. It promotes continuous improvement based on an extrapolation of past trends. This can be effective over the short and longer term but it may not be path breaking because it may produce little change in the underlying beliefs and assumptions that guide behaviour. New ways of acting are likely to be bound by current thinking and known routines.

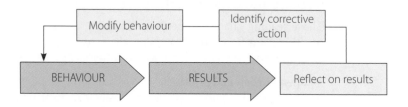

Figure **2.3** *Single-loop learning*

When leaders' behaviour produces positive feedback, through continuous improvement, existing practices tend to be reinforced. A leader under pressure to deliver better margins might seek ways of doing things more efficiently by improving the fit between the internal elements of the organization. For example, training might be identified as a way of improving the fit between workers' skills and the skills they need to operate the existing manufacturing system efficiently, and a reconfiguration of departmental structures might be seen as a way of eliminating jurisdictional disputes that disrupt the manufacturing process. While these and similar actions can deliver efficiencies, it is also possible that short-term gains might be eroded if leaders' actions lock the system into a path that involves producing the same products (albeit more efficiently) using existing technologies for customers in traditional markets and lock out the possibility of acting in ways that can facilitate the exploitation of new opportunities as and when they arise.

Double-loop learning

Double-loop learning (Figure 2.4) occurs when leaders are able to think outside the box by reflecting on outcomes, identifying and challenging the assumptions and beliefs that underpinned the decisions and actions that led to these outcomes, and, where appropriate, revising their assumptions in ways that open the possibility of experimenting with new ways of behaving.

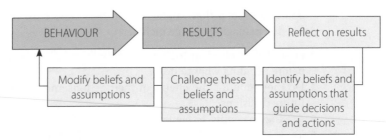

Figure **2.4** *Double-loop learning*

For example, at a strategic level, leaders at the Midland Bank in the UK were the first to challenge the business model that assumed that the only way to relate to retail customers was via an expensive branch network, and this radical thinking led to the launch of First Direct, the first telephone bank.

At a less strategic level, after reflecting on how people reacted to the introduction of a new performance management system, leaders might attempt to empathize with those affected and understand why they resisted the change. Viewed from this perspective, leaders might realize that their leadership style could be part of the problem and this might prompt them to challenge some of the assumptions they make about the motivation and commitment of subordinates. Covey (1992) contends that while leaders think they are objective and see things as they are, they actually see what they have been conditioned to see. In the performance management example, a newly appointed HR director might have drawn on past experience in a different organization and not recognized how assumptions based on this experience are not valid in the current situation. Covey (1992, p. 29) argues that:

> The more aware we are of our basic paradigms, maps or assumptions, and the extent to which we have been influenced by our experience, the more we can take responsibility for those paradigms, examine them, test them against reality, listen to others and be open to their perceptions, thereby getting a larger picture and a far more objective view.

One area that often escapes attention is the assumptions that leaders make about time. Huy (2001) argues that leaders' time perspective affects how they prioritize issues, allocate resources and the urgency they attribute to activities. Leaders who have a short time perspective are more likely to choose actions that produce immediate, visible results and pay less attention to longer term outcomes, whereas leaders with a longer time perspective are more likely to work towards achieving long-term, lasting outcomes. It is possible that when leaders are unaware that they have a short time perspective, they will be more vulnerable to path dependencies (discussed in Chapter 1) that can lead to inefficiencies over the longer term.

Double-loop learning challenges accepted ways of thinking and behaving and provides a new understanding of situations and events. This understanding can offer leaders the possibility of avoiding inefficient path dependencies and the need to invest energy and resources to counter negative reactions and unnecessary resistance from other stakeholders. (Single- and double-loop learning are examined in more detail in Chapter 29.)

Some questions that might help leaders reflect on how they learn from the process of managing change include:

- Do those involved in the change anticipate how others will respond to events before deciding what to do?
- Do they monitor the effects of their actions and use this information to guide future decisions?
- Are they receptive to feedback from others?
- To what extent do they view their own and others' mistakes as opportunities for learning?
- Do they attempt to identify and challenge the assumptions that underpin their behaviour?
- Are they aware of how decisions that produce positive outcomes in the short term may undermine performance over the long term?

Improving leader performance

It has been argued that leaders can learn to be more effective if they step back and monitor what is going on – paying particular attention to how others react to what they do and how their decisions impact immediate and longer term outcomes – and use these observations to guide their behaviour. But all too often this does not happen, because leaders:

- are so bound up in a frenetic range of activities that they have little time or no opportunity for observation and reflection
- are so committed to a course of action that they fail to recognize evidence that challenges their worldview
- harbour beliefs about the competence and motives of others that makes it easy for them to dismiss their feedback
- are insulated from information about the impact of their decisions by organizational structures, policies and management practices that impede upward communication and foster a climate of organizational silence (see Morrison and Milliken, 2000)
- are so bound up in and entrapped by a path that progressively limits their scope for decision making that they become path dependent to the exclusion of path-breaking behaviour, because they are too involved to adopt an outward-looking perspective.

Leaders need to be aware that these barriers can make it difficult for them to disengage from an immediate 'doing' mode; they need to work hard to adopt an 'observing' mode and bring a critical perspective to bear on their everyday practice.

When leadership is viewed as a process and when events, decisions, actions and reactions are seen to be connected, leaders are more likely to be able to take action and intervene in ways that can break inefficient patterns and move the change process in a direction that has a higher probability of delivering superior outcomes.

Summary

This chapter has built on the ideas discussed in Chapter 1 and presented a process model of change that draws on teleological and dialectical theories. It provided a conceptual framework that those leading change can use to identify the issues they need to address if they are to secure desired outcomes. It can also be used to identify the kinds of questions that will help them reflect on how well they are doing and what else they could do to improve performance.

The model conceptualizes the management of change as a purposeful, constructed but often contested process that involves attending to seven core activities:

1 recognizing the need for change and starting the change process
2 diagnosing what needs to be changed and formulating a vision of a preferred future state
3 planning how to intervene in order to achieve the desired change
4 implementing plans and reviewing progress
5 sustaining the change
6 leading and managing the people issues
7 learning.

These activities are presented as separate elements of the change process because the decisions and actions associated with them tend to dominate at different points in the process and there is a logical sequence connecting them. However, in practice, the boundaries are not always clear-cut. For example, the recognition of a need for change is based on an initial diagnosis of the situation, and attempts to implement plans for change that lead to unintended consequences also contribute to an unfolding diagnosis. Also, the sequence of the elements specified in the model is not linear. The change process is often iterative, in the sense that some issues (such as diagnosis) can be addressed more than once. Also, some issues can be addressed simultaneously with others. For example, learning can occur at any or every point in the process and people issues need to be addressed throughout. This said, all the activities, such as diagnosis, planning and implementing, are important and need to be attended to by those leading a change.

When managing change is viewed as a process and when events, decisions, actions and reactions are seen to be connected, those leading the change are more likely to be able to take action and intervene in ways that can break inefficient patterns and move the change process in a direction that is more likely to deliver superior outcomes.

Figure 2.5 summarizes the model, displays the seven elements of the process, and highlights examples of questions that those leading the change might consider in order to help them reflect on how well they are doing and what they could do to improve their performance. The way in which Chapters 1–29 relate to this model is presented in the Introduction to Part I.

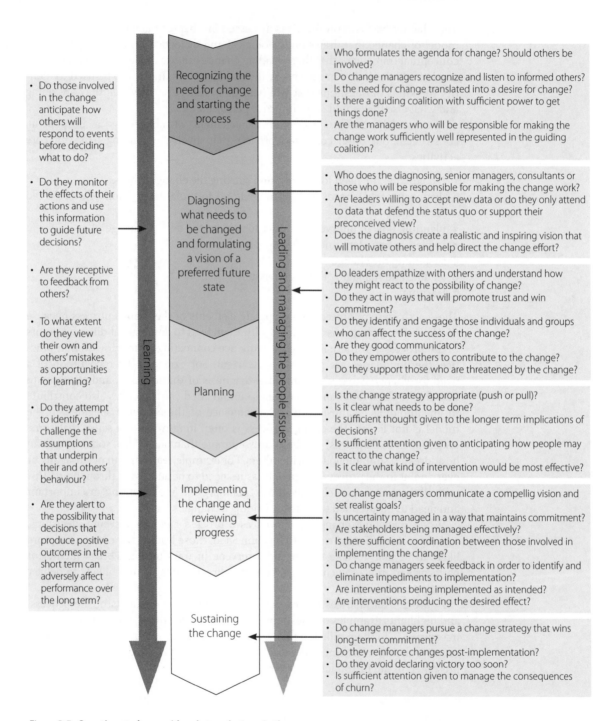

Figure **2.5** *Questions to be considered at each stage in the process*

References

Argyris, C. and Schön, D. (1978) *Organizational Learning*. London: Addison-Wesley.

Beckhard, R. and Harris, R. (1987) *Organizational Transitions: Managing Complex Change* (2nd edn). Reading, MA: Addison-Wesley.

Buchanan, D.A., Fitzgerald, L. and Ketley, D. (eds) (2007a) *The Sustainability and Spread of Organizational Change*. London: Routledge.

Buchanan, D.A., Fitzgerald, L. and Ketley, D. (2007b) Sustaining change and avoiding containment: Practice and policy. In D.A. Buchanan, L. Fitzgerald and D. Ketley (eds) *The Sustainability and Spread of Organizational Change*. London: Routledge.

Buchanan, D.A. and Storey, J. (1997) Role taking and role switching in organizational change: The four pluralities. In I. McLoughlin and M. Harris (eds) *Innovation, Organisational Change and Technology*. London: International Thompson.

Burke, W.W. (2002) *Organization Change: Theory and Practice*. Thousand Oaks, CA: Sage.

Burnes, B. (2004a) Kurt Lewin and the planned approach to change: A re-appraisal, *Journal of Management Studies*, 41(6): 977–1002.

Burnes, B. (2004b) Kurt Lewin and complexity theory: Back to the future?, *Journal of Change Management*, 4(4): 309–25.

Clegg, C.W. (2000) Sociotechnical principles for system design, *Applied Ergonomics*, 31: 463–77.

Clegg, C.W. and Walsh, S. (2004) Change management: Time for change, *European Journal of Work and Organization Psychology*, 13(2): 217–39.

Covey, S.R. (1992) *The 7 Habits of Highly Effective People: Powerful Lessons in Personal Change*. London: Simon & Schuster.

Dawson, P. (2003) *Organisational Change: A Processual Approach*. London: Chapman.

Egan, G. (1996) *Change Agent Skills B: Managing Innovation and Change*. Englewood Cliffs, NJ: Prentice Hall.

Ford, W.M. and Greer, B.M. (2006) Profiling change: An empirical study of change process patterns, *Journal of Applied Behavioral Science*, 42(4): 420–46.

Hendry, C. (1996) Understanding and creating whole organisational change through learning theory, *Human Relations*, 48(5): 621–41.

Huy, Q.N. (2001) Time, temporal stability and planned change, *Academy of Management Review*, 26(4): 601–23.

Kantor, R.M., Stein, B.A. and Jick, T.D. (1992) *The Challenge of Organizational Change*. New York: Free Press.

Kotter, J.P. (1995) Leading change: Why transformation efforts fail, *Harvard Business Review*, 73(2): 59–67.

Lewin, K. (1947) New frontiers in group dynamics. In D. Cartwright (ed.) (1952) *Field Theory in Social Science*. London: Social Science Paperbacks.

Lewin, K. (1951) *Field Theory in Social Science*. New York: Harper & Row.

Lippet, R., Watson, J. and Wesley, B. (1958) *The Dynamics of Planned Change*. New York: Harcourt Brace, Jovanovich.

Locke, E.A. and Latham, G.P. (1984) *Goal Setting: A Motivational Technique that Works*. Englewood Cliffs, NJ: Prentice Hall.

Morrison, E.W. and Milliken, F.J. (2000) Organizational silence: A barrier to change and development in a pluralistic world, *Academy of Management Review*, 25(4): 706–25.

Nadler, D.A. (1987) The effective management of organizational change. In J.W. Lorsch (ed.) *Handbook of Organizational Behaviour*. Englewood Cliffs, NJ: Prentice Hall.

Nadler, D.A. (1993) *Feedback and Organizational Development: Using Data Based Methods*. Reading, MA: Addison-Wesley.

NHS Modernisation Agency (2002) *Improvement Leaders' Guide to Sustainability and Spread.* Ipswich: Ancient House Printing Group.

Schein, E.H. (1996) Kurt Lewin's change theory in the field and in the classroom: Notes towards a model of management learning, *Systems Practice*, 9(1): 27–47.

➕   *Visit* **www.palgrave.com/companion/hayes-change-management4** *for further learning resources*

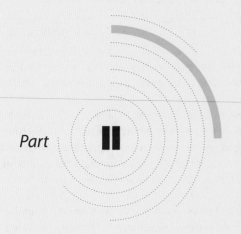

RECOGNIZING THE NEED FOR CHANGE AND STARTING THE CHANGE PROCESS

Introduction to Part **II**

Part II takes a closer look at recognizing the need for change and starting the change process.

Chapter **3** *Patterns of change*

In order to survive and prosper, all systems, whether they are work groups or entire organizations, need to recognize and respond to changes that can affect the supply of inputs or the demand for outputs. Some systems are much better at this than others. They are proactive and search out potential threats and opportunities. They prepare for destabilizing events that might occur, and they actively seek out possibilities to initiate changes that could provide a competitive advantage. Others are much more reactive and only respond when there is a clear and pressing need to respond.

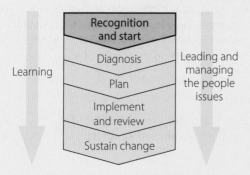

Until recently, almost all received models of change were incremental and cumulative. These models assume that organizations adapt to opportunities and threats by engaging in a process of continuous incremental change. The gradualist paradigm describes this response. Many argue that continuous adaptation is the most effective way of changing because it helps the organization maintain alignment with its (changing) external environment, but, in reality, this pattern of change is the exception rather than the norm. The way most organizations respond to changing circumstances is best described by the punctuated equilibrium paradigm.

The essence of punctuated equilibrium is that systems evolve through the alternation of periods of equilibrium, in which persistent 'deep structures' only permit limited incremental change, and periods of revolution, in which these deep structures are fundamentally altered. The earlier the need for change is recognized, the more options managers have when deciding how to respond. When they are forced to react to an urgent and pressing need for change, they are relatively constrained in what they can do.

Four types of change, depending on whether it is reactive or proactive and incremental or continuous, are identified and their implications for change management practice are discussed.

Chapter 4 *Recognizing a need or opportunity for change*

Chapter 4 reviews a range of external and internal sources of change and explores some of the issues that affect an organization's ability to recognize the opportunity or need for change. Sources of change are considered first. The PEST acronym and Stebel's cycle of competitive behaviour are introduced as tools that can help identify external sources of change, and Greiner's organizational life cycle is presented as a useful model that highlights internal sources.

Sensing a need for change and formulating a change agenda begin when individuals notice and respond to what they perceive to be significant external or organizational events. Discrepancies between actual and desired levels of performance signal a need for change but problems can arise when discrepancies are not recognized because attention is restricted to a narrow range of indicators. Some of the indicators that need to be monitored are reviewed.

The final part of the chapter focuses attention on issues that can affect the formulation of the agenda for change. While formulating the change agenda is often restricted to senior managers, people located at multiple levels in the hierarchy may be well placed to make a valuable input. However, their effort to contribute may not be sufficient to guarantee that the organization will address the issues they identify as important.

Chapter 5 *Starting the change*

Chapter 5 considers some of the issues associated with starting the change process. Most important is translating the need for change into a desire for change. Organizational members are not powerless pawns, unable to affect change, but independent actors able to intervene in ways that can make an important difference. To do this, they need confidence in their own ability to affect outcomes, the motivation to pursue change, concepts and theories that will help them understand and manage the change process, and a range of change management skills.

A second issue that must be addressed is deciding, at least in the first instance, who will lead the change. The change agent could be an insider, a member of the system or subsystem that is the target for change, or an outsider. There is some evidence suggesting that change efforts are most successful when led (pulled) by users rather than (pushed) by technical experts. The impact of confidence and trust on the quality of the change relationship is also considered.

Chapter 6 *Building change relationships*

Chapter 6 examines the importance of building effective relationships between those leading and those involved in the change. The strengths and weaknesses of five different modes of facilitating change are reviewed:

1 *Advising:* involves change agents drawing on their own knowledge and experience and telling clients what they should do to resolve their problem.
2 *Supporting:* involves listening empathetically; withholding judgement and helping clients to express the feelings and emotions that impede clear and objective thinking about their problem. The prime focus is the client rather than the problem.
3 *Theorizing:* involves the change agent presenting others with a theory relevant to their problem and helping them to use the theory to understand the problem and plan remedial action.
4 *Challenging:* involves confronting the foundations of people's thinking in order to identify beliefs and values that may be distorting the way they view the situation.

5 *Information gathering:* involves helping others collect data they can use to evaluate and reinterpret the situation.

☑ *Exercise* **Part II** *Useful questions for reviewing your approach to recognizing the need for change and starting the change process*

In Chapter 2, after discussing each stage in the process model of change management, your attention was drawn to a number of questions that might help you assess how well a change is being (or was) managed. All these questions are summarized in Figure 2.5 and the questions relating to recognizing the need for change and starting the change process are listed below:

- Who formulates the agenda for change? Should others be involved?
- Do change managers recognize and listen to informed others?
- Is the need for change translated into a desire for change?
- Is there a guiding coalition with sufficient power to get things done?
- Are those who will be responsible for making the change work sufficiently well represented in the guiding coalition?

Reflect on and review these questions and, after reading the four chapters in Part II, revise this list and generate your own set of useful questions that you might find it helpful to refer to when you are leading a change.

Chapter **3**   **Patterns of change**

Open systems theory (discussed in Chapter 1) provides a useful conceptual framework for viewing organizations as a system of interrelated components that transact with a larger environment. Irrespective of whether the focal system is a work group, department or organization, it is embedded within a larger system and is dependent on this larger system (its external environment) for the resources, information and feedback it requires in order to survive. In its simplest form, an organization can be portrayed as an open system that actively relates with its environment, receiving various inputs that it transforms and exports as outputs (Figure 3.1). In the case of an organization that produces goods or services for external customers, the revenue generated from the sale of these outputs may be used to fund the acquisition of new inputs, such as labour, raw materials, equipment and facilities, which can then be used to produce more outputs. Feedback from customers and other external stakeholders can signal a need to modify the way it produces the goods and services it exports, or a need to develop new products to satisfy changes in the marketplace, and these changes can affect the organization's requirement for inputs from the environment. Changes in the price and availability of inputs can also affect an organization's strategy.

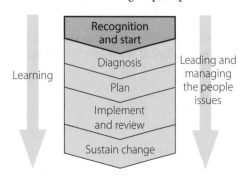

Most organizations operate within a dynamic environment and to prosper in this changing world they need to be aware of and respond to emerging opportunities and threats. Example 1.3 on Nokia highlights the consequence of failing to recognize important shifts in the external environment.

This chapter examines how an organization can respond to opportunities and threats. It is argued that the ideal response is a continuous stream of incremental adaptations that ensure that the organization is always aligned with its environment, but in reality this is the exception. The rule is that, because of internal forces

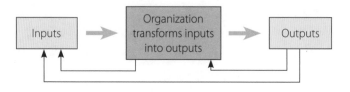

Figure **3.1** *An organization transacting with its environment*

that promote inertia, many organizations are slow to adapt to changing circumstances. The result is strategic drift and a growing misalignment with their external environment that eventually forces them to engage is some form of radical change.

Adapting to change: the gradualist paradigm

The gradualist paradigm posits that organizations adapt to opportunities and threats by engaging in a process of continuous incremental change. Their response is evolving and, over time, these continuous changes cumulate to transform the organization (Figure 3.2).

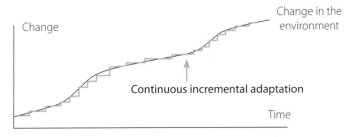

Figure **3.2** *The gradualist paradigm: continuous evolutionary change*

Brown and Eisenhardt (1997) support this view and cite companies such as Intel, Walmart, 3M, HP and Gillette, suggesting that for them the ability to change rapidly and continuously is not just a core competence but is at the heart of their cultures. They refer to Burgelman (1991) and Chakravarthy (1997), who suggest that continuous change is often played out through product innovation as companies change and sometimes transform through a process of continually altering their products. HP is identified as a classic case. The company changed from an instruments company to a computer firm through rapid, continuous product innovation, rather than through a sudden discontinuous change.

Continuous change, when it occurs, involves constant updating of work processes and social practices. Weick and Quinn (1999) argue that this leads to new patterns in how an organization organizes itself in the absence of a priori intentions on the part of some change agent. It is emergent, in the sense that there is no deliberate orchestration of change. It is continuous and is the outcome of the everyday process of management. They cite Orlikowski (1996), who suggests that continuous change involves individuals and groups accommodating and experimenting with everyday contingencies, breakdowns, exceptions, opportunities and unintended consequences, and repeating, sharing and amplifying them to produce perceptible and striking changes.

Brown and Eisenhardt (1997) studied product innovation in six firms in the computer industry at a time of rapid product development associated with the Pentium processor, multimedia, the internet and the convergence of telephony with consumer electronics. Three of their case studies related to firms with a record of successful product innovation and business performance and three related to firms with a relatively poor record of developing multi-product portfolios. They identified three characteristics of the firms that were able to manage change as a continuous process of adjustment: semi-structures that facilitated improvisation, links in time that facilitated learning, and sequenced steps for managing transitions.

Weick and Quinn (1999) echo these findings and observe that the distinctive quality of continuous change is the idea that small continuous adjustments, created simultaneously across units, can cumulate and create substantial change. They describe the three related processes associated with continuous change as improvisation, translation and learning:

- *Improvising:* facilitates the modification of work practices through mutual adjustments in which the time gap between planning and implementing narrows towards the point where planning (composition) converges with implementation (execution).
- *Translation:* refers to the continuous adaptation and editing of ideas as they travel through the organization.
- *Learning:* involves the continuous revision of shared mental models, which facilitates a change in the organization's ability to be responsive.

Weick and Quinn (1999, p. 372) suggest that:

> organizations produce continuous change by means of repeated acts of improvisation involving simultaneous composition and execution, repeated acts of translation that convert ideas into useful artifacts that fit purposes at hand, or repeated acts of learning that enlarge, strengthen, or shrink the repertoire of responses.

While Burke (2002) accepts the possibility that more that 95 per cent of organizational changes are, in some way, evolutionary and gradually unfold over time in response to changing circumstances, he challenges Orlikowski's assumption that a continuous stream of incremental changes can lead to fundamental change. Burke (2002, p. 69) asserts that most organizations require some kind of discontinuous 'jolt' to the system to overcome the inertia that limits change:

> Organisation change does occur with continuous attention and effort, but it is unlikely that fundamental change in the deep structure of the organization would happen.

The punctuated equilibrium paradigm: an alternative view of how organizations change

The essence of the punctuated equilibrium paradigm is that systems (organizations) evolve through the alternation of periods of equilibrium, in which persistent 'deep structures' only permit limited incremental change, and periods of revolution, in which these deep structures are fundamentally altered (Figure 3.3). This pattern of change is very different to that presented by the gradualist paradigm, which argues that organizations can be fundamentally changed by a continuous stream of gradual adaptations.

Gould (1978) was one of the first to challenge the notion of incremental, cumulative change. He is a natural historian with an interest in Darwin's theory of evolution. Traditionalists assert that evolution involves a slow stream of small changes (mutations) that are continuously being shaped over time by environmental selection. While Gould accepts the principle of natural selection, he rejects the proposi-

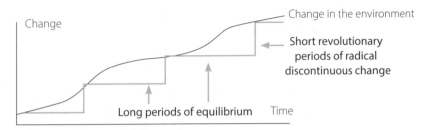

Figure **3.3** *Punctuated equilibrium*

tion that change is gradual and continuous. Gould (1978, p. 15) asserts that the evidence points to 'a world punctuated with periods of mass extinction and rapid origination among long stretches of relative tranquility'. Some of his essays focus on the two greatest 'punctuations'. After 4 billion years of almost no change, there was the Cambrian explosion of life (about 600 million years ago) and, after another longish period of very slow change, the Permian extinction wiped out half the families of marine invertebrates (225 million years ago).

Gersick (1991) has studied models of change in six domains – individual change, group development, organization development, history of science, biological evolution, and physical science – and found support for the punctuated equilibrium paradigm in every one. According to Gersick (1991, p. 12), the paradigm has the following components: 'relatively long periods of stability (equilibrium), punctuated by compact periods of qualitative, metamorphic change (revolution)'. Gersick (1991, p. 12) goes on to assert that in all the models she studied across the six domains:

> the relationship of these two modes is explained through the construct of a highly durable underlying order or deep structure. This deep structure is what persists and limits change during equilibrium periods and is what disassembles, reconfigures, and enforces wholesale transformation during revolutionary periods.

Deep structure

Gersick (1991, p. 16) refers to 'deep structure' as the fundamental choices an organization makes that determine the basic activity patterns that maintain its existence. She argues that deep structures are highly stable because the trail of choices made by a system (organization) rule out many options and rule in those that dependent on each other – 'early steps in the decision tree are the most fateful'. She also argues that the activity patterns of a system's deep structure reinforce the system as a whole through mutual feedback loops. This argument is similar to that advanced by Sydow et al. (2009) (see Chapter 1), which suggests that self-reinforcing sequences lead to the development of a pattern of events, decisions and actions that begin to dominate and divert attention away from alternative ways forward.

Tushman and Romanelli (1985) identify five key domains of organizational activity that might be viewed as representing an organization's deep structure. These are organizational culture, strategy, structure, power distribution, and control systems. Romanelli and Tushman (1994) assert that it takes a revolution to alter a system of interrelated organizational parts when it is maintained by mutual dependencies among the parts, and when competitive, regulatory and technological systems outside the organization reinforce the legitimacy of the managerial choices that produced the parts.

Greenwood and Hinings (1996) offer a slightly different perspective based on neo-institutional theory, but the core argument is the same; there is a force for inertia that limits the possibility for incremental change, and this resistance to change will be strongest when there is a network of tightly coupled mutual dependencies. Greenwood and Hinings' (1996, p. 1023) argument is that a major source of resistance to change stems from the 'normative embeddedness of an organization within its institutional context'. Organizations must accommodate institutional expectations in order to survive. They illustrate this point with reference to the way institutional context has influenced the structure and governance of accounting firms. They were (and most still are) organized as professional partnerships, not because that form of governance facilitated efficient and effective task performance, but because it was defined as the appropriate way of organizing the conduct of accounting work.

The parameters offered by such an archetypal template provide the context for convergent change. Greenwood and Hinings (1996, p. 1025) suggest, for example, that an accounting firm operating as a professional partnership could, as it grows, introduce some form of representative democracy in place of the traditional, broadly based democratic governance. This kind of incremental change could be achieved because it is perceived to be consistent with prevailing core ideas and values. However, a move towards a more a bureaucratic form of authority and governance might encounter strong resistance because it is perceived to be inconsistent with the prevailing template. Such a radical change would involve the organization moving from one template to another.

These templates work in the same way as Gersick's deep structures. However, the degree of embeddedness and strength of these templates may vary between sectors, and this will affect the power of the template to limit the possibility for incremental cumulative change in any particular organization. In the case of the accounting profession, the partnership organizational form, with its commitment to independence, autonomy and responsible conduct, is supported by a strong network of reciprocal exchanges between professional associations, universities, state agencies and accounting firms. The outcome is a situation where individual accounting firms are tightly coupled to the prevailing archetypal template. Greenwood and Hinings (1996) argue that radical change in tightly coupled fields will be unusual, but if it does happen, it will not be a gradual process. It is more likely to take the form of a discontinuous revolutionary change. However, in loosely coupled fields, it will be easier to achieve radical change through a process of continuous adjustment that unfolds over a period of time. But loose coupling can contain change. Weick and Quinn (1999) suggest that when interdependencies are loose, continuous adjustments can be confined within subunits and remain as pockets of innovation and will not cumulate to produce fundamental change across the organization. This problem is discussed in more detail in Chapter 28.

Equilibrium periods

Gersick (1991, p. 16) introduces the analogy of a playing field and the rules of the game to describe an organization's deep structure, and the game in play to describe activity during an equilibrium period. How a game of football is played may change over the course of a match, but there is a consistency determined by the nature of the playing field and the rules of the game. The coach and the players can intervene and make changes that will affect team performance, but they cannot intervene to change the nature of the playing field or the rules of the game (the deep structure). In terms of organizational change, during periods of equilibrium, change agents can intervene and make incremental adjustments in response to internal or external perturbations, but these interventions will not fundamentally affect the organization's deep structure.

According to the punctuated equilibrium paradigm, in equilibrium periods, organizations are resistant to change because of forces of inertia that work to maintain the status quo. Gersick argues that so long as the deep structure is intact, it creates a strong inertia to prevent the system from generating alternatives outside its own boundaries. Furthermore, these forces for inertia can pull any deviations that do occur back into line. Gersick (1991) identifies three sources of inertia: cognitive frameworks (similar to the cognitive biases discussed in Chapter 1), motivation (similar to the increasing returns and commitments to past decisions also discussed in Chapter 1) and obligations.

Organizational members often develop shared cognitive frameworks and mental models that influence the way they interpret reality and learn. Shared mental models can restrict attention to thinking 'within the frame'. With regard to change, attention may be restricted to searching for ways of doing things better. In periods of equilibrium, assumptions about the organization's theory of business (Drucker, 1994) often go unchallenged and organizational members fail to give sufficient attention to the possibility of doing things differently or even doing different things. (See Hodgkinson and Healey, 2008, for details of studies that have considered the role of mental representations in organizational inertia and strategic adaptation.)

Motivational barriers to change are often related to the fear of loss, especially with regard to the sunk costs incurred during periods of equilibrium (see, for example, the discussion of set-up costs and learning in Chapter 1). Gersick (1991, p. 18) refers to the fear of losing control over one's situation if the equilibrium ends and argues that this contributes heavily to the human motivation to avoid significant system change. Thaler and Sunstein (2009) draw on the work of Samuelson and Zeckhauser (1988) to argue that for lots of reasons people prefer to stick with their current situation.

Obligations can also limit change. Tushman and Romanelli (1985, p. 177) note that even if a system can overcome its own cognitive and motivational barriers against realizing a need for change, the networks of interdependent resource relationships, such as relationships with suppliers, and value commitments generated by its structure will often prevent it being able to achieve the required change. This view, at least in part, adds support to Greenwood and Hining's (1996) proposition that the normative embeddedness of an organization can limit change.

Episodes of discontinuous change occur when inertia, that is, the inability of organizations to change as rapidly as their environment, triggers some form of revolutionary transformation.

Revolutionary periods

Gersick (1991) asserts that the definitive element of the punctuated equilibrium paradigm is that organizations do not shift from one 'kind of game' to another through incremental steps. According to Romanelli and Tushman (1994), this is because resistance to change prevents small changes in organizational units from taking hold and substantially influencing activities in related subunits. Consequently, small changes do not accumulate incrementally to transform the organization.

Weick and Quinn (1999) note that punctuated equilibrium theorists posit that episodes of revolutionary change occur during periods of divergence, when there is a growing misalignment between an organization's deep structure and perceived environmental demands. They report that the metaphor of the firm implied by episodic change is an organization that comprises a set of interdependencies that converge and tighten (become more closely aligned) as short-term adaptations are pursued in order to achieve higher levels of efficiency. This focus on internal alignment deflects attention away from the need to maintain alignment with the external environment and, consequently, the organization is slow to adapt to environmental change. Inertia maintains the state that Lewin (1947) described as stable, quasi-stationary equilibrium until misalignment reaches the point where major changes are provoked. The only way forward is for the organization to transform itself. Gersick (1991, p. 19) argues that the transformation of deep structures can only occur through a process of wholesale upheaval:

> According to this logic, the deep structures must first be dismantled, leaving the system temporarily disorganized, in order for any fundamental change to be accomplished. Next, a subset of the system's old pieces, along with some new pieces, can be put back together into a new configuration, which operates according to a new set of rules.

This process of revolutionary change and organizational transformation provides the basis for a new state of equilibrium. However, because of forces of resistance that inhibit continuous adaptation, this new equilibrium gives rise to another period of relative stability that is followed by a further period of revolutionary change. This process continues to unfold as a process of punctuated equilibrium.

Those who subscribe to the punctuated equilibrium paradigm argue that revolutionary episodes may affect a single organization or a whole sector. An example of a whole sector that was faced with the need to change its deep structure is the electricity supply sector in the UK. When the Conservative government decided to privatize the industry, this created a new playing field and a new set of rules for all the utility companies in the sector. Marks & Spencer is an organization that was faced with the need to reinvent itself when, even after a long period of incremental change, it found itself misaligned with its environment and performing less well than other leading retailers (Example 3.1).

Example **3.1** *Marks & Spencer*

Marks & Spencer was founded by Michael Marks as a penny bazaar in Leeds and grew to become a multinational retailer with over 700 stores in the UK and 360 stores spread across 40 other countries worldwide. Up until 1998, the company had enjoyed a long period of uninterrupted growth and financial success. Its core business centred on providing customers with good quality, classic (rather than highly fashionable) and affordable clothing.

At the end of 1998, this pattern of success was dramatically interrupted by a 23 per cent fall in half-year profits. A number of factors contributed to this change in fortunes but the main problem was that the company lost touch with what customers wanted. As the company expanded into overseas markets, it based its operations on the tried-and-tested formula that had worked well in the UK, without paying sufficient attention to local customer requirements. In the UK, the company was slow to recognize and respond to market changes. At the top end, new competitors such as Gap, Next and Oasis began to poach customers by offering them up-to-date fashions at prices that were not too dissimilar for those charged by M&S for their less inspiring classical ranges. At the bottom end, discount stores such as Matalan and supermarkets such as Tesco and Asda (with its highly successful 'George' range) began to make inroads into M&S's market share by offering customers a well-designed range of value-for-money clothing. The *Financial Times* (16 January 1999) reported that M&S had been too complacent and ignored changes in its domestic market, and on 1 November 2000, BBC Two's *The Money Programme* reported a fall in customer satisfaction from 71 per cent in 1995 to 45 per cent in 1999.

Support for the punctuated equilibrium paradigm

Numerous case histories offer support for the punctuated equilibrium paradigm. Pettigrew (1987) reports a study of change in ICI over the period 1969–86. He found that radical periods of change were interspersed with periods of incremental adjustment and that change in core beliefs preceded changes in structure and business strategy. Tushman et al. (1986) examined the development of AT&T, General Radio, Citibank and Prime Computers and observed periods during which organizational systems, structures and strategies converged to be more aligned with the basic mission of these organizations. They also observed that these equilibrium periods were punctuated by brief periods of intense and pervasive change that led to the formulation of new missions and then the initiation of new equilibrium periods. The first direct test of the paradigm was Romanelli and Tushman's (1994) empirical study of microcomputer producers, the key elements of which are summarized in Research report 3.1.

Research report **3.1** *Study of microcomputer producers*

Romanelli, E. and Tushman, M.L. (1994) Organizational transformation as punctuated equilibrium: An empirical test, *Academy of Management Journal*, 37(5): 1141–66.

Hypotheses
According to the punctuated equilibrium model, radical and discontinuous change of all or most organizational activities is necessary to break the grip of strong inertia. This provides the basis of Romanelli and Tushman's first hypothesis:

1 Organizational transformations will most frequently occur in short, discontinuous bursts of change involving most or all key domains of organizational activity.

Resistance to change is critical to punctuated equilibrium theory in that it establishes the key condition that supports revolutionary transformation. Resistance prevents small changes in organizational subunits from taking hold or substantially influencing activities in related subunits. This gives rise to their second hypothesis:

2 Small changes in individual domains of organizational activity will not accumulate incrementally to yield a fundamental transformation.

Their final hypothesis addressed how organizational transformation is stimulated. Since the punctuated equilibrium model posits strong inertia as the common state of organizational affairs, they hypothesized that:

3 Inertia will be broken by a severe crisis in performance, major changes in the organization's environment, and the succession of its chief executive officer (CEO).

Method
Romanelli and Tushman studied the life histories of 25 minicomputer producers founded in the USA between 1967 and 1969. The firms were selected to maximize organizational similarities on dimensions of

organizational age and the environmental characteristics the organizations faced during founding and later in their lives.

Data were collected for all the years of the organizations' lives from a variety of sources, including information required by the Securities and Exchange Commission, annual reports, prospectuses, and industry and business press reports. They found that detailed information about strategies, structures and power distributions was available for all organizations throughout their lives. However, they also found that organizations reported information about cultures and control systems infrequently and inconsistently. Consequently, Romanelli and Tushman dropped the culture and control system domains of activity from further analysis and focused their attention on structure, strategy and power distributions.

Fundamental organizational transformations, which could be either revolutionary or non-revolutionary, were identified as occurring whenever substantial changes were observed in the strategy, structure and power distribution domains of organizational activity. Revolutionary transformations were defined as occurring whenever changes in all three strategy, structure and power distributions occurred within any

two-year period. NB: Two years was selected because some of the data were presented for corporate fiscal years and some for calendar years; however, they found that the majority of the revolutionary transformations actually occurred within a single year.

Non-revolutionary transformations were identified in two ways. First, whenever there were substantial changes over a period longer than two years and, second, when small changes accumulated to a 30 per cent change and when all three domains exhibited this level of change.

Results

The key findings of the study were that:

- A large majority of organizational transformations were accomplished via rapid and discontinuous change.
- Small changes in strategies, structure and power distribution did not accumulate to produce fundamental transformations. This finding provides additional evidence that fundamental organizational transformations tend to occur in short, discontinuous bursts.
- Triggers for transformations were major environmental changes and CEO succession.

The nature of change confronting most organizations

Dunphy (1996) argues that planned change is triggered by the failure of people to create a continuously adaptive organization, the kind of organization that is sometimes referred to as a 'learning organization'. Weick and Quinn (1999) propose that the ideal organization would resemble the successful self-organizing and highly adaptive firms that Brown and Eisenhardt (1997) found in the computer industry. However, while some organizations might achieve this ideal and become so effective at double-loop collective learning (see Chapters 2 and 29) that they are rarely misaligned with their environment, most do not. The majority of organizations, if they survive long enough, experience episodic change that cycles between relatively long periods of continuous incremental improvement punctuated by short periods of discontinuous revolutionary change.

There are three main categories of organizations that may not experience periods of discontinuous change:

1 The kinds of self-organizing and continuously changing learning organizations identified by Brown and Eisenhardt.
2 Companies operating in niche markets or slow-moving sectors where they have not yet encountered the kind of environmental change that requires them to transform their deep structures.

3 Organizations that are able to continue functioning without transforming themselves because they have sufficient 'fat' to absorb the inefficiencies associated
with misalignment.

With these exceptions, most organizations experience change as a pattern of punctuated equilibrium.

According to the punctuated equilibrium paradigm, organizations experience
two types of change:

1 *Incremental change:* this occurs during the relatively long periods of equilibrium
and is associated with the extrapolation of past trends, doing things better, and
securing efficiencies (see the discussion of path dependency in Chapter 1).
2 *Transformational change:* this occurs during periods of disequilibrium when the
organization, because of the effect of inertia and a failure to recognize the need
for change, becomes so misaligned with its external environment that it cannot
continue as before.

The studies undertaken by Tushman and colleagues (summarized in Nadler and
Tushman, 1995) suggest that most companies not only go through periods of incremental and transformational change, but that:

• this pattern of change repeats itself with some degree of regularity
• patterns vary across sectors, for example periods of discontinuity may follow a
30-year cycle in cement, but a 5-year cycle in minicomputers
• in almost all industries, the rate of change is increasing and the time between
periods of discontinuity is decreasing.

This last point is important because it predicts that all managers will be confronted
with an ever greater need to manage incremental and transformational change.
Not all organizations are able to successfully negotiate episodes of discontinuity
and those that fail to adapt may drop out or be acquired by others. Foster and
Kaplan (2001) provide chilling evidence of the consequences of failing to adapt.
They refer to changes in the Forbes top 100 companies between 1917 and 1987.
Out of the original 100 companies, only 18 were still in the list in 1987 and 61 no
longer existed.

The possibility of anticipating change

Sometimes, it is relatively easy to anticipate the need for change. For example,
companies operating in the European Union can, if they pay appropriate attention,
anticipate the impact of new regulations currently being discussed in Brussels.
Companies competing in markets where margins are being squeezed can anticipate the need to secure greater efficiencies or generate new income streams. There
are, however, occasions when organizations are confronted with changes that are
difficult to anticipate, for example the 2008 credit crunch, the effects of the 9/11
terrorist attacks, or the SARS epidemic of 2002–03.

Some organizations are much better at anticipating the need for change than
others. They are proactive. They search out potential threats and opportunities.
They prepare for destabilizing events that might occur or anticipate changes they
could initiate to gain competitive advantage. Other organizations are much more
reactive and only act when there is a clear and pressing need to respond.

Whether the need is for incremental or transformational change, the earlier the need is recognized, the greater the number of options managers will have when deciding how to manage it. Whenever managers are forced to react to an urgent and pressing need to change, they are relatively constrained in what they can do. For example:

- *There is less time for planning:* Careful planning takes time, something that is more likely to be available to those who are proactive and anticipate the need for change.
- *There is unlikely to be sufficient time to involve many people:* Involving people and encouraging participation in the change process can aid diagnosis, reduce resistance and increase commitment, but this also takes time.
- *There will be little time to experiment:* Early movers not only have time to experiment, they may also have the time to try again if the first experiment fails. When there is a pressing need for change, it is more difficult to search for creative solutions.
- *Late movers may have little opportunity to influence shifts in markets and technologies:* Early movers may have the opportunity to gain a competitive advantage by not only developing but also protecting, for example through patents, their new products or technologies.

A typology of organizational change

Combining two of the dimensions of change discussed so far, the extent to which change involves incremental adjustment or transformational change and the extent to which the organization's response to an opportunity or threat is proactive or reactive, provides a useful typology of organizational change (Figure 3.4).

	Incremental	Transformational
Proactive	Tuning	Reorientation
Reactive	Adaptation	Re-creation

Figure **3.4** *Types of organizational change*
Source: Adapted from Nadler et al., 1995, p. 24

Nadler et al. (1995) identify four types of change:

1 *Tuning:* change that occurs when there is no immediate requirement to change. It involves seeking better ways of achieving and/or defending the strategic vision, for example improving policies, methods, procedures; introducing new technologies; redesigning processes to reduce cost, time to market and so on; or developing people with required competences. Most organizations engage in a form of fine-tuning much of the time. This approach to change tends to be initiated internally in order to make minor adjustments to maintain alignment between the internal elements of the organization and between the organization's strategy and the external environment.

2 *Adaptation:* an incremental and adaptive response to a pressing external demand for change. It might involve responding to a successful new marketing strategy adopted by a competitor or to a change in the availability of a key resource. Essentially, it broadly involves doing more of the same but doing it better in order to remain competitive. An example of adaptive change might be what happens when one company, for example Nestlé, is forced to respond to a competitive move by another, for example Mars, which may have either increased the size or reduced the price of some of its confectionary products. This kind of change is not about doing things in fundamentally different ways nor is it about doing fundamentally different things.

While tuning and adaptation can involve minor or major changes, they are types of change that occur within the same frame; they are bounded by the existing paradigm. Reorientation and re-creation, on the other hand, are types of change that, to use Gersick's analogy, target the playing field and the rules of the game rather than the way a particular game is played. They involve transforming the organization and bending or breaking the frame to do things differently or to do different things.

3 *Reorientation:* involves a redefinition of the enterprise. It is initiated in anticipation of future opportunities or problems. The aim is to ensure that the organization will be aligned and effective in the future. It may be necessary to modify the frame but, because the need for change has been anticipated, this could involve a relatively gradual process of continuous frame bending. Nestlé offered a good example of reorientation in the mid-1980s. At a time when it was doing well, it embarked on a major change programme to ensure that it would remain aligned to its environment over the medium term. It initiated a top-down review to decide which businesses it should be in. Should it, for example, be in the pet foods business, continue to manufacture baked beans at a time when margins on that product were diminishing, or, as a major consumer of cans and glassware, supply its own or buy them in on a just-in-time basis? It also embarked on a major project to re-engineer the supply chain across the business and a bottom-up analysis of the added value contributed by each main activity. British Gas provides another example. After it had been privatized as a monopoly supplier of gas, the company was referred to the Monopolies and Mergers Commission. It was obvious to the top team that when the commission delivered its report, the company would be forced to change and might even be broken up. In order to prepare for this, a team of 10 senior managers was created to explore and test possible scenarios and help the organization develop the capability to respond to the inevitable, but at that time unspecified, changes it would have to face. In those cases where the need for change is not obvious to all and may not be seen as pressing by many, senior management (as in the British Gas example) may need to work hard in order to create a sense of urgency and gain widespread acceptance of the need to prepare for change.

4 *Re-creation:* a reactive change that involves transforming the organization through the fast and simultaneous change of all its basic elements. Nadler and Tushman (1995) state that it inevitably involves organizational frame breaking and the destruction of some elements of the system. It can be disorienting. An often cited example of this kind of change is that introduced by Lee Iacocca when he became the new CEO at Chrysler. He embarked on a process of revolutionary change that involved replacing most of the top team, withdrawing the

company from the large car market, and divesting many foreign operations. Case study 14.1 on Asda offers another example of this kind of reactive change.

The most common type of change is incremental, either fine-tuning or adaptation, but it is not unusual for a single organization, such as UK Coal, to be involved in more than one type of change at the same time (Example 3.2).

Example **3.2** *UK Coal: the simultaneous pursuit of adaption and reorientation*

The state-owned coal industry in the UK was privatized in 1994–95. At that time, UK Coal operated about 20 deep mines and the same number of opencast mines. By 2004, turnover was down by half and the number of mines had reduced by more than 50 per cent. The main reason for the closure of many of UK Coal's deep mines was the exhaustion of economically viable reserves. New mines were not developed to replace those that had been closed because the continuing downward trend in world coal prices had undermined the business case for new investment.

The exhaustion of economically viable reserves was not the only problem. Other problems included environmental opposition to the burning of coal with high sulphur content. Imported coal was more attractive to major customers (the power generators) on this count as well as on price. Another factor was the considerable capital investment required to develop a new deep mine.

The change strategy

The reduction in the number of deep and opencast mines encouraged UK Coal to begin looking for ways of improving the company's operating efficiency. One way of achieving this was to reduce the overhead cost of its central corporate headquarters by making each mine more autonomous and delegating to each unit a wider range of activities than used to be the case. Alongside this restructuring, UK Coal introduced a continuous improvement programme across all the remaining deep mines in order to make them more efficient and ensure their long-term survival.

Confronted with ever diminishing opportunities to grow the mining business, UK Coal also began to reappraise its assets and consider how it might revise its theory of business. It decided to explore the possibility of redefining the company as a land and property management and mining company. This reorientation involved many changes, including bringing new senior managers into the organization with competences in the area of land and property management.

Implications of these different types of change for change management practice

Different types of change can affect the focus for change efforts, the sequence of steps in the change process, and the locus for change, as discussed below.

The focus for change efforts

With incremental change, the aim is to improve the internal alignment between existing organizational components in order to do things better and improve the efficiency of the organization (Figure 3.5).

With transformational change, the aim is to seek a new configuration of organizational components in order to realign the organization with its changing environment. As noted above, this often leads to doing things differently or doing different things (Figure 3.6).

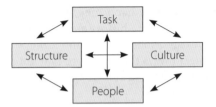

Figure **3.5** *Incremental change for internal alignment*

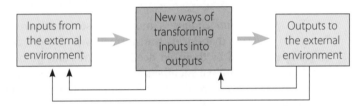

Figure **3.6** *Transformational change for external alignment*

The sequence of activities required to achieve a desired outcome

Inertia can be an important barrier to change. As an organization moves through a period of equilibrium, interdependencies between work roles, departments, processes, technologies, customers and suppliers tighten, ideologies that prescribe the best way of operating become more widely accepted, and the fear of losing benefits associated with the status quo strengthens the resistance to change. Thus, the first step in the change process involves equilibrium breaking, a step that Lewin (1947) referred to as 'unfreezing' (discussed in Chapter 2). This unfreezing creates the conditions that facilitate transitioning, moving the organization to a new state (Figure 3.7).

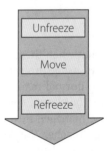

Figure **3.7** *Lewin's three-step process*

With most types of change, there will be resistance from some stakeholders and unfreezing will be an essential first step in the change process. However, in a minority of cases, where constantly adapting organizations (of the type identified by Brown and Eisenhardt, 1997) are operating in high-velocity environments, the issue might not be overcoming inertia and unfreezing the organization but reviewing and redirecting the continuous process of change that is already underway. Weick and Quinn (1999, p. 379) suggest that the appropriate change sequence required to redirect this kind of continuous change starts with 'freezing' in order to take stock and highlight what is happening, then moving on to 'rebalancing', a process that involves reinterpreting history and resequencing patterns so that they unfold with fewer blockages, followed by 'unfreezing' to resume improvisation, translation and learning 'in ways that are more mindful of sequences, more resilient to anomalies, and more flexible in their execution'.

The locus for change

Nadler and Tushman (1995) argue that an important factor determining how change will be managed is the intensity, that is, level of trauma and dislocation, of the change. With reference to the typology of change presented above:

- *Transformational change* is more intense than incremental change. Gersick (1991) observes that during transformational change, since organizations are no longer directed by their old deep structures and do not yet have future directions, organizational members (including senior managers) experience uncertainty, often accompanied by powerful emotions (see the discussion of Bridges' model in Chapter 13).
- *Reactive change* is also more intense than proactive change. Nadler and Tushman (1995) contend that during reactive change, everybody is aware that failure may threaten survival. Furthermore, organizational members may find that their efforts are constrained by time pressures, and often by a shortage of resources.

They go on to argue that tuning is the least intense, followed by adaptation. There is a jump in intensity associated with reorientation but the highest level of intensity is associated with re-creation (Figure 3.8).

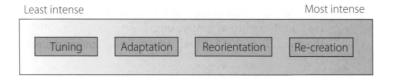

Figure **3.8** *Intensity of change*

The main thrust of their argument is that when the intensity of change is low, it can usually be managed by local leaders using project management and other forms of implementation associated with normal management processes. As the intensity of change increases, so does the burden of change management until it reaches a point where it cannot easily be managed through normal management processes. When the intensity of change reaches this level, senior management often create special structures and roles to aid the process and they may even appoint an internal or external change agent to facilitate the change. Nadler and Tushman (1995, p. 32) refer to this approach to change management as 'transition management':

> It involves mechanisms specially created for the purpose of managing a specific change ... the senior team plays a supporting role, and the organization continues to be run as it was before. If the change is intense enough, it may appear on the senior team's agenda as one of a number of important items to be reviewed and managed over time.

However, as the intensity of changes increases still further, change management is no longer just one of the items on the senior team's agenda, it *is* the senior team's agenda and the CEO assumes responsibility for directing the change rather than delegating it to others.

New patterns of change

Gersick's (1991) multi-level and multi-domain exploration of punctuated equilibrium suggests that this pattern of change is not new. What is new is how people are experiencing it. When the pace of change was slower, a good number of people could spend their entire working life in organizations that were never significantly misaligned with their environment. Consequently, their experience of organizational change might have been confined to incremental fine-tuning and adaptation. However, with the increasing pace of change, many more organizations have experienced periods of strategic drift (Johnson et al., 2008) and misalignment with their environment, to the point where the only way forward requires some form of radical transformation.

The management of change poses many challenges for managers. Burnes (2005, p. 85) observes that:

> Managing and changing organizations appears to be getting more rather than less difficult, and more rather than less important. Given the rapidly changing environment in which organizations operate, there is little doubt that the ability to manage change successfully needs to be a core competence for organizations.

Many, and some argue the majority of, change projects fail to achieve their intended outcomes. One reason for this is the failure to recognize the need for change early enough. Recognizing the need for change and starting the change relationship will be considered in more detail in Chapters 4–5.

This chapter ends with a series of case studies of organizations adapting to changing circumstances. You are invited to reflect on the content of this chapter and consider how it applies to these cases.

Case studies **3.1–3.4** *Types of change*

Read the following four case studies and use the typology of change in Figure 3.9 to identify the type of change described in each case.

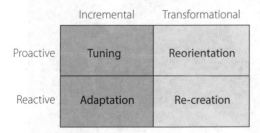

Figure 3.9 *Types of organizational change*
Source: Adapted from Nadler et al., 1995, p. 24

Case study **3.1** *The BBC*

After a long period of stability, during which the BBC had developed a reputation for honest reporting and programmes of outstanding quality, the corporation had become complacent. Staff believed that the BBC was financially secure and was the best programme maker and broadcaster in the world. But then the world began to change and the BBC was slow to respond.

The situation when John Birt came to the BBC

John Birt came to the BBC as deputy director-general in 1987 and was appointed director-general in December 1992. In his autobiography, *The Harder Path* (2000), he reports that he was surprised to learn that there was little hard information about the BBC's basic business. He described the culture within the BBC as a kind of imperialism, where every regional commander in every part of the corporation acquired a full fleet of facilities, irrespective of need. The result was a vast excess of facilities, and Birt commented: 'We could have covered Wimbledon, the World Cup and a world war, and still have had unused resources to spare.' He also found that staff utilization was low and that in some areas there was between 25 and 50 per cent more staff than necessary. Part of the problem was that facilities, overheads and support services were funded by the centre and not charged to particular programmes. One result of this was that nobody had the slightest idea how much it cost to make a programme.

Until the mid-1980s, the corporation was able to survive in spite of its inefficiencies because, for a period of 60 years, its income from the licence fee had grown, on average, 4 per cent per annum. But this changed in 1985, because of a new political climate.

Political pressures for change

In 1979, Margaret Thatcher and a Conservative government came to power with an agenda for change that included plans to privatize much of the public sector. Thatcher viewed the BBC as a bloated bureaucracy that was overmanned, inefficient and, therefore, ripe for reform.

In 1985, the government froze the licence fee (paid to the BBC by everybody in the UK who owns a radio or TV), in order to force the corporation to become more efficient. Although the licence fee remained constant or was reduced in value over the next decade, costs continued to rise. Thatcher's intention of delivering a 'rude shock' to the BBC did not have the intended immediate impact because Birt's predecessor had begun his term of office with a huge cash surplus, which he spent on funding the growing gap between licence fee income and costs. When this surplus was used up, the BBC started borrowing, until, in 1992, it faced a deficit of £100 million. Birt recognized that this situation could not continue and major changes were required.

© IMAGE SOURCE

Technological developments and new market pressures

The problem was further complicated by a wave of technological developments that threatened to undermine the BBC's traditional ways of working. The biggest challenge came from the development of digital technologies that opened up the possibility of many more channels, better technical quality, video-on-demand and interactivity. There was also increased competition from new players, for example Rupert Murdoch's launch of BSkyB.

Birt's strategy for change

Birt felt that he had no option other than to introduce radical reforms as quickly as possible in order to ensure the BBC's survival.

Case study **3.2** *Leicester Royal Infirmary*

Leicester Royal Infirmary is one of the largest teaching hospitals in England, with 1,100 beds and 4,200 staff. By the late 1980s, it had a reputation for being well run and was near the top of the NHS efficiency league tables. However, although the hospital was at the forefront of change – for example it was one of the first hospitals to introduce general managers in the mid-1980s, it was an early adopter of clinical directorates that focused on delivering specialized areas of clinical care in 1986, and it gained NHS trust status, and greater independence from the Department of Health, in 1993 – there were growing pressures for further change.

The new pressures for change

The city of Leicester had three acute hospitals located close to each other and integrated by a common medical school. When the opportunity of gaining more independence presented itself, the original proposal was that all three hospitals would become a single NHS trust. The Department of Health rejected this proposal and in the end three separate trusts were established. This created the possibility for competition between the three hospitals. For example, the district health authority (the body that purchased services from providers – hospitals – on behalf of the community) adopted a policy of service rationalization, which raised the prospect of the Leicester Royal Infirmary losing contracts to one of the other hospitals.

The NHS internal market, introduced in 1991, led to another competitive pressure from the primary care sector, as community based doctors (those who were GP fundholders with delegated budgets to purchase certain elective services) began 'shopping around' the three hospitals to obtain the most cost-effective and best quality provision. Purchasers also began to put considerable pressure on the hospitals to reduce patient waiting times. In addition, the introduction of national targets to improve efficiency placed new demands on all hospitals to make year on year savings.

The change strategy

The Leicester Royal Infirmary was much better placed than most hospitals to face these challenges and the leadership team proactively sought additional funding from the government to embark on a major change

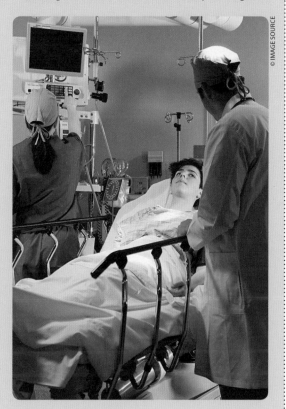

© IMAGE SOURCE

programme (see McNulty and Ferlie, 2002). Because of its earlier success in eliminating inefficiencies, there were few easy targets for further cost cutting. McNulty and Ferlie (2002) quote one member of the trust board as saying: 'I believe that there is no way we could improve the effectiveness and efficiency of this hospital simply by trying to do better that which we already do.'

Leister Royal Infirmary, like hospitals generally, was organized according to functional principles. However, early experiments that involved introducing process-based principles of organizing led to some dramatic improvements in parts of the organization. (Functional and process-based organization structures are discussed in Chapter 21.) In neurology, for example, the introduction of a single visit clinic reduced the time from visit to diagnosis from 12 weeks to one day, and in hearing services the time to fit a hearing aid was reduced from 14 months to 6 weeks.

These early successes encouraged the hospital to embark on an ambitious organization-wide programme of business process re-engineering. It was introduced in 1994 as a top-down programme to redesign two of the hospital's core processes: patient visits and diagnostic tests. The aim was to transform the organization from one characterized by fragmented functional thinking, which directed attention and activity towards narrow departmental priorities, to one where everybody worked together across functional boundaries to achieve wider organizational goals.

Case study **3.3** *McDonald's*

McDonald's is the world's largest fast-food restaurant chain. In 2004, it operated 1,250 outlets in the UK, of which 35 per cent were franchised. McDonald's experienced rapid growth in the UK market from the early 1970s until the late 1990s. However, from the late 1990s, it began to experience a slowdown in growth leading, in 2000, to a fall in total sales and market share.

Over the previous 45 years, its core business has been selling burgers, fries and soft drinks. Over this period, McDonald's had only introduced occasional and relatively minor changes to its menu. Some commentators have suggested that because of its track record of sustained success, McDonald's was slow to recognize and respond to changes in its external environment.

Several factors appear to have contributed to the change in the company's fortunes:

- Greater competition from new entrants into the market, including new chains of coffee shops and sandwich bars.
- A desire on the part of consumers for a wider choice of food.
- A greater awareness of the importance of leading a healthy lifestyle and eating healthy foods.
- New evidence on the causes of obesity.
- Media interest that has publicized possible links between certain kinds of 'fast food' and obesity.

An additional threat that received media attention was the possibility that the UK government might introduce restrictions on advertising to children. There were also rumours that it might consider imposing new taxes on those foods deemed to be 'unhealthy'.

McDonald's response to the new situation

In 2004, McDonald's broadened its food offering and focused more attention on healthy eating, with the launch of 'Salads Plus'. This was the biggest change to the McDonald's menu since it started business in the UK in 1974. The menu strategy involved the simultaneous introduction of eight new items to the menu: Caesar salad, bacon ranch salad, mixed salad, Quorn sandwiches, chicken filled sandwiches, yogurt and berry pots, fresh apples and muffins.

This major change to the product line involved a series of related changes:

- The introduction of new cooking equipment in all 1,250 outlets.
- Training 70,000 staff to cook and serve the new products.
- Training restaurant managers how to order and store new raw ingredients, and how to manage the introduction of the new menu in a way that enhanced profitability.
- Preparing managers at all levels, who had a wealth of experience managing in a steady-state environment, to lead the introduction of these changes.

Case study **3.4** *GNER*

GNER was a train operating company and part of Sea Containers Ltd, an entrepreneurial Bermuda-registered company with regional operating offices in London, Genoa, New York, Rio de Janeiro, Singapore and Sydney. GNER started business in 1996 when it won a seven- (later extended to nine-) year franchise to operate the InterCity East Coast routes from London to all major cities on the eastern side of the UK. From 2005, the franchise for the following 10 years was to be awarded on the basis of open competition. For GNER, it was a 'win or die' situation. The only way it could retain its business was to submit the winning bid. If it was unsuccessful, all the company's assets would be transferred to a new operator.

The company's response was to establish a new development team, headed by a director of development, charged with preparing the company's bid for the East Coast franchise. The bid was successful and GNER won the franchise up until 2015. The company decided to build on this experience and grow its business through bidding for other railway franchises as and when opportunities presented themselves. Its first venture was to join forces with the MTR Corporation, which runs the highly successful mass transit railway in Hong Kong, to bid for the Integrated Kent Franchise that includes the commuter rail services between southeast England and London and the new high-speed line from London to the Channel Tunnel. This first bid for new business was unsuccessful as was a second for the South Western franchise.

The change strategy

GNER's change strategy was to develop the existing East Coast railway and generate additional revenue through the provision of enhanced services. Plans included rebuilding all the electric fleet carriages,

introducing, what was at the time, an innovative on-board wireless internet service on all trains and increasing the number of daily intercity services to London from 53 to 80. Alongside this development of the InterCity East Coast business, the company planned to grow by acquiring more franchises in the UK. It was anticipated that these would include different types of railway (intercity, regional and commuter), each with different risk patterns, and a portfolio of franchises with different expiry dates that would help to provide the company with greater stability.

© PHOTODISC/GETTY IMAGES

Exercise **3.1** *The nature of the changes that confront your organization*

You might find it useful to reflect on the nature of the changes over the past year that have confronted the total organization or part of the organization you know best. If you do not have much work experience, think about other organizations you are familiar with, such as your university, a football club, a church, mosque or similar organization:

- Overall, would you describe the main type of change as incremental or transformational?
- In terms of the organization's typical response to change, think back and consider how the organization responded to change over the past few years. How does this compare with the organization's current way of responding to change?
- Is the organization's typical response to change reactive or proactive?

Summary

- It has been argued that the ideal way for organizations to respond to change is for them to engage in a continuous stream of incremental adaptations that ensure they will always be aligned with the external environment. This corresponds to the 'gradualist paradigm', which posits that this kind of evolving change can be cumulative and can lead to organizational transformation without the need for a discontinuous jolt to trigger a radical change.
- While the ideal pattern of change might be incremental and cumulative, the reality for many organizations appears to be a pattern of episodic change, which involves alternating between periods of equilibrium, where the focus for change is 'doing things better' through a process of continuous tinkering, adaptation and modification, and periods of discontinuous change, which involve a break with the past and doing things differently or doing different things. This pattern of change is referred to as 'punctuated equilibrium'.
- Some organizations are much better at recognizing the need for change than others. The earlier the need for change is recognized, the greater the number of options managers will have when deciding how to manage it. Whenever managers are forced to react to an urgent and pressing need for change, they are relatively constrained in what they can do.
- Nadler et al. identified four types of change – tuning, adaptation, reorientation and re-creation. Each of these types has implications for change management practice because they can affect the focus for change efforts, the sequence of steps in the change process, and the locus for change.

References

Birt, J. (2000) *The Harder Path: The Autobiography*. London: TimeWarner.

Brown, S.L. and Eisenhardt, K.M. (1997) The art of continuous change: Linking complexity theory and time-paced evolution in relentlessly shifting organizations, *Administrative Science Quarterly*, 42(1): 1–34.

Burgelman, R.A. (1991) Intraorganizational ecology of strategy making and organizational adaptation: Theory and field research, *Organizational Science*, 22(2): 239–62.

Burke, W.W. (2002) *Organizational Change: Theory and Practice*. Thousand Oaks, CA: Sage.

Burnes, B. (2005) Complexity theories and organizational change, *International Journal of Management Reviews*, 7(2): 73–90.

Chakravarthy, B. (1997) A new strategy framework for coping with turbulence, *Sloan Management Review*, 38(2): 69–82.

Drucker, P.F. (1994) The theory of the business, *Harvard Business Review*, 72(5): 95–104.

Dunphy, D. (1996) Organisational change in corporate settings, *Human Relations*, 49(5): 541–52.

Foster, R.N. and Kaplan, S. (2001) *Creative Destruction: Why Companies that are Built to Last Underperform in the Market – and How to Successfully Transform Them*. New York: Currency.

Gersick, C.J. (1991) Revolutionary change theories: A multilevel exploration of the punctuated equilibrium paradigm, *Academy of Management Review*, 16(1): 10–36.

Gould, S.J. (1978) *Ever Since Darwin: Reflections in Natural History*. London: Burnett Books.

Greenwood, R. and Hinings, C.R. (1996) Understanding radical organizational change: Bringing together the old and the new institutionalism, *Academy of Management Review*, 21(4): 1022–54.

Hodgkinson, G.P. and Healey, M.P. (2008) Cognition in organizations, *Annual Review of Psychology*, 59(1): 387–417.

Johnson, G., Scholes, K. and Whittington, R. (2008) *Exploring Corporate Strategy*. London: Prentice Hall.

Lewin, K. (1947) New frontiers in group dynamics. In D. Cartwright (ed.) (1952) *Field Theory in Social Science*. London: Social Science Paperbacks.

McNulty, T. and Ferlie, E. (2002) *Reengineering Health Care: The Complexities of Organisational Transformation*. Oxford: Oxford University Press.

Nadler, D.A. and Tushman, M.L. (1995) Types of organizational change: From incremental improvement to discontinuous transformation. In D.A. Nadler, R.B. Shaw and A.E. Walton (eds) *Discontinuous Change: Leading Organizational Transformation*. San Francisco, CA: Jossey-Bass.

Nadler, D., Shaw, R.B. and Walton, A.E. (1995) *Discontinuous Change: Leading Organizational Transformation*. San Francisco, CA: Jossey-Bass.

Orlikowski, W.J. (1996) Improvising organisational transformation over time: A situated change perspective, *Information Systems Research*, 7(1): 63–92.

Pettigrew, A.M. (1987) Context and action in the transformation of the firm, *Journal of Management Studies*, 24(6): 649–69.

Romanelli, E. and Tushman, M.L. (1994) Organizational transformation as punctuated equilibrium: An empirical test, *Academy of Management Journal*, 37(5): 1141–66.

Samuelson, W. and Zeckhauser, R.J. (1988) Status quo bias in decision making, *Journal of Risk and Uncertainty*, 1: 7–59.

Sydow, J., Schreyögg, G. and Koch, J. (2009) Organizational path dependence: Opening the black box, *Academy of Management Review*, 34(4): 689–709.

Thaler, R.H. and Sunstein, C.R. (2009) *Nudge: Improving Decisions about Health, Wealth and Happiness*. London: Penguin.

Tushman, M.L. and Romanelli, E. (1985) Organizational evolution: A metamorphosis model of convergence and reorientation. In B. Staw and L. Cummings (eds) *Research in Organization Behavior*, vol. 7. Greenwich, CT: JAI Press.

Tushman, M.L., Newman, W. and Romanelli, E. (1986) Convergence and upheaval: Managing the unsteady pace of organization evolution, *California Management Review*, 29(1): 29–44.

Weick, K.E. and Quinn, R.E. (1999) Organizational change and development, *Annual Review of Psychology*, 50: 361–86.

II

Chapter **4**

Recognizing a need or opportunity for change

Many of the opportunities and threats that trigger change can be found in an organization's external environment, but some originate from within the system itself. This chapter reviews a range of external and internal sources of change and explores some of the issues that affect an organization's ability to recognize the opportunity or need for change.

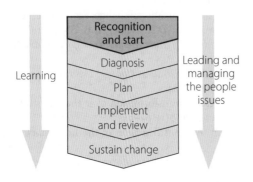

External sources of change

Some managers appear to be better than others when it comes to identifying opportunities and threats in the external environment. Successful entrepreneurs seem to be particularly good at this and use intuition to identify opportunities in situations where many others see only chaos, contradictions and confusion (Allinson et al., 2000). There are, however, some useful analytical tools that everybody can use to help them search the external environment for opportunities and threats.

The acronym PEST refers to an analytical tool that focuses attention on political, economic, sociocultural and technological trends that managers need to be aware of:

- *Political factors:* include new legislation in areas such as environmental management, consumer protection and employment; regulation of markets in areas such as banking, telecommunications and broadcasting; fiscal policies and so on. Organizations that operate in international markets need to be aware of how legislative changes or changes in the level of political stability in different parts of the world might influence their operations.
- *Economic factors:* include issues such as the ongoing impact of the credit crunch, exchange rates, cost of borrowing, change in levels of disposable income, cost of raw materials, security of supplies, new competitors and the trade cycle.
- *Sociocultural factors:* include demographic trends such as a fall in the birth rate or an ageing population. They also include shifting attitudes towards education, training, work and leisure, which can have knock-on effects on the availability of trained labour, consumption patterns and so on. Cultural factors can also affect business ethics and the way business is done in different parts of the world.
- *Technological factors:* include issues such as the levels of investment that competitors are making in research and development and the outcome of this

investment; the availability of new materials, products, production processes, means of distribution and so on; the rate of obsolescence and the need to reinvest in plant and people.

Managing change in practice **4.1** *Mick Yates: The implications of big data*

Mick Yates is responsible for international markets at dunnhumby, the global leader in helping businesses make better, more customer-focused business decisions. In 1997, Mick founded www.leader-values.com, one of the internet's most visited leadership development sites. Until mid-2001, he was company group chairman of Johnson and Johnson's consumer business in Asia-Pacific, based in Singapore. Prior to this, he spent 22 years at Procter & Gamble, latterly as regional vice president based in Hong Kong and then in Japan. In all, he has spent 11 years as a regional CEO of Asian businesses.

Mick offers some useful insights into how new developments can affect the agenda for change. Watch the video on the book's website at **www.palgrave.com/ companion/hayes-change-management4**, which shows him talking about the impact of big data and how it can change the way an enterprise makes decisions, how departments within an organization talk to each other, and how the business interacts with its customers.

Strebel (1996) developed a model that managers can use to anticipate technological and economic changes in the environment and to help them initiate changes that will enable their company to remain one step ahead of the competition. He argues that there is an evolutionary cycle of competitive behaviour and that different phases of the cycle are marked by break points. He also suggests that, given proper attention to competitive trends, these break points can be predicted in advance. The two phases of the cycle are innovation and efficiency (see Figure 4.1).

The start of the innovative phase of the cycle is characterized by a sharp increase in divergence between what competitors are offering and begins when an innovation by one competitor is seen to create a new business opportunity. This triggers others to innovate and gives rise to a greater variety in the offerings (products and services) available to customers. This process continues until there is little scope for further innovation that offers suppliers or customers much in the way of added value. At this point, the divergence of offerings begins to decline as the best features of past innovations are imitated by competitors.

The next phase of the cycle begins when one or more providers begin to turn their attention to efficiency rather than innovation. Cost reduction is seen as the route to maintaining market share and increasing profit. They achieve this by improving systems and processes to reduce delivered cost. While each phase of the cycle can present opportunities for some, it can also pose threats for others. In the efficiency phase of the cycle, only the fittest survive and inefficient competitors are driven out of business.

When most of the opportunities for gaining competitive advantage from improving efficiency have been exploited, attention might switch once again to innovation, and the cycle will repeat itself. Strebel (1996) notes that convergence, when organizations turn their attention to efficiencies, is usually easier to anticipate than divergence, because it involves a move towards greater similarity in

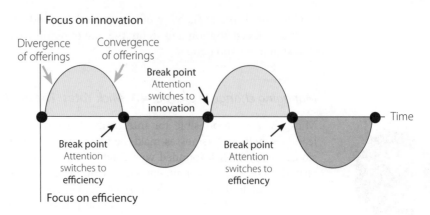

*Figure **4.1** Strebel's cycle of competitive behaviour*

Source: The Change Pact: Building Commitment to Ongoing Change, Strebel, P., Pearson Education Limited

existing products and services, whereas divergence is based on potential new offerings and their existence might not be known until a competitor offers them to customers.

So far this discussion has focused attention on the alignment of the organization with its external environment, but managers also need to consider internal alignment and how internal misalignments can trigger change.

Internal sources of change

Greiner (1972) cautions managers about the danger of only attending to the external environment and the future. He asserts that, for many organizations, the most pressing problems are rooted more in the organization's past decisions than present events and external dynamics. His view is that organizations evolve through five predictable stages of development and each stage brings with it a set of alignment-related issues that have to be managed if the organization is to be effective. Each phase of Greiner's organization life cycle involves a prolonged period of evolutionary growth during which changes tend to be small and incremental, and these phases create their own crisis (due to internal misalignments) that end with a period of turmoil and revolution. Whereas Romanelli and Tushman (1994) believe that periods of discontinuous revolutionary change are triggered by changes in the external environment, Greiner argues that it is internal problems that trigger crises and cause discontinuous change (see Figure 4.2). The way these crises are managed determines whether the organization will survive and move forward to the next phase of evolutionary growth. Managers need to be aware of where their organizations, and the component parts within the organization, are in terms of the five stages of development, and recognize the kinds of problems that need to be addressed.

According to Greiner (1972), each evolutionary period is characterized by a dominant management style, and each revolution is characterized by a dominant management problem that must be resolved if the organization is to continue to grow. The five phases are:

1 *Growth through creativity leading to a crisis of leadership:* At first, most organizations are preoccupied with identifying a market and creating a product. The founders are typically entrepreneurial and technically oriented and the organization's structure, systems and culture tend to be informal. But as the organization grows, the need for more knowledge about the efficiencies of manufacturing, more professional systems for maintaining financial control, and more formal approaches for managing and developing people lead to a crisis of leadership. A new approach to managing and leading the business is required, but the founders may not be qualified to provide this. Sometimes, the only effective way forward is for the founders to bring in a strong business manager from outside; for example, Larry Page and Sergey Brin, the founders of Google, brought in Eric Schmidt to run the company.

2 *Growth through direction leading to a crisis of autonomy:* During the second phase of growth, organizations often differentiate activities and develop a functional organizational structure, along with a clear hierarchy, more formal communication systems, and more sophisticated accounting, inventory and manufacturing systems. Although this new level of order and direction delivers efficiencies, as the organization continues to grow, it eventually becomes less effective; for example, long communication chains delay decision making and set procedures prevent competent people taking initiatives. This leads to demands for greater autonomy.

3 *Growth through delegation leading to a crisis of control:* Delegation brings many benefits. Employees at lower levels are motivated and managers operating in a decentralized organization structure can act faster. Eventually, however, they begin to lose sight of organization-wide goals, develop parochial mindsets, and begin to work too independently. This gives rise to a need for greater coordination across the organization.

4 *Growth through coordination leading to a crisis of 'red tape':* Formal systems and procedures are introduced in order to facilitate greater coordination. While these measures align separate functions, departments and work groups around corporate goals, the creeping bureaucratization of the organization eventually stifles initiative and strangles growth.

5 *Growth through collaboration:* Greater spontaneity is encouraged through developing interpersonal competences, matrix and network structures and associated systems that enable people to work together in ways that rely more on social control and self-discipline than formal control and close monitoring from above.

Figure 4.2 shows Greiner's five phases of evolutionary growth, during which there is a continuous stream of low intensity incremental changes, mapped onto the pattern of punctuated equilibrium illustrated earlier in Figure 3.3. The periods of equilibrium are punctuated by periods of revolutionary change that have to be successfully negotiated if the organization is to survive and prosper.

According to Greiner, when organizations come to the end of one of the evolutionary phases and enter a period of crisis (revolution), the critical task for change managers is to be aware of the organization's history and its current phase of development, and identify the new set of organization practices that will provide the way forward into the next period of evolutionary growth.

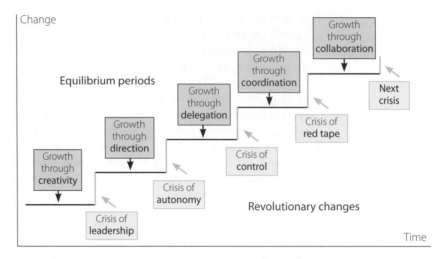

Figure **4.2** *Internal factors that can trigger discontinuous change*
Source: Adapted with permission from Greiner, 1972, p. 41

Recognizing the need for change

A failure to recognize the need for change can lead to internal and external misalignments that can undermine organizational effectiveness. Hickman and Silva (1984) observe that most ailing organizations are blind to their own problems and argue that, in most cases, they are not suffering because they are unable to resolve their problems, they are suffering because they cannot *see* their problems. Organizations need to develop what Egan (1988) refers to as a 'culture of vigilance', but vigilance can be dented by a number of factors, such as cognitive biases, retrospective rationality and the need to justify past decisions, and short time perspectives that encourage managers to stick with a winning formula too long and pay insufficient attention to how the situation may change over a longer time frame (see the examples of Nokia, FiReControl and Direct Banking in Chapter 1).

Organizational path dependence and the trap of success

Nadler and Shaw (1995) offer support for Sydow et al.'s (2009) notion of organizational path dependence when they observe that one of the paradoxes of organizational life is that success often sets the stage for failure. This is because when organizations are successful, managers become locked into the patterns of behaviour that produced the original success. These patterns become codified or institutionalized and are rarely questioned. Nadler and Shaw elaborate their argument with the proposition that success often leads to growth and growth leads to complexity and greater differentiation. As this happens, attention shifts away from how the organization relates to the environment – it is taken for granted that this relationship will be successful – and is switched to managing the new and more complex relationships within the organization. Customers and suppliers receive less attention and the competitive gains of rival organizations, for example in terms of reduced costs or shorter time to market, receive insufficient attention (as happened to M&S, and discussed in Example 3.1). Where this complacency and internal focus lead to declining performance, the organization may behave as if the solution is to do more of what led to success in the past. Nadler and Shaw (1995, p. 11) refer to the organization becoming 'learning disabled'. Managers become incapable of looking outside, reflecting on success and failure, accepting new ideas and developing new insights. If unchecked, the ultimate outcome of this trap of success can be what they refer to as the 'death spiral' (Figure 4.3).

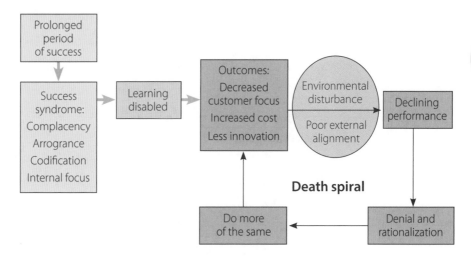

Figure **4.3 The trap of success**

Source: Adapted from Nadler and Shaw, 1995, p. 11

Improving the organization's ability to sense the need for change

Sensing a need for change and formulating a change agenda begin when individuals notice and respond to what they perceive to be significant external or organizational events. Pitt et al. (2002) observe that sometimes the signals or events that cause individuals to sense that an issue is important or urgent may be relatively weak but, based on their intuition and context-specific experience, some individuals are able to anticipate the implications of these signals.

Attending to indicators of effectiveness

Managers are responsible for ensuring that the organization, or the part of the organization they manage, performs effectively. Discrepancies between actual and desired levels of performance signal a need for change, but problems can arise when discrepancies are not recognized because managers restrict their attention to a narrow range of indicators and fail to pay attention to others that may be equally or even more important.

Exercise **4.1** Indicators of effectiveness

Before reading on, make a note, in the space provided below, of the indicators that you believe are used to assess whether or not your organization – and your department or unit within the organization – is effective. If you are a student with little work experience, do the same for your department or the university as a whole.

Indicators of effectiveness

Organization

Department/unit

When you have completed this chapter, you might like to review these indicators and consider whether any of them need to be revised.

Some of the factors that managers might need to take into account when assessing performance include:

- *Purpose:* Many commercial organizations use profit as one of the main indicators of effectiveness, but this indicator might not apply to all organizations. While financial viability may be necessary for the survival of organizations such as religious orders, universities, hospitals or charities, profit might not be viewed as a critical indicator of effectiveness. The effectiveness of hospitals in the British NHS, for example, might be judged on indicators such as waiting times and mortality rates rather than 'profit'. Change managers need to attend to performance indicators that reflect the purpose of their organization.

- *Stakeholder perspective:* Different stakeholders often use different indicators to assess an organization's effectiveness. Profit might be more important to shareholders than to workers. Suppliers, customers, employees and people in the wider community affected by the products and services (and pollution) produced by an organization will all have their own views on what should be taken into account when assessing whether or not it is effective. When John Birt joined the BBC, he felt that programme makers were neglecting some of the corporation's key stakeholders and this neglect was threatening the organization's survival (see Case study 3.1).

- *Level of assessment:* Effectiveness can be assessed at different levels, for example the organization, subunit or individual employee. Only paying attention to overall performance might result in major inefficiencies within the organization going undetected.
- *Alignment:* Assessments of effectiveness need to be aligned up, down and across the organization. Indicators of individual and group effectiveness need to be aligned with indicators of departmental effectiveness, which, in turn, need to be aligned with indicators of organizational effectiveness.
- *Time perspective:* It has already been noted that, in some cases, profitability can be a useful indicator of organizational effectiveness. However, just because organization A is currently more profitable than organization B does not mean that A is the most effective organization. Organization B might be incurring higher costs and lower profits today in order to invest in new plant, product development and staff training in the belief that this will help to secure survival and growth over the longer term. The implication of this is that organizational leaders need to take account of the time perspective when assessing the effectiveness of particular departments or the organization as a whole.
- *Benchmarks:* Often, effectiveness is assessed in terms of some output-to-input ratio, such as the number of units produced per man-hour. It is assumed that any increase in output with constant or decreasing inputs represents greater effectiveness and vice versa. When making this kind of assessment, reference needs to be made to a standard or benchmark. For example, all producers within a given product category or industrial sector may have experienced efficiency gains because of the introduction of a new and widely available manufacturing system. In this context, the assessment of whether one particular producer has maintained or improved its effectiveness might need to include a comparison of this producer's performance relative to the performance of others. A company may have improved its output-to-input ratio, and therefore improved its efficiency, but may have achieved smaller improvements than other comparable producers. In these circumstances, the company may be deemed to be more efficient than it used to be but less effective than comparable companies.
- *Constraining and enabling factors:* Account also needs to be taken of any constraints that inhibit performance, or enabling factors that boost performance relative to comparable other organizations. The new manufacturing system referred to above might produce levels of toxic emissions greater than the levels permitted by environmental regulations. These regulations may only apply to a minority of producers located in a particular region or country. In these circumstances, while a producer faced with strict environmental regulations might not improve output-to-input ratios as much as some of its competitors, it might achieve considerable success in modifying its production processes in a way that enables it to adopt the new manufacturing technology and improve efficiency enough to produce sufficient profit to survive. A failure to respond in this way may have resulted in the company going out of business. In terms of its ability to minimize the effect of the constraint imposed by environmental legislation, it might be deemed to be an effective organization.

Example **4.1** *Horizontal misalignments identified in a large snacks and confectionery manufacturing company*

The indicators used to assess the performance of different functions, such as production and marketing and sales, in a large snacks and confectionery manufacturing company were not aligned with each other. One consequence was that managers working in different parts of the company often lost sight of the overall goal of the organization and focused their attention on the achievement of more immediate goals related to functional performance. For example, in the face of strong price competition, marketing and sales sought to secure increased sales (related to their goal of maximizing revenue from sales) by offering customers fast delivery and customized products. While this strategy helped sales and marketing achieve its own performance targets, it undermined the effectiveness of manufacturing and distribution. In order to customize products and offer an immediate and flexible response to satisfy customers' just-in-time delivery requirements, the manufacturing function had to introduce short product runs, make greater use of

overtime working, and hold higher stocks of work in progress. The distribution function also had to hold higher inventories of finished goods and, because of unpredictable demand, make more deliveries that involved part loads. The cost of meeting these new manufacturing and distribution requirements was greater than the net benefits achieved from the increased sales revenue, and threatened the organization's overall effectiveness. Figure 4.4 provides some examples of functional misalignment.

An investigation of this problem revealed a number of other misalignments indicated by the double-headed arrows shown in Figure 4.4. As can be seen from this example, it is not uncommon for organization subunits and individual employees to be rewarded for behaving in ways that have little to do with overall organizational effectiveness. Unless organizational leaders are alert to the need to monitor internal alignment, problems may go unrecognized for some time.

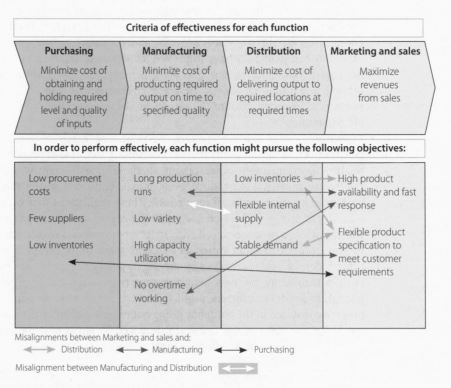

Figure **4.4** *Examples of functional misalignment*

Summarizing the discussion so far, those assessing effectiveness need to take account of:

- purpose and desired outcomes
- the stakeholder perspective from which the assessment is made
- level of assessment
- alignment of the various indicators used at different levels and across different functions
- specified time frame – short, medium or long term
- benchmark standard
- any special constraints or enabling factors that affect performance.

When any of these factors are ignored, those assessing performance may fail to spot problems and identify the need for change in good time.

The balanced scorecard

Many organizations have adopted the balanced scorecard to help managers widen the criteria they use to assess performance. Kaplan and Norton (2004, p. ix) developed the balanced scorecard after observing that managers and others focus their attention on those aspects of performance that are measured and give little or no attention to those aspects of organizational functioning that are not measured, and the primary measurement system in most organizations was financial accounting:

> which treated investments in employee capabilities, databases, information systems, customer relationships, quality, responsive processes, and innovative products and services as expenses in the period in which they were incurred.

In their view, these financial reporting systems fail to measure or provide a basis for managing the value created by the organization's intangible assets.

While the balanced scorecard includes financial measures to provide a useful summary of the results of actions previously taken, they are supplemented by measures of three other aspects of organizational functioning that can be important drivers of future financial performance: customer-related measures, internal business process measures, and measures of the infrastructure that facilitates long-term growth and improvement. The scorecard approach enables managers to review performance from these four perspectives against short- and long-term objectives:

1 *Financial perspective:* focuses attention on the financial objectives of the organization and helps managers track financial success in terms of variables such as return on investment, cash flow, and shareholder value. It encourages managers to think about how the organization should appear to its shareholders.
2 *Customer perspective:* helps managers to think about customer objectives and how the organization should appear to customers.
3 *Internal process perspective:* helps managers to focuses attention on operational goals and the key processes necessary to deliver customer objectives and satisfy shareholders.
4 *Learning and growth perspective:* focuses attention on the intangible drivers of future success such as skills, training, organizational culture, leadership, systems and databases.

Figure 4.5 illustrates the kind of dashboard that can be constructed using the balanced scorecard approach. The ways in which the balanced scorecard can be used as a change management tool are discussed in Chapter 26.

Perspective	Objectives	Measures	Targets	Need for change
Financial				
Customer				
Internal process				
Learning and growth				

*Figure **4.5** A balanced scorecard*

Diversity in the top team

It is often argued that when top teams are populated by executives with diverse backgrounds, they are more likely to be sensitive to a wider range of internal and external issues that could impact on future performance than when they are drawn from similar backgrounds, and will therefore be less likely to be learning disabled and caught in the trap of success. This proposition is based on the assumption that functional conditioning (current and past functional experience) affects cause-and-effect beliefs and directs attention to issues related to these beliefs. Various studies support the validity of this view. For example, Cohen and Ebbesen (1979) found that goals that are salient during a task amplify the salience of information related to these goals, suggesting that executives who work or have worked in various functional areas will be influenced by the information and issues related to their various and different past experiences. However, Chattopadhyay et al. (1999), in a study of 371 executives working in 58 businesses across 26 industrial sectors, found little support for this view. A key finding of their study was that the beliefs of other members of the top team had a much greater effect on collective sense making than members' own functional experience. This raises the possibility that groupthink, where people become so focused on maintaining group cohesion that they lose their ability to think independently and make good, sound judgements (discussed in Chapter 29), could undermine the top team's ability to recognize the need for change.

Change tool 4.1 can be used to challenge your thinking about the indicators you and others use to assess your unit's performance and the quality of your unit's alignment with suppliers and customers. This kind of analysis can alert you to:

- the need to reconsider the criteria you use to judge your own unit's performance
- changes that will improve the quality of the alignment between your unit and the 'customers' who receive whatever it is you export as outputs
- changes you might need to negotiate with your suppliers to improve the value of the inputs you receive from them.

Change tool **4.1** *Alignment check between your unit and your customers and suppliers*

Think of your organization, department or work group in terms of a process that transforms inputs into outputs.

Step 1

Identify the major inputs and outputs and make a note of them in the space provided below. Depending on the time available, focus on one or more inputs *and* one or more outputs.

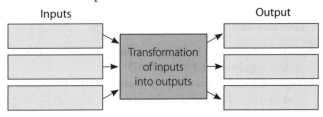

Step 2

Select one *input* and identify the work group, department, or external supplier that provides it.

Step 3

Assess how effective you think this supplier is:

- List the indicators *you* use to assess the effectiveness of the supplier.
- Against each indicator, note *your* assessment of how effective the supplier is (use a five-point scale, where 1 = very ineffective and 5 = very effective).

Step 4

Think about how members of the supplying organization, department or work group rate their own effectiveness:

- List the indicators you think *they* use to assess their own effectiveness.
- Against each indicator, note how you think *they* rate their own effectiveness.

Indicators I use to assess the effectiveness of the supplier	My assessment	Indicators they use to assess their effectiveness	Their assessment

Step 5

Compare the two lists. Do they suggest any actual or potential problems that could undermine the effectiveness of your unit? If so, specify below.

Now repeat steps 2–5 for one of your *outputs.*

Step 6

Select one *output* and identify the work group, department, or external customer that receives it.

Step 7

Assess how effective you think your unit is:

- List the indicators *you* use to assess the effectiveness of your unit (with respect to the supply of the focal output).
- Against each indicator, note *your* assessment of how effective you think your unit is (use a five-point scale, where 1 = very ineffective and 5 = very effective).

Step 8

Think about how members of the receiving work group, department or organization rate the effectiveness of *your* unit:

- List the indicators you think *they* use to assess your unit's effectiveness.
- Against each indicator, note how you think *they* rate the effectiveness of your unit.

Indicators I use to assess the effectiveness of my unit	My assessment	Indicators customers use to assess the effectiveness of my unit	Their assessment

Step 9

Compare the two lists. Do they suggest any actual or potential problems that could undermine the effectiveness of your unit?

If you do not have sufficient work experience to complete this exercise as specified above, you can use it as a template for a mini research study. Interview a manager (or the owner of a small business such as a café) and identify the criteria they use to assess the quality of whatever it is they provide for their customers. Then ask them to put themselves in their customers' shoes and speculate about the criteria customers use to assess the quality of the product or service they receive. Consider whether this process helps the manager identify any discrepancies in the criteria they and their customers use, and whether such discrepancies signal a need for change. You could extend this exercise by interviewing one or more customers to check out whether the manager really is aware of the criteria customers use to assess their performance.

Shaping the agenda for change

According to Pitt et al. (2002), issues emerge and are shaped to form the 'agenda for change' through various forms of individual initiative. While agenda-forming initiatives are often restricted to senior managers at the top of the organization, people located at multiple levels in the hierarchy can also make a valuable contribution. Thompson (2012) echoes this view and asserts that those employees who interact directly with customers can be the first to learn about product shortcomings or pick up on what competitors are doing to increase their market share. He goes on to argue that people throughout the organization can have valuable insights about opportunities for change but, all too often, these potential contributions are lost.

Pitt et al. (2002) assert that if ideas and concerns are to have any impact on what the organization does, they must receive some minimal level of collective attention and be recognized as having sufficient priority to deserve further consideration. Personal concerns compete for collective attention and interpretation:

> Whether, and how fast a concern crystallizes into an issue or item *on the agenda* depends on who is involved and the opportunities they have to interact and construct the issue through conversation and debate. (Pitt et al., 2002, p. 157)

Political behaviour to promote self-interest and strong ideologies that marginalize minority or dissenting views and promote groupthink are some of the factors that can affect which issues emerge as part of the agenda for change. Thompson (2012) observes that recognizing and using the valuable information that is scattered around the organization is one of the key business challenges of the modern age.

The role of playmakers

The individuals who influence the organizational agenda are referred to by Pitt et al. (2002) as 'playmakers', a term they borrow from football, where it refers to the restless, energetic midfield role that links play, energizes the team and 'makes things happen'. They argue that these playmakers do not always have to form an exclusive elite. Top managers can encourage other organizational members to perform playmaker roles by seeking out relevant opinions from those who are close to the realities of the operating environment; however, in many organizations, this does not happen – see the discussion of organizational silence in Chapter 11.

Based on a study in a manufacturing company, Pitt et al. (2002) identified a number of roles that people from various parts of the organization can play to influence the agenda for change. These are:

- *Upward-facing advocates:* they promote ideas and concerns via rational arguments. Those who opt to play this kind of role are most effective when they are perceived as experts and are able to present persuasive technical evidence and well-crafted arguments. Describing his approach to influencing the top team, a systems manager who acted as an upward-facing advocate said:

  > Senior people like to measure things. Arguments about change are easier to sustain if you can quantify things. If you want to justify something, get clear measurements of feasibility and benefits, proof on paper. (Pitt et al., 2002, p. 161)

- *Upward-facing emotive champions:* they use emotion and polemics rather than rational arguments to manage impressions and champion issues. Those who adopt this approach are often motivated by self-interest allied to a genuine concern for the future of the organization. Pitt et al. (2002, p. 161) cite a manager who adopted this approach to influencing the change agenda:

> I went to a meeting and really stirred it up. I told them what they were saying was ludicrous. I came back and said to my manager that lunatics have taken over the asylum. I created a major issue.

This approach can involve risks but the person quoted above felt so strongly about the issue that he was prepared to speak up.

- *Democratic brokers:* they facilitate lateral communication among peers. They tend to be respected organizational members with perceived expertise who function as interpreters, ideas brokers and opinion canvassers. They use their nodal position in communication networks to originate and trade concerns with peers. Because they bring together different groups and interests, brokers can make a particularly valuable contribution by promoting diverse interpretations of situations that can point to opportunities or threats that might not be identified by a narrow group of senior managers acting alone. Pitt et al. (2002, p. 165) refer to a planning manager who described a situation in which he acted as broker with his peers in various departments:

> We bounce problems off each other all the time. What's expected of us and how it fits in with where the company's going. How we want to restructure it, where people actually fit in. A lot is about communication ... trying to ... influence our peers. Its about networking ... talking to people, bouncing ideas off them.

Pitt et al. (2002, p. 164) report that in the company they studied, notwithstanding the examples referred to above, the locus of playmaking was narrowly demarcated and tended to be confined to a select few:

> Although newcomers and junior staff were in theory free to contribute to issue debates, older and wiser hands tended to be ambivalent or dismissive when they did so, thereby limiting interpretive diversity in practice.

Widening the opportunity for organizational members to engage in playmaking can greatly improve an organization's ability to recognize the need to take action to either minimize threats or exploit new possibilities.

Case study 4.1 on the Active Sports Equipment Company provides a good example of how people located at different points in the organization have the potential to make a valuable contribution to the formulation of the change agenda.

Case study **4.1** *The Active Sports Equipment Company*

The Active Sports Equipment Company (ASE) is a small to medium-sized manufacturer of high-quality sports equipment. It was founded 35 years ago and currently employs around 50 people to manufacture a specialist piece of sporting equipment. Current turnover is £4 million and 65 per cent of output is exported worldwide. The founder of the company is a mechanical engineer. He established ASE to produce a

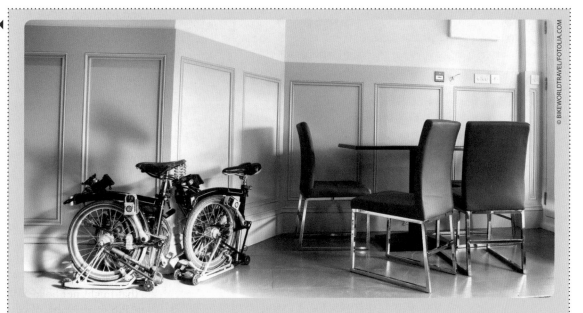

specialist piece of sports equipment based on his own original and highly innovative design. He is still the managing director and his obsessive concern with the details of design and engineering excellence dominate the culture of the company.

This concern for engineering excellence has served the company well, and it has built itself an enviable reputation as *the* standard by which all other sporting equipment in this specialist category is judged, despite the fact that the basic design of ASE's product has evolved little over the years. Recently, however, a number of challenges to this dominant position have emerged as other sports equipment manufacturers have sought to enter what they regard as an attractive market with newer designs. These newcomers compete effectively on price and many aspects of performance and specification, although they still fail to match ASE's product on ease and speed of assembly and the compactness of the fold for transportation. Much of the success of the ASE product is based on its well-engineered and robust construction that enables it to be folded and unfolded easily and quickly. However, it is with such challenges in mind that ASE introduced a number of innovations, the most significant of which was the option of a number of titanium parts that deliver important weight-saving advantages.

But what about the future? ASE might continue to focus on its core competence and seek to retain its current competitive advantage by further improving the design of its product. Product and production engineering are highly valued within the company. There is no doubt that it is engineering that has created the ASE brand and made it what it is today, but there is the risk that engineering alone may not guarantee that the current record of success will be sustained.

A number of other possibilities are deserving of attention:

- Some managers see opportunities for improving the effectiveness of the company by reviewing the way it functions. Like many small and medium-sized enterprises, ASE appears to have pursued a rather informal approach to the development of its own internal organization. This reflects the priority given to the development of product and production processes in the early years. Since then, staff roles have been redefined and new ones created on an ad hoc basis to reflect the changing demands on the business. There may be advantages to be gained from improving internal communication and planning processes or reviewing the way the organization is structured. Such changes might lead to superior performance by improving internal alignment.
- Other managers are aware of opportunities in the marketplace. A marketing manager was recruited two years ago but this appointment has not had much impact on the company's overall culture,

which continues to be engineering led. More attention to marketing issues might help to ensure that if and when customer needs change, this will be recognized by those who control the strategic agenda.

- Related opportunities might involve building alliances between product engineering and marketing to extend the product range and exploit the ASE brand.

- People working in the production departments are also aware of opportunities to reduce manufacturing costs, but are reluctant to voice these because they suspect they may lead to job losses.

If you were a manager in ASE aware of some of these issues, would you actively try to influence the company's strategic agenda? If not, why not? If you would, how would you attempt to do this?

Source: This case study is based on contributions from Andy Shrimpton.

Problems relating to the recognition of the need for change are more likely to arise in those organizations where alternative perspectives and interpretations are ignored or suppressed than in those organizations where they are actively sought out and debated. Such debates will not necessarily lead to major changes, but at least they ensure that the possibility of new threats or opportunities is properly considered. There are many examples of companies that have continued to exploit, for many years, whatever it is that has provided them with a competitive advantage. This can be a healthy state of affairs so long as care is exercised to avoid complacency and the trap of success.

Summary

This chapter considered some of the factors that can affect the recognition of a need for change. Sources of change are considered first. The PEST acronym and Strebel's cycle of competitive behaviour were introduced as tools that can help identify external sources of change, and Greiner's organizational life cycle was presented as a useful model that highlights internal sources.

Sensing a need for change and formulating a change agenda begins when individuals notice and respond to what they perceive to be significant external or organizational events. Discrepancies between actual and desired levels of performance signal a need for change but problems can arise when discrepancies are not recognized because attention is restricted to a narrow range of indicators. Some of the indicators that need to be monitored were reviewed. These include:

- organizational purpose and desired outcomes
- the stakeholder perspective from which the assessment is made
- level of assessment – total organization, department, work group or individual
- the alignment of the various indicators used at different levels and across different functions
- specified time frame – short, medium or long term
- benchmark standard
- special constraints or enabling factors that affect performance.

The balanced scorecard illustrates an approach to assessing performance that attends to a wide range of factors.

The final part of the chapter focused attention on issues that can affect the formulation of the agenda for change. While formulating the agenda for change is often restricted to senior managers, people located at multiple levels in the hierarchy may be well placed to make a valuable input. However, their contribution may not be sufficient to guarantee that the organization will address the issues they identify as important.

References

Allinson, C.W., Chell, E. and Hayes, J. (2000) Intuition and entrepreneurial performance, *European Journal of Work and Organizational Psychology*, 9(1): 31–43.

Chattopadhyay, P., Glick, W.-H., Miller, C.C. and Huber, G.P. (1999) Determinants of executive beliefs: Comparing functional conditioning and social influence, *Strategic Management Journal*, 20(8): 763–89.

Cohen, C. and Ebbesen, E. (1979) Observational goal and schema activity: A theoretical framework for behavior perceptions, *Journal of Experimental and Social Psychology*, 15: 305–29.

Egan, G. (1988) *Change-Agent Skills B: Managing Innovation and Change*. San Diego, CA: University Associates.

Greiner, L.E. (1972) Evolution and revolution as organizations grow, *Harvard Business Review*, 50(4): 37–46.

Hickman, C.R. and Silva, M.A. (1984) *Creating Excellence*. New York: New American Library.

Kaplan, R.S. and Norton, D.P. (2004) *Strategy Maps: Converting Intangible Assets into Tangible Outcomes*. Boston, MA: Harvard Business School Press.

Nadler, D.A. and Shaw, R.B. (1995) Change leadership: Core competency for the twenty-first century. In D.A. Nadler, R.B. Shaw and A.E. Walton (eds) *Discontinuous Change: Leading Organizational Transformation*. San Francisco, CA: Jossey-Bass.

Romanelli, E. and Tushman, M.L. (1994) Organizational transformation as punctuated equilibrium: An empirical test, *Academy of Management Journal*, 37(5): 1141–66.

Pitt, M.R., McAulay, L. and Sims, D. (2002) Promoting strategic change: 'Playmaker' roles in organizational agenda formulation, *Strategic Change*, 11: 155–72.

Strebel, P. (1996) Breakpoint: How to stay in the game, *Financial Times Mastering Management*, 17: 13–14.

Sydow, J., Schreyögg, G. and Koch, J. (2009) Organizational path dependence: Opening the black box, *Academy of Management Review*, 34(4): 689–709.

Thompson, D. (2012) *Oracles: How Prediction Markets Turn Employees into Visionaries*. Boston, MA: Harvard Business School Press.

Chapter **5**   **Starting the change**

This chapter considers some of the issues associated with starting the change process. Most important is translating the need for change into a desire for change. Organizational members may be reluctant to pursue change because they lack confidence in their own and others' ability to make a difference. This chapter (and book) adopts a 'voluntaristic' perspective and argues that, in most cases, organizational members are not powerless pawns, unable to affect change, but are independent actors able to intervene in ways that can make an important difference. To do this, they need concepts and theories that will help them understand the process of changing and ways of intervening, but they also need to believe in their own and others' ability to affect outcomes. The final part of this chapter looks at who should lead the change and how they can build effective change relationships. Chapter 6 goes on to examine how the way change agents relate with those involved in a change can affect outcomes.

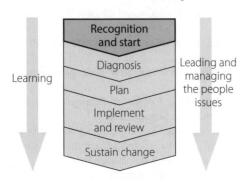

Beliefs about change agency

Change agency refers to the ability of a manager or other agent of change to affect the way an organization responds to opportunities and threats. One approach to the study of change and change management portrays the manager and other organizational members as pawns affected by change rather than as agents who can initiate and secure change. This approach is referred to by Wilson (1992) as 'determinism'.

The deterministic view

The deterministic view is that the ability of the manager to influence change is limited because the main determining forces lie outside the organization and the realms of strategic choice for managers (see the discussion of predetermined change trajectories in Chapter 1). Wilson (1992, p. 42) notes that advocates of this approach view organizations as interdependent elements of a much greater open system and they regard the characteristics of the wider organization–environment linkages as the key determinant of strategic change. For example, no matter how good the CEO of an organization might be, when faced with a dramatic downturn in the trade cycle or unfavourable exchange rates, they may be able to do little to improve the immediate fortunes of the organization. Greenwood and Hinings

(1996) echo this view when they discuss how, in some circumstances, an organization's institutional context can limit the possibilities for change, especially when the organization is embedded in a wider system that has tightly coupled relationships. Mellahi and Wilkinson (2004) note that one of the points that classical industrial organization and organizational ecology scholars can agree on is the deterministic role of the environment that constrains management action.

The voluntarist view

The voluntarist view supports the notion of constructed trajectories discussed in Chapter 1 and rejects the assumption that managers are powerless. Advocates of this perspective argue that managers and other organizational members are the principal decision makers who determine the fate of the organization. The strategic choice framework (Child, 1972, 1997) highlights the ability of managers to exercise choice and provides an example of how the voluntarist approach can work. It challenges the view that there is an ideal type of organization and one best way of managing. It recognizes functional equivalents and the possibility of equifinality, whereby organizational outcomes can be achieved in a variety of different ways. One of the key factors that determines the effectiveness of an organization is the quality of the strategic choices made by members of the dominant coalition. This approach emphasizes the role of human agency and asserts that managers can intervene to affect change in ways that will either promote or undermine organizational effectiveness.

Raynor et al. (2009), however, sound a note of caution about seeking insight into how those leading a change should act from 'success studies', because every success cannot be attributed to human agency. Chance factors can also affect outcomes. They argue that some of the companies cited in management bestsellers such as *In Search of Excellence* (Peters and Waterman, 1982) and *Good to Great* (Collins, 2001) may just have been lucky. Raynor et al. demonstrate how easily we can succumb to the temptation to 'explain' seemingly significant outcomes that are entirely random by describing an experiment conducted by one of them at the beginning of her strategic management class. She starts the class by asking all the students in the room to stand up and instructs each of them to toss a coin. If the toss comes up tails, they are to sit down, but if it comes up heads, they are to remain standing:

> Since there are around 70 students in the class, after six or seven rounds there is only one student left standing. With the appropriate theatrics, I approach the student and say, 'How did you do that? Seven heads in a row! Can I interview you in *Fortune*? Is it the T-shirt? Is it the flick of the wrist? Can I write a case study about you?' (Raynor et al., 2009, p. 18)

This example illustrates that chance is a factor that cannot be ignored. Nonetheless, there is still evidence that managers do act in ways that contribute to the success of their organizations. For example, Pettigrew and Whipp (1991) report the outcome of a study of firms in four sectors – automobile manufacture, book publishing, merchant banking and life assurance – and conclude that there are observable differences between the ways that leaders in higher performing firms manage change compared to those in lesser performing firms.

From the perspective of change agency, the deterministic view offers a perspective that is too fatalistic. While, in some situations, there may be external forces that exercise a powerful effect on organizational performance, there will almost always be scope for managers to intervene in ways that will promote the organization's interests. Burnes (2004, p. 198) argues that despite the constraints they face, managers have a far wider scope for shaping decisions than most organization theories acknowledge. He asserts that 'the scope for choice and the development of political influence is likely to be more pronounced where change, particularly major change, is on the managerial agenda'.

Problems can arise, however, when managers and others do not believe in their own ability to act as agents of change. As a consequence, they may fail to behave proactively. Their response, and therefore the response of the organization, may be to react passively in response to external forces for change.

Voluntarism and change agency

Two assumptions underpinning the approach to managing change adopted in this book are that managers can make a difference and can learn to manage change more effectively. Effective change managers require, and can be helped to acquire:

- confidence in their own ability to make a difference
- the motivation to change
- conceptual models and action tools/interventions
- change management skills.

These factors are now explored in more detail.

Confidence in their own ability to affect outcomes

Some managers may have the conceptual knowledge and required skills to equip them to intervene and make a difference, but they may fail to act because they have insufficient faith in their own ability to affect outcomes. While optimism and over-confidence can be a problem and result in unnecessary risk taking (for example Thaler and Sunstein, 2009, found that 90 per cent of all drivers think they are above average when they are behind the wheel), change managers can often be ineffective because they lack the confidence to act in ways that enable them to exercise the control necessary to achieve desired outcomes. May (1969) argued that in many walks of life, people are hypnotized by their own feelings of powerlessness and use this as an excuse for doing nothing. He describes the central core of modern human neuroses as the undermining of people's experience of themselves as responsible, and the sapping of their will and ability to make decisions. According to May (1969, p. 184):

> the lack of will is much more than merely an ethical problem: the modern individual so often has the conviction that even if he *did* exert his 'will' – or whatever illusion passes for it – his actions wouldn't do any good anyway.

This inner feeling of impotence is a critical problem for some managers and can undermine their ability to act as agents of change. There are two explanations for this:

1 *Locus of control:* Rotter (1966) developed the concept of locus of control after observing that some people seemed to attribute outcomes to luck rather than to factors over which they had some control. Locus of control reflects the degree to which people believe that their own behaviour determines what happens to

them. Those who attribute outcomes to their own efforts are referred to as 'internals' and those who attribute outcomes to external factors, such as luck, fate, other people, the state of the economy or other factors over which they have no control, are referred to as 'externals'. In the context of change management, those who are overcommitted to a deterministic view of change may be inclined to believe that the locus of control is external to themselves and the organization and may therefore develop the view that there is little they can do to influence events. Those who think this way are less likely to attempt to adopt a proactive approach to the management of change than those who have a more internal view about the locus of control.

2 *Learned helplessness:* Locus of control is related to Seligman's (1975) theory of learned helplessness, which argues that a person's expectation about their ability to control outcomes is learned. It suggests that managers may begin to question their ability to manage change if, when confronted with a new problem or opportunity, old and well-tried ways of managing fail to deliver desired outcomes. Furthermore, if their early attempts to experiment with alternative ways of managing are equally unsuccessful, this questioning of their own ability may develop into an expectation that they are helpless and the associated belief that there is little they can do to secure desired outcomes. Seligman argues that this expectation will produce motivational and cognitive deficits:

- *Motivational deficits* involve a failure to take any voluntary actions designed to control events following a previous experience with uncontrollable events. If managers believe that they cannot exercise any control over outcomes, they will not even be motivated to try.
- *Cognitive deficits* involve a failure to learn that it is possible to control what happens. If managers believe that they cannot affect outcomes in a particular set of changing circumstances, this belief may stop them recognizing opportunities to exercise control, even if there is evidence that their own behaviour has actually had an important impact on outcomes.

The theory of learned helplessness suggests that the incentive for managers and others to initiate activity directed towards managing change will depend on the (learned) expectation that their action can produce some improvement in the problematic situation. If they do not have any confidence in their own ability to manage the change and achieve any improvements, they will not try to exercise influence. Both individuals and organizations can develop the expectation that there is little they can do to secure desirable outcomes when confronted by change. However, individuals and organizations can also learn that they can affect their own destiny, and they can learn how to exercise this influence.

The motivation to change

Pugh (1993) argues that those who are most likely to want to change are those who are basically successful but are experiencing tension or failure in some particular part of their work. This group will have the confidence and the motivation to change. The next most likely to change are the successful because they will have the required confidence, but because of their success, they may be satisfied with the status quo and lack the motivation to change. Individuals, like organizations, can fall into the trap of success (see Chapter 4). The least likely to understand and accept the need for change are the unsuccessful. While they may be the ones who need to change most, they are also the ones who are likely to lack confidence in their own ability to improve their predicament. Consequently, they may prefer the status quo (the devil they know) to the possible outcome of a failed effort to change (the devil they don't).

Change readiness is important. Jones et al. (2005) define readiness as the extent to which employees hold positive views about the need for change and believe that the change will yield positive outcomes for themselves and the wider organization. By (2007) studied the management of change in the UK tourism industry and found support for Armenakis et al.'s (1993) proposition that successful implementation is positively correlated with the level of change readiness.

Case study 5.1 illustrates that it can be difficult to translate a need for change into a desire for change, especially when a company has enjoyed a sustained period of success.

Case study **5.1** *Failure to convince others of the need for change at AT&T*

There are many instances where those who recognize the need for change want to embrace it but cannot because they are unable to convince others that the change is necessary. Werther (2003) illustrates this with the example of AT&T's telephone manufacturing division (Western Electric) following deregulation of the telecommunications sector in the USA. Prior to deregulation, consumers had no choice other than to lease their telephones from one of the Bell operating companies (another part of AT&T). These local operating companies were regulated monopolies, allowed to earn up to a set maximum return on their assets. This regulated monopoly situation encouraged AT&T to pursue a high reliability, high-cost strategy for the manufacture of its telephone instruments. This strategy was attractive for a number of reasons:

1 The cost of the phones was included as part of the asset base on which the local operating company's returns were calculated. This offered no incentive for them to persuade Western Electric to reduce its manufacturing costs.

2 Western Electric's market was protected from the threat of low-cost phones produced elsewhere because customers had to lease their phones from the local Bell company.

3 High-quality, high-cost phones were more reliable. This reduced the cost of repairs and service for the operating company and also reduced the number of complaints to the regulator about the quality of service.

All this changed after deregulation. Customers were allowed to purchase and install their own telephones and were attracted to the many low-cost instruments that began to flood the market. This had a dramatic effect on Western Electric's share of the market and convinced senior management of the need to switch from a high reliability, high-cost manufacturing strategy to one that focused on producing low-cost phones. Werther reports that this proposed switch was fiercely resisted by engineers, managers and assemblers across the company because they believed that the company should remain committed to its traditional policy of producing high-quality if expensive phones. Their resistance was so strong that the company was forced to outsource the production of low-cost phones overseas.

What could senior managers have done to persuade engineers, managers and assemblers to support the required change?

©GETTY

This case study illustrates the importance of translating the need for change into a desire for change on the part of all those who can affect the success of the change project. Stephen Elop, the new CEO at Nokia, attempted to do this with his 'burning platform' message, when he broadcast the fact that fierce competition from Apple and Google had inflicted serious damage on Nokia's market share and revenue streams (Constantinescu, 2011; see Examples 1.3 and 9.3). His aim was to disconfirm the widely held view among employees that Nokia was a secure and prosperous company, and his use of a burning platform analogy was intended to create sufficient anxiety to motivate staff to accept that the only way forward was to embrace radical change. He followed this up by announcing a new strategy that would involve working with Microsoft to build a new mobile ecosystem.

Pitt et al. (2002) refer to how senior managers can adopt a downward-facing evangelist playmaker role to win subordinates' attention and commitment. In their study, they found evidence to suggest that spreading a message via potent, emotive symbols can be more effective than rational appeals. Pitt et al. (2002, p. 163) cite the case of a technical director who needed to win support for a proposed change to improve hygiene standards. His message was that the company is in a high-risk business (producing ingredients for the processed food industry) and that 'the bottom line is life and death – if you get it wrong you are going to kill people'. There are, however, circumstances where alternative ways of winning support might be more effective, such as involving change recipients at an early stage in the process, providing emotional support, and rewarding behaviours that facilitate the change. These are considered in more detail in Chapter 12.

It is not unusual to discover that some people have a greater readiness for change than others. This has implications for deciding where to initiate the change effort. When faced with the possibility of alternative starting points, the change agent might decide to start working with those who appear to be the most receptive to change and have the confidence and motivation to engage in the change process. Early successes in some parts of the organization can inspire others to get involved.

Conceptual models

Change managers can acquire a range of concepts and theories they can use to manage change. Essentially, they fall into two categories: process models that are concerned with the *how* of change management, and diagnostic models that focus on identifying *what* it is that needs to be changed. Change managers need concepts and theories that will help them to:

- identify the kind of change that confronts them, for example incremental or discontinuous
- understand the process of changing
- identify what needs to be attended to – through a process of diagnosis and goal setting, which are covered in Part III – if they are to achieve desired outcomes.

Process models have been considered in Chapters 1 and 2 and types of change in Chapter 3. Diagnosis involves the application of the many theories that exist about the behaviour of individuals and groups in organizations, about organizational processes such as power and influence, leadership, communication, decision making and conflict, and the structure and culture of organizations. These individual, group and organizational performance models can be used to help managers to identify what needs to be changed in order to protect or improve organizational effectiveness. Organizational-level diagnostic models are considered in Chapter 7.

In addition to the conceptual tools that can help change managers to understand the change process and diagnose what needs to be changed, they also need to be familiar with a range of different types of intervention they can use to secure a desired change. These are considered in Chapters 16–23.

Change managers also need to have some basis for deciding which interventions to use in specific circumstances, taking account of contingencies such as the pace of change, the power of stakeholders to resist and so on. Models that can be used for this purpose are considered in Chapter 24.

Change management skills

While conceptual understanding is necessary, it is not sufficient to guarantee that change agents will be able to secure desired changes. When managers are acting as change agents, they need to be able to communicate, offer leadership, work with teams, confront, negotiate, motivate, and manage relationships with others. Change agency requires these and many other skills that managers use in everyday life. Sometimes, change agents are less effective than they might be because they fail to recognize the importance of some of these skills or they fail to apply them when required.

Starting the change process

After persuading others of the need for change, it is necessary to decide who will, at least in the first instance, facilitate the change. The change agent could be an insider, a member of the system or subsystem that is the target for change, or an outsider. An insider might be chosen in situations where:

- the person responsible for managing the unit or subsystem that is to be the (initial) target for change is committed to acting as change agent
- it is agreed that a particular insider has the time, knowledge and commitment to manage the change more effectively than an outsider
- the system does not have the resources to employ an outsider
- issues of confidentiality and trust prohibit the use of an outsider
- it proved impossible to identify a suitable outside consultant.

An outsider might be chosen where:

- there is nobody on the inside who has the time or competence to act as facilitator/change agent
- it is felt that all the competent insiders have a vested interest in the outcome and therefore might be less acceptable to other parties than a neutral outsider.

Deciding who will manage the change can have an important impact on the outcome of the change process. Often, it is automatically assumed that the lead will be a technical expert rather than the manager (user) who will be responsible for making the change work post-implementation. Clegg (2000) challenges this assumption and advocates that users should play a more central role. In Chapter 2, reference is made to the fragmented nature of many change projects. This can result in the separation of diagnosis, planning and implementation from use and maintenance. This separation can allow technical experts leading the change to focus too much attention on technical issues, such as designing a technically superior system, rather than on the needs of users. Clegg cites the example of the way a successful change project was led by a senior user at Lyons Confectionery to support his case that users need to be more centrally involved (Example 5.1).

Example **5.1** *Leading change at Lyons Confectionery*

Lyons Confectionery makes confectionery products for sale through retail outlets across the UK. Products are distributed using a fleet of several hundred delivery vans. The sales director (who was the lead user responsible for this function) was keen to improve various aspects of the performance of the van sales and delivery operation. He identified inaccuracies and delays in the feedback of information from shops as an important source of inefficiencies. This information was provided by the drivers and was an essential input for deciding manufacturing plans, inventory levels and delivery schedules.

The sales director thought that it would be possible to improve the quality and speed of information flow, but rather than starting by bringing in an information technologist to develop a new information technology (IT) system, he decided to spend time with his team working out how they wanted the new way of working to operate. Their starting point was to think about how the whole van sales and delivery operation could be changed for the better before thinking about how this could be supported by new IT. They undertook a total rethink of the drivers' role.

Should they, for example, continue working in their existing delivery role or could their role be expanded to include sales? They even thought about making the drivers into franchise holders, running their own businesses at the interface between the bakery and the retail outlets.

The project team included the regional sales managers, some delivery drivers and depot workers, and people from sales administration, customer services and manufacturing (all the groups linked in the process), and they were advised by the company's IT specialist (along with other experts from departments such as accounts). In other words, it was the prospective users of the new system who pulled through the new working arrangements (and technology) that they needed to meet their operational needs. The team, taking advice from the IT specialist, decided that hand-held computers could deliver the required improvements, and it was the team of prospective users who organized the trials of various hand-held computers available on the market.

Clegg (2000) reports that this proved to be one of the most successful change projects he ever witnessed.

© IMAGE SOURCE

Establishing a change relationship

Where the change agent is a member of the target system, entering the change relationship may not be too difficult so long as everybody can agree that there is:

- a problem or opportunity that requires attention
- a need to engage in some form of preliminary data gathering in order to determine what further action is required.

A brand manager who is unhappy with the time it takes to introduce a change in the way a product is packaged may enlist the support of others to benchmark their performance against that of leading competitors. Similarly, a manager of a sports centre might set up a meeting with staff to consider possible reasons why an increasing proportion of existing members are failing to renew their membership.

Because the change agent is an insider and known to others, many of the issues that could be problematical and require careful attention when introducing an external consultant/change agent (such as building trust and confidence) can often be managed informally and without too much difficulty.

Where the change agent is an outsider – a senior manager or somebody from another part of the organization or from outside – the establishment of a change relationship can be a more complex process due to some of the reasons outlined below.

Issues that can affect the quality of the relationship

One of the key issues is the ability to build trust and confidence. Some individuals and groups are less comfortable than others when it comes to being open and discussing their affairs with outsiders. This might be because they fear that it could be difficult to communicate the nature of their problem or opportunity to others and that others may view them as incompetent or foolish. Alternatively, it may be because they fear that seeking help will threaten their autonomy and make them too dependent on others. The early stages of the relationship-building process can be critical because clients quickly form impressions about the change agent's competence, ability to help, friendliness and inferred motives. Margerison (2000) likens the change agent's early encounters with the client to 'knocking at doors which are half open and seeing them either close in your face, or open fully'. Lines et al. (2005) argue that trust and trustworthiness have a direct bearing on the change agent's access to knowledge and cooperation. When clients feel that they can trust the change agent, they are more likely to be open, share information and avoid defensive behaviours. Normally, this takes time, particularly if the change agent is completely new to the situation, as building trust is an incremental process. Lines et al. define trust as a state that depicts how individuals and groups view other individuals and social units. They argue that it is based on the processing of numerous experiences, normally over a long period of time. This is particularly pronounced in individuals and groups who feel vulnerable (and many do in times of change), as they will process *any* information or experience they feel has a bearing on the extent to which they can trust the change agent. Morgan and Zeffane (2003) view organizational change as a critical event that can either create trust or destroy a long-standing trusting relationship in an instant.

Managing change in practice **5.1 Colin Ions: The role of HR in acquisitions and mergers**

Colin Ions set up the consulting arm of DLA Piper, one of the world's largest law firms. Prior to moving into consulting, he had a 30-year career in the engineering and brewing industries and was group HR director for Courage, a major division of Scottish and Newcastle.

In his video on the role of HR in mergers and acquisitions, Colin argues that HR managers can make a strong contribution to change so long as they are on the right agenda and 'get into the mind of the CEO'. People in the business have to have confidence that the HR function understands what the CEO and the top team are trying to do with the enterprise and that they have a strong business focus. He goes on to discuss four factors that can affect the value of the HR contribution. Watch the video on the book's companion website at **www.palgrave.com/companion/hayes-change-management4** and consider whether you agree.

In terms of competence and ability, some clients want a change agent (who could be an HR practitioner) who has sufficient expertise to be able to 'see a way through' and tell them what to do. They might expect the change agent to undertake a diagnostic study and prepare a written report. In these circumstances, the competence they are seeking from the change agent is related to the 'content' of the problem or opportunity. Others might want a more collaborative relationship and expect the change agent to work with them to help them learn how to solve their own problems. The competence that is valued in this type of relationship is related more to the process of problem solving and managing change rather than the content of a problem. The important point to make at this stage is that both parties need to reach some agreement about the role of the external consultant/change agent.

In terms of friendliness and approachability, what many clients want is a helper who, on the one hand, is sympathetic to their needs and values but, on the other hand, sufficiently neutral to offer objective comment, feedback and other assistance.

Finally, in relation to inferred motives, it is important that clients believe that the change agent is 'on their side' and is 'working for them', as they will be more likely to share sensitive information and be receptive to feedback or suggestions about helpful processes and so on. However, where the change agent is seen as untrustworthy, incompetent or 'not for them', the clients will be much more likely to react defensively and resist any attempt to influence their thinking. Van Buren and Safferstone (2009) observe that many newly appointed change managers feel under pressure to secure quick wins and this often comes across as a drive to secure an individual (personal) quick win. They argue that to be successful, leaders need to work with others to achieve 'collective' quick wins.

Building effective change relationships is considered in more depth in Chapter 6, but from the perspective of the client developing a relationship with an external change agent. We will see that this can take time and sometimes clients test the helper's competence, attitudes, perceived role and trustworthiness by presenting them with what they regard as a safe or peripheral problem. If they are satisfied with the change agent's performance, the client may move on to present what they believe to be the real problem.

External change agents need to pay careful attention to two additional issues: identifying the client and clarifying the issues to be addressed.

Identifying the client

From the perspective of the change agent, an issue that must be managed carefully is the identification of the client. The person who invites an outsider into a situation may not be the person or group that becomes the focal client. The change agent needs to be ready to amend the definition of the client if a preliminary diagnosis suggests that the problem is not confined to one group or unit, but involves multiple units, several levels of the hierarchy, or people outside the organization such as customers, suppliers, trade associations or unions. Problems can arise when external change agents define the client as the person/group who invited them into the situation. If they are blind to the need to redefine who the client is, they may inadvertently end up working to promote or protect a sectional interest rather than the effectiveness of the organization.

One way of defining the client is in terms of the person or persons who 'own' the problem and are responsible for doing something about it, for example the sales director in the Lyons Confectionery example discussed earlier. Cummings and Worley (2001) define the client as those organizational members who can directly impact the change issue, whether it is solving a particular problem or improving an already successful situation. This definition is more likely to identify the client as a group or the members of a subsystem rather than as an individual. Cummings and Worley specify the client in terms of all those who can directly impact on the change, because, they argue, if key members of the client group are excluded from the entering and contracting process, they may be reluctant to work with the change agent.

The author learned about this from direct experience. He was invited by the personnel director of an international oil company to help with a problem in a distant oil refinery. He was flown to the nearest major airport, put up in a hotel and, next morning, flown by a small plane to the refinery's own airstrip. Eventually, he found himself in a meeting room in the refinery with all the senior managers. After some brief introductions, the refinery manager started the meeting by asking the consultant why he was there. It was clear that the personnel director had not involved the refinery manager in the decision to engage an external consultant. This was strongly resented and by the time the consultant had arrived at the refinery, there was little he could do to build an effective working relationship with the management team. However, some months later, the same refinery manager approached the consultant and invited him back to the refinery to work on a different problem. On this occasion, it was his problem and his decision to involve an outsider. The rejection first time round had nothing to do with the consultant's competence. The refinery manager had been unhappy that somebody else had decided he had a problem and, without any consultation, had decided he needed external help to resolve it.

Clarifying the issue

The symptoms or problem presented to an external change agent may not be the real issue that needs to be addressed. Those who seek help from consultants often present the difficulty as somebody else's problem. The head of HR of a manufacturing company invited a consultant to meet the finance director over lunch. The problem that the finance director, who was also the deputy chairman of the board, wanted to talk about was to do with the poor state of communication between the board and senior management. He defined the problem in terms of the quality of the senior managers. Eventually, after the consultant had met the board, they redefined the problem as stemming from within the board itself, where there were conflicting views regarding the role of the board and political issues affecting how it functioned.

Another issue is that problems are often presented in terms of their implied solutions, such as: 'We need help to

- improve the appraisal system
- build a more cohesive team
- improve communications.'

The communications problem, for example, might be further defined as a need to improve the communication skills of certain individuals. However, a preliminary investigation conducted by a change agent may suggest that while communications could be improved, an important factor contributing to the problem is the structure of the organization and the effect this has on communication networks. In such a situation, improving the communication skills of selected individuals or replacing existing members with others might do little to resolve the underlying structural problem.

Change agents need to keep an open mind about the nature of the problem until there has been some kind of preliminary investigation. However, it is important that the change agent also pays careful attention to the felt needs of the client and what they believe the problem to be.

Exercise **5.1** *Starting the change process*

Think of an occasion when you acted as a change agent. It might have been at work or elsewhere; for example, if you live in a flat with other students, it might have involved persuading others to keep the flat clean, share the cooking, or regulate spontaneous parties and overnight guests. Did the change go smoothly from the start or did you hit problems initiating the change process? If you did hit problems, did they relate to any of the issues considered in this chapter?

Reflect on this experience and make a note of any learning points that might help you to avoid similar problems in the future.

Summary

This chapter discussed three of the main issues associated with starting the change process:

1. Translating the need for change into a willingness to pursue change: This chapter adopts a 'voluntaristic' perspective and argues that organizational members are not powerless pawns, unable to affect change, but are independent actors able to intervene in ways that can make an important difference. To do this, they need:
   - *Confidence in their own ability to affect outcomes:* While optimism and over-confidence can be a problem, some change managers and others are ineffective because they fail to act in ways that enable them to exercise the control necessary to achieve desired outcomes:

- The locus of control reflects the degree to which people believe in their own ability to make things happen. Those who attribute outcomes to their own efforts (internals) tend to have confidence in their own ability to make a difference.
- Seligman's theory of learned helplessness proposes that a person's expectation about their ability to control outcomes is learned. It suggests that organizational members may begin to question their ability to manage change if, when confronted with a new problem or opportunity, old and well-tried ways of managing fail to deliver desired outcomes.
- *The motivation to pursue change:*
  - Those who are most likely to want to change are those who are basically successful but who are experiencing tension or failure in some particular part of their work. This group will have the confidence and motivation to change.
  - The next most likely to change are the successful because they will have the required confidence. However, because of their success, they may be satisfied with the status quo and lack the motivation to change.
  - The least likely to understand and accept the need for change are the unsuccessful. While they may be the ones who need to change most, they are also the ones who are likely to lack confidence in their own ability to improve their predicament.
- *Concepts and theories that will help them understand and manage the change process:* These include concepts and theories that will help them to:
  - identify the kind of change that confronts them, for example incremental or discontinuous
  - understand the process of changing
  - identify what needs to be attended to – through a process of diagnosis and goal setting – if they are to achieve desired outcomes.
- *Change management skills:* While conceptual understanding is necessary, it is not sufficient to guarantee that change agents will be able to secure desired changes. When managers are acting as change agents, they need to be able to communicate, offer leadership, work with teams, confront, negotiate, motivate and manage relationships with others.

2 Leading the change process: After persuading others of the need for change, it is necessary to decide who will, at least in the first instance, facilitate the process. The change agent could be an insider, a member of the system or subsystem that is the target for change, or an outsider. There is some evidence suggesting that change efforts are most successful when led (pulled) by users rather than (pushed) by technical experts.

3 Establishing an effective change relationship:
- The quality of the relationship between the change agent and others is highly dependent on factors such as confidence and trust.
- Associated issues for the change agent include being clear about who the client is, and keeping an open mind about the precise nature of the problem, while seeking to clarify the issues of concern to the client.

References

Armenakis, A.A., Harris, S.G. and Mossholder, K.W. (1993) Creating readiness for organizational change, *Human Relations*, 46(6): 681–703.

Burnes, B. (2004) *Managing Change: A Strategic Approach to Organisational Dynamics.* Harlow: Pearson.

By, R.T. (2007) Ready or not … , *Journal of Change Management*, 7(1): 3–11.

Child, J. (1972) Organizational structure, environment and performance: The role of strategic choice, *Sociology*, 6(1): 1–22.

Child, J. (1997) Strategic choice in the analysis of action, strategies, organizations and environment: Resprospect and prospect, *Organization Studies*, 18(1): 43–76.

Clegg, C.W. (2000) Sociotechnical principles for system design, *Applied Ergonomics*, 31: 463–77.

Collins, J. (2001) *Good to Great: Why Some Companies Make the Leap … and Others Don't.* New York: HarperCollins.

Constantinescu, S. (2011) Leaked: Nokia's memo discussing the iPhone, Android, and the need for drastic change, IntoMobile, 8 February, www.intomobile.com/2011/02/08/leaked-nokias-memo-discusses-need-for-drastic-change/.

Cummings, T.G. and Worley, C.G. (2001) *Organization Development and Change* (7th edn). Cincinnati, OH: West.

Greenwood, R. and Hinings, C.R. (1996) Understanding radical organizational change: Bringing together the old and the new institutionalism, *Academy of Management Review*, 21(4): 1022–54.

Jones, R.A., Jimmieson, N.L. and Griffiths, A. (2005) The impact of organizational culture and reshaping capabilities on change implementation success: The mediating role of readiness for change, *Journal of Management Studies*, 42(2): 361–86.

Lines, R., Selart, M., Espedal, B. and Johansen, S.T. (2005) The production of trust during organizational change, *Journal of Change Management*, 5(2): 221–45.

Margerison, C.J. (2000) *Managerial Consulting Skills.* Aldershot: Gower.

May, R. (1969) *Love and Will.* New York: W.W. Norton.

Mellahi, K. and Wilkinson, A. (2004) Organisational failure: A critique of recent research and a proposed integrative framework, *International Journal of Management Reviews*, 5/6(1): 21–41.

Morgan, D.E. and Zeffane, R. (2003) Employee involvement, change and trust in management, *International Journal of Human Resource Management*, 14(1): 55–75.

Peters, T. and Waterman, R.H. (1982) *In Search of Excellence: Lessons from America's Best-run Companies.* New York: Harper & Row.

Pettigrew, A. and Whipp, R. (1991) *Managing for Competitive Success.* Oxford: Blackwell.

Pitt, M.R., McAulay, L. and Sims, D. (2002) Promoting strategic change: 'Playmaker' roles in organizational agenda formation, *Strategic Change*, 11: 155–72.

Pugh, D. (1993) Understanding and managing organisational change. In C. Mabey and B. Mayon-White (eds) *Managing Change.* London: Paul Chapman/Open University.

Raynor, M.R., Ahmed, M. and Henderson, A.D. (2009) Are 'great' companies just lucky?, *Harvard Business Review*, 84(4): 18–19.

Rotter, J.B. (1966) Generalized expectancies of internal versus external control of reinforcements, *Psychological Monographs: General and Applied*, 80(1): 1–28.

Selegman, M.E.P. (1975) *Learned Helplessness.* San Francisco, CA: W.H. Freeman.

Thaler, R.H. and Sunstein, C.R. (2009) *Nudge: Improving Decisions about Health, Wealth and Happiness.* London: Penguin.

Van Buren, M.E. and Safferstone, T. (2009) The quick win paradox, *Harvard Business Review*, 87(1): 54–61.

Werther, W.B. (2003) Strategic change and leader-follower alignment, *Organizational Dynamics*, 32(1): 32–45.

Wilson, D. (1992) *A Strategy for Change.* London: Routledge.

Chapter 6

Building change relationships

Some of the issues that can affect the quality of a change relationship, such as confidence and trust, were discussed in Chapter 5. This chapter focuses on five modes of intervening and discusses the importance of change agents demonstrating a genuine respect for the people they are working with.

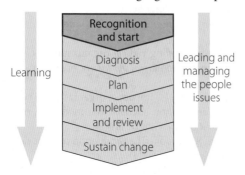

When people think about change agents, they often only think about external consultants, but within organizations, there are many people who occupy roles that are almost exclusively concerned with facilitating change. These people include systems analysts, business development advisers and project managers, to name but a few. There are also many managers who, as part of their normal day-to-day responsibilities, intervene to facilitate change. They contribute to the introduction of new working practices, finding ways of reducing costs, helping staff to develop better relationships with customers, helping others to identify and exploit opportunities offered by changing circumstances, or assisting colleagues who are experiencing problems that are affecting their performance or general wellbeing. Throughout this chapter, all those who facilitate change will be referred to as change agents or helpers and those who are being helped – whether colleagues, subordinates, or clients in the more conventional sense – will be referred to as clients.

Much has been written about the skills required by change agents. Greiner and Metzger (1983) refer to a wide range of skills but argue that consulting and facilitating change are essentially human enterprises and, irrespective of whether the problem being addressed concerns a new accounting system or the need for better strategic planning, the success of the project will be largely determined by the quality of change agents' interactions with the client or client group. Margerison (2000) echoes this view and highlights the importance of personal and interpersonal skills. It is these skills that will be the focus of attention in this chapter.

Intervention styles

Change agents can intervene to help in many different ways. The intervention style indictor below has been designed to help you to identify what your preferred approach to facilitating change would be. You might find it useful to complete it now and refer back to your intervention style profile as you read on. It will provide you with a point of reference when thinking about how you might improve the effectiveness of your helping interventions in future.

✓ *Exercise* **6.1** *The intervention style indicator*

Five scenarios (problem situations) are presented and, for each case, there are five examples of how a change agent/helper could respond. For *each* of the five responses to each case, circle the number on the scale that most closely reflects the probability that you would use that response. For example:

Never use ➡ | 1 | ② | 3 | 4 | 5 | ⬅ Definitely use

There are no right or wrong answers.

II

Scenario A

A newly appointed supervisor has complained to you that her subordinates are hostile, moody, only hear what they choose to hear, and often fail to obey instructions. She likened their behaviour to rebellious school children who are determined to 'break' the new teacher. Her account placed all the blame for the rapidly deteriorating situation onto her subordinates. You had not expected this kind of conversation because she had joined the company with glowing references and a 10-year record of successful people management. In addition, her work group has never been the source of problems before. All of them have been with the company for at least 10 months, most are well qualified and two have recently been through the company's assessment centre and have been identified as having potential for promotion.

How likely is it that you would use each of the following responses? Circle one number on each of the five scales.

1 Introduce the supervisor to a theory that might help her better understand the situation. For example, you might explain the basics of transactional analysis and ask her to (a) apply it to her problem and consider whether her subordinates see her as a controlling parent dealing with a group of inexperienced children rather than an adult interacting with other competent adults, and (b) speculate how she might apply the theory to improve the situation.

A1 Never use ➡ | 1 | 2 | 3 | 4 | 5 | ⬅ Definitely use

2 Tell her that she has failed to recognize the quality of her subordinates, she is undervaluing the contribution they can make, and she needs to delegate more and give them greater responsibility.

A2 Never use ➡ | 1 | 2 | 3 | 4 | 5 | ⬅ Definitely use

3 Listen carefully and attempt to see the problem through her eyes in the hope that, by being supportive, you can encourage her to open up and tell her story, which, in turn, may help her to develop a better understanding of the problem and what needs to be done about it.

A3 Never use ➡ | 1 | 2 | 3 | 4 | 5 | ⬅ Definitely use

4 Suggest to her that it may not only be her subordinates who hear what they choose to hear, and ask her if she has really paid attention to all the messages she has been sent by the members of her work group.

A4 Never use ➡ | 1 | 2 | 3 | 4 | 5 | ⬅ Definitely use

5 Help her to get to the bottom of the problem by assisting her to gather more information, which she can use to develop a better understanding of what is going on and what can be done to improve matters.

A5 Never use ➔ | 1 | 2 | 3 | 4 | 5 | ◀— Definitely use

Scenario B

You have been approached by the head of a strategic business unit in your organization with a request for help. She has been in post for six months and has come to the view that the way her top team is working together is adversely affecting performance.

How likely is it that you would use each of the following responses? Circle one number on each of the five scales.

1 Offer to collect information from people who are affected by how well the team is performing and feed this back to her and her senior colleagues to help them review their performance and agree what they need to do to improve matters.

B1 Never use ➔ | 1 | 2 | 3 | 4 | 5 | ◀— Definitely use

2 Offer to bring in a trainer to run a workshop for her top team, which would introduce them to the concept of team roles and help them use Belbin's model of team roles to diagnose how well they are working together and what they might do to improve their performance.

B2 Never use ➔ | 1 | 2 | 3 | 4 | 5 | ◀— Definitely use

3 Adopt a supportive approach and encourage her to talk about her concerns in order to help her clarify her own thoughts and feelings and develop for herself a better understanding of the situation.

B3 Never use ➔ | 1 | 2 | 3 | 4 | 5 | ◀— Definitely use

4 Interview all members of her top team and the people who are affected by how well the team is performing in order to prepare a report that lists a set of recommendations that she should implement to improve the situation.

B4 Never use ➔ | 1 | 2 | 3 | 4 | 5 | ◀— Definitely use

5 Focus attention on her behaviour and consider whether this might be contributing to the problem. This approach might involve challenging some of the assumptions she is making and/or drawing attention to discrepancies between what she says she does and what you observe her doing.

B5 Never use ➔ | 1 | 2 | 3 | 4 | 5 | ◀— Definitely use

Scenario C

You are the HR manager of a large utility company. An employee (a 40-year-old widower) was recently promoted and moved from a busy office in the city, where he had spent most of his working life, to manage a small but strategically important office in a relatively isolated small town. He has come to see you because he is unhappy with the new job. He misses his friends, does not enjoy being the boss in a situation where he has no colleagues he can relate to, and he reports that the people who live locally are cliquish, aloof and unfriendly.

How likely is it that you would use each of the following responses? Circle one number on each of the five scales.

1 Tell him there is a vacancy at his old grade in the department he used to work in and indicate that you think the best solution would be for him to move back.

C1 Never use → | 1 | 2 | 3 | 4 | 5 | ← Definitely use

2 Explore how he feels about the situation without passing judgement or jumping to conclusions. Make sure that you really understand why he is unhappy and do everything you can to help him clarify his own feelings about what the problem might be. You might listen hard to what he has to say and then reflect back to him the essence of what you think you heard. For example: 'What you seem to be saying is ... Have I got it right?'

C2 Never use → | 1 | 2 | 3 | 4 | 5 | ← Definitely use

3 Help him adopt a balanced problem-solving approach and encourage him to thoroughly explore every aspect of the problem and, where necessary, gather information that might help him identify and evaluate possible solutions; for example, by helping him to identify opportunities to meet new people.

C3 Never use → | 1 | 2 | 3 | 4 | 5 | ← Definitely use

4 Give him the kind of feedback that might push him into taking a new initiative, for example by telling him that you have listened to what he has said and not once heard him mention anything he has actually done to try to make new friends; in fact, all he seems to do is moan about others and complain that they do nothing to make him welcome. You might try to encourage him into action by asking him if he has thought about what he might do that would make others want to get to know him better.

C4 Never use → | 1 | 2 | 3 | 4 | 5 | ← Definitely use

5 Lend him a copy of Dale Carnegie's book *How to Win Friends and Influence People* (1936) and suggest that if he could master some of the techniques and skills it contains, he might more easily make new friends.

C5 Never use → | 1 | 2 | 3 | 4 | 5 | ← Definitely use

Scenario D

The CEO of a fast-growing software company has approached you for help following the second time in 12 months that a project team has failed to deliver a major project within budget and on time. She told you that, on both occasions, similar problems appear to have been associated with the failures. She also told you that relationships between members of the project team have deteriorated and they all appear to be blaming each other for the failures.

How likely is it that you would use each of the following responses? Circle one number on each of the five scales.

1 Interview the CEO and the manager in charge of the project team to ensure that you have a good understanding of what happened before advising the CEO what she should do to ensure that future projects will be managed more efficiently and effectively.

D1 Never use ➤ 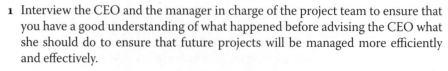 ◄— Definitely use

2 Run a workshop on new approaches to managing projects and use the models presented to help team members review the way they managed the last two projects and identify lessons they might use to inform the way they will manage the next project.

D2 Never use ➤ | 1 | 2 | 3 | 4 | 5 | ◄— Definitely use

3 Talk to each member of the team individually in order to help them express any frustrations, anxieties or other feelings that might be inhibiting their ability to make an objective assessment of the situation.

D3 Never use ➤ | 1 | 2 | 3 | 4 | 5 | ◄— Definitely use

4 Interview all members of the project team and other stakeholders in order to identify key issues related to the failures and then convene a workshop where you can feed this information back and use it to stimulate a discussion of the problem and help them explore ways of improving their performance.

D4 Never use ➤ | 1 | 2 | 3 | 4 | 5 | ◄— Definitely use

5 Work with the CEO to help her clarify the issues she wants to raise with the project team, and then facilitate a meeting where she can confront members with her concerns.

D5 Never use ➤ | 1 | 2 | 3 | 4 | 5 | ◄— Definitely use

Scenario E

A colleague has come to you for help. He does not want to be an autocratic boss and believes that people work best when they are given the freedom to get on with their jobs. However, his department is beginning to gain a reputation for not getting it right. He has explained that while he always tries to pursue an open-door policy, there are some people who never cross his threshold. Consequently, he is badly informed and avoidable mistakes have been made. He is obviously upset and you suspect that he has just had a rather fraught meeting with his manager about this.

How likely is it that you would use each of the following responses? Circle one number on each of the five scales.

1 Share with him a similar problem you once had and tell him what you did about it. Also, suggest that there can come a time when democracy has to go out of the window and you have to read the riot act, which is what he should do now.

E1 Never use ➤  ◄— Definitely use

2 Tell him about a theory you are familiar with, which argues that the best style of leadership might vary from one situation to another, and suggest that one way

forward might be for him to consider whether his current style appears to be a 'best fit', or whether the theory would suggest an alternative leadership style.

E2 Never use ➔ [1 | 2 | 3 | 4 | 5] ◄— Definitely use

3 On the basis of what you have observed, challenge his view that he always operates an open-door policy. You might, for example, tell him that you have heard that he is never around when he is needed, and that, while he might believe he is approachable, others see him as aloof and distant. You might follow this up by asking him to consider how true this is.

E3 Never use ➔ [1 | 2 | 3 | 4 | 5] ◄— Definitely use

4 You can see that he is upset, so decide that the best thing you can do is to sit him down with a cup of coffee and let him get it off his chest.

E4 Never use ➔ [1 | 2 | 3 | 4 | 5] ◄— Definitely use

5 Help him identify some specific circumstances where things have gone wrong, and then question him about a number of these problems to sort out precisely what happened and whether there are any patterns he could do something about.

E5 Never use ➔ [1 | 2 | 3 | 4 | 5] ◄— Definitely use

SCORING

In the grid below, all the available responses to each case have been arranged into columns that reflect five different styles of helping.

- Taking each scenario in turn, enter the *number you circled* for each response alongside the appropriate response code in the grid. For example, for case A, you may have circled ② for response A1, so enter '2' in the square for A1, and you may have circled ⑤ for response A2, so enter '5' in the square for A2, and so on.

NB: For cases B to E, the response codes are presented in different sequences and are *not* arranged in order from 1 to 5.

- Calculate the total score for each column and enter this in the box provided. The total score for each column indicates your relative preference for the different helping styles.

Response grid									
	Theorizing		Advising		Supporting		Challenging		Information gathering
Scenario A	A1		A2		A3		A4		A5	
NB: From B to E, the response codes are not arranged in order from 1 to 5									
Scenario B	B2		B4		B3		B5		B1	
Scenario C	C5		C1		C2		C4		C3	
Scenario D	D2		D1		D3		D5		D4	
Scenario E	E2		E1		E4		E3		E5	
TOTAL									

You should now have a score for all five modes of intervening. Note whether your scores are equally spread across all five intervention styles, or whether your response pattern indicates that you prefer to use one or two approaches more than the other modes of intervening.

You might find it useful to keep this information to hand and refer back to it at relevant points during the chapter.

The goal of intervening

Change agents intervene to facilitate change. Blake and Mouton (1986) describe their interventions as 'cycle-breaking endeavours'. They argue that behaviour tends to be cyclical in character, that is, sequences of behaviour are repeated within specific time periods or particular contexts or settings. Some of these patterns of behaviour are advantageous to the client or client group but some do little to promote their interests and may even be harmful (see the discussion of path dependence in Chapter 1). They go on to argue that individuals, groups or larger client systems such as entire organizations may engage in behaviour cycles by force of habit. They may not be conscious of the possibility of harmful or self-defeating consequences. They may be aware that things are not going well, but they may not understand why or what they could do to improve matters. The change agent's function is to help clients identify and break out of these damaging kinds of cycles.

This cycle-breaking endeavour can take many forms. It can be prescriptive or collaborative. Egan (2004) argues that problem management and opportunity development are not things that change agents do *to* clients. He advocates a collaborative approach that involves clients achieving their goals through the facilitation of the change agent. However, much of the help offered by external consultants and internal change agents is not collaborative in nature, as we will see below.

The five modes of intervening featured in the intervention style indicator – advising, supporting, theorizing, challenging and information gathering – are now discussed.

Prescriptive mode of intervening: advising

The mode of intervening referred to as 'advising' on the intervention style indicator is prescriptive. Many change agents intervene by giving advice and telling others what to do in order to rectify problems or develop opportunities. Change agents who adopt this mode of intervening assume that they have a greater level of relevant expertise than their clients and can discern their real needs. They also appear to assume that clients lack the necessary competence to either make a sound diagnosis or plan corrective actions for themselves.

In many circumstances, consultants or change managers can see a solution because they are more experienced than their clients, but if they intervene by offering advice and telling people what to do, they deprive them of the opportunity to learn how to solve the problem for themselves. Clients can become dependent on the change agent and the next time they experience a difficulty, they have to seek help again.

Often, clients actively seek advice, especially when they are under great pressure to find a solution and/or when they have tried to solve the problem a number of different ways to no avail. Steele (1969) argues that the needs and attitudes of the client and the change agent may propel the change agent towards exclusive occupancy of the role of expert in their relationship, and in those circumstances where the client accepts the change agent as expert, there may be some benefits. However, he also identifies some costs. One is increased dependency and the other has to do with the change agent's neglect of clients' knowledge about their own problem. Even where clients do not attempt to withhold this knowledge, the helper may choose to ignore it:

> The client often has great wisdom (intuitive if not systematic) about many aspects of his own situation, and an overweighing of the consultant's knowledge value may indeed cause poorer choices to be made than if there were a more balanced view of that which each can contribute to the situation. (Steele, 1969, p. 193)

Moreover, although clients often seek advice, there are circumstances when they may reject any advice they are offered. For example, they are likely to reject advice when they lack confidence in the expertise of the change agent, or when it is offered by a change agent who appears to be insensitive to their needs.

Collaborative modes of intervening

The other four modes of intervening – supporting, theorizing, challenging and information gathering – are non-prescriptive. Change agents adopting these approaches work with clients to help them develop opportunities or manage their own problems rather than intervene by telling them what they should do.

A number of factors can contribute to clients being ineffective opportunity developers or problem managers. Emotional states such as anger or insecurity may undermine their ability to function normally. They may lack the information they need to understand the problem or develop a plan for change. They may be locked into an ideology or set of beliefs that inhibit their ability to respond effectively. They may not have access to concepts and models that can help them identify the cause-and-effect relationships that maintain the status quo or the opportunities for change. There is also the possibility that they have already tried to introduce changes and their efforts have failed to deliver desired outcomes. All these conditions can contribute to clients lacking confidence in their own ability.

Seligman's (1975) theory of learned helplessness, mentioned in Chapter 5, states that when individuals are subjected to events that are uncontrollable, that is, when the probability of an outcome is the same, irrespective of how they respond, they will develop expectations of non-contingency between response and outcome. The theory suggests that the incentive for clients to initiate activity directed towards resolving a problem depends on their expectation that responding will produce some improvement to the problematic situation. If clients have no confidence in their own ability to achieve any improvement, they will not try. Hiroto (1974) illustrated this effect with an experiment that exposed one group of college students to loud controllable noises they could terminate by pressing a button four times and a second group to uncontrollable noises that were terminated independently of what they did. A third group was not exposed to any noise. All subjects were then tested in a situation in which it was possible for them to exercise control over noise termination. Hiroto found that the groups that had either been subjected to controllable noise or no noise learned to terminate the noise in the later test situation, whereas subjects who had previously been subjected to uncontrollable noise failed to terminate noises during later tests.

Abramson et al. (1978) distinguish between universal helplessness – where the client believes that the problem is unsolvable by anyone – and personal helplessness – where the client believes that the problem is solvable, for example by the helper but not by the self. The danger with the prescriptive/advising approach to helping is that it can promote a sense of personal helplessness in the client and the client may become dependent on the help of others.

Egan (2004) discusses the notion of 'empowerment' in the helping relationship. He notes that some people come to believe, sometimes from an early age, that there is nothing they can do about certain life situations. They engage in disabling self-talk (see Ellis, 1977) and tell themselves that they cannot manage certain situations and they cannot cope. Egan's position is that whether clients are victims of their own doing or the doings of others, they can and must take an active part in managing their own problems, including the search for solutions and efforts towards achieving those solutions. He also argues that helpers can do a great deal in facilitating people to develop a sense of agency or self-efficacy. They can help clients to challenge self-defeating beliefs and attitudes about themselves and the situation, to develop the knowledge, skills and resources they need to succeed, and to encourage them to take reasonable risks and support them when they do. The function of the change agent, according to Egan, is to encourage clients to apply a problem-solving approach to their current situation and to learn from this experience, so that, over the longer term, they will apply this approach again to future situations.

The collaborative modes of intervening discussed below involve supporting clients, providing them with concepts and theories to help them make sense of situations and identify what can be done to improve matters, challenging and confronting their assumptions, attitudes and behaviors, and helping them identify and acquire the information they need to manage the situation more effectively.

Supportive approach

The supportive mode of intervening involves the change agent working with others to help them clarify their views and express feelings and emotions that impede objective thinking about a problem or opportunity.

Margerison (2000) refers to change agents helping clients to give themselves permission. In the first instance, this involves clients giving themselves permission to talk about difficult issues, which leads on to giving themselves permission to act rather than to worry. He reports that in his consulting experience, an effective intervention has sometimes been to just listen and help managers to open up difficult areas and talk about matters they have so far avoided. He observes that clients appear to experience this kind of intervention as a great relief. Change agents adopting a supportive mode of intervening listen empathetically, withhold any judgement and help clients develop for themselves a more objective view of the situation. It is assumed that this new level of awareness will often be sufficient to help them go on and solve the problem for themselves.

Supportive interventions have many similarities with the way client-centred counsellors and social workers work with their clients (Rogers, 1958). They listen, reflect and sometimes interpret what clients have to say about themselves and their relationship with others and the situation, but they do not intervene or develop any active strategies for dealing with clients' problems. It is a person-centred, as opposed to a problem-centred, approach to helping. Example 6.1 will help to clarify how this approach can be effective. Blake and Mouton (1986) describe a case in which a consultant working at the Hawthorne Works plant of Western Electric in the USA used a supporting approach to help a shop-floor worker.

Example 6.1 *Using a supportive approach*

The consultant overheard the worker complaining, in an emotional tone, about his supervisor and decided to intervene. He asked what had been going on and was told, in the same emotional tone: 'The bosses are not worth a damn because when you have a rise coming to you, they will not give it.' The worker went on to tell the consultant that he thought the place stank and he wanted to get out. The consultant's response was to avoid siding with either the worker or the supervisor, but to invite the worker into his office to 'talk it over'. As the interaction progressed, the worker unloaded his feelings about his supervisor. Then he began to ramble from one complaint to another. He had been refused a rise, and because he was at the top of his grade, he

could not advance any higher. He complained about the machine setters who did everything they could to protect their own position and stop others learning anything that would help them to improve the work they did.

Throughout this diatribe, the consultant maintained his neutral stance and refrained from making any evaluation of the worker's complaints. He assumed the role of active listener and did little more than reflect his sympathetic understanding by repeating what he had been told. For example, in response to the complaint about the machine setters, he said: 'I see, they seem to be pretty selfish about their knowledge of screw machines.'

In this case, the consultant's strategy was to allow the worker to vent his anger because he believed that until he had done this, he would be too frustrated to think clearly. It appeared to work. Slowly, as the tension eased, the conversation moved away from gripes towards problem solving. The consultant confined his interventions to supportive listening and clarifying, but eventually the worker (client) began to work through his problems for himself.

Supportive modes of intervening can be effective but there are situations where this approach to helping clients develop a better understanding of their situation may not be sufficient to produce change. In these circumstances, other modes of intervening might be required, but supporting can still have an important role to play in the early stages.

Theorizing approach

The theorizing approach involves change agents identifying theories and conceptual models that are pertinent to clients' problem situation, presenting these to clients and helping them learn to use them to facilitate a better understanding of their situation in an analytical cause-and-effect fashion. The change agents then build on this understanding and use it to help clients identify what they can do to move towards a more desirable state of affairs.

This mode of intervening might be adopted when change agents feel that some kind of theoretical framework could help clients to organize their thoughts and provide the basis for a fresh appraisal of their predicament. For example, the stakeholder grid discussed in Chapter 10 might be used to help a management team identify important stakeholders and develop strategies for winning their support, or the Burke-Litwin causal model of organizational performance (Chapter 7) might be used to focus attention on important cause-and-effect relationships that affect performance. Change agents can also use theories to facilitate the discussion of potentially delicate or sensitive issues. For example, a discussion of Belbin's (1993) team roles might provide a relatively safe and non-threatening way of exploring how members of a management team work together. This theory-based approach can also provide a way of exploring and testing implicit assumptions and values in a way that avoids direct confrontation, and it can provide a basis for increasing the client's capacity for independent action. Force-field analysis (introduced in Chapter 2) also offers an approach that clients can use to help understand their predicament and identify a viable course of action, as shown in Example 6.2.

Example **6.2** *Using force-field analysis*

Bill had been recruited by a large multinational auto components manufacturer to transform the organization's manufacturing capability so that the company could regain its previous world-class status and ensure its survival in an increasingly competitive environment. Sometime after his appointment, he began to worry about his lack of progress. The senior managers of the operating divisions located in several countries around the world were resisting his efforts to introduce change. An external consultant met Bill when he was working on another project in the company. They talked about the problem for 20 minutes and Bill suggested a further conversation, which happened the following week.

The story Bill told revealed a complex set of related problems but eventually he focused on an immediate goal, which was to engage more effectively with senior managers and persuade them to provide him with detailed information about the current situation in the manufacturing units for which they were responsible. Initially, Bill focused on why managers should provide him with this information. He needed it to be able to assess how well the group was doing in relation to leading competitors and to assess the company's strengths and weaknesses in terms of its current manufacturing technology. He also wanted to be in a position to identify opportunities for rationalization and areas where efforts to introduce new technologies might be productive. He expressed a genuine desire to help divisions raise their performance and felt that the information he was seeking would help him make this contribution. He also felt that the information would be valuable to managers for their own use within their own divisions. Given all these powerful reasons why the provision of this information was in the company's best interests, he failed to understand why divisional managers insisted on keeping him at arm's length and were resistant to his requests for information.

In terms of Lewin's force-field (1951), Bill had focused his attention on the driving forces. His initial plan for achieving his goal was to further increase these driving forces by enlisting the support of the CEO and asking him to instruct the divisional managers to comply with his requests for detailed information. At this point, the consultant introduced Bill to force-field analysis, suggesting that before he pursued this course of action, Bill might consider some of the restraining forces. Why were the divisional managers resisting his requests and was there anything Bill could do to lower this resistance? (In Chapter 2, it was noted that Lewin favoured action directed towards reducing restraining forces.) The consultant suggested that Bill might find it helpful to view the situation through the eyes of the divisional managers. As he did this, Bill began to speculate about whether they truly understood his role and what he was trying to achieve. He also recognized the possibility that they feared that the detailed reporting he was requesting could threaten their autonomy, unfavourable comparisons might be made between the divisions, and the information – in its raw form – might be misinterpreted by others at corporate headquarters, who might access it when making decisions about resources, promotions and bonuses. He also recognized that he had not involved the divisional managers in specifying the information requirements, nor had he given them the opportunity to discuss the information that would be of help to them in their own businesses. There was also a possible problem relating to the cost of collecting this information. Who was to pay for it? This analysis helped

►

Bill develop a better understanding of the situation and provided a good basis for planning action to achieve his goal.

Bill decided that his first initiative would not be to appeal to the CEO to increase pressure on the divisional managers to comply with his requests. He didn't rule this out, but decided that actions directed towards reducing the restraining forces might be more productive, especially bearing in mind that achieving this particular goal was only one part of his overall plan for change. The consultant continued to work with Bill to help him prioritize the forces he wanted to work on and to identify specific actions he could take to achieve his aim. In this case, it transpired that all Bill's priorities for action involved reducing the power of selected restraining forces. It is not essential that plans should only be based on reducing the power of restraining forces, but plans that only involve actions to increase the power of driving forces might deserve another look.

Blake and Mouton (1986) argue that theories can help clients free themselves from blind reliance on intuition, hunch, common sense and conventional wisdom and enable them to see situations more objectively. Theories can be applied to all classes of problems in a wide range of situations, so long as the theory is valid and clients are willing and able to internalize it and make it a personally useful source of guidance. Theory-based interventions might be less effective than other approaches if the change agent introduces clients to a theory they perceive to be invalid, irrelevant or too complicated, or if the client is unreceptive to the possibility of using theory as a basis for managing problems. Even valid, user-friendly theories may be rejected, for example when clients are emotionally charged. In such circumstances, a supportive mode of intervening might be used before adopting a theory-based approach to helping.

Challenging approach

The challenging mode of intervening has great potential for facilitating change. It involves the change agent confronting the foundations of the client's thinking in an attempt to identify beliefs, values and assumptions that may be distorting the way situations are viewed. Blake and Mouton (1986, p. 210) observe that:

> Values underlie how people think and feel and what they regard as important and what is trivial. Sometimes guidance from a particular set of values is sound – things go smoothly, results are good. Sometimes values cause problems – they are inappropriate, invalid, or unjustified under the circumstances. Often people who must work in concert hold different values; failure to achieve agreement in such situations results in antagonisms, disorder or outright chaos.

An assumption underlying this challenging mode of intervening is that effective action can be undermined by clients' inability or unwillingness to face up to reality. They may not be aware of some aspects of their behaviour or its consequences, or they rationalize or justify their behaviour and in so doing create or perpetuate an unsatisfactory situation. Challenging interventions are designed to call attention to contradictions in action and attitude, or challenge precedents or practices that seem inappropriate. The aim of this approach is not only to challenge values and assumptions but also identify alternatives that might facilitate the exploitation of opportunities, or lead to the development of more effective solutions to problems, as we will see in Example 6.3.

Example **6.3** *Using a challenging approach*

The head teacher of a successful primary school had worked hard to improve the school's external reputation and had invested a great deal of effort in building a good team spirit among his staff. When one of them applied for a job elsewhere, the head teacher interpreted this as a sign of disloyalty. He communicated his reaction to the individual concerned and made his disapproval public by excluding him from management team meetings. The deputy head intervened. He reminded the head about his own early career progress and pointed out how this was no different from the progress the teacher who had applied for the job elsewhere was seeking. The deputy pointed out that the head had rarely stayed in one job for more than three years, whereas this individual had already been in post and had performed satisfactorily for almost four years. He asked the head how he thought others would interpret his action and what effect it was likely to have on the team spirit he prized so highly. Eventually, the head accepted that the teacher's application was a timely and appropriate step to take, and that he had not only overlooked the career development needs of this individual but had given insufficient attention to the career development of all his staff. He also accepted that his response had been inconsistent with the management culture he was trying to create.

Great care needs to be exercised when change agents adopt a challenging style. Egan (2004) argues that confrontation can be strong medicine and, in the hands of the inept, can be destructive. Effective challenges are those which are received by clients as helpful invitations to explore aspects of a problem from a new perspective. Change agents adopting this approach ask questions or provide feedback that draws the client's attention to inappropriate attitudes, values, discrepancies and distortions, but they avoid telling the client how they should think or act. Challenges that clients perceive as personal attacks or a public unmasking of possible inadequacies are likely to be met with some form of strong defensive reaction and will rarely be effective. Even when a challenging style of intervention promises to be effective, this promise may not be realized if change agents are inept at challenging and confronting.

Information-gathering approach

The information-gathering approach to helping involves change agents assisting clients to collect data they can use to evaluate and reinterpret a problem situation. Hayes (2002) illustrates this with the example of a sales trainer (Example 6.4).

The assumption underlying this approach is that information deficiencies are an important cause of malfunctioning. Helpers' objectives are to guide clients so that they arrive at a better level of awareness of the underlying causes of a problem and to help them to identify what action is required to resolve it. Many change agents adopting this approach assume that any information they might present will be less acceptable and less likely to be understood than information that indi-

---

Example **6.4** *Using an information-gathering approach*

A trainer in the sales department of a machine tool company was faced with a demotivated young representative who had recently lost three important accounts. The trainer suggested that he got in touch with the buyers he used to deal with and ask them why they had changed suppliers. The trainer suspected that it was because the representative had not been attentive to their needs but he felt that it would be more effective if the representative discovered this for himself and then decided what he needed to do about it.

© PHOTODISC/GETTY IMAGES

---

viduals or groups generate for themselves. Another assumption often made by change agents adopting this approach is that clients will be less resistant to proposals and action plans they generate for themselves. Pascale and Sterin (2005) point to 'positive deviance' as an example of an intervention that relies on helping others to gather and use information for themselves. It involves helping clients to identify and investigate examples of innovation and superior performance in order to share their findings and use them as a basis for exploring ways of spreading this best practice. For example, one department in a hospital was identified as being a positive deviant because it had a very low incidence of the MRSA super-bug. Staff from other parts of the hospital visited the department and interviewed staff and patients to identify possible causes and actions they could take to control the problem in their departments. Pascale and Sterin argue that because the process of information gathering is undertaken by members of the client system, ownership is high, and because the innovators who are responsible for superior performance are members of the same system ('just like us'), disbelief and resistance are easier to overcome.

Sometimes, change agents might be more directly involved in the collection of data but when this happens, they are often working on behalf of their clients and they feed the information back to them for them to use to develop a better understanding of their problem and explore ways of improving the situation.

Developing collaborative relationships

Collaborative modes of intervening are most effective when change managers have a genuine respect for the people they are working with. This requires that they:

- *Signal that the other's viewpoint is worth listening to:* This reflects their willingness to commit to working with others. It also suggests a level of openness to their point of view. Too often, even when change managers go through the motions of asking others for their views, they are not really committed to listening. If collaborative working is to be effective, change managers need to respect others' views and clearly signal this respect.
- *Suspend critical judgement:* If change managers are really committed to working collaboratively with others, they need to keep an open mind and avoid reaching

premature conclusions. Egan (2004) and Reddy (1987) assert that this does not mean that they should signal approval of everything they hear or observe, rather it involves communicating that their point of view has been heard and understood. The act of suspending judgement, and trying to understand the other's viewpoint, can encourage the client to explore their position. It avoids pushing them into defensive positions and gives them the freedom to change their view.

✓ Exercise **6.2** *Monitoring your respect for others*

Next time you are involved in a helping relationship, observe yourself. Open up a second channel and monitor what you are *thinking* when you are relating with a client (remember that by 'client', we are referring to anyone on the receiving end of the change). What does this tell you about your respect for others and their points of view?

- Are you able to suspend critical judgement?
- Do you believe that the client's point of view is worth listening to?

According to Reddy (1987), suspending judgement and keeping an open mind do not come naturally. He argues that we have been conditioned to persuade others to our point of view. At school, there is nearly always a debating society but rarely a listening club. It may be that we often fail to keep an open mind because if we listen, we may end up agreeing, and if we agree, we may appear to have lost. However, the aim of a collaborative helping relationship is not to win. Signalling to others that their views are worth listening to and suspending judgement can encourage them to believe that the change agent is prepared to help them to achieve the best outcome, whatever that might be.

Prescriptive versus collaborative modes of intervening

It has been argued that the most effective way of helping others is to help them to help themselves, and that this will normally involve adopting a collaborative mode of intervening. There may, however, be occasions when a more prescriptive style might be appropriate. Clients may be faced with a critical problem that, if not resolved quickly, could have disastrous consequences. If the change agent has the expertise to help them avoid this disastrous outcome, it might be appropriate to adopt a prescriptive mode to provide the required help fast. While this kind of intervention is only likely to provide a 'short-term fix', it might be effective if it can buy time to help clients to develop the competences they require to manage similar situations they might encounter in the future.

Mode of intervening and the stage of the helping relationship

The most effective mode of intervening can vary over the course of a helping relationship. The supportive mode that involves the use of empathetic listening to help clients develop a new level of understanding might be especially effective at the beginning of the helping process. As well as helping clients clarify their thinking about an opportunity or problem, it can contribute to the development of trust and a supportive relationship between change agent and client. However, as the helping relationship develops, it might be necessary for change agents to modify their initial approach and begin to adopt a more challenging, information-gathering or theorizing style of facilitation. They may need to confront clients about discrepancies between what they say and what they do, provide them with feedback, or help them gather new information for themselves that will help them view their problem from a different perspective. It might also be beneficial to introduce clients to theories and conceptual frameworks that will facilitate their diagnosis and action planning. In other words, any one approach, used in isolation, might not always lead to an adequate level of understanding about a problem or to the development and implementation of plans to move towards a preferred future. It might be necessary to draw on a number of different modes of intervening as clients' needs change. Egan (2004) argues that helpers should be competent in all the approaches to helping discussed in this chapter because they are all interdependent. For example, helpers who specialize in challenging may be poor confronters if their challenges are not based on an empathic understanding of the client, or if they confront clients too early in the helping relationship.

Helping skills

The focus of attention in this chapter has been on intervention styles and how they can be applied to facilitate change over the course of the helping relationship. Passing reference has also been made to some of the specific helping skills that change agents need to use to intervene effectively. These 'helping skills' are not a special set of skills reserved exclusively for the helping relationship (Hopson, 1984). Helping involves the appropriate use of a wide range of 'everyday and commonly used' interpersonal skills. Some of these are:

- self-awareness
- establishing rapport and building relationships
- empathy
- listening to facts and feelings
- probing for information
- identifying themes and seeing the bigger picture
- giving feedback
- challenging assumptions.

These and many other relevant interpersonal behaviours are considered in detail in *Interpersonal Skills at Work* (Hayes, 2002).

Exercise 6.3 is designed to help you reflect on the discussion so far and your experience of being a client.

✓ Exercise **6.3** *Identifying effective helping behaviours*

The aim of this exercise is to use your own experience to identify effective helping behaviours. Think of a number of occasions when others have tried to help you.

1 Identify people whose behaviour towards you was very helpful.
   - What did they do that you found helpful?
   - How did you respond to this behaviour? (Why was it helpful?)

Record your observations below.

List of helpful behaviours	Explain why the behaviours are helpful

2 Identify people who, while trying to help, behaved towards you in ways you found *un*helpful.
   • What did they do that you found unhelpful?
   • How did you respond to this behaviour? (Why was it unhelpful?)

List of unhelpful behaviours	Explain why the behaviours are unhelpful

Reflect on your findings and consider how they relate to the modes of intervention referred to in this chapter. Does your experience highlight any skills not discussed but which appear to have an important bearing on the outcome of the helping relationship?

Summary

The goal of intervening is not about planning or action but about achieving results – system-enhancing outcomes such as innovations realized, problems managed more effectively and opportunities developed, or new organization-enhancing behaviours put in place.

Blake and Mouton describe intervening as a 'cycle-breaking endeavour'. This chapter considered five modes of intervening to facilitate change:

• *Advising:* involves change agents drawing on their own knowledge and experience and telling clients what they should do to resolve their problem.

- *Supporting:* involves listening empathetically; withholding judgement and helping clients to express the feelings and emotions that impede clear and objective thinking about their problem. The prime focus is the client rather than the problem.
- *Theorizing:* change agents present clients with a theory relevant to their problem and help them to use the theory to understand the problem and plan remedial action.
- *Challenging:* involves confronting the foundations of clients' thinking in order to identify beliefs and values that may be distorting the way they view the situation.
- *Information gathering:* involves helping clients to collect data they can use to evaluate and reinterpret the situation.

In many circumstances, consultants or change managers can see a solution because they are more experienced than their clients/subordinates and this encourages them to intervene by giving advice and telling others what to do. However:

- Telling people what to do may deprive them of the opportunity to learn how to solve the problem for themselves.
- Clients can become dependent on the change agent and the next time they experience a difficulty, they have to seek help again.

While acknowledging that advising may be an appropriate mode of intervention in some circumstances, this chapter highlighted the benefits of those approaches that help clients to help themselves.

Helpers are most effective when they demonstrate a genuine respect for the people they are working with. They can do this by:

- signalling that the other person's viewpoint is worth listening to
- suspending critical judgement.

Helping involves the appropriate use of a wide range of 'everyday and commonly used' interpersonal skills.

References

Abramson, L.Y., Seligman, M.E.P. and Teesdale, J.D. (1978) Learned helplessness in humans: Critique and performulations, *Journal of Abnormal Psychology*, 87(1): 49–74.

Belbin, R.M. (1993) *Team Roles at Work*. Oxford: Butterworth Heinemann.

Blake, R.R. and Mouton, J.S. (1986) *Consultation: A Handbook for Individual and Organization Development*. Reading, MA: Addison-Wesley.

Carnegie, D. (1936) *How to Win Friends and Influence People*. New York: Simon & Schuster.

Egan, G. (2004) *The Skilled Helper: A Problem Management and Opportunity Development Approach to Helping*. Pacific Grove, CA: Brooks/Cole.

Ellis, A. (1977) The basic clinical theory of rational-emotive therapy. In A. Ellis and G. Grieger (eds) *Handbook of Rational-emotive Therapy*. Monterey, CA: Brooke/Cole.

Greiner, L.E. and Metzger, R.O. (1983) *Consulting to Management*. Englewood Cliffs, NJ: Prentice Hall.

Hayes, J. (2002) *Interpersonal Skills at Work*. Hove: Routledge.

Hiroto, D.S. (1974) Locus of control and learned helplessness, *Journal of Experimental Psychology*, 102(2): 187–93.

Hopson, B. (1984) Counselling and helping. In C. Cooper and P. Makin (eds) *Psychology for Managers*. Leicester: British Psychological Society.

Lewin, K. (1951) *Field Theory in Social Science*. New York: Harper & Row.

Margerison, C.J. (2000) *Managerial Consulting Skills*. Aldershot: Gower.

Pascale, R.T. and Sterin, J. (2005) Your company's secret change agents, *Harvard Business Review*, 83(5): 72–81.

Reddy, M. (1987) *The Manager's Guide to Counselling at Work*. London: British Psychological Society/Methuen.

Rogers, C.R. (1958) The characteristics of a helping relationship, *Personnel and Guidance Journal*, 37(1): 6–16.

Seligman, M.E.P. (1975) *Helplessness*. San Francisco, CA: W.H. Freeman.

Steele, F.I. (1969) Consultants and detectives, *Journal of Applied Behavioural Science*, 5(2): 193–4.

Visit **www.palgrave.com/companion/hayes-change-management4** *for further learning resources*

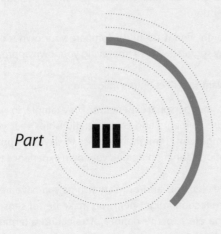

Part III DIAGNOSING WHAT NEEDS TO BE CHANGED

Introduction to Part III

Part III takes a closer look at diagnosing the need for change.

Chapter 7 Diagnosis

Organizational diagnosis is a process of research into the functioning of an organization that leads to recommendations for improvement.

The first part of this chapter examines the role of models in organizational diagnosis and introduces an exercise designed to help raise your awareness of the implicit models you use when thinking about organizations and assessing the need for change.

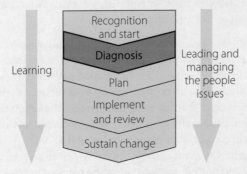

The second part considers the relative merits of component and holistic models. Component models focus on particular aspects of organizational functioning, such as motivation, decision making, group dynamics and organization structure, whereas holistic models consider the system as a whole. A useful starting point can be to use holistic models to provide an overall assessment before focusing attention on specific issues that appear to be the problem. Combining, in some additive manner, the specific assessments provided by a range of component models can provide an incomplete or misleading view of the health of the total system.

The main body of the chapter presents four holistic models that can be used to aid diagnosis:

1 Kotter's integrative model of organizational dynamics highlights the importance of alignment and explores the factors that determine organizational effectiveness in the short, medium and long term.

2 The McKinsey 7S model illustrates how change tools can be developed to identify areas of misalignment that require further investigation.

3 Weisbord's six-box model is an open systems model that draws attention to informal as well as formal aspects of organizational functioning.

4 The Burke-Litwin causal model of organizational performance and change draws attention to the causal weight of the various elements of the organization and indicates how

the requirement for different types of change can affect which elements of the organization might need to be a focus for attention.

When you have read this chapter, you might find it useful to compare your own model with these four and consider whether they suggest ways of improving your own approach to diagnosis.

To refine your own model, you might want to reflect on the following:

- How do the models presented relate to your personal experience? For example, to what extent do they accommodate or ignore elements and causal relationships that your experience has led you to believe are important? It might be unwise to slavishly apply a model that ignores aspects of organizational functioning that your own experience tells you are significant.
- Do any of the available models include elements and/or relationships you have never previously considered but which, on reflection, might help you make better sense of your own experience? You need to be alert to the danger of rejecting alternative models too hastily. You might find that a model that is quite different from your own personal model can provide useful new insights. Even if you decide not to adopt an alternative model in its entirety, you might decide to incorporate some aspects of it into your own model.

Three characteristics of a 'good' model are:

- relevance to the issues under consideration
- ability to identify critical cause-and-effect relationships
- ability to focus attention on elements that change managers can affect.

Chapter 8 *Gathering and interpreting information*

This chapter examines the process of gathering and interpreting information for the purpose of diagnosis. Attention is focused on five main steps:

1 *Selection of an appropriate conceptual model for diagnosis:* Conceptual models play a key role in the diagnostic process, because they help us decide which aspects of organizational behaviour require attention and provide a focus for information gathering. They also provide a basis for interpreting the information that has been collected. When selecting a model for diagnosis, the first point that has to be considered is the extent to which the model is relevant to the issue(s) under consideration, for example loss of market share, dysfunctional intergroup conflict, high labour turnover and so on.

2 *Clarification of information requirements:* Once a diagnostic model has been selected, the change manager can identify the items of information that will be required to assess how an organization (unit or work group) is performing.

3 *Information gathering:* Factors that might determine the method of data collection – interviews, questionnaires, projective methods, observations and unobtrusive measures – are considered, together with ways of sampling people, activities and records that will provide sufficient information to provide a representative picture of what is going on.

4 *Analysis:* Once information has been collected, it needs to be analysed. Some qualitative and quantitative analytical techniques are reviewed. Qualitative techniques are used to explain why people think and behave in certain ways, whereas quantitative techniques are used to count the numbers of people who think or behave in certain ways. Qualitative techniques are best used to answer why questions, whereas quantitative techniques are best used to answer what, when and who questions.

5 *Interpretation:* Issues that need to be considered when interpreting data are reviewed. Collecting information is not an innocuous or benign activity. Attention is drawn to the political issues associated with data collection, which need to be kept in mind as they can frustrate attempts to gain an accurate impression of organizational functioning.

✓ *Exercise* **Part III** *Useful questions for reviewing your approach to diagnosing the need for change*

In Chapter 2, after discussing each stage in the process model of change management, your attention was drawn to a number of questions that might help you assess how well a change is being (or was) managed. All these questions are summarized in Figure 2.5 and the questions relating to diagnosing the need for change are listed below:

- Who does the diagnosing: senior managers, consultants or those who will be responsible for making the change work?
- Are leaders willing to accept new data or do they only attend to data that defend the status quo or support their preconceived view?
- Does the diagnosis create a realistic and inspiring vision that will motivate others and help direct the change effort?

Reflect on and review these questions and, after reading the two chapters in Part III, revise this list and generate your own set of useful questions that you might find it helpful to refer to when you are leading a change.

III

Chapter **7**   # Diagnosis

Organizational diagnosis is a process of research into the functioning of an organization that leads to recommendations for improvement (Postma and Kok, 1999). The first part of this chapter examines the role of models in organizational diagnosis, and introduces the Site Security and Secure Escorts case study and an exercise on diagnostic model building to raise your awareness of the implicit models you use when thinking about organizations and assessing the need for change. The second part considers the relative merits of component and holistic models, and reviews four holistic models that have been widely used by change agents.

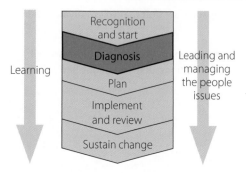

Diagnosis is not a one-off activity. The Site Security and Secure Escorts case study presented below illustrates how diagnosis is often a multi-stage iterative process that begins with the initial recognition of problems or opportunities but does not stop there. As you read the case, note how the diagnosis evolved over time. You might find it interesting to pay attention not only to the different phases in the diagnosis but also to who was involved, what they paid attention to and how they collected data.

Case study **7.1** *Site Security and Secure Escorts*

Site Security and Secure Escorts (SSSE) is a company wholly owned by what will be referred to here as CP Security Services. The parent company provides a wide range of security services in the UK and abroad, including risk assessment and management, site security and secure escort services, cash transit (armoured vehicles) and high-value courier services, detention centres and prison escorts, and technical security systems. SSSE provides manned guard and secure escort services across a range of sectors, including pharmaceuticals, financial services, telecommunications, defence and utilities, to provide protection from theft, vandalism, industrial espionage, terrorism and attacks from radical activists motivated by issues such as animal rights.

A new CEO was appointed to SSSE and tasked to grow the business and improve profitability. His first task was to familiarize himself with the current state of affairs and identify what could be done to improve the situation. He spent a lot of time out of his office meeting people. He had almost daily conversations with most managers at head office and, with his director of operations, visited clients and met SSSE staff working on clients' premises. His aim, using conversations, observations and management reports, was to identify key issues and begin to formulate an agenda for change. He did not embark on this process with a 'clean sheet'. When he joined SSSE, he brought with him, based on his previous experience of managing similar businesses, his own subjective model

▶

© BRAND X PICTURES

of how organizations work and the key cause-and-effect relationships that determine effectiveness, and used this to direct his attention and interpret what he saw, heard and read about the organization.

He quickly realized that a number of clients were unhappy with the quality of service provided by SSSE. This not only threatened to undermine his plan to grow the business and increase margins but also raised the possibility that SSSE would lose existing business as and when contracts came up for renewal. His initial diagnosis pointed to several factors that appeared to be contributing to this state of affairs:

- *Staff shortages:* Following 9/11 and the aggressive tactics employed by some animal rights activists, there had been a sharp increase in the demand for site security. This was accompanied by a related demand for new recruits to be more thoroughly vetted, a time-consuming process that reduced supply just when the demand for new staff was growing.
- *Management style:* The company's management style was top-down command and control. While this had been effective in the past when management could easily impose sanctions for poor performance, it was proving less effective in the tight labour market. There was evidence that it was having a negative impact on motivation and some employees were paying less attention to performance standards and were ignoring operating procedures, because they were confident, given the rising demand for staff, they would not be dismissed.

- *Management structure:* The number of supervisors had not increased in line with the number of new contracts, and so supervisors were overstretched. This was exacerbated by the fact that, in order to fulfill immediate contractual requirements for guards and escorts, supervisors had to stand in and personally cover for staff shortages.
- *Ineffective management information systems:* Decision making was highly centralized but inadequately supported by the quality of available management information. For example, managers located at headquarters did not have access to up-to-date information on operations, making it difficult for them to schedule work effectively.

The CEO shared and debated this assessment with senior colleagues. This debate produced some additional data and one minor reinterpretation and provided the basis for a searching discussion of what could be done to improve the situation. One suggestion was to explore ways of improving the performance of existing staff, but it was recognized that before this possibility could be pursued there was a need for more information. The operations director agreed to co-opt a site supervisor and conduct two focus groups with guards and escorts drawn from several sites. Their report indicated that while the guards and escorts raised different points specific to their roles, a number of common themes emerged. For example, both groups indicated that they often felt bored on the job, which lacked any meaningful challenge, and some remarks hinted that when not directly supervised, they read newspapers or did puzzles rather than give their full attention to their duties. They also felt undervalued. They realized there was a growing demand for personnel who had the level of security clearance required by SSSE's clients, but they felt that this 'scarcity factor' was not reflected in their rates of pay. These findings prompted the management team to initiate a more detailed diagnosis of the roles people were required to perform, with a view to redesigning their jobs in ways that would improve their motivation and the quality of their work. A consultant was employed to facilitate this step in the process. He introduced managers to Hackman and Oldham's (1980) job characteristics theory and helped them to use the job diagnostic survey to gather more information (see the theorizing mode of intervening discussed in Chapter 6).

Another suggestion for improvement was to take a detailed look at the way the organization was structured and the prevailing management style, and to consider alternatives that might address some of the issues uncovered by the initial diagnosis. The consultant who had been brought in to help with the redesign of the jobs performed by guards and escorts was asked to facilitate a workshop on organization design. This led to the senior management team exploring the possible benefit of introducing team working on client sites, with self-managed teams being delegated responsibility for monitoring their own performance as well as executing the task. Hackman's book *Leading Teams* (2002) guided much of this work.

You might find it useful to think about the following questions before moving on:

1 What were the main steps in the diagnosis and who was involved at each stage?
2 Was there anything that influenced what the CEO paid attention to?
3 What were the main sources of information that informed the diagnosis?
4 How was information obtained?

Ideas relating to the last two questions will be discussed in Chapter 8, but what follows in this chapter will address issues relating to the first two questions. In the SSSE case, the diagnosis evolved through several stages and gradually involved more people in the process. It began with a wide-ranging review by the new CEO, which he then shared with his top team. They elaborated his initial diagnosis and went on to identify issues that required more detailed investigation. One of these was investigated by the operations director and a site supervisor. They identified two more specific issues that seemed to be important. The top team reviewed their findings, decided which issue to pursue first and engaged an external consultant to work with a team of managers to redesign some jobs. The diagnosis did not stop there. When it came to implementing the redesigned jobs, some of the proposed changes were rejected by the guards and this triggered another phase of diagnosis.

Using models to aid diagnosis

The CEO in the SSSE case did not start his diagnosis with a 'clean sheet'. He brought with him an implicit model of how organizations like SSSE work and this affected what he paid attention to and how he interpreted what he discovered.

Organizational behaviour, at all its different levels, is a complex phenomenon. It is impossible for anyone to pay attention to, or understand the interactions between, the many elements or variables that can have an effect on how an organization functions. Consequently, we tend to simplify the real world by developing models that focus attention on:

- a limited number of *key elements* that we feel offer a good representation of the real world

- the ways these elements interact with each other, sometimes referred to as *causal relationships* or laws of effect
- the *outputs* produced by these interactions, which provide the basis for evaluating performance and assessing effectiveness.

We all develop our own implicit theories or conceptual models about how organizations function, and we use these models to:

- guide the kind of information that we attend to
- interpret what we see
- decide how to act.

Like the CEO in the SSSE case, we develop these models on the basis of our personal experience, either as members of an organization or external observers of organizational behaviour. Sometimes, these models provide a good basis for understanding what is going on and predicting what kinds of actions or interventions would produce the desired change. Often, however, they are highly subjective and biased; they overemphasize some aspects of organizational functioning and completely neglect others. Consequently, they do not always provide a useful guide for the management of change.

The aim of the first part of this chapter is to help you develop a greater level of awareness of your own model of organizational functioning. This will help you assess whether the model you use is consistent with or relevant to the problems or opportunities you need to address. It will also help you compare your implicit model with alternatives and point to ways of modifying it to improve its utility. Making your implicit models more explicit can be of benefit to all the people involved in managing a change. It can provide an opportunity for them to share their models, debate their relative merits, and move towards the development of a shared model that can be used to provide a basis for joint diagnosis and concerted action.

Exercise 7.1 is designed to help you become more aware of your implicit model of how organizations function. It is written for readers with some work experience but can easily be modified for readers who have little or no work experience. In place of steps 1 and 2, imagine that you are a consultant retained by the CEO of a large retailing organization and have been tasked to provide her with an assessment of the strengths and weaknesses of the company. She has given you authority to go anywhere, speak to anyone and access any company data you may require. The company has a network of large out-of-town superstores selling food and related products. It is one of the largest retailers in the UK and has a long history of successful trading but over the past three years its shares have underperformed. Your task is to produce a list of the bits of information you would seek out or attend to in order to diagnose the 'health' of the organization. Enter the information that you would attend to in Table 7.2 before step 3 of Exercise 7.1. Try and identify at least 25.

✅ Exercise **7.1** *Raising awareness of your implicit model of organizational functioning*

This exercise is based on a procedure for collaborative model building devised by Tichy and Hornstein (1980) and involves five steps. The first step requires you to prepare a short assessment of the current state of your organization. The next four steps involve reflecting on how you arrived at this assessment in order to tease out the main features of your implicit model of organizational functioning.

Step 1   Assess the current state of your organization

Prepare a short note that describes your organization (either the total organization or an important unit that you are familiar with) and assesses or diagnoses its current state. Make reference to the issues you feel require attention, which could be problems or opportunities. If you feel there is a need for some kind of change to ensure that these issues will be managed more effectively, justify this view.

Do *not* explain the kinds of interventions you think may be necessary to bring about any required changes. The aim of this exercise is to diagnose the current state of the organization (and assess whether it is and will continue to perform effectively), not to provide a prescription of actions required to improve matters.

Step 2   Identify the information you used to make this assessment

Think about the things you considered when making your assessment in the first step of this exercise. Identify and list the 'kinds of information' you attended to. Focus on the information you did actually attend to, rather than the information you think you 'should' have considered. If possible, identify at least 25 different entries and record them in the space provided in Table 7.2. Table 7.1 provides some examples of the types of information that people might attend to when assessing the state of their organization. These are only offered to stimulate your thinking; your own list may contain none of these.

Table **7.1** *Examples of the kind of information that might be attended to*

Quality of boss–subordinate relationships	Production/operations systems	The way activities and staff are grouped together	Awareness of competitive threats
Effectiveness of coordinating mechanisms	Quality of communications	Level of commitment to the organization	Training and staff development
Knowledge management	Reward systems	Costs	Inventory levels
Margins	Staff turnover	Customer satisfaction	Cash flows
The extent to which people feel challenged in their present jobs	Match between staff competences and task requirements	Extent to which staff understand the central purpose of the organization	Awareness of possible future sources of income/ revenue
The way the business is financed	Attitudes towards quality assurance	The way conflicts are managed	Level of bureaucracy
Effectiveness of IT system	Number of levels in the hierarchy	Marketing procedures and policies	Management accounting systems

Table **7.2** *Information you attended to*

Step 3 Developing categories for organizing your diagnostic information

Some of the types of information you used to make your assessment might be related and it might be possible to group them together into a number of more inclusive categories:

• Do this by grouping related kinds of information into the category boxes provided below. Typically, people identify 4–12 categories, but there are no restrictions on the number of categories you might identify.
• When you have categorized your information, describe the rationale you used for including information in each category.

These categories reflect the main elements or variables of your diagnostic model.

Category name:	Category name:
Items included in category:	Items included in category:
Briefly state rationale for including items in this category:	Briefly state rationale for including items in this category:

Category name:	Category name:
Items included in category:	Items included in category:
Briefly state rationale for including items in this category:	Briefly state rationale for including items in this category:

Category name:	Category name:
Items included in category: Briefly state rationale for including items in this category:	Items included in category: Briefly state rationale for including items in this category:

Category name:	Category name:
Items included in category: Briefly state rationale for including items in this category:	Items included in category: Briefly state rationale for including items in this category:

Use additional category boxes if required.

Step 4 Specifying relationships between categories/elements

The categories identified above reflect the elements of your implicit diagnostic model. Step 4 of the model-building process focuses on the interdependencies and causal relationships between the elements. These can be identified by considering whether a change in any one element will have an effect on any other element:

- Using the format of Table 7.3, list the elements (categories) identified in step 3 down the left-hand column and across the top of the table.
- Take each element down the left-hand column in turn and assess the impact a change in this element might have on every other element, using a three-point scale, where 0 = no or slight impact, 1 = moderate impact and 2 = high impact.
- Sum the scores for each row.
- Rank the scores (1 = highest). The rank order of the elements indicates your assessment of the key drivers of performance.

Table **7.3** *Interdependencies between elements*

Effect of change on	1	2	3	4	5	6	7	8	9	10	11	12	Σ sum	Rank order
Elements														
1	–													
2		–												
3			–											
4				–										
5					–									
6						–								
7							–							
8								–						
9									–					
10										–				
11											–			
12												–		

NB: Although elements might be interrelated and affect each other, one element, for example A, can have a greater effect on another, for example B, than vice versa. This is illustrated in Table 7.4, where element A has a high impact on element B (score = 2), but element B has only a moderate impact (score = 1) on element A.

Table **7.4** *An example of a matrix of interdependencies*

Categories	A	B	C	D	E	Sum	Rank
A	–	②	1	0	2	5	2
B	①	–	1	0	1	3	4
C	0	1	–	0	1	2	5
D	0	0	2	–	2	4	3
E	2	1	1	2	–	6	1

Your implicit model can be represented diagrammatically:

- Draw a circle for each of the elements you identified in Table 7.1.
- Label each circle with the name of the element it represents.
- Draw lines between those elements that have a moderate or high impact on each other. Use a solid line to show a strong (high-impact) relationship between elements, with the arrowhead indicating the direction of a cause-and-effect relationship, and a dotted line to show a moderate link. Do not join elements that have only a slight or no impact on each other.
- Insert the rank order of each element to indicate its impact on other elements.

The model represented by Table 7.4 is presented diagrammatically in Figure 7.1.

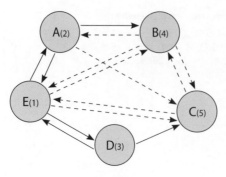

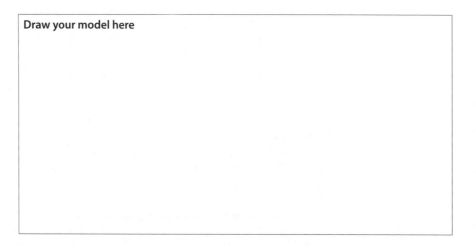

Figure **7.1** *A causal map of a diagnostic model*

Draw your model here

    The rest of this chapter presents a range of models of organizational functioning that are widely used to aid diagnosis. When you have read to the end of this chapter, you might find it useful to compare your own model with these alternatives and consider whether they suggest ways of improving your model.

    To refine your own model, you might want to reflect on the following:

- How do the models presented relate to your personal experience? For example, to what extent do they accommodate or ignore elements and causal relationships that your experience has led you to believe are important? It might be unwise to slavishly apply a model that ignores aspects of organizational functioning that your own experience tells you are significant.
- Do any of the available models include elements and/or relationships that you have never previously considered but which, on reflection, might help you make better sense of your own experience? You need to be alert to the danger of rejecting alternative models too hastily. You might find that a model that is quite different from your own personal model can provide useful new insights. Even if you decide not to adopt an alternative model in its entirety, you might decide to incorporate some aspects of it into your own model.

Giving proper consideration to these issues can help to refine and improve your personal model of organizational functioning.

Component versus holistic models

Component models focus on particular aspects of organizational functioning, such as motivation, decision making, group dynamics, organization structure and so on, whereas holistic models consider the system as a whole. Nadler and Tushman (1980, p. 262) acknowledge the utility of component models but caution against combining, in some additive manner, the specific assessments they provide because they may produce an incomplete or misleading view of the organization. They argue that the systemic nature of organizations implies that:

> there are properties of the whole that cannot be understood by simply adding together the component parts. Indeed, part of the dynamic of the whole concerns the nature of the interaction among the different components of organizational behaviour.

This echoes the essence of the ancient Indian story of six blind men encountering an elephant. Each one touched a different part of the elephant's body. The blind man who felt a leg said the elephant was like a pillar; the one who felt its tail said it was like a rope; the one who felt its trunk said it was like a tree branch; the one who felt its ear said it was like a fan; the one who felt its belly said it was like a wall; and the one who felt its tusk said it was like a spear. When they shared the descriptions of what they had discovered, they learned little about the nature of the whole system (the elephant).

The new CEO in the SSSE case started his diagnosis by reviewing the organization as a whole and it was only later, after specific problems had been identified, that he and his team began to use component models to drill down and explore particular issues. When interviewed after the change, the CEO revealed his thinking about the nature of organizations and how he used this to guide his search for understanding what was going on in SSSE. The model presented in Figure 7.2 shows the main elements of his model and the cause-and-effect relationships between them.

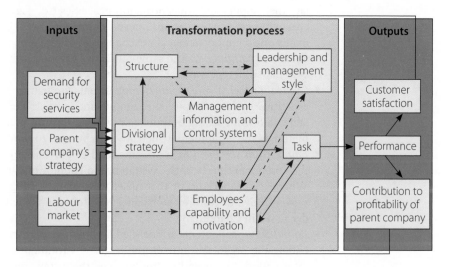

*Figure **7.2** The CEO's model of causal relationships affecting the performance of SSSE*

Open systems theory

Open systems theory provides a framework that views an organization as a system of interrelated components that transact with a larger environment. From the perspective of open systems, some of the main characteristics of organizations are that they are:

- *Embedded within a larger system:* Organizations are dependent on the larger system (environment) for the resources, information and feedback they require in order to survive.
- *Able to avoid entropy:* Through the exchange of matter, energy and information with the larger environment, organizations can forestall entropy, the predisposition to decay. They can even increase their vitality over time. People are partially closed systems, in that while they can import food, water and air to breathe, there are parts of the human body that cannot be renewed or replaced. Groups and organizations, on the other hand, have the potential for indefinite life. In their simplest form, as illustrated by Figure 7.3, organizations can be portrayed as open systems in a dynamic relationship with their environment, receiving various inputs they transform in some way and export as outputs. In order to survive, organizations need to maintain favourable input–output transactions with the environment.

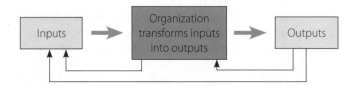

*Figure **7.3 The organization as an open system***

- *Regulated by feedback:* Systems rely on information about their outputs to regulate their inputs and transformation processes (see Figure 7.3). Feedback loops also exist between the various internal components of the system. Thus, changes in any one component can affect changes in other components.
- *Subject to equifinality:* The same outcomes can be produced by configuring the system in different ways.
- *Cyclical in their mode of functioning:* Events are patterned and tend to occur in repetitive cycles of input, throughput and output. For example, the revenue generated from selling outputs can be used to fund inputs such as labour, raw materials and equipment, which are then be used to produce more outputs.
- *Equilibrium seeking:* Open systems tend to gravitate towards a state where all the component parts of the system are in equilibrium and a steady state exists. Whenever changes occur that upset this balance, different components of the system move to restore the balance. (Note the links with Lewin's field theory, discussed in Chapter 2.)
- *Bounded:* Open systems are defined by boundaries. External boundaries differentiate the organization from the larger environment and regulate the flow of information, energy and matter between the system and its environment. Internal boundaries differentiate the various components of the system from each other and regulate the inputs and outputs of subsystems.

While recognizing the utility of component models, this chapter presents four holistic (total system) models that have been widely used for diagnosing the need or opportunity for change:

1   *Kotter's integrative model of organizational dynamics:* highlights the importance of alignment and explores the factors that determine organizational effectiveness in the short, medium and long term.
2   *The McKinsey 7S model:* illustrates how change tools can be developed to identify areas of misalignment that require further investigation.
3   *Weisbord's six-box model:* draws attention to informal as well as formal aspects of organizational functioning.
4   *The Burke-Litwin causal model of organizational performance and change:* draws attention to the causal weight of the various elements of the organization and indicates how the requirement for different types of change can affect which elements of the organization might need to be a focus for attention.

Kotter's integrative model of organizational dynamics

Open systems theory predicts that changes to any one of the internal or external elements of an organization's system will cause changes to other elements. This implies that in order to understand the performance of an organization, one must view it as a system of interconnected choices (Siggelkow, 2001). Kotter (1980) elaborated this proposition when he developed his integrative model of organizational dynamics. His model comprises seven major elements; a set of key organizational processes plus six structural elements, as shown in Figure 7.4.

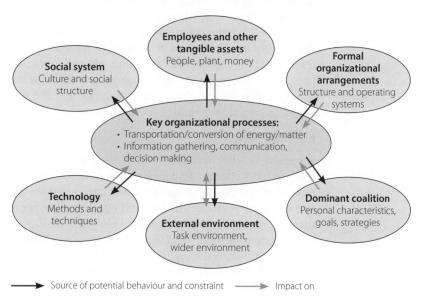

Figure **7.4** *Kotter's integrative model of organizational dynamics*
Source: Kotter, 1980, p. 282

There are two interdependent sets of organizational processes; one set relates to the transportation or conversion of energy and matter, and the other to information gathering, decision making and communication. There are, of course, many more specific processes that can be labelled according to their purpose, such as market research, product development or manufacturing processes.

The six structural elements in Kotter's model are:

1 *external environment*: including the immediate task-related environment and the wider environment, which includes public attitudes, the political system and so on
2 *employees and other tangible assets:* such as buildings, plant, inventories and cash
3 *formal structures:* these specify the grouping of activities and hierarchical arrangements, job design and operating systems
4 *social system:* including the organization's culture and social structure
5 *technology (or technologies):* associated with the organization's core products
6 *dominant coalition:* the objectives and strategies of those who control policy making.

A distinguishing feature of this model is that it highlights which aspects of organizational functioning impact effectiveness over the short, medium and long term.

Short term

In the short term, an organization's effectiveness can be defined in terms of the nature of the cause-and-effect relationships that link all the elements of the system together. For example, if demand for a major product begins to slump, leaders in some organizations will recognize this and take corrective action much faster than leaders in other organizations. An organization's response will be influenced by the quality of its information-gathering and decision-making processes and by how quickly these processes can affect other elements in the organization to adjust matter/energy conversion and transportation processes in ways that will maintain their efficiency. Adjustments might involve cutting production, finding new customers, or reducing prices in order to minimize any build-up of stocks of finished goods. Any delays in reacting to changes will result in a wasteful use of resources. In the short term, therefore, effective organizations are those that have key processes characterized by high-quality decision making and matter/energy efficiency that help to ensure that resources are used to best advantage. Chapters 21 and 22 look at interventions designed to improve business processes.

Medium term

Kotter argues that over the medium term, which he defines as a few months to a few years, the effective organization is one that is capable of maintaining its short-term effectiveness. He suggests that organizations do this by maintaining the key process elements in an efficient and effective state because it is this that enables them to ensure that the six structural elements are aligned to each other. Sustained misalignment (sometimes referred to as 'poor fit') leads to levels of waste that will eventually threaten the organization's survival. He suggests that what constitutes a misaligned relationship between any two or more structural elements is often 'intuitively obvious', and cites several examples to illustrate the point:

• If the goals and strategies championed by the organization's dominant coalition are based on inaccurate assumptions about the task environment, the dominant coalition and the task environment are obviously misaligned.

- If the size of the workforce or the organization's other tangible assets are not sufficient to take advantage of the economies of scale inherent in the organization's technologies, the two elements are obviously misaligned.
- If the level of specialization called for in formal organizational arrangements is inconsistent with the skills of the workforce, then again the two elements are misaligned.

The most common sources of misalignment are changes in the external environment and growth. Kotter argues that organizational systems correct misalignments by taking the path of least resistance; they move towards the solution that requires the minimum use of energy. This usually involves realigning around the element or elements of the organization that are most difficult and expensive to change (or emerge as the driving force over the longer term). However, if the organization can afford the waste associated with misalignment, minor examples of poor fit could go uncorrected for some time. This argument suggests that, over the medium term, the focus of change management is to ensure that the elements of the organization are appropriately aligned.

Long term

Over the longer term (6–60 years), Kotter predicts that it is the organization's driving force and adaptability of the six structural elements that will be the underlying determinant of effectiveness. He notes that, over time, one or more of the structural elements, for example the external environment, technology, the employees or the dominant coalition, typically begin to exert more influence on key organizational processes than the other elements. This element (or elements) emerges as the driving force that shapes the development of the company. He argues that because of the nature of the interdependence among all the elements and the equilibrium-seeking disposition of systems, if one or two elements emerge as the driving force, the natural tendency is for the others to follow. They adapt to the 'driving force' in order to maintain internal alignment. The founder and managing director of ASE (see Case study 4.1) illustrates this point. His obsessive concern with engineering excellence dominated the organization's culture and shaped its strategy and management practices for many years. This argument suggests that the driving force can create a 'deep structure' within an organization that can be a source of inertia and inhibit change (see the discussion of this point in Chapters 1 and 3).

The key to an organization's prosperity and long-term survival is its ability to adapt in order to maintain external alignment. According to Kotter, this adaptability is a function of the state of its structural elements. These can range on a continuum from highly constraining and hard to align with other structural elements to unconstraining and easy to align with. He provides examples of structural states that do and do not facilitate system adaptation, shown in Table 7.5. The more an organization's structural elements look like those in the left-hand column of Table 7.5, the more difficult it will be for the organization to adapt. Adaptability is important because it determines whether or not the organization will be able to maintain the required degree of alignment over the long term. Over the longer term, therefore, the focus of change management is to ensure that the structural elements of the organization are as adaptable as possible.

*Table **7.5** Examples of element states that do and do not facilitate system adaptation*

Factors	States that are highly constraining and hard to align with, thus inhibiting adaptation	States that are not constraining and are easy to align with
Technology	Organization possesses a single complex technology, which is rapidly becoming outdated and requires large amounts of capital for equipment	Organization possesses the most advanced technologies for its products, services and administrative systems, along with a number of alternative technologies it might need in the future
Social system	Key norms are not supportive of organizational flexibility; little trust found in relationships; total power in the system is low; morale is low; little sense of shared purpose	Key norms are supportive of organizational flexibility; high trust found in relationships; total power in the system is high; morale is high; high degree of shared purpose
Employee and other tangible assets	Plant and equipment are run-down; employees, especially middle managers, are unskilled; organization has some highly specialized human skills and equipment it doesn't need anymore	Plant and equipment in top-notch shape; employees, especially middle managers, are highly skilled; organization possesses equipment and people with skills it doesn't need now but may need in the future
Organizational arrangements	Formal systems are not sophisticated but are applied in great detail, uniformly across the organization	Different kinds of formal systems exist for structuring, measuring, rewarding, selecting and developing different types of people working on different tasks; formal systems also exist to monitor change in the organization and its environment and to change the formal systems accordingly
Dominant coalition	A small, homogeneous, fairly untalented group with no effective leadership; all about the same age	A large, heterogeneous but cohesive group of reasonably talented people who work well together and have plenty of effective leadership; members are of different ages
External environment	The organization is dependent on a large number of externalities, with little or no countervailing power Demand for products and services is shrinking; supplies are hard to get; regulators behave with hostility and inconsistency Public angry at the firm; economy in bad shape; political system isn't functioning well; overall, the environment is hostile	The organization has a limited number of strong dependencies, with a moderate amount of countervailing power over all dependencies Demand for products and services is growing; supplies are plentiful; regulators behave consistently and fairly Public likes the organization; economy is in good shape; political system is functioning well; overall, the environment is benevolent

Source: Kotter, 1980, pp. 292–3

The McKinsey 7S model

The McKinsey 7S model highlights seven interrelated elements of organizations (Figure 7.5), which, when aligned, make an important contribution to organizational effectiveness (Pascale and Athos, 1981). It can be used to identify relationships that are misaligned and point to elements of the organization that need to be changed.

The seven elements are:

1 *Strategy:* Purpose of the business and the way the organization seeks to enhance its competitive advantage.
2 *Structure:* Division of activities; integration and coordination mechanisms; nature of informal organization.

3 *Systems:* Formal procedures for measurement, reward and resource allocation; informal routines for communicating, resolving conflicts and so on.

4 *Staff:* The organization's human resources, its demographic, educational and attitudinal characteristics.

5 *Style:* Typical behaviour patterns of key groups, such as managers and other professionals, and the organization as a whole.

6 *Shared values and superordinate goals:* Core beliefs and values and how these influence the organization's orientation to customers, employees, shareholders and society at large. Figure 7.5 shows shared values at the centre of the model.

7 *Skills:* The organization's core competences and distinctive capabilities.

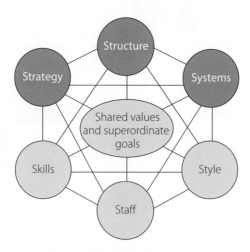

Figure **7.5   The McKinsey 7S model**
Source: Waterman et al., 1980, p. 14

Change managers using the 7S model can draw on their knowledge of the organization's seven elements (based on the first phase of the diagnosis) to construct a 7S matrix (see Change tool 7.1) and use the matrix to assess the degree of alignment between the elements. For example, using a five-point scale, the change manager can assess the extent to which shared values are aligned with the organization's strategy, structure, systems, staff, skills and so on. This analysis will point to areas where it might be necessary to draw on component models to design an intervention to change an element in order to improve fit. However, introducing a change to improve the fit between two specific elements might create misalignments elsewhere, but the model provides a framework for reviewing each change and taking further action as required.

Weisbord's six-box model

Weisbord (1976) presents his systemic model as a 'practice theory' that synthesizes knowledge and experience from change agents. It provides a conceptual map of six elements or boxes that can be used to apply any (component) theories to the assessment of these elements in a way that can reveal new connections and relationships

⚒ *Change tool **7.1** The 7S matrix*

Strategy	Structure	Systems	Staff	Style	Shared values	Skills
Describe strategy	Strategy/ structure alignment	Strategy/ systems alignment	Strategy/ staff alignment	Strategy/ style alignment	Strategy/ vales alignment	Strategy/ skill alignment
	Describe structure	Structure/ systems alignment	Structure/ staff alignment	Structure/ style alignment	Structure/ values alignment	Structure/ skills alignment
		Describe systems	Systems/ staff alignment	Systems/ style alignment	Systems/ values alignment	Systems/ skills alignment
			Describe staff	Staff/style alignment	Staff/ values alignment	Staff/skills alignment
				Describe style	Style/ values alignment	Style/skills alignment
					Describe shared values	Values/ skills alignment
						Describe skills

between them (Figure 7.6). It is an open systems model that recognizes the importance of organization–environment relationships but focuses most attention on what needs to be done internally to ensure that the organization becomes and/or remains a high performance organization able to adapt to external changes.

Weisbord (1976) argues that the effectiveness of an organization's functioning depends on what goes on in and between the six boxes. There are two aspects of each box that deserve attention: the formal and the informal. He argues that the formal aspects of an organization, for example stated goals or the structure as represented by an organization chart, might bear little relation to what happens in practice. Attention needs to be given to the frequency with which people take certain actions in relation to how important these actions are for organizational performance (see Change tool 29.2). This leads to a consideration of why people do what they do, and what needs to be changed to promote more effective behaviour. Leadership is seen to have a role to play in coordinating what goes on in the other five boxes.

Weisbord (1976) suggests that a useful starting point for any diagnostic exercise is to:

- focus on one major output (of a unit or the total organization)
- explore the extent to which the producers and the consumers of the output are satisfied with it
- trace the reasons for any dissatisfaction to what is happening in or between the six boxes that represent the unit or organization under consideration (a similar methodology underpins Change tool 4.1).

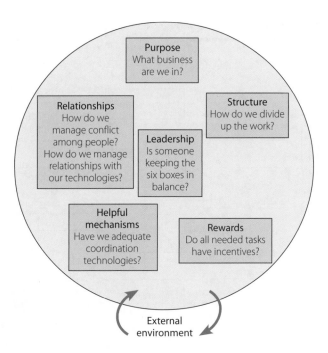

Figure **7.6 *Weisbord's six-box model***
Source: Weisbord, 1976, p. 9

The Burke-Litwin causal model of organizational performance and change

The Burke-Litwin (1992) model points to the relative weight of the elements of organizational functioning and the causal linkages that determine the level of performance and affect the process of change. The model also differentiates between two types of change: 'transformational change' that occurs as a response to important shifts in the external environment, and 'transactional change' that occurs in response to the need for more short-term incremental improvement. These features distinguish this model from the others considered in this chapter.

The model comprises 12 interrelated elements (Figure 7.7). It is an open systems model in which the inputs are represented by the external environment element at the top of the figure, and the outputs by the individual and organizational performance element at the bottom. Feedback loops go in both directions: the organization's performance affects its external environment and the external environment affects performance. The remaining 10 elements represent the process of transforming inputs into outputs, and reflect different levels of this process. Strategy and organizational culture, for example, reflect aspects of the whole organizational or total system. Work unit climate is an element associated with the local unit level, and motivation, individual needs and values, and tasks and roles are individual-level elements.

The model is presented vertically (rather than across the page from left to right) to reflect causal relationships and the relative impact of elements on each other. Burke and Litwin posit that those elements located higher in the model, such as

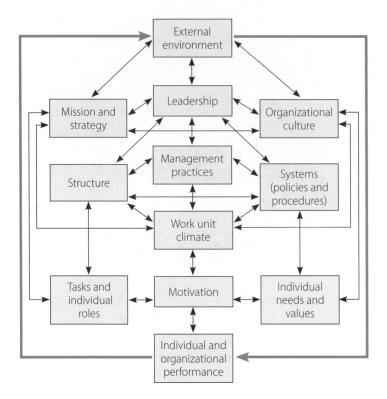

*Figure **7.7** The Burke-Litwin causal model of organizational performance and change*
Source: Burke and Litwin, 1992, p. 528

mission and strategy, leadership, and organizational culture, exert greater impact on other elements than lower elements do on higher elements. In other words, although elements located lower down in the model can have some impact on those above them, the position in the model reflects the 'weight' or net causal impact.

This said, the model does not prescribe that change should always start with elements at the top of the model. It is a predictive rather than a prescriptive model. It specifies the nature of causal relationships and predicts the likely effect of changing certain elements rather than others. The decision about where to intervene first might be influenced by whether the aim is to secure transformational or transactional change. The model elaborates these two distinct sets of organizational dynamics. One is associated with organizational transformation and the need for a fundamental shift in values and behaviour, while the other is associated with behaviour at the more everyday level.

Transformational change is required when an organization has to respond to the kinds of environmental discontinuities considered in Chapter 3. This kind of change involves a paradigm shift and completely new behaviours. Instead of changes designed to help the organization do things better, the organization needs to do things differently or do different things. This calls for the principles, assumptions and values that underpin the implicit and explicit rules guiding behaviour to be revised. It involves a change in the organization's culture. It also calls for a change in the organization's mission and strategy, and for managers at all levels to provide a lead and behave in ways that clarify the new strategy and encourage others to act in ways that will support it. Where the need is for this kind of change, attention should be focused on the transformational elements highlighted in Figure 7.8.

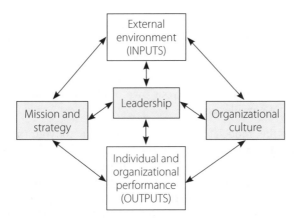

Figure **7.8** *The transformational factors*
Source: Adapted from Burke and Litwin, 1992, p. 523

Transactional change is associated with fine-tuning, with how the organization functions within the existing paradigm. It emphasizes single- rather than double-loop learning, as in the model of organizational learning discussed in Chapters 1 and 29. The focus of attention needs to be the structures, management practices and systems that affect the work climate, which in turn impacts on motivation and performance at the unit and the individual level.

Interventions designed to bring about organizational transformation that target 'higher level' elements in the model will eventually and inevitably have an impact on all other elements in the system because of their weight and relative impact. If, however, the target of interventions is primarily the elements in the lower part of the model, aimed at achieving what Burke and Litwin refer to as 'transactional change', the impact is more likely to remain at local unit level. Interventions targeted at this type of element might have relatively little, if any, impact on overall organizational culture and strategy. Burke and Litwin (1992) present an impressive (if selective) summary of studies that provide empirical support for the causal linkages hypothesized by their model.

Revising your personal model of organizational functioning

This chapter has presented a brief summary of some widely used holistic models of organizational functioning and has identified some of the main differences between them. You are advised to develop a 'healthy scepticism' towards the utility of specific models and constantly reassess which is most appropriate for the purpose at hand.

Characteristics of a good model

All the models that have been considered are simplifications of the real world. None are guaranteed to accommodate all circumstances, provide a reliable basis for understanding why things are the way they are, or identify actions that can be taken to produce a desired outcome. Depending on circumstances and purpose, some theories or models might have greater utility than others.

Three characteristics of 'good' diagnostic models are that they:

1 are relevant to the particular issues under consideration
2 help change agents to recognize cause-and-effect relationships
3 focus on elements they can influence.

At the end of Exercise 7.1, it was recommended that, after reading this chapter, you reflect on and review your own model of organizational functioning. Points you might consider are:

• How the models presented above relate to your personal experience. For example, to what extent do they accommodate or ignore elements and causal relationships that your experience has led you to believe are important? It might be unwise to slavishly apply a model that ignores aspects of organizational functioning that your own experience tells you are significant.

• Do any of these models include elements and/or relationships that you have never previously considered but which, on reflection, might help you to make better sense of your own experience? You need to be alert to the danger of rejecting alternative models too hastily. You might find that a model that is quite different from your own personal model can provide useful new insights.

Summary

Organizational diagnosis is a process of research into the functioning of an organization that leads to recommendations for improvement. The first part of this chapter examined the role of models in organizational diagnosis and introduced an exercise designed to help raise your awareness of the implicit models you use when thinking about organizations and assessing the need for change.

The second part of the chapter considered the relative merits of component and holistic models. Component models focus on particular aspects of organizational functioning such as motivation, decision making, group dynamics, organization structure and so on, whereas holistic models consider the system as a whole. It is recommended that a useful starting point can be to use holistic models to provide an overall assessment before focusing attention on specific issues that appear to be the problem. Combining, in some additive manner, the specific assessments provided by a range of component models can provide an incomplete or misleading view of the health of the total system.

The main body of the chapter presented four holistic models that can be used to aid diagnosis:

1 Kotter's integrative model of organizational dynamics highlights the importance of alignment and explores the factors that determine organizational effectiveness in the short, medium and long term.
2 The McKinsey 7S model illustrates how change tools can be developed to identify areas of misalignment that require further investigation.
3 Weisbord's six-box model is an open systems model that draws attention to informal as well as formal aspects of organizational functioning.

4 The Burke-Litwin causal model of organizational performance and change draws attention to the causal weight of the various elements of the organization and indicates how the requirement for different types of change can affect which elements of the organization might need to be a focus for attention.

You might find it useful to compare your own model with the four holistic models presented in this chapter and consider whether they suggest ways of improving your own approach to diagnosis.

References

Burke, W.W. and Litwin, G.H. (1992) A causal model of organizational performance and change, *Journal of Management*, 18(3): 523–45.

Hackman, J.R. (2002) *Leading Teams.* Boston, MA: Harvard Business School Press.

Hackman, J.R. and Oldham, G.R. (1980) *Work Redesign.* Reading, MA: Addison-Wesley.

Kotter, J.P. (1980) An integrative model of organizational dynamics. In E.E. Lawler, D.A Nadler and C. Cammann (eds) *Organizational Assessment.* New York: Wiley.

Nadler, D.A. and Tushman, M.L. (1980) A congruence model for organizational assessment. In E.E. Lawler, D.A. Nadler and C. Cammann (eds) *Organizational Assessment.* New York: Wiley.

Pascale, R. and Athos, A. (1981) *The Art of Japanese Management.* New York: Warner Books.

Postma, T. and Kok, R. (1999) Organizational diagnosis in practice: A cross-classification analysis using the DEL-technique, *European Management Journal*, 17(6): 584–97.

Siggelkow, N. (2001) Change in the presence of fit: The rise, the fall, and the renaissance of Liz Claiborne, *Academy of Management Journal*, 44(4): 838–57.

Tichy, N.M. and Hornstein, H.A. (1980) Collaborative model building. In E.E. Lawler, D.A. Nadler and C. Cammann (eds) *Organizational Assessment.* New York: Wiley.

Waterman, R.H., Peters, T. and Philips, J.R. (1980) Structure is not organization, *Business Horizons*, 23(3): 14–26.

Weisbord, M.R. (1976) Organizational diagnosis: Six places to look for trouble with or without a theory, *Group and Organization Studies*, 1(4): 430–47.

Chapter **8**

Gathering and interpreting information

Diagnosing the need for change involves a process of gathering, analysing and interpreting information about individual, group and organizational functioning. This chapter examines the main steps in this process. These are:

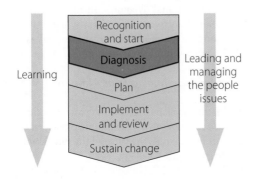

1 selecting a conceptual model for diagnosis
2 clarifying information requirements
3 information gathering
4 analysis
5 interpretation.

The final section considers how diagnostic information, once interpreted, can be used to begin the process of action planning. The SWOT analysis and force-field analysis are introduced as useful frameworks for planning what needs to be done.

Selecting a diagnostic model

It was noted earlier that organizational behaviour, at all its different levels, is a complex phenomenon and it is impossible for managers to pay attention to every aspect of organizational functioning. We cope with this complexity, sometimes unconsciously, by developing or adopting conceptual models that simplify the real world and focus attention on a limited number of elements and relationships. Some of the explicit models of organizational functioning available to change agents relate to how the organization functions as a total system. Others, known as component models, focus on selected elements of the overall system, such as leadership, structure, job design, competences and so on. A range of holistic models was considered in Chapter 7, and most good texts on organizational behaviour critically review a wide range of component models.

Conceptual models play a key role in the diagnostic process because they help us to decide which aspects of organizational behaviour require attention and provide a focus for information gathering. They also provide a basis for interpreting the information that has been collected.

When selecting a model for diagnosis, the first point to consider is the extent to which the model is relevant to the issue(s) under consideration, for example loss of market share, dysfunctional intergroup conflict, high labour turnover and so on. An effective model is one that identifies specific elements and/or cause-and-effect relationships that contribute to the problem or opportunity, and also indicates which of these have most weight (or effect) on other aspects of organizational functioning and performance. Evidence, from personal experience or published research, about the ability of a conceptual model to explain and predict cause-and-effect relationships can help the change manager to select an appropriate model for diagnosis. However, the ultimate aim of organizational diagnosis is more than improving our understanding of why something is the way it is. It also involves using this understanding to plan action to improve organization effectiveness. Thus, if a diagnostic model is to have any practical utility, it needs to highlight aspects of organizational functioning that, either directly or indirectly, the change manager can work on.

Clarifying information requirements

Exercise 7.1 invited you to think about the information you would use in order to diagnose the current state of your organization. This information was then categorized and used to help you make explicit your personal model of organizational functioning.

This process can be reversed. When a diagnostic model has been selected, the change manager can identify the items of information that will be required to assess how an organization (unit or group) is performing and to distinguish what is going well and what is going not so well. Two examples illustrate what this involves.

The 7S model focuses attention on seven aspects of organizational functioning – strategy, structure, systems, staff, style, shared values and skills (see Figure 7.5). A change manager using this model will need to identify the kind of information required to describe each element. For example, under 'strategy', they may seek information about how the organization goes about matching its resources with the opportunities, constraints and demands in the environment, how it plans to develop in the future, and how it goes about creating and maintaining a competitive advantage. Under 'structure', a change manager may seek information about formal and informal arrangements for grouping and coordinating activities, defining responsibilities, and establishing reporting relationships. An organization's structure might be described in terms of functions, divisions, a matrix or a network.

The 12 elements of the Burke-Litwin causal model of organizational performance, discussed in Chapter 7, are defined in Table 8.1, together with examples of the kinds of questions that might be used to elicit information about each element. The examples are taken from a diagnostic exercise used by the BBC in 1993. The survey instrument included a minimum of four questions relating to each element of the model. Respondents were invited to respond to the questions on a five-point scale. The way a change manager can use this kind of information to identify what might need to be changed is considered later in this chapter.

Change tool 8.2, at the end of the chapter, which looks at a force-field approach to opportunity development or problem management, provides another example of how a model can help to clarify the kind of information you need to collect.

When clarifying information requirements, those undertaking a diagnosis also need to take account of how easy or difficult it will be to collect the desired information and, later, how they can analyse it.

Table **8.1** *Examples of questions asked in a BBC staff survey*

	Elements	Indicative questions
External environment	Any outside condition or situation that influences the performance of the organization. Includes such things as marketplaces, world financial conditions, political/governmental circumstances and so on	Regarding the pace of change, what would you say the organization as a whole is experiencing – from static to very rapid change?
Mission/strategy	What organizational members believe is the central purpose of the organization and how the organization intends to achieve that purpose over an extended time	How widely accepted are the organization's goals among employees?
Leadership	Executive behaviour that encourages others to take needed actions	To what extent do senior managers make an effort to keep in touch with employees at your level in the organization?
Culture	'The way things are done around here' – the collection of overt and covert rules, values and principles that guide behaviour and have been strongly influenced by history, custom and practice	To what extent are the standard ways of operating in the organization difficult to change?
Structure	The arrangements of functions and people into specific areas and levels of responsibility, decision-making authority and relationships	To what extent is the organization's structure clear to everyone?
Management practices/action	What managers do in the normal course of events to use human and material resources to carry out the organization's strategy	To what extent does your manager communicate in an open and direct manner?
Systems	Standardized policies and mechanisms that facilitate work. They typically manifest themselves in the organization's reward systems and in control systems such as goal and budget development and human resource development	To what extent are the communication mechanisms in the organization effective, for example grapevine?
Climate	The current collective impressions, expectations and feelings of the members of local work units. These affect members' relations with supervisors, with one another and with other units	Where you work in the organization, to what extent is there trust and mutual respect among employees?
Task requirements and individual skills	The behaviour required for task effectiveness, including specific skills and knowledge required for people to accomplish the work assigned and for which they feel directly responsible – the job–person match	How challenged do you feel in your present job?
Motivation	Aroused behavioural tendencies to move towards goals, take needed action and persist until satisfaction is attained	To what extent do you feel encouraged to reach higher levels and standards of performance in your work?
Individual needs and values	The specific psychological factors that provide desire and worth for individual actions and thoughts	(From disagree strongly to agree strongly) I have a job that matters.
Performance	The outcomes or results, with indicators of effort and achievement. Examples include productivity, customer or staff satisfaction, profit and service quality	To what extent is the organization currently achieving the highest level of employee performance of which they are capable?

Information gathering

The information-gathering stage of the process begins with a series of planning decisions relating to which methods of data collection to employ and whether data can/should be collected from every possible source or from a representative sample of the total population of sources. In Case study 7.1 on SSSE, data were collected via observations, conversations (informal interviews), focus groups (group interviews), questionnaires (job diagnostics survey) and reading reports, and various people, including a sample of customers, were involved in this process.

A number of different techniques or methods can be used to collect information, including individual and group interviews, questionnaires, projective methods such as drawings and collages, observation, and the use of secondary data, sometimes referred to as 'unobtrusive measures'. Cummings and Worley (2001) provide a useful discussion of most of these methods. Their main features are summarized below, including the use of sampling.

Interviews

Individual and group interviews are a rich source of information about what is going on in an organization. People can be asked to describe aspects of the organization and how it functions, and to make judgements about how effectively the organization, or an aspect of it, functions and how they feel about this – their affective reaction. For example, after describing how the appraisal system operates in an organization, some employees might judge it to be ineffective but indicate that they are quite happy about this because the ineffective system works to their personal advantage.

Individual interviews have some added advantages. Respondents might be persuaded to share private views they may be reluctant to express in a more open forum. The interaction between interviewer and respondent can offer the possibility that respondents might be stimulated to articulate and make explicit vague feelings and views they had not previously formulated at a conscious level.

Interviews are adaptive. If respondents raise issues the interviewer had not anticipated, the interview schedule can be modified to allow these emerging issues to be explored in more detail. The interview also offers the opportunity for the interviewer/change agent to build rapport and develop trust with respondents and motivate them to develop a constructive attitude towards the change programme.

Interaction between respondents in a group interview can generate information that might not be forthcoming in an individual interview. For example, if individuals from different units or levels in the organization express different views, these differences might promote a useful discussion of why the conflicting perceptions exist and what problems or opportunities they might point to.

There are, however, a number of potential problems associated with using the interview to collect information. Interviews can be time-consuming and costly, although group interviews less so than individual interviews.

Coding and interpreting responses can be a problem, especially when interviews are unstructured. Coding and interpretation can be simplified by adopting a more structured approach, asking all respondents the same set of predetermined questions and limiting the use of open-ended questions. However, the gains from adopting a more structured approach need to be balanced against the potential loss of rich data that can be gleaned from a more unstructured conversation, for example where the interviewer leads off with some general open-ended questions and then follows the respondent's chain of thought.

Bias is another problem that can arise from the way interviewers organize the order of topics to be covered and the way they formulate questions. Special care needs to be taken to avoid the use of leading questions that signal to the respondent that there is a desired response.

Questionnaires

Questionnaires are sometimes referred to as 'self-administered interviews'. They are designed to obtain information by asking organizational members (and others) a predetermined set of questions about their perceptions, judgements and feelings. Using questionnaires to collect diagnostic information can be more cost-effective than using interviews, because they can be administered simultaneously to large numbers of people without the need to employ expensive interviewers. Also, they can be designed around fixed response-type questions that ease the burden of analysis.

However, they do have a number of disadvantages. They are non-empathic. When using questionnaires to collect information, it can be difficult for change managers to build rapport and communicate empathy with respondents. This can have an adverse effect on respondents' motivation to give full and honest answers to the questions asked.

Questionnaires are also much less adaptive than interviews. Interviewers can modify their approach in response to the interviewee's reaction to questions and can explore unanticipated issues. The format of the questionnaire, on the other hand, has to be decided in advance. Problems can arise because respondents fail to understand or misinterpret the meaning of questions. Important questions may also be omitted from the questionnaire – a difficult problem to resolve once the questionnaire has been administered.

Another problem is self-report bias. Questionnaires (like interviews) collect information from people who may, either deliberately or otherwise, bias their response. Responses to questions are based on respondents' perceptions of the situation. These perceptions may be based on incomplete or false information. There is also a tendency for respondents to present their own behaviour in the most positive light and protect their own interests. The design of the questionnaire can also bias responses. For example, people may fall into a pattern of answering co-located questions in a similar manner, or their attention may wander and they may take less care when answering questions towards the end of the questionnaire.

Projective methods

Projective methods such as drawings and collages can be a useful way of collecting information about issues that people may find difficult to express in other ways. Fordyce and Weil (1983) suggest that asking subgroups to prepare a collage around themes, such as 'how do you feel about this team?' or 'what is happening to the organization?', and present and explain it to the total group in a plenary session helps organizational members to express and explore issues at a fairly deep and personal level. A similar procedure is to invite individuals to prepare and share drawings that show certain aspects of organizational life. For example, individuals might be asked to draw a circle for each member of their group, making the circles larger or smaller depending on the influence they have over the way the group works. They may also be asked to elaborate their drawing by locating the circles for different members of the group in terms of how closely they need to work together to get the job done. A further elaboration might be to ask them to join the circles with blue lines where the people they represent have a personally close relationship and with red lines if they are far apart in terms of communication, rapport and empathy.

These kinds of approaches to surfacing information can be good icebreakers and can provide an easy route to the discussion of sensitive issues that are rarely discussed openly. However, while they may be well received by some groups, others may reject them as childish games.

Observations

Observing behaviour as it occurs is one approach to collecting information that avoids self-report bias. One of the key issues associated with this approach is deciding how the observation can be organized to focus attention on required behaviour and avoid being distracted or swamped by irrelevant information. When collecting information about behaviour in a group setting, for example, the degree of structure for observing and recording can vary from using broad categories such as leadership or communication to the use of detailed category sets such as the interaction process analysis framework developed by Bales (1950).

An advantage of this approach to information collection is that the observer may recognize patterns of behaviour that those being observed may be unaware of and are therefore unable to report in interviews or in their responses to questionnaires. Another advantage is that observations relate to current behaviour and are less likely than self-reports to be contaminated by historical factors. Observation is also an adaptive approach to collecting information. What is observed might cue the observer to explore connected aspects of current practice. Some of the disadvantages of this approach include problems associated with coding and interpretation, cost and possible observer bias.

Unobtrusive measures

In many organizational settings, large amounts of information are collected as a normal part of day-to-day operations, which relate to various aspects of organizational functioning, such as costs, downtime, wastage rates, absenteeism, labour turnover, delivery times, margins, complaints, number and type of meetings and so on. This kind of information is referred to as 'unobtrusive', because the fact that it is being collected for diagnosis is unlikely to prompt any specific response bias. It is also likely to be readily accepted by organizational members and, because of the nature of many of the records that contain this kind of information, it may be easy to quantify.

However, even when records are maintained, it may be difficult to access information in the required form. For example, information about individuals, such as the outcome of performance appraisals, increments awarded, absenteeism and sickness rates, may all be contained in each individual's personal record but may not be available in any aggregate form for all members of a particular department.

Sampling

Sometimes, for example when collecting information from members of a relatively small work group, it may be possible to include every member of the group in the survey. However, when a diagnostic exercise involves collecting information about a whole department, or the total organization, it may be necessary to consider ways of sampling people, activities and records in a way that will provide sufficient information to provide a representative picture of what is going on.

Important issues that need to be considered when drawing a sample relate to sample size, relative to the total population, and composition. For example, how many people should be interviewed, events observed or records inspected, and which individuals, events or records should be included in the sample? The answer to the size or 'how many' question depends on the degree of confidence required in the findings and, if the information is to be subjected to statistical analysis, the type of analysis to be used. The answer to the composition or 'which' question depends on the complexity of the total population. If the total population is relatively homogeneous, the selection of members to be included in the sample might be done on a random basis, using random number tables, or by selecting every nth member of the total population. If, however, the total population contains different subgroups, it might be important to ensure that all of them are represented in the sample. This involves segregating the total population into a number of mutually exclusive subpopulations and drawing a sample from each. The composite sample that results from this process is referred to as a 'stratified sample'.

Analysis

Once information has been collected, it needs to be analysed. For example, in response to a question such as 'How challenged do you feel in your present job?', only some of those surveyed might have offered a positive response. The change agent may want to know what proportion of the sample responded in this way compared to those who responded in the same way in other organizations, in order to be able to assess whether the lack of challenging work is a problem. It might also be useful to consider whether there is any relationship between those who do not feel challenged and the unit they work in or their level in the hierarchy. Analytical procedures organize information in ways that can provide answers to diagnostic questions. Analytical techniques are often classified as 'qualitative' or 'quantitative'. Qualitative techniques are used to explain why people think and behave in certain ways rather than to count the numbers of people who think or behave in certain ways. Quantitative techniques focus on pieces of information that can be counted and are best used to answer what, when and who rather than why questions.

Qualitative techniques

Qualitative techniques tend to be more concerned with meaning and underlying patterns than with scientific tests. Content analysis and force-field analysis are two examples of qualitative analytical techniques frequently used in organizational diagnostic exercises.

Content analysis

Content analysis attempts to summarize respondents' comments into meaningful categories. This involves identifying comments or answers that tend to recur most frequently and grouping them in ways that provide a set of mutually exclusive and exhaustive categories or themes. For example, in response to a question such as 'What do you like best about your work?', a number of responses might refer to working with friendly colleagues, considerate supervisors and having the opportunity to communicate with co-workers while doing the job. All these comments might be regarded as referring to a common theme, the 'social aspects' of the job. A different set of comments might refer to the degree of challenge offered by the work, the opportunity to be creative and the freedom to experiment with new methods. All these comments might be regarded as referring to different aspects of the 'nature of the work' itself. These two categories might then be used as a basis for analysing the content of all the information collected from respondents. When a set of categories is exhaustive, it is possible to allocate every response to a category, and when it is mutually exclusive, each item of information will fall into one particular category. After all responses have been classified, one way of determining the importance of the different categories is to identify those that have been referred to most often.

NUD*IST is one example of a software tool that can be used for coding and analysing qualitative data, and provides a relatively easy method of comparing the responses from different respondents to particular questions.

Force-field analysis

Force-field analysis, discussed in Chapter 2, also involves categorizing information. The distinctive feature of force-field analysis is that it involves organizing the categories into two broad types – those relating to forces or pressures for change and those relating to forces or pressures supporting the (problematic) status quo and resisting change.

It was noted in Chapter 2 that Lewin (1951) viewed the level of behaviour in any situation as the result of a force-field comprising a balance of the forces pushing for change (some different level of behaviour) and the forces resisting that change. Diagnosing situations in terms of driving and restraining forces can provide a useful basis for developing action plans to secure the desired change. When the forces pushing in one direction exceed the forces pushing in the opposite direction, the dynamic equilibrium changes. The level of behaviour can be changed towards a more desirable state by increasing the strength of forces for change (the driving forces) in the desired direction or by diminishing the strength of restraining forces (Figure 8.1).

Change tool 8.2, at the end of this chapter, provides a step-by-step approach you can use to apply force-field analysis to an opportunity development or problem management issue with which you might have to deal.

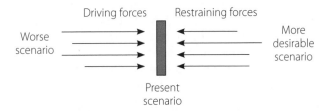

Figure **8.1** *A force-field*

Quantitative techniques

Quantitative techniques focus on data that have numerical significance and involve counting and measuring to answer what, when and who type questions. Some of the basic techniques most frequently used by change agents when analysing quantitative information are means, standard deviations, correlation coefficients and difference tests. The mean is a measure that indicates the average response or behaviour. For example, over the past year, the eight employees in department X might have averaged 5 days' sick leave. The standard deviation indicates the extent to which there is high or low variation around this mean, for example six members of the department may have had no sick leave, whereas the other two may have had 20 days each. Correlation coefficients measure the strength of the relationship between variables, for example sick leave might be inversely related to job satisfaction. Difference tests indicate whether the scores achieved by one group, for example an average of 5 days' sick leave for members of department X, are significantly different from those achieved by members of other groups – different departments in the same organization or some benchmark score or industry norm. More details on these and other techniques can be found in any standard text on statistics.

Interpretation

Conceptual models provide a basis for interpreting diagnostic information and identifying what needs to be changed to achieve a more desirable state of affairs.

Change managers using the 7S model (described in Chapter 7) can construct a 7S matrix (see Change tool 7.1) that can be used to point to those areas where internal misalignment may be a problem.

The results of the 1993 staff survey in the BBC, which was designed around the Burke-Litwin causal model of organizational performance, indicated some priorities for change. The elements most in need of change were structure, leadership and factors affecting motivation, but there was also evidence that there was scope for improvement in many other areas. A brief summary of the results of this survey is presented in Figure 8.2.

Change tool 8.2, at the end of this chapter, provides another example of how diagnostic information can be used to identify what action needs to be taken to improve organizational performance.

Political considerations

Collecting information is not an innocuous or benign activity, because people will have concerns about who will use the data and for what purpose, and how they will analyse and interpret them. Nadler (1977) argues that the collection and distribution of information can change the nature of power relationships. Data collection can generate energy around the activities or behaviours that are being measured for a number of reasons. For example:

- It may result in information that an individual or group has previously withheld in order to secure some political advantage being widely distributed, thereby undermining their power and influence.
- It opens up the possibility of comparing the current performance of an individual or group with their own past performance, the performance of others, or some benchmark. These possibilities might be perceived as threatening, especially where there is a link between performance and rewards.

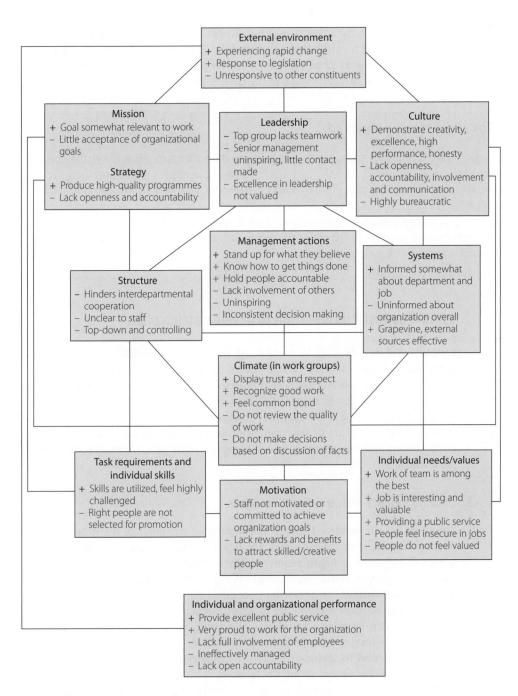

Figure **8.2** *Results of the 1993 BBC staff survey*

The energy generated by data collection can be directed towards assisting or undermining the change agent's attempt to diagnose the need for change. How the energy will be directed will be influenced by the perceptions people have about the possible future uses that may be made of the data. If, for example, employees expect the information collected in a diagnostic survey to be used in an open, non-threatening and helpful manner, they may be motivated to provide accurate information. If, on the other hand, they expect it to be used in a punitive manner, they may attempt to withhold or distort data. This point is illustrated in Example 8.1. Change managers need to be alert to the possibility that they will encounter resistance even at this early stage in the change process.

● *Example* **8.1** *The effect of being observed*

A group of employees worked together to assemble a range of complicated large steel frameworks. Their method of working varied depending on whether or not they were being observed by anyone who might influence the rate they were paid for the job. The group had discovered that by tightening certain bolts first, the frames would be slightly sprung and all the other bolts would bind and be difficult to tighten. When they used this method, they gave the impression they were working hard all the time. When they were not being observed, they followed a different sequence of tightening bolts and the work was much easier and the job could be completed in less time (Porter et al., 1975).

Using diagnostic information to develop action plans

Planning will be discussed in more detail in Chapter 15, but this section demonstrates how diagnostic information can be used as a basis for formulating action plans. SWOT analysis and force-field analysis provide useful frameworks for using diagnostic information to identify what needs to be changed.

Anybody can do a SWOT analysis (Change tool 8.1), but doing it with others can provide a richer picture of how the group or organization fits with its operating environment and the issues that need to be attended to in order to secure future performance.

⚒ *Change tool* **8.1** *Using a SWOT analysis*

Strengths are the positive tangible and intangible attributes of the group, department or organization. Weaknesses are negative factors that can undermine the group, department or organization's ability to attain desired goals. The PRIMO-F framework (people, resources, innovation, marketing, operations, finance) offers a useful set of headings for reviewing strengths and weaknesses, but in some situations it might be more appropriate to adapt this framework to include particularly relevant factors, such as scalability – the ability to rapidly expand or contract operations, or develop a bespoke framework more suited to the circumstances. It can also be useful to include a catch-all category such as 'other' to ensure that difficult-to-categorize factors are not ignored.

Opportunities are external factors that offer the possibility for benefit and threats are the factors that can jeopardize existing ways of working, limit possibilities and derail future plans. The PEST (political, economic, sociocultural, technological) headings can provide a useful set of categories for exploring opportunities and threats.

A simple 2 × 2 matrix can provide a basic framework for plotting the findings and identifying issues that require attention (Table 8.2).

*Table **8.2** A simple SWOT template*

Strengths	Weaknesses
1	1
2	2
3	3
4	4
Opportunities	Threats
1	1
2	2
3	3
4	4

Table 8.3 presents a more sophisticated template, which incorporates the PRIMO-F and PEST categories and offers the possibility of assessing the relative impact of each strength, weakness, opportunity and threat.

*Table **8.3** A more detailed SWOT template*

Strengths	Major	Significant	Marginal	Weaknesses	Major	Significant	Marginal
People				People			
1				1			
2				2			
3				3			
Resources				Resources			
1				1			
2				2			
3				3			
Innovation				Innovation			
1				1			
2				2			
3				3			
Marketing				Marketing			
1				1			
2				2			
3				3			
Operations				Operations			
1				1			
2				2			
3				3			
Finance				Finance			
1				1			
2				2			
3				3			
Other				Other			
1				1			
2				2			
3				3			

Opportunities	Major	Significant	Marginal	Threats	Major	Significant	Marginal
Political 1 2 3				Political 1 2 3			
Economic 1 2 3				Economic 1 2 3			
Sociocultural 1 2 3				Sociocultural 1 2 3			
Technology 1 2 3				Technology 1 2 3			
Other 1 2 3				Other 1 2 3			

Once the strengths, weaknesses, opportunities and threats that need to be addressed have been identified, they can be transposed onto the template in Table 8.4. The final steps in the process involve exploring ways of developing and making best use of strengths and using them to exploit opportunities, and finding ways of reducing weaknesses and containing threats.

Table **8.4** *Using SWOT to develop action plans*

Internal factors			
Strengths	**Ways to exploit**	**Weaknesses**	**Ways to reduce**
1 2 3 4 5	1 2 3 4 5	1 2 3 4 5	1 2 3 4 5
External factors			
Opportunities	**Ways to exploit**	**Threats**	**Ways to reduce**
1 2 3 4 5	1 2 3 4 5	1 2 3 4 5	1 2 3 4 5

The value of change tools such as the SWOT analysis is that they can help to ensure that those leading change do not adopt a blinkered approach and ignore key data. The danger of those at the top adopting a blinkered approach is illustrated by the rise and fall of the building society Northern Rock, as shown in Example 8.2.

Example **8.2** *Northern Rock*

Until 2007, Northern Rock was seen by insiders, customers and many in the wider financial community as a successful financial services company offering mortgage products to the UK market and providing a portfolio of savings products. Initially, like other traditional building societies, Northern Rock relied on its savings products to fund much of its lending but, over time, it started to source more and more of its funding through wholesale borrowing on capital markets, bonds and securitized loans. These new sources of funding provided a platform for expansion and the development of a new profitable business model that involved lending higher risk mortgages products (loans of more than 100 per cent of the property value) and making these loans available to a wider customer base, including some customers who, by traditional industry standards, would not have been judged as able to afford the repayments. While property values continued to increase, this business model was very successful and Northern Rock continued to expand. Customers were attracted by the more than 100 per cent mortgages because they provided surplus funds they could use to furnish their new properties or for some other purpose, such as the purchase of a new car.

Those in Northern Rock who were responsible for managing the agenda for change appeared to focus their attention on opportunities for generating profit and failed to pay much attention to potential threats. Adopting a SWOT approach might have provided a diagnostic framework that would have helped those caught up in the (apparent) runaway success of the business be alert to potential threats alongside the opportunities that appeared to dominate their thinking. Some signs of potential threats were there but they appeared to have little impact on the thinking of those leading the business. These included an increase in consumer debt and the possibility that this was affecting the Northern Rock customer demographic more than that of most other high-street lenders, associated concerns about affordability, and concerns about the future growth of property values.

III

Force-field analysis is another change tool that can be used as a stand-alone tool for diagnosis. It can also be used as a framework for analysing the findings from any diagnostic exercise to develop an action plan. Example 6.2 showed how a change agent used force-field analysis to become aware of restraining forces as well as driving forces. Change tool 8.2 provides further guidance on how to develop practical goals to manage these driving and restraining forces and formulate an action plan.

Change tool **8.2** *A force-field approach to opportunity development or problem management*

1 Think about a problem you have to manage or an opportunity you could develop and imagine a more desirable scenario you would like to reach. Use this as a basis for identifying a concrete goal you wish to achieve, and write it in the box on the right-hand side of the page. (If you are struggling to come up with an example from your own experience, you could look ahead to Example 9.2, and apply force-field analysis to it.)

2 List the driving forces that are pushing towards the more desirable scenario in the left-hand column. In the right-hand column, list the restraining forces that are blocking the achievement of your goal.

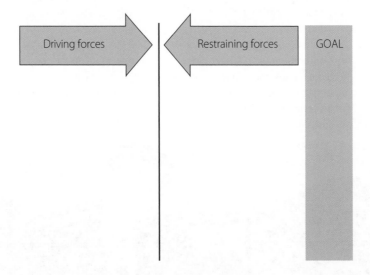

3 Review your list of driving and restraining forces and highlight those that are powerful, in terms of either pushing for or resisting change, and manageable, that is, you anticipate you will be able to affect the power of the force.

Driving forces: Review each of the driving forces you have highlighted on a separate sheet, starting with the most important, and brainstorm all the steps you could take to *increase* the effect of the force. Do not confine yourself to 'sensible' ideas. List everything that comes to mind. Do not evaluate any of these action steps until you have brainstormed action steps to reduce the effect of the restraining forces.

Restraining forces: Now do the same for the most important restraining forces, but this time brainstorm all the steps you could take to *reduce* the effect of each restraining force.

Now review all the action steps:

1 Eliminate those action steps that are totally impractical, but only after you are sure they cannot be 'twisted' or 'adapted' to provide a useful contribution.

2 Identify the 'best of the rest'. Consider whether some action steps can contribute to the strengthening of more than one driving force or the erosion of more than one restraining force. An alternative approach to distilling out the most useful action steps is to group similar actions together and identify those from each group that seem most practical.

3 Finally, list those action steps that deserve serious consideration below.

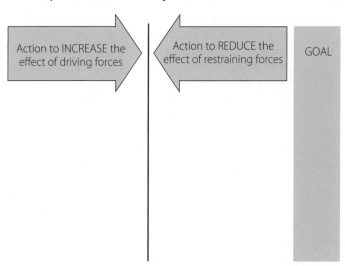

The final step involves re-evaluating the action steps from a cost–benefit perspective. The plan has to be practical and some of the proposed action steps might be too expensive in terms of time or other resources. It may be necessary to amend the plan at this stage in order to improve its viability. However, it may also be necessary to include new elements to mould individual action steps into an integrated plan. Give some thought to timescale and milestones against which progress can be assessed. Milestones are important because they provide early warning if the plan is not working and signal the need for renewed effort or the implementation of contingency plans.

You might find it useful to reflect on the content of this and Chapter 7 and review your (and others') use of diagnostic information (Exercise 8.1).

✓ Exercise **8.1** *Evaluating your use of diagnostic information*

Think about a recent occasion when you (or somebody working close to you) have attempted to introduce and manage a change. The change could have been in your work organization or elsewhere, such as your university social club.

1 Reflect on the extent to which this change initiative was based on an accurate diagnosis of the need for change.

2 Consider to what extent this was related to:
   • the appropriateness of the (implicit or explicit) diagnostic model used
   • the nature of the information collected
   • the way in which it was interpreted.

3 Reflect on the steps you or others might take to help improve the quality of the way the need for change is diagnosed in your unit, department or elsewhere.

Summary

This chapter examined the process of gathering and interpreting information for the purpose of diagnosis. Attention was focused on five main steps:

1 *Selection of an appropriate conceptual model for diagnosis:* Conceptual models play a key role in the diagnostic process because they help us decide which aspects of organizational behaviour require attention and provide a focus for information gathering. They also provide a basis for interpreting the information that has been collected. When selecting a model for diagnosis, the first point to consider is the extent to which the model is relevant to the issue(s) under consideration, for example loss of market share, dysfunctional intergroup conflict, high labour turnover and so on.

2 *Clarification of information requirements:* Once a diagnostic model has been selected, the change manager can identify the items of information that will be required to assess how an organization (unit or work group) is performing.

3 *Information gathering:* Factors that might determine the method of data collection – interviews, questionnaires, projective methods, observations and unobtrusive measures – were considered, together with ways of sampling people, activities and records that will provide sufficient information to provide a representative picture of the current situation.

4 *Analysis:* Qualitative and quantitative analytical techniques were reviewed.

5 *Interpretation:* Issues that need to be considered when interpreting data were reviewed. Collecting information is not an innocuous or benign activity. Attention was drawn to the political issues associated with data collection that can frustrate attempts to gain an accurate impression of organizational functioning.

References

Bales, R.F. (1950) *Interaction Process Analysis: A Method for the Study of Small Groups.* Cambridge, MA: Addison-Wesley.

Cummings, T.G. and Worley, C.G. (2001) *Organizational Development and Change* (7th edn). Cincinnati, OH: South Western.

Fordyce, J.K. and Weil, R. (1983) Methods for finding out what is going on. In W. French, C.H. Bell and R. Zawacki (eds) *Organization Development: Theory, Practice and Research*. Plano, TX: Business Publications.

Lewin, K. (1951) *Field Theory in Social Science*. New York: Harper & Row.

Nadler, D. (1977) *Feedback and Organization Development: Using Data-based Methods.* Reading, MA: Addison-Wesley.

Porter, L.W., Lawler, E.E. and Hackman, J.R. (1975) *Behavior in Organizations*. New York: McGraw-Hill.

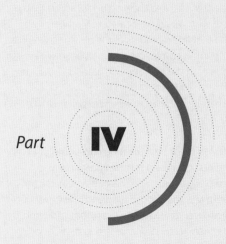

Part **IV**

LEADING AND MANAGING THE PEOPLE ISSUES

Introduction to Part **IV**

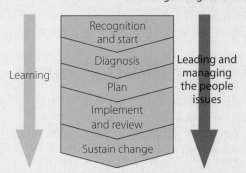

Leaders need to attend to people issues throughout the whole change process. A common mistake many leaders make is to treat the early stages of recognizing the need for change and diagnosing what needs to be changed as technical activities that can be managed with no reference to those who might be affected by the change. It is not unusual for 'expert' change agents to decide when and where change is required and to define change objectives without taking into account the concerns of stake-holders or recognizing the ways in which they can contribute to or sabotage the change process. The Triumph case, which is described in two parts, illustrates how people issues can affect whether the change will succeed or fail.

💼 *Case study* **Part IV** *Triumph: sourcing components from cost-competitive countries, Part 1*

A slowdown in the growth of profits in 2009–10 led a large US producer of outdoor power equipment (referred to here as Triumph) to review its operations and explore what could be done to improve profitability. Two possibilities were identified. One was to adopt some of the lean manufacturing processes developed by Toyota to eliminate waste and the other was to source more of its components from cost-competitive countries.

Here, in the first part of the case, attention is focused on the sourcing project (the lean manufacturing project did not start until mid-2012). The opportunity for sourcing from cost-competitive countries was

identified by the deputy head of procurement. She persuaded her boss, the director of procurement, that sourcing components from cost-competitive countries could deliver benefits for their department and the company as a whole. He was quickly convinced and tabled the proposal at a meeting of the executive team. The CEO was impressed and tasked the director of procurement with undertaking an exploratory study and to report back as soon as possible. The outcome was a recommendation to set up a small procurement office in Mumbai, India. A business plan was prepared and approved by the executive committee, the head of product development was asked to set up and chair a ▶

161

steering committee to oversee the project, and the purchasing director was told to set up a task force to progress the project.

The director of procurement recognized the importance of populating the steering committee with people likely to support the project. It was not his committee but he recommended the appointment of two second-tier managers from the manufacturing function who he knew would champion the new venture.

Careful attention was given to planning. The task force sought input from those working on procurement at HQ and from managers in all the manufacturing units. They also collected information from managers working in product development, quality and logistics, and visited potential suppliers in India. At every stage of the process, they reported back to the steering committee and eventually produced a detailed plan for the new procurement unit, including proposals for how the unit would be structured (it would mirror the structure of the purchasing

department at HQ) and the job specifications for the eight staff who would be located in Mumbai. It was proposed that five members of the new unit would be current Triumph employees who had been working in procurement in the USA and had a good knowledge of the company, and three would be recruited locally to ensure that the unit had sufficient experience of doing business in India.

Before starting work in India, the five existing Triumph staff spent time meeting colleagues in all the departments that would receive and/or use the imported components, and the staff who had been recruited in Mumbai (two Indians and one German) were flown over to the USA to learn about Triumph, its products, manufacturing processes, systems and procedures.

Before reading on, list those 'people issues' you thought had been managed in a way that could help the change to succeed. Now identify any 'people issues' that might not have been managed as well as they could have been.

Case study **Part IV**   *Triumph: sourcing components from cost-competitive countries, Part 2*

In September 2011, the members of the new unit started work in India to develop links with potential suppliers. During this early phase, there were many occasions when they needed information about technical specifications, production schedules and so on from colleagues working for Triumph in the USA but, to their surprise, they found that their requests were often dealt with slowly and information was sometimes withheld. They began to feel that US-based staff regarded them as outsiders and no longer members of the 'home team'.

This reaction was very different to the way they had been received when they were in the USA setting up the operation. At that point, sourcing from cost-competitive countries was the 'flavour of the month', it was being championed by top management and everybody seemed to be supporting the project. But as the project was being implemented, this enthusiasm seemed to evaporate. Appeals to members of the steering committee to bring their influence to bear on those who seemed to be dragging their feet had little effect. This began to undermine the morale of those

working in India, especially the five US expatriates. Without the support they received from the three locally based members of the Mumbai team, this could have been an even more difficult time for them. The head of the unit decided to fly back to the USA to secure the support necessary to get the project back on track.

Within a few days, he identified a number of problems:

- A new CEO had been appointed and she had new priorities that were dominating the top team's agenda. While the top team still supported the sourcing project, they had less time to champion it across the organization.
- Early on, when senior managers were communicating a strong message that the sourcing project was a priority for the top team, managers across the company complied and went along with it but, with the benefit of hindsight, it appeared that they were never fully committed. When the top team's attention was diverted elsewhere, this lack of commitment began to surface.

- Support remained strong in the purchasing department because they had much to gain. Sourcing from low-cost countries would help the department meet its objective to reduce procurement costs.
- Support elsewhere was weak because they had little to gain and could lose out if the project was not 100 per cent successful. Managers in the manufacturing units had reservations because they felt that it might be more difficult for Indian suppliers to meet their just-in-time delivery requirements and production could be halted because shipments were delayed at some point in their journey from distant locations across India. They also feared that they might have to insure against this possibility by increasing inventory levels. Quality assurance was another department that felt that it had much to lose and little to gain from the new sourcing policy. Staff feared that unknown Indian suppliers might not be able to provide the near zero defect rate they enjoyed from existing suppliers.
- When the head of the Mumbai unit turned to the steering committee for help, he found that there was little that this group of managers could (or were willing to) do. While membership of the committee represented all interested and affected departments, the individual managers appointed to the committee were not always sufficiently powerful in their home departments to influence opinion. They also had conflicting interests. As members of the steering committee, they could appreciate the value of the project for the organization as a whole, but they were also under pressure from colleagues to protect the interests of their home departments.

This two-part case study provides many examples of how people-related issues affected the success of the project. These issues will be looked at in more depth in the five chapters that make up Part IV. A short synopsis of each chapter is presented below, together with a paragraph indicating how the content relates to the Triumph case.

Chapter 9 The role of leadership in change management

The first part of Chapter 9 draws on theory to identify seven tasks that leaders need to perform in order to ensure change success. These are:

1 *Sense making:* Making sense of the world and identifying the opportunities and threats that require attention.
2 *Visioning:* Identifying a vision of what a more desirable state of affairs might look like and what needs to be done to move towards this better future.
3 *Sense giving:* Communicating the vision to a wider audience and responding to feedback as required to win commitment to the change.
4 *Aligning:* Promoting a shared sense of direction so that people can work together to achieve the vision.
5 *Enabling:* Removing obstacles and creating the conditions that empower others to implement the change.
6 *Supporting:* Recognizing and responding to the concerns of those affected by the change.
7 *Maintaining momentum and sustaining the change:* Showing commitment and 'walking the talk' to keep people focused on the change.

While it is recognized that a strong vision can make a valuable contribution to the success of a change initiative, some factors that might render the vision unfit for purpose are reviewed. Attention is also given to communicating the vision in a way that will align people behind it.

The second part of the chapter focuses attention on distributed leadership. It can be dangerous to focus too much attention on individual leaders. Within organizations, the growth of matrix and network structures and the move from functional to more process-oriented organizational forms are creating circumstances where traditional command and

IV

control cultures are being eroded and managers increasingly have to collaborate with others, over whom they have no direct authority, in order to get things done.

Link to the Triumph case: Sense making, visioning and sense giving had a role to play. The deputy head of procurement saw an opportunity to reduce costs. She shared her idea with her boss, convinced him of its merit and he took it to the CEO and the executive committee and won their approval to take the project forward. The second part of the case also illustrates that when leadership tasks such as aligning, enabling, supporting and maintaining momentum are not performed effectively, this can undermine the success of a change initiative.

Chapter 10 *Power, politics and stakeholder management*

Chapter 10 explores the politics of organizational change and points to the importance of enlisting support from key stakeholders. Organizations are conceptualized as a collection of constituencies, each pursuing their own objectives:

- Individuals and groups attempt to influence each other in the pursuit of self-interest.
- When there is a conflict of interest, it is the power and influence of those involved that determines the outcome rather than logical and rational argument.
- In order to ensure the successful introduction of change, it is essential that change managers secure the assistance of powerful stakeholders and build a critical mass of support for the change.

Political behaviour tends to be more intense in times of change because individuals and groups perceive the possibility of upsetting the existing balance of power. Some may be motivated to defend the status quo, whereas others may perceive change as an opportunity to improve their position. Consequently, those leading change need to be alert to these political dynamics, especially the possibility that others may be motivated to act in ways that undermine their efforts to bring about change.

Link to the Triumph case: Part 1 showed how the director of procurement and his deputy worked hard to secure the support of powerful stakeholders (the CEO and members of the executive committee) and build a critical mass of support for the change by doing what they could to ensure that the steering committee was populated by influential people from across the organization who were likely to support the project. Part 2 demonstrated how members of the task force and the team that were to lead the project in India also invested a lot of time enlisting the support of others who would be affected by the change. However, as time passed and the situation changed, many of those affected by the change, including members of the steering committee, developed new priorities and conflicts of interest that eroded support for the change.

Chapter 11 *Communicating change*

The quality of communications can have an important impact on the success or otherwise of a change. It can, for example, affect whether the need for change is recognized in good time and whether people will be motivated to support the change. Chapter 11 explores the value of a clear communication strategy and examines some of the issues that those leading a change need to consider when formulating a coherent approach to communicating change.

Link to the Triumph case: Part 2 revealed that the CEO moved on and a new CEO was appointed and she had new priorities that began to dominate the top team's agenda. Consequently, while some members of the executive committee continued to support the sourcing project, they had less time to champion it across the organization and circumstances forced them to take their 'eyes off the ball'. Managers across the organization, who were also developing new priorities that undermined their commitment, recognized that this gave them more freedom to pursue their own interests and invest less effort in the procurement project. The director of procurement contributed to this problem because he failed to detect this dip in support. Communication was also a problem for the leader of the team in India and he experienced problems maintaining his relationship with colleagues back in the USA.

Chapter **12** *Motivating others to change*

A key challenge for leaders is motivating others to support change. Efforts often fail because those leading the process pay insufficient attention to winning the support of those who can affect the outcome of the change. Chapter 12 considers how the general level of commitment in an organization can affect the level of support for change, identifies some of the most common sources of resistance to change, and explores the utility of expectancy theory for assessing and managing resistance to change.

Link to the Triumph case: Early on, the CEO and other senior managers were motivated to support the project and their enthusiasm persuaded others to throw their weight behind it, but this motivation was not sustained. Within the procurement department, members were highly motivated to be selected to work on the sourcing project in India, because they had been told that it would raise their profile in the company and help them secure advancement. Later, as support for the project waned, the project leader was even more highly motivated to make the project a success, but others began to feel that it would not deliver the promised benefits. Low motivation could be a major threat to the eventual success of the project.

IV

Chapter **13** *Supporting others through change*

Chapter 13 addresses the way organizational members experience change. It examines the response to change, irrespective of whether the change is viewed as an opportunity or a threat, as a progression through a number of stages of psychological reaction. It also considers how an understanding of the way individuals react to change can help managers to plan and implement organizational change in ways that will maximize benefit and minimize cost for the organization and those affected by the change.

Link to the Triumph case: As 'back home' support for the project began to evaporate, members of the Mumbai team started to feel isolated and abandoned. It was difficult for everybody, especially the American expats, and three of them, after the initial excitement, experienced serious problems adjusting to their new circumstances. It was largely because of the support they received from their colleagues (and their families) who were already living in India that they were able to continue working in Mumbai.

💼 *Case study* **Part IV** *Triumph: sourcing components from cost-competitive countries, Conclusion*

The sourcing project is still limping along but it is not delivering the benefits that had been anticipated at the start. If you were the director of procurement, what could you have done differently that would have helped to ensure the success of the project? Think about this question as you read through Chapters 9–13, and try to identify sections from the chapters to give reasons for your answer.

✓ *Exercise* **Part IV** *Useful questions for reviewing your approach to leading people through change*

In Chapter 2, after discussing each stage in the process model of change management, your attention was drawn to a number of questions that might help you assess how well a change is being (or was) managed. All these questions are summarized in Figure 2.5 and the questions relating to leading people through change are listed below:

- Do leaders empathize with others and understand how they might react to the possibility of change?
- Do they act in ways that will promote trust and win commitment?
- Do they identify and engage those individuals and groups who can affect the success of the change?
- Are they good communicators?
- Do they empower others to contribute to the change?
- Do they support those who are threatened by the change?

Reflect on and review these questions and, after reading the five chapters in Part IV, revise this list and generate your own set of useful questions that you might find it helpful to refer to when you are leading a change.

Chapter **9**

The role of leadership in change management

Leadership is widely regarded as the key enabler of the change process but there appears to be considerable debate about what constitutes good leadership. Drawing on Northouse (2004), leadership is defined here as a process that involves influencing others to achieve desired goals.

This chapter reviews the role of leadership, explores the proposition that, in times of change, managerial work is increasingly a leadership task, examines what leaders have to do to deliver successful change, and considers the view that leadership needs to be viewed as a collective process.

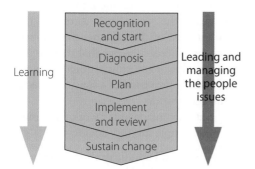

Management and leadership

Tichy and Devanna (1986) and Kotter (1990) highlight a tension between management and leadership. They argue that management is concerned with maintaining the existing organization, whereas leadership is concerned with change. In other words, management is about 'doing things right' and leadership is about 'doing the right things' (Bennis and Nanus, 1985, p. 21). Table 9.1 draws on the work of Kotter to summarize the main differences between management and leadership. They both involve deciding what needs to be done, developing the capacity to do it, and ensuring that it is done. However, while management is concerned with order and consistency, leadership is concerned with new directions and change.

Managerial work, in times of change, is increasingly a leadership task

While management and leadership are distinct activities, they are complementary and both are necessary for success in a changing business environment. Bolden (2004) argues that it can be confusing to think about managers and leaders as though they are different people and, to a large extent, incompatible. For example, some talk about leaders as dynamic, charismatic individuals with the ability to inspire others, and managers as uninspiring bureaucrats who just focus on the task in hand. Bolden (2004, p. 7) asserts that such a view does not coincide well with the lived experience of being a manager. People are generally recruited into 'management', rather than 'leadership', positions and are expected to complete a multitude of tasks, ranging from day-to-day planning and implementation to longer term strategic thinking. None of these are done in isolation.

Table **9.1** *The focus of management and leadership*

Management	Leadership
1 Deciding what needs to be done	
Management involves planning and goal setting, formulating steps for achieving goals, and identifying the resources that will be required – *planning and budgeting*	Leadership involves *developing a vision* that sets the direction for change and developing strategies that will deliver the changes required to achieve the vision
2 Developing the capacity to achieve it	
Management involves creating organizational structures and work roles that will facilitate the achievement of goals, appointing qualified people, communicating plans and delegating appropriate levels of responsibility – *organizing and staffing*	Leadership involves *communicating the new direction* in a way that enables people to understand what needs to happen if the vision is to be achieved and creating the conditions necessary to align their efforts to deliver the vision
3 Ensuring that it is done	
Management involves monitoring performance, identifying deviations from plans and taking corrective action – *controlling and problem solving*	Leadership involves *motivating and inspiring* people to achieve the vision

Kotter (1999) argues that managers are the people who are in the best position to provide the leadership required to ensure that a change will be successful. However, if they are to provide this leadership, they need to recognize that their role involves a dual responsibility, for management – keeping the system operating effectively – and for leadership – revitalizing and renewing the system to ensure that it will remain effective over the longer term. The thrust of the argument developed in Chapter 3 is that not only is the pace of change increasing, but that there is also a shift in emphasis towards managing discontinuous or transformational change. An implication of this shift is that leadership, and the provision of a sense of direction, has become a more important part of managerial work.

Kotter (1990, p. 104) illustrates the point that managerial work, in times of change, is increasingly a leadership task with a simple military analogy:

> A peacetime army can usually survive with good administration and management up and down the hierarchy, coupled with good leadership concentrated at the top. A wartime army, however, needs competent leadership at all levels.

In a wartime army, platoon leaders and company commanders still have to manage, but successful outcomes in combat situations are highly dependent on the quality of the leadership they provide. Leadership cannot just be concentrated at the top of the organization. This theme will be developed later in this chapter when the distributed aspect of leadership is discussed in more detail.

The role of leadership

There is growing evidence that 'what leaders do' can have a powerful effect on follower behaviour and the success of change initiatives. There has been much discussion on what leadership entails. Kotter (1990) describes leadership in terms of creating a vision, communicating and aligning people to achieve the vision, and motivating and inspiring them by appealing to their needs, values and emotions. Higgs and Rowland (2000, 2011), after reviewing earlier work, report five behaviours associated with successful change implementation:

1 creating the case for change
2 ensuring that change is based on an in-depth understanding of the issues
3 engaging others and building commitment
4 developing effective plans and good monitoring practices
5 facilitating and developing the capability of those involved.

Ancona et al. (2007) refer to four capabilities: sense making, relating, visioning and inventing. Inventing involves conceiving, designing, and putting into practice new ways of working. Yates (2009) offers a 4E framework:

1 envisioning a values-driven set of goals and strategies
2 enabling their achievement by selecting appropriate methods, tools and people
3 empowering others by developing trust and interdependence between leaders and followers
4 energizing everybody to drive the change.

Yates argues that the moment a leader flags or shows a lack of resolve, the team will lose energy and results will suffer. Subordinates' perceptions of leaders' behaviour can have a powerful impact on leader effectiveness. Gilley et al. (2009) studied subordinates' perceptions of effective leader behaviour and identified, in order of importance, three factors related to support for change – the leader's ability to motivate others, communicate effectively and build teams. Oreg et al. (2011) reviewed 700 studies of change recipients' reactions to change and reported that when they perceived the process to be participative and supportive, with open lines of communication, and when managers were perceived to be competent and fair, they were more likely to react positively towards the change.

What managers (and others) do when leading change

Drawing on these ideas, it is possible to identify seven tasks that leaders need to perform in order to ensure change success (Table 9.2). They are discussed in detail below.

*Table **9.2** Key leadership tasks*

Sense making	Make sense of the world and identify the opportunities and threats that require attention
Visioning	Identify a vision of what a more desirable state of affairs might look like and what needs to be done to move towards this better future
Sense giving	Communicate the vision to a wider audience and respond to feedback as required to win commitment to the change
Aligning	Promote a shared sense of direction so that people can work together to achieve the vision
Enabling	Remove obstacles and create the conditions that empower others to implement the change
Supporting	Recognize and respond to the concerns of those affected by the change
Maintaining momentum and sustaining the change	Show commitment and 'walk the talk' – demonstrating that they are prepared to change their behaviour as well – to keep people focused on the change

Sense making

Leaders need to be able to make sense of the world around them and develop cognitive maps – mental representations of their environment that show what they perceive to be more or less important – to help them identify those issues that require attention. This is not always easy because leaders (and others) have a conservative tendency to interpret what is going on in terms of what has gone on in the past. Colville et al. (2013, p. 1213), discussing sense making in the context of counterterrorism, suggest that 'a sensible event often resembles one that has happened before'. They refer to the 9/11 Commission Report (2004), which found that members of the intelligence community were on the *alert* for signs of the past, but were unprepared for and *unaware* of signals of an emerging, changing present. Various accounts of what happened suggest that the CIA failed to attend to reports that potential terrorists were learning to fly because this story did not fit with pre-existing cognitive maps about how terrorists operate.

Näslund and Pemer (2012) make a similar point following their exploration of 'dominant stories' in two Scandinavian companies. Organizational members tell stories about characters, situations and their perceptions of cause-and-effect relationships in order to help make sense of their everyday experience. Over time, dominant stories emerge and serve as collective frames that both enable and restrict sense making. Stories that fit with the dominant story are perceived as convincing and those that do not are viewed as implausible or even unthinkable, and therefore have little impact. Consequently, organizations find it easier to change in a direction that is congruent with the dominant story.

Ancona et al. (2007, p. 95) suggest that leaders can improve their sense making by seeking data from multiple sources, checking whether different people have different perspectives, and using early observations to design small experiments to test ideas. It is important to note, however, that while sense making might be an essential first step, it is not a one-off activity. Situations change and leaders need to be continually alert to how new developments might impact the agenda for change.

Visioning

While sense making and visioning are separate activities, they are closely linked and it is essential that those exercising leadership formulate a vision based on a realistic assessment of the situation and the needs and priorities of key stakeholders. Colville et al. (2012, p. 8) view sense making as the act of cueing a story in the form of a frame (cognitive map) that provides leaders with a recipe that serves both as a scheme of interpretation (this is the meaning of the situation) and a scheme for action (this is what we should do next). Based on their interpretation of the current situation and emerging threats and opportunities, leaders can begin to identify their vision of what a more desirable state of affairs might look like and what needs to be done to move towards this better future. There is wide acceptance that a strong vision, informed by an in-depth understanding of the context, can make a valuable contribution to the success of a change initiative.

According to Kotter (1996), a good vision needs to be:

- *imaginable:* conveys a picture of what the future will look like
- *desirable:* appeals to the long-term interests of employees, customers, shareholders and stakeholders
- *feasible:* comprises realistic, attainable goals
- *focused:* clear enough to provide guidance in decision making

- *flexible:* general enough to allow individual initiatives and alternative responses in light of changing conditions
- *communicable:* easy to communicate; can be successfully explained within five minutes.

There is no set formula for how leaders should formulate a vision. Some leaders work on their own to develop a vision before presenting it to others as a clear and formulated picture of a preferred future (as did the CEO in Example 1.5, the Direct Banking case, when he announced his intention to introduce voice automation and routing in order to drive down costs). Others begin to share their ideas almost as soon as they become aware of a need or opportunity for change, and encourage others to contribute to visioning what a better future might look like. The extent to which others are allowed to participate can vary but there is considerable evidence that participation does contribute to change success. Oreg et al. (2011) identified 14 studies that assessed the effect of participation and found that it was associated with a sense of agency and control over the change, lower levels of stress, higher readiness to accept change, and overall support for the process.

Irrespective the extent to which the recipients of change and other stakeholders are allowed to contribute to formulating the vision, there is considerable agreement (Kotter, 1990; Yates, 2009) that a vision is more likely to be achieved when it is compatible with the values of all those who will be involved in and affected by its implementation.

As explained in Example 9.1, when Birna Einarsdóttir took over as CEO of Íslandsbanki after the Icelandic economy imploded, she worked hard to involve others in building a new vision for the bank that would enjoy widespread support.

IV

Example **9.1** *Involving staff in developing a new vision for Íslandsbanki*

As a society, Iceland was in a state of economic and social crisis after 2008. The impact of the banking collapse in Iceland cannot be underestimated. Íslandsbanki was founded on the ruins of its predecessor, Glitner, which was taken over by a winding down committee. Íslandsbanki's management team, under the leadership of Birna Einarsdóttir, its new CEO, faced a considerable challenge; to rebuild a collapsed bank and create an institution able to gain the trust of the society in which it operated. Her strategic vision was to create a common direction for all Íslandsbanki's employees and create an internal culture of organizational purpose that would contribute positively to the dual purpose of organizational and societal recovery.

Einarsdóttir described the situation in 2008 as one where the bank had '100,000 angry customers, 1,000 troubled employees and no balance sheet'. She decided that, despite the crisis situation and the uncertainty it created, it was important to generate a

shared vision of the way forward. The critical component of this vision emerged as an organizational culture of common purpose that became a guiding principle for all the bank's staff members.

While there were riots and protests in the streets in central Reykjavik, all employees of Íslandsbanki were invited to participate in a full-day strategy workshop on a Saturday in early January 2009. At this workshop, a group of 650 employees, organized into eight different work streams, worked on the strategy of the new Íslandsbanki. The eight work streams were: 'Our values', 'Internal and external communications', 'Competition', 'Rebranding', 'Trust and transparency', 'Customers first', 'Improved work processes' and 'The best workplace'. The CEO described the situation as:

a unique opportunity to start from scratch, building a new vision, culture and values, learning from prior mistakes made, but at the same time building on the strengths and experience of the bank's 100 years of banking history.

▶

◄   This workshop and extensive project-based follow-up work marked an important turning point for the bank. Since then, employees have been deeply engaged and involved in the annual review of the bank's strategy and an important outcome is a strong culture, which facilitates service and innovation, support and collaboration, and open and candid communications.

This is perhaps an unusual case, but it does demonstrate that visioning can be an inclusive process.

While Kotter (1995) argues that visions that ignore the legitimate needs and rights of some stakeholders and favour certain stakeholders over others may never be achieved, there are circumstances where leaders may be forced to give preference to the interests of some over others. These circumstances will be discussed in Chapter 10.

Conger (1990) suggests that sometimes visions can be flawed because leaders become so committed to a project or a belief that they only attend to information that supports their own position and fail to recognize signals that point to, for example, changes in customer requirements or the limited availability of necessary resources. A history of past successes can contribute to this condition. In Chapter 4, reference is made to the 'trap of success', where past experience promotes a sense of self-belief and arrogance, which can encourage leaders to plough ahead without giving sufficient consideration to key aspects of the situation, or the concerns raised by others.

Bruch et al. (2005) argue that leadership decisions about the 'right thing to do' (the vision) need to be made before deciding 'how to do the change right', otherwise ongoing debates about 'does the change make sense?' will rob the project of its energy and weaken the implementation process.

Sense giving

Communicating the vision is sometimes referred to as 'sense giving'. Gioia and Chittipeddi (1991, p. 442) define sense giving as: 'the process of attempting to influence the sense making and meaning construction of others towards a preferred construction of organizational reality'. Leaders disseminate a vision to stakeholders and constituents in order to communicate their interpretation of a new and better reality and to influence others to adopt this view of the world.

Shaping the vision: reciprocal cycle of sense making and sense giving

A leader often starts by communicating with senior colleagues before engaging with a wider audience. However, it is rarely a one-way process – even when leaders have not involved others in the initial formulation of the vision – because, once communicated, their vision will almost inevitably trigger what Gioia and Chittipeddi (1991) refer to as a 'sequential and reciprocal cycle' of sense making and sense giving. The recipients of the leader's message engage in their own sense making, digesting and interpreting what they have heard in order to anticipate the implications of the leader's new vision for themselves and their unit or organization. The leader's vision may trigger an immediate enthusiastic and positive response but often the recipients, after trying to make sense of what they have heard, may feel a need to engage in their own sense-giving activity that involves giving feedback to leaders. This feedback may be in the form of a request for further clarification, a bid to modify and shape the leader's original vision or even to challenge their proposition that there is a need for a new vision in the first place.

The nature of the reciprocal sequence of sense giving and sense making can have an important impact on the quality of the vision. When leaders genuinely encourage feedback and challenge, there is a good chance that the vision that eventually emerges will be robust and fit for purpose. There are circumstances, however, where leaders receive little, if any, feedback on their proposed vision. This may happen if others fear repercussions if they challenge any aspect of the leader's vision, or if they have become too dependent on and trusting in the leader's judgement. Some writers argue that charismatic leaders who have dominant personalities can promote this kind of unquestioning dependence. A lack of challenge can also develop in those circumstances where the leadership team becomes so committed to a single ideology that they engage in what Janis (1972) described as 'groupthink'.

Translating the vision into a desire for change

Just because change recipients understand the leader's vision does not mean that they accept it and will be committed to achieving it. Sense giving is most effective when the outcome is not just that others recognize a need for change but when the potential recipients go on to translate this recognition into a desire for change. There are a number of things that leaders can do that will affect whether or not this will happen.

Winning trust

Translating the recognition of a need for change into a desire for change is more likely to happen when the potential recipients of change trust their leaders and feel that leaders respect their views (Oreg et al., 2011). Leaders can help to develop this kind of respect by seeking feedback and encouraging others to voice their views, and signalling to them that they believe that their views are worth listening to and they (the leaders) will do their best to keep an open mind until they have understood what they have to say. But sometimes, leaders, although they may appear to listen, may be perceived as giving insufficient attention to or trivializing the views of others. This is illustrated by a case reported by Werkman (2010) in Example 9.2.

IV

● *Example **9.2** Reorganizing the emergency response function in a Dutch police organization*

The chief commissioner and top management team of a Dutch police organization felt that the internal culture was characterized by fragmentation and lack of cooperation, and the introduction of a new regional emergency response (ER) function, which required police officers from different units and departments to work together, would help to strengthen organization identity. The change required officers to work shifts in districts other than their own with colleagues from different units, some of whom were new to this work and drawn from specialized units such as the criminal investigation department. A project team was appointed to lead the change and worked hard to communicate the intended change to all those who would be affected.

Police officers understood what they were being asked to do but were opposed to the proposed change. They felt that it was being driven by financial considerations and management had failed to appreciate the detrimental effect that the proposed changes would have on the existing fast and effective ER, which was tailored to the needs of local communities. They voiced their concerns to members of the project team and senior managers. They argued that colleagues from other districts would have insufficient local knowledge about the problems ▶

civilians were experiencing, and members of the local population would have less confidence and trust in officers they did not know. They also argued that because officers from other districts and departments would be unfamiliar with the area, it would take them longer to arrive at an incident, and inexperienced specialists would need training before they could work effectively. The police officers who normally did ER work also feared that specialists who did not work shifts would not be motivated to provide a good 24/7 emergency response.

The police officers did all they could to engage with members of the project team and senior managers in an attempt to influence their sense making and persuade them to revise their vision in a way that recognized the importance of providing a high-quality emergency response for local communities, but senior managers were not convinced by, and trivialized, their arguments. This was, in part, because they felt that rank-and-file officers had a history of resisting change and acting out of self-interest, and this was one of the factors that had helped to create the negative and fragmented organizational culture they were trying to change. Another problem was that members of the project team and senior managers feared that if they withdrew their plans and 'gave in' to the police officers, this might undermine the hierarchy of senior–subordinate relationships and lead to a loss of face and position.

The outcome was that having interpreted the situation from their own perspective and having decided that adjusting the intended change or their approach to the change process was not an option, senior managers and the project team proceeded to introduce the change as planned.

Highlighting benefits

Example 9.2 also demonstrates the importance of the perceived costs and benefits associated with the change. Rank-and-file police officers felt that the change threatened something they valued, the service offered to local communities, and promised few, if any, benefits. Oreg et al. (2011) report that a key determinant of whether change recipients will accept or resist change is the extent to which they perceive the change as beneficial or harmful. Leaders can be more effective if they communicate a compelling vision that is aligned with change recipients' values and promises to deliver personal benefit. While crafting the vision so that it appeals to change recipients can produce more support for a change, Conger (1990) sounds a note of caution and argues that leaders need to be careful not to present information in ways that make their vision appear more realistic and more appealing than it really is.

Promoting perceptions of competence

Oreg et al. (2011) and Neves (2011) refer to studies that identify change recipients' perceptions of their leader's competence, and therefore their ability to affect outcomes and achieve desired goals, as a factor that can affect their commitment to a proposed change. This points to the importance of leaders doing everything they can, not only to develop the competences and build the relationships with significant others that will help them deliver successful change, but also to ensure that they are seen to be competent and well connected by those involved in the change. This said, Conger (1990) sounds another note of caution and asserts that leaders should not communicate a vision in ways that foster an illusion of control when the reality is that things are out of control. In Chapter 5, the need to create a sense of confidence in order to promote a readiness to change is discussed, but this has to be done ethically. Sometimes, information is manipulated in a way that encourages employees and other stakeholders to make decisions that are neither in their own nor the organization's best interest.

Demonstrating that the status quo is unsustainable

Kotter (1995), writing about why transformation efforts fail, discusses the difficulties often encountered by leaders when trying to drive people out of their comfort zones and create a readiness for change. One approach he advocates to address this problem is to act in ways that create a sense of urgency. Stephen Elop, the new CEO of Nokia, did just that when he used a 'burning platform' analogy to communicate the urgency of the situation facing the company, as outlined in Example 9.3.

IV

Example **9.3** *Stephen Elop's burning platform memo*

In early February 2011, some days before announcing his plans to reverse setbacks at Nokia, in an internal memo to staff (which was leaked), Stephen Elop (Constantinescu, 2011) wrote:

> There is a pertinent story about a man who was working on an oil platform in the North Sea. He woke up one night from a loud explosion, which suddenly set his entire oil platform on fire. In mere moments, he was surrounded by flames. Through the smoke and heat, he barely made his way out of the chaos to the platform's edge. When he looked down over the edge, all he could see were the dark, cold, foreboding Atlantic waters.
>
> As the fire approached him, the man had mere seconds to react. He could stand on the platform, and inevitably be consumed by the burning flames. Or, he could plunge 30 meters in to the freezing waters. The man was standing upon a 'burning platform,' and he needed to make a choice.
>
> He decided to jump. It was unexpected. In ordinary circumstances, the man would never consider plunging into icy waters. But these were not ordinary times – his platform was on fire. The man survived the fall and the waters. After he was rescued, he noted that a 'burning platform' caused a radical change in his behaviour.
>
> We too, are standing on a 'burning platform,' and we must decide how we are going to change our behaviour.
>
> Over the past few months, I've shared with you what I've heard from our shareholders, operators, developers, suppliers and from you. Today, I'm going to share what I've learned and what I have come to believe.
>
> I have learned that we are standing on a burning platform.
>
> And, we have more than one explosion – we have multiple points of scorching heat that are fuelling a blazing fire around us.

He then proceeded to outline the problems confronting Nokia, the 'multiple scorch points', together

▶

◀ with his views about why the company had found itself in this difficult situation, before setting the scene for a major change initiative:

> We are working on a path forward — a path to rebuild our market leadership. When we share the

new strategy on February 11, it will be a huge effort to transform our company.

A few days later, he announced the new strategic partnership with Microsoft and the intention to develop the Windows Phone operating system as the new smartphone platform.

Sensing the need or opportunity for change, formulating a vision of a better future, and communicating this vision to those who will be the recipients of change are essential early steps, but leaders also need to work hard to create the conditions that will empower people to deliver the desired change.

Aligning

An important aspect of sense giving is communicating in a way that promotes a shared sense of direction and aligns people so that they can work together to achieve the vision. Kotter (1996) argues that a central feature of modern organizations is interdependence, where no one has complete autonomy, and most members of the organization are tied to many others by their work, technology, management systems and hierarchy. Kotter argues that these linkages present a special challenge when organizations attempt to change because unless individuals line up and move together, they will get in each other's way and fall over one another. Kühl et al. (2005) argue that managers throughout the organization have to engage in 'lateral leadership' to create a shared understanding, influence the political process and develop trust. Some of the most effective leaders have the ability to identify those who might be able to support or sabotage an initiative, network with them and communicate in a credible way what needs to be done. Aligning people in this way empowers them, even people at lower levels of the organization. When there is a clear, and shared, sense of direction, committed stakeholders, including subordinates, are more likely to feel able to take action without encountering undue conflict with others or being reprimanded by superiors.

Enabling

Communicating a clear and compelling vision and aligning people to support it can help inspire change recipients and those involved in implementing the change to overcome the inevitable barriers they will encounter as the initiative unfolds. But leaders need to do more. Ancona et al. (2007, p. 99) argue that: 'even the most compelling vision will lose its power if it floats, unconnected, above the everyday reality of organizational life'. They assert that to transform a vision of the future into a present-day reality, leaders need to create the conditions that will help facilitate implementation.

Kotter (1995) argues that even when those involved in the change understand and support the new direction, an 'elephant' may appear and block their path. Sometimes, the elephant is in their imagination and may require the leader to challenge their worldview or work with them to develop the confidence they require to proceed with the change. At other times, the elephant may be a very real, tangible barrier to change, which involves complex organization structures, narrow work roles, lack of access to relevant information, misaligned performance measures, and incentives that reward people for maintaining their old ways of working. Leaders need to take action to remove these barriers in order to create the conditions that will empower people to deliver change.

Drawing on the work of Hackman (2002), Higgs and Rowland (2011), Oreg et al. (2011) and others, it is possible to identify a number of ways in which leaders can create the conditions that will enable people to contribute to change implementation. Leaders can enable people to deliver change by:

- Ensuring that everybody is clear about what needs to be done.
- Creating clear structures and frameworks that enable people to work together to achieve a common purpose. This could involve revising organizational structures or making departmental boundaries more permeable to facilitate the sharing of information and other resources.
- Designing and delegating tasks that are aligned with people's values and provide sufficient challenge to make their work meaningful.
- Where possible, designing work for teams rather than individuals, thereby enhancing members' sense of collective responsibility for change outcomes.
- Providing access to information that some may believe should be restricted, so that individuals and groups are able to make decisions without always having to seek information and permission from others.
- Developing feedback mechanisms that individuals and groups can use for themselves to monitor their own progress and learn from their successes and failures.
- Encouraging those involved in the change to generate and discuss explanations for how well the change is progressing.
- Creating alignment at the top so that senior managers communicate consistent messages to others and adopt a common approach to implementing the change.

Supporting others during the change

Sometimes, it is easier for leaders to identify and communicate benefits for the organization than it is to communicate benefits for the individual, but those affected by a change have a pressing need to understand how the change will affect them personally. It is important, therefore, to recognize and respond to these concerns. Even when a leader is convinced that the individual will enjoy benefit from the change, some of those affected may not share this view and, even if they do, may still experience a feeling of loss or lack of control over what will happen to them. This kind of reaction can motivate them to hold on to the status quo rather than let go and embrace the change. Providing opportunities for dialogue so that those affected can explore and understand what will be involved can help to address these concerns. A related issue is a fear that following the change, those affected may not be able to deliver the required level of performance. Providing training opportunities in anticipation of the change, on-the-job support during implementation, and making it safe to admit mistakes and seek assistance can all help to boost confidence and help people to embrace the change.

Maintaining momentum and sustaining the change

There is often a tension between 'keeping the show on the road' (maintaining production) and introducing changes that will deliver improved performance over the longer term because implementing changes can be costly in terms of time and other resources. When employees are under pressure to maintain output, immediate demands can squeeze out the change agenda. Leaders need to be careful to act

IV

in ways that help to maintain the momentum of change and ensure that hard-won gains do not evaporate. When people can observe their leaders' active involvement in and commitment to the change, there is every chance they will be motivated to persist with the change even when confronted by problems that might otherwise have undermined their commitment. However, a common problem is that having identified the need for change, created and communicated a vision and set the change in motion, leaders turn their attention elsewhere and those working to deliver the change perceive a lack of support from the top. Whelan-Berry and Sommerville (2011), drawing on work by Schein (1999), Hesselbein (2002) and Cameron and Green (2004), argue that leaders need to 'walk the talk' throughout the implementation process if they are to be effective drivers of change. Kotter and Heskett (1992) make a similar point and argue that leaders need to demonstrate the behaviours they want others to model.

It is also important that leader support is not restricted to the senior managers who may have initiated the change. They need to involve other leaders down the line and hold them accountable for implementing the change in their departments and work groups. Managers and supervisors at all levels need to be committed and equally involved in 'walking the talk' to ensure that adequate attention and resources are focused on the task.

Sometimes, implementing a change can be a lengthy process and there is a danger that, over the course of time, people will lose their initial sense of urgency and divert their attention to more pressing, day-to-day operational issues. Kotter (1995) argues that one way of minimizing this risk is for those leading the change to seek out short-term wins and plan for visible (interim) performance improvements that can be celebrated along the way. However, while advocating the celebration of early wins, Kotter cautions against declaring victory too soon because this can kill momentum.

Managing change in practice **9.1** *Jo North: Start with the end in mind*

Jo North is the managing director of The Big Bang Partnership Ltd, a commercial consultancy that works with businesses to help them innovate and grow. Previously, she was deputy managing director and customer service director of East Coast Mainline Company Ltd, commercial director of Northern Rail, and director of sales and marketing at FirstGroup, UK Bus.

In her video, 'Start with the end in mind', on the book's companion website at **www.palgrave.com/companion/hayes-change-management4**, Jo highlights what she sees as four key leadership tasks. Compare Jo's list with the tasks included earlier in Table 9.2. Is one list better that the other or do they cover much the same ground?

Leadership style

Hackman (2002) argues that too much attention has been given to the importance of leadership style and asserts that leaders can be successful using those behaviours or styles that make the most sense to them personally, given the properties of the situation, the state of the team, and their own idiosyncratic skills and preferences.

Early work on leadership styles suggested that some styles were superior to others. For example, Lewin et al. (1939) studied the effect of leadership styles in classroom situations and concluded that democratic leadership was more effective than an autocratic style. Later work by academics at Ohio State University identified two dimensions of leader behaviour that appeared to influence performance (Fleishman et al., 1955). They were 'consideration', the extent to which supervisors have relationships that are characterized by mutual trust, respect for subordinates' ideas and consideration of their feelings, and 'initiating structure', which reflects the extent to which the leader is inclined to define and structure the work of subordinates. Fleishman et al.'s (1955) findings suggested that effective leaders were those who attributed high importance to both consideration and structure. This provided the conceptual basis for Blake and Mouton's (1964) managerial grid, which pointed to 'team management' as the most effective leadership style.

Situational leadership challenged the notion that there is one leadership style that will be best for every manager in all circumstances. Fiedler (1967), Adair (1973) and Hersey and Blanchard (1977) are just some of those who proposed theories suggesting that the most effective style depends on situational factors, such as the people, the task, and the organizational context.

Charismatic leadership

The development of new models of leadership was, at least in part, prompted by research evidence, which indicated that traditional, sometimes referred to as 'transactional', leadership models – that focus on goal setting, direction, support and reinforcement – only accounted for a relatively small percentage of variance in performance outcomes (Bryman, 1992). Accumulated research on the new models, on the other hand, has found that charismatic and transformational leadership are positively associated with a range of important organizational outcomes, such as job satisfaction, motivation, morale and performance, across many different types of organizational setting (see Avolio et al., 2009).

Charismatic leadership highlights the power of the emotional interaction between leaders and followers. Bass (1985, p. 35) coined the term 'idealized influence' to describe 'leaders who by the power of their person have profound and extraordinary effects on their followers'. They have the ability to motivate followers to achieve goals they may not have considered achievable. Drawing on Podsakoff's model of transformational-transactional leadership, Antonakis (2012) suggests that they do this by communicating a vision in a way that inspires others, setting challenging goals and articulating high performance expectations, challenging followers to rethink their ideas and look at old problems in new ways, promoting cooperation and teamwork to get people working towards the same goal, setting an example and leading by doing rather than telling, and providing individualized support.

Conger (1991, p. 31) argues that a distinguishing feature of charismatic leaders is that they communicate in ways that inspire others. To illustrate what this involves, he uses the story of two stonemasons who, while working on the same project, were asked what they were doing. The first replied: 'I am cutting stone'; the second: 'I am building a great cathedral.' Conger asserts that the second mason was able to describe his work in a more far-reaching and meaningful way. He argues that leaders need to embody this same ability – 'the capacity to articulate an organization's mission and communicate it in ways that inspire'. This requires

IV

two distinct skill categories. The first is 'framing', the ability to define the purpose of the organization in a meaningful way. The second is the ability to use symbolic language to give emotional power to the message, which Conger refers to as 'rhetorical crafting'. While the basic message provides the sense of direction, it is the rhetoric that heightens its motivational appeal and determines whether it will be sufficiently memorable to influence the day-to-day decision making of those involved in the change.

Adopting an appropriate leadership style can help facilitate change but there is considerable support for the view that there is no one best style. An argument developed in Chapter 6 is that there are many ways in which change leaders can work with others to facilitate change and the most effective way might be different at different points in the change relationship. Also, in Chapter 14, it is argued that the change leader's purpose (bottom line or building capability) and timescale can affect their approach to leading change, and Figure 14.1 summarizes some of the factors that support either directive or collaborative change strategies.

Distributed leadership

It is important that charismatic leaders are not defined and glorified as heroic individuals who, by the power of their personality, are able to lead change single-handed. In many organizations, there has been a move from deep hierarchies, in which leader–subordinate relationships are clearly defined, towards new organizational forms, where cross-functional teams, networks and communities of practice require an approach to leadership that is capable of being dissociated from organizational hierarchies. Even in traditional hierarchical organizations, leadership, at least to some extent, has to be cascaded down the hierarchy. Gilley et al. (2009) observe that while it may be top management that develops the organization's vision, mission and corporate-wide change initiatives, it usually falls to middle managers to develop the shorter term operational plans that give life to top management directives, and it is frontline managers who shoulder the main burden of implementing these plans. In other words, many organizational members contribute to the leadership process.

Often, the initiator of change might be an individual or a small group. These initiators might be viewed as the ones leading the change, but Kotter (1999) argues that this leadership has to be multiplied and shared if the change is to be successful. Throughout the system, all managers have to accept that they have a leadership role to play. They have to contribute to creating a vision, aligning relationships and inspiring others. Oxtoby et al. (2002) support this view and argue that not only does a system of leadership need to cascade down the organization in the form of a distributed network of key players, each providing leadership in their part of the organization, but also that to be effective, this network needs to share a common vision of the organization's purpose that is clear, consistent and inspiring. Developing and maintaining this common approach is not always easy.

Spillane (2006) likens leadership to a two-partnered dance. While it is possible to focus attention on the actions of a single partner, to understand the performance of the dance it is necessary to pay attention to the interactions of all the dancing partners. Collinson (2005) notes that many studies of leadership have only concentrated on leaders' traits and styles and have either ignored or underestimated the importance of relations between leaders and followers. Bolden (2004) points to an increasing awareness of the importance of social relations, the need for leaders to be given authority by followers, and the realization that no one individual is the ideal leader in all circumstances. This line of thinking has led to the development of less formalized models of leadership, which accommodate the possibility that leadership is not the exclusive preserve of a single manager or even a cohort of senior managers. Bolden observes that individuals at all levels in an organization (not just managers) can exercise leadership influence over colleagues and thus influence the overall direction of the organization. This perspective shifts attention away from the individual 'heroic' leader to a more collective process of sense making and direction giving.

The collective nature of leadership

In much of the literature on organizational change, the role of the CEO as leader receives considerable attention. Research evidence on the link between the CEO's leadership style and organizational performance is mixed. Avolio et al. (2009) refer to some studies that found that the charisma of the CEO was not related to subsequent organizational performance, whereas others found the opposite. This may be because, in many situations, leadership needs to be viewed as a collective process. Pascale and Sterin (2005) point out that when individuals stand out as champions of change, there is a danger that this will generate unconstructive dependence from other members of the organization. They argue that leadership needs to come from within a community. Denis et al. (2001) also caution against the glorification of individual heroes. Organizations are becoming more complex and pluralistic. Their external boundaries are becoming increasingly blurred as they engage in a variety of collaborative arrangements and outsource many of their operations. Within organizations, the growth of matrix and network structures and the move from functional to more process-oriented organizational forms are creating circumstances where traditional command and control cultures are being eroded and managers are increasingly having to collaborate with others, over whom they have no direct authority, in order to get things done.

IV

Coherence

One of the key problems associated with managing change in pluralistic settings is the development of sufficient coherence. Denis et al. (2001) argue that in situations where power is diffused and there are divergent objectives, change initiatives need to be led by a collective leadership group rather than a single individual.

On the basis of their research in healthcare organizations (see Research report 9.1), Denis et al. (2001) argue that major change in pluralistic organizations is more likely to be achieved under unified collective leadership, in which members of a 'leadership constellation' (collective leadership group) play complementary roles and work together harmoniously. In many countries, there are conventions or legally binding codes of practice that explicitly formalize the collective nature of strategic leadership by separating the posts of CEO and president or chair of the company's board of directors, but often the membership of the leadership constellation is wider than this, with members having different but complementary roles. For example, some may focus their attention on the management of external relations, whereas others may manage relationships with particular internal constituencies. Collective leadership is essential where a single individual is unable to formulate and implement a vision that is acceptable to a sufficient body of powerful stakeholders. Collective leadership offers the possibility of bringing together the range of skills and experience required to formulate an acceptable vision as well as the ability to influence others in a manner perceived to be legitimate.

Fragility

While Denis et al. (2001) argue that unified collective leadership is necessary in pluralistic settings, they found that leadership constellations are always fragile. They define 'fragility' with reference to three types of 'coupling':

1 *Strategic coupling:* the internal harmony between members of the leadership constellation (Figure 9.1). Constellations can become disconnected when divergent views emerge about what is important and these differences lead to conflicts within the constellation.

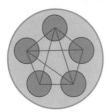

Figure **9.1** *Strategic coupling*

2 *Organizational coupling:* reflects the relationship between members of the leadership constellation and their organizational constituencies, which in turn relates to the perceived conformity between the objectives of leaders, as reflected by their behaviour, and the interests of constituents (Figure 9.2). If members of the leadership constellation lose touch with their constituents, the constituents will begin to feel that their views are not being properly represented by their leaders. This can reduce leaders' ability to influence constituents and may even threaten their membership of the leadership constellation, because leaders rule, at least in part, by the consent of the led. Thorpe and Gold (2010, p. 5) illustrate this point with the example of an Indian chief, who when asked why he was the leader, replied because he had followers. He explained that if, when hunting buffalo on the great plain and the track forked left and right, he rode left and the braves followed him, he was reaffirmed as the leader; but if he rode right and the braves did not follow him, he would no longer be the leader.

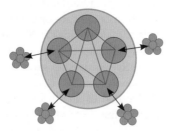

Figure **9.2** *Organizational coupling*

Denis et al. (2001, p. 825) argue that:

> In a context of fluid power relationships, the judgements of others concerning the appropriateness of one's behaviour are crucial for long-term survival in a leadership position. Actions that tend to enhance survival prospects are called credibility enhancing, and those that tend to diminish them are

credibility draining. Changes in credibility directly or indirectly affect the capacity of an individual or leadership group to act in the future. Increased credibility widens the scope for action. Reduced credibility diminishes it and may lead to leader turnover.

This has implications for the effectiveness of different leadership styles. Denis et al. suggest that if a constellation is tightly coupled and covers all power bases, members of the constellation may find that behaving in an aggressive, secretive and authoritarian manner is an effective way of getting things done in the short term, but they suggest that in the long term, these tactics can drain credibility. There may be a need, especially over the long term, to balance forceful leadership action with maintaining a necessary level of approval from those being led.

3 *Environmental coupling:* the degree of coherence between the leadership constellation's vision and aspirations and the demands and constraints imposed by powerful external stakeholders (Figure 9.3). Constellations can break down if they become so detached from their environments that performance begins to decline. This happens when concerns about performance lead to pressures from the company's board or other powerful external stakeholders for members of the constellation to be replaced.

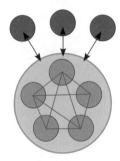

*Figure **9.3** Environmental coupling*

Denis et al. (2001) argue (see Research report 9.1, below) that it can be difficult to maintain harmony at all three levels. Sometimes, too much attention is directed towards developing a close alignment between the aspirations of internal stakeholders (organizational coupling) and insufficient attention is given to the impact of external demands (environmental coupling). Accommodating different interests is easier when there is a degree of organizational slack, but when resources are limited, there is less opportunity for accommodations and compromises. In these circumstances, the stability of leadership constellations and their ability to deliver change may depend on some of the personal and interpersonal skills of members. Denis et al. (2001) refer to the importance of a tacit knowledge of how things can be done in the organization (social embeddedness) and creative opportunism – the ability to see opportunities to reconcile a range of aspirations with environmental pressures. Other factors might also be important. Hollenbeck and Hall (2004) highlight the effect of self-efficacy, that is, leader self-confidence, on leader performance, and while Ferris et al. (2000) agree that tacit knowledge and self-efficacy are important, they also point to the importance of a number of other social skills such as social intelligence, emotional intelligence, ego resilience and self-monitoring.

IV

Research report **9.1** *Collective leadership and strategic change in healthcare organizations*

Denis, J.-L., Lamothe, L. and Langley, A. (2001) The dynamics of collective leadership and strategic change in pluralistic organizations, *Academy of Management Journal*, 44(4): 809–37.

The study was designed to examine leadership from a process perspective, focusing attention on what leaders do to mobilize others in a system of interrelationships. They set out to examine the dynamic construction, deconstruction and reconstruction of leadership roles over time.

Method

The study was partly planned and partly opportunistic, and was partly deductive (inspired by theory) and partly inductive (inspired by data). A case study approach was adopted because this enabled the researchers to trace processes in their natural contexts and study the temporal sequence of events.

The research process

Five cases were studied over a 10-year period. The first involved a hospital that was negotiating with a medical school to acquire a teaching mission. The data drew the researchers' attention to the importance of collective leadership and the link between leaders' tactics and their capacity to remain in leadership positions. In this case, after an earlier change initiative had failed, a new leader emerged and mobilized the leadership team to pursue the teaching mission. But the united leadership team moved too fast for many others in the hospital and an election led to the team being dissolved and replaced, slowing down the once rapid change process.

The second case, which involved a small hospital developing a new emergency care service, was planned to replicate and test the conceptual model that was emerging from the first study. A new leader replaced the management team, built credibility with the board and achieved internal and external support for the new mission, but a group of physicians put in place to implement the development of the emergency service pushed to develop it more extensively than the CEO and the board felt was possible. Conflict led to the departure of the physicians and a halt to the project.

Building on their emerging model of collective leadership, the third case focused on how a new CEO positioned himself within an existing leadership constellation.

Over the course of these three case studies, four observations emerged as important:

1 Periods of substantive change tend to be associated with complementary and united leadership constellations.

2 Leadership constellations are fragile because of the possibility of disconnections between members (strategic coupling), between members of the leadership constellation and their organizational bases (organizational coupling), and between the leadership constellation and environmental demands and constraints (environmental coupling).

3 Because of this difficulty of maintaining alignment at all three levels, change occurs in a cyclical fashion as opposing forces are reconciled on a sequential, rather than a simultaneous, basis. For example, after a leadership constellation has developed a commitment to change, it may need to seek support from external stakeholders. This may not be easy (problems with environmental coupling) and might require the leadership constellation to make concessions. This may lead to problems within the leadership constellation (strategic coupling). The resolution of these differences may, in turn, require further compromise, creating problems for some members with their organizational constituents (organizational coupling). These problems may have to be resolved before the change can progress.

4 Leadership affects political positions. The way others perceive and judge a leader's actions, such as conceding or failing to deliver on promises, affects their credibility and survival in a leadership role.

Denis et al. went on to observe that four factors – slack resources, internal social embeddedness, creative opportunism, and a combination of time, stakeholder inattention and the protection of formal position – could help to create sufficient temporary stability to allow substantive change to become irreversible before political changes made it impossible.

Four years after the start of the project, moves to consolidate the teaching hospital network in Quebec presented a new opportunity to extend the research to more complex cases. Two further cases were studied, each involving the merger of three hospitals. Denis et al. found that increasing the number of pluralistic dimensions made it much more difficult to establish a unified leadership constellation, achieve anything more than partial coupling, break free from a cycle of shifting alliances, and manage the sequential attention to different goals.

Denis et al. concluded that greater complexity increases the need for counterbalancing sources of stability, such as slack resources, internal social embeddedness, creative opportunism, and time, inattention and the protection of formal position, if substantive change is to be achieved.

Exercises 9.1 and 9.2 draw on many of the points discussed in this chapter. Exercise 9.1 is a three-step process designed to help you improve your approach to leading change. The first step can be completed as a stand-alone exercise.

✅ Exercise **9.1** *Improving your approach to leading change*

This exercise is designed to help you improve your approach to leading change. It is divided into three parts. You will be able to complete the first part immediately, but the next two steps may take a little time:

1 The first step involves reflecting on how leaders known to you behave when trying to introduce a change. The leaders you think about may be managers at work, members of your family, people who are involved in other aspects of your social life, or those who exercise leadership in a club or religious organization (church, mosque or temple) you are affiliated to.

   Use the following checklist as an aide-mémoire:

   1 *Sense making:* To what extent did they appear to recognize the need or opportunity for change in good time? Did they appear to take account of the views of others at this stage?
   2 *Visioning:* To what extent did they appear to formulate a vision of a better future based on an in-depth understanding of the situation?
   3 *Sense giving:* Did they communicate a vision to a wider audience in a way that won their commitment to achieving the vision?
   4 *Aligning:* To what extent did they communicate a shared sense of direction so that everybody involved in the change – other leaders and change recipients down the line – could work together to achieve the vision?
   5 *Enabling:* To what extent did they identify and remove obstacles that got in the way of change?
   6 *Supporting:* To what extent did they recognize and respond to the concerns of those affected by the change?
   7 *Maintaining momentum and sustaining the change:* Did they demonstrate a continuing commitment to the change and do whatever was necessary to keep others focused on implementing and sustaining the change?

Based on the above, identify what it was they did that helped to secure change and what they might have done better.

2 The second step involves monitoring your own behaviour and identifying what you do when trying to influence others to change. Do not change what you normally do. The aim of this step is to increase your awareness of your normal

IV

approach. Use the same approach to assess your own behaviour as you did to assess what others did when leading change. You might find it helpful to record your observations on a copy of the aide-mémoire you used for the first part of this exercise.

3 The final step involves experimenting with new behaviours. After reflecting on what you have observed others doing, how you normally behave when leading change, and the ideas and concepts introduced in this chapter, identify how you could change your behaviour in a way that will help you to be more effective when trying to introduce change.

You might not be able to complete this step immediately but do your best to seek out opportunities to experiment with new leadership behaviours as soon as possible.

Exercise 9.2 invites you to consider two leaders – one who you judge to be an effective change manager and one who you judge to be less effective – and consider whether effective leaders are more likely to attend to the leadership behaviours discussed in this chapter.

✓ *Exercise **9.2** Profiling effective leader behaviour*

Identify two change managers who have been key figures in attempting to introduce and manage change in your organization, your family, or some other aspect of your professional, social or religious life. One should be a person who you judge to have been very successful at managing change, and the other should be someone who you judge to have been much less successful.

Assess their approach to managing change using the checklist for leading change presented in Exercise 9.1. Consider whether there is any evidence to suggest that successful change managers are those who attend to the leadership behaviours discussed in this chapter.

Summary

The first part of the chapter drew on theory to identify seven tasks that leaders need to perform in order to ensure change success. These are:

1 *Sense making:* Making sense of the world and identifying the opportunities and threats that require attention.
2 *Visioning:* Identifying a vision of what a more desirable state of affairs might look like and what needs to be done to move towards this better future.
3 *Sense giving:* Communicating the vision to a wider audience and responding to feedback as required to win commitment to the change.
4 *Aligning:* Promoting a shared sense of direction so that people can work together to achieve the vision.
5 *Enabling:* Removing obstacles and creating the conditions that empower others to implement the change.
6 *Supporting:* Recognizing and responding to the concerns of those affected by the change.
7 *Maintaining momentum and sustaining the change:* Showing commitment and 'walking the talk' to keep people focused on the change.

While it is recognized that a strong vision can make a valuable contribution to the success of a change initiative, some of the factors that might render the vision unfit for purpose have been reviewed. These include leaders making unrealistic assessments of opportunities and constraints and formulating the vision in a way that does not address the needs and concerns of key stakeholders.

The need to communicate the vision in a way that will align people behind it was discussed, along with the contribution that charisma and the emotional interaction between leaders and followers can make to energizing people to achieve the change. Attention was also given to what leaders can do to facilitate the implementation of the vision and embed the change.

The second part of the chapter focused attention on distributed leadership. The danger of focusing too much attention on individual leaders was discussed. Within organizations, the growth of matrix and network structures and the move from functional to more process-oriented organizational forms are creating circumstances where traditional command and control cultures are being eroded and managers are increasingly having to collaborate with others, over whom they have no direct authority, in order to get things done.

Denis et al. argue that in situations where power is diffused and there are divergent objectives, change initiatives need to be led by a collective leadership group rather than by a single individual. Special attention is given to:

- coherence and the importance of unified collective leadership
- fragility – leadership constellations tend to be fragile because of the possibility of disconnections between members of the leadership constellation (strategic coupling), between members of the leadership constellation and their constituents (organizational coupling), and between the leadership constellation and environmental demands and constraints (environmental coupling).

In various chapters, attention is given to some of the aspects of leadership discussed here. For example:

- recognizing the need for change: Chapters 2, 4 and 9
- identifying and reviewing change goals: Chapters 9, 10, 25 and 26
- communicating a sense of direction: Chapters 9, 10, 11, 25 and 26
- formulating a change strategy: Chapters 2, 14 and 25
- involving others: Chapters 2, 5, 10, 14, 16, 19, 20 and 27
- motivating people: Chapters 5, 9, 10 and 12
- providing support: Chapters 6 and 13
- creating an organizational context conducive to change: Chapters 26 and 28.

The next four chapters in Part IV explore various aspects of leadership in more detail.

References

9/11 Commission Report (2004) Available at http://www.9-11commission.gov/report/911Report.pdf.

Adair, J. (1973) *Action-centred Leadership*. New York: McGraw-Hill.

Ancona, D.M., Thomas, W., Orlikowski, W.J. and Senge, P.M. (2007) In praise of the incomplete leader, *Harvard Business Review*, 85(2): 92–100.

Antonakis, J. (2012) Transformational and transactional leadership. In D. Day and J. Anto-nakis (eds) *The Nature of Leadership* (2nd edn). Thousand Oaks, CA: Sage.

Avolio, B.J., Walumbwa, F.O. and Weber, T.J. (2009) Leadership: Current theories, research, and future directions, *Annual Review of Psychology*, 60(1): 421–49.

Bass, B.M. (1985) *Leadership and Performance beyond Expectations.* New York: Free Press.

Bennis, W. and Nanus, B. (1985) *Leaders: The Strategy for Taking Charge.* New York: Harper & Row.

Blake, R.R. and Mouton, J.S. (1964) *The Managerial Grid.* Houston, TX: Gulf.

Bolden, R. (2004) *What is Leadership?*, research report. Leadership South West: University of Exeter.

Bruch, H., Gerber, P. and Maier, V. (2005) Strategic change decisions: Doing the right change right, *Journal of Change Management*, 5(1): 97–107.

Bryman, A. (1992) *Charisma and Leadership in Organizations.* Newbury Park, CA: Sage.

Cameron, E. and Green, M. (2004) *Making Sense of Change Management: A Complete Guide to the Models, Tools and Techniques of Organizational Change.* London: Kogan Page.

Colville, I., Brown, A.D. and Pye, A. (2012) Simplexity: Sensemaking, organizing and storytelling for our time, *Human Relations*, 65(1): 5–15.

Colville, I., Pye, A. and Carter, M. (2013) Organizing to counter terrorism: Sensemaking amidst dynamic complexity, *Human Relations*, 66(9): 1201–23.

Collinson, D. (2005) Leading questions: Questions of distance, *Leadership*, 1(2): 235–50.

Conger, J.A. (1990) The dark side of leadership, *Organizational Dynamics*, 19(2): 44–5.

Conger, J.A. (1991) Inspiring others: The language of leadership, *Academy of Management Executive*, 5(1): 31–45.

Constantinescu, S. (2011) Leaked: Nokia's memo discussing the iPhone, Android, and the need for drastic change, IntoMobile, 8 February, http://www.intomobile.com/2011/02/08/leaked-nokias-memo-discusses-need-for-drastic-change/.

Denis, J.-L., Lamothe, L. and Langley, A. (2001) The dynamics of collective leadership and strategic change in pluralistic organizations, *Academy of Management Journal*, 44(4): 809–37.

Ferris, G.R., Perrewe, P., Anthony, W.P. and Gilmore, D.C. (2000) Political skills at work, *Organizational Dynamics*, 28(4): 25–37.

Fiedler, F. (1967) *A Theory of Leadership Effectiveness.* New York: McGraw-Hill.

Fleishman, E.A., Harris, E.F. and Burtt, H.E. (1955) *Leadership and Supervision in Industry*, Columbus, OH: Ohio State University.

Gilley, A., McMillan, H.S. and Gilley, J.W. (2009) Organizational change and the characteristics of leadership effectiveness, *Journal of Leadership and Organizational Studies*, 16(1): 38–47.

Gioia, D.A. and Chittipeddi, K. (1991) Sensemaking and sensegiving in strategic change initiation, *Strategic Management Journal*, 12(6): 433–48.

Hackman, J.R. (2002) *Leading Teams: Setting the Stage for Great Performances.* Boston, MA: Harvard Business School Press.

Hersey, P. and Blanchard, K. (1977) *Management of Organizational Behavior.* Englewood Cliffs, NJ: Prentice Hall.

Hesselbein, F. (2002) The key to cultural transformation. In F. Hesselbein and Johnston, R. (eds) *On Leading Change: A Leader to Leader Guide.* San Francisco, CA: Jossey-Bass.

Higgs, M. and Rowland, D. (2000) Building change leaders capability: The quest for change competence, *Journal of Change Management*, 1(2): 116–30.

Higgs, M. and Rowland, D. (2011) What does it take to implement change successfully? A study of behaviours of successful change leaders, *Journal of Applied Behavioural Science*, 47(3): 309–35.

Hollenbeck, G.P. and Hall, D.P. (2004) Self-confidence and leaders performance, *Organizational Dynamics*, 33(3): 254–69.

Janis, I.L. (1972) *Victims of Groupthink: A Psychological Study of Foreign Policy Decisions and Fiascos*. Boston, MA: Houghton-Mifflin.

Kotter, J.P. (1990) What leaders really do, *Harvard Business Review*, 68(3): 103–11, reproduced in J.P. Kotter (1999) *On What Leaders Really Do*.

Kotter, J.P. (1995) Leading change: Why transformation efforts fail, *Harvard Business Review*, 73(2): 59–67.

Kotter, J.P. (1996) *Leading Change*. Boston, MA: Harvard Business School Press.

Kotter, J.P. (1999) *On What Leaders Really Do*. Boston, MA: Harvard Business School Press.

Kotter, J. and Heskett, J. (1992) *Corporate Culture and Performance*. New York: Free Press.

Kühl, S., Schnelle, T. and Tillmann, F.J. (2005) Lateral leadership: An organisational change approach, *Journal of Change Management*, 5(2): 177–89.

Lewin, K., Lippitt, R. and White, R. (1939) Patterns of aggressive behavior in experimentally created social environments, *Journal of Social Psychology*, 10: 271–99.

Näslund, L. and Pemer, F. (2012) The appropriated language: Dominant stories as a source of organizational inertia, *Human Relations*, 65(1): 89–110.

Neves, P. (2011) Building commitment to change: The role of perceived supervisor support and confidence, *European Journal of Work and Organizational Psychology*, 20(4): 437–50.

Northouse, P.G. (2004) *Leadership: Theory and Practice* (3rd edn). London: Sage.

Oreg, S., Vakola, M. and Armenakis, A. (2011) Change recipients' reactions to organizational change: A 60-year review of quantitative studies, *Journal of Applied Behavioral Science*, 47(4): 461–524.

Oxtoby, B., McGuiness, T. and Morgan, R. (2002) Developing organisational change capability, *European Management Journal*, 20(3): 310–20.

Pascale, R.T. and Sterin, J. (2005) Your company's secret change agents, *Harvard Business Review*, 83(5): 72–81.

Schein, E. (1999) How to set the stage for a change in organizational culture. In P. Senge, A. Kleiner, C. Roberts et al. (eds) *The Dance of Change: The Challenges to Sustaining Momentum in Learning Organizations*. New York: Currency Doubleday.

Spillane, J. (2006) *Distributed Leadership*. San Francisco, CA: Wiley.

Thorpe, R. and Gold, J. (2010) Leadership and management development: The current state. In J. Gold, R. Thorpe and A. Mumford (eds) *Gower Handbook of Leadership and Management Development*. Aldershot: Gower.

Tichy, N.M. and Devanna, M.A. (1986) *The Transformational Leader*. Chichester: Wiley.

Werkman, R. (2010) Reinventing organization development: How a sensemaking perspective can enrich OD theories and interventions, *Journal of Change Management*, 10(4): 421–38.

Whelan-Berry, K.S. and Somerville, K.A. (2010) Linking change drivers and the organizational change process: A review and synthesis, *Journal of Change Management*, 10(2): 175–93.

Yates, M. (2009) Developing leaders in a global landscape. In D. Giber, S.M. Lam and M. Goldsmith (eds) *Best Practices in Leadership Development Handbook: Case Studies, Instruments, Training*. San Francisco, CA: Pfeiffer/Wiley.

IV

Chapter 10

Power, politics and stakeholder management

This chapter explores the politics of organizational change and points to the importance of enlisting the support of key stakeholders. Political behaviour tends to be more intense in times of change because individuals and groups perceive the possibility of upsetting the existing balance of power. Some may be motivated to defend the status quo, whereas others may perceive change as an opportunity to improve their position. Consequently, change managers need to be alert to these political dynamics, especially the possibility that others may be motivated to act in ways that undermine their efforts to bring about change.

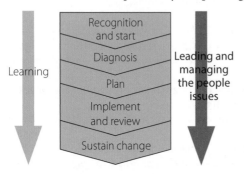

In Chapter 9, some key leadership tasks were identified and the importance of promoting a shared sense of direction, removing obstacles, and creating the conditions that empower others to implement a change were considered. In this chapter, attention is focused on what leaders can do to influence those who are in a position to slow or undermine the change. Attention is also given to:

- What leaders can do to increase their ability to influence others.
- Identifying which stakeholders should be taken into account by those leading the change.
- Ethical considerations.
- A conceptual framework, based on life cycle, resource dependence and prospect theory, that leaders can use to decide how best to manage stakeholders.
- The stakeholder grid, a useful tool for mapping the power of stakeholders and their predisposition to support or oppose the change.

Organizations as political arenas

Leaders need to understand and manage the politics of organizational change. Most organizations are not well-integrated entities within which everybody works harmoniously together. Companies and other institutions are becoming more complex and pluralistic and, as was noted in Chapter 9, the growth of matrix and network structures and the move from functional to more process-oriented organizational forms are creating an environment where traditional command and control cultures are being eroded and managers are increasingly having to collaborate with others, over whom they have no direct authority, in order to get things done.

Most organizations can be conceptualized as a collection of constituencies, each pursuing their own objectives. This view presents organizations as political arenas within which individuals and groups attempt to influence each other in the pursuit of self-interest. Those who adopt this political perspective argue that when there is a conflict of interest, it is the power and influence of the individuals and groups involved that determine the outcome of the decision process, not logic and rational argument. This perspective submits that those responsible for managing change cannot afford to ignore issues of power and influence.

Nadler (1987) argues that political behaviour tends to be more intense in times of change because individuals and groups perceive the possibility of upsetting the existing balance of power. Some may be motivated to defend the status quo, whereas others may perceive change as an opportunity to improve their position (see McNulty, 2003). Pettigrew (1972) also argues that some may engage in political action for ideological reasons, especially when they fear that a change may be inconsistent with their values.

Change managers need to be alert to these political dynamics, especially the possibility that others may be motivated to act in ways that undermine their efforts to bring about change. These others may resist change not only because they feel threatened by the anticipated future state, but also because they feel threatened by the processes used to secure change. For example, some organizational members may be concerned that the collection of information for diagnosis could weaken their position because they may be asked to disclose information they had previously protected in order to secure some political advantage.

Given that different constituents or stakeholders are likely to act in ways that maximize their power and their ability to secure preferred outcomes, change managers need to be alert to the identity of important stakeholders and their predisposition to either support or resist the change. They also need to know how to influence stakeholders in order to persuade them to support the change.

Power and influence

McClelland (1975) defines power as the ability to change the behaviour of others. It is the ability to cause others to perform actions they might not otherwise perform. Those in authority are those who are seen to have a legitimate right to influence others, but power is not always legitimate. Sometimes, individuals and groups who do not have legitimate authority are able to exercise considerable influence and may even have more power than legitimately appointed managers. Change managers need to ensure that they do not overlook or ignore powerful individuals or groups just because they do not have any formal authority to influence a proposed change.

✓ *Exercise* **10.1** *Sources of power and influence*

Think about a change you have tried or would like to introduce (at work, home or elsewhere). Who are the people who were/are able to facilitate or block your efforts to implement this change? Why were/are they able to exercise this influence; what is the basis of their power?

Power is inherent in any relationship in which one person or group is dependent on another. Emerson (1962, p. 32) observes that:

> the power to control or influence the other resides in control over the things he values, which may range all the way from oil resources to ego support. In short, power resides implicitly in the other's dependence.

Review your answer to the questions posed in Exercise 10.1 and consider whether those who were able to influence your efforts to implement a change were able to do so because you (and others) were dependent on them in some way.

Acquiring and exercising power and influence

Leaders and other organizational members can increase their ability to influence others by promoting their reputation for delivering successful change, taking steps to increase others' dependence on them, minimizing their dependence on those they are seeking to influence, building collaborative relationships and negotiating advantageous agreements. Based on his work with product development engineers in a large automotive and aerospace company, Hayes (1984) observed that politically competent managers were those who paid attention to these factors.

Promoting their reputation

Change recipients are more likely to follow leaders when they perceive them to be competent and able to deliver benefit. This points to the importance of leaders doing everything they can to not only develop the competences they need to deliver successful change but also to ensure that they are seen to be competent by change recipients. People pay more attention to leaders when they perceive them to be motivated, competent and capable of affecting outcomes.

Increasing others' dependence on the leader

Leaders can increase their ability to influence targeted others by doing whatever they can to increase these others' dependence on them. They can assess others' dependence on them by:

- taking stock of what it is the targeted others seek from them, for example information, contacts or some other resource
- assessing how important these resources are to them
- exploring how readily the targeted others can obtain these resources from elsewhere.

This appraisal will provide some indication of how dependent the targeted others are on the leaders. But it is not sufficient for leaders to know that others are dependent on them. In order to exercise power, others have to be aware that they are dependent on those leading the change.

Increasing others' sense of dependence

Leaders can make others aware of their dependence in a number of ways. For example, they can threaten to withhold some vital resource. However, such heavy-handed measures may frighten the dependent others and provoke them into searching for alternative sources, which, if successful, could reduce their dependence on those leading the change. It may also provoke them into seeking out counterdependencies, which they could use against leaders as bargaining points. Heavy-handed approaches may promote the kind of win–lose climate, which can easily deteriorate into one where everybody loses. Ideally, the objective of any awareness-raising exercise should be to raise an awareness of dependency but to do so within a climate that supports mutual help and cooperation.

If, through their interactions with others, leaders can convince them that they need the information or other resources that they (the leaders) can provide, this will increase their ability to influence target others. Whether or not leaders actually control or are the only available source of that resource is less relevant than the impression they manage to create. Leaders' ability to 'define reality' for others and convince them that they are dependent on them can be an effective way of enhancing their power. However, another note of caution may be in order. While bluff and concealment can help bolster a leader's power, if discovered, this approach could seriously undermine trust and limit the leader's ability to influence others in the future.

Minimizing leaders' dependence on those they are seeking to influence

It is not sufficient for leaders to promote impressions of their competence and take steps to increase others' dependence on them. They also need to do whatever they can to minimize their dependence on others. To do this, they need to identify who the 'significant others' are they need to influence (this will receive more attention later in this chapter) and why and to what extent they are dependent on them.

Once they are aware of the basis of their dependency, they can begin to think about what they can do to minimize it. For example, they can:

- search for alternative sources of the resources they require
- challenge existing working agreements where they suspect that others are exercising power over them because of dependency relationships which may have prevailed in the past, but which no longer reflect the current situation. As available resources, market conditions or any number of other factors change, so do the nature of dependency relationships and therefore the distribution of power.

Building collaborative relationships

Another possibility for improving the leader's ability to influence others involves building better working relationships with those they are dependent on in order to enlist their help to implement the change:

- Building closer relationships offers leaders the possibility of identifying information and other resources that others may require and that the leader could, but currently does not, provide, thereby establishing a basis for negotiation and trade.
- Often, projects are starved of resources, not because somebody has intentionally withheld them but because those controlling the resources are not aware that the leader requires them. Improved communication between those involved can help eliminate this kind of problem.
- Better relationships also offer the possibility of others using their networks to influence third parties that are inaccessible to the leader and/or championing the leaders' cause to a much wider audience.

IV

Negotiating advantageous agreements

Most working agreements are based on some degree of reciprocity or interdependence. Leaders who are good at influencing others are likely to be aware of this and able to assess, realistically, what it is they can offer to others and what it is they need from them. They will be able to set this alongside an equally realistic assessment of what others have to offer them and what they need from others, and use these assessments to negotiate working agreements up, down and across the organization that will support their efforts to implement change.

Interactions between those attempting to lead a change and others who can affect the outcome do not have to occur within the fixed framework of a zero-sum ('I win, you lose') game, and it is not always necessary for leaders to seek ways of eroding the power of others in order to progress a change. More political awareness and a willingness to involve others in the context of an increasing-sum game can often lead to better outcomes and a more successful change.

Improving your ability to influence others

Sometimes, those leading a change are unaware of their potential ability to influence others because they have never attempted to consciously assess how dependent they are on others and compare this with the extent to which others are dependent on them. Thinking about relationships in terms of relative dependencies can point to ways in which leaders can shift the balance of power in their favour. Exercise 10.2 is designed to help you do this.

☑ *Exercise* **10.2** *Checklist for the acquisition and exercise of power*

- Think about those situations in which you are *satisfied* with your ability to influence others. Using the checklist presented below, build a profile of what you typically do *to acquire and use power* in those situations.
- Next, think about those situations in which you are *dissatisfied* with your ability to influence. Repeat the procedure and build a profile of what you do when you are less successful.
- Compare the two profiles and look for differences in your behaviour. Differences between the two profiles might point to possibilities for changing your behaviour in ways that will improve your ability to influence others.

Did you take steps to:

1 Promote your reputation as somebody who can deliver change?
2 Increase others' dependence on you by:
   - Taking stock of what resources others want from you?
   - Assessing how important these resources are to them?
   - Exploring whether they can obtain the resources you provide from other sources?
   - Raising others' awareness of their dependence on you?
3 Minimize your dependence on others by:
   - Taking stock of what you need from others?
   - Searching for (and establishing) alternative sources of supply?

- Challenging historic assumptions about your dependence on others when situations have changed?
4 Build collaborative relationships with others and:
  - Identify new ways in which you could help target others?
  - Communicate your needs with those others you can trust in order to encourage them to provide the resources you require?
  - Enlist the help of others to influence third parties inaccessible to you?
5 Use all the above to negotiate advantageous agreements with others?

Stakeholders

Leaders need to be able to identify those stakeholders who can influence the outcome of the change. Freeman (1984) defines a stakeholder as any individual or group who can affect or is affected by the achievement of the organization's objectives. In the context of evaluating corporate performance, Clarkson (1995) widened the traditional definition to include the government and the communities that provide infrastructure and markets – whose laws must be obeyed, and to whom taxes and other obligations may be due – as well as traditional stakeholder groups such as employees, shareholders, investors, customers and suppliers. Stakeholders other than employees can exercise considerable influence over the outcome of many change initiatives, but often the success of a project is highly dependent on support from other organizational members. Several examples illustrate this point.

IV

McNulty and Ferlie (2002) attribute the lack of success of a project to change the care process for patients in the accident and emergency (A&E) department of a large UK hospital to the change agent's failure to generate sufficient support for the change from senior doctors and nurses. Clinical staff viewed the attempt to introduce change as interference from 'outside' by people who lacked adequate experience and understanding of the department's work. They were suspicious of the change agent's objectives, and believed that the project failed to address the core problems of the department and was more concerned with achieving cost savings rather than improving services provided to patients. McNulty and Ferlie also report that A&E doctors viewed the process-based philosophy behind the initiative as a threat to the established function of the A&E department, in the broader context of the hospital, and doctors' roles within the department.

In a large manufacturing company, a change was blocked by a senior manager who was not immediately involved in any of the departments directly affected by the change but who was pursuing a separate agenda that was inconsistent with the proposed change. The proposal was to drive down costs by centralizing procurement in order to gain economies of scale. It had many supporters but the senior manager who opposed it did so because he favoured the company adopting a more decentralized structure.

While internal stakeholders can exercise considerable influence, external stakeholders can also be important. Local residents in a UK city were offended – to the point of rioting in the streets – when a large leisure company decided to rebrand its bingo halls as 'Mecca Bingo'. The problem arose because the company failed to recognize the impact of demographic changes, which resulted in many of its bingo halls being located in neighbourhoods with predominantly Islamic populations.

Another example involved the Bank of Scotland when some customers, including West Lothian Council with a £250 million account, threatened to close their accounts in protest at the bank's proposed joint business venture with US evangelist Pat Robertson. Customers were unhappy with the proposal after he proclaimed that Scotland was a 'dark land' and a stronghold of homosexuality. These examples illustrate the point that it is not always easy to identify all the individuals and groups who may be affected by a change or who have the power to influence the outcome of the change.

Which stakeholders should be taken into account by those leading change?

Jones and Wicks (1999) identify two divergent approaches to stakeholder management: normative (also referred to as ethical) and instrumental.

Ethics-based theories

According to ethics-based theories, the interests of all stakeholders have intrinsic value and should be taken into account when formulating strategy and planning and implementing change. Berman et al. (1999) note that ethics-based theories hold that many stakeholder claims are based on fundamental moral principles unrelated to stakeholders' instrumental value to the organization. Those who subscribe to normative theories argue that moral commitments should provide the basis for managing stakeholder relationships rather than the desire to use stakeholders to promote managerial interests.

While pressures from investors and analysts might make it difficult for managers to address the concerns of all stakeholders, because investors may fail to see any connection between 'doing good' and financial performance, adopting an ethics-based approach can make business sense over the longer term. Fombrun et al. (2000, p. 90) assert that:

> Sustained corporate citizenship creates reputational capital and so provides a platform from which other opportunities may spring. The supportive social relationships that a company builds through its citizenship programmes today put it in a more favourable position to take advantage of opportunities that emerge tomorrow. In contrast, companies that fail to invest in corporate citizenship today may lack the relationships and reputational capital that they need to exploit emerging opportunities tomorrow.

Reputational capital

While there may not be any clear and immediate correlation between corporate *social* performance and corporate *financial* performance, Fombrun et al. (2000) argue that by 'doing good' and addressing the concerns of a wide range of stakeholder groups, it is possible for organizations to generate reputational gains that will improve their ability to attract resources, enhance performance and build competitive advantage. For example:

- committed employees can help to build reputational capital when they convey the merits of the company to customers, friends and neighbours
- satisfied customers can promote a positive image of the company

- activist groups are more likely to endorse organizations that promote safe working practices, pollution prevention, philanthropy and equal employment opportunities
- the media is more likely to feature positive stories about organizations that are seen to be behaving in a socially responsible way
- joint venture partners will be more inclined to collaborate with companies that are viewed as good corporate citizens.

Ignoring stakeholder interests, either through carelessness or in order to improve the bottom line, can seriously damage the organization's reputation and undermine long-term success. For example:

- Delta Airlines ended its strategic alliance with Korean Airlines after it was cited for safety violations.
- Primark, the Irish clothing retailer operating in eight countries across Europe, began to pressurize its suppliers to improve safety after hundreds of workers died following the collapse of a factory in Bangladesh.
- When News International was accused of phone hacking, police bribery and exercising improper influence in the pursuit of attention-grabbing stories, public pressure and advertiser boycotts led to the closure of *The News of the World* in 2011, one of the company's leading titles, and News Corporation (News International's parent company) was forced to abandon its bid to take over BSkyB.
- In the banking sector, attempts to inflate or deflate interest rates and manipulate LIBOR (the London Interbank Offered Rate) in order to profit from trades led to criminal investigations, massive fines and the dismissal of senior bankers. In 2013, regulators in more than 10 countries were investigating the rigging of LIBOR and other interest rates and there was speculation that the cost of litigation, penalties and loss of confidence could drive down finance industry profits for years to come.

Instrumental theories

The basic premise of instrumental theories of stakeholder management is that managers will only attend to the interests of stakeholders to the extent that those stakeholders can affect their interests. They posit that managers are selective in who they attend to and are not motivated by a concern for the welfare of stakeholders in general. Managerial interests vary, and may range from parochial concerns such as status or the end of year bonus, to more strategic concerns such as marketplace success and organizational survival. In most formulations of the instrumental approach, however, managerial interests are equated with the firm's financial performance and shareholders' satisfaction. Schein (1996, p. 15) refers to a tacit set of assumptions that CEOs and their immediate subordinates appear to share worldwide:

> This executive worldview is built around the necessity to maintain an organization's financial health and is preoccupied with boards, investors, and capital markets. Executives may have other preoccupations but they cannot get away from having to worry about the financial survival and growth of their organization.

At lower levels in the organization, however, many managers may be more concerned with managing relationships with different stakeholders who can have a more immediate impact on the performance of their department.

Implicit in the instrumental perspective is the assumption that change managers will abandon modes of dealing with stakeholders that prove to be unproductive. Berman et al. (1999) argue, for example, that while a firm might try to improve sales by adopting a total quality management approach that involves investing considerable effort in improving relationships with workers and suppliers, it might reassess its commitment to this strategy if it fails to deliver results. Similarly, an organization might adopt an employee share ownership scheme in the hope that it will motivate organizational members to work more effectively, but might abandon the scheme if it has little effect on performance.

The instrumental approach to stakeholder management is highly pragmatic. In the context of change management, regardless of the purpose of the change, it dictates that the change manager will focus attention on those relationships that will affect the success of the change.

Balancing corporate interests and stakeholder concerns

Shell provides a good example of an organization that has worked hard to integrate commerce and good citizenship. In 1995, the company's reputation was severely damaged following its proposal to sink the Brent Spar oil storage platform in deep water, rather than break it up on land, and the accusation that it was despoiling the Ogoni people's homeland in southeastern Nigeria. Mirvis (2000) reports how the company's 50-strong committee of managing directors 'held up a mirror' and examined the Shell Group's culture. What they found raised doubts about the viability of Shell's traditional culture that gave primacy in decisions to analysis and hard facts and had a tendency towards insularity and arrogance when dealing with many stakeholder groups, including nongovernmental organizations and the public. This triggered the development of a culture that valued the engagement of the global public in a two-way conversation over profits and principles and the measuring and reporting of the company's social and environmental record alongside its financial performance.

A life cycle approach to stakeholder management

Jawahar and McLaughlin (2001) offer an approach to managing stakeholders that draws on resource dependence theory, prospect theory and organizational life cycle models. Their underlying premise is that an organization faces different pressures and threats at different stages in its life cycle. Thus, over time, certain stakeholders will become more important than others because of their ability to satisfy critical organizational needs. Their theory identifies which stakeholders will be important at different stages in the organizational life cycle and indicates how the organization will attempt to deal with each of its primary stakeholders at every stage.

The contribution of resource dependence theory

Resource dependence theory conceptualizes the organization as being dependent on the resources in its environment for survival and growth. Jawahar and McLaughlin (2001) extend this theory to stakeholder management and propose that organizations will pay most attention to those stakeholder groups who control resources critical to the organization's survival. In the context of change management, resource dependence theory indicates that change managers will be motivated to attend to those stakeholders who control the resources that are critical to the change project's success. The different levels of attention they devote to different groups of stakeholders are manifest in the form of different stakeholder management strategies. Following Carroll (1979), Clarkson (1995) and others, it is possible to identify four ways of managing stakeholders:

1 *Being proactive:* doing a great deal to address stakeholder issues
2 *Accommodating:* a positive but less active approach for dealing with stakeholder issues
3 *Defending:* doing only the minimum required to address stakeholder issues, for example attending to employee concerns only to the extent required by employment legislation
4 *Ignoring:* ignoring or refusing to address stakeholder issues.

The contribution of prospect theory

Prospect theory also helps to explain why, sometimes, change managers are selective about which stakeholders they attend to, whereas on other occasions they will be more inclined to address the concerns of all (or many) stakeholders. Prospect theory posits that, relative to whatever reference point is used to evaluate an outcome, which might be the current position or a level of benefit that an individual hopes to achieve, outcomes evaluated as losses are weighted more heavily than similar amounts of outcome evaluated as gains. Central to prospect theory is the notion that the actual (objective) and psychological (subjective) values attributed to an outcome can and do differ. Bazerman (2001) illustrates this with the observation that the pain associated with losing $1,000 is generally perceived to be greater than the pleasure associated with winning a similar amount.

The work of Kahneman and Tversky (1979) suggests that the way people react to situations depends on whether the outcomes are framed in terms of gains or losses. They hypothesize that when outcomes are framed in terms of gains, individuals will be risk averse, and avoid acting in ways that might threaten the anticipated gain, but when outcomes are framed in terms of losses, they will be more prepared to pursue a risky option if this offers the possibility of avoiding or minimizing the anticipated loss.

Bazerman (2001) provides an example of how this might work in practice. He describes a plant closure problem. When managers are presented with a positively framed version of the problem, the majority select plan A, the option with the 'certain' outcome (Table 10.1).

Table **10.1** *Positive frame*

Plan A		Plan B
'Certain' (no risk) outcome Selected by the majority		High-risk outcome
Save one of three plants and 2,000 of 6,000 jobs	*versus*	1 in 3 chance of saving all three plants and all 6,000 jobs, but a 2 in 3 chance of saving no plants and no jobs

However, when managers are presented with a negatively framed version of the same problem, the majority select plan D, which is the risky option (Table 10.2).

Table **10.2** *Negative frame*

Plan C		Plan D
'Certain' outcome framed in terms of what will be lost		High-risk outcome Selected by the majority
Lose two of the three plants and 4,000 jobs	*versus*	2 in 3 chance of losing all three plants and all 6,000 jobs, but a 1 in 3 chance of losing no plants and no jobs

Both sets of alternative plans are *objectively* the same. Plan A (saving one of three plants and 2,000 of 6,000 jobs) offers the same objective outcome as plan C (losing two of the three plants and 4,000 of the 6000 jobs), and plan B offers the same objective outcome as plan D.

Based on contributions from resource dependence theory and prospect theory, Jawahar and McLaughlin (2001) take the first step towards the development of their descriptive stakeholder theory by proposing two theorems:

1 In the absence of threats, a 'gain frame' will be adopted, and those leading the change will follow a risk-averse strategy and actively address all stakeholder issues. They will actively address all stakeholder issues because doing so is likely to persuade them all to support the change.

2 In the presence of threats, a 'loss frame' will be adopted, and those leading the change will pursue a risky strategy that involves addressing the concerns of only those stakeholders who are relevant to the immediate loss threat, while defending or denying any responsibility for the concerns of other stakeholders. For example, if a firm is in danger of being forced into administration, senior managers might do everything possible to address the concerns of creditors, while giving little attention to the concerns of employees.

The contribution of organizational life cycle models

Life cycle models posit that a change proceeds through a sequence of stages. Jawahar and McLaughlin (2001) argue that, at each stage, the threats and opportunities that could affect the success of the change may vary, so the resources required to support the change will also vary. This led them to argue that at any given life cycle stage, certain stakeholders become more important than others because they control the resources required at that stage in the process.

Jawahar and McLaughlin's stakeholder theory

Drawing on contributions from all three theories, Jawahar and McLaughlin argue that if, at any stage in the change project life cycle, the fulfilment of critical resource requirements is threatened, change managers will adopt a loss frame and focus their attention on those stakeholders who control the critical resources and interact with them in a proactive or accommodating manner. In those stages where the flow of resources is not threatened, decision makers are likely to adopt a gain frame, pursue a risk-averse strategy, and actively address the concerns of all stakeholders.

Change managers must not assume that if they engage in the kind of stakeholder analysis suggested below, they will have identified, once and for all, the key constituents who require attention. Power relationships and the ability of various individuals and groups to influence events will change over time, thus it may be necessary to review and manage stakeholder relationships on a continuing basis.

IV

Managing stakeholders

Building on the key player matrix developed by Piercy (1989), Grundy (1998) suggests a useful approach for managing stakeholder relationships. The first part of the process involves a stakeholder analysis to identify important stakeholders and assess their power to influence and their attitude towards the proposed change. The second part involves developing a strategy for persuading influential stakeholders to support the change.

Case study **10.1** *Merger of two hospitals: stakeholder brainstorm*

Familiarize yourself with this case and list all the individuals and groups who can affect or might be affected by the outcome of the change.

This is a real case. Imagine that you are the recently appointed human resources (HR) director of a new acute hospital. You have been in the post for four weeks. The hospital has been formed from the merger of two hospitals (A and B) in the same city. The new chief executive (CE) was appointed five months ago. He was previously CE of hospital B. You moved to your post from another hospital elsewhere in the NHS. You were the last of the directors to be appointed. The board is in place but the structure of the new hospital has not yet

been finalized. The two parts of the new organization continue to operate much as they did before the merger. However, the CE feels that the HR and finance functions need to be reorganized as quickly as possible, and expects that these two functions will help facilitate the merger of other parts of the new hospital.

You have been tasked with merging the HR departments of hospitals A and B and achieving an annual saving of £140,000 on the HR budget. The HR staff obviously have high expectations about what you will deliver. Almost everybody wants the merger of the two departments to be completed quickly, but with minimum disruption to the status quo. There are

▶

© CORBIS

important differences in the culture and structure of hospitals A and B, reflected in the way their HR departments operate. A potential problem is that the staff in both HR departments, and line managers in their respective former hospitals, appear to be happy with the way things are operating at present and would like their way of working to be the template for the new merged department.

Some of the main differences between the two original hospitals are shown in Table 10.3.

You recognize that it may be necessary to slim down the HR establishment if you are to achieve the £140,00 cost savings. Additional issues that might influence your approach to managing this change are:

1 The two former heads of the HR functions, who are still leading the two departments, have different philosophies about the nature of HR.
2 Since the two hospitals were merged, there has been a rapid rise in the number of grievances registered by staff across the new organization, especially from

Table **10.3** *Differences between the two hospitals*

Hospital A	Hospital B
Decentralized structure. Two big, largely autonomous directorates (surgery and medicine), each with its own operational director	Centralized structure. Many small departments led by general managers who report directly to the CE
Fragmented culture, medical staff and managers are separate groups	Collaborative culture, medical staff and managers work closely together
The HR department is only responsible for personnel information and employee relations. Training and development is located under nursing	All the HR functions, including training and development, are centralized within one department
The HR department employs a small group of staff who tend to stay within their own department and act as professional advisers to the operational managers. Operational managers are responsible for much of the HR management within their own departments	The HR department is 'staff rich'. HR staff work closely with operational managers, accompany them to meetings, take notes for them and assume responsibility for much of the day-to-day HR activity
Line managers hold personnel files in operational departments	HR holds personnel files centrally

staff required to work alongside colleagues from the other former hospital. Most of these grievances relate to the differences in terms and conditions that apply across the new hospital. For example, there are differences in the protection agreements that safeguard an individual's pay and conditions when their work is regraded, and there are differences in holiday entitlements that led to problems when members of the two former hospitals started working together. This has had a marked effect on the day-to-day workload of sections of your staff.

3 Managers across the new organization are seeking help from HR on issues related to the merger. This presents you with two related issues. First, it adds to the HR workload problem. At a time when HR needs to allocate resources to managing its own internal merger, it has to respond to new demands from client departments. Second, managers across the new hospital, depending on where they worked previously, have different expectations regarding the support HR should provide.

You are required to develop a plan to bring together the two HR departments in order to:

- Create a new HR function that will promote excellent HR practice.
- Deliver efficiency gains of £140,00 p.a.

With this in mind, brainstorm a list of stakeholders.

Identifying the power and commitment of stakeholders

Grundy (1998) outlines three steps for identifying the power and commitment of stakeholders:

1 He refers to the first step as the 'stakeholder brainstorm'. This involves identifying all those who might be affected by and/or could affect the outcome of the proposed change.

2 The second step involves assessing how much power and influence each group of stakeholders has. This can be quite difficult in practice:
- There may be people with little influence over organizational issues in general but who have considerable influence over a particular issue related to the change.
- There may be individuals who express support for the change but who cannot be relied on because their supportive efforts are undermined by other people in their departments.
- There may be people who have exercised little influence in the past but who have more power than anticipated or who have recently acquired the ability to influence others.

3 The third step involves assessing stakeholders' attitudes towards the proposed change. Again, this can be difficult. For example:
- There may be individuals or groups who appear to support the proposal in public but who work against it behind the scenes.
- There may be others who misunderstand the proposed change but would be supportive if they were better informed.

Attitudes can range from positive, through neutral to negative. Shaw and Maletz (1995) describe those who proactively work to prevent the change effort from succeeding as 'blockers', and those who proactively work to ensure that it succeeds as 'sponsors'.

The two dimensions of 'attitude' and 'power' are brought together in the stakeholder grid presented in Change tool 10.1 below.

IV

Case study **10.2** *Merger of two hospitals: stakeholder mapping*

Developing the merger case presented in Case study 10.1, imagine that your initial vision for the new HR function is one where:

- There will be a core group of HR professionals working on strategic HR issues. Most day-to-day operational matters will be devolved to line managers. The HR department will only work on operational issues where there are clear benefits from providing a centralized service. These benefits could be cost savings or service quality.
- Training and development will be moved from nursing to HR, but some delivery – especially the day-to-day aspects of work-based training – will be based in operational departments.
- The HR function will be restructured. Instead of the two existing departments (based in the former hospitals), each providing a full range of services, work will be reallocated into two broad portfolios

and will be managed on a new hospital-wide basis. You (the new HR director) will manage one of these portfolios and the other will be managed by one of the heads of the two former HR departments.

- You want to co-locate most staff on a single site but you feel this might be easier to achieve if everybody moved to a new location on one of the existing sites in order to avoid the feeling that one of the former departments has been 'taken over' by the other. However, you also feel it is necessary for HR to have a 'presence' on each site but you feel that on one of the sites this should be limited to a small number of staff who will work alongside line managers as advisers.

Before you begin to test out this vision with others or start to develop a plan to move from the current situation to your vision for the HR function, think about the others who may have a stake in the change and how they might react using Change tool 10.1.

The stakeholder grid is a useful tool that can be used to identify stakeholders in terms to their power and predisposition to support or oppose the change (Change tool 10.1).

Change tool **10.1** *Stakeholder grid*

Locate all the stakeholders who can affect or might be affected by the outcome of the change onto the stakeholder grid below.

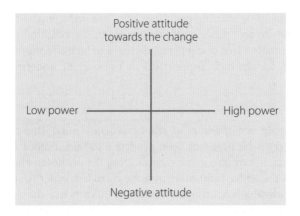

Influencing stakeholders to support the change

The second part of the process described by Grundy (1998) involves the change manager acting in ways that will ensure maximum support for the change. This might involve:

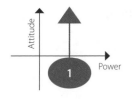

1 *Winning the support of those who oppose the change and have the power to influence the outcome:* Changing powerful blockers into sponsors might be achieved by providing them with information that could persuade them to be more supportive, involving them in the change process in order to give them more control over the outcome, or bargaining with them to win their support.

   Listening to why they oppose the change and indicating a willingness to at least consider revising the change plan can be an effective way of winning their support. Sometimes, change managers are so concerned with being right that they lose sight of their original goal. Ford and Ford (2009) argue that stubbornly pushing things through without even trying to understand the blockers' viewpoint can waste a valuable opportunity to engage the sceptics.

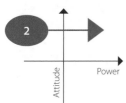

2 *Increasing the influence of already supportive stakeholders:* This might be achieved, for example, by working to secure their appointment to decision-making groups that regulate matters related to the proposed change.

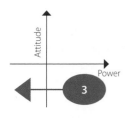

3 *Reducing the influence of powerful blockers:* This might be achieved in a number of ways. For example, managers can challenge the arguments blockers use to oppose the change. They can also take steps to marginalize them from the decision-making process by working to ensure that they are not members of the committee or group that has to sanction the change, or transferring them to another part of the organization.

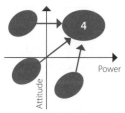

4 *Building a coalition of supportive stakeholders who will be prepared to work together to support the change:* This might involve communicating an inspiring vision that highlights mutual benefits and encourages independent groups of stakeholders to align themselves with the change manager's purpose.

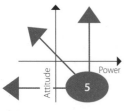

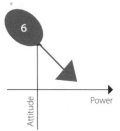

5 *Fragmenting existing coalitions who are antagonistic towards the change.* This might involve picking off key players in the coalition and providing them with information that could persuade them to be more supportive, or bargaining with them to win their support (as in 1 above) or undermining their case (as in 3 above).

6 *Bringing new sponsors or champions into play:* This could involve persuading 'players' who have not been proactive to take a more active part in influencing events. It may also involve publicizing the proposed change within the company or in the wider community, via the media, in order to seek support from powerful individuals or groups who may be unknown to the change manager. However, this kind of intervention is not without risk because it could also attract the attention of unknown others who may be opposed to the change.

Another possibility that the change manager might consider is reformulating the change in a way that will make it more acceptable to a wider range of stakeholders.

Case study 10.3 *Merger of two hospitals: managing stakeholder relationships*

1 Review the stakeholder map you produced in Change tool 10.1 and indicate how you would attend to the concerns of stakeholders. Which stakeholders would you:
  • *address proactively:* do a great deal to address their concerns? Indicate with a 'P' on your stakeholder map.
  • *accommodate:* take a less active approach to dealing with their concerns? Indicate with an 'A' on your stakeholder map.

  • *ignore:* do the legal minimum or refuse to address their concerns? Indicate with an 'I' on your stakeholder map.
  Reflect on how the project might unfold and consider whether any stakeholders you decided to ignore might become more important at a later date.
2 What steps would you take to increase support or reduce opposition for your proposed way of managing the merger?

An important point to remember is that as a change project unfolds and circumstances change, the identity of key stakeholders may also change. This can have implications for how you decide to manage stakeholder relationships over the short term because some stakeholders who may be unimportant today could become much more important in the future. If they feel that their interests have been disregarded in the past, they may be reluctant to support the change manager in the future.

Managing relationships between stakeholders

There is evidence suggesting that the way one set of stakeholders is managed can affect how other stakeholders will react to a change. For example, the way redundancies are managed can impact the commitment and motivation of survivors. There is a widely held view that if leavers are seen to be treated badly, this will adversely affect the motivation and commitment of those who have kept their jobs.

Early work on 'survivor syndrome' (see Brockner, 1992; Doherty and Horsted, 1995) focused attention on how the good treatment of leavers can help to maintain the support of survivors. However, while there is evidence to support this proposition, a more recent study has shown that managing stakeholders to maintain commitment can be a more complex process than it may appear. Sahdev (2004) found that focusing too much attention on pleasing leavers can have a negative effect on the behaviour of survivors (see Research report 10.1).

Research report **10.1** *Perceptions of fair treatment*

Sahdev, K. (2004) Revisiting the survivor syndrome: The role of leadership in implementing downsizing, *European Journal of Work and Organizational Psychology*, 13(2): 165–96.

Sahdev's qualitative study compared the effects of two different approaches to managing redundancies. She studied two organizations, Barclaycard and SKF UK (a leading provider of bearings, seals and lubrication systems), over a four-and-a-half-year period, collecting data from company documents, one-to-one interviews and focus groups. In both organizations, downsizing was accompanied by a transformation change.

Barclaycard, anticipating greater competition, had proactively embarked on a three-year re-engineering programme designed to reduce costs and deliver better service to customers. It involved a big investment in new technology, the redesign of roles and responsibilities, and the introduction of a matrix structure. As part of the change, 1,100 employees were made redundant. Guided by state-of-the-art knowledge (including research on survivor syndrome), the company focused strongly on accommodating leavers by pursuing a transparent redundancy process, applying fair decision rules, and providing substantial support for leavers in terms of outplacement and redundancy packages.

While the majority of those who were made redundant felt they had been fairly treated, employees who were retained felt let down by the company. The new technology did not deliver the promised high service levels. Response speeds were too slow, making it difficult to satisfy customer needs. Customer service advisers also failed to achieve their targets, creating high levels of anxiety. Employees began to question the rationale for the change and the capability of senior management to handle the re-engineering programme. Senior managers were rarely visible

throughout the change process and many employees felt that the changes were implemented mechanistically, with little regard for those who had to make them work. Furthermore, the way senior managers announced the impending downsizing created false expectations. Everyone assumed that they could take the severance package and many started to make plans for 'life after Barclaycard'. Unfortunately, lots of applications for voluntary redundancy were rejected and many of those who did not want to be part of the new world were forced to stay on.

The outcome, contrary to the company's expectations, was that while every effort had been made to manage the redundancy process in a positive and supportive way, this approach had failed to retain the commitment and support of those employees who were retained. Sahdev attributes this to the lack of attention given to survivors' needs.

SKF UK was pushed into a major change programme because, compared with other SKF sites, the UK operation was a high-cost, low-quality producer of ball bearings. In order to avoid closure, the company embarked on a lean manufacturing transformation programme. This involved shifting responsibility down the hierarchy to blue-collar workers directly involved in the manufacturing process, and empowering them to take whatever actions might be necessary to eliminate waste and improve quality. Managers were supportive and engaged with the production operatives to ensure that they had the resources to manage the many day-to-day challenges they faced. Management also made a significant investment in educating the entire workforce to acquire new skills, for which they received extra pay. Overstaffing was addressed through a voluntary redundancy programme, which targeted those workers who had been with the company for a long time and who genuinely wanted to take early retirement rather than retrain and adopt the new ways

IV

of working. The severance scheme was generous and allowed people to leave with dignity.

Compared to the survivors in Barclaycard, those who stayed on in SFK were more committed to the company. Sahdev suggests that this was because, while SKF gave people the choice of leaving with a generous severance package, the company also gave high priority to the needs of those who chose to stay. Barclaycard, on the other hand, paid too much attention to the leavers and insufficient attention to winning the commitment of those who were retained.

Sahdev's study suggests that changes such as downsizing need to be managed in a way that directly attends to the needs of all stakeholder groups including leavers and survivors. Focusing attention on leavers, while necessary, is not sufficient to ensure the commitment of those who are retained.

Reflect on the issues discussed in this chapter and addressed in Case studies 10.1–10.3 and consider how they apply to the management of stakeholders in your organization in Exercise 10.3.

✓ Exercise **10.3** *Stakeholder management*

Think about a recent change you have observed at work, college or elsewhere and, with the advantage of hindsight:

- identify the stakeholders involved in the change
- classify them according to their power to influence and their attitude towards the change
- assess the extent to which the person managing the change was aware of these stakeholders and took proper account of them when managing the change.

Summary

This chapter explored the politics of organizational change and pointed to the importance of enlisting support from key stakeholders.

Organizations are conceptualized as a collection of constituencies, each pursuing their own objectives:

- Individuals and groups attempt to influence each other in the pursuit of self-interest.
- When there is a conflict of interest, it is the power and influence of those involved that determines the outcome rather than logical and rational argument.
- In order to ensure the successful introduction of change, it is essential that change managers secure the assistance of powerful stakeholders and build a critical mass of support for the change.
- Stakeholders are any individuals or groups who can affect or are affected by a change.

Political behaviour tends to be more intense in times of change because individuals and groups perceive the possibility of upsetting the existing balance of power. Some may be motivated to defend the status quo, whereas others may perceive change as an opportunity to improve their position. Consequently, change managers need to be alert to these political dynamics, especially the possibility that others may be motivated to act in ways that undermine their efforts to bring about change.

Power is inherent in any relationship in which one person or group is dependent on another. Sometimes, those leading a change are unaware of their potential ability to influence others because they have never attempted to consciously assess how dependent they are on others and compare this with the extent to which others are dependent on them. Thinking about relationships in terms of relative dependencies can point to ways in which leaders can shift the balance of power in their favour.

Leaders can increase their ability to influence others by taking steps to increase others' dependence on them and minimizing their dependence on those they are seeking to influence.

Jones and Wicks (1999) identify two divergent theoretical positions regarding stakeholder management:

1 *Normative*: all stakeholders should be taken into account. Moral commitments should provide the basis of managing stakeholder relationships rather than the desire to use stakeholders to promote managerial interests.
2 *Instrumental*: managers will only attend to the interests of stakeholders to the extent that they can affect their interests.

Jawahar and McLaughlin's (2001) instrumental theory of stakeholder management provides a conceptual framework for identifying and managing stakeholders. It draws on:

1 *Resource dependence theory:* organizations are dependent on the resources in their environment for survival and growth.
2 *Prospect theory:* outcomes that are evaluated as losses are weighted more heavily than similar amounts of outcome that are evaluated as gains. Individuals will be risk seeking in the loss domain and risk averse in the gain domain.
3 *Organizational life cycle models:* the pressures that threaten the success of a change project will vary with the stages of the project life cycle. Consequently, the resources required will also vary with life cycle stages.

Based on contributions from resource dependence theory and prospect theory, Jawahar and McLaughlin (2001) propose two theorems:

1 In the absence of threats, a 'gain frame' will be adopted, and the organization will follow a risk-averse strategy and actively address all stakeholder issues.
2 In the presence of threats, a 'loss frame' will be adopted, and the organization will pursue a risky strategy that involves addressing the concerns of only those stakeholders who are relevant to the immediate loss threat, while defending or denying any responsibility for the concerns of other stakeholders.

Based on contributions from life cycle models, Jawahar and McLaughlin argue that if at any stage in the organizational (or change project) life cycle, the fulfilment of critical resource requirements is threatened, organizational decision makers will adopt a loss frame and interact with those stakeholders who control the critical resources in a proactive or accommodating manner and with other stakeholders in a defensive manner. In those stages where the flow of resources is not threatened, decision makers are likely to adopt a gain frame, pursue a risk-averse strategy and actively address the concerns of all stakeholders.

The following points emerged as important:

IV

- At any given stage in a change project, certain stakeholders emerge as more important than others because of their potential to satisfy critical organizational needs.
- It is possible to identify which stakeholders are likely to be more or less important at each stage.
- The strategy that will be used to deal with each stakeholder will depend on the importance of that stakeholder relative to other stakeholders.

The stakeholder grid was introduced as a useful tool for identifying the power of stakeholders and their predisposition to support or oppose the change.

References

Bazerman, M. (2001) *Judgement in Managerial Decision Making* (5th edn). Chichester: Wiley.

Berman, S.L., Wicks, A.C., Kotha, S. and Jones, T.M. (1999) Does stakeholder orientation matter? The relationship between stakeholder management models and firm financial performance, *Academy of Management Journal*, 42(5): 488–506.

Brockner, J. (1992) Managing the effects of layoffs on others, *California Management Review*, 34(4): 9–27.

Carroll, A.B. (1979) A three-dimensional conceptual model of corporate social performance, *Academy of Management Review*, 4(4): 497–505.

Clarkson, M.B. (1995) A stakeholder framework for analyzing and evaluating corporate social performance, *Academy of Management Review*, 20(1): 92–117.

Doherty, N. and Horsted, J. (1995) Helping survivors stay on board, *People Management*, 1(1): 26–31.

Emerson, M. (1962) Power dependence relations, *American Sociological Review*, 27(1): 31–41.

Fombrun, C.J., Gardberg, N.A. and Barnett, M.L. (2000) Opportunity platforms and safety nets: Corporate citizenship and reputational risk, *Business and Society Review*, 105(1): 85–106.

Ford, J.D. and Ford, L.W. (2009) Decoding resistance to change, *Harvard Business Review*, 87(4): 99–103.

Freeman, R.E. (1984) *Strategic Management: A Stakeholder Approach*. Boston, MA: HarperCollins.

Grundy, T. (1998) Strategy implementation and project management, *International Journal of Project Management*, 16(1): 48–50.

Hayes, J. (1984) The politically competent manager, *Journal of General Management*, 10(1): 24–33.

Jawahar, M. and McLaughlin, G.L. (2001) Toward a descriptive stakeholder theory: An organizational life cycle approach, *Academy of Management Review*, 26(3): 397–414.

Jones, T.M. and Wicks, A.C. (1999) Convergent stakeholder theory, *Academy of Management Review*, 24(2): 206–21.

Kahneman, D. and Tversky, A. (1979) Prospect theory: An analysis of decisions under risk, *Econometrica*, 47(2): 263–91.

McClelland, D.C. (1975) *Power: The Inner Experience*. New York: Irvingston.

McNulty, T. (2003) Redesigning public services: Challenges of practice for policy, *British Journal of Management*, 14: S31–45.

McNulty, T. and Ferlie, E. (2002) *Reengineering Health Care: The Complexities of Organizational Transformation*. Oxford: Oxford University Press.

Mirvis, P.H. (2000) Transformation at Shell: Commerce and citizenship, *Business and Society Review*, 105(1): 63–84.

Nadler, D.A. (1987) The effective management of organizational change. In J.W. Lorsch (ed.) *Handbook of Organizational Behaviour*. Englewood Cliffs, NJ: Prentice Hall.

Pettigrew, A.M. (1972) Information control as a power resource, *Sociology*, 6(2): 187–204.

Piercy, N. (1989) Diagnosing and solving implementation problems in strategic planning, *Journal of General Management*, 15(1): 19–38.

Sahdev, K. (2004) Revisiting the survivor syndrome: The role of leadership in implementing downsizing, *European Journal of Work and Organizational Psychology*, 13(2): 165–96.

Schein, E.H. (1996) The three cultures of management: The key to organizational learning, *Sloan Management Review*, 38(1): 9–20.

Shaw, B.R. and Maletz, M.C. (1995) Business processes: Embracing the logic and limits of reengineering. In D.A. Nadler, R.B. Shaw and A.E. Walton (eds) *Discontinuous Change: Leading Organizational Transformation*. San Francisco, CA: Jossey-Bass.

IV

Chapter ⑪)))) **Communicating change**

Communication plays an important role in all the 'people issues' discussed in Part IV of this book, such as leading, managing stakeholders, motivating and supporting others. For example, leaders need to be effective communicators because, among other things, they have to convey a compelling vision of a better future, inspire and motivate others to implement the changes, align their efforts by communicating a shared understanding of what needs to be done, and provide the feedback required to sustain the change.

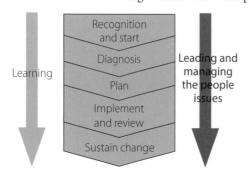

This chapter explores the value of a clear communication strategy and examines some of the issues that need to be considered when formulating a coherent approach to communicating change. It also examines some of the features of communication networks, such as directionality, role, content and channels, explores some of the factors that can deprive managers of access to vital information, and considers how change communication can affect perceptions of fairness and justice.

Case study 11.1 illustrates how inattention to communication issues can disrupt the best-laid plans for change.

Case study **11.1** *Connect2*

Connect2 (as it will be referred to here) was an advertising agency located in Sydney, Australia. It was founded by a talented and ambitious graduate who successfully expanded the business from an original client base of 1 to 45 over a 10-year period. The business focused on investor relations and developed a strong reputation for designing and producing annual and interim reports. The production process, from receipt of the client's brief to delivery of the printed report, was clear, simple and worked effectively. Project managers were good at developing and maintaining close relations with clients and always ensured that clients' expectations were met and, where possible, exceeded. The business employed 27 staff who worked well together as a tightly knit group. While the owner ran a

tight ship and had his finger on the pulse of every project, he was approachable and did not micromanage. He led from behind and did everything he could to empower his staff to act in the best interests of Connect2 and its clients. Employees enjoyed their work and, when required, were happy to put in extra hours to meet tight deadlines.

In 2011, the owner was persuaded to sell the company to two experienced businessmen. The people who worked for Connect2 expected the new owners to make changes. Most were prepared for this but some were concerned that they could lose out and even lose their jobs. Much of this early anxiety was allayed when the new owners told them there would be no redundancies and they were intending to ►

expand the business. For a few weeks, nothing seemed to change and the new owners said little about their plans. After a while, this lack of information became a new source of concern.

Behind the scenes, however, the new owners were busy. Their vision was to grow the business into a media powerhouse. They were in the process of acquiring two other companies, one a successful public relations (PR) agency and the other a video production company, and their intention was to merge all three into a single organization offering a wide range of advertising, marketing and PR services. Their first step was to expand Connect2 to provide the core management infrastructure for the new company. They hired eight new business development managers to work on expanding the client base and appointed two new managers to functional roles, one to head finance and the other to head HR. They also had plans to appoint a creative director.

Before the negotiations to acquire the PR and video production companies were finalized, the new owners of Connect2 employed the services of a consultant to help them interview candidates for the new business development and functional management roles and they invited her to facilitate an intensive one-week induction for the newly appointed staff. It was only at this point that the two most senior Connect2 project managers were briefed on the new developments and brought in to familiarize the newcomers with the company's current processes. Soon after their induction, the business development managers, who were highly incentivized, began to visit potential clients to seek new business. It was at this point that things began to go wrong. The changes had not been properly communicated to Connect2 staff and they had not been given any opportunity to comment on them. Consequently, the owners were taken by surprise when they discovered that existing staff did not have the skills or experience they required to deliver the new services that were to be provided to new clients. They were also unaware that the company's existing business processes were unable to accommodate the new volumes of work that were anticipated.

Another problem was that the new owners had done little to facilitate communication between new and existing staff and this resulted in misunderstandings about roles and responsibilities. The business development managers expected the project

© IMAGESOURCE

managers to assume responsibility for processing all the new work they brought in without checking that the project managers had the time or other resources to cope with this additional work. They also failed to recognize that part of the project managers' role had historically involved managing relationships with the company's existing clients. This generated conflicts and bad feelings when the business development managers visited existing clients to sell new services without informing the respective project managers. There was also little communication with existing clients or suppliers about the changes. Existing clients were confused about who was managing their accounts and felt less confident about giving their business to Connect2. Nobody had taken the time to reassure suppliers that Connect2 wanted to retain their services or to explore opportunities of securing better terms if Connect2 increased their business with them.

Within the company, the staff who had been with Connect2 before it had been sold were unhappy because the old closely knit culture, clear sense of direction and tried-and-tested processes had given way to confusion about the company's goals, a lack of clarity regarding roles, responsibilities and reporting

IV

relationships, and frustration that their efforts were undermined by business processes that were no longer fit for purpose. Even when they were motivated to do what they could to satisfy clients, there was little support for initiative taking. Morale plummeted and commitment evaporated. It was not long before the two senior project managers resigned and took some of Connect2's long-standing clients with them. Key staff in the editorial and other departments also resigned, further undermining the effectiveness of some key processes, and the new business development managers were unhappy because they had to spend more time on site managing some of

their own projects in order to deliver promised outcomes to clients.

At this point, the purchase of the PR company was finalized but morale was so low within Connect2 that attempts to merge the two companies failed and they had to be managed as two separate businesses. Plans to purchase the video production company were put on hold. A year later, the PR company was sold and recently Connect2 ceased trading.

Before reading on, list some of the communication problems in this case and think about how they could have been managed more effectively.

Source: This case is based on contributions from Jolene Roelofse.

The need for a communication strategy

In the Connect2 case, the new owners appeared to focus most of their attention on communicating with each other and the new staff they had recruited, and gave very little attention to communicating with existing staff or clients. This is the result of a common problem: the failure to develop a coherent change communication strategy. In many cases, leaders act on impulse and interact with those who seem important at the time, without thinking through how the way they communicate could affect the outcome of the change.

The first step in developing a change communication strategy is for those leading the change to study the situation, identify the key issues, and formulate a set of communication goals that will address them. The issues that will be identified as important will vary from situation to situation but, in the Connect2 case, one was the need to assess whether the company could support the envisioned new business streams. Addressing this issue would involve gathering and interpreting information about the capabilities and experience of existing staff and investigating whether the organization's operational infrastructure is able to cope. Another issue was to understand how the planned changes might affect the morale and commitment of those occupying key roles. It appears that the new owners were not good at seeking out information or listening to others. Understanding these issues would point to related communication goals such as formulating and conveying a vision that key stakeholders will perceive to be attractive and achievable.

With communication goals such as these in mind, leaders can begin to think about how best to communicate the change. Without clear communication goals, it is difficult for leaders to identify the information they and others need, and how this information is to be acquired and exchanged. Clear goals also help leaders identify key stakeholders, what information they have and how they can be encouraged to share this with others, particularly those leading the change, and what information stakeholders need and how best this can be conveyed to them.

Clampitt et al. (2000) observe that implicit communications strategies often emerge without much conscious thought. For example, those leading change can:

- Communicate about anything but, because of time constraints and perceptions about the sensitivity of certain pieces of information, they cannot communicate about everything, so, implicitly or explicitly, they make choices about communication content. Ideally, these choices will be informed by a well-articulated set of communication goals, but all too often they are not.

- Unconsciously act in ways that impact on the shape of communication networks. They may communicate with some organizational members but not with others. This may be for good reason or it may be simply because they are co-located with some colleagues, and frequently have the opportunity to exchange ideas with them, but rarely communicate with others who work on a different floor or in another building. When everybody meets together, those who are not co-located with the leaders may recognize that others are better informed, and they might form the opinion that this is because they are members of an in-group from which they have been deliberately excluded. When leaders act in ways that create this impression, they can unintentionally generate negative feelings that undermine the motivation to support a change.

These difficulties can be minimized if leaders give more attention to developing a well-thought-out strategy for communicating the change. Kotter (1995), writing about the importance of communicating a compelling vision, asserts that in many change programmes, this is undercommunicated by a factor of ten. He also observes that communicating a vision involves more than the spoken and written word. Organizational members, and other stakeholders, observe those responsible for managing the change for indications of their commitment. It is important, therefore, that leaders 'walk the talk' and communicate their enthusiasm for the vision by example.

When developing a change communication strategy, leaders might find it helpful to consider the importance of factors such as directionality, role, content and channel.

Directionality

The management of change is often experienced as a top-down process, with those responsible for managing the change informing others lower down the organization about the need for change, what is going to happen and what is required of them. Allen et al. (2007) argue that the reason why many organizations encounter difficulties in reducing employee uncertainty during change is because of this one-way, top-down pattern of communication. Effective change communication is two-way. Upward communication is essential because it provides change managers with valuable information that can help them clarify the need for change and, later, help them develop and implement plans for change. Beer (2001) identifies the poor quality of upward communication as one of his six 'silent killers' that block change and learning.

Directionality and content

O'Reilly and Pondy (1979) list some of the consequences of directionality on the content of messages. Senders transmitting messages up the organization hierarchy send information they perceive to be relevant and which reflects favourably on their performance, or that of their unit. Where possible, they screen out information that reflects unfavourably on them. Consequently, people further up the organization may not receive all the information they need to understand what is going on.

Senders transmitting messages down the organization have a tendency to screen out any information they perceive to be not directly relevant to subordinates' roles. This 'need-to-know' attitude can lead to problems when change managers fail to pass on information that might have helped others to understand the need for change or feel more involved in the change process (see the discussion of the 'withhold and uphold' communication strategy below).

Directionality and accuracy, confidence and time

Even when those leading the change have every intention of passing on all relevant information, if they transmit this information top down in a one-way direction, it may well be misunderstood. Back in 1951, Leavitt and Mueller conducted a now classic experiment to test the hypothesis that feedback increases the accuracy of communication. One person (the leader) communicated geometrical patterns (see sample in Figure 11.1) to a number of recipients who were told that the experiment was to test their ability to understand instructions. They were instructed to draw the pattern and to work as rapidly as possible. The experiment was repeated to test four conditions of feedback. The first condition was 'zero feedback'. The leader sat behind a screen to describe the diagram and the recipients were not permitted to ask questions. The second condition was 'visible audience', in which the leader could see the recipients and observe their reactions to the message but no questions were allowed. The third condition was 'yes-no', in which members of the visible audience were permitted to answer yes or no in response to questions from the leader. The fourth condition was 'free feedback', in which recipients were permitted to ask questions, interrupt and make statements.

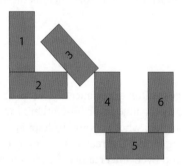

Figure **11.1** *Sample problem*

The results showed that the accuracy of recipients' diagrams increased steadily from the zero feedback to the free feedback conditions, indicating that two-way communication produces better understanding of the message than one-way communication. They also showed that recipients were more confident they had understood the message the more they were able to engage with the sender, but two-way communication, when recipients had more freedom to interact with the sender, took much longer than one-way communication. Another interesting observation was that senders felt more exposed when engaging in two-way communication. In the free feedback condition, some recipients behaved in a hostile or aggressive way, making comments such as 'That's impossible', 'Are you purposely trying to foul me up', and 'You said left, it has to be right.'

While two-way communication has many advantages, in some circumstances leaders may conclude that it is not always better than one-way communication. Leaders may opt for two-way communication when accuracy is important, they want others to have confidence they understand the issues being communicated, and time is not an issue. But one-way communication might be preferred when accurate understanding is not judged to be a critical requirement, time is limited, or the leader wants to avoid being challenged in public.

Lateral communication and performance

The quality of lateral communication can also have a powerful impact on an organization's level of performance and its ability to innovate and change. Brown and Eisenhardt (1997), Orlikowski (1996) and Tjosvold (1998) all argue that intense and open lateral communication is an essential requirement for continuous improvement. This information sharing contributes to the identification of issues and the development of new possibilities. Hargie and Tourish (2000, p. 7) assert that 'when groups work in isolation, with people sharing minimal information … the locomotive of change slows to a crawl'. They report finding that poor interdepartmental communication is linked to feelings of isolation and dissatisfaction and low levels of involvement in the decision-making process. In Hargie and Tourish's (2000, p. 7) opinion, 'poor information exchange exacerbates uncertainty, increases alienation and produces a segmented attitude to work that is inimical to the spirit of innovation'.

IV

Organizational silence and a lack of upward communication

Morrison and Milliken (2000, p. 720) argue that 'despite "knowing" that they should encourage upward communication, leaders may do just the opposite and adopt attitudes and behaviours that create a climate of silence'. They argue that many organizations are caught in an apparent paradox, in which most employees know the truth about certain issues and problems but are afraid to voice that truth to their superiors. They refer to the widespread withholding of opinions and concerns as 'organizational silence' and assert that it can be a major barrier to organizational change and development. In Chapter 4, the importance of ensuring that multiple and divergent views contribute to the decision-making process was highlighted in the context of formulating the agenda for change, but Morrison and Milliken refer to several studies (for example Moskal, 1991; Ryan and Oestreich, 1991) indicating that, in practice, employees often feel compelled to remain silent and refrain from voicing their views. The dynamics that limit upward communication and give rise to organizational silence are summarized in Figure 11.2.

According to Morrison and Milliken (2000), a climate of silence in organizations will develop when:

- Leaders fear negative feedback from subordinates and try to avoid it (see the findings from Leavitt and Mueller cited above) or, if this is not possible, dismiss it as inaccurate or attack the credibility of the source.
- Senior managers hold a particular set of implicit beliefs about employees and the nature of management that make it easy for them to ignore or dismiss feedback. These beliefs are that:
  - employees are self-interested, untrustworthy and effort averse

- management knows best and therefore subordinates should be unquestioning followers, especially since they are self-interested and effort averse and therefore unlikely to know or care about what is best for the organization
- dissent is unhealthy and should be avoided, and unity, agreement and consensus are indicators of organizational health.

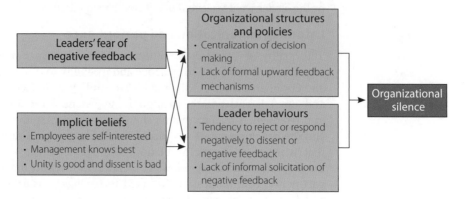

Figure **11.2** *Dynamics giving rise to organizational silence*
Source: Adapted from Morrison and Milliken, 2000

Effect of these beliefs and the fear of feedback on structures, policies and practices

Morrison and Milliken (2000) argue that in organizations where the dominant ideology reflects the belief that employees are self-interested, leaders know best and disagreement is bad, this will give rise to structures, policies and leader behaviours that create an environment that discourages upward communication. Examples of structures and policies that inhibit upward communication include:

- centralized decision-making procedures that exclude most employees
- an absence of formal feedback mechanisms for soliciting employee feedback on decisions after they have been made.

Examples of leader behaviours that have a similar effect include:

- a tendency to reject employees' concerns about a proposed change because they are viewed as 'resistance' motivated by self-interest rather than a true concern that the change may be bad for the organization (see Example 9.2, the Dutch police case)
- a general unwillingness on the part of managers to seek informal feedback from subordinates, for reasons that include those discussed above.

Morrison and Milliken (2000) point out that these barriers to upward communication can exist at many different levels in the organization. While it may only be top management that can impose company-wide structures and policies that foster organizational silence, leaders at all levels can discourage upward communication by the way they design the part of the organization they are responsible for, and by reacting negatively to unsolicited inputs from subordinates and failing to seek feedback from employees on issues that affect performance. However, even when middle managers do not share the implicit beliefs held by their superiors, top management attitudes can still encourage leaders down the line and many other supervisors to behave in ways that foster silence. For example, leaders down the line may choose to respond to senior managers' lack of openness to dissenting views by filtering out some of the information they receive from their subordinates before passing it up the organization. Their subordinates, in turn, notice this apparent disregard for their views and respond by not voicing their own concerns and those reported to them by their subordinates. In this way, the conditions that encourage a climate of silence trickle down the organization.

The implications of organizational silence

Organizational silence can compromise decision making and elicit undesirable reactions from employees. It deprives decision makers of the opportunity to consider alternative perspectives and conflicting viewpoints. Evidence shows that this can adversely affect creativity and undermine the quality of decision making. Also, blocking negative feedback can inhibit organizational learning, because it affects the ability of managers to detect and correct the causes of poor performance. Morrison and Milliken (2000) suggest that decision makers may not receive important information because employees only pass on the information they think their managers want to hear.

The damage that refusing to listen to negative feedback from subordinates can have is illustrated by what happened at HBOS, a failed UK bank (Example 11.1).

IV

Example **11.1** *Poor upward communication at HBOS*

Masters (2012) reports that long before HBOS failed, the bank had an 'us and them' culture and a dysfunctional reporting structure that made it almost impossible for risk managers to share and discuss serious risk-related issues with top managers. Paul Moore, the former head of group regulatory risk, describes how the bank's culture was threatening for members of his team. Senior executives were resistant to challenge, didn't turn up for meetings, were rude and swore at risk managers, and Moore himself was fired after he warned that the bank was taking excessive risks. Masters observed that the reporting structures made matters worse because the staff in the operational divisions who were responsible for risk reported to line managers in the business side of the bank rather than to the central risk group.

Leaders not only need to be receptive to negative feedback but also need to seek it out. It is all too easy to dismiss negative feedback as disruptive resistance to change rather than view it as potentially useful feedback.

The conditions that foster organizational silence can have destructive outcomes for employees, with knock-on effects for the organization:

- Employees may feel undervalued, which may affect their commitment and lead to lower motivation, satisfaction, psychological withdrawal or the decision to quit.
- When discouraged from speaking up, employees may feel that they lack sufficient control over their working environment. This can trigger attempts to regain some control by acting in ways that are destructive to the organization, including, in some extreme cases, engaging in sabotage.

Morrison and Milliken (2000) argue that when top management adheres to the assumptions that foster silence, it makes it difficult to respond to the diversity of values, beliefs and other characteristics that are features of pluralistic organizations. The more these differences 'pull' the organization in divergent directions, the more senior managers may 'push' against these forces because they view difference as a threat that has to be suppressed.

Role

The communication of change can also be affected by the roles organizational members occupy. The nature of an 'inter-role relationship' is important; a person might communicate certain things to a colleague that they would not communicate to an external consultant, an auditor, a member of another department, their boss, a subordinate or a customer. This issue will be discussed in more detail when the effect of trust and power on the quality of interpersonal relationships is considered.

Isolates

The requirements of a role can be an important determinant of whether the role occupant will be an 'isolate' or a 'participant' in the organization's affairs. Some roles are potentially more isolating than others: a finance officer may be better networked within the organization than a salesperson responsible for a remote territory; an employee working at a given point on an assembly line may have relatively few opportunities to communicate with others compared with somebody working in an open-plan office. Some of the interventions considered in Chapter 29 are designed to create opportunities for dialogue, sharing and the provision of feedback, which are so important in situations characterized by uncertainty and change. When planning to communicate with people about a proposed change, it is important to take account of those who occupy isolated roles. People who feel they have been neglected or excluded are more likely to be alienated than those who feel they are in a position to participate in the change.

Boundary spanners

Some members of the organization occupy 'boundary-spanning roles' that enable them to transfer information from one constituency to another. For example, people in sales, customer support and product development occupy roles that link the organization with the wider environment. Within the organization, there are also roles that straddle the boundaries between internal constituencies. The occupants of these boundary-spanning roles may have access to important information that could be used to identify emerging problems or opportunities or provide feedback on how the change is affecting different parts of the organization. MacDonald (1995) argues that critical information is often imported into organizations through informal and individual contacts and that the boundary spanners who acquire this information may not be the people who can use it as a basis for managing change. They may have to pass their information on to others who are in a better position to respond. However, these 'others' may not recognize the importance of the information or may receive a message that is different from that which the originator of the message intended to convey.

Gatekeepers

Distortion can occur because information is passed on to others by 'gatekeepers'. Gatekeepers are those who are in a position to interpret and screen information before transmitting it to others. Almost everybody in the organization is a gatekeeper to some extent, but some roles offer their occupants considerable power to control the content and timing of the information that is passed on to decision makers. Change managers need to be aware of who controls the flows of information that are important to them. One way of reducing dependence on some gatekeepers is to build an element of redundancy into the communication network by establishing additional sources of information, thereby reducing recipients' dependence on a single source (gatekeeper) who is in a position to filter or delay the onward transmission of information.

Playmakers

In Chapter 4, three different kinds of 'playmaker' roles are discussed. Pitt et al. (2002) borrowed this term from football, where it refers to the restless, energetic, midfield role that links play, energizes the team and 'makes things happen'. They argue that playmakers are the individuals who are motivated to seek out opinion from those who are close to the realities of the operating environment and pass it on to those who are in a position to formulate the change agenda.

The effect of trust on the quality of interpersonal communication

Trust can have an important effect on the quality of the information that is exchanged, especially between people who occupy different roles, for example between managers leading a change and the recipients of the change. Lines et al. (2005) argue that whether change agents gain access to the knowledge and creative thinking they need to solve problems depends largely on how much people trust them. O'Reilly and Pondy (1979) refer to studies that show that a lack of trust is associated with a tendency for senders to withhold unfavourable but relevant information while passing on favourable but irrelevant information. There is also evidence that senders are guarded in what they are prepared to share with those who are able to influence what happens to them.

Change managers often have to seek out information from others (see Chapter 8), but this is not always an easy task. Interpersonal interactions are complex social encounters in which the behaviour of each party is influenced by the other. An often-used model of information gathering presents the process solely in terms of an information seeker (change manager) getting information from respondents (organizational members). This model is an oversimplification because it fails to take full account of the interactive nature of the encounter (Figure 11.3).

Figure **11.3** *An oversimplified model of the interview*

Organizational members are aware that change managers are observing what they say and do and may be making judgements about them and their future role. Consequently, they may not openly and honestly answer all the questions they are asked. They may attempt to manage the way they respond so as to maximize their personal benefit from the interaction rather than help those leading the change achieve their purpose.

A better representation of the interaction between change managers and organizational members is illustrated in Figure 11.4. Change managers are likely to structure the situation and behave in ways they feel will best project their definition of the purpose of the encounter and the role they want to assume in the interaction. This behaviour not only says a lot about how change managers wish to be seen, but also about their evaluation of other organizational members and the role they are expected to play. Change managers attempt to influence others' interpretation of the situation and to focus their attention on those issues which they (the change managers) regard as important, and much of what takes place at this stage involves this type of cognitive scene setting.

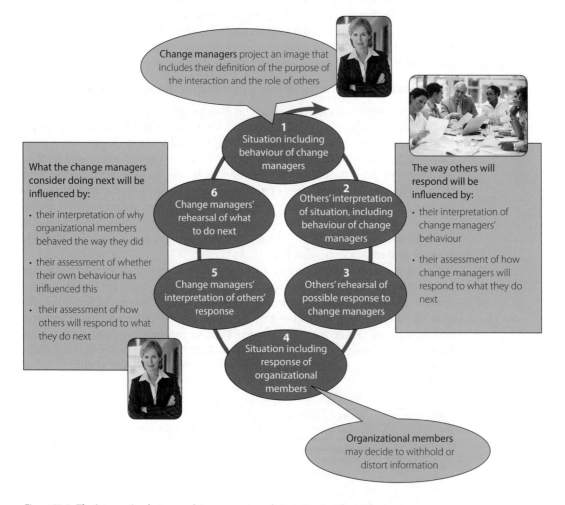

Figure **11.4** *The interaction between change agents and organizational members*

At stage 2 in Figure 11.4, organizational members seek to understand what it is that change managers are projecting and what implications this has for them. Do the change managers, for example, appear to see the encounter as an information-gathering exercise designed to provide them with the information they need to determine what has to be changed? Or do they see it as the first step towards involving organizational members in the management of the change process?

Organizational members might detect a difference between the performance change managers consciously and deliberately give, and what Mangham (1978) refers to as the information they 'give off'. Change managers may attempt to perform in a way that gives others the impression they are committed to a shared approach to managing the change; however, they may actually 'give off' verbal and nonverbal signals that contradict this intended impression. Thus, as the interaction progresses through stages 3 and 4, organizational members may decide to cooperate and give change managers the information they are seeking, or they may decide to distort or withhold information until they are more confident about the change managers' intentions.

At stage 3, organizational members have to decide, on the basis of their interpretation of the situation, how to respond to change managers. Mangham (1978) observes that people not only act but react to their own actions. They react to their own behaviour on the basis of the actual or anticipated reaction of others. They can anticipate others' reactions through a process of mental simulation or rehearsal. They can try out, in their own minds, a few pieces of behaviour and test them for fit. Mangham even suggests that they can simulate several stages into alternative futures for an interaction, a form of mental chess in which various moves and their consequences are tested.

Once organizational members have decided what to do and have responded to the change managers' initial behaviour, the situation changes. At stage 4, both parties are faced with a situation that includes the most recent behaviour of organizational members. If change managers failed to make their purpose explicit (at stage 1), organizational members may misinterpret their behaviour and act in ways that change managers either did not anticipate or feel are inappropriate to the situation.

In stage 5, change managers have to assess this situation and attempt to understand the meaning of organizational members' behaviour. Their interpretation of their response offers a basis for assessing the relevance and validity of any information communicated by them. Good interviewers/information gatherers have the ability to empathize with the other party; they can assume the other's role in the interaction, putting themselves in the other's shoes and replaying in their mind the situation faced by them. This helps them to interpret the other's behaviour, including their answers to questions. Unfortunately, this is a skill that many of those leading change have not developed, so all too often they misinterpret the significance of the other's response to their questioning.

On the basis of their interpretation of the situation, including organizational members' behaviour, change managers can rehearse in their mind possible next moves (stage 6) before deciding what to do and/or say. This then forms part of the unfolding scene to which other organizational members will have to respond, and so the process continues.

The point of this example is that factors such as mutual trust and perceptions of others' intent will influence how both parties will interpret what they see and hear. It will also influence the quantity and quality of the information that each is prepared to offer. Those leading change need to give careful thought to how others will interpret their actions, as their interpretation will not only affect what they are prepared to communicate but also how they will behave in response to information passed to them by change managers.

Content

Allen et al. (2007) argue that one reason why many organizations encounter difficulties in reducing employee uncertainty during change is because change managers often focus on providing employees with information regarding strategic issues. They acknowledge this might be important at first but argue that later in the change process, employee concerns are likely to shift to more personal and job-related issues. The consequence of failing to address personal concerns is illustrated in Example 11.2.

Example **11.2** *PCBtec*

PCBtec (as it will be referred to here) designs and manufactures printed circuit boards for customers in the automotive and aerospace industries. The company's headquarters and main manufacturing facility are located near Blois and it has a design team based in Toulouse. In 2011, the owners started merger talks with a leading supplier of components to the aerospace industry. Two weeks after the start of talks, the brother of an employee overheard two senior managers talking about the merger when he was on a train travelling from Blois to Paris.

When the employee told his workmates what his brother had overheard, rumours about the merger quickly spread and, before the end of the morning, a colleague confronted their supervisor to demand more information. This was the first she had heard about it so she sought out her manager, who was also surprised by the rumour. He rang his director and the top team quickly recognized that they had to do something about the situation. Their concern was that their automotive sector customers might be worried if they heard the rumour because they might fear that the new merged company would focus on aerospace and cease supplying automotive customers.

© PHOTODISC/GETTY IMAGES

A site-wide meeting was called for the end of the day, at which the CEO confirmed that merger talks were in progress but, as yet, nothing had been agreed. He went on to explain how important it was not to unsettle suppliers and customers and outlined how best they might respond if outsiders enquired about what was happening. The meeting focused on what they could do to help manage the company's external relationships and almost nothing was said about how a merger would affect them personally.

The meeting did little to stop the rumours because people continued to worry about how the merger would affect them. Their main concern was jobs. Everybody was worried but those who were involved in manufacturing circuit boards for automotive customers feared that this part of the business could be discontinued or sold off and they could be made redundant. They did everything they could to signal their concern but the top team failed to respond until, five months later, all staff were informed, via a short message on the company's intranet, that talks had broken down and the merger was off.

Everybody was relieved but also felt that they had been badly let down by their managers. The way top management had communicated with them about the merger had changed the psychological contract and there had been a significant shift in the company's culture. Before the rumoured merger, most employees identified with the company and believed that it was like a family that looked after its own. They were highly committed and willing to put in the effort required to ensure the company's success. Five months later, this had all changed. Most shared the view that the owners and top managers believed that employees were just hired hands who were expendable whenever things became difficult.

Not long after, the CEO announced that merger talks had been resumed and that a deal had been agreed. He asked for volunteers to join a joint task force to plan the integration of the two companies. Nobody volunteered and departmental managers had to be instructed to nominate individuals.

Managers' apparent disregard for their employees' personal interests seriously undermined their commitment to PCBtec and their motivation to support the management's change agenda. Sometimes, this kind of problem arises not because those leading a change do not care about their staff but because they are too preoccupied by other pressing issues. Developing a change communication strategy can help leaders keep track of all the communication issues they need to attend to.

Unfamiliar content

MacDonald (1995) distinguishes between internal and external information and draws attention to the importance of attending to information from outside the organization and integrating this with the information that is routinely available to organizational members in order to facilitate organizational learning. A common problem, however, is that this external information is often unfamiliar, and responding to it frequently leads to disruption and uncertainty. For example, in the case presented in Chapter 30, the European Working Time Directive was incorporated into English law in October 1998 and it was known that it would restrict the number of hours doctors could work, but little was done to accommodate the 48-hour week until it was finally imposed in 2009. It was only then that hospital managers began to realize that it would compromise the quality and continuity of care given to patients and undermine the quality of training given to junior doctors.

Organizational members tend to prefer the more familiar internal information that is easier to integrate into the mental models they use for making sense of the situation confronting them.

Perceptions of fairness and justice

The content of communications about the change can affect perceptions of fairness and justice that, in turn, will affect how stakeholders will respond to the change. For example, organizational members expect to receive adequate and accurate information in good time before decisions are implemented, thus giving them an opportunity to voice their concerns and have an input to the decision process. If they perceive that the change is being managed in a way that is unfair, this perception may have an adverse effect on their morale, organizational commitment and performance.

Colquitt et al. (2001) identify a number of ways of thinking about organizational justice, which are important to bear in mind when thinking about the content of any communications about the change:

- *Distributive justice:* the equity of outcomes.

IV

- *Procedural justice:* fair process. After studying dispute resolution procedures, Thibaut and Walker (1975) found that disputants were more prepared to give up control of the decision about outcomes if they had had sufficient control over the process used to reach the decision, especially over the presentation of their arguments and the time they had to present their case.
- *Informational justice:* the explanations provided to people that convey information about why particular procedures were used or why the outcomes were distributed in a particular fashion. The discussion of realistic merger previews in Chapter 25 provides a useful insight into how the provision of information affects the way people respond to change.
- *Interpersonal justice:* how people are treated by those executing procedures or determining outcomes. Greenberg (1990) studied how people reacted to a pay cut and found that when employees were treated with dignity by managers who were sensitive to how the changes would affect them, and when managers explained and justified the changes and demonstrated that they were being applied consistently and without bias, they reacted better than employees who were not treated in this way.

Greenberg (1990) investigated the effect of adequate explanations on perceptions of inequity by observing employee theft rates and labour turnover when rates of pay were temporarily cut by 15 per cent. His findings suggest that paying careful attention to the way the content of a communication is presented can have a powerful effect on perceptions of fairness and justice, which in turn affects how employees respond (Research report 11.1).

Research report 11.1 *Communicating bad news*

Greenberg, J. (1990) Employee theft as a reaction to underpayment inequity: The hidden cost of pay cuts, *Journal of Applied Psychology*, 75(5): 561–8.

Participants in the study were employees working for 30 consecutive weeks in three manufacturing plants owned by the same parent company. Following the loss of two large manufacturing contracts, two of the three plants lost work and the company responded by cutting wages. The third plant was unaffected and wage rates remained unchanged.

- In plant A (the adequate explanation condition), employees were called to a meeting and informed by the company president that their pay was going to be cut by 15 per cent for a period expected to last 10 weeks. They were told that management seriously regretted the need to reduce their pay, but they were taking this action to avoid layoffs, and all plant employees, including managers, would share in the pay cuts. The reasons for the decision were carefully explained and information about cash flows was shared to reassure everybody that the need for pay

cuts was only temporary. The meeting lasted 90 minutes and most of the time was given over to answering questions.

- In plant B (the inadequate explanation condition), the meeting lasted 15 minutes. Employees were informed about the pay cut, that it was expected to last for 10 weeks and was being imposed because of the loss of contracts. There was no expression of apology or remorse and the basis for the decision was not clearly described.
- In plant C (the control condition), the loss of the contracts had no effect and rates of pay remained unchanged.

Following the pay cuts in plant B, where the explanation had been inadequate, pilfering increased threefold compared to levels of pilfering in the control plant. In plant A, where a full and sensitive explanation had been provided, thefts also increased, but not as much as in plant B. There were, however, significant differences in turnover rates. In plant B, turnover was 23 per cent, whereas in plants A and C, it was 5 per cent or less.

Equity theory posits that motivation is correlated with an individual's perception of equity and fairness, and the data in this study support the theory's predictions regarding likely responses to underpayment and demonstrate the mitigating effects of adequate explanations on feelings of inequity.

Channel

Information and meaning can be communicated in many different ways: written communication via hard copy, electronic communication via email, texts, tweets and blogs, videoconferencing, telephone, face-to-face communication on a one-to-one, one-to-group or group-to-group basis and so on. O'Reilly and Pondy (1979) suggest that written communication may be effective when the sender and receiver have different vocabularies or problem orientations, because it gives them more time to study and understand the message, and oral communication may be most effective when there is a need to exchange views, seek feedback, and provide an immediate opportunity for clarification. They note, however, that while organization members may prefer certain channels, and certain forms of communication may have clear advantages in specific circumstances, external factors may limit the freedom to select a particular channel. For example, distance may prohibit face-to-face interaction, budget constraints may demand the use of written communication rather than videoconferencing, and time constraints may rule out the use of lengthy meetings. Clampitt et al. (2000) echo this efficiency/effectiveness dilemma. They note that while it may be more *efficient* to send an email to all employees outlining a major change, it may not be the most *effective* way to create employee buy-in. They argue that face-to-face communication is a more persuasive channel because it provides a dynamic and effective way of dealing with people's concerns. However, face-to-face communication costs the organization more in terms of time and energy than a lean medium like email.

IV

Communication strategies

These features of communication networks such as directionality and content provide a useful backdrop for comparing the advantages and disadvantages of various communication strategies. On the basis of their experience in several organizations and a review of the literature, Clampitt et al. (2000) identified five basic strategies. Sometimes, the communication strategy in any particular setting closely resembles one of these, but sometimes it is a hybrid and includes a blend of elements from more than one. The five basic strategies are:

1 *Spray and pray:* Clampitt et al. (2000) use this term to describe a communication strategy that involves showering employees with all kinds of information in the hope they will feel informed and have access to all the information they require. It is based on the assumption that more information equals better communication, which in turn contributes to improved decision making. It is also based on an implicit assumption that all organizational members are able to differentiate between what is significant and what is insignificant. In practice, some employees may only attend to the information related to their own

personal agendas, while others may be overwhelmed by the amount of information they are confronted with – they cannot see the wood for the trees.

2 *Tell and sell:* This involves change managers communicating a more limited set of messages they believe address the core issues related to the proposed change. First, they tell employees about these key issues and then sell them the wisdom of their approach to managing them. Clampitt et al. (2000) observe that change managers who adopt this kind of strategy often spend a great deal of time planning sophisticated presentations but devote little time and energy to fostering meaningful dialogue and providing organizational members with the opportunity to discuss their concerns. They also assume that they (the change managers) possess much of the information they need and tend to place little value on input from others.

3 *Underscore and explore:* Like the 'tell and sell' approach, this involves focusing attention on a limited set of fundamental issues linked to the change but, unlike that approach, change managers give others the creative freedom they need to explore the implications of these issues. Those who adopt this approach are concerned not only with developing a few core messages but also with listening attentively for potential misunderstandings and unrecognized obstacles.

4 *Identify and reply:* This strategy is different from the first three, in that the primary focus is organizational members' concerns. It is a reactive approach that involves a lot of listening in order to identify and then respond to these concerns. It is essentially directed towards helping employees make sense out of the often confusing organizational environment, but it is also attentive to their concerns because it is assumed that organizational members are in the best position to know what the critical issues are. However, this may not always be the case. Clampitt et al. (2000) suggest that often they may not know enough to even ask the right questions.

5 *Withhold and uphold:* This involves withholding information until necessary. When confronted by rumours, change managers uphold the party line. There may well be special circumstances where commercial or other considerations require information to be shared on a need-to-know basis but there are also change managers whose implicit values are secrecy and control whatever the circumstances. Some of those who adopt this strategy assume that information is power and they are reluctant to share it with anyone. Others assume that most organizational members are not sophisticated enough to grasp the big picture.

The 'spray and pray' strategy provides employees with all the information they could possibly desire, while the 'withhold and uphold' strategy provides the absolute minimum information. Both strategies can make it difficult for employees to frame and make sense of the intended change and its consequences. The other three strategies pay more attention to prioritizing and managing content to provide guidance for those involved in the change and, to varying degrees, attend to employee concerns. Clampitt et al. (2000) argue that, in most cases, the 'spray and pray' and 'withhold and uphold' strategies are the least effective and the most effective is 'underscore and explore'. This is because it incorporates elements of the 'tell and sell' strategy and allows change managers to shape the change agenda, and it also incorporates aspects of the 'identify and reply' strategy that responds to employees' concerns.

Auditing the effectiveness of the communication strategy

Hargie and Tourish (2000) recommend the regular auditing of communications. This requires those leading the change to have a clear idea about their communication objectives in order to assess the extent to which they are being achieved. Some of the questions they might need to ask are:

• Who is communicating with whom?
• What issues are they talking about?
• Which issues receive most attention and arouse most anxiety?
• Do people receive all the information they require?
• Do people understand and use the information they receive?
• Do people trust and have confidence in the information they receive?
• From what sources do people prefer to get their information?
• Which channels are most effective?

Often, the discussion of change communication tends to focus exclusively on the 'what, when, who and how' of communication from the perspective of the change manager communicating to others, but it is important to note, as discussed earlier in this chapter, that there are also issues associated with how change managers perceive, interpret and use information provided by others.

There are no magic formulae about the 'what, when, who and how' of communication that can provide ready answers for all situations. In some circumstances, change agents may advocate a policy of complete openness about all issues to everybody as soon as possible. In other circumstances, information might be highly restricted because it is deemed to be commercially sensitive, or it might be decided that information should not be widely shared until after certain high-level decisions have been made. Counterarguments might focus on the difficulty of keeping the need for change secret and the importance of not losing control of communications to the informal grapevine. The five strategies, considered above, highlight some of the options available to change managers. What is important is that adequate attention is given to ensuring that all relevant information is sought and attended to by change managers, and that they pay careful attention to the information they need to communicate to others. When Maersk Line, the largest container shipping company in the world, launched a major change programme to make the organization more customer centric (see Example 26.1), those leading the change used a detailed stakeholder analysis to develop a communication plan for all major stakeholder groups. The plan specified responsible parties, the information to be communicated, and the timing of communications. Stakeholder analysis and change tools such as the stakeholder grid are discussed in Chapter 10.

✓ Exercise 11.1 *Assessing the quality of communications*

Think about a recent attempt to introduce and manage change at work, in your university department or elsewhere and reflect on how the quality of communication helped or hindered the change process:

• Did those leading the change communicate effectively to all those involved in or affected by the change?
• If not, to what extent was this related to the factors discussed in this chapter, such as directionality, role, content and channel?

IV

- What do you think the change manager(s) could have done differently that might have improved the quality of communications?

Case study 11.2 provides an opportunity for you to explore the relevance of the ideas discussed in this chapter.

Case study **11.2** *Galaxy*

Galaxy, as it will be referred to here, is a German company producing a wide range of heating, air-conditioning, refrigeration, cooking and laundry appliances for home and commercial use. Most of its 30,000 employees are located in the older EU states and the company has an annual turnover of €40 billion. Galaxy has always been focused on making a good return on investments and growing shareholder value and has pursued this goal by prioritizing product innovation, investment in new technology, and developing the capability of its staff.

Galaxy has managed to maintain the competitive position of its European manufacturing facilities in the face of growing competition from companies manufacturing in low-cost countries. However, two years ago, the board recognized that this competitive position could not be sustained and that eventually much of its manufacturing capacity would have to be moved to cheaper locations.

Galaxy already has manufacturing facilities in India and China but these were built to produce a new range of products and did not involve the relocation of work from existing plants in Europe. Over the next four years, this situation will change. The company plans to close seven plants in Germany, France, Denmark, Italy and the UK, with the loss of 12,000 jobs, and expand production elsewhere in the world.

The first closure will involve a German plant that produces refrigeration equipment. A new

manufacturing facility has been acquired in China and within nine months it will be ready to commence production of a limited range of high-volume products that have few parts and are relatively easy to assemble. As the capability of the Chinese workforce is developed, the full range of products manufactured at the German plant will be relocated, but it will be two years before all production, including the more complex, high-value products, can be moved. Consequently, while some staff will be laid off in nine months, others will need to be retained for up to two years.

Sixty-five per cent of the output of the plant targeted for closure is sold within Germany but the company estimates that the reduction in production costs associated with the move to China will more than outweigh the cost of transporting the refrigeration equipment back to the German market. One concern, however, is how customers will react to the company moving jobs abroad. Employees were shocked by the news that their plant is to be closed and are planning to do everything they can to resist the closure. Employees elsewhere in the company are aware that more plants are likely to be closed.

Imagine that you have been asked to advise Galaxy about how to manage the closure of the refrigeration plant in Germany:

- What are the communication issues?
- How do you think they should be addressed?

Summary

The quality of communications can have an important impact on the success or otherwise of a change programme. It can, for example, affect whether the need for change is recognized in good time and can have a major impact on the quality of collective learning. This chapter has considered the features of communication networks that relate to the management of change, reviewed a number of communication strategies, explored some of the factors that can deprive change managers of access to vital information, discussed the effect of interpersonal relations on the quality of communication, and considered how change communication can affect perceptions of fairness and justice.

Four features of communication networks have been considered:

1 *Directionality:*
  - The management of change is often experienced as a top-down process, with those responsible for managing the change informing others lower down the organization about the need for change, what is going to happen, and what is required of them.
  - Effective change communication calls for a stream of upward communication that provides change managers with the information they require in order to clarify the need for change, and develop and implement a change programme.

2 *Role:*
  - The nature of what is communicated can be affected by the roles that organizational members occupy.
  - The nature of an inter-role relationship is important; a person might communicate certain things to a colleague they would not communicate to an external consultant, an auditor, a member of another department, their boss, a subordinate or a customer.

3 *Content:*
  - It is important to give careful consideration to the potential relevance of information that at first sight may appear to be of little consequence. MacDonald (1995) distinguishes between internal and external information and draws attention to the importance of attending to information from outside the organization and integrating this with the information that is routinely available to organizational members in order to facilitate organizational learning.
  - It is also important to pay attention to issues of fairness and justice when deciding what to communicate.

4 *Channel:*
  - Information and meaning can be communicated in many different ways. It is important to select a channel that is fit for purpose.

IV

The chapter also discussed the need for those leading change to continuously monitor and review the effectiveness of their approach to communicating change.

References

Allen, J., Jimmieson, N.L., Bordia, P. and Irmer, B.E. (2007) Uncertainty during organizational change: Managing perceptions through communication, *Journal of Change Management*, 7(2): 187–210.

Beer, M. (2001) How to develop an organization capable of sustained high performance: Embrace the drive for results-capability development paradox, *Organizational Dynamics*, 29(4): 233–47.

Brown, S.L. and Eisenhardt, K.M. (1997) The art of continuous change: Linking complexity theory and time-paced evolution in relentlessly shifting organizations, *Administrative Science Quarterly*, 42(1): 1–34.

Clampitt, P.G., DeKoch, R.J. and Cashman, T. (2000) A strategy for communicating about uncertainty, *Academy of Management Executive*, 14(4): 41–57.

Colquitt, J.A., Conlon, D.E., Wesson, M.J. et al. (2001) Justice at the millennium: A meta-analytic review of 25 years of organizational justice research, *Journal of Applied Psychology*, 86(3): 425–45.

Greenberg, J. (1990) Employee theft as a reaction to underpayment inequity: The hidden cost of pay cuts, *Journal of Applied Psychology*, 75(5): 561–8.

Hargie, O. and Tourish, D. (2000) *Handbook of Communication Audits for Organisations*. London: Routledge.

Kotter, J.P. (1995) Leading change: Why transformation efforts fail, *Harvard Business Review*, 73(2): 59–67.

Leavitt, H.J. and Mueller, R.A.H. (1951) Some effects of feedback on communication, *Human Relations*, 4: 401–10.

Lines, R., Selart, M., Espedal, B. and Johansen, S.T. (2005) The production of trust during organizational change, *Journal of Change Management*, 5(2): 221–45.

MacDonald, S. (1995) Learning to change: An information perspective on learning in the organization, *Organizational Science*, 6(5): 557–68.

Mangham, I.L. (1978) *Interactions and Interventions in Organizations*. Chichester: Wiley.

Masters, B. (2012) HBOS had 'threatening' culture, says ex-head of risk, *Financial Times*, 30 October.

Morrison, E.W. and Milliken, F.J. (2000) Organizational silence: A barrier to change and development in a pluralistic world, *Academy of Management Review*, 25(4): 706–25.

Moskal, B.M. (1991) Is industry ready for adult relationships?, *Industry Week*, 24(4): 18–25.

O'Reilly, C.A. and Pondy, L.R. (1979) Organizational communication. In S. Kerr (ed.) *Organizational Behavior*. Columbus, OH: Grid Publications.

Orlikowski, W.J. (1996) Improvising organisational transformation over time: A sustained change perspective, *Information Systems Research*, 7(1): 63–92.

Pitt, M., McAulay, L. and Sims, D. (2002) Promoting strategic change: 'Playmaker' roles in organizational agenda formulation, *Strategic Change*, 11(3): 155–72.

Ryan, K.D. and Oestreich, D.K. (1991) *Driving Fear out of the Workplace: How to Overcome the Invisible Barriers to Quality, Productivity and Innovation*. San Francisco, CA: Jossey-Bass.

Thibaut, J. and Walker, L. (1975) *Procedural Justice: A Psychological Analysis*. Hillsdale, NJ: Erlbaum.

Tjosvold, D. (1998) *Team Organization: An Enduring Competitive Advantage*. New York: John Wiley.

Chapter 12

Motivating others to change

A key challenge for leaders is motivating others to support change, and as we saw in Chapter 11, the way the change is communicated can have a large impact on this. Choi (2011) observes that change will only be successful and persist over time when individuals alter their on-the-job behaviours in ways that support the change. He argues that employees have to be at the centre of organizational change but asserts that change efforts often fail because those leading the process pay insufficient attention to winning the support of those who can affect the outcome of the change.

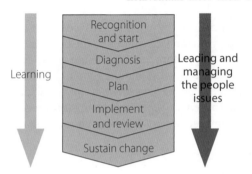

It was noted in Chapter 7 that organizations, like all open systems, seek to maintain a state of equilibrium; they tend to gravitate to a condition where all the component parts of the system are aligned with each other. Intentionally intervening to change the organization by modifying one or more components of the system can disturb this state of equilibrium and create pressure to restore it. Restoration can be achieved by either realigning other components with those that have been changed, or resisting the change and seeking to re-establish the status quo. When organizational members are one of the components that has been changed and they feel that the change, for example to reporting relationships, tasks, technologies, performance evaluation criteria or headcount, is disturbing the status quo in a way that disadvantages them, they will be motivated to resist the change and maintain or restore the status quo.

Those leading the change need to do whatever they can to win the support of change recipients. This may not be too difficult when they can point to either the benefits that will follow successful implementation of the change or a significant loss of benefits following no change, but just because leaders anticipate this pattern of costs and benefits does not mean that those who will be affected by the change will share this assessment. Motivating others to support change when those affected are unlikely to enjoy any benefit is much more difficult. There may be scope for working together to discover alternative ways forward, finding ways of minimizing the losses that seem inevitable, or providing support for those who feel they will lose out.

This chapter will:

- Consider some of the factors that can influence whether or not individuals and groups will support change.

- Explore the benefit of viewing resistance as valuable feedback rather than an unwelcome threat that has to be managed.
- Review some of the steps that change leaders can take to motivate others to change.
- Draw on expectancy and equity theories to provide a change tool that leaders can use to help them achieve this.

Organizational commitment and support for change

Several studies have found that employees who are committed to their organization are willing to exert effort on its behalf and are more accepting of the need for change (Oreg et al., 2011). Begley and Czajka (1993) also found that organizational commitment can serve as a buffer, dampening the detrimental effects of change-related stress. Furthermore, organizational members' past experience of change can affect their level of commitment to the organization and their willingness to support further change.

Over 50 years ago, Argyris (1960) first defined the 'psychological contract' as the perceptions of both parties to the employment relationship and the obligations of each which are implied in this relationship. More recently, Guest et al. (1996) referred to it in terms of perceptions of fairness, trust and the extent to which the 'deal' is perceived to have been delivered. It is an unwritten set of expectations between all organization members and those who represent the organization, and incorporates concepts such as fairness and reciprocity. For example, organizations may expect employees to:

- be loyal
- keep trade secrets
- work hard and do their best for the organization.

In return, employees may expect that they will:

- receive an equitable level of remuneration
- be treated fairly and with dignity
- have some level of security of employment
- have some level of autonomy
- have an opportunity to learn and develop.

If employees feel that their managers have kept their side of the psychological contract, they are likely to respond by displaying a high level of commitment to the organization. If, on the other hand, they feel that the organization has failed to keep its side of the bargain, they may respond by redefining their side of the psychological contract. They may invest less effort in their work, be less inclined to innovate, and less inclined to respond to the innovations or changes proposed by others.

☑ *Exercise* **12.1** *Violations of the psychological contract*

Think of an incident at work or university when the organization/management fell short of what might have been reasonably expected of them in their treatment of you or another individual or group of employees/students.

In the space below, list any effects this incident had on the level of commitment of those who felt they had been let down.

You might also consider the effect on others. People observe how colleagues are treated and this affects their views about how they may be treated in the future if they are involved in some kind of change. Note, in the space below, any 'ripple effect' this incident had on the commitment of others and their willingness to support change.

IV

Managers often expect that those who have been retained after a programme of redundancies will be relieved and grateful and will respond with higher levels of commitment and performance. Research on survivor syndrome and perceptions of fair treatment (see Doherty and Horsted, 1995) suggests that this may not be the case. Survivors may respond in a number of ways, ranging from shock, anger, animosity towards management, guilt, concern for those gone, anxiety, fear of losing their job in the future, or to relief they still have a job. Some research (Sahdev, 2004, cited in Chapter 10) also suggests that if survivors feel that leavers have been treated too generously relative to their own situation, they may feel that they have been treated unfairly and this can have an adverse effect on their motivation and commitment.

The PCBtec example (Example 11.2) illustrates how easily managers can, sometimes unintentionally, damage the psychological contract.

Commitment to a job and the willingness to support change

While there is evidence that employees who are committed to their organizations are more likely to support change than those who are not, the situation is complicated when employees are also committed to (and satisfied with) their job. Van Dam (2005) found that employees who reported high job satisfaction were more reluctant to change than those who were less satisfied. This reluctance might be because they do not want to do anything that could threaten the benefits their job provides.

What leaders see as resistance others might interpret as support

People react to change in different ways. Dialectical theories focus on the conflicting goals of different parties that result in one challenging another's attempt to secure a particular outcome. Sometimes, these challenges are powerful enough to block or radically transform the change. Often, however, a change proposal might be challenged because one party sees problems that another has missed or because they anticipate that the change will not deliver sufficient benefit to justify the costs involved. This kind of challenge might not be intended to derail the change. In Chapter 9, reference is made to a sequential and reciprocal cycle of sense making and sense giving that is triggered when leaders communicate their vision of a better future. Recipients of the leader's message engage in their own sense making, digesting and interpreting what they have heard and anticipating the implications of the leader's new vision for themselves, their unit or the organization. They then offer feedback to their leaders. This can be in the form of a request for further clarification, a bid to modify and shape the leader's original vision, or even to challenge their proposition that there is a need for a new vision in the first place. Those giving this kind of feedback may see themselves as making well-intentioned contributions to the proposed change rather than opposing the new initiative for personal advantage.

Problems can arise, however, when leaders too quickly interpret this kind of feedback as negative resistance and a threat that has to be managed. As noted in Chapter 11, responding negatively to feedback from others can undermine their morale, damage organizational commitment, and erode their support for the change. Ford and Ford (2010), while not denying that some reactions to change can be detrimental, argue that much of what might be perceived as resistance can have functional value and should be viewed as feedback. For example, when leaders genuinely encourage feedback on their vision, there is a good chance that the vision that eventually emerges will be more robust and fit for purpose.

Factors that can undermine support for change

Kotter and Schlesinger (1979) identify four main reasons why organizational members might attempt to modify or resist a proposal for change. These are lack of trust, low tolerance for change, different assessments of the need for and consequences of the change, and parochial self-interest.

Low trust

Misunderstandings can be a frequent source of resistance. Stakeholders often resist change because they do not understand the implications it may have for them. Such misunderstandings may lead them to perceive that the change will cost them more than they will gain and are most likely to arise when trust is lacking between change leaders and the stakeholders who feel that they will be affected by the change. Lines et al. (2005) note that several studies have linked trust to levels of openness in communication and information sharing, levels of conflict, and the acceptance of decisions or goals. When organizational members do not trust change managers, they are likely to resist any change they propose.

Managers and change agents often fail to anticipate this kind of resistance, especially when they are introducing a change they perceive will be of benefit to those involved. A consultant was asked by the CEO of a chemical company to investigate why the workforce had rejected a productivity agreement that senior management believed offered considerable advantage to the organization and the process workers. It turned out that the message that had been communicated to the workforce was, in some important respects, different to the proposal the senior management team had agreed to make (see Chapter 11 on communication problems). These differences had arisen as the proposal had been passed down the management chain. However, this communication problem had been compounded by the fact that the process workers felt that the offer was too good to be true and that management was intent on manipulating them in some way.

Low tolerance for change

Stakeholders also resist change when they are concerned they will not be able to develop the new skills and behaviours that will be required of them. All people are limited in their ability to change, but some are more limited than others. Even when those affected by a change understand the need for it, they may be emotionally unable to make the transition. Perceived loss can affect people in different ways but often involves some element of denial and a reluctance to 'let go'.

Different assessments

Kotter and Schlesinger (1979) suggest that another common reason why some stakeholders resist change is that they assess the situation differently from those initiating the change and see more costs than benefits resulting from it, not only for themselves but also for the organization or other constituencies that are important to them. Kotter and Schlesinger argue that managers who initiate change sometimes assume that they have all the relevant information required to conduct an adequate organization analysis and that those who will be affected by the change have the same facts. Often, neither assumption is correct. Also, those initiating change often fail to take account of how the change might affect stakeholders who are not organizational members. External stakeholders can be an important source of resistance. This problem was discussed in Chapter 10.

Furthermore, Zaltman and Duncan (1977) point to how selective attention and retention can prevent individuals or groups appreciating that the current state of affairs is unsatisfactory. The mental models that influence how they perceive, interpret and make sense of their environment can have a strong effect on how organizational members assess their circumstances and whether or not they perceive any problems. The mental models that guide their sense making can also affect the kind of solution they will favour if a problem is perceived to exist. It is not unusual for resistance to occur, even when organizational members and their managers have a shared view of the nature of a problem, because both parties have conflicting views about what should be done to resolve it.

Parochial self-interest

People resist change when they think it will cause them to lose something of value. It is not uncommon for stakeholders to focus on their own best interests rather than those of the organization. Indeed, Pugh (1993) suggests that, all too often, managers fail to anticipate resistance because they only consider change from a rational resource allocation perspective and fail to appreciate that many organizational members are much more concerned about the impact it will have on them personally.

Oreg et al. (2011) cite a number of studies that suggest that a key determinant of resistance to change is the extent to which potential change recipients perceive the change as personally beneficial or harmful. What can happen when a change is seen to offer little personal benefit is illustrated in Example 12.1.

● *Example* **12.1** *Legal templates*

Recent times have been difficult for many small and medium-sized law firms, especially those specializing in commercial law. The recession, an associated slowdown in mergers and acquisitions, a trend towards companies using more in-house lawyers, and competition from other providers, such as auditors, who are offering services that used to be the exclusive preserve of law firms, have combined to depress turnover and squeeze margins.

One firm responded to this slowdown by initiating merger talks with two similar-sized practices. The first merger was completed in late 2011 and the second in 2012. They created a new practice, referred to here as SBP, with 36 partners, 179 lawyers and 150 administrative staff and trainees. Like many law firms, the partners each led their own individual unit with two or more lawyers working with them.

The managing partners of SBP agreed that they needed to search for ways of reducing costs and winning more business. While working on a long-term plan to develop a new business model, they pursued a more immediate initiative to improve effectiveness by sharing knowledge and best practice across the firm. They recognized that, following the mergers, the new partnership had a wealth of knowledge that could be drawn on to improve the quality of the legal products and services they provided. The first target for change was the document templates that partners and their associates used. The plan was for each lawyer to review the templates they used, identify those that might be of value to colleagues, and upload them to a new knowledge database that would be available to all.

To begin with the plan was implemented as intended but, after the good start, the managing ▶

partners turned their attention elsewhere. Once the lawyers sensed that the pressure was off, the flow of new templates began to slow and eventually stopped altogether. The problem was their motivation. Reviewing their documents, identifying templates that might be useful to others and uploading them to the new database were time-consuming activities, and the time allocated to this work was not recognized as billable hours, the key performance measure used by the firm. The problem was further exacerbated by the firm's informal culture of intergroup competition, which was based on the prestige of the work the lawyers did for clients. This competition undermined the incentive for partners and their associated lawyers to share with others any information that could help them secure the most prestigious work.

From the perspective of the managing partners, their plan for change promised benefits for the whole firm, but from the perspective of individual lawyers, the change involved cost and little, if any, personal benefit.

IV

This personal impact can take many forms. It might include how the change will affect ways of working, job opportunities, career prospects, job satisfaction and so on, and how it might undermine or enhance an individual's power and status, and the prestige of the groups to which they belong.

Zaltman and Duncan (1977) view threats to power and influence as one of the most important sources of resistance to change. They observe that the prospect of a merger often gives rise to fears on the part of individuals, groups and even entire organizations that they will lose control over decision making. They also note that managers, even senior managers, may resist the use of certain approaches to the management of change if they feel that these may undermine their power and authority. They illustrate this with an example of head teachers who were resistant to the use of a survey feedback approach to organization development because it enabled teachers and district-level personnel to have access to data and use them to propose solutions to problems. Some head teachers were concerned that this approach would increase the power of teachers and undermine their own power to influence how the schools were managed.

Resistance and the need to motivate people to change

Change leaders can act in a number of ways to minimize resistance and increase the motivation of change recipients to support the change. We discuss some of these below.

Education and persuasion

One of the most frequently used ways of minimizing resistance is to present rational arguments and technical evidence to educate people about the need for change. Zaltman and Duncan (1977) refer to 'educative' strategies as those that provide a relatively unbiased presentation of the facts in order to provide a rational justification for action. This approach is based on the assumption that organizational members and other stakeholders are rational beings capable of discerning fact and adjusting their behaviour accordingly when the facts are presented to them.

A related approach is to persuade people to change by appealing to their emotions, presenting passionate arguments, and biasing the message to increase its appeal (see the reference to downward-facing evangelistic managers in Chapter 5). Most advertising is persuasive in nature. When the level of commitment to change is low, persuasive approaches are likely to be more effective than rational educative strategies. Persuasive approaches can increase commitment by stressing (realistically or falsely) either the benefits of changing or the costs of not changing. The way a persuasive argument is framed is important. Thaler and Sunstein (2009, p. 36) argue that people are more likely to be persuaded to change if attention is focused on what they will lose by not changing rather than on what they will gain if they do change. This is because people are loss averse: 'Roughly speaking, losing something makes you twice as miserable as gaining the same thing makes you happy.' However, if a persuasive message is so false/biased as to deceive the change target, the approach is better classified as manipulative (see below).

Nadler (1993) builds on Lewin's notion of 'unfreezing' (discussed in Chapter 2) and argues that one of the most effective ways of motivating people to change is to expose or create a feeling of dissatisfaction with the current state. This can be accomplished via education or persuasion, but if change recipients feel they are being blamed, they may react defensively and try to save face by justifying their current work practices and denying the need to change. A more effective approach is to avoid apportioning blame, while pointing to the potential losses if alternative practices are not adopted and/or highlighting the benefits that will flow from the adoption of alternative practices.

Involvement

Nadler (1993) argues that another effective way of surfacing and creating dissatisfaction with the current state and motivating people to change (unfreezing) is to involve them in the collection, analysis and presentation of information. Information that people collect for themselves is more believable than information presented to them by external experts or other advocates of change.

A potential benefit of participation and involvement is that it can excite, motivate and help to create a shared perception of the need for change within a target group. When change is imposed, the change target is likely to experience a lack of control and feel the 'victim' of change. The more people are involved, the more likely they are to feel that the change is something they are helping to create. In addition to increasing motivation, participation and involvement can also produce better decisions because of the wider input and can help to sustain the change once implemented because of a greater sense of ownership.

The classic study by Coch and French (1948) demonstrated that workers are much more accepting of a change in work practices when they are involved in the planning of the change (Research report 12.1).

Q Research report **12.1** *Effect of group participation on resistance to change*

Coch, L. and French, J.R. (1948) Overcoming resistance to change, *Human Relations*, 1(4): 512–32.

Coch and French designed one of the first experiments to explore the effect of group participation on resistance to change. They observed, in the Harwood Manufacturing Company, that changing people's jobs and rates of pay often led to drops in performance and higher levels of grievances, aggression and labour turnover.

They examined the effect of two different ways of including workers in the design of the change. The first involved participation through representation and the second involved the participation of the whole group. The effects of these two methods were compared with the outcome of the normal procedure for introducing change.

The normal way of introducing change was for management to define the new job and then set the new rate of pay before calling a meeting to inform the workers why the change was necessary (a response to competitive pressures) and what it would involve. Questions were answered before the meeting was closed.

The first experimental treatment (participation through representation) involved a group meeting with all operators before any changes had been designed. Managers explained the need for change and encouraged discussion before proposing a six-stage process that involved studying the job as it was being done, eliminating all unnecessary work, training representative operators in the new methods, setting the new piece rates using time studies of these operators, explaining the new job and pay rates to all operators and, finally, involving the representatives in training all the other operators. Coch and French report that this approach was successful and that the representatives referred to 'our job' and 'our rate'. The second experimental treatment was applied to two groups. It was similar to the first but involved all operators rather than just representatives.

Results

There was little improvement in the performance of the control group, where change had been introduced in the normal way, and resistance to the change developed almost immediately. However, there was significant improvement in the performance of both experimental groups – participation through representation and participation of the whole group – and the changes were introduced without any significant resistance. The rate of performance improvement was higher when all operators participated in designing the change.

Coch and French conducted a second experiment 10 weeks after the control group involved in the first experiment had been dispersed to other jobs in the company. The members of the original group were brought together again and transferred to a new job using the total participation procedure – no reference was made to their previous behaviour on being transferred. The results were in sharp contrast to the results when they had been moved to new work using the company's normal procedure. Performance improved and there was no resistance.

The first set of experiments indicated that:

- performance improvement was directly proportional to the amount of participation
- the rate of turnover and aggression was inversely proportional to the amount of participation.

The second experiment with members of the original control group suggested that the results depended on the experimental treatment (amount of participation) rather than personality factors or differences in skill level.

IV

Coch and French's findings suggested that participation led to the acceptance of new practices because it encouraged the group to 'own' them as a group goal. This ownership offered the bonus of new group norms that helped to implement and sustain the changes.

Lines (2004) conducted a study of change management in a national telecommunications firm that also demonstrates a link between participation and the acceptance of change. The findings indicated a strong positive relationship between participation, goal achievement and organizational commitment and a strong negative relationship between participation and resistance.

Involvement can be encouraged at any stage of the change process and can include all of a target group or only a representative sample. Organizational members might be invited to participate in the initial diagnosis of the problem, the development of solutions and the planning of implementation strategies, in the actual implementation of the change plan and/or in the evaluation of the effectiveness of the change. Some of these possibilities will be discussed in more detail in Chapter 24 when different types of intervention are considered.

Some managers have an ideological commitment to participation and involvement, whereas others feel that it threatens their power and authority and is almost always a mistake. Kotter and Schlesinger (1979) maintain that both attitudes can lead to problems because neither is realistic. They argue that where change initiators do not have all the information they need to design and implement a change, or when they need the wholehearted commitment of the change target, involving others can make good sense. However, involvement does have some costs. It can be time-consuming and, if those who are involved have less technical expertise than those leading the change, it can result in a change plan that is not as good as it might have been. Factors that can affect the decision to involve others are discussed in Chapter 15.

Facilitation and support

Kotter and Schlesinger (1979) suggest that when fear and anxiety lie at the heart of resistance, an effective approach to motivating change is to offer facilitation and support. They suggest that this might involve the provision of training in new skills, giving time off after a demanding period, or simply listening and providing emotional support.

Nadler (1993) refers to the need to provide time and opportunity for people to disengage from the current state. This can be especially helpful when they feel a sense of loss associated with the letting go of something they value or feel is an important part of their individual or group identity. He also refers to the value of group sessions that provide organizational members with the opportunity to share their concerns about the change. However, he acknowledges the possibility that such sessions might also have the effect of increasing rather than reducing resistance by, for example, becoming an opportunity to simply air grievances.

Ceremonies and rituals that mark transitions can also help people to let go of the past and begin to think constructively about the future. When staff had to transfer to new roles following the closure of an old generating plant at a large UK power station, they made a coffin that they paraded around the plant before burning it in the furnace. After work, they all went out for a meal together to talk about old times. It was a bit like a funeral followed by a wake. Rituals can help people manage the sense of loss that is often associated with change. They can also be used to symbolize the need for change. Bridges (1993) advocates that managers shouldn't just talk about what is wrong with the current situation and why it has to end, they should create actions to dramatize the need for change. Example 12.2 illustrates this point.

● *Example* **12.2** *Actions can speak louder than words*

When René McPherson was appointed CEO at the Dana Corporation, he found that the organization was choked with rules. There were rules for everything and there were so many rule books and manuals that often employees couldn't find the rules that applied to a particular circumstance. His priority was to change the culture of the organization and introduce a few universal principles that would empower employees to work more effectively.

Bridges (1993) describes how he chose action rather than words to convey his point. At the start of a management meeting, he piled all the rule books and manuals into a stack more than 60 cm high and swept them onto the floor and then held up a single sheet of paper on which he had typed all the new corporate principles.

The provision of emotional support can be particularly effective in circumstances where feelings undermine people's ability to think clearly and objectively about a problem. Some examples of facilitation and support will be considered in Chapter 13.

Negotiation

People can be motivated to change by rewarding those behaviours that will facilitate the change. The explicit provision of additional rewards is a useful approach when the change target is unlikely to perceive any obvious gains associated with the original change proposal.

Kotter and Schlesinger (1979) suggest that negotiated agreements can be a relatively easy way to avoid resistance when it is clear that someone, who has sufficient power to resist a change, is going to lose out if the change is implemented. The problem associated with this approach is that others who may have been content to go along with the change may then see the possibility of improving their lot through negotiation. The long-term effect can be to increase the cost of implementing changes and increase the time required to negotiate the change with all interested parties.

Manipulation and co-option

Manipulation is the covert attempt to influence others to change and it can involve the deliberate biasing of messages, as considered above. It can also involve co-option. Kotter and Schlesinger (1979) note that co-opting usually involves giving an individual or group leader a desirable role in the design or implementation of the change. The aim is not to seek access to any expertise they may have, but to secure their endorsement. While this approach may be quicker and cheaper than negotiation, it runs the risk of those who are co-opted feeling that they have been 'tricked' into supporting the change. Also, those who are co-opted may exercise more influence than anticipated and steer the change in a direction not favoured by the change initiators.

IV

Explicit and implicit coercion

The ability to exercise power exists when one person or group is dependent on another for something they value. Coercive strategies involve change managers using their power to grant or withhold valued outcomes in order to motivate people to change. While the result may be a willingness to comply and go along with the change, the change target's commitment to the change may be low. Consequently, compliance may only be sustained so long as the change manager continues to monitor the situation and maintains the threat of withholding valued outcomes. In spite of the risks of long-term resentment and the possibility of retaliation that are often associated with coercive change strategies, there may be occasions where their use is appropriate. These may include situations where the target group has a low perceived need for change, where the proposed change is not attractive to the target group, and where speed is essential.

Goal setting

Hundreds of studies have shown that goal setting can affect levels of performance and there are strong arguments that they can also affect the motivation to support change. Seijts and Latham (2012) argue that attractive goals can affect priorities, effort, persistence, and the search for effective ways of working. For example:

- Most employees and other stakeholders have multiple demands on their time. Presenting them with compelling goals for change can help them set priorities and focus their attention on implementing the change.
- Goals can affect the effort that people are willing to invest in the change. When those involved have high self-efficacy and anticipate that they will be able to deliver whatever performance is required (referred to below as 'effort to performance expectancy'), challenging goals will be more motivating than easy goals.
- Goals that are attractive (perceived to deliver benefit) and challenging motivate those involved to persevere and continue working to implement the change.
- When it is not immediately obvious what needs to be done, attractive and challenging goals can motivate those involved to draw on their repertoire of knowledge and experience to develop and implement strategies that will deliver the required performance.

Expectancy theory and the motivation to support or resist change

When change recipients anticipate that a change could provide them with some benefit, they may well be motivated to support it, but whether this possibility will actually be translated into positive action will depend on their expectation that the change will deliver the promised benefit. Expectancy theory considers how expectations influence motivation. It offers a useful conceptual framework for assessing whether a stakeholder is likely to support or resist an impending change. Expectancy theorists (for example Vroom, 1964; Porter and Lawler, 1968) argue that behaviour is a function of two factors: the attractiveness of outcomes and expectancies about the achievement of valued outcomes:

1 *Outcomes:* These can be evaluated in terms of their value or attractiveness. Vroom (1964) refers to this as 'valence'. If stakeholders expect the change to reduce the availability of valued outcomes, they are likely to offer resistance. If,

on the other hand, they expect it to increase the availability of valued outcomes, they are more likely to offer support.

2 *Expectancies:* Stakeholder motivation will be influenced by their expectations about the likelihood that they will actually receive valued outcomes in practice. The theory focuses attention on two expectancies about the future:

- *effort to performance expectancy:* This refers to the person's expectation that they can perform at a given level, in other words, that their efforts will lead to successful performance.
- *performance to outcome expectancy:* This refers to a person's expectation that some level of performance will lead to desired outcomes, or the avoidance of negative outcomes.

From a motivational perspective, it is the expectation or belief about the relationship between effort, performance and valued outcome that will determine whether a stakeholder will be motivated to support or resist a change. The basic elements of this theory are illustrated in Figure 12.1.

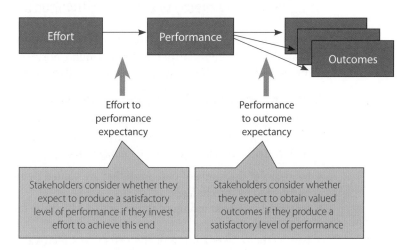

*Figure **12.1** The expectancy model of motivation*

Equity of treatment

The model can be extended to include stakeholder expectations about the equity of outcomes in the changed situation. If stakeholders believe that comparable others will receive more favourable treatment (in terms of valued outcomes) as a result of the change, this will affect their assessment of the attractiveness of the outcomes they expect to receive. Some stakeholders who expect, in absolute terms, to receive a net increase in valued outcomes may still resist the change because they feel they are being treated unfairly relative to comparable others.

Understanding and competence

The model can be extended still further to include key factors that may affect effort to performance expectancies. These include the stakeholder's understanding of the nature of the required performance, and the rules that govern how a performance should be produced, as well as the competences required to deliver a satisfactory level of performance (Figure 12.2). These will be discussed below.

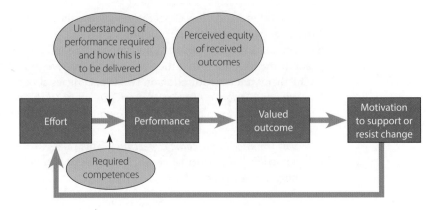

Figure **12.2** *An expectancy model of the motivation to support or resist change*

Using expectancy theory to enhance motivation and support for change

Those leading change can use expectancy theory to assess and improve the perceived attractiveness of outcomes and build positive expectations about the relationship between effort and performance and the achievement of outcomes.

Assessing the availability of valued outcomes

The first step in assessing how stakeholders will respond to change is to identify how the change will affect the availability of valued outcomes in the changed situation. In order to do this, the change manager needs to:

- be aware of the kinds of outcomes that are valued by the stakeholders who will be affected by the change
- have some understanding of the extent to which the current situation provides these outcomes
- have some understanding of the extent to which valued outcomes will be (at least potentially) available in the changed situation.

This assessment will provide a useful first indication of the extent to which stakeholders will support or resist the change. It will also indicate the extent to which they are likely to be motivated to perform in ways that will contribute to organizational effectiveness in the changed situation.

When people are confronted by an impending change, they often fear that they will lose some of the outcomes they value in the existing situation. However, they may also anticipate some gains. These gains might be more of the outcomes they already enjoy or some completely new benefits. In order to anticipate how stakeholders will feel about a change, it is necessary to empathize with them in order to construct a balance sheet of what (we think) they will perceive as gains or losses.

Different people value different outcomes. Even the same person may value different outcomes at different points in time. The more we know about stakeholders, the better placed we will be to construct the balance sheet. Listed below are some broad headings that might suggest the kinds of outcomes that could be important to stakeholders. This list is not exhaustive and it is important to remember that different kinds of stakeholders may value different kinds of outcomes:

- Pay
- Working conditions
- Interesting/meaningful work
- Autonomy
- Opportunity for competition or collaboration
- Opportunities to be creative
- Power and influence
- Belonging/involvement
- Location
- Security
- Working with considerate supervisors
- Satisfaction
- Challenge
- Achievement
- Recognition
- Status
- Openness/sharing
- Opportunity to use knowledge and skills
- Flexible working arrangements.

Each of these headings can be elaborated to include a more detailed list of associated outcomes. For example, under the heading of pay, employees might feel that the impending change is likely to reduce the availability of a valued outcome because they will be required to work longer hours or at a faster rate for the same pay. On the other hand, the change might be viewed as enhancing valued outcomes if it leads to a regrading that will boost pay. This might also be the case if it offers a shift to annualized hours that will eliminate unpredictable variations in weekly pay and provide a guaranteed annual income that can be used, for example, to secure a bank loan or a mortgage.

Change tool 12.1 *Assessing the availability of valued outcomes*

1 Think about a recent or impending change at work or elsewhere (at home, in a social club you belong to and so on), and identify a key stakeholder affected by the change.
2 List all the valued outcomes you believe the stakeholder receives in the current situation. Review the list and indicate whether you feel that the change will produce a gain (✓), no change (?) or a loss (✗) for each outcome.

Valued outcome in existing situation	✓	?	x	Rank

3 Next, extend the list by adding any new outcomes you anticipate will be available to the stakeholder in the changed situation and indicate your assessment of whether the stakeholder will view them as a gain (✓), neutrally (?) or as a loss (✗).

New outcome in changed situation	✓	?	✗	Rank

4 Finally, review the content of the full table and rank how you think the stakeholder will value the outcomes. In the column headed 'Rank', enter the 1 next to the most valued outcome, 2 next to the second most valued and so on.

5 In order to make an overall assessment of the potential net gain or loss for the stakeholder, it is necessary to take account of the number of gains and losses identified in the above table, and the relative importance of the different valued outcomes to the stakeholder. The ranking is intended to provide a basis for weighting the significance of each gain and loss. Taking all this into account, assess whether the stakeholder is likely to view the net effect of the change as a gain or a loss.

6 Consider whether those leading the change were/are aware of how the change was/is likely to affect the availability of outcomes valued by the selected stakeholders.

7 Consider whether this information might have improved the way the change was/is being managed.

Expectancies about effort–performance and performance–outcome relationships and equity of net benefits

Although the change manager may see potential net gains for the people affected by the change, the individuals concerned may not share this assessment. As discussed above, whether stakeholders will be motivated to support or resist the change will depend on their expectations about:

- their ability to deliver a satisfactory level of performance in the changed situation
- whether a satisfactory (or even exceptional) level of performance will lead to the achievement of valued outcomes in the changed situation
- whether the net benefits accruing to them will be equitable when compared to the net benefits accruing to comparable others in the changed situation.

In order to understand better the extent to which stakeholders will resist or support change, the change manager needs to consider these three additional issues.

Anticipate stakeholder effort–performance expectancies

There will be less resistance, and therefore more support, in those situations where stakeholders expect to be able to deliver a satisfactory level of performance in the changed situation. Individuals or groups are more likely to resist a change when they expect that, irrespective how hard they work, the change will undermine their ability to produce a satisfactory level of performance.

Diagnosis of potential misunderstandings

In order to anticipate how the change might affect stakeholder expectations about their ability to produce a satisfactory level of performance in the changed situation, those leading the change need to take into account misunderstandings that might arise about the processes and procedures that will apply in the changed situation. Stakeholders may assume that any new rules that define the nature of a satisfactory level of performance, or new rules that regulate working practices, may undermine their ability to produce a satisfactory level of performance.

Example: Individuals may assume that in the changed situation they will have less autonomy and will be required to work in a group setting. They may also fear that in this group setting their performance will be dependent on inputs from others who are poor or unreliable performers. Their fears may be well founded, but may also be based on misunderstandings about the nature of the change or the other people they may have to work with.

Possible action

Those leading the change may be able to reduce resistance from this source by:

- helping people develop a clear understanding of how the change will affect the way they will be required to work – *education*
- helping them understand the consequences these new processes and procedures may have for their ability to deliver a performance – *education and persuasion*
- providing them with an opportunity to be involved in the planning of the change. This might reassure them that the change will be managed in a way that will minimize those factors that could undermine their ability to deliver a satisfactory level of performance – *participation and involvement*.

Diagnosis of impact of change on relevance of competences

Those leading the change may also need to take into account the relevance of existing competences in the changed situation.

Example: In those situations where a stakeholder's core competences become more highly valued, the individual is more likely to support the change. However, where core competences are perceived to be less relevant (or even redundant), the change is more likely to be resisted because stakeholders may fear they will not be able to produce a satisfactory level of performance.

Possible action

Those leading the change may be able to reduce the resistance from this source by:

- considering possibilities for redeploying people to roles that will better utilize existing competences – *planning*
- involving people in identifying possibilities for redeployment – *participation*
- providing training to develop more relevant competences – *training and development*.

Anticipate stakeholder performance–outcome expectancies

There will be less resistance, and more support, for a change in those situations where stakeholders expect that the delivery of a satisfactory level of performance will be linked to the achievement of valued outcomes. In those situations where they expect the change to undermine the achievement of valued outcomes, they are more likely to resist the change and be less motivated to perform in the changed situation.

Diagnosis

In order to anticipate how the change might affect stakeholder expectations about the relationship between performance and the achievement of valued outcomes, those leading the change need to empathize with them in order to develop a better understanding of this.

Example: If an individual values promotion and expects that in the changed situation there will be a closer link between advancement and level of performance, they may support the change and be motivated to perform well in the changed situation. If, however, the individual expects the change to weaken this link, it will increase the possibility that the change will be resisted.

Possible action

Those leading the change may be able to reduce resistance from this source by:

- Considering ways of modifying the change to strengthen the links between performance and the achievement of valued outcomes – *planning*
- Persuading individuals that the change will actually strengthen these links – *persuasion*
- Involving stakeholders in the diagnosis, planning and implementation of the change. This might reassure them that the change will be managed in a way that will strengthen links between performance and valued outcomes – *participation*.

Anticipate stakeholder perceptions of equity

Finally, there will be less resistance (and more support) in those situations where stakeholders feel they are being treated equitably relative to others, that is, their net benefits (or losses) compared to those enjoyed by comparable others. Where they feel they are being treated unfairly, they may be more likely to resist the change.

Diagnosis

In order to anticipate the effects of perceived equity on the level of resistance or support for change, those leading the change need to identify those who may regard themselves as being treated inequitably.

Possible action

Those leading the change may be able to reduce resistance from this source by:

- helping people who feel this way recognize all the potential gains available to them and ensuring that they fully understand the possible losses if the change is not implemented – *education and persuasion*
- exploring possibilities for improving the availability of valued outcomes for those who feel they have received inequitable treatment – *planning*
- exploring the possibility of redistributing costs and benefits between those affected by the change in order to produce greater equity – *planning*
- involving stakeholders in the diagnosis, planning and implementation of the change. This might reassure them that the change will be managed in a way that will maximize equity of treatment – *participation*.

Translating theory into practice

Drawing on the ideas discussed in this chapter and the other chapters in Part IV, review the situation at the Douglas refinery (Case study 12.1). The CEO of Prosper, the company that owns the refinery, has asked a consultant to review the case and recommend how the situation might be managed from this point forward. He has also asked the consultant to identify any lessons that will help the management team manage similar situations in the future.

Case study **12.1** *Managing change at the Douglas refinery*

Located in the Republic of Ireland, the Douglas refinery had originally been commissioned in 1959 and was one of four refineries owned by McPherson Oil. The Douglas refinery is the smallest of these four refineries, employing 150 staff and producing transport fuels such as diesel, petrol and jet fuel. McPherson Oil was acquired by Prosper, a private equity company, in 2009. The new owners invested new capital, recruited a new CEO and other key managers, and tasked the new Prosper management team to restructure and reposition the business in order to enhance profitability.

Over the next three years, two new refineries were acquired and three of the existing refineries were expanded, but there was little new investment in the Douglas refinery. While the Douglas refinery was making a small profit, the new management team did not (and still does not) see it as a core asset. Members of the Prosper management team and a group of consultants undertook a strategic review that explored possibilities for transforming and expanding the Douglas refinery. The refinery manager was informed of the review and asked to provide answers to specific questions about the operation of the site, but she was not a member of the review team. She was instructed not to inform any employees at the Douglas refinery about the review. The review process was completed in the autumn of 2011 and concluded that, because there were only limited opportunities for transforming and expanding the Douglas refinery, it should be sold.

The refinery manager was informed of this decision but instructed not to tell other employees, including members of the Douglas refinery management team, until after possible buyers had been approached. The Prosper management team decided on this course of action in order to prevent staff at the Douglas site feeling insecure about their future, believing that any

© BRAND X

IV

feelings of insecurity could trigger actions that might interrupt operations and/or encourage staff to look for alternative employment. They feared that any disruption would make it more difficult to secure a sale. The Prosper management team was particularly concerned about the possibility of losing staff because, despite the recent downturn in the Irish economy, a chemical company was expanding its facilities on an adjacent site and seeking to recruit process workers, some supervisors and at least one manager.

Four weeks after the decision to sell the Douglas refinery, a local newspaper published an article reporting rumours of a pending sale. Employees were shocked and angered by this 'announcement' and confronted their managers who, until the article had been published, knew nothing about it. The refinery manager immediately contacted the CEO at Prosper HQ in Switzerland and was told to deny the rumour until a consultant (who was a co-opted member of the strategic review team) had visited the site and assessed the situation. Despite this instruction, the refinery manager decided to take the site HR manager into her confidence and inform him about the strategic review and the decision to sell off the refinery. She did this because she felt that the Prosper management team's approach to managing change was creating problems that were difficult for her to manage and she felt a need to discuss the situation with somebody she could trust.

They both recognized that the other members of the refinery management team would be upset when they found out they had not been kept informed about the strategic review and the decision to sell the refinery. Even so, they felt they had no option other than to follow instructions from the CEO and deny any knowledge of the decision to sell the refinery. However, they did inform other members of the Douglas refinery management team that a representative of the Prosper management team (the consultant) would be on site within 24 hours to help clarify the situation.

Imagine that you are the consultant. The CEO has asked you to assess the situation as quickly as possible and report back with recommendations for how the change should be managed from this point forward. You have also been asked to identify any lessons that will help the management team manage similar situations in the future.

The CEO has informed you (the consultant) that only one of the possible buyers who had been approached has shown any interest in the Douglas refinery. While this potential buyer might be willing to acquire the refinery, it has indicated that it is not willing to pay the asking price. This is because Douglas is a simple refinery that can only process part of each barrel of oil it purchases. In addition to the transport fuels that it produces and sells to end users, it also produces a number of intermediate products that it has to sell to other refineries for further processing. The market for some of these intermediate products is predicted to fall and it is this that is putting off prospective buyers. Nonetheless, the Prosper management team is keen to sell the Douglas refinery even if it has to accept a price lower than anticipated. But in order to secure the sale, the Douglas refinery must be kept working as normal.

Because there is some doubt about the pending sale, the Prosper management team has explored other possibilities. Two have been identified. The first is to close the refinery and sell off the site, making everybody redundant. The second involves retaining the site, closing the refinery and developing the site as a terminal. This option would involve making up to 100 staff redundant. However, it is possible that work could be found for between 40 and 60 of these employees if they were willing to retrain and cooperate with managers to develop new work streams on the Douglas site, which would support operations elsewhere within the Prosper group of companies.

Until the current crisis, employees at the Douglas site have been committed to the refinery and have responded well to new initiatives. Communications have been good and employees have felt able to make suggestions and seek information from their managers. Because there are only 150 employees on site, it has always been possible to discuss key issues face to face via team and departmental meetings. In addition, bimonthly meetings between managers and union and other employee representatives have ensured good two-way communication.

The rumour published in the local paper has undermined trust and damaged commitment. This could make it more difficult to retain staff and keep the refinery operating as normal and could, if the refinery is not sold, adversely affect their willingness to work with managers to transform the site from a refinery into a terminal and commit to the development of new streams of business that could be located on the Douglas site.

Summary

This chapter considered how the general level of commitment in an organization can affect the extent to which organizational members will support new initiatives:

- people's past experience of change can affect their level of commitment to the organization and their willingness to support further change
- the psychological contract is an unwritten set of expectations between all organization members and those who represent the organization and incorporates concepts such as fairness, reciprocity and a sense of mutual obligation. If employees feel that the organization has failed to keep its side of the 'bargain', they may respond by redefining their side of the psychological contract and invest less effort in work, be less inclined to innovate and less inclined to respond positively to changes.

While there is evidence that employees who are committed to their organizations are more likely to support change than those who are not, the situation is complicated when employees are also committed to (and satisfied with) their job because they do not want to do anything that could threaten the benefits their job provides. A key determinant of resistance to change is the extent to which potential change recipients perceive the change as personally beneficial or harmful.

Resistance to change can be viewed as feedback which can have functional value. Those leading change need to be careful not to always interpret negative feedback as resistance and a threat to change success.

A number of factors can affect whether or not people will support a change. These are:

- low trust
- low tolerance for change
- different assessments about costs and benefits
- parochial self-interest.

Leaders can do a number of things to minimize resistance, including persuasion, participation, facilitation and support, negotiation, manipulation and co-option, explicit or implicit coercion, and goal setting.

This chapter also discussed expectancy theory and the motivation to support or resist change. Expectancy theory considers how expectations influence motivation and provides a basis for assessing whether a stakeholder is likely to support or resist an impending change. Whether stakeholders will be motivated to support or resist the change will depend on their expectations about:

- their ability to deliver a satisfactory level of performance in the changed situation
- whether a satisfactory, or even exceptional, level of performance will lead to the achievement of valued outcomes in the changed situation
- whether the net benefits accruing to them will be equitable when compared to the net benefits accruing to comparable others in the changed situation.

References

Argyris, C. (1960) *Understanding Organizational Behavior*. Homewood, IL: Dorsey Press.

Begley, T.M. and Czajka, J.M. (1993) Panel analysis of the moderating effects of commitment on job satisfaction, intention to quit and health following organizational change, *Journal of Applied Psychology*, 78(4): 552–6.

Bridges, W. (1993) *Managing Transitions: Making the Most of Change*. Reading, MA: Addison-Wesley.

Choi, M. (2011) Employees' attitudes towards organizational change: A literature review, *Human Resource Management*, 50(4): 479–500.

Coch, L. and French, J.R. (1948) Overcoming resistance to change, *Human Relations*, 1(4): 512–32.

Doherty, N. and Horsted, J. (1995) Helping survivors stay on board, *People Management*, 1(1): 26–31.

Ford, J.D. and Ford, L.W. (2010) Stop blaming resistance to change and start using it, *Organizational Dynamics*, 39(1): 24–36.

Guest, D., Conway, N., Briner, R. and Dickman, M. (1996) *The State of the Psychological Contract in Employment*. London: Institute of Personnel and Development.

Kotter, J.P. and Schlesinger, L.A. (1979) Choosing strategies for change, *Harvard Business Review*, 57(2): 106–14.

Lines, R. (2004) Influence of participation in strategic change: Resistance, organisational commitment and change goal achievement, *Journal of Change Management*, 4(3): 193–215.

Lines, R., Selart, M., Espedal, B. and Johansen, S.T. (2005) The production of trust during organizational change, *Journal of Change Management*, 5(2): 221–45.

Nadler, D. (1993) Concepts for the management of organisational change. In C. Mabey and B. Mayon-White (eds) *Managing Change* (2nd edn). London: Paul Chapman.

Oreg, S., Vakola, M. and Armenakis, A. (2011) Change recipients' reactions to organizational change: A 60-year review of quantitative studies, *Journal of Applied Behavioral Science*, 47(4): 461–524.

Porter, I. and Lawler, E.E. (1968) *Managerial Attitudes and Performance*. New York: Irwin.

Pugh, D. (1993) Understanding and managing organisational change. In C. Mabey and B. Mayon-White (eds) *Managing Change* (2nd edn). London: Paul Chapman.

Sahdev, K. (2004) Revisiting the survivor syndrome: The role of leadership in implementing downsizing, *European Journal of Work and Organizational Psychology*, 13(2): 165–96.

Seijts, G.H. and Latham, G.P. (2012) Knowing when to set learning goals versus performance goals, *Organizational Dynamics*, 41(1): 1–6.

Thaler, R.H. and Sunstein, C.R. (2009) *Nudge: Improving Decisions about Health, Wealth, and Happiness*. London: Penguin.

Van Dam, K. (2005) Employee attitudes toward job changes: An application and extension of Rusbult and Farrell's investment model, *Journal of Occupational and Organizational Psychology*, 78(2): 253–72.

Vroom, V.H. (1964) *Work and Motivation*. London: Wiley.

Zaltman, G. and Duncan, R. (1977) *Strategies for Planned Change*. London: John Wiley.

Chapter **13**

Supporting others through change

Leaders need to be alert to how others are being affected by change, to understand what they may be experiencing, and to know what they can do to support those who are vulnerable, anxious or have doubts about their ability to cope. This chapter addresses the way organizational members experience change, irrespective of whether they view it as an opportunity or a threat. It examines the individual's response to change as a progression through a number of stages of psychological reaction. It also considers how an understanding of the way individuals react to change can help those leading the change to plan and implement it in ways that will maximize benefit and minimize cost for the organization and individual organizational members.

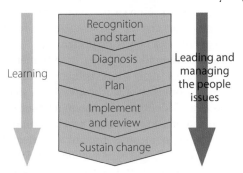

Organizational change involves contextual or situational factors, such as technology, structures, systems and required competences. This is well understood, but it also involves a series of personal transitions for all those affected. Bridges (1980) suggests that while many managers are wise about the mechanics of change, they are often unaware of the dynamics of the transition.

Personal transitions are important because, although some situational factors can be changed relatively quickly, the new organizational arrangements may not work as planned until the people involved let go of the way things used to be and adjust to the new situation. Commenting on the factors that can undermine the successful implementation of change, Bridges (1991, p. 3) claims: 'It isn't the changes that do you in, it's the transitions.'

The nature of personal transitions

Individuals, like organizations, can be confronted with both incremental and discontinuous changes. Some changes happen slowly, for example ageing. This process of gradual incremental change rarely presents any abrupt challenges to the assumptions people make about how they relate to the world around them. But this is not the case for all types of change. A sudden merger, and the announcement that key personnel will have to reapply for their jobs in the new organization, will raise many questions in the minds of those affected about what the future will hold for them. This is an example of a change that poses a serious challenge to an individual's 'assumptive world'. Parkes (1971) argues that this assumptive world is the only world of which we are aware. It includes everything we know or think we know. It affects our interpretation of the past and our expectations of the future, our plans and our prejudices. Any or all of these may need to change as a result of an organizational change, whether or not these changes are perceived as gains or losses.

When changes are lasting in their effects, take place over a relatively short period of time, and affect large areas of the assumptive world, they are experienced as personal transitions. Those leading a change might perceive the promotion of a team member to team leader as a simple and quickly accomplished organizational change. However, from the perspective of the individual who is promoted, the personal transition associated with this change might be a more protracted process. It might be difficult for the newly promoted team leader to let go of their former role as team member, and the close friendships this involved with some colleagues and the distant, businesslike relationships it involved with others. The newly promoted team leader might feel isolated in the new role and be unsure about how to behave towards others, especially subordinates who used to be both colleagues and close friends. It might take some time and quite a lot of experimenting to discover a style of managing that works. In some cases, the individual may be so unhappy with the new role that they might give up the struggle and resign, leaving the change manager with the job of finding a new team leader.

Loss of employment, for example through redundancy or early retirement, is another example of a personal transition. Parkes (1971) suggests that the loss of a job deprives a person of a place of work, the company of workmates and a source of income. It also removes a familiar source of identity, self-esteem and sense of purpose. Adjustment to this change will require, for example, new assumptions about the way each day will be spent and sources of income. It might also affect the individual's faith in their capacity to work effectively and earn a living. This kind of disruption to their assumptive world will cause an individual to set up a cycle of changes aimed at finding a new fit between self and the changed environment.

Even the loss of a job that was wanted but not secured can be difficult to cope with because a person's assumptive world contains models of the world as it is and also as it might be. People who might be promoted to a managerial level rehearse in their mind the world they hope to create. They engage in a kind of anticipatory socialization aided by the rich imagery of their comfortable new office, challenging assignments and respectful subordinates. It may be almost as hard to give up such expectations and fantasies as it is to give up objects that actually exist. Thus, the people who are not promoted may actually lose something important and may have to make new assumptions about how things will be in the future.

Marks (2007, p. 724) observes that in many work organizations, discontinuous transitions have become a way of life: 'an acquisition, followed by a downsizing, a restructuring, a change in strategy, a subsequent restructuring, another wave of downsizing and so on'. He argues that the effects of stressful events are cumulative and the costs of ongoing change mount. He refers to O'Toole (1995), who notes that persistent discontinuous change is not a natural condition of life, and that resistance is to be expected. He echoes Burke (2002), when he goes on to argue that the phenomenon of resistance to change is not necessarily that of resisting the change per se but is more accurately a resistance to losing something of value to the person – loss of the known and tried in the face of being asked, if not forced, to move into the unknown and untried.

The personal cost of coping with transitions

Personal transitions require those affected to engage in some form of coping behaviour. Holmes and Rahe (1967) developed a social readjustment rating scale that attributed mean values to the degree of adjustment required after individuals experience a series of life events. The scale was originally constructed by telling 394 subjects that marriage had been given an arbitrary value of 50 and asking them to attribute a score to 42 other life events, indicating whether each life event would require more or less adjustment than marriage. The mean values attributed to the 43 events included in the social readjustment rating scale ranged from 100 for death of a spouse to 11 for a minor infringement of the law (see Table 13.1). 'Social readjustment' was defined in terms of the amount and duration of change in one's accustomed pattern of life following a life event, irrespective of the desirability of the event. Various retrospective and prospective studies using the social readjustment rating scale, reported by Holmes and Masuda (1973), found that the magnitude of life change is highly significantly related to the time of illness onset. An example of a prospective study of this relationship is one that involved recording the life changes experienced by 2,500 officers and enlisted men aboard three US navy cruisers. It was found that there was a clear correlation between life changes experienced in a given period before the cruisers put to sea and the onset of illness during the period at sea. The studies reported by Holmes and Masuda indicate that the higher the score over the past 12 months, the greater the likelihood of illness onset over the next 12 months.

IV

Table **13.1** *The social readjustment rating scale*

Rank	Life event	Mean value
1	Death of spouse	100
2	Divorce	73
3	Marital separation	65
4	Jail term	63
5	Death of close family member	63
6	Personal injury or illness	53
7	Marriage	50
8	Dismissed from work	47
9	Marital reconciliation	45
10	Retirement	45
11	Change in health of family member	44
12	Pregnancy	40
13	Sexual difficulties	39
14	Gain of a new family member (child or 'oldster' moving in)	39
15	Business readjustment	39
16	Change in financial state	39
17	Death of close friend	37
18	Change to a different line of work	36

Rank	Life event	Mean value
19	Change in number of arguments with spouse	35
20	Taking on a large mortgage (for example for house purchase)	31
21	Foreclosure of mortgage or loan	30
22	Change in responsibilities at work	29
23	Son or daughter leaves home	29
24	Trouble with in-laws	29
25	Outstanding personal achievement	28
26	Spouse beginning or ceasing work	26
27	Begin or end school (formal education)	26
28	Change in living conditions	25
29	Revision of personal habits (dress, manners, associations and so on)	24
30	Trouble with boss	23
31	Change in work hours or conditions	20
32	Change in residence	20
33	Change in schools/college	20
34	Change in recreation	19
35	Change in religious activities	19
36	Change in social activities	18
37	Taking on medium-level loan (for TV, computer and so on)	17
38	Change in sleeping habits (amount, time of day and so on)	16
39	Change in number of family get-togethers	15
40	Change in eating habits	15
41	Holidays	13
42	Christmas	12
43	Minor violations of the law	11

Source: Adapted from Holmes and Rahe, 1967, p. 215

This relationship between life change and illness susceptibility may be moderated by individual differences in the ability to cope with personal transitions. People may perceive the same event and/or assess their ability to cope with it in different ways. This can be influenced by many factors, including past experience of the event and personality variables such as hardiness, self-esteem, self-reliance and so on.

You might find it interesting to use the social readjustment rating scale (Table 13.1) to assess the amount of life change you have experienced in the past 12 months. Total the values of the life change events you have experienced over this period. A life crisis is defined by Holmes and Rahe as 150 or more life change units in any one year:

- a mild life crisis is defined as 150–199 life change units
- a moderate crisis is 200–299 life change units
- a major life crisis is defined as more than 300 life change units.

The relationship between life change and illness susceptibility highlights the personal cost associated with adjusting to change, irrespective of whether the change is viewed as desirable or undesirable. It also points to the possibility that different people may react to the same organizational change in different ways, because for some it is an isolated event, whereas for others it is one of a number of changes, at work and elsewhere, that could push them towards a major life crisis.

Adjusting to organizational change

As previously discussed, when individuals adjust to organizational changes that are lasting in their effects, take place over a relatively short period of time, and affect large areas of the assumptive world, they experience a process of personal transition. Exercise 13.1 invites you to reflect on how you have reacted to a change that involved a personal transition. The information generated by this exercise will enable you to compare your reactions with the typical pattern of reaction described by the stage model of transition presented later in this chapter.

✓ *Exercise* **13.1** *Your experience of a transition*

Think of a change that was lasting in its effects, took place over a relatively short period of time, and affected the assumptions you made about how you related to the world around you. Examples of this kind of change could be redundancy, a change in employment, promotion, relocation, bereavement, illness or accident that affected your mobility or some other aspect of your functioning, marriage, or the birth of your first child. For the purpose of this exercise, the change need not be an organizational change.

IV

Answer the following questions:

Entry:

1 When did you realize that the transition was to take place?
2 How did you know?
3 What did you feel at the time?
4 What did you do/how did you behave?

During the transition:

1 Did your feelings and/or behaviour change during the transition?
2 Are you able to identify any stages that highlighted differences in the way you reacted to the change? If so, what were these stages?

Exit:

1 When did you realize that your transition had ended? How did you know?

Think about your answers to the questions posed in Exercise 13.1 when the stages of psychological reaction to a change are considered below.

The process of personal transition

Organizational change involves the ending of something and the beginning of something else. For example, it might involve the introduction of a new organizational structure, a more automated production process, revised procedures, the merger of two units, the closure of a plant, a redundancy programme, job transfers, a new project, or a promotion. While these changes might be carefully planned and happen on a predetermined date, it might be some time before those involved have adapted to their new circumstances. Managers need to develop an understanding of how people respond to change. They need to know the course of events associated with the process of transition and the kinds of actions they can engage in to facilitate adaptation.

A model of change as a personal transition

The model presented below is based on the work of Bridges (1980, 1991). It conceptualizes a personal transition as beginning with an ending and then going on to a new beginning via a neutral zone (see Figure 13.1). These three phases are not separate stages divided by clear boundaries. Phases can overlap and an individual can be in more than one phase at any one time. Bridges sees the movement through a transition as being marked by a change in the dominance of one phase as it gives way to the next.

Endings involve letting go of the old situation and the personal identity that went with it. It is impossible to fully engage in a new role or have a new purpose until those involved have let go of the old role or old purpose. For example, as noted above, a promotion, especially when it is in the same work group, involves letting go of the role of group member and internalizing the new role of group leader. Fink et al. (1971), drawing on the work of Lewin, argue that every human system has within it forces for the maintenance of the status quo and forces for growth. While these forces tend to operate against each other, the balance between maintenance and growth is constantly shifting. Endings are often associated with a predominance of maintenance forces that manifest themselves in a resistance to change and a reluctance to let go.

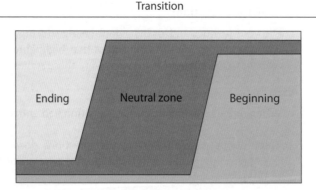

Figure **13.1** *Bridges' model of transition*
Source: Bridges, 1991, p. 70

The neutral zone is the in-between state. It involves a recognition of the need to change and uncertainty about the nature of more desirable end states. It is a period of disorientation, self-doubt and anxiety, but it can also be a period of growth and creativity in which new opportunities are identified. However, there is a danger that people may be so uncomfortable with the ambiguity and disorientation associated with this stage of transition that they push prematurely for certainty and closure. Consequently, they may lock on to the first opportunity that offers any promise of a more satisfactory state of affairs and, in so doing, lock out the possibility of a creative search for better alternatives.

Beginnings involve reorientation to a new situation and the development of a new identity. Initially, the forces for growth predominate but eventually, as the new situation is more clearly defined and a new identity is internalized, these become balanced again with forces for maintenance.

The stages of psychological reaction

People going through change experience a variety of emotional and cognitive states. Transitions typically progress through a cycle of reasonably predictable phases described below. This applies to all kinds of transitions: voluntary and imposed, desirable and undesirable. There is a widely held view that, in each case, the person experiencing the transition will have to work through all the stages if the transition is to be successfully completed. Understanding this process can help individuals and managers.

Figure 13.2 has been developed by Hayes and Hyde (1996) from an earlier version that originally appeared in *Transitions: Understanding and Managing Personal Change* by Adams et al. (1976). The cycle reflects variations in self-efficacy and belief in a person's ability to exercise control over the situation. The seven transition stages shown in Figure 13.2 are discussed below.

IV

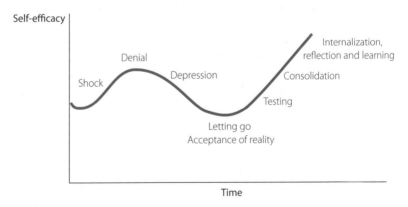

Figure **13.2** *Transition phases*

Awareness/shock

When people have little warning of changes, they often experience the initial phase of a transition as a shock. Depending on the significance of the change for them, they may feel overwhelmed and paralysed. Feelings of anxiety and panic can undermine their ability to take in new information, think constructively and plan. This leads to a state of immobilization. People behave as though they are on 'autopilot' and show little response to new developments. While their mood may be more positive if the transition is perceived as a desirable gain, for example winning first prize on the lottery, they may still experience a state of immobilization and have difficulty planning and taking constructive action. In those circumstances where people develop a gradual awareness of a pending change, they often focus on what they might lose and engage in 'worry work' that diverts their attention from other matters that might require their attention. The intensity of this phase will be influenced by the degree of preparedness and the desirability of the transition – immobilization will be greater when the transition is unexpected and unwanted.

Denial

This phase is characterized by a retreat from the reality of change. Negative changes may be denied or trivialized and attention may be displaced onto other, more immediate but less important matters. Energy and activity are devoted to the known and the familiar and any perceived threat to the status quo is managed by behaving in habitual ways. Clinging to the past and refusing to consider the need to change can lead to a reduction in anxiety. Anything or anyone who challenges this false sense of security is likely to provoke an angry response. Resistance to change is at its highest at this point. Positive changes may induce euphoria together with an unwillingness to consider any possible negative consequences. In some cases, denial may be functional if it provides the opportunity to recharge 'emotional batteries' and helps a person face up to the need to change.

Depression

Eventually, the reality of the change becomes apparent and the individual acknowledges that things cannot continue as they are. In terms of Bridges' model, this corresponds to the start of the neutral zone. This provokes depression often associated with a feeling that the situation is beyond one's control. This phase may be characterized by anger, sadness, withdrawal and confusion. This depressed mood occurs, even in changes that were initially enthusiastically embraced, whenever practical difficulties are encountered. It is in the depression phase therefore that the change really starts to be experienced as stressful. If the change was a voluntary one, this may be the point at which the person gives up. In involuntary changes, the person may seek to leave the situation.

Letting go

This phase involves accepting reality for what it is. It implies a clear letting go of the past. This may be experienced as a 'little death' and often entails a process of mourning. It can help at this point to remember that the lowest ebb is the turn of the tide.

Testing

A more active, creative, experimental involvement in the new situation starts to take place. New ways of behaving and being are tried out. More energy is available but anger and irritability may be easily aroused if the new behaviour is not successful. This phase may involve trial-and-error behaviour or a more active plan, do, study, act cycle (see Chapter 21). As some patterns are found that seem to work, this phase gradually gives way to the next.

Consolidation

Out of the testing process come some new ways of being and behaving that are gradually adopted as the new norm. This corresponds to the beginning stage in Bridges' model. This stage progresses in parallel with testing but, to begin with, there is often more testing and rejecting than testing and consolidating. It involves reflecting on new experiences and assessing whether they offer a basis for a constructive way forward. Sometimes there is little consolidation. Early experiments with new roles and relationships are rejected and the person experiencing the transition learns little from the experience. When consolidation occurs, it involves reflecting on the new experience (the outcome of a test) and using any learning to build on this and inform the choice of further 'testing' experiences.

Internalization, reflection and learning

The transition is complete when the changed behaviour is 'the norm' and happens subconsciously, and is the new natural order of things. Ideally, the past has been left behind and little or no 'unfinished business' remains. Reflection is a cognitive process involving reflecting on what all the activity and emotion have really meant. It is at this point that learning and personal growth, which may benefit future transitions, may be recognized.

At this point, you might find it interesting to reflect on the answers you gave to the questions in Exercise 13.1. Does the stage model of psychological reaction presented above provide a useful conceptual framework for understanding the process of adjustment you went through?

Some observations on the stage model of transition

Each individual's experience of a transition will be influenced by a number of factors. These include the importance of the transition, whether it is perceived as a gain or loss, the intensity of its impact, the existence of other simultaneous transitions (and the magnitude of any associated life crises), personal resilience and so on. Thus, it follows that there can be no absolutely standard pattern of reaction. These are some possible variations:

- The wave (shown in Figure 13.2) can be shallower or deeper and the overall shape of the curve may be skewed one way or the other. For example, if the change is perceived as a desirable opportunity, the individual might find it easier to let go of the past, whereas if it is perceived as a threat or loss, the individual might be reluctant to let go and resist the change for as long as possible.
- The time taken to pass through all the phases can vary greatly. Just as some people take longer than others to come to terms with the loss of a loved one, so organizational members can vary in terms of the time it takes for them to adjust to a work-related transition.
- Although presented as a purely linear process, people may regress and slip back to an earlier stage in the process.
- People can get stuck at any phase and not complete the cycle. They may, for example, continue to deny the need to change or fail to recognize the new opportunities associated with the change.

Where multiple transitions are involved, people handle the situation in different ways. Some people keep the transitions firmly compartmentalized and deal with one at a time; others throw their energy into one as a displacement activity to get away from another, which is therefore held in denial; in other cases, one major transition predominates and swamps the others.

Implications for individuals and change managers

Hayes and Hyde (1996) summarize some of the implications for individuals and change managers going through a transition.

For individuals:

- it takes time for them to make the adjustments required in transitions
- it can help them to know that their own experience is normal, it will involve ups and downs, and it will eventually come to an end
- the process can be managed: there are things they can do to facilitate their own transitions.

For change managers:

- it is important to recognize that there will often be a time lag between the announcement of a change and an emotional reaction to it: it is easy to mistake the apparent calm of the immobilization and denial phases for acceptance of the change
- because any given change will have different implications for different individuals or groups, different parts of the organization will progress through the cycle at different rates and in different ways
- change managers need to be aware that they will probably be at a different stage to other organizational members. They tend to know about the change before others, so it is not unusual for them to have reached an acceptance of change long before others. This can create potential for ineffective communication
- the cycle cannot be avoided, but there is much that change managers can do to facilitate people's passage through it.

Facilitating progress through a transition

Here, we outline some of the interventions change managers can implement to help facilitate other people's progress through a transition. When discussing ways of helping organizational members to adapt to discontinuous changes such as a merger, acquisition, downsizing or restructuring, Marks (2007) suggests that those leading the change can intervene in ways that, on the one hand, weaken the forces that encourage them to hold on to the status quo and, on the other hand, strengthen the forces for accepting the new situation. He argues that leaders can weaken forces that maintain the status quo by conveying empathy and understanding and letting people know that they are aware that circumstances are difficult for them. They can also engage people and help them to understand that the change is necessary (as Elop did when he sent his 'burning platform' memo to all staff at Nokia – see Example 9.3).

Marks (2007) suggests that leaders can help people accept the new reality that might, for example, follow a restructuring by energizing those affected by the change and getting them excited about the possible benefits that might be available after the change, and by clarifying expectations about what will be required of them in the post-change situation. One way of doing this is to involve them in designing that bit of the change that will affect them, thereby helping them to develop a sense of control.

Often, leaders need to help others progress through the stages of psychological reaction discussed above in order to stop them becoming stuck at a particular point in the process. The interventions presented below are grouped in relation to each stage of the transition process. What follows is not meant to be a prescriptive list of what the change manager should do. It is a set of suggestions, based on observations and anecdotal evidence of what seems to have worked in practice, supplemented by managers' reports about what they have done that appeared to help others to manage their personal transitions. These suggestions might alert you to some of the issues that have to be managed and possible ways of intervening that might be appropriate in a particular set of circumstances.

Shock

The shock reaction associated with the announcement/discovery of a change affecting an individual's assumptive world can sometimes be minimized by:

- preparing the ground and creating a climate of receptivity to change by providing timely information and opportunities to be involved in relevant decision making.

If this is not possible, the change manager might consider possible ways of announcing the change. Anecdotal evidence suggests that the following points might be worth considering:

1 *Announcing the change:*
   - It often helps to show empathy and understanding for how people will feel, for example: 'I know this will be upsetting for you and I feel very sad about it myself, but … .'
   - Should questions be encouraged?
2 *Who should make the announcement:*
   - This might be a senior manager, in order to signal the importance of the change and the organization's concern for the people involved.
   - Alternatively, it might be decided that a relatively junior manager should make the announcement because they have a better relationship with those affected.
3 *Timing:*
   - Should the announcement be made simultaneously to all staff or should some be told before others?
   - Should people be told as soon as possible or should the announcement be delayed?
4 *Method:*
   - Should it be done face to face, via a video link, by email or by letter?
   - In face-to-face encounters, it is important to keep calm and avoid becoming defensive or aggressive in the face of questions.
5 *Content:*
   - Should a consistent message be given to all?
   - How much information should be communicated?
   - Should the message be kept as simple as possible?
   - Should explanations be given about why the change is necessary?

IV

It is important to allow time for people to digest the information and share their feelings with others.

When people are in shock, leaders need to recognize that:

- performance might be temporarily impaired and, in some circumstances, this might lead to dangerous or costly consequences, which could influence the timing of the announcement
- some people might need more support than others.

Denial

Those leading change need to diagnose what it is that is being denied, for example the change isn't necessary, is not real, does not affect me and so on. They can help those in denial by:

- gently and supportively confronting what is being denied
- repeating the message
- drawing people's attention to relevant examples, evidence and experience that demonstrate that the change is happening
- arranging demonstrations of what the change will involve, if possible
- establishing and keeping to a timetable to provide milestones and evidence of change
- finding ways to ensure that they have to engage with the reality of the change
- taking early action if at all possible. The longer the gap between the announcement of a change and the change taking effect, the easier it is for an individual to ignore that the change is really happening
- breaking the ice by getting people to do practical things related to the change.

Depression

Leaders can intervene in order to help others understand and accept the situation by:

- providing support
- listening
- adopting an accepting and non-critical reaction to their expression of feelings.

They can also help others to work on their feelings about the situation by:

- helping them to get it off their chest
- providing space to grieve
- providing appropriate opportunities to vent emotion.

Leaders can also help them to identify opportunities to move on by:

- not letting them wallow in feeling bad: gently confronting and challenging
- helping them to identify other things they are good at
- providing further information about the change to help them envisage what the future will be like
- helping them to identify options and possible benefits
- helping them to focus their attention on the things they can do or can influence
- where possible, providing opportunities for the exercise of influence, for example consultation and involvement.

Letting go

Leaders can help people let go of the past by:

- explaining the need for change in terms of benefits rather than problems associated with past practice. Rubbishing the past can provoke a defensive reaction
- providing challenging targets associated with the movement towards a more desirable state
- drawing attention to deadlines
- eliminating the symbols of the past in the workplace, for example changing the stationery and logo after a merger
- reminiscing in a way that leads to a process of taking the best forward from the past
- marking the ending by rituals and ceremonies, wakes and leaving parties
- letting people take souvenirs and mementoes home, for example taking part of a now redundant uniform or a sample of what they used to produce. Disengaging people from the past does not necessarily require all evidence of it to be stamped out.

Testing

Some of the ways in which those leading change can encourage testing include:

- creating the space, time and resources required to test
- promoting creative thinking
- helping people to identify options
- encouraging risk taking and experimentation
- discouraging premature closure by suggesting that they should try to identify more than one possibility before making a decision
- avoiding punishing those who make mistakes
- creating new processes, tools and competences that will help people to help themselves
- eliminating the drivers of old behaviours
- acting as a mentor
- praising and supporting successes
- encourage networking and cross-fertilization
- providing feedback.

Consolidation

Consolidation can be facilitated by:

- reviewing performance and learning (more on this below)
- helping others to identify the desirable characteristics of the new state
- recognizing and rewarding achievement
- getting them to help others and share their experience
- helping them to build on successes
- broadcasting their successes.

Reflecting, learning and internalization

Reflecting, learning and internalization can be facilitated by:

- helping them to review the experience of change – asking questions, running review workshops and so on
- conducting formal post-implementation reviews
- getting them to tell stories and share their experience.

Managing change in practice **13.1** *Debbie Middleton: Motivational coaching to help people navigate transitions*

Debbie Middleton has been in the recruitment and HR consultancy business for 27 years and for the last 7 she has been running Middleton Green Executive Resourcing – an independent, bespoke service specializing in helping organizations to attract, retain and develop talent.

In her video, 'Motivational coaching to help people navigate transitions', Debbie talks about what happens when people are forced to let go of their current job and move to a different role within the same organization, or when they are released from their job and made redundant. Part of her role is to help them navigate this kind of transition. For many who are made redundant, the journey can be much longer than it used to be and while it can lead to them securing a job similar to the one they left, often it involves moving to a different kind of work, self-employment or even early retirement.

When the transition takes time and early attempts to secure a new job are unsuccessful, it can undermine self-esteem and self-confidence. An important part of Debbie's role in this phase of the transition involves motivational coaching to strengthen their resolve and, as they move into the testing phase of the transition, helping them develop new competences, search for opportunities and be prepared to experiment with the unfamiliar.

Another part of her role is to help those managers who employ her clients to support them as they adjust to their new circumstances and not to confuse lack of confidence with lack of talent.

Visit the companion website at **www.palgrave.com/companion/hayes-change-management4** to watch the video and learn more about what Debbie does.

Summary

This chapter has addressed the way organizational members experience change:

- Organizational change not only involves a change in situational factors, such as technology, structures and systems, but also a series of personal transitions for all those affected.
- New structures and systems may not work as planned until organizational members let go of the way things used to be and adjust to the new situation.

Incremental and discontinuous changes:

- Individuals, just like organizations, can be confronted with incremental or discontinuous changes.
- Incremental changes do not present any serious challenge to the assumptions we make about how we relate to the world around us, but discontinuous changes do.
- Discontinuous changes are those that are perceived to be relatively lasting in their effects, take place over a relatively short period of time, and affect large areas of an individual's assumptive world.

There is a personal cost of coping with transitions. Studies have found a link between the magnitude of life changes – irrespective of the desirability of the changes – and illness susceptibility and this relationship can be moderated by individual differences, for example hardiness and self-esteem, and past experience.

The process of personal transition involves a number of stages of psychological reaction:

- *Awareness/shock:* when awareness is sudden, the individual can be overwhelmed – anxiety can undermine the ability to think constructively and plan, leading to a state of immobilization.
- *Denial:* individuals cling to the past in order to reduce anxiety – attention is focused on the known and the familiar.
- *Depression:* following acknowledgement that things cannot continue as they are, individuals experience a feeling of loss of control. This can lead to depression, anger, sadness, withdrawal and confusion.
- *Letting go:* the need to change is accepted.
- *Testing:* experimental involvement in new situations begins to occur. Frustration is experienced when experiments fail. As some experiments appear to work, the individual begins to consolidate successes.
- *Consolidation:* this stage progresses in parallel with testing and leads to new ways of behaving and being.
- *Reflection, learning and internalization:* the transition is completed when the changed behaviour is accepted as normal.

An individual's experience of a transition will be influenced by a number of factors:

- the importance of the transition
- whether it is perceived as a gain or a loss
- the existence of other simultaneous transitions
- personal resilience.

There are a number of implications for managers. They should:

- Recognize that there will often be a time lag between the announcement of a change and an emotional reaction to it. It is easy to mistake the apparent calm of the initial awareness and denial phases for acceptance of the change.
- Realize that different individuals or groups will progress through the cycle at different rates and in different ways, because the change might affect them differently.
- Be aware that they may be at a different stage to other organizational members. They tend to know about the change before others, so it is not unusual for them to have reached an acceptance of change long before them.

References

Adams, J., Hayes, J. and Hopson, B. (1976) *Transitions: Understanding and Managing Personal Change.* London: Martin Robertson.

Bridges, W. (1980) *Transitions.* Reading, MA: Addison Wesley.

Bridges, W. (1991) *Managing Transitions: Making the Most of Change.* Reading, MA: Addison Wesley.

Burke, R.J. (2002) Organizational transitions. In C.L. Cooper and R.J. Burke (eds) *The New World of Work.* Malden, MA: Blackwell.

Fink, S.L., Beak, J. and Taddeo, K. (1971) Organisational crisis and change, *Journal of Applied Behavioral Science*, 7(1): 15–37.

Hayes, J. and Hyde, P. (1996) Transitions workshop, unpublished manual. Hyde Management Consulting.

Holmes, T.H. and Masuda, M. (1973) Life change and illness susceptibility. In J.P. Scott and E.C. Senay (eds) *Separation and Depression*. Washington DC: American Association for the Advancement of Science.

Holmes, T.H. and Rahe, R.H. (1967) The social readjustment rating scale, *Journal of Psychosomatic Research*, 11(2): 213–18.

Marks, M. (2007) A framework for facilitating adaptation to organizational transition, *Journal of Organizational Change Management*, 20(5): 721.

O'Toole, J. (1995) *Leading Change*. San Francisco, CA: Jossey-Bass.

Parkes, C.M. (1971) Psycho-social transitions: A field of study, *Social Science and Medicine*, 5: 101–15.

> ✚   Visit **www.palgrave.com/companion/hayes-change-management4** *for further learning resources*

Part **V** # PLANNING AND PREPARING FOR CHANGE

Introduction to Part **V**

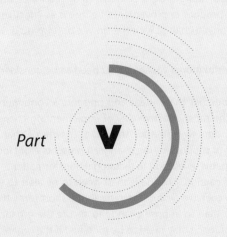

The 11 chapters in Part V take a closer look at planning and preparing for change. Chapter 14 provides the big picture and explores different change strategies, Chapter 15 focuses on the development of a change plan, Chapter 16 provides an overview of different types of intervention, Chapters 17–23 take a more detailed look at specific interventions, and Chapter 24 reviews some of the factors that need to be considered when selecting which intervention to use in a given situation.

Before reading the chapters in Part V, you are invited to complete the tasks in the case studies presented at the end of this part Introduction. After reading Chapters 14–24, review your approach and consider whether a different intervention might have been more effective.

Chapter **14** *Shaping implementation strategies*

Chapter 14 opens with an overview of how the dominant change strategies have changed over time, but notes that while tough top-down strategies continue to be popular, there has been renewed interest in more collaborative strategies.

The strengths and weaknesses of the three approaches to managing change identified by Beer are reviewed:

1 Economic strategies focus on the drive for economic value through tough, top-down, results-driven action. These actions involve the imposition of technical solutions to those problems that are seen to undermine organizational effectiveness. While economic strategies might deliver short-term results, they may not guarantee longer term success.

2 Organization development (OD) strategies focus on creating the capabilities required to sustain competitive advantage and high performance. OD strategies emphasize the importance of shared purpose, a strong culture, bottom-up change and involvement rather than financial incentives as the motivator for change. This approach can improve shareholder value but it has been criticized on the grounds that it is too indirect and takes too long, especially when the need for change is urgent.

3   Beer describes a third way, a combined economic/OD strategy. He asserts that while both economic and OD strategies can produce improvements, neither is as effective as one that combines top-down, results-driven change with the slower, bottom-up development of organizational capability.

Attention is also given to some of the situational variables that need to be considered when shaping a change strategy.

The final part of the chapter draws together these ideas and presents a contingency model that leaders can use to identify the most effective way of implementing change. The model is based on three variables: time available for the change, type of change (incremental or discontinuous), and level of support for the change. It presents eight ideal type strategies, which range from participative evolution to dictatorial transformation.

The chapter concludes with a note of caution. Change leaders need to be alert to the longer term consequences of adopting a coercive change strategy. In the short term, they may feel that they have no option other than to impose change to secure the organization's survival, but, at some point, this approach may need to be modified if the organization's long-term prosperity is to be assured.

Chapter 15 *Developing a change plan*

Those leading a change need to plan how they will move from the pre-change state to the state that will exist after the change. During this period, many of those involved will have to keep the old system going while learning how to work with the new system and develop the work roles and relationships that will have to be in place when the new system is up and running.

This chapter looks at some of tasks that need to be incorporated in the change plan. These include:

* Deciding who will be in charge during the transition phase.
* Avoiding unnecessary fragmentation. While it is important to appoint capable people to lead the transition, it is also important to ensure that they keep in close contact with others who were involved at earlier stages in the process and those who will have to live with the consequences of the change.
* Identifying what needs to be done if the change is to be successful.
* Using multiple and consistent leverage points for change. If only one component of the system is changed, this could trigger forces that will work to realign all the components of the system and re-establish the status quo. One way of avoiding this is to use multiple and consistent leverage points for achieving change.
* Producing an implementation plan that takes account of change participants' perceptions of the proposed change and the clarity (or lack of clarity) of the end state.
* Scheduling activities.
* Ensuring that adequate resources are allocated to the change and that an appropriate balance is maintained between keeping the organization running and implementing the changes necessary to move to the desired future state.
* Implementing reward systems that encourage experimentation and change.
* Developing feedback mechanisms that provide the information required to ensure that the change programme moves forward in a coordinated manner, especially where the plan calls for consistent change in a number of related areas.

Chapter **16** *Types of intervention*

Change efforts can be less successful than they might be because those responsible for managing the change are unaware of the full range of available interventions. Chapter 16 explores a range of different interventions from two perspectives.

The first approach considers interventions from the perspective of who does the intervening, and four main types of intervention are discussed that involve:

- experts applying scientific principles to solve specific problems
- groups working collaboratively to solve their own problems
- experts working to solve system-wide problems
- everybody working together to improve the capability of the whole system.

The second approach considers interventions from the perspective of the problems they are designed to address. Four categories of intervention are identified:

- Human process interventions focus on the development of better working relationships and the processes people use for communicating, problem solving, decision making and so on.
- Technostructural interventions are typically associated with shifts from rigid and bureaucratic to more adaptive and cost-efficient organizational forms, and address such issues as the division of labour, coordination between departments, processes used to produce goods and services, and the design of work.
- Human resource interventions focus on people management practices and how they can be used to integrate employees into the organization. They address issues such as how to attract and retain competent people, set goals and reward people, develop employee competences, and plan and develop careers.
- Strategic interventions address issues such as the formulation and implementation of strategy, ensuring that strategy is aligned with organizational structure and culture and that all three are aligned with the external environment, and seeking and maintaining competitive advantage.

These different perspectives draw attention to different aspects of organizational life and have implications for the focus of change efforts and how change is managed. Factors to be considered when deciding which interventions to use are discussed in Chapter 24.

Chapter **17** *Action research*

Action research is based on the premise that people learn best and are more willing to apply what they have learned when they manage the problem-solving process for themselves. The learning process involves:

- observing what is going on
- developing hypotheses that specify cause-and-effect relationships and point to actions that could help manage the problem more effectively
- taking action
- collecting data to evaluate the effect of the action and test the hypothesis.

The client group is often helped by a facilitator who works with members to help them design their own fact-finding procedure, work on the data they have collected, plan what to do, take action and then evaluate their actions in such a way that they can test their cause-and-effect hypotheses and learn from what they did.

Chapter **18** *Appreciative inquiry*

Appreciative inquiry involves the generation of a shared image of a better future and considers what the future would be like if the best of what is became the norm. Whereas action research promotes learning through attending to dysfunctional aspects of organizational functioning, appreciative inquiry seeks to accentuate the positive rather than eliminate the negative. Attention is given to:

- discovering the best of …
- understanding what creates the best of …
- amplifying the people or processes that create the best of … .

Chapter **19** *Training and development*

Chapter 19 considers how training can help to re-establish alignment between the competences of organizational members and other elements of the system such as task and structure. Attention is directed towards the main elements of an effective approach to training: a training needs analysis, which involves a systems-level review, a task analysis and a person analysis; the design and delivery of the training intervention; and the evaluation of the training intervention.

Chapter **20** *High performance management*

High performance management involves developing and implementing a bundle or system of people management practices that are internally consistent, aligned with other business processes, and aligned with the organization's business strategy. The practices that are often targeted are those that affect performance by improving employees' knowledge and skills and motivating them to engage in discretionary behaviours that draw on their knowledge and skill. Attention is also give to modifying organizational structures in ways that enable employees to improve the way they perform their jobs.

Chapter **21** *Business process re-engineering*

Business process re-engineering (BPR) involves switching attention away from fragmented functional thinking towards cross-functional processes. Some view it as involving a fundamental rethink and radical redesign of organization-wide processes but, in practice, it is often used to achieve incremental piecemeal improvements. BPR can be highly politicized and often involves jurisdictional disputes when, as a result of the process re-engineering, organizational members are required to let go of activities or decisions they value.

Chapter **22** *Lean*

Lean is a customer-focused process that aims to provide customers with precisely what they want, free of defects, exactly when they want it. It involves people in the workplace developing a detailed understanding of how the work is done, searching out the root causes of waste, and identifying more effective ways of delivering value to end users.

Some practitioners view lean as a set of tools and techniques that can be applied to eliminate waste, whereas others view it as a philosophy that involves acting in accordance with guiding principles and overarching aims to create a 'lean enterprise'. The original five guiding principles are:

1 precisely specify value for each product or product family
2 identify value streams for each product to expose waste
3 make value flow without interruption
4 let customers pull value from the producer
5 pursue perfection by searching out and eliminating further waste.

Chapter **23** *Culture profiling*

Cultural profiling can be used to pre-screen merger partners and, later in a merger process, guide the integration of the merging units. It is an intervention that draws on social identity and acculturation theory to diagnose how a proposed merger or acquisition can threaten employees' organizational identities and exacerbate 'us-and-them' dynamics, and to explore how, in the light of employees' preferences for combining cultures, practices and systems, mergers can be managed in a way that will promote rather than undermine people synergies.

Chapter **24** *Selecting interventions*

Chapter 24 examines the factors that need to be considered when selecting which type of intervention to use. Three factors, diagnosed problem, level of change target, and depth of intervention required, are combined to provide a three-dimensional model to aid choice. Two additional factors are also referred to: the time available to implement the change, and the efficacy of interventions. The three-dimensional model is used to classify interventions and while many are named (and can be researched online), only a few are discussed in any detail (see Chapters 16–23).

☑ *Exercise* **Part V** *Useful questions for reviewing your approach to planning and preparing for change*

In Chapter 2, after discussing each stage in the process model of change management, your attention was drawn to a number of questions that might help you assess how well a change is being (or was) managed. All these questions are summarized in Figure 2.5 and the questions relating to planning and preparing for change are listed below:

- Is the change strategy appropriate, for example push, pull, or a blend of both?
- Is it clear what needs to be done?
- Is sufficient thought being given to the longer term implications of decisions?
- Is sufficient attention being given to anticipating how people may react to the change?
- Is it clear what kind of intervention(s) would be most effective?

Reflect on and review these questions and, after reading the 11 chapters in Part V, revise this list and generate your own set of useful questions that you might find it helpful to refer to when you are leading a change.

Case studies: *selecting and designing interventions*

Before reading the 11 chapters of Part V, you are invited to complete the tasks in the following four case studies. Imagine that you are a consultant and have been invited to design an intervention to address the issues raised in each case:

- Case study V.1 involves improving the effectiveness of primary healthcare centres in southwest India.
- Case study V.2 involves increasing the motivation and flexibility of the workforce of a large dairy company operating in the UK.
- Case study V.3 involves improving the treatment offered by the trauma orthopaedic care department of a large UK NHS hospital.
- Case study V.4 involves reducing absenteeism in the elderly care sector of Silkeborg Council in Denmark.

After reading Chapters 14–24, you might find it useful to review your approach to designing an intervention for each of the following cases. You might also consider the nature of your change strategy in the light of the strategies considered in Chapter 14.

Case study **V.1** *Designing an intervention to improve the effectiveness of primary healthcare centres in southwest India*

A senior health official in an Indian state government has approached you for advice. The state has a rapidly growing population and a high demand for primary healthcare, but a tight budget, which means that every effort has to be made to improve the effectiveness of the existing provision. There will only be limited resources to cope with the growing demand for primary healthcare services. The existing provision is good when benchmarked against World Health Organization standards and exceptionally good when compared with countries at a similar stage of development and with most other states within India.

There are about 500 primary healthcare centres spread across the state, many in isolated rural areas. Their role is to offer medical care, mother and child welfare, family planning, improvements in environmental sanitation, control of communicable disease, health education and school health. In addition, they are required to collect statistics and provide a referral service. Each centre is managed by a chief medical officer and has approximately 60 staff. Typically, there is a main facility that accommodates

clinics, operating theatres for minor surgery, three wards for short-stay patients and a pharmacy. Various outreach services may also be located at satellite sites in the community served by a centre.

Until now, attempts to improve the effectiveness of primary healthcare provision have been limited to sending chief medical officers and other doctors who have been identified as candidates for promotion on a lengthy training programme at the state's Institute for Management in Government. The senior health official who has approached you for advice believes that there has been relatively little transfer of learning back into the primary healthcare centres and the heavy investment in training has had little effect on performance.

1 Design an intervention that will improve the capability of the staff working in the health centres in order to improve the effectiveness of the services they provide.
2 Identify issues that might affect the success of your proposed intervention and explain how you would address these issues.

Case study **V.2** *Designing an intervention to increase the motivation and flexibility of the workforce in a large dairy company*

The new CEO and the director of HR of a large dairy company have sought your advice regarding the kind of intervention that might be effective in helping them to involve employees in order to motivate them to work more flexibly and support the modernization of the dairies.

The Danish-owned company began production in the UK six years ago following the acquisition of a number of British dairies. It now employs 2,400 people at six dairies and one other plant that produces fruit drinks. The past few years have been a difficult time for the dairy industry in the UK and many companies have gone out of business. Supermarkets are selling milk at very competitive prices, presenting a fierce challenge to the doorstep delivery business, and the abolition of the Milk Marketing Board has led to a sharp increase in the price of raw milk.

After the new CEO was appointed, he initiated a restructuring of the UK business, creating strategic business units serving particular segments of the market and major customers such as the large supermarket chains. The company has also invested heavily in state-of-the-art processing and packaging equipment. But further action is still needed to ensure the company's success.

Labour requirements fluctuate considerably as the demand for dairy products varies over the week and over the year. Operations managers cope with peak periods by making extensive use of overtime working. Many of the workers at the company's processing sites are low paid and make a living wage by working overtime. It is not unusual for workers to work 50–70 hours over a six-day week. There is always plenty of overtime at peak times such as Christmas, but in order

© PHOTOALTO

to ensure that overtime is available at other times, employees operate machines inefficiently.

Managers experience great difficulty persuading employees to work flexibly or accept new practices. Over the years, they have used supplementary payments as a way of getting things done. There are over 90 different rates of pay and no formal grading system to justify differences. The state of industrial relations varies across sites, ranging from good to difficult. Absenteeism is high, running at about 10 per

cent. The company needs a skilled and well-motivated workforce able and ready to react flexibly to customers' demands and willing to support the modernization of the dairies.

1 Design an intervention that will involve employees in order to motivate them to work more flexibly and support the modernization of the dairies.
2 Identify issues that might affect the success of your proposed intervention and explain how you would address these issues.

Case study **V.3 Designing an intervention to improve the treatment offered by the trauma orthopaedic care department in a large UK NHS hospital**

The general manager responsible for orthopaedic services in a large acute NHS hospital has sought your advice regarding the kind of intervention that might be effective in helping to improve the treatment offered to patients who are admitted for trauma orthopaedic care.

Trauma orthopaedic care, which typically involves an emergency admission via the A&E department and immediate treatment for a condition such as a broken leg, and elective orthopaedic care, which involves non-emergency treatment such as a hip replacement operation, are provided by separate departments located in neighbouring hospitals within the same city. Because of a government initiative to reduce waiting times for elective treatments, extra resources have tended to be allocated to elective care rather than to trauma services. The situation confronting trauma

orthopaedic care has worsened over the past three years because the department has had to cope with an 11 per cent increase in emergency admissions. This has undermined the department's ability to provide the quality of care that it, and other stakeholders, believe patients should receive. While the hospital recognizes that trauma services are underresourced and has agreed to appoint more orthopaedic surgeons and increase their access to operating theatres, everybody recognizes that these changes will not be in place for some time. As a result, staff morale is low.

Several orthopaedic surgeons and departmental managers are highly motivated to change what they refer to as a 'desperate situation' in trauma orthopaedic care. They are particularly concerned to improve patient care for one of the largest groups of patients, those admitted with a broken neck or femur. There are approximately 800 such admissions each year and the average patient stay is 24 days.

The department has a traditional structure with four wards, each headed by a ward sister (a senior nurse who acts as ward manager). Occupational therapists and physiotherapists work with patients to facilitate their rehabilitation. Doctors, nurses, occupational therapists and physiotherapists maintain their own care notes and treatment plans. Many patients with this condition are elderly and require support in the community post discharge. Social workers, who work for the local authority's social services department, assess this need and arrange social care packages.

1 Design an intervention that will improve the situation in trauma orthopaedic care. This could include delivering outcomes such as improved patient care and reduced length of stay in hospital.
2 Identify issues that might affect the success of your proposed intervention and explain how you would address these issues.

Case study **V.4** *Designing an intervention to reduce absenteeism in the elderly care sector of Silkeborg Council, Denmark*

An area manager responsible for the care of the elderly in Silkeborg has approached you for advice. Absenteeism is a problem for all departments of Silkeborg Council. The average number of working days lost over the first six months of the year was 9.25 – an annual rate of just under 20 days per employee. One of the departments in which absenteeism is especially high is elderly care.

Over a period of several years, the council had taken a variety of initiatives to reduce absenteeism. In the area of elderly care, these have included:

- analysing the reasons for lost time
- introducing a 'stop-lift' policy to improve practices in moving and handling in order to reduce lost time caused by back injuries
- helping group leaders develop their supervisory skills
- educating the management team in the area of supervision and leadership
- helping the management team and care staff to work together to develop an absenteeism policy.

An important element of the new absenteeism policy is that illness should be regarded as a common concern for both employer and employee rather than a private issue for the employee alone. If people are off sick frequently, or for a prolonged period of time, their managers should engage in a dialogue with them about work, health and satisfaction to explore ways of improving the situation for individuals and the department.

These various initiatives have produced short-term improvements but little long-term change.

1 Design an intervention that will help the elderly care department provide a better service for patients and the wider community by ensuring that the 250 frontline staff are present more of the time and making a full contribution to the department's work.
2 Identify issues that might affect the success of your proposed intervention and explain how you would address them.

© THINKSTOCK

Chapter 14

Shaping implementation strategies

Sometimes, those leading change give insufficient attention to developing a change strategy that will be fit for purpose. If they have a successful record of leading change, they may assume that what worked in the past will work again in the current situation. This might not be the case.

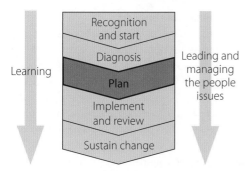

This chapter begins with a historical overview of change strategies and the values and assumptions that underpin them. After exploring the strengths and weaknesses of three frequently used approaches to managing change, some of the situational variables that need to be considered when shaping a change strategy are reviewed. The final part of the chapter draws together these ideas and presents a contingency model that leaders can use to identify the most effective way of implementing change.

Before reading on, look at Case study 14.1 on Asda and think about how you would have managed the situation if you had been the newly appointed CEO. Make a note of the essential features of your proposed change strategy. After you have read this chapter, revisit your proposed strategy for managing change at Asda and consider whether, in the light of the ideas presented, it would have been as effective as it could have been.

Case study **14.1** *Asda: a winning formula*

Asda was the first company in the UK to invest in large, out-of-town superstores, selling food and related products, and offering ample free car parking. Asda was created in 1965 as a subsidiary of Associated Dairies. It started business by opening a string of large discount stores in converted mill and warehouse premises. In the early days, shoppers were offered a limited range of competitively priced products. When Asda went public in 1978, it was the third largest food retailer in the UK, selling an ever widening range of products. Its success continued to be based on high volumes, low margins and good value for money.

A change of strategy: the pursuit of higher margins

In 1981, Asda began to shift towards a new strategy focused on raising margins. A range of new initiatives involved seeking efficiencies to reduce costs and introducing more high-margin products such as prepared foods and a wider range of non-food items. There was also a drive to expand in the south of England where customers had greater spending power. However:

- This expansion policy was slow to get off the ground, partly because planning permissions for large retail developments were more difficult to secure in the south, since the price of land was significantly higher

▶

and many of the best sites were already being developed by competitors.

- Sales were less than anticipated because Asda's value-for-money image and its somewhat austere store layouts tended to be unattractive to relatively wealthy southern customers who were used to shopping in more upmarket stores. Asda attempted to brighten up some of its stores and further distance itself from its 'pile 'em high, sell 'em cheap' image but this did not generate the anticipated contribution to operating profits.
- Long-standing customers in the north appeared to be confused by what Asda was beginning to offer them and many switched their allegiance to new cut-price retailers who were more focused on offering value for money.

Diversification

Additionally, towards the end of the 1970s, senior management had begun to consider the possibility that saturation may limit future growth in food retailing and the decision was taken to diversify into non-foods by acquiring other companies. Some of the most notable acquisitions included Wades Department Stores, with over 70 prime high-street sites, in 1977, and Allied Retailers (Allied Carpets, Ukay Furniture and Williams Furnishings) in 1978; unfortunately this acquisition did not make the anticipated contribution to profitability because the recession in the early 1980s led to heavy discounting. Ukay furniture fared worst

and was sold in 1982. While the recession hit Allied Carpets, it continued to make modest profits and by 1985 had improved to the point where it was decided to expand this side of the business.

Moreover, in 1985 Asda merged with the MFI furniture group, but this merger, the biggest in British retailing up to that point, was another disappointment. Asda-MFI attributed the poor performance to one-off problems, such as a new range of kitchens that failed to sell. It was anticipated that the problems would be short-lived but performance failed to pick up as expected. Finally, in 1986, Asda launched Asdadrive, a car retailing business at sites adjacent to six of its superstores, with the intention of rolling it out to about 75 per cent of all sites.

Refocusing on the core business

Following the merger with MFI, Asda-MFI's shares significantly underperformed. In 1987, the company surprised the market with a major change of strategy. Instead of continuing with the policy of diversification, it decided to refocus on the Asda superstores. The Asda-MFI merger ended with a management buyout of MFI, although Asda then bought a 25 per cent stake in this new company. Asdadrive and most of the associated fresh foods business were also disposed of and it was the intention to get rid of the Allied Carpets business. However, following the collapse of the equity market, it proved impossible to obtain the anticipated profit from the sale of Allied Carpets, so the business was retained and later expanded with the acquisition of Marples in 1989.

In order to develop the core business, it was decided to invest up to £1 billion over a period of three years. Most was earmarked for accelerating the opening of new stores, especially in the south, but there were other demands. Asda had lagged behind its competitors in a number of areas:

- *Own-label products:* They had all invested heavily in own-label products, which offered higher margins and better value to customers, whereas Asda had only started to introduce them in the mid-1980s, and on a much smaller scale.
- *Computerized point of sale equipment:* Competitors had invested heavily in technology that improved stock control and provided better customer service at checkouts.

- *Centralized distribution networks:* The competition had also developed centralized distribution networks for fresh foods that pushed down costs, enabled stores to receive fewer just-in-time deliveries from vehicles carrying full loads, and reduced the requirement for store-related warehousing space.
- *Store refurbishment:* Asda had neglected many of its stores, which were beginning to look tired and in urgent need of refurbishing.

Asda recognized the need for investment in all these areas.

A leap forward that contributed to a major debt problem

In 1989, a consortium that was planning to buy Gateway agreed that, if its bid was successful, it would sell 62 superstores to Asda for £705 million. This was seen as an attractive proposition. It offered Asda the possibility of making up for lost ground and regaining its old position as the third largest British food retailer. It also promised to double the number of Asda stores in the south of England and contribute an extra £1 billion to sales. Asda bought the stores in October 1989.

However, Asda's performance following the purchase of the Gateway stores was poor. Profits were down and Asda's stake in MFI contributed a loss. Allied-Marples was also in trouble. Asda had net debts of over £900 million. From the end of 1989, Asda's share price began to slide compared with major competitors and, in September 1991, it dropped a further 29 per cent. The announcement of a rights issue (an invitation to existing shareholders to purchase additional shares) at the end of the month led to another massive fall in the share price.

The appointment of Archie Norman

Archie Norman was offered the role of CEO in October 1991 and took up his appointment in December. By the time he arrived, Asda was fast running out of cash. He found a company that was bureaucratic, hierarchical and highly centralized. There was a large HQ located in the new custom-built Asda House. Directors had little contact with their subordinates. The culture was risk averse. People at all levels appeared to be intimidated by their bosses and told them what they thought they wanted to hear. They also seemed reluctant to take any initiatives that would call attention to themselves. Morale was low.

Norman also found that the trading department was dominant. Buyers, located at Asda House, determined what the stores would sell but they had little contact with store managers. The new CEO had concerns about the quality of management and the apparent unwillingness, throughout the organization, to make best use of the talent that existed. Store managers felt ignored and found it impossible to have any meaningful input to thinking at Asda House. There were also problems within stores themselves. Vertical communication was poor and customers were not valued.

If you had been Archie Norman in December 1991, what would have been your strategy for change?

A historical overview of change strategies

In the first half of the twentieth century, the dominant change strategy was a Tayloristic top-down search for efficiencies, which involved experts, such as experienced managers and methods engineers, applying their working knowledge and scientific principles to analyse problems and identify solutions that they then implemented/imposed with little, if any, consultation. The main focus of their expert attention was technostructural problems and the changes they implemented ranged from new work methods and job redesign to organization-wide production systems.

In the late 1930s and 1940s, a series of studies on autocratic and democratic leadership produced findings suggesting that participation and involvement led to improved outcomes, which stimulated the development of a new approach to managing change, known as organization development (OD), based on these values. Burnes and Cooke (2012) report that proponents of OD saw bureaucracy and autocratic top-down management as 'choking the life out of organizations' and believed that the solution was a more bottom-up participative approach. In the 1960s, sensitivity training, sometimes referred to as T-groups, was widely used to improve managers' self-awareness and develop their interpersonal skills so that they would be better able to work effectively with others to solve problems. This early strand of OD quickly gave way to using action research (see Chapter 17) and other forms of participative management to secure change in organizations. Several writers (for example Lewin, 1947; French and Bell, 1990; Bargal et al., 1992; Coghlan, 2011; Boje et al., 2011; Burnes and Cooke, 2012) have identified some of the important values and assumptions that underpin OD:

- Situations are unique and those trying to bring about change need to understand this, in order to decipher what is going on and decide what needs to be done.
- Change works best when it is a collaborative process that allows those involved to engage in discussion, debate and experimentation.
- Organizational renewal is supported by collective learning and joint problem solving.
- Organizational members support what they have helped to create.
- Change is most effective when it takes place at the level of the group.
- Change will only be sustained when the individuals and groups involved change their behaviour.
- Developing the competences that enable group members to identify and solve future problems is as important as finding the solution to the immediate problem.

Guided by the assumptions that change works best when it involves participation and takes place at the group level, most early OD interventions were small scale and localized but, as time passed, more large-scale OD change initiatives, such as total quality management (TQM), began to emerge. Burnes (2009) attributes this to the recognition that divisional and company-wide structures and large-scale production and process technologies often hindered the success of more localized change initiatives. So, while human processes still held central stage, the focus began to shift from group learning to organization learning.

In the last quarter of the twentieth century, the relatively stable economic environment following the end of the Second World War began to be disrupted by a series of factors, such as hikes in oil and other commodity prices, the development of new technologies, and the growth of low-cost competitors based in emerging economies. These disruptions placed new demands on organizations to adjust quickly to changes in the external environment. This shifted the need away from localized, relatively slow, incremental change strategies to organization-wide transformational strategies. Survival emerged as an imperative. Burnes and Cooke (2012) cite French and Bell's (1990, p. 351) description of how this shift affected the values of those leading change: top managers now focus less on people-oriented values and more on 'the bottom line and/or the price of stock ... [consequently] some executives have a "slash and burn" mentality'.

Nevertheless, although organization-wide, top-down imposed change strategies became more important again, some organizations continued to favour small-scale incremental change, especially, but not exclusively, when the requirement was for localized change. While some commentators had forecast the demise of OD, Burnes and Cooke (2012) suggest that it is enjoying a renaissance in the twenty-first century. A new generation of scholars have re-evaluated the work of Kurt Lewin and recognized the importance of human processes, while others are giving attention to different theoretical perspectives, such as social constructionism, which looks at the socially created nature of reality, and complexity theories, which consider how order, structure and pattern arise from extremely complicated, apparently chaotic systems. These developments are encouraging practitioners to develop new approaches to OD, such as appreciative inquiry (Chapter 18), which focus on dialogue between individuals, groups and other constituencies and address issues at the subsystem level and the whole system.

Three approaches to managing change

Beer (2001), a leading US consultant and professor at Harvard Business School, has researched the change strategies used by companies and has identified two well-tried approaches, economic and organization development, but argues that the most effective strategy is a third way that combines the best of both.

Economic strategies

Economic strategies focus on the drive for economic value through tough, top-down, results-driven action. These actions involve the imposition of technical solutions to those problems that are seen to undermine organizational effectiveness. There are a wide range of such solutions, including restructuring, re-engineering, drives for efficiencies and layoffs. Often, large groups of consultants are employed to help top management drive the changes into the organization. Sometimes, a new CEO or other senior executive might be appointed to act as a 'turnaround' manager, as in the case of Asda outlined above.

There are many examples where economic strategies have led to improved shareholder returns. Many believe that they made a major contribution to the success of Lord Hanson and his colleagues at Hanson Trust, where the policy was to purchase underperforming assets and turn them around, taking whatever measures necessary to reform the business, including mass redundancies. However, economic strategies have been criticized on the grounds that they often destroy human commitment. Consequently, while they might deliver short-term results, they may not guarantee longer term success.

Organization development strategies

Organization development (OD) strategies focus on creating the capabilities required to sustain competitive advantage and high performance. Beer and others identify some of these capabilities as:

- coordination and teamwork
- commitment and trust
- competence – both technical and leadership
- open communications
- creativity
- the capacity for constructive conflict
- learning.

OD strategies emphasize the importance of shared purpose, a strong culture, bottom-up change and involvement rather than financial incentives as the motivator for change. This approach can improve shareholder value but it has been criticized on the grounds that it is too indirect and takes too long, especially when the need for change is urgent.

The BBC offers good examples of the implementation of both economic and OD strategies. During the 1990s, the dominant strategy was economic (Example 14.1), but when Greg Dyke was appointed director-general in 2000, he began to pursue more of an OD strategy (Example 14.2 below).

Example **14.1** *The implementation of an economic strategy at the BBC*

After a long period of sustained success during which the BBC established itself as the world's leading public broadcaster, it began to become complacent. It knew that it was the best in the field and, because of the way it was funded via a compulsory licence fee, felt financially secure. But then the world began to change and the BBC was faced with a range of pressing problems. These are discussed in Case study 3.1, but the essential features are summarized here. They included:

- *A new political climate:* In 1979, Margaret Thatcher and a Conservative government came to power with an agenda for change that included plans to transform the public sector. Although the BBC was not the new government's first target, Thatcher viewed it as a bloated bureaucracy that was overmanned, inefficient and ripe for reform. The government (like many before and since) was also unhappy with the BBC's editorial policy and was particularly irritated by what it perceived as unpatriotic reporting of issues such as Northern Ireland and the Falklands War.

- *Wide-ranging technological change:* This was probably the biggest challenge and came from the development of digital technologies that opened up the possibility of many more channels, better technical quality, video-on-demand and interactivity.
- *Increased competition:* This came from new players and the launch of BSkyB.

In order to fend off the possibility of privatization, protect the licence fee, which the government had reduced in real terms, and prepare the BBC for the digital world, John Birt, director-general of the BBC between 1992 and 2000, introduced a range of tough reforms. His mission was to make the BBC the best managed organization in the public sector. At the time he was appointed, it was almost impossible to determine how much it cost to make a programme or use an in-house facility such as a studio. The core values were about quality rather than cost.

Birt was determined to make the organization more efficient. He introduced 'Producer Choice' and created

© GETTY

▶

an internal market that shifted the balance of power away from programme makers to managers and accountants. Departments became cost centres that had to break even, and producers were required to reduce the cost of programme making by using external suppliers whenever they could provide a more cost-effective service than in-house providers. This top-down drive to introduce new structures and systems slashed the cost of making programmes, but the reorganization led to nearly 10,000 people being made redundant or opting to leave the organization.

By the time Birt retired in 2000, his strategy for change had delivered results that secured the future of the BBC. He had gained the confidence of the government and other opinion formers – the public sector equivalent of shareholders – and had successfully introduced a range of 'technical' solutions that helped to secure the licence fee for a further six years, plus extra funding to develop new digital services. However, his change strategy had neglected the social system. He had done little to win the hearts and minds of the majority of staff. His reforms fragmented what had been a collaborative organization. People became much more focused on achieving their own targets, and were inclined to 'play safe' rather than take risks and innovate.

When Greg Dyke succeeded John Birt as director-general at the BBC, he inherited an efficient organization but detected a climate of fear and was worried about whether this increased efficiency had been won at the expense of other factors that would begin to have a negative impact on the BBC's performance. Example 14.2 describes what he did next.

Example **14.2** *The implementation of an OD strategy at the BBC*

Efficiency was still on Greg Dyke's agenda but he pursued it via a more inclusive approach. He also began to pursue a bottom-up strategy to identify what inspired people and develop the capabilities required to ensure that the BBC retained its position as the world's leading public broadcaster. He introduced a new vision. In place of trying to make the BBC the best managed organization in the public sector, his vision was to turn the BBC into the most creative organization in the world, where people enjoy their work and feel supported and powered to excel.

In February 2002, he launched the 'One BBC – Making it Happen' initiative. While he had some ideas about how to make it happen, he wanted the detailed plans to emerge from within the organization. The aims of 'Making it Happen' were to:

- put audiences at the heart of the BBC
- inspire creativity
- develop current leaders and nurture those of the future
- provide an environment where people feel valued and encouraged to give their best
- cut through the bureaucracy and build greater collaboration between divisions.

Dyke decided that he and the executive team would take every opportunity to demonstrate their commitment to the process. For example, they brought together the top 400 managers for two days to create a collective sense of responsibility for leading change. Dyke also led many discussions with other members of staff and introduced the notion of the 'big conversation'. He was determined to consult with a critical mass of employees.

In order to promote buy-in and ownership, this process was managed by in-house staff rather than external consultants. The first phase involved a search for 'quick wins'. These included modest changes such as refurbishments and reward schemes that recognized people when they made a special contribution. In the news division, for example, one of the first winners was a travel desk clerk. The second phase involved 10,000 staff, a third of the entire workforce, participating in 180 half-day workshops. Local managers and their staff were invited to 'Just Imagine' what the organization could be like and to identify what needed to be changed in order to make it happen. In each of the BBC's 17 divisions, 'Make it Happen' teams were established to coordinate the 'Just Imagine' sessions and introduce change at the local level. For example, in the news division, various measures were introduced to improve the working climate and encourage staff to take risks and perform to a high standard. The change plan also included a number of simple, inexpensive measures designed to address other issues that emerged from the 'Just Imagine' sessions, including 'back to the floor' days for managers and short secondments to enable staff to better understand what was happening in other departments.

In addition to what was happening within divisions, there were organization-wide initiatives that emerged from the 'Making it Happen' process. These included providing a more thorough induction to all new staff, a shift away from the extensive use of short-term contracts in an attempt to build more commitment, and a big investment in leadership and management training.

The third way: a combined economic/OD strategy

Beer (2001) asserts that while both economic and OD strategies can produce improvements, neither is as effective as one that combines top-down, results-driven change with the slower bottom-up development of organizational capability. With the benefit of hindsight, it could be argued that change at the BBC was successful because it did embrace Beer's combined strategy – but implemented sequentially rather than simultaneously. However, change at the BBC was not planned as a combined strategy. This emerged because Dyke recognized a need to address issues that had not been addressed by his predecessor. The real challenge for those leading change is to implement a combined strategy simultaneously.

Beer (2001) argues that change strategies that are capable of delivering sustained high performance require:

1 *The development of a compelling and balanced business and organization development direction:* This requires the CEO to lead change at the top and create an effective executive team that can speak with one voice and articulate a coherent story about why and what type of change is needed. This story is more likely to win the support of key stakeholders when it not only provides an explanation of why the change is necessary but also offers an inspiring vision of a preferred future, which includes a business direction that will lead to the achievement of key results, and an overview of the organizational capabilities required to achieve and sustain this vision.

2 *The management of key stakeholders in order to buy time to develop organization capability:* Often, but not always, this will involve managing shareholder expectations. Making overambitious commitments to shareholders about the achievement of economic results can push change managers into short-term cost-cutting strategies rather than longer term strategies designed to create the capability required to generate revenue, or achieve other outcomes required to sustain organizational success.

3 *The adoption of a sociotechnical approach that involves the development of down the line managers:* When tightly prescribed change programmes are rolled out across the organization, they typically focus on improving the technical system, and the interaction between the technical and social system tends to be ignored. Problems can arise when this type of programmatic change strategy fails to:
   • respond to local conditions, that is, it ignores the uniqueness of the situation
   • adequately involve local managers in a way that enables them to take real responsibility for moving the organization forward

- provide local managers with the opportunity to reflect on and learn from their experience of managing change.

Beer (2001, p. 242) argues that

> top-down initiatives undermine one of the key capabilities needed for sustained performance – down-the-line leaders who can lead a process of organizational learning.

He advocates the management of corporate change on a unit-by-unit basis with a high involvement of local staff because this:

- enables organizational members to engage with senior managers and contribute to shaping the change process
- facilitates the development of down the line leaders.

Top management's reluctance to adopt a combined approach

Beer's (2001) research suggests that CEOs and their top teams tend to have a mindset that promotes a top-down drive for results. The three key aspects of this mindset are discussed.

The importance given to shareholder interests

Shareholders have gained considerable power relative to employees, and even customers. Low share prices lead analysts, the financial community at large and board members to press CEOs for change. Those who do not respond risk being fired. Consequently, the top team is focused on the need to maximize economic value. Guerrera (2009) reports that former GE chief Jack Welch, widely recognized as the father of the shareholder value movement, now challenges this approach. He claims that it is a 'dumb idea' for analysts and executives to focus so heavily on quarterly profits and share price gains, and that more attention should be given to increasing a company's long-term value. Shareholder value should be regarded as a result, not a strategy. He goes on to argue that more attention needs be given to employees, customers and products. Nonetheless, many executives still appear to give high priority to achieving short-term improvement in shareholder value. Their attention to shareholder interests echoes Schein's (1996) view that chief executives and their immediate subordinates tend to see themselves as lonely embattled warriors championing the organization in a hostile economic environment. They develop elaborate management information systems to stay in touch with what is going on in the organization and impose control systems to manage costs. They view people as 'resources' and regard them as costs rather than human assets. People and relationships are merely a 'means to the end of efficiency and productivity, not an end in themselves', and their attitude is that 'if we must have human operators, so be it, but let's minimize their possible impact on the operations and their cost to the enterprise' (Schein, 1996, p. 16).

The assumption that the organization's technical rather than social system is the prime determinant of performance

Change strategies are designed to improve the organization as a technical system, and interventions such as business process re-engineering, TQM and performance management tend to be viewed as technical solutions. Beer (2001) extends this argument to include the introduction of new human resource management systems such as performance appraisal, succession planning and training programmes. They are implemented without too much thought being given to how they might affect roles, responsibilities, relationships and the power, status, self-esteem and security of individuals and groups across the organization. This neglect can erode trust, commitment and communication.

The assumption that there is little to be gained from dialogue with employees

When top teams are planning and implementing transformational change, they often overrely on top-down communication. Beer (2001, p. 238) notes how the thoughts and feelings of the CEO and the top team can be shaped by pursuing a 'drive' strategy:

> To avoid the dissonance aroused by the opposites of tough, top-down action to lay off employees and sell businesses on the one hand, and the need to gain commitment to change on the other, they distance themselves from employees. They begin to assume that employees are part of the problem.

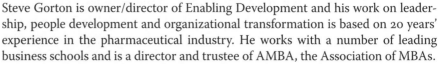

Managing change in practice **14.1** *Steve Gorton: Soft skills for hard results*

Steve Gorton is owner/director of Enabling Development and his work on leadership, people development and organizational transformation is based on 20 years' experience in the pharmaceutical industry. He works with a number of leading business schools and is a director and trustee of AMBA, the Association of MBAs.

Steve argues that those managers who are too focused on a top-down approach will be less successful than those who do everything they can to win the hearts and minds of all those involved in or affected by the change. Visit the book's companion website at **www.palgrave.com/companion/hayes-change-management4** and watch him talking about this in detail. What are the key points he is making? Do you think that most managers share his views?

Ford and Ford (2009, p. 100) argue that rather than regarding questions and complaints as resistance, change managers might benefit from viewing this 'feedback' as a resource:

> Even difficult people can provide valuable input when you treat their communications with respect and are willing to reconsider some aspects of the change you're initiating.

Morrison and Milliken (2000) suggest that senior managers are more likely to discourage upward communication when they believe that employees are self-interested and effort averse and are therefore unlikely to know or care about what is best for the organization. This kind of thinking can lead to a situation where top managers are deprived of vital information that can signal a need for further change or provide feedback about the effectiveness of change initiatives that have already been implemented (see Chapter 11). It can also lead to a situation where the top team begins to rely on outside consultants and new managerial hires. Beer notes that when this happens, it can further alienate people down the line, leading to an erosion of trust and the capabilities required for high performance such as coordination, commitment, communication and learning.

Beer (2000) and Beer and Nohria (2000) summarize the main differences between economic and OD strategies and highlight the main features of combined strategies:

- *Leadership:* Economic strategies involve top-down leadership, OD strategies involve participative leadership, and combined economic and OD strategies involve senior managers setting the direction and then engaging people throughout the organization.
- *Focus:* Economic strategies focus on changing structures and processes (the technical systems), OD strategies focus on changing the organization's culture (the social systems), and combined economic and OD strategies focus simultaneously on changing technical and social systems.
- *Process:* Economic strategies are programmatic and involve the development and implementation of plans, OD strategies are more emergent and encourage experimentation, and combined economic and OD strategies involve plans that accommodate spontaneity.
- *Reward systems:* A feature of economic strategies is a reliance on extrinsic motivation and the use of financial incentives, OD strategies rely on intrinsic motivation and the development of commitment, and combined economic and OD strategies use financial incentives and other extrinsic motivators but only to reinforce change rather than to drive it.
- *Use of consultants:* Economic strategies involve using consultants to analyse problems and prescribe solutions, OD strategies involve using consultants as facilitators to help managers diagnose problems and shape their own solutions, and combined economic and OD strategies involve using consultants who are experts but are able to use their expertise to empower organizational members.

✅ Exercise **14.1** *A change strategy for Asda*

With regard to Case study 14.1 at the start of the chapter, reflect on the strategy you would have adopted if you had been Archie Norman at Asda. Would your strategy have been primarily an economic strategy that involved a drive to maximize economic value, a development strategy that focused on developing organizational capabilities, or a combined drive and development strategy?

Situational variables that can shape an implementation strategy

The strategy Archie Norman implemented at Asda was a combined drive (for economic value) and development (of organizational capability) strategy. When he arrived, the company was facing bankruptcy and there was an urgent need to generate cash to ensure short-term survival as well as transform the business in ways that would ensure its long-term success. His approach to managing change was 'tough'; at times he was very directive and many people ended up leaving, but he also encouraged people at all levels to participate in the process of transforming the business. Norman went to great lengths to involve others and to ensure that managers down the line engaged with their subordinates. He also integrated careful planning with a willingness to let the details of the change strategy emerge over time.

There is no simple formula for designing implementation strategies based on Beer's 'third way'. After studying the merger of the Swedish pharmaceutical company Astra AB with the British company Zeneca, Eriksson and Sundgren (2005) concluded that while there are benefits from combining economic and OD theories, the ideal balance between the two may vary from case to case. Kotter and Schlesinger (1979) argue that successful change strategies are those that are internally consistent and compatible with key situational variables. In practice, many managers vary their approach to managing change at different stages of the change process. For example, some may decide not to involve others in the preliminary diagnostic phase, but might draw more people into the latter stages of problem definition and the specification of a more desirable future state. They may then move on to involve many more in the details of implementing the change plan. Factors that might lead to a variation in approach over time will receive more attention below.

Some of the main situational variables that have to be taken into account when shaping a change strategy are:

- *Stability of the external environment:* When the focal unit (work group, department, organization) is embedded in a stable environment, incremental adjustment might be an effective change strategy, but when the environment is unstable and the organization (or other focal unit) has to cope with external discontinuities, then a more transformational strategy might be called for.

- *Urgency and stakes involved:* The greater the short-run risks to the organization if the current situation is not changed quickly, the more change managers may have to adopt a directive strategy. Involvement and participation take time, and this time might not be available if the need for change is urgent.

- *Level of support:* If support for change is low, those initiating the change need to consider whether resistance could be reduced by adopting a more collaborative strategy. If this is unlikely, then a more top-down coercive strategy might need to be considered.

- *Degree to which other stakeholders trust those leading the change:* The more other stakeholders trust those leading the change, the more likely they are to be prepared to follow their direction. When trust is low, time is short, and those leading the change have more power than those who will be affected by the change, a more directive change strategy might work, but when the change is not urgent and the balance of power is unclear, then a more collaborative strategy could help to improve levels of trust.

- *Clarity of desired future state:* Reference has already been made to two different types of change: blueprint change and emergent change (see Chapter 2). Blueprint changes are those where the desired end state can be clearly specified from the start, whereas emergent changes are those where the need for change is recognized but it is difficult to anticipate what a more desirable future state will look like. Depending on other factors, such as the balance of power, it may be easier to adopt a more directive approach to implementation when confronted with a blueprint-type change. When the need for a change is recognized but there is uncertainty about what needs to be changed or what a better future might look like, a process of collaborative incremental adjustment might be most effective. Incremental change strategies often involve repeated cycles of hypothesizing about what needs to be done, planning how to achieve it, taking action, and reflecting on what happened. This process is more successful when those leading the change seek input and feedback from others.

- *The extent to which change managers have the required data for designing and implementing the change:* The more change managers anticipate that they will need information from others to help design and implement the change, for example when there is little clarity about what a desired end state will look like, the more they will have to adopt a collaborative approach and seek inputs from others.
- *Degree to which change managers have to rely on the commitment and energy of others to implement the plan:* The more change managers are dependent on the energy and commitment of others to engage in discretionary behaviours to make the change plan work, the more attention they need to give to winning the commitment and support of those they have to rely on. One way of achieving this is to adopt a more collaborative approach.
- *Alignment of values:* Burnes and Jackson (2011) report findings which suggest that when the values of those initiating the change are aligned with those affected by the change, the change initiative is more likely to be successful. When values are misaligned, support may be limited and, because it is difficult to modify people's values in the short term, those initiating the change may feel that the only way forward is to adopt a more directive approach.
- *Variations over time:* Balogun and Hailey (2008) echo Kotter and Schlesinger's (1979) view that the focus of a change strategy may vary over time. For example, in the short term, the critical requirement might be to secure the organization's survival. In order to do this, it might be necessary to adopt a tough top-down, results-driven strategy that involves radical cuts and closures, or it may be necessary to redefine the purpose of the organization. Over the longer term, the focus may switch to a more incremental strategy of fine-tuning and the major concern may become continuous improvement. This change in focus may involve a move from a directive to a more collaborative approach to implementation.
- *Divisibility:* Where the change is divisible and quick action is required, an effective approach might be to direct a part of the organization to adopt a small-scale trial before making a decision about how to proceed. If it is decided to go ahead, speed may be less of an issue and commitment might be more important. Consequently, at this stage, a less directive approach may be adopted.
- *Need for coordination:* Coordination may become a problem if a number of separate and incompatible change initiatives begin to emerge at different points across the organization. In some cases, coordination from the top may be an essential ingredient of an effective change strategy, even if many of the initiatives originate at lower levels in the organization.

Whatever the overall strategy those leading the change decide to adopt, they might want to consider the best starting point for the change. Balogun and Hailey (2008) discuss the benefit of restricting a change to a pilot site in the first instance. A pilot site might be a single unit or a completely new site. At Asda, for example, three existing stores were selected for the early experimental phase of the change. An alternative approach could be to pilot the change at a new site, with new staff. New sites can provide effective test beds for initiatives that might be resisted elsewhere because of ingrained traditional attitudes and practices. Once a change initiative has been proven on the pilot site, other parts of the organization might find it more difficult to resist the change. However, this is not always the case (see the discussion of 'spread' in Chapter 28).

A contingency model

Kotter and Schlesinger (1979) argue that one of the most common mistakes made by change agents is they often rely on a single approach to implementing change, regardless of the situation. They refer to:

- the autocratic manager whose only approach is to coerce people
- the people-oriented manager who typically tries to involve and support people
- the cynical manager who always tries to manipulate others
- the intellectual manager who relies too much on education as an influence strategy
- the lawyer-type boss who typically tries to negotiate and bargain.

There are a number of alternative change strategies that leaders can adopt. As we saw above, Beer discusses the advantages of economic and OD strategies and asserts that a combined economic and OD strategy will often be the most effective. Dunphy and Stace (1988) advocate a contingency approach and offer a model to aid choice that combines two dimensions: type of change (incremental and discontinuous) and mode of change (collaborative and coercive). Burnes (2009) offers an alternative model based on environmental turbulence/scale of change and speed of change.

The model presented in Figure 14.1 is based on three variables, time available for the change, type of change (incremental or discontinuous) and level of support for the change.

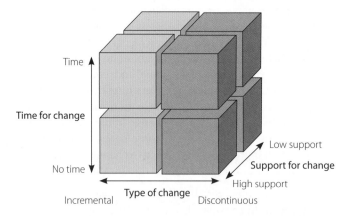

Figure **14.1** *A three-dimensional model to aid choice of change strategy*

Incremental change strategies

Figure 14.2 identifies four change strategies that might be effective when the need is for incremental adjustment.

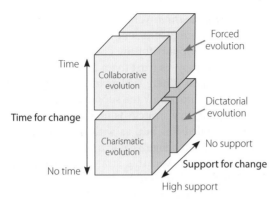

Figure **14.2** *Incremental change strategies*

1 *Collaborative evolution:* An incremental collaborative change strategy that can be effective when the change target (organization, department or work group) is broadly aligned with its environment but there is still a requirement for some minor adjustment, when the need to implement the change is not urgent (so there is time to involve others), and when key stakeholders recognize and accept the need for change.

2 *Charismatic evolution:* Another incremental strategy that can be effective even when the need for change is urgent and there is insufficient time to involve those affected, so long as charismatic leaders can communicate a compelling vision and others trust them to deliver that which they have promised.

3 *Forced evolution:* A directive approach that draws on the leaders' legitimate authority to force others to accept the change. This strategy can be effective when there is a need for incremental adjustment, there is no pressing demand for immediate change but leaders judge it will be difficult to generate sufficient support for the change. Because the need for change is not urgent and time is on their side, those leading the change can avoid a rushed, heavy-handed approach when imposing their authority. But this strategy will only work if key stakeholders eventually come to recognize and respect the leaders' authority. If they do not, those leading the change may have to adopt a more coercive approach and use their power to impose the change.

4 *Dictatorial evolution:* A top-down push strategy that can be used when there is an urgent need for incremental adjustment and key stakeholders are resisting the change. The effectiveness of this coercive approach will depend on the balance of power between those wanting to impose the change and those resisting this move.

Transformational change strategies

Figure 14.3 identifies four change strategies that might be effective when the need is for transformational change.

1 *Collaborative transformation:* Even in turbulent times, such as the years following the 2008 credit crunch, organizations can sometimes anticipate the need for transformational change in sufficient time to be able to adopt a collaborative transformational change strategy. But this approach will only be effective if change recipients recognize and accept the need for change.

2 *Charismatic transformation:* When there is a sudden and urgent need for transformational change and insufficient time to involve employees, leaders may still be able to win their support for the change if they can communicate a compelling vision and if employees trust them to deliver the promised outcome.

3 *Forced transformation:* Where leaders have anticipated the need for transformational change but do not enjoy the support of important stakeholders, they may judge that a collaborative strategy is unlikely to be successful and a more directive approach is called for. But, as with the forced evolution discussed above, because the need for change is not urgent, they can avoid a rushed, heavy-handed approach. However, this strategy will only work if key stakeholders eventually come to recognize and respect the leaders' authority.

4 *Dictatorial transformation:* Transformational changes, such as mergers and major restructuring, often cut across the entrenched interests of key stakeholders. When those affected by the change anticipate few benefits or fear harmful outcomes, they are unlikely to support the change. In such circumstances, those leading the change may feel that their only option is a strategy which relies on implicit or explicit coercion.

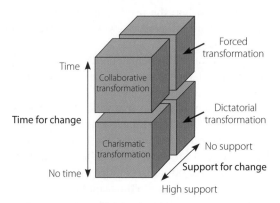

Figure **14.3** *Transformational change strategies*

Change leaders need to be alert to the longer term consequences of adopting a coercive change strategy. In the short term, they may feel that they have no option other than to impose change to secure the organization's survival, but, at some point, this approach may need to be modified if the organization's long-term prosperity is to be assured.

✓ *Exercise* **14.2** *Change strategies*

1 In your experience, which is the most frequently used change strategy? What are the reasons for this?

2 In your opinion, can a change strategy that combines a top-down drive for results *and* the development of organizational capability offer a better chance of achieving sustained high performance than one that focuses on either results or capability? Why?

3 Identify a recent change in your organization, or another organization you are familiar with, maybe because it has attracted press attention, and critically assess the effectiveness of the strategy used to implement it.

Summary

This chapter opened with an overview of how the dominant change strategies have changed over time but noted that while tough top-down strategies continue to be popular, there has been renewed interest in more collaborative strategies.

The strengths and weaknesses of the three approaches to managing change identified by Beer were reviewed:

1 *Economic strategies:* focus on the drive for economic value through tough, top-down, results-driven action. These actions involve the imposition of technical solutions to those problems that are seen to undermine organizational effectiveness. While economic strategies might deliver short-term results, they may not guarantee longer term success.

2 *Organization development (OD) strategies:* focus on creating the capabilities required to sustain competitive advantage and high performance. Beer and others identify some of these capabilities as:
   • coordination and teamwork
   • commitment and trust
   • competence (technical and leadership)
   • open communications
   • creativity
   • the capacity for constructive conflict
   • learning.

   OD strategies emphasize the importance of shared purpose, a strong culture, bottom-up change and involvement rather than financial incentives as the motivator for change. This approach can improve shareholder value but it has been criticized on the grounds that it is too indirect and takes too long, especially when the need for change is urgent.

3 *The third way, a combined economic/OD strategy:* Beer asserts that while both economic and OD strategies can produce improvements, neither is as effective as one that combines top-down, results-driven change with the slower, bottom-up development of organizational capability.

Attention was also given to some of the situational variables that need to be considered when shaping a change strategy.

The final part of the chapter drew these ideas together and presented a contingency model that leaders can use to identify the most effective way of implementing change. The eight ideal type strategies included in this model are:

• collaborative evolution
• charismatic evolution
• forced evolution
• dictatorial evolution
• collaborative transformation
• charismatic transformation
• forced transformation
• dictatorial transformation.

The chapter concluded with a note of caution. Change leaders need to be alert to the longer term consequences of adopting a coercive change strategy. In the short term, they may feel that they have no option other than to impose change to secure the organization's survival, but, at some point, this approach may need to be modified if the organization's long-term prosperity is to be assured.

References

Balogun, J. and Hailey, V.H. (2008) *Exploring Strategic Change*. London: Prentice Hall.

Bargal, D., Gold, M. and Lewis, M. (1992) The heritage of Kurt Lewin: Introduction, *Journal of Social Issues*, 48(2): 3–13.

Beer, M. (2000) Cracking the code of change, *Harvard Business Review*, 78(3): 133–41.

Beer, M. (2001) How to develop an organization capable of sustained high performance: Embrace the drive for results-capability development paradox, *Organizational Dynamics*, 29(4): 233–47.

Beer, M. and Nohria, N. (2000) *Breaking the Code of Change*. Boston, MA: Harvard Business School Press.

Boje, D., Burnes, B. and Hassard, J. (eds) (2011) *The Routledge Companion to Organizational Change*. London: Routledge.

Burnes, B. (2009) *Managing Change* (5th edn). Harlow: Prentice Hall.

Burnes, B. and Cooke, B. (2012) The past, present and future of organization development: Taking the long view, *Human Relations*, 65(11): 1395–429.

Burnes, B. and Jackson, P. (2011) Success and failure in organizational change: An exploration of the role of values, *Journal of Change Management*, 11(2): 133–62.

Coghlan, D. (2011) Organization development and action research: Then and now. In D. Boje, B. Burnes and J. Hassard (eds) *The Routledge Companion to Organizational Change*. London: Routledge.

Dunphy, D. and Stace, D. (1988) Transformational and coercive strategies for planned organizational change: Beyond the OD model, *Organization Studies*, 19(3): 317–34.

Eriksson, M. and Sundgren, M. (2005) Managing change: Strategy or serendipity – reflections from the merger of Astra and Zeneca, *Journal of Change Management*, 5(1): 15–28.

Ford, J.D. and Ford, L.W. (2009) Decoding resistance to change, *Harvard Business Review*, 87(4): 99–103.

French, W.L. and Bell, C.H. (1990) *Organization Development* (4th edn). Englewood Cliffs, NJ: Prentice Hall.

Guerrera, F. (2009) Welch slams the obsession with shareholder value as a 'dumb idea', *Financial Times*, 13 March.

Kotter, J. and Schlesinger, L. (1979) Choosing strategies for change, *Harvard Business Review*, 57(2): 106–14.

Lewin, K. (1947) Group decisions and social change. In T.L. Newcomb and E.L. Hartley (eds) *Readings in Social Psychology*. New York: Henry Holt.

Morrison, E.W. and Milliken, F.J. (2000) Organizational silence: A barrier to change and development in a pluralistic world, *Academy of Management Review*, 25(4): 706–25.

Nadler, D. and Shaw, R. (1995) Change leadership. In D. Nadler, R. Shaw and A.E. Walton (eds) *Discontinuous Change*. San Francisco, CA: Jossey-Bass.

Schein, E.H. (1996) The three cultures of management: The key to organizational learning, *Sloan Management Review*, 38(1): 9–20.

Chapter **15** **Developing a change plan**

Developing a change plan involves thinking through what needs to happen if a change target (work group, department or organization) is to be moved towards a desired end state.

Where this desired end state is known in advance, it might be possible to develop a 'blueprint' plan, which specifies a whole range of things, such as who will lead the change, what needs to be done, a timeline for implementation, and the provision of the resources at each step along the way. However, where it is difficult to define the desired end state in advance, blueprint planning may not be possible and the plan for change will have to be more tentative and flexible. This kind of flexible plan has to evolve over time.

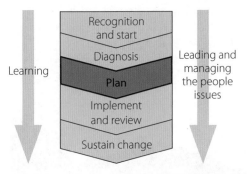

Sometimes, planning happens as a standalone, clearly bounded activity, but often the boundaries between planning and implementation and diagnosis and planning are blurred. Even when this is the case and planning is closely entwined with other activities, there are still a number of planning-related issues that require attention.

This chapter begins by looking at the development of high level plans and then goes on to discuss what has to be done to translate these high level intentions into detailed plans. Attention is focused on eight tasks:

1 appointing a transition manager
2 identifying what needs to be done
3 producing an implementation plan, with clear targets and goals, which can indicate progress and signal any need for remedial action
4 using multiple and consistent leverage points for change
5 scheduling activities
6 ensuring that adequate resources are allocated to the change and that an appropriate balance is maintained between keeping the organization running and implementing the changes necessary to move to the desired future state
7 implementing reward systems that encourage experimentation and change
8 developing feedback mechanisms that provide the information required to ensure that the change programme moves forward in a coordinated manner, especially where the plan calls for consistent change in a number of related areas.

Developing a high level plan for change

Example 2.1 on Concrete Flags, discussed in Chapter 2, illustrates a common problem. The plan for change failed to take account of the need to maintain internal alignment. Plans focused on developing new products and markets and installing a new production technology, but failed to consider the implications of the change for the operatives whose job was to manufacture and dispatch the new 'dream patios'. Case study 15.1 offers another example of how high level plans can evolve after a need for change has been recognized.

Case study **15.1** *Planning for change at Bairrada Wines*

Bairrada Wines (as it will be referred to here) is a small family-owned Portuguese winery that uses traditional methods to produce excellent wine from its own grapes. For many years, demand outstripped supply, so in 1999 it was decided to plant more vines. It was 2003 before the additional output was available for sale but, once again, all the wine was quickly sold. Encouraged by this, the founder/owner acquired more land and planted more vines to increase production, and profits continued to increase until the last quarter of 2008. It was then that the economic downturn began to affect sales. However, although revenue fell, the winery was still making a profit and the banks were happy to continue lending to Bairrada Wines, even though they were closing their doors to many similar businesses. This created a false sense of security and it was not until 2009 that the founder/owner and the CEO recognized that the recession was not a temporary downturn and they had to take action if they were to survive and prosper in the new hostile economic climate.

Although times were getting harder, the business was continuing to make a modest profit and had few debts, so the founder/owner and the CEO decided that the situation did not call for them to impose any draconian cuts. They felt that sudden radical change could do serious damage to the winery's culture and the high level of staff commitment that, over the years, had contributed to the success of the business. Their view was that the best way forward was to involve the management team and as many employees as possible in developing a plan that would secure the long-term success of the business.

After several meetings of the management team, a plan began to emerge. It was decided that more needed to be done to secure the future market for their wine. Over 75 per cent of output was sold within

Portugal and no effort had been made to develop export markets. The 25 per cent of the wine that had been sold for export had been sold to foreign buyers who had sought out the winery. But in 2009, the Portuguese economy was in free fall and local sales were predicted to fall over the long term. So, it was decided to begin exhibiting at those wine fairs that attracted foreign buyers and to do more travelling to visit buyers in selected export markets such as Germany and the UK.

© PHOTODISC/GETTY IMAGES

Attention was also given to reducing costs. Labour costs accounted for a high proportion of the company's annual spend so this was an obvious target, but because most employees had been with the company for many years, redundancy was a costly option and letting people go could undermine the commitment of those who were retained. However, one senior member of the administrative department was 12 months off qualifying for early retirement, so a possibility was to explore her willingness to switch to a part-time contract until then. It was also decided to explore other possibilities for moving staff to part-time work.

Savings could also be made if winery and vineyard workers could be persuaded to work more flexibly. It was already accepted practice that the agricultural workers would work in the winery when, because of weather conditions or the time of the year, there was little or no work in the vineyard. But this arrangement did not work the other way round. Winery workers did not normally work outside and seasonal workers were employed at harvest and for pruning. It was anticipated that the proposal to temporarily relocate some of the winery workers to the vineyards at peak times would be resisted, but it was decided that this option needed be explored. The management team acknowledged that they would have to communicate a compelling vision of the required changes if they were to secure the support for more flexible working, an approach Dibella (2007) identified as effective when the appeal of a necessary change is low (see Figure 15.2 below).

Opportunities for cost savings were also identified within the winery. Elaborating aged wine is a traditional process, and in the winery many of the steps in the process, such as pump over, pressing, run off and racking, involved little mechanization, but it was decided to engage a consultant to investigate possibilities of reducing costs without affecting quality. With this exception, it was decided to curtail all capital investment, so plans to construct a new water purification plant and purchase additional land for planting new vineyards were put on hold.

The founder/owner and CEO felt that the management team had helped them to develop a good plan for change that involved working on several levers for change simultaneously.

Before reading on, review the change plan developed by the founder/owner and senior managers at Bairrada Wines:

1 Is the change plan based on an appropriate strategy for change (see ideas discussed in Chapter 14)?
2 Does the change plan address the main problems confronting the business?
3 Does the plan take account of all the issues that could affect the outcome or are there important omissions?
4 Would an alternative approach deliver superior outcomes?
5 If 'Yes', outline the essential elements of your alternative plan.

The proposed changes needed to be presented to the board of directors, so the CEO prepared a paper that outlined the plan and detailed all the actions that required approval. The CEO and management team considered the required approval as a formal step and did not anticipate any problems. It was a huge surprise, therefore, when the plan was not approved and the founder/owner, who owned 40 per cent of the shares, was released from the role of company president. He was outvoted by his children and other family members who, together, owned the other 60 per cent of the shares.

The board, which comprised the other family members, was not happy with the proposed plan. It wanted fast action to restore the previous level of profitability and came up with a new strategy, which involved laying off five managers and supervisors and replacing them with two new managers who would be tasked to work alongside the CEO to cut costs as quickly as possible.

The plan for change that had been developed by the management team was not implemented because the founder/owner and the CEO had paid insufficient attention to the other family members who were on the board. The founder/owner was taken completely by surprise when they rejected the plan because, during the good times, they had shown little interest in how the business was managed and had done little to help shape the company's strategy. The founder/owner also reported that he had never before observed them acting as a cohesive group.

Source: This case is based on contributions from Eva Perez.

This case illustrates how carefully thought-out plans for change may not be implemented as anticipated if those leading the change fail to take account of the concerns and interests of all powerful stakeholders. In this case, the founder/owner and the CEO, based on their past experience, had been completely unaware of the threat posed by other members of the board to their plans.

Translating high level intentions into detailed plans

Beckhard and Harris (1987) define the period of time between the identification of the need for change and the achievement of a desired future state as the 'transition state'. Often, key phases of this state are unique and different from either the pre-change state or the post-change state. For example, if an organization recognizes that it needs to improve the way it manages information and, after exploring a number of possibilities, decides to move to an enterprise resource planning integrated information system, it will experience a period of transition. There will come a point when the organization continues to rely on the old system while the new one is being developed, installed and debugged. During this period, people affected by the change will have to keep the old system going while learning how to work with the new system and develop the work roles and relationships that will have to be in place when the new system is up and running.

It is not unusual for many types of change to disrupt normal work practices and undermine existing systems of management. Nadler (1993) argues that during this period, control is one of the major challenges facing management. To abandon previous management systems before new ones have been developed can frustrate any attempt to manage the change unless some form of temporary management system is put in place. Nadler refers to the need for 'transition devices'. These include the appointment of a transition manager, the development of a plan for the period of transition between the old state and the proposed future state, the allocation of specific transition resources such as budgets, time and staff, and the development of feedback mechanisms to facilitate monitoring and control. These, along with some other planning issues, will be considered below.

☑ Exercise 15.1 *Reflect on and review a past plan for change*

Reflect on a change that you tried to introduce at work or elsewhere:

- Did you have an explicit plan for achieving the desired change?
- Did it work?
- Why was this?
- Could you have done anything to improve your plan?

Appoint a transition manager

It is not always obvious who should be in charge during the transition phase. Should the person in charge of the pre-change state continue to be in charge during the transition? Should management responsibility pass to a temporary project manager or the person who will be in charge post-transition? Beckhard and Harris (1987) suggest that there is no cut-and-dried answer to this question. Typically, the transition state is characterized by high levels of ambiguity and conflict and the individual (or group) tasked with managing the transition needs the:

- *clout* to mobilize the resources necessary to keep the change moving. In situations where resources are scarce, those responsible for keeping the old system going may resist giving up the staff time and other resources required to develop the new system. The transition manager needs the power and authority to ensure that resources are allocated as required
- *respect* of the existing operational leadership and those who are working on the development of the new system
- *ability* to get things done in ways that will win support and commitment rather than resistance and compliance.

Depending on the nature of the change, there may be several possible candidates for the transition management role. A senior person in the organization may step in and take control. A project manager may be appointed on a temporary basis (see the discussion of this possibility in Chapter 5). The person in charge of the pre-change state may be given responsibility for the transition in addition to their current operating role. A task force or temporary team may be established. Where a team approach is adopted, consideration needs to be given to team composition. It might include representatives from the constituencies affected by the change, a diagonal slice of staff representing different levels of the organization, 'natural leaders' (people who have the confidence and trust of large numbers of their colleagues), or a group who are drawn together because of their technical skills (see the discussion of the composition of the buy team tasked to plan an acquisition in Chapter 25).

Avoid unnecessary fragmentation

The problem with some of these options, such as the appointment of a temporary project manager, is that they can fragment the change process. Clegg and Walsh (2004) observe that many change processes appear to be designed with little reference to the powerful logic underlying business process thinking. They refer to software development projects that are often managed through various sequential stages including, for example, strategy, feasibility, conceptual design, detailed design, programming, implementation, use and maintenance. Even when change projects involve fewer steps, they may still be fragmented, with recognition, initial diagnosis and visioning being undertaken by one (often senior) group who then hand over to others for more detailed work and implementation, who in turn hand over to users who have to make the changes work. Clegg and Walsh (2004) suggest that this can give rise to a number of problems:

- the different people involved at each stage can make different assessments and prioritize different objectives, resulting in confusion, conflict and waste
- feedback loops are limited
- consequently, opportunities to influence and learn from each other are restricted.

So while it is important to appoint a capable person to lead the transition, it is also important to ensure that this transition manager keeps in close contact with others involved at an earlier stage in the process and the post-transition manager who will have to live with the consequences of the change.

Identify what needs to be done

Once a change objective has been identified, attention needs to be given to what has to be done to achieve the change. The Awakishi diagram could prove helpful for this purpose (Change tool 15.1).

Change tool **15.1** *The Awakishi diagram*

The Awakishi diagram (Newman, 1995) is a useful tool to stimulate thinking about what needs to be done. Let us assume that the change involves the closure of a plant to achieve cost savings. An individual (or group) could brainstorm ideas about what needs to be done to achieve this goal. The brainstorm might generate a large number of issues requiring attention, which can be grouped into categories. The most important categories provide the main 'bones', which connect to the spine of the skeleton (see Figure 15.1). These could be plant to be closed, surplus equipment, inventories and people.

Using these bones as prompts, the other things that will need to be done can be identified and prioritized. For example, what needs to happen in order to identify which plant to close, which equipment to dispose of, and which people to let go? Attention can then be given to what needs to be done to actually close the target plant, dispose of surplus equipment, and manage the relocation/severance of surplus staff. Attention can also be given to issues such as stakeholder management, communications and so on.

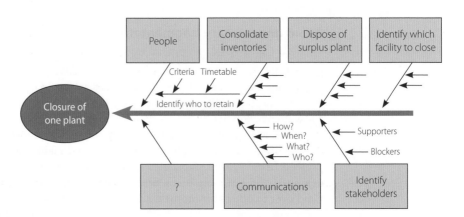

Figure **15.1** *Using the Awakishi diagram as a change tool: plant closure*

Develop an implementation plan

Two factors will influence the change plan:

1 Change participants' perceptions of the proposed change in terms of its appeal and the likelihood that it will happen.
2 Clarity of the desired end state – is the change a 'blueprint change', where the desired end state is known, or an emergent change, where the desired end state is, as yet, unknown?

Change participants' perceptions

Dibella (2007) points to four scenarios regarding change participants' perceptions of the appeal and likelihood of the change occurring, and suggests how these perceptions might affect the way a change manager responds (Figure 15.2).

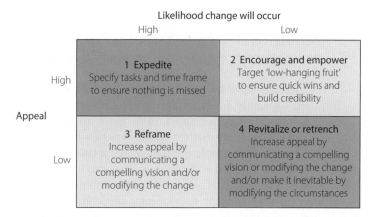

Figure **15.2** *Change participants' perceptions of the appeal and likelihood of the change*
Source: Dibella, A.J. (2007) Critical perceptions of organisational change, *Journal of Change Management*, 7(3/4): 231–42, reprinted by permission of the publisher Taylor & Francis Ltd (www.tandfonline.com)

1 *Participants view the change as desirable and consider it inevitable:* Here, the change manager's task is to expedite the change. There will be little resistance so the main requirement is to develop an implementation plan that lays out critical tasks and time frames. This will help to avoid the possibility that, because the change is viewed as inevitable, those involved may relax and overlook the need to complete some necessary tasks.
2 *Participants view the change as desirable but are not convinced it will happen:* Thus, the change manager needs develop a plan that will encourage and empower others by acting in ways that will shift their perceptions and increase their conviction that the change will be accomplished. Dibella (2007) suggests this can be achieved by developing a change plan that focuses, first, on achieving small victories by addressing the 'low-hanging fruit'. This will help to secure early successes that will build credibility.
3 *Participants do not view the change as desirable but anticipate that it is inevitable:* This fits the stereotypical condition where resistance to change is expected. Dibella (2007) suggests that, overtly or covertly, participants will strive to alter the conditions and make it less inevitable by reducing their engagement. Delaying tactics, for example, might hold back the change until it is eclipsed by a crisis or some other initiative that diverts attention elsewhere. Here, change managers need to focus attention on reframing and making the change more desirable. There may be features of the change that can be modified to make it more appealing. As a minimum, the change manager will need to communicate a compelling vision.
4 *Participants perceive the change to be undesirable and unlikely to happen:* Here, there is no clear incentive for participants to engage in the change. They may be openly defiant and act in ways that will test the change manager's credibility. Dibella (2007) suggests that the change manager's options include revitalization, modifying the change to make it more appealing, or retrenchment, altering the

environment to make it seem more inevitable. One possibility for altering the environment might be to recruit a set of champions or advocates into the process, who view the change in more positive terms, or remove some of the most resistant participants from the scene (see the discussion of stakeholder management in Chapter 10).

Clarity of the end state

Planning is easier when the desired end state is known. With a blueprint change, it is normally relatively easy to define the change goal, but sometimes it is not possible to articulate a clear vision of what the end state will look like. There are circumstances, described in Chapter 2, where a need for change might be recognized – because, for example, the organization is losing market share or failing to innovate as fast as its competitors – but it may be far from obvious what needs to be done to improve matters. There may be a broadly defined goal and a direction for change, for example improving competitiveness, but it may not be possible to provide a detailed specification of what this end state will look like. Here, change needs to be viewed as an open-ended and iterative process that emerges or evolves over time. Rather than developing a single grand plan to achieve a clearly defined end state, the change manager might need to think in terms of developing a series of smaller but reasonably well-defined plans. After each step in the implementation process, the step itself and the direction of the change can be reviewed, and the plan for the next step in the process firmed up (Figure 15.3).

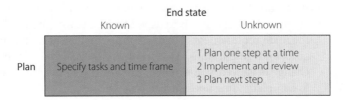

Figure **15.3** *Clarity of end state and content and structure of the plan*

Quinn (1993) suggests that this kind of incremental approach to planning and implementing change can have advantages even when change managers do have a view of where they want the organization to be. He argues that taking small steps, reflecting on progress, and building on the experience gained can be effective because it:

- improves the quality of the information used in key decisions
- helps overcome the personal and political pressures resisting the change
- copes with the variety of lead times and sequencing problems associated with change
- builds the overall awareness, understanding and commitment required to ensure implementation.

Based on his observations of senior managers in Xerox, GM and IBM, Quinn (1993, p. 83) concludes that often, in practice, by the time change plans begin to crystallize, elements of them have already been implemented. He reports that by consciously adopting this kind of incremental process, change managers can build sufficient momentum and gain sufficient commitment to change plans 'to make them flow towards flexible and successful implementation.'

While recognizing the importance of planning, Nadler and Tushman (1989) caution against developing an uncompromising commitment to an implementation plan. Early actions will have unintended consequences, some welcome, some not, and it is inevitable that some unforeseen opportunities as well as problems will be encountered. They assert that to ignore unanticipated opportunities just because they are not in the plan could be 'foolish'. Planned change involves learning and constant adjustment. Planning needs to be balanced with what they refer to as 'bounded opportunism'. Change managers should not feel compelled to respond to every problem, event or opportunity, because doing so could involve adopting courses of action that are inconsistent with the intent of the change, but, within certain boundaries, being opportunistic and modifying plans can deliver benefits.

Beckhard and Harris (1987) identify seven characteristics of effective transition plans. Effective plans are:

1 *purposeful:* the planned activities are clearly linked to the change goals and priorities
2 *task specific:* the types of activities involved are clearly identified rather than broadly generalized
3 *integrated:* the discrete activities are linked
4 *temporal:* events and activities are timetabled
5 *adaptable:* there are contingency plans and ways of adapting to unanticipated opportunities and problems
6 *agreed:* by top management, and other key stakeholders, as required
7 *cost-effective:* to avoid unnecessary waste.

This list might be extended to include some of the issues considered below, for example the provision of adequate resources and rewards for desired behaviours.

Use multiple and consistent leverage points for change

It was noted earlier that organizations are equilibrium-seeking systems. If only one component of the system is changed, this can trigger forces that will work to realign all the components of the system and re-establish the status quo. One way of avoiding this is to use multiple and consistent leverage points for achieving change. For example, if it is decided to change the structure of an organization, it may be necessary to modify other elements of the system at the same time, such as culture and career management systems, in order to secure the intended benefits (see Example 15.1).

● *Example* **15.1** *Matrix structures*

Managers in an auto components manufacturing company decided that, in order to improve performance, they needed to introduce a new structure that would be more responsive to the complex technical issues associated with production and the unique project requirements of their customers (see Figure 15.4). This kind of dual focus has long been recognized as a requirement in the aerospace industry, where products are technically complex and customers very demanding.

In this case, the promise of improved performance was not realized because the transition plan did not incorporate multiple and consistent leverage points for change. It failed to recognize the need, when

▶

introducing the new structure, to adjust a range of other elements of the wider organization, such as the organization's systems and culture.

Matrix structures will only be effective if they are supported by organizational systems concerned with planning, controlling, appraising and rewarding that serve the needs of the functional and customer project dimensions of the new structure. If appraising and rewarding are left in the hands of functional managers, such as the heads of engineering and production, the managers responsible for the customer-related projects might find that they have little influence over the members of their project teams who also report to a functional manager. In the auto components manufacturing company, team members gave priority to the demands of their functional managers because they continued to exercise most influence over their career and reward package. The new systems failed to accommodate the new dual focus.

There was also no attempt to modify the pre-change organization culture to ensure it would be compatible with the new matrix approach to management. In this case, there was a rigid bureaucratic tradition, a belief in the sanctity of the unity of command, and a commitment to immediate departmental objectives. This culture undermined attempts to achieve the dual strength of technical competence and customer focus. A matrix organization will only be effective when members are aware of and willing to work towards

these broad goals and have the skills and competence to expand their contribution to embrace responsibility for managing the relationship between their subtask and the broader organizational purpose.

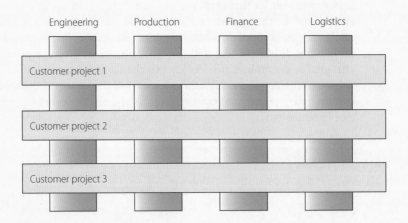

Figure **15.4 *A matrix organization structure***

Schedule activities

Any plan for change will involve managing a long list of things that will need to be done in order to make the proposed change a reality. There will be different lead times associated with the various tasks, interdependencies between them and resource and other constraints. All these things need to be taken into account when developing an implementation plan. Careful scheduling can help to ensure that all the necessary actions occur when required. This process can be accomplished with the help of critical path analysis (Change tool 15.2).

Change tool 15.2 *Critical path analysis*

Critical path analysis is a useful tool for scheduling and identifying resource requirements. It focuses attention on:

- the tasks that need to be completed
- the order in which they have to be undertaken
- dependencies between activities. It may not be possible to start some activities until others have been completed, whereas others might not be dependent on the completion of other tasks and can be started at almost any time – so long as they are completed when required by later stages in the change process (see task 8 below)
- the resources needed to complete the project and when they will be required
- milestones to monitor progress
- the shortest time to complete the project to specification and within budget
- possible ways of shortening this project time if circumstances require – crashing the critical path.

Drawing the critical path

The first step is to list all the tasks that need to be undertaken, the time required to complete each task, and the dependencies between tasks. A simple table can help.

Task	Duration	Start date	Completed by
Task 1	5 days	To be completed first	Day 5
Task 2	3 days	On completion of task 1	Day 10 (2-day float)
Task 3	5 days	On completion of task 1	Day 10
Task 4	5 days	Any time	Day 15 (10-day float)
Task 5	5 days	On completion of task 3	Day 15
Task 6	3 days	On completion of tasks 4 and 5	Day 21 (3-day float)
Task 7	2 days	On completion of tasks 4 and 5	Day 17
Task 8	1 day	Any time	Day 22 (21-day float)
Task 9	5 days	On completion of task 7	Day 22

The data can be used to create a diagram (see Figure 15.5), in which the arrows show the activities and time required to complete each task. Circles show the beginning and end of tasks. The numbers in each circle shows the required end date, and the milestones for the critical path (in bold).

The coloured arrows in Figure 15.5 show the critical (longest) sequence of dependent tasks and the shortest time to complete the project. Unless tasks on the critical path are started and completed on time, it will take longer than necessary to complete the overall project. The table above and Figure 15.5 also show those tasks that have spare or 'float' time. For example, task 8 can be started any time as long as it is completed by day 22.

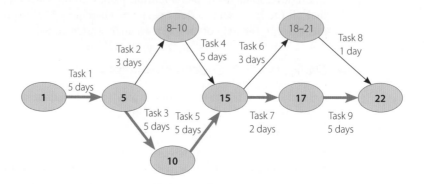

Figure **15.5** *A critical path analysis*

Crashing the critical path

If part of the project is delayed, or it is necessary to complete the project quickly for some other reason, the critical path analysis will indicate how this might be achieved. Just throwing extra resources at every task to speed things along may be less effective than targeting extra resources at those tasks that are part of the critical path.

Provide resources for the transition

There is always a cost associated with change. For example, there may be a need for training, new equipment, the development of software, the design of new structures, and staff time to do all this. When the need for change is anticipated, it is more likely that the resource requirements will have been foreseen. However, when change is imposed as an urgent response to a pressing problem, the organization may find itself stretched. Sometimes, it may be so stretched that it cannot resource the change and has no option but to go out of business. In less pressing circumstances, it is not unusual for management to assume that much of the staff burden of change will be borne by employees working longer and harder. While people often rise to the challenge in the short term, goodwill cannot be relied on forever. Where change is a constant feature of organizational life, this needs to be recognized and the required resources made available.

Nadler and Tushman (1989) suggest that one of the most scarce resources is senior staff time and when senior managers are so overloaded they are unable to invest sufficient time – to attend planning meetings, make presentations, attend special events, get involved in training and so on – change initiatives are more likely to fail.

Reward transition behaviours

Where people are required to continue working with the pre-change system, in order to 'keep the show on the road' and maintain operations, while simultaneously developing the new system, they might give insufficient attention to the change. This can happen because existing control systems reward current practice and offer little incentive for development work. Consequently, people are discouraged from investing their time in this work and from experimenting with new behaviours that might be required in the future. Steps need to be taken to ensure that transition behaviour is not penalized and every opportunity to reward this kind of behaviour needs to be explored. Example 12.1 on the introduction of legal templates illustrates this point.

Develop feedback mechanisms

A key requirement for maintaining control in the transition phase is the development and installation of new feedback devices and control systems that will facilitate the monitoring of progress towards the desired future state. Nadler (1993) is a particularly strong advocate of customized feedback mechanisms during the transition phase, because the feedback processes that managers normally use to collect information about how the organization is functioning might be less appropriate during this period. Additional sources of feedback might include organization-wide surveys, focus group discussions, and feedback from individual organizational members. Bruch et al. (2005) argue that a comprehensive system for monitoring and reporting is essential to maintain people's attention on the change. This point receives more attention in Chapter 26.

Using Oakland's figure of eight framework to prepare and review plans for change

Oakland (2013) has developed a figure of eight framework for change that can provide a useful template for assessing whether early preparation and future planning for implementation will lead to a successful change (see Figure 15.6).

Those leading change can use the top ring of the model to determine whether their plan gives sufficient attention to generating a readiness for change. For example, does it include actions that will help to create a shared appreciation of and commitment to the need for change, and is attention given to helping change recipients develop an understanding of the priorities for change?

The bottom ring of Oakland's model can be used to help plan for implementation. Any and every change requires the implementation of new, or modification of existing, processes. The organization and resources need to be assembled around this new process architecture; systems and controls need to be aligned to ensure that people understand their responsibilities, accountabilities and who they need to keep informed; and this understanding needs to drive the new behaviours that will be required to deliver the change.

The figure of eight framework can help those leading change understand the consequences of not attending to each element of the model. Figure 15.7 shows

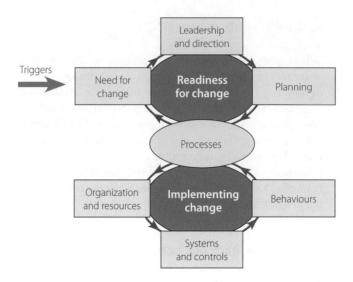

Figure **15.6** *Oakland's figure of eight framework for successful change*
Source: Oakland, 2013

what could happen if insufficient attention is given to the three elements in the top circle. Leaders can use the signs and symptoms listed in the right-hand column to identify the strengths and weaknesses of their plans for change.

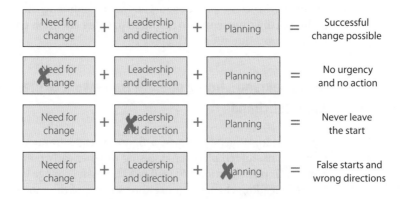

Figure **15.7** *Readiness to change*
Source: Oakland, 2013

If the need for change is not properly understood, there will be no urgency and no action; if leaders provide insufficient direction, the change will not get started; and if early planning is inadequate, there will be false starts and unanticipated consequences.

Figure 15.8 illustrates what could happen if insufficient attention is given to the four elements in the bottom circle.

If insufficient attention is given to how processes will have to change, effort will be wasted on non-core activities. There could also be paralysis and frustration if leaders fail to give enough attention to organization and resources because people

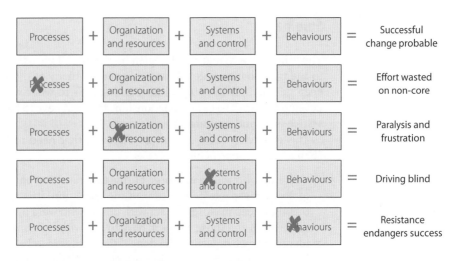

Processes	+	Organization and resources	+	Systems and control	+	Behaviours	=	Successful change probable
✗ocesses	+	Organization and resources	+	Systems and control	+	Behaviours	=	Effort wasted on non-core
Processes	+	O✗anization a✗ resources	+	Systems and control	+	Behaviours	=	Paralysis and frustration
Processes	+	Organization and resources	+	✗stems a✗ control	+	Behaviours	=	Driving blind
Processes	+	Organization and resources	+	Systems and control	+	✗aviours	=	Resistance endangers success

Figure **15.8 *Implementing change***
Source: Oakland, 2013

will not understand their new roles and responsibilities. Implementation could be undermined if the systems and controls required to run the new processes are not in place (driving blind), or if insufficient attention is given to the way people will have to behave in order to make the change work.

Managing change in practice **15.1 *John Oakland: Figure of eight framework to prepare and review plans for change***

John Oakland is chairman of Oakland Consulting plc and Emeritus Professor of Business Excellence and Quality Management at Leeds University Business School.

For over 30 years, he has researched and consulted in all aspects of quality management and business improvement in thousands of organizations. He is also the author of several bestselling books, including *Total Organizational Excellence, Total Quality Management, Oakland on Quality Management, Statistical Process Control* and *Production and Operations Management.* Oakland Consulting, in its original form, was created by Professor Oakland in 1985 and now operates throughout the world, helping organizations in all areas of business improvement.

Visit the book's companion website at **www.palgrave.com/companion/hayes-change-management4** to watch John Oakland talking about how he has used this figure of eight framework in his consulting work with a wide range of organizations.

☑ *Exercise* **15.2 *Seven symptoms of poor planning***

Think about a change you have observed, experienced or led at work or in some other organizational setting such as a sports club or university society.

Was there any evidence of Oakland's seven symptoms of poor planning (as shown in Figures 15.7 and 15.8)? How could the plan for change have been improved?

Summary

Those leading a change need to plan how they will move from the pre-change state to the post-change state. During this period, many of those involved will have to keep the old system going while learning how to work with the new system and develop the work roles and relationships that will have to be in place when the new system is up and running.

This chapter looked at some of the tasks that need to be incorporated in the change plan. These include:

1 Deciding who will be in charge during the transition phase. While it is important to appoint capable people to lead the transition, it is also important to ensure that they keep in close contact with others who were involved at earlier stages in the process and those who will have to live with the consequences of the change.

2 Identifying what needs to be done if the change is to be successful.

3 Producing an implementation plan that takes account of change participants' perceptions of the proposed change and the clarity (or lack of clarity) of the end state.

4 Using multiple and consistent leverage points for change. If only one component of the system is changed, this could trigger forces that will work to realign all the components of the system and re-establish the status quo. One way of avoiding this is to use multiple and consistent leverage points for achieving change.

5 Scheduling activities. Critical path analysis is a useful tool at this stage.

6 Ensuring that adequate resources are allocated to the change and that an appropriate balance is maintained between keeping the organization running and implementing the changes necessary to move to the desired future state.

7 Implementing reward systems that encourage experimentation and change.

8 Developing feedback mechanisms that provide the information required to ensure that the change programme moves forward in a coordinated manner, especially where the plan calls for consistent change in a number of related areas.

References

Beckhard, R. and Harris, R.T. (1987) *Organizational Transitions: Managing Complex Change*. Reading, MA: Addison-Wesley.

Bruch, H., Gerber, P. and Maier, V. (2005) Strategic change decisions: Doing the right change right, *Journal of Change Management*, 5(1): 97–107.

Clegg, C. and Walsh, S. (2004) Change management: Time for change?, *European Journal of Work and Organizational Psychology*, 13(2): 217–39.

Dibella, A.J. (2007) Critical perceptions of organisational change, *Journal of Change Management*, 7(3/4): 231–42.

Nadler, D.A. (1993) Concepts for the management of organizational change. In C. Mabey and B. Mayon-White (eds) *Managing Change*. London: Paul Chapman/Open University.

Nadler, D.A. and Tushman, M.L. (1989) Organizational frame bending: Principles for managing reorientation, *Academy of Management Review*, 10(3): 194–204.

Newman, V. (1995) *Made-to-measure Problem Solving*. Farnham: Gower.

Oakland, J. (2013) *Managing Change in Practice: John Oakland*, video, available on the companion website to this book.

Quinn, J.B. (1993) Managing strategic change. In C. Mabey and B. Mayon-White (eds) *Managing Change*. London: Paul Chapman/Open University.

Chapter 16

Types of intervention

Change efforts can be less successful than they might be because those responsible for managing the change are unaware of the full range of interventions that are available. Cummings and Worley (2001, p. 142) define interventions as 'a set of sequenced planned actions or events intended to help an organization increase its effectiveness'. They are deliberate acts that disturb the status quo. This chapter reviews some of the main types of intervention.

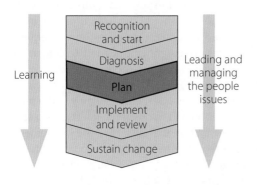

The first section considers interventions from the perspective of who does what (Weisbord, 1989). Using this approach, four main types of intervention are identified that involve:

1 experts applying scientific principles to solve specific problems
2 groups working collaboratively to solve their own problems
3 experts working to solve system-wide problems
4 everybody working to improve the capability of the whole system for future performance.

The second section introduces an alternative typology that classifies the types of intervention on the basis of the issues they address (Cummings and Worley, 2001). Again, four main types of intervention are identified, focusing on:

1 human process issues
2 technology/structural issues
3 human resource issues
4 strategic issues.

A number of specific interventions are briefly considered under each of these headings, and a selection of interventions are discussed in more detail in subsequent chapters.

A classification of interventions based on who does what

Weisbord (1989) observes that there has been a continuous development of new types of intervention over the past century and suggests that an important development (already discussed in Chapter 14) was the recognition that collaborative interventions that involved organizational members diagnosing and solving their own problems could be an effective way of achieving improvements in performance. Another trend he observed was a shift away from interventions that focused on localized small-scale problems towards interventions that targeted system-wide issues. He mapped these developments onto a timeline, as shown in Figure 16.1.

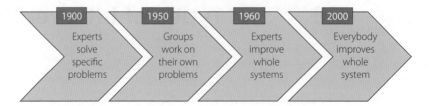

Figure **16.1** *Developments in interventions over the past century*

The use of technical experts to solve problems

Fredrick W. Taylor published his *Principles of Scientific Management* in 1911, in which he advocated a systematic experimental approach to problem solving. His principles involved a careful analysis of tasks and experimentation to determine, from the perspective of efficiency, how the task should be divided into segments and how the work in each segment should be done. One of the most frequently quoted examples of Taylor's work involves an assignment at the Bethlehem steel plant designed to find the most efficient way of moving 100lb pigs (slabs) of iron from a loading dock into a railroad truck (a bogie). He enlisted the help of a pig iron handler called Schmidt and studied him, while, on instruction, he moved the pigs in different ways. The outcome was an ideal approach to doing the job that also specified rest periods and included an incentive system that rewarded the job holder for working efficiently. The new approach increased productivity by 280 per cent.

Taylor's approach led to the widespread use of experts to solve problems, such as methods engineers to identify the most efficient way of accomplishing a task and time and motion analysts to set standard times for the completion of each segment of the work. Although, at the beginning of the twentieth century, experts like Taylor were mainly used to solve small-scale problems, others were also working on the development of organization-wide manufacturing systems, such as the introduction of the assembly line in 1913 by Henry Ford.

Today, many organizations continue to employ experts to solve specific and systemic problems, for example to develop a new payments system or design a new information management system. Experts are often brought in from outside a business unit or the organization to help when there is only the occasional need for a specific kind of expertise (and thus a permanent in-house expert cannot be justified), when the need is for cutting-edge expertise that might only be obtained from specialist departments or external consultants, or when a solution has to be found urgently and the quickest approach is to buy in external help. Expert help can be invaluable but when experts adopt a prescriptive approach (see Chapter 6), members of the target system may not agree with their diagnosis of the problem and therefore may not be committed to implementing the prescribed solution. Also, members of the system may not learn how to solve the problem for themselves, so, should it reoccur, they will continue to be dependent on the expert for the solution. This is much less of a problem when the external expert acts as a facilitator to help those involved in the change develop the capability to manage this and similar problems for themselves rather than as a technical expert who prescribes solutions.

Interventions that involve groups working on their own problems

In 1944, the Research Center for Group Dynamics at MIT was established, and Kurt Lewin and his associates began to produce evidence that supported the proposition that the behaviour, attitudes, beliefs and values of individuals are all based in the groups to which they belong. This led to the realization that groups can exert a strong influence over whether individuals will accept or resist change. A consequence was the development of new kinds of interventions that involved all members of a work group working together to solve problems. Interventions focused on changing the group's norms, roles and values.

Cartwright (1951) summarized eight principles, which emerged from the early research on group dynamics, and which influenced the design of this type of group-focused collaborative intervention. The first five are concerned with the group as a medium of change and how the group is able to exert influence over its members. The final three focus on the potential benefits of making the group the target for change, even when the prime aim is to change individual behaviour. Evidence suggests that by changing the standards, style of leadership and structure of a group, it is possible to change the behaviour of individual group members. The eight principles are:

1 **If the group is to be used as a medium of change, those people who are to be changed and those who are to exert influence for change must have a strong sense of belonging to the same group.**

This implies that where the change agents are regarded as part of the group, and a strong 'we' as opposed to an 'us and them' feeling exists, those trying to bring about change will have more influence over others. Cartwright cites research findings that show that there is greater change in members' opinions when discussion groups operate with participatory rather than supervisory leadership.

2 The more attractive a group is to its members, the greater the influence it will exert over its members.

When individuals find a group attractive and want to be members of the group, they are more ready to be influenced by other members of the group. Attractiveness promotes cohesiveness and a willingness, on the part of members, to conform with others when conformity is a relevant matter for the group.

A group is more attractive to members the more it satisfies their needs. Some of the ways that group attractiveness can be increased include:

- increasing the liking of members for each other
- increasing the perceived importance of the group goal
- increasing the prestige of the group in the eyes of others.

3 A group has most influence over those matters that attract members to it.

Research evidence suggests that in attempts to change attitudes, values or behaviour, the more relevant they are to the basis of attraction to the group, the greater the influence the group is able to exert on them. This helps to explain, for example, why a member of a local branch of a trade union might be willing to follow a union recommendation to engage in industrial action to influence the outcome of a pay negotiation but refuse to join a wider political protest targeted at government policies. While some members might be attracted by the union's political agenda, others might not share the union's political affiliation. However, all may be attracted by the role the union can play in protecting their interests in the workplace.

4 The greater the prestige of a member in the eyes of other group members, the greater the influence that member can exert.

The relevance of this principle, in the context of change management, is that the person who has greatest prestige and exerts most influence may not be the manager or formal leader designated by the organization. Also, in peer groups, the most influential person may not be the person who behaves in ways that are valued by superiors. For example, in a classroom situation, the teacher's pet may have low prestige in the eyes of other members of the class and will therefore have low influence over them.

5 Efforts to change individual members or subparts of a group, which, if successful, would have the effect of making them deviate from the norms of the group, will encounter strong resistance.

In many groups, the price of deviation is rejection. Consequently, especially where group membership is valued, there is pressure to conform to the norms of the group. This principle helps to explain why training interventions that involve taking individuals from different groups and training (changing) them often have a poor record in terms of transfer of learning back to the workplace when compared with training interventions that are directed at all members of a natural work group. Where the focus is on changing an individual, the individual may be reluctant to continue to behave differently after training for fear of rejection. Where the intervention is targeted at the whole group, this problem is less likely to arise.

6 It is possible to create strong pressures for change in a group by establishing a shared perception of the need for change, thus making the source of pressure for change lie within the group.

When groups are presented with 'facts' by an outsider, for example a manager, an internal or external consultant, even where, to the outsider, the facts 'prove' the case for change, the facts may not be accepted by the group. The group may reject the facts because it does not own them.

When groups collect and test their own facts, they are more likely to accept the evidence. Cartwright notes that there appears to be all the difference in the world between those cases where external consultants are hired to do a study and present a report and those in which a technical expert collaborates with the group to help members conduct their own study. Often, external reports are not acted on, but are left to gather dust rather than stimulate lasting change.

> 7 **Information relating to the need for change and the consequences of change, or no change, must be shared by all relevant people in the group.**

This principle is about getting people talking about the need for change. Changes can be blocked unless action is taken to improve communication. Evidence suggests that where the prospect of change creates feelings of threat, mistrust or hostility, people avoid communicating openly and freely about the issues that concern them. Just at the point when the need for communication is at its highest, people act defensively and communicate less.

> 8 **Changes in one part of the group or system produce strain in other parts of the group or system that can be reduced only by eliminating the initial change or bringing about readjustments in the related parts.**

This principle is about alignment. For example, a training programme that has produced changes in one subgroup, say nurses working on a hospital ward, will have implications for other subgroups working above, below and around them as part of the total group of people dealing with patients on that ward.

Many group-based interventions draw on these principles. Most aim to deliver improvements by locating decision making and problem solving as close to information sources as possible, increase members' sense of self-direction and self-control, and help everybody involved manage their problem solving according to relevant objectives rather than embedded past practices (Friedlander and Brown, 1974).

Action research offers an example of how a facilitator can work with a group to help members develop this kind of approach to problem solving. In the first instance, a change agent (who could be a consultant or experienced manager) intervenes to help the group design its own fact-finding procedures and plan and evaluate its actions in such a way that members learn from their actions and become more competent at managing problems. Eventually, as members become more competent, the facilitator becomes redundant and the group assumes responsibility for managing its own problems. This kind of intervention is discussed in more detail in Chapter 17.

Team building is also used to improve goal setting, develop more effective working relationships, and clarify members' roles and responsibilities.

Process analysis and process consultation aim to help organizational members improve their understanding of how they work with others to accomplish tasks. A facilitator works with a group as it goes about its normal business and then, from time to time, calls time out and helps participants reflect on issues, such as how they share information, make decisions, set priorities, influence each other, and review their performance.

Intergroup interventions have also been developed. Often, one or more groups are required to work together to accomplish important tasks. Sometimes this kind of interaction works well but sometimes it can be difficult because each group sees itself without fault and the other as inefficient or hostile. Negative stereotypes develop and communication becomes difficult. Beckhard (1969) describes a method for managing differences between groups (Change tool 16.1).

Change tool **16.1** *Beckhard's process for improving intergroup relations*

1 The first step involves the leaders, or the total membership, of two groups meeting to agree to commit some time and effort to working together to develop a joint understanding about the issues causing friction.
2 The two groups meet in separate rooms. Their first task is to develop a list that summarizes their attitudes and feeling about the other group, which might include their perceptions of what the other group is like and the way members behave. They do not have to reach a consensus about the items on their list.
3 Their second task is to develop another list that summarizes what they think the other group might be saying about them.
4 The groups then come together to share their lists. They start by sharing their first list – what they think about the other group. They have to listen to each other without comment at this stage. They then share their second lists – what they thought the other group would write about them.
5 The groups return to their separate rooms to discuss their reactions to what they have heard and to prepare a new list of issues they think both groups should work on. Beckhard reports that in this meeting, group members discover that at least some of the issues on their first list reflected misunderstandings that were cleared up by simply sharing information. Their lists of key issues for attention are usually much shorter than their original lists.
6 The two groups then meet, compare their lists of issues and make one joint list that reflects their agreed views about importance and immediacy. They then begin working together to agree what needs to be done.

Another intervention for improving intergroup relations is the organization mirror (Change tool 16.2). This intervention helps a unit or department to see itself as others see it and to use this new awareness to improve its working relationships with other groups. Essentially, data are gathered from other units or departments and fed back to the focal unit for consideration. Typically, members of the other groups are present when the data are fed back and participate in the analysis and discussion.

Change tool **16.2** *Organization mirror*

Before the mirror meeting

The person facilitating the process works with the focal group to help members understand how they fit into the business and identify the other units that are affected by what they do. Representatives of these 'outsider' groups are invited to meet the focal group and provide feedback. The facilitator may interview these representatives before the meeting to gain a sense of the key issues and brief them on the process.

The mirror meeting

The leader of the focal group welcomes the representatives of 'outsider' groups and invites them to give their feedback. The outsiders sit in an inner circle with members of the focal group forming a second outer circle – a configuration often referred to as a 'fishbowl'. Those on the outside listen as those in the fishbowl share their views about the focal group. Members of the focal group observe and listen but do not intervene.

The two groups then change places and members of the focal group, now in the fishbowl, talk about and seek to understand what they have heard, asking for clarification if required. The aim, so far, is to uncover problems, not to work on them.

The next step begins by prioritizing the issues that have been uncovered and identifying what needs to be done to improve the effectiveness of the focal group. This is done by subgroups, each comprising members of the focal and outsider groups.

The total group then convenes to share views, formulate action plans, and agree who needs to do what by specific dates; some actions may require joint work by insiders and outsiders.

The use of experts to solve systemic problems

Following the impact of von Bertalanffy's (1955) seminal paper on the theory of open systems in physics and biology, social scientists began to pay more attention to organizations as systems of interrelated units that transact with a larger environment. (Some of the main implications of systems thinking for organizations are summarized in Chapter 7.) This led to the development of a new class of intervention and accelerated the shift away from solving isolated problems to looking at more systemic issues. Organizations began to employ experts such as operational researchers and systems analysts to lead this approach to problem solving.

During the Second World War, operations researchers had begun to use mathematical modelling techniques to improve military capabilities and later these methods were applied to improve the efficiency of tasks such as scheduling air crews to the physical extraction of mineral ores from deep mines. Industrial engineers were also busy designing manufacturing and other technical systems for a wide range of organizations.

In the UK, social scientists at the Tavistock Institute of Human Relations (founded in 1946) began to develop interventions based on sociotechnical theory that involved changing the social and technical systems together. Much of their work was based on the principle that, in any situation, there is rarely one single social system (work relationship structure) that can be used to accomplish a given task. Usually, a number of such systems can be used to operate the same technology, thus there is an element of choice in designing work organization (see Trist, 1969). This prompts the question of which social system will provide the optimum conditions and contribute most to the outcomes valued by various stakeholders. The ground-breaking work on sociotechnical systems was undertaken by Trist and Bamforth (1951) in the UK coal mining industry. Their study (see Research report 16.1) demonstrates how the introduction of a new technology, in this case, a new technology for coal-getting, had a profound negative impact on miners and their social system.

Research report **16.1** *Sociotechnical systems*

Trist, E.L. and Bamforth, K.W. (1951) Some social and psychological consequences of the longwall method of coal-getting, *Human Relations*, 4(1): 3–38.

The introduction of the longwall method of coal-getting into UK mines failed to achieve the level of performance improvements that had been anticipated. Trist and Bamforth investigated the impact of the new technology on the social quality of work at the coalface. Their research method involved following and maintaining relatively continuous contact with 20 coalface workers over two years. Group discussions with all grades of manager provided additional data.

Their findings indicated that the 'room-and-pillar' method, which preceded the longwall system, provided workers with greater social balance than the more mechanized system. The outstanding feature of the room-and-pillar system was its emphasis on autonomous small groups. It was common practice for two colliers – a hewer and his mate – to make their own contract with colliery management and work their own small section of the coalface, with the assistance of a 'trammer' who loaded the hewn coal into tram-tubs and removed it from the coalface. This group had responsibility for the complete coal-getting task, was self-regulating and could set its own targets, adjusting work rate to take account of age, stamina and changing working conditions. The choice of workmates was also made by the men themselves.

The introduction of coal cutters and mechanical conveyers required radically different work relationships. Colliers worked in units of 40 or more men along a single long coalface, and their work was broken down into a series of component operations that followed each other in rigid succession over three shifts. In the first shift, two men worked across the top of the coalface boring holes for explosives. Another two men used a cutter to undercut the coal to a depth of 2 m, 15 cm from the floor. Four more men removed the coal from this 15 cm undercut, making a gap so that the coalface could drop when the explosive shots were fired. Finally, temporary 'noggins' were inserted in this gap so that the coalface would not sag while it was left standing during the next shift. While all this was happening, two more men dismantled the conveyor belt and got it ready for moving.

During the second shift, two men moved and rebuilt the conveyor belt close to the new face. A separate team of eight reinforced air and haulage ways and ripped down the remaining roof of the old face to make the new working area safe. When all this had been done, the explosive shots were fired to collapse the coalface.

The third shift of 20 'fillers' worked independently of each other to extract all the coal from their designated section of the coalface. This had to be completed before the cycle could begin again, but many factors could make this difficult.

There were many close interdependencies between all the above tasks. Failure to achieve 100 per cent performance on any task seriously disrupted the cycle, but despite this interdependence, workers were only qualified to perform their own task, had little or no contact with others, and had no sense of belonging to a whole work group. Trist and Bamforth documented many of the problems that workers had to contend with in this situation of 'dependent isolation' – where they were split off from any sense of belonging to either a shift or a total production group – and observed that one of the ways the miners adapted was to adopt a norm of low productivity.

Trist (1969) reports that the early 'conventional' longwall system eventually gave way to a 'composite' system, in which miners were multiskilled and worked in self-selected autonomous teams responsible for allocating themselves to the various jobs management required the team to undertake. This increased flexibility allowed an oncoming shift to take up the production cycle at whatever point the previous shift had left it and carry on with whatever jobs had to be done next. This sociotechnical approach produced impressive improvements in both performance and the quality of work life for the miners.

This kind of development gave rise to a proliferation of other interventions in different settings that were directed towards systemic issues such as managing the organization's relationship with its environment and helping to promote a better alignment of the elements within the organization. While most early systemic interventions were led by experts, many of those that were developed later integrated representatives of the target system into the process of managing change. This development has been taken a stage further in whole system interventions.

Whole system interventions to improve capability for future performance

Weisbord (1989) refers to whole system interventions in which everybody is involved in whole system improvement as the most recent category of intervention to be developed. While examples of this type of intervention, such as Weisbord's strategic search conference, are relatively new, another form of system-wide intervention, survey feedback, has been extensively used for over 60 years.

Rensis Likert and colleagues at the Survey Research Centre at the University of Michigan developed the survey feedback intervention. It involves using surveys to systematically collect information from members of an organization (or a department within an organization). After it has been collated, it is fed back to all those who participated in the survey. It is this feeding back of information that differentiates survey feedback interventions from attitude surveys. Attitude surveys are usually commissioned by senior managers who use the information generated to monitor what is going on and make decisions. Survey feedback is a more collaborative intervention, which French and Bell (1978) describe as a procedure for giving groups at all levels in the organization objective data about how the system functions so that they can use the data to improve selected aspects of the system.

The process starts with senior managers working with a facilitator to design the survey. They may develop their own survey instrument, which may be informed by one of the diagnostic models discussed in Chapter 7, or adopt a commercially available one and use it to collect information from all, or a sample, of organization members. The BBC used the Burke-Litwin model (discussed in Chapter 7) to design a survey instrument; examples of some of the questions are presented in Table 8.1.

With this kind of survey, the facilitator receives and tabulates the results and starts the process by sharing the data with top managers. After the top management group has worked on the data, identified issues that need attention and started to make plans to deliver improvements, each member of this senior group cascades the survey data to the next level and introduces and discusses the data with members of their own work groups. Members of these groups, after reviewing and working on the data, continue to cascade the process down the organization by working on the data with their own groups, and so the process continues.

Cummings and Worley (2001) observe that sometimes this process can be reversed and occur as a bottom-up rather than a top-down process. In this case, the process starts by feeding back the data to work groups or departments lower down the organization and members of these groups work on the data to address issues over which they have some control. They are also invited to discuss issues that are beyond their power and authority to resolve and forward suggestions for improvement up the organization to their managers. The next step involves these managers sharing and working on these suggestions with peers in their own (more senior) work groups, and so the process unfolds up the organization.

Cummings and Worley (2001, p. 134) describe the guidelines used to brief the facilitators who were tasked to roll out a large survey feedback intervention in the telecommunications industry in California. The key points of these guidelines, together with observations from French and Bell (1978) and Bowers and Franklin (1972), are summarized in Change tool 16.3.

⚒ *Change tool* **16.3** *Facilitator brief for survey feedback intervention*

This brief addresses two issues: pre-meeting preparation and facilitation of problem solving during meetings.

Pre-meeting preparation

- Distribute copies of the feedback report to members before the meeting so that they can think about the findings in advance. This will give them time to identify any discrepancies between the way they see the situation and the picture presented by the survey's findings or confirm their view that there are problems that need to be addressed.
- Think about substantive issues in advance. Although the facilitator should not lead the discussion and tell others what the important issues are, it can be helpful if they have formulated a view about what the data suggest is important. This might relate to the group's strengths and weaknesses or the circumstances it has to contend with. Given this preparation, as the meeting progresses, if the group focuses attention on just one issue, or if issues are being avoided, the facilitator might be able to gently nudge the group to at least consider whether there are other issues that merit their attention.
- If you anticipated that the group is likely to deny the validity of some of the data and/or be defensive, consider how you might persuade members to confront these difficult issues.
- Plan how you will introduce the meeting. You might explain that the first step is to review that data before moving on to using the data to identify issues and develop plans for managing these issues and resolving problems.

Using the feedback for problem solving

1 Consider the best way the group can review the data contained in the feedback report. It might be helpful to discuss the data in digestible chunks, stopping at appropriate points to see if anybody wants to comment or seek clarification before moving on.
2 Facilitate discussion of the data by asking questions such as:
   - Do you have any questions about what the data mean?
   - Does anything in the data surprise you?
   - What does the data tell you about how we are doing as a group/department?
3 Help the group to understand the meaning of the data by sharing your observations about how they are working on the feedback.
   - What I hear some of you saying is … . Do you all agree with that?
   - Is it a problem that needs to be addressed?
4 Help generate possibilities for action by asking:
   - What are some of the things we can do to resolve the problem?
5 Keep the group focused on what members can do to deliver improvements. Many groups find it easier to discuss what other groups or senior managers need to do rather than consider what they can do. Some statements and questions that might help are:

- There may be lots of things that others need to do but what does the data say about this group and what we need to do?
- What are the things under our control that we can do something about?

6 Be prepared for problem-solving discussions that are only loosely related to the data from the survey. A group may not be motivated to systematically go through the data and may pick on issues that are of particular concern or use these issues to trigger discussion of related issues not raised by the survey feedback. While it is important to consider the survey data, some discussion of other issues might be helpful, insofar as it helps the group to understand itself better and engage in constructive problem solving. But it is important to keep the group focused on what members can do to deliver improvements and try to ensure that it does not focus on some 'easy' issues as an excuse for not confronting others that may be important but difficult.

Additionally, 'whole system in the room' and other interventions that have a conference format have gained popularity over the past 30 years. Five principles that underpin the whole system approach are summarized below:

1 *Parallel organization versus 'whole system in the room' approaches:* The effectiveness of attempts to introduce change, especially at the strategic level, is dependent on the actions and behaviours of everybody affected by the change. Therefore, wherever practicable, everybody should be involved in the change process. A typical intervention used to develop a shared vision and an agreed strategic plan is to set up a temporary parallel organization involving representatives from different groups (and levels) across the regular organization to work together in various committees and task forces to produce the desired output. It is assumed that this kind of approach creates a wide feeling of involvement and gains the commitment of all organizational members. Often, however, only the representatives and those close to them feel involved. While this minority may become excited and passionate about the changes, others may feel left out and unable to influence developments. This can undermine their commitment to the vision and strategic plan produced by this process.

   An alternative approach, embedded in the whole system in the room or conference model, involves a significant part of the whole system rather than a parallel organization of representatives. This permits everybody to contribute. It is not uncommon to accommodate 500 or more members of the organization in a single conference. In large organizations, several conferences may be required, with some mechanism for integrating the findings from the different meetings at key stages.

2 *Problem-solving versus preferred future approaches:* Lippitt (1983) argues that trying to 'fix the past' by problem solving depletes energy, whereas focusing attention on planning for a new future releases energy. Dannemiller and Jacobs (1992) report that when Lippitt compared a problem-solving group and a group using a 'preferred futures' approach, the latter group envisioned the future they preferred and developed plans to achieve it, whereas the former group restricted itself to problem identification and action planning. Lippett also found that the preferred futures approach was associated with higher levels of energy, greater ownership of the situation, and more innovative and future-oriented goals and plans. The focus of whole system approaches tends to be on what the organization might become, rather than the current problems that need to be solved.

3 *Organizational biographies: understanding the past and present as a basis for exploring a preferred future:* All too often, organizational members are unaware of the assumptions and consistent patterns that guide how they interpret and respond to situations (see the discussion on this point in Chapter 1), yet these assumptions and consistent patterns may blind them to threats and opportunities and lead them to develop unrealistic strategic plans. What an organization is today has been influenced by the way organizational members have interpreted and responded to opportunities and threats in the past. But organizations are not victims of the past. It is possible to learn from past experience and use this learning to challenge and modify assumptions, identify new possibilities, and what needs to happen if these possibilities are to become reality. An element of many interventions, therefore, is the development of a better understanding of where the organization has come from, where it is today, and how it moved from where it was to where it is.

4 *Overcoming resistance to change:* Change occurs when organizational members experience a tension that results from a discrepancy between their awareness of current reality and their desired future state (Fritz, 1984). They are motivated to reduce the tension by acting in ways that will help the organization move towards the more desired future state. The conference method is designed to create this necessary tension across the whole organization. Dannemiller and Jacobs (1992) advance this view and adapt Gleicher's change formula to argue that change (C) will occur when the product of dissatisfaction with the present situation (D), a vision of what is possible (V), and practical first steps towards reaching the vision (F) are greater than the cost of change/resistance (R): $C = (D \lor F) > R$.

The conference method involves a process that openly explores organizational members' satisfaction with the status quo, develops a clear vision of future possibilities, and identifies practical first steps in order to motivate people to change.

5 *Open systems planning:* Jayaram (1977) and others strongly advocate open systems planning. In the conference method, external stakeholders, such as suppliers and customers, are invited to contribute their views about the organization's current performance and the opportunities and threats it will have to respond to in the future. This kind of input enriches the database available to organizational members. Essentially, large group methods involve getting people together to deal with issues of importance. These issues might relate to problems affecting performance in a particular organizational unit, managing relationships with customers or suppliers, or the future of the whole system. Alban and Bunker (2009) suggest that they tend to be most effective where the issue affects the whole system, it is important to the organization's future, it would benefit the organization to have broader ownership of the issues, and where new and creative ideas are required. Large group methods can help promote bottom-up change but they can also form part of a management-led initiative and do not need to take away management's responsibility for charting the way forward.

Change tool 16.4 illustrates a template for this kind of 'whole system in the room' intervention.

🔍 *Change tool* **16.4** *A conference method for developing a 'preferred future'*

The conference method is a process involving one or more meetings of organizational members, and other stakeholders as appropriate, to:

- examine key issues affecting the organization's future from a variety of perspectives
- learn from each other
- develop a shared understanding.

This shared understanding can be used either to facilitate real-time decision making by the organizational members participating in the conferences, or as an input to guide the decision making of a smaller strategic planning group.

Elements of the conference method

The details of the process will differ depending on circumstances, and will normally be decided by an in-company design team, facilitated by a consultant. However, the elements of the process typically include the following steps:

1 *Past:* development of a shared understanding of the organization's strengths and weaknesses and opportunities and threats at an agreed point in time, say three years ago.
2 *Present:* exploration of the organization's current strengths, weaknesses, opportunities and threats, as perceived by organizational members and external stakeholders.
3 *Lessons about change:* assessment of how the change (from past to present) was managed. Key questions might be: What did we get right? What might we have done better?
4 *Futures:* development, by a number of subgroups, of a range of alternative visions of the future, based on the views of organizational members and external stakeholders.
5 *Criteria:* examination and critique of these alternative visions to identify the criteria that should be used for selecting a 'preferred future'. (Justifying choice when voting for preferred futures can help to surface criteria.)
6 *Shared vision:* generation of a shared vision of what a preferred, achievable future would be like.
7 *Implementation plan:* development of a shared understanding about the best way of managing the change required to move to the desired future state, taking account of lessons learned from reviewing the management of past changes (step 3).

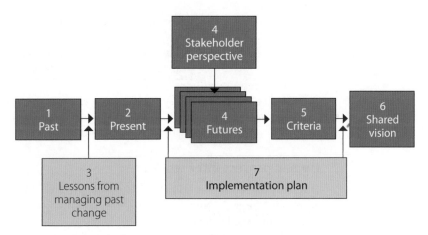

Figure **16.2** *A conference method for developing a 'preferred future'*

The past 100 years have seen many developments in the types of intervention available to change agents, but all four types considered so far can be used to good effect in appropriate circumstances. The next section reviews interventions from a different perspective.

A classification of interventions based on focal issues

Cummings and Worley (2001) offer an alternative typology for classifying interventions based on the kinds of issues they are designed to resolve. Figure 16.3 shows the four main types of intervention. Systemic interdependencies are indicated by the double-headed arrows. Specific interventions within each of the four types can differ in terms of their intended target: individual, group or whole organization. For example, under the heading of 'human resource issues', there might be some interventions, such as those concerned with reward systems, that could be targeted at all three levels, whereas other interventions, such as those concerned with performance appraisal, might only be targeted at the individual and group levels.

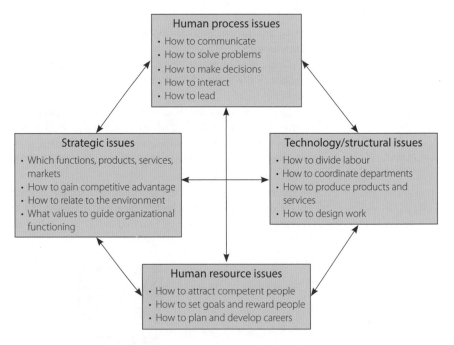

Figure **16.3** *Cummings and Worley's typology of interventions based on focal issues*

Source: Cummings, T.G. and Worley, C.G. (2001) *Organizational Development and Change* (7th edn), South Western, a part of Cengage Learning Inc. Reproduced with permission, www.cengage.com/permissions

Human process interventions

Human process interventions focus on people and the processes by which they accomplish organizational goals, such as communication, problem solving, decision making and leadership.

Friedlander and Brown (1974, p. 326) observe that most human process interventions are based on three assumptions:

1 Sharing information can be valuable, especially where it has previously been unshared but has a potential impact on organizational processes, for example covert feelings.
2 Confronting and working through differences between people who must work together can enhance collaboration.
3 Participation in decision making can lead to increased commitment.

Several human process interventions have already been mentioned. Team development and action research involve working with groups. Intergroup interventions, such as Beckhard's process for improving group relations and the organization mirror, focus on managing the interface between groups, and survey feedback is a whole system intervention that involves groups discussing diagnostic data and planning action steps. Culture profiling (discussed in Chapter 23) can be used to help manage relations between groups and alongside strategic interventions that involve selecting merger or acquisition partners, while coaching and counselling can be used with individuals. Action research and appreciative inquiry (another human process intervention) are discussed in more detail in Chapters 17 and 18.

Technostructural interventions

Technostructural interventions focus on the three areas of structure, task methods and job design and are intended to affect the content of work, work methods, the way work is divided between organizational members, and employee involvement.

One group of interventions relates to the design of organizations and includes activities such as downsizing and re-engineering. Downsizing interventions are aimed at reducing the size of the organization. Structural design encompasses interventions that aim to identify and move towards more effective ways of structuring activities. It often involves moving towards more process-based and network-based structures in order to provide the flexibility to cope with increasing turbulence and uncertainty. Business process re-engineering and lean involve a fundamental rethink and radical redesign of business processes to achieve a transformational improvement in performance. They often involves the use of IT systems to help organizational members control and coordinate work processes more effectively. These interventions are considered in more detail in Chapters 21 and 22.

Some structural interventions are designed to increase employee involvement in order to enhance their commitment and performance. They often involve moving decision making downwards in the organization, closer to where the work is done. To achieve this, employees, at all levels, have to be provided with the power, information, knowledge and skills required to act effectively. Interventions of this type include:

- General interventions designed to improve the quality of work life such as job enrichment and self-managed teams.
- Interventions of various types that involve the creation of a parallel structure that operates in tandem with the formal organization to provide alternative settings, such as awaydays, project groups or quality circles, in which organizational members can address problems and search for solutions.
- High involvement organization redesign, which is designed to increase employee involvement. This entails a joint manager-worker redesign of the organization to promote high levels of involvement and performance.

Several types of intervention involve the redesign of jobs. Engineering approaches focus on efficiency and job simplification, motivational approaches focus on enriching the work experience and are designed to motivate employees to work more effectively, and sociotechnical approaches focus on integrating the technical and social aspects of work and often involve the introduction of self-managed work groups.

Human resource management interventions

Human resource management (HRM) interventions focus on personnel practices such as selection, training and development, goal setting, performance appraisal, incentives, internal promotion systems, career development and so on, and how they can be used to integrate people into the organization. There are many HRM interventions.

Training interventions are used to achieve or re-establish alignment between the competences of organizational members and other elements of the organization, such as tasks, technologies and structures, which have been changed. Training interventions are discussed in more detail in Chapter 19.

Performance management interventions focus on how goal setting, performance appraisal and reward systems can contribute to organizational effectiveness by aligning members' work behaviour with business strategy and workplace technology. High performance management is a performance management intervention that embraces a wide range of people management practices and aims to make them internally consistent with each other and aligned with the organization's strategy. High performance management is discussed in more detail in Chapter 20.

There are many other HRM interventions. Examples include:

- Career planning and development interventions that help employees manage their own careers and prepare them to respond to the uncertainties and lack of job security that are increasingly a feature of organizational life.
- Workforce diversity interventions that respond to the different needs, preferences and expectations of the various groups of employees who bring different resources and perspectives to the organization.
- Employee wellness and stress management interventions that promote the well-being of organizational members and contribute to the development of a productive workforce.

Strategic interventions

Strategic interventions link the internal functioning of the organization with the wider environment. They aim to align business strategy with organizational culture and the external environment.

The whole system in the room interventions can focus on many issues but are often used to help organizational members assess their organization's strengths, weaknesses, opportunities and threats and use this assessment as a basis for visioning a better future.

Mergers and acquisitions are interventions that involve combining separate units to create new entities that can add value by achieving financial synergies, economies of scale, access to resources, market penetration and so on. Some of the issues involved when identifying acquisition targets and merger partners and integrating the two units to create a new organizational entity are discussed in Chapter 25.

Strategy mapping is an intervention based on the balanced scorecard and is used to aid strategy development, communicate the strategy to those who will be involved in its implementation, and monitor its implementation. It can be an effective way of closing the loop between formulating and implementing strategy because it provides those formulating strategy with feedback about whether it is having the kind of impact that was anticipated.

Transorganizational development is an intervention that focuses on the creation of beneficial partnerships (joint ventures and strategic alliances) with other organizations to perform tasks or solve problems that are beyond the capability of a single organization. For example, in a large city, several agencies may have to learn to work together to tackle the problems associated with drug addiction.

☑ *Exercise* **16.1** *Types of intervention*

Review some of the change programmes that have been pursued within your organization, or one that you have read about in the press or elsewhere, and consider the types of intervention used. Did they all tend to fall within one or two of the categories reviewed in this chapter or were a wide range of different types of intervention employed?

Summary

Interventions are 'a set of sequenced planned actions or events intended to help an organization increase its effectiveness' (Cummings and Worley, 2001, p. 142). They purposely disrupt the status quo in order to move the organization towards a more effective state.

This chapter presented two contrasting typologies to provide a brief overview of the wide range of interventions available to change agents.

The first focuses attention on who does the intervening and what it is they do to bring about change. Four classes of intervention were discussed:

1 *Experts applying scientific principles to solve specific problems:* Experts tend to be brought in when there is only an occasional need for a particular expertise within a business unit and/or when there is a need for cutting-edge expertise. Problems can arise if:
   - the expert disregards local knowledge
   - insiders are reluctant to share their knowledge and experience with the expert
   - the expert's diagnosis and prescription for change are resisted by insiders
   - insiders may become too dependent on the expert.
2 *Groups working collaboratively to solve their own problems:* Coch and French (see Research report 12.1) demonstrated that people are much more accepting of change when they are involved in the process of planning and implementing the change. Action research is one example of how a facilitator can work with a group to help it solve its own problems.
3 *Experts working to solve system-wide problems:* Experts such as operations researchers, systems analysts and manufacturing systems engineers typically focus on changing the technical system. Trist and Bamforth were the first to recognize the importance of changing the social and technical systems together – the sociotechnical systems approach.

4 *Everybody working to improve the capability of the whole system for future perfor-mance:* The most recent development has been whole system interventions in which everybody is involved in whole system improvement.

The second typology classifies interventions in terms of the issues they address. Again, four main types of intervention were identified:

1 *Human process issues:* Human process interventions focus on the development of better working relationships and the processes people use for communicating, problem solving, decision making and so on.
2 *Technology/structural issues:* Technostructural interventions are typically asso-ciated with shifts from rigid and bureaucratic to more adaptive and cost-efficient organizational forms, and address such issues as the division of labour, coordi-nation between departments, processes used to produce goods and services, and the design of work.
3 *Human resource issues*: Human resource interventions focus on people manage-ment practices and how they can be used to integrate employees into the organ-ization. They address issues such as how to attract and retain competent people, set goals and reward people, develop employee competences, and plan and develop careers.
4 *Strategic issues:* Strategic interventions address issues such as the formulation and implementation of strategy, ensuring that strategy is aligned with organiza-tional structure and culture and that all three are aligned with the external envi-ronment, and seeking and maintaining competitive advantage.

These different typologies of interventions draw attention to different aspects of organizational functioning.

References

Alban, B. and Bunker, B.B. (2009) Let your people take you higher, *People Management*, 15(5): 22–5.
Beckhard, R. (1969) *Organization Development: Structures and Models.* Reading, MA: Addison-Wesley.
Bowers, D.G. and Franklin, J.L. (1972) Survey guided development: Using human resource measures in organizational change, *Journal of Contemporary Business*, 1(3): 43–5.
Cartwright, D. (1951) Achieving change in people: Some applications of group dynamics theory, *Human Relations*, 4(2): 381–92.
Cummings, T.G. and Worley, C.G. (2001) *Organizational Development and Change* (7th edn). Cincinnati, OH: South Western.
Dannemiller, K.D. and Jacobs, R.W. (1992) Changing the way organizations change: A revolution of common sense, *Journal of Applied Behavioural Science*, 28(3): 480–98.
Friedlander, F. and Brown, L.D. (1974) Organization development, *Annual Review of Psychology*, 25: 313–41.
French, W.L. and Bell, C.H. (1978) *Organization Development* (2nd edn). Englewood Cliffs, NJ: Prentice Hall.
Fritz, R. (1984) *The Path of Least Resistance.* Salem, MA: Stillpoint.
Jayaram, K. (1977) Open systems planning. In T.G. Cummings and S. Srivastva (eds) *Management of Work: A Socio-technical Systems Approach.* San Diego, CA: University Associates.
Lippitt, R. (1983) Future before you plan. In R.A. Ritvo and A.G. Sargent (eds) *The NTL Managers' Handbook.* Arlington, VA: NTL Institute.

Taylor, F.W. (1911) *Principles of Scientific Management*. New York: Harper & Brothers.

Trist, E.L. (1969) On socio-technical systems. In W.G. Bennis, K.D. Benne and R. Chin (eds) *The Planning of Change*. New York: Holt, Rinehart & Winston.

Trist, E.L. and Bamforth, K.W. (1951) Some social and psychological consequences of the longwall method of coal-getting, *Human Relations*, 4(1): 3–38.

Von Bertalanffy, L. (1955) General systems theory. In *General Systems: Yearbook of the Society for the Advancement of General Systems Theory*, 1: 1–10.

Weisbord, M. (1989) *Building Productive Workplaces: Change Strategies for the 21st Century*. Blue Sky Videos.

V

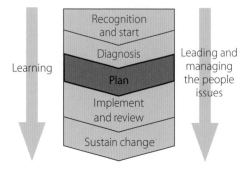

Chapter **17**   **Action research**

Action research is the basic model underpinning most organizational development interventions. It involves the application of scientific methods (fact finding and experimentation) to organizational problems and underpins the generic process model of change presented in Chapter 2.

Lewin developed the action research model in the 1940s when he identified the need for social scientists to base their theory building on research into practical problems. Early projects involved Coch and French (1948) working with employees at the Harwood Manufacturing Company to overcome resistance to change and Lewin working in the community to reduce violence between Catholic and Jewish teenage gangs (see Marrow, 1969). These early projects involved social scientists collaborating with members of social systems to understand and take action to resolve problems. The action research methodology helped members to apply scientific methods to guide their actions and helped social scientists to develop knowledge about social processes that they could generalize to other situations.

Dickens and Watkins (1999) observe that Lewin originally conceived of action research as a process that involved cycling back and forth between an ever deepening surveillance of the problem situation and a series of research-informed action experiments. These experiments formed an important part of the process. Action research is based on the traditional scientific paradigm that involves experimental manipulation and observation of the effects of the manipulation. However, as Dickens and Watkins note, there are important differences between action research and traditional science. Action research, unlike traditional science, does not attempt to set tight limits and controls on the experimental situation. Also, action research uses information to guide behaviour in order to solve immediate problems, whereas traditional science involves studying information for the purpose of learning and typically ends at the point of discovery. Over time, this dual focus on problem solving and theory building has changed, as those concerned with facilitating change have focused more of their attention on improving organizational functioning within a particular context rather than helping social scientists contribute to the development of theoretical understanding. However, over the past few years, a growing body of social scientists have been using action research as the basis for developing theory. Brydon-Miller et al. (2001) refer to Lewin's (1951, p. 169) assertion that 'there is nothing so practical as a good theory' as a major influence on their work. Brydon-Miller et al. (2001, p. 15) argue that:

332

action research goes beyond the notion that theory can inform practice, to a recognition that theory can and should be generated through practice, and ... that theory is really only useful insofar as it is put in the service of a practice focused on achieving positive social change.

Action research and organizational learning

Hendry (1996) reviews the role of learning in the management of change and refers to Lewin's three-stage process of change as a learning process. The motive force for learning and change is cognitive dissonance and the experience of disconfirmation. As discussed in Chapter 2, the initial questioning and unlearning associated with this 'unfreezing' experience provide the motivation for individuals and groups to engage in the information gathering, diagnosis and experimentation that leads to new learning.

Individuals, groups and whole systems are constantly faced with the need to learn and change in order to adapt to changing circumstances. Those who are best able to adapt are those who are able to learn from their experiences. Kolb (1984) elaborated Lewin's model and articulated a theory of experiential learning that conceptualizes learning as a four-stage cycle, which translates experience into concepts that are used to guide the choice of new experiences (Figure 17.1).

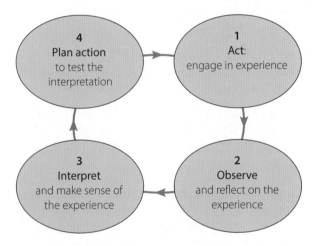

Figure **17.1** *The experiential learning model*

Stage 1 involves engaging in immediate concrete experience in order to provide the basis, at stage 2, for observation and reflection. At stage 3, these observations are interpreted and assimilated into a 'theory' from which new implications for action can be deduced. These implications or hypotheses then serve as guides when planning, at stage 4, how to act to create new experiences. If individuals and groups are to be effective learners and action researchers, they must be able to:

- involve themselves fully, openly and without bias in their experiences
- reflect on and observe these experiences from many perspectives
- create concepts that integrate their observations into logically sound theories
- use these theories to make decisions and solve problems.

Role of the facilitator

This process can be facilitated by a change agent. Shepard (1960) advocated a collaborative relationship between consultant and client. His view was that the role of the consultant is to 'help' the client or client group to design their fact-finding procedures and plan their actions in such a way that they can learn from them in order to discover better ways of organizing.

The role of the change agent as facilitator rather than prescriber of solutions has received considerable attention. Action learning (Revans, 1980), for example, advocates an approach to learning that involves solving real problems. Mumford (1985) made the point that those who wish to assist learners should do so by helping them to learn from exposure to problems and each other. The role of the facilitator/ trainer is to help learners to formulate their own plans for action and test them through implementation.

Over the past 60 years, action research has spawned many related action strategies that have been applied to individual learners, groups, organizations and even wider networks of institutions (see the special edition of *Management Learning*, edited by Raelin, 1999, and the special issue of *Human Relations*, edited by Eldon and Chisholm, 1993). In addition to the classical model of action research, Raelin (1999) refers to five other models: participatory research, action learning, action science, developmental action inquiry, and cooperative inquiry. Appreciative inquiry is also regarded by many as a contemporary development of the classical action research model. This will receive separate and detailed attention in Chapter 18.

The participative nature of action research

All these action strategies are inherently participative. According to Raelin (1999, p. 117), facilitators and members of the target system

> mutually open themselves up to an inquiry process that seeks to 'unfreeze' the assumptions underlying their actions. Their methodologies are experimental and predominantly conducted in group settings.

Reason and Bradbury (2001, p. 1) define action research as

> a participatory, democratic process concerned with developing practical knowing in the pursuit of worthwhile human purposes ... It seeks to bring together action and reflection, theory and practice, in participation with others, in the pursuit of practical solutions to issues of pressing concern to people, and more generally the flourishing of individual persons and their communities.

Most of those who advocate a collaborative approach to problem solving in organizations do so because they believe that much of the information relevant to resolving problems is widely disseminated throughout the organization. Participation increases the likelihood that those who hold important information will share it with others. Collaborative approaches to problem solving also build commitment and facilitate the implementation of actions designed to resolve the problem.

Blake and Mouton (1983) report one of the early examples of action research to illustrate the importance of participation. This is described in Example 17.1.

Example 17.1 *Action research at the Harwood Manufacturing Company*

The Harwood Manufacturing Company was planning to recruit older workers to ease the labour shortage, created by the Second World War, at its pyjama factory in rural Virginia. The proposal was fiercely resisted by supervisors who feared that older workers would be inefficient and difficult to manage. The director of personnel responded by providing supervisors with scientific 'proof' that older workers did possess the skills and aptitude necessary to perform effectively. But the supervisors rejected the evidence and were not persuaded. However, rather than moving ahead and imposing the new hiring policy, the director of personnel decided to try to change attitudes by involving the supervisors in a research project designed to investigate the efficiency of older workers.

The study focused on older workers already employed in the plant. Some had been with the company for many years and others had been employed more recently for social reasons, for example because they had been widowed. Members of staff were given full responsibility for designing the project and deciding how to collect the data. The findings of the study were a surprise to the supervisors. They found that it was not age but a range of other factors that were the main determinants of performance. Blake and Mouton report that while the supervisors had rejected 'expert' evidence, they were convinced by their own findings. Their involvement in the project helped them to unlearn some of the beliefs they had held to be true and changed their attitudes towards the employment of older workers.

The process of action research

The classical model of action research involves collecting and analysing data about the nature of a problem, taking action to bring about a change, and observing the effects of the action in order to inform further actions to improve the situation. Sometimes, the process starts following the identification of a problem by a senior member of the organization who has the power and influence to make things happen. However, this top-down approach is not the only way of introducing action research methodologies into organizations. Sometimes, group members are aware that a problem exists but, for a variety of reasons, find it difficult to manage the problem more effectively. This may motivate them to take the initiative and seek help from an external facilitator. Whatever the starting point, Lewin (1946) argued that an essential prerequisite for action research is a 'felt need', an inner realization that change is necessary. Unless the group are willing to work on their problem, this kind of collaborative intervention is unlikely to succeed.

Following the identification of an issue that requires attention, action research involves successive cycles of action and evaluation. Each cycle comprises five steps. Succeeding cycles begin with the collection and analysis of data to evaluate the consequences of the action taken at the end of the preceding cycle (Figure 17.2). The five steps are:

1 *Data gathering for diagnosis:* Involves collecting data about the problem. Several methods of collecting data have been discussed in Chapter 8, such as interviews, questionnaires, observations and reference to performance data and other records that are collected as a normal part of day-to-day operations. The choice of method needs to be influenced by the nature of the problem and the people involved. For example, the 'organization mirror' (see Change tool 16.2) is a technique that might be appropriate when the problem involves the quality of rela-

tionships between a group and other organizational units or external parties such as suppliers and customers. These other units reflect back to the focal group their perceptions and information about its performance. They act as a mirror and provide the group with their view of the situation. Data can be collected by the whole focal group in a meeting with representatives of other units, or by a designated person interviewing others on behalf of the group.

2 *Data feedback to client group:* Often, members of the focal (problem-solving) group are delegated to investigate particular aspects of the problem or an external facilitator collects data on behalf of the group. Consequently, in order for the process to be truly collaborative, data need to be fed back to all group members.

3 *Discussion of the data and diagnosis of the problem:* One of the defining features of action research is that system members collaborate with each other and with an external facilitator to review the data, clarify issues and formulate hypotheses about cause and effect.

4 *Action planning:* Involves identifying possible interventions to improve the situation and selecting a preferred way forward.

5 *Implementation of action plan:* Involves taking action to improve the situation.

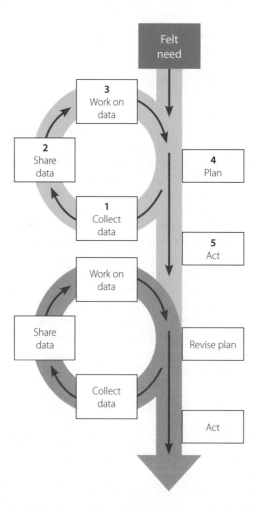

Figure **17.2** *The action research process*

Following the first cycle of the process, the original hypothesis about cause and effect and the action taken to improve the situation are evaluated through a further cycle of data gathering, feedback and analysis. This evaluation might suggest ways of refining the original hypothesis, or the implementation of alternative actions, or it might prompt the formulation of a completely different hypothesis regarding the nature of the problem. And so the process continues. Example 17.2 provides an example of how the process can unfold in practice.

Example **17.2** *Action research at Freedman House*

Freedman House is a 10-bed voluntary hostel for ex-offenders who have recently been released from prison. The initial energy for the Freedman House project had come from probation officers who worked in the community to rehabilitate offenders. They were aware that of the 250 people from their city who were committed to prison each year, over 20 per cent had no fixed abode. Many had been to prison before and homelessness was identified as a factor contributing to their recidivism.

One of the probation officers noticed that there were two uninhabited houses near the city centre that had been boarded up for some considerable time. He thought they might provide the possible basis for a hostel and brought the idea to a volunteer group attached to the local probation office. The group agreed to establish a working party, which eventually obtained planning permission to convert the houses into a hostel. Their next step was to call a public meeting, elect a management committee and launch a fundraising campaign. The committee worked with enthusiasm, but because cash was short, it was impossible to employ contractors to undertake all the necessary work, so members and volunteers did much of the work to convert the houses. Eventually, a warden was appointed, the first residents selected and the hostel opened.

Unfortunately, this was a short honeymoon, soon to end with the premature departure of the first warden. The hostel had to close until a replacement could be found. Two candidates were interviewed and one was appointed. Soon after accepting the post, the successful candidate announced that he would not be able to take up the appointment. Time was short. The hostel was empty and it was decided, that rather than embark on a new round of advertising and interviewing, the unsuccessful candidate would be offered the job, which he accepted.

A few months after the hostel was reopened, the office holders of the management committee decided it was time to take stock and identify priorities to carry the project forward. A national charity concerned with the welfare of offenders agreed to sponsor a consultant to facilitate this work. The office holders had an initial meeting with the consultant, where they provided him with a brief history of the project and outlined, in broad terms, the kinds of issues they felt needed to be addressed. While a number of the group were familiar with action research, some were not and had expected the consultant to introduce them to 'best practice' and offer advice. This minority was a little uncomfortable with the consultant's proposal that he would act as a catalyst to help them move forward, but as the meeting progressed, they warmed to the idea and it was agreed that the group would take the proposal to the next meeting of the full management committee. The full committee agreed to embark on the project and mandated the lead group of office holders to work with the consultant to begin data gathering.

The lead group and consultant discussed the kind of information they would need to help themselves and the full committee understand how the 'system' currently operates, identify problems, and explore what could be done to improve matters. They also thought about what they needed to do to gather this information and who should be involved. Because all the group had 'day jobs' elsewhere, they invited the consultant to take the lead collecting data and agreed that he would interview all office holders, the warden, two members of the committee who were not office holders, an external stakeholder (a member of the voluntary group attached to the probation service) and two groups of residents (those under 20 and older residents). Interviews with the warden and management committee focused on the goals of the hostel, the hostel organization, strengths and weaknesses, decision making, communications and 'important issues'. Interviews with residents focused on the goals of the hostel, their expectations before arrival, what it was like now, and what they would change.

The way the process unfolded is shown below in Figure 17.3. A number of issues emerged from the initial feedback meeting. These were:

- *Finance:* It was felt that raising funds to keep the hostel going would be more difficult than it had been to establish the 'exciting new project' in the first place.
- *The relationship between the management committee and the warden:* A majority of the management committee felt that their role was to closely supervise the warden and the general running of the hostel. They also felt that the warden frequently stepped out of role and assumed too much responsibility, thus preventing the management committee from managing. The warden, on the other hand, felt that the management committee was bureaucratic, unwieldy and too reluctant to delegate. It was decided that this issue needed to be one of the first they would work on.
- *The management committee's contact with residents:* Some committee members felt that it was their right to 'drop in' to see how things were going at the hostel. The warden felt that this was inappropriate and insensitive. Other members of the committee supported the warden on this point, and data from residents indicated that they perceived committee members to be authority figures – most were magistrates, probation officers and so on – and felt uncomfortable when they were around.
- *The liaison officer's role:* One member of the committee had been designated as liaison officer responsible for communications between the committee and the warden and residents. It transpired that there were almost as many views about the role of the liaison officer as there were members of the committee. A clear brief had never been agreed and a complicating factor was that many probation officers on the committee had clients who were residents in the hostel.
- *Original vision versus current reality:* Some members of the committee were becoming disappointed with the project because they had had to compromise on some of their aims. Others were more pragmatic and reasonably satisfied that, at last, the hostel was 'up

and running' and appeared to be 'ticking over' with few problems.

- *The future role of the management committee:* Early on, everybody had been involved in lots of talking, planning and fundraising. As the project progressed, attention shifted to making things happen. Following the launch (and relaunch), attention shifted again to ensuring things worked as required, but the committee was much bigger than needed to manage this task.

There was insufficient time to work on all these issues at the first meeting, so attention was focused on the management committee's relationship with the warden, their contact with residents and the role of the liaison officer. As a first step, it was agreed that only the liaison officer would visit the hostel on a regular basis. However, it was agreed that he could visit unannounced, at least on some occasions, in order to reassure the committee that all was well. With regard to the warden's role, it was anticipated that reducing visits from committee members would allow the warden more freedom to get on with managing day-to-day matters. The committee also asked the liaison officer to work with the warden to review their relationship and how this might be changed to improve the way the hostel was managed. Figure 17.3 shows the action research process in diagrammatic form.

Taking action to improve relations between the warden, liaison officer and management committee was not an easy or comfortable process, but some progress was made. The warden wrote and circulated a frank report for the committee, in which he aired a number of delicate issues that, up until then, had been avoided by all parties. The committee responded by arranging a special meeting with the warden and sharing some of their concerns about the way he ran the hostel and related to members of the committee.

Working on these issue raised a number of concerns, chief of which was that the warden might 'take umbrage' and leave, but almost everybody felt that the free discussion at the special meeting and the respectful way in which it was managed produced some positive outcomes. It helped to improve relationships, reassure the committee that the warden was both competent and committed to the committee's strategy, and reassured the warden that he had the committee's support for what he was trying to do.

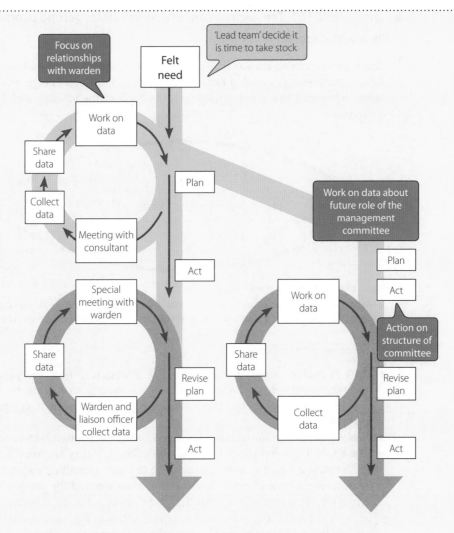

Figure **17.3** *The action research process at Freedman House*

While this was happening, the management committee also met to work on some of the other issues identified at the first meeting of the full committee. Attention was focused on the future role of the management committee. It was agreed that the project had entered a new phase and the existing, large management committee was no longer appropriate.

Instead, there was a need for a smaller core group supported by a wider network of 'friends', and a separate subcommittee focused on fundraising to finance day-to-day operating expenses.

It was at this point that the consultant began to withdraw, leaving the original lead team to take matters forward.

The action research process sometimes focuses on natural work groups and sometimes brings together people who do not have close working relationships. In both settings, but especially the latter, the aim is not always to get members of the group to work together to identify and solve problems. A useful framework for managing meetings in a way that encourages maximum involvement is provided by the Axelrod meeting canoe (Change tool 17.1).

🖌 *Change tool* **17.1** *The Axelrod canoe: a blueprint for getting people involved in meetings*

The meeting canoe, shown in Figure 17.4, is a blueprint for making meetings dynamic and energy creating rather than spirit sapping and energy draining. The canoe represents the opening up phase, the body of the meeting and the closing down phase.

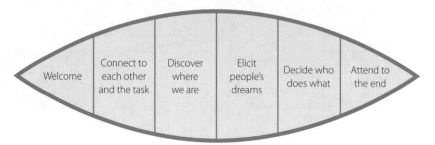

Figure **17.4** *The meeting canoe*

Source: Axelrod, R.H., Axelrod, J.B. and Jacobs, R.W. (2004) *You Don't Have to Do it Alone: How to Involve Others to Get Things Done*, Berrett-Koehler Publishers Inc., San Francisco, CA. All rights reserved, www.bkconnection.com

The steps are as follows:

1 *Start by making people feel welcome:* Pay attention to how you greet people, make them feel welcome. Also pay attention to seating arrangements. A circle or semicircle may work better that seating people in rows with senior people at a top table.

2 *Find ways to create connections among people:* Conversations help us to connect. Find a way to get everybody to engage with others. If they are strangers or semi-strangers, you might start by asking them to share something about themselves that others may not know, or initiate a quick once round the group with people saying why they are there or what they hope to get out of the meeting.

3 *Discover the way things are: build a shared picture of the current situation:* How you do this will depend on the purpose of the meeting. If the purpose is to explore alternative futures, you might begin by asking people to explain where they fit in and what their job is in order to help them understand better how the system currently operates. If the purpose is to solve a particular problem, you might start by encouraging people to talk about how the problem impacts on them and their bit of the organization.

4 *Elicit people's dreams: build a shared picture of where you want to go:* One way of doing this is to get people to pretend it is five years on and ask them what they would like to be telling outsiders about what the organization has become. For example, what is it like working here or what it is like being one of our customers? Pay attention to the themes that emerge. Is there a shared picture?

5 *Decide who does what to create the future you've agreed on:* Clarify how decisions will be made – consensus, majority vote or by the leader. Identify what needs to be done. Sometimes brainstorming can help. Finally, decide who will do it.

6 *Attend to the end:* Put as much thought and attention into saying goodbye as you did to saying hello. You might end by reviewing decisions and agreements, so that everyone is sure what has been decided and what the next steps are.

Results from action research

Action research is widely acknowledged as an effective means of bringing about change. Reference has already been made in Example 17.1 to the Harwood Manufacturing Company project, illustrating how it can be used to overcome resistance to changes proposed by senior management. Greenwood et al. (1993) reported a successful action research project in the Xerox Corporation, which involved employees persuading senior management to radically change their proposal to outsource the manufacturing of selected components (Example 17.3).

Example **17.3** *Action research at Xerox*

During the 1980s, the Xerox Corporation introduced a series of major changes in response to a decline in market share and profits. One outcome of this process was the development of an employee involvement programme at the Webster plants, the company's major US manufacturing facility. Sometime later, this was integrated with a quality improvement programme and was jointly administered at plant level by local managers and members of the union. They received training in group problem solving so that they could be involved in the programme as internal consultants and facilitators. This high level of collaboration provided the context for a successful action research project.

As part of a competitive benchmarking programme, Xerox decided to outsource the production of parts that could be manufactured externally at lower cost. The first outsourcing decision targeted the production of wire harnesses. Benchmarking and cost comparison studies indicated that the company could save $3.2 million a year by outsourcing production and shutting down the wire harness department. It was anticipated that an immediate outcome of this outsourcing decision would be the loss of 180 jobs, but the union feared that this might be just the beginning of a major programme of redundancies as the competitive benchmarking exercise was rolled out to include a wider range of components, and local managers also recognized that their jobs were at risk.

Greenwood et al. (1993) reported that after several weeks of discussions with top union and management officials, it was decided to institute a cost study team, comprising six workers and two members of management. The team was established to determine whether Xerox could cut its manufacturing costs

sufficiently to meet the outside bid and thus save the jobs. Inputs were sought from many sources including industrial engineers, cost accountants and a social psychologist. Greenwood et al. describe the outcome of this action research intervention as spectacular. The team was able to demonstrate cost savings sufficient to persuade senior management to retain wire harness production within the company. The exercise was successfully extended to include four other cases and led to 900 jobs being saved.

© GETTY

Greenwood et al. (1993) also reported other benefits following the action research project at Xerox. Management developed greater trust in workers' abilities and this led to them promoting a variety of other initiatives involving workers in new plant design and the restructuring of the research and development programme for discovering new products and new manufacturing methods. Union leaders and workers experienced a raised level of confidence in their own ability to make an intellectual contribution to the solving of manufacturing problems. In terms of contributing to theory, the cost study teams learned how conventional forms of allocating indirect costs to industrial products could lead management to make decisions against the economic interests of the company and workers. Greenwood et al. also assert that their analysis led to a theoretical reformulation of the relations between worker participation and productivity.

Summary

Lewin created action research as a vehicle for using communities and work organizations as laboratories for field experiments designed to help scientists develop theories about social processes and members of the focal community to understand and manage their circumstances more effectively. During the 1960s, organization development practitioners began to use action research as a basis for intervening to promote change in organizations.

Action research is based on the premise that people learn best and are more willing to apply what they have learned when they manage the problem-solving process for themselves. The learning process involves:

- observing what is going on
- developing hypotheses that specify cause-and-effect relationships and point to actions that could help manage the problem more effectively
- taking action
- collecting data to evaluate the effect of the action and test the hypothesis.

The client group is often helped by a facilitator who works with members to help them design their own fact-finding procedure, work on the data they have collected, plan what to do, take action, and then evaluate their actions in such a way that they can test their cause-and-effect hypotheses and learn from what they did.

It is a collaborative process because:

- many people may have information relevant to the problem
- their 'rich knowledge' about issues might be different to an outside consultant's understanding of reality
- involvement promotes psychological ownership of the problem
- involvement facilitates the implementation of the action that has been planned.

According to the typology presented in Figure 16.3, action research is a human process intervention that addresses processes such as learning, problem solving, communication and decision making.

A wide range of change management interventions are rooted in action research methodologies, insofar as they involve some form of fact finding and action taking designed to improve the way problems are managed. Many also reflect the principles of interactive or participatory action research, insofar as they involve organizational members in the problem-solving process in order to promote the kind of learning that will support the ongoing development of their group or organization.

References

Axelrod, R.H., Axelrod, J.B. and Jacobs, R.W. (2004) *You Don't Have to Do it Alone: How to Involve Others to Get Things Done.* San Francisco, CA: Berrett-Koehler.

Blake, R.R. and Mouton, J.S. (1983) *Consultation: A Handbook for Individual and Organization Development* (2nd edn). Reading, MA: Addison-Wesley.

Brydon-Miller, M., Greenwood, D. and Maguire, P. (2001) Why action research?, *Action Research*, 1(1): 9–14.

Coch, L. and French, J.R. (1948) Overcoming resistance to change, *Human Relations*, 1(4): 512–32.

Dickens, L. and Watkins, K. (1999) Action research: Rethinking Lewin, *Management Learning*, 30(2): 127–40.

Eldon, M. and Chisholm, R.F. (1993) Emerging varieties of action research: Introduction to the special issue, *Human Relations*, 46(2): 121–42.

Greenwood, D.J., Whyte, W.F. and Harkavy, I. (1993) Participatory action research as a process and as a goal, *Human Relations*, 46(2): 175–93.

Hendry, C. (1996) Understanding and creating whole organizational change through learning theory, *Human Relations*, 49(5): 621–41.

Kolb, D.A. (1984) *Experiential Learning.* Englewood Cliffs, NJ: Prentice Hall.

Lewin, K. (1946) Action research and minority problems, *Journal of Social Issues*, 2(4): 34–46.

Lewin, K. (1951) *Field Theory in Social Science.* New York: Harper.

Marrow, A.J. (1969) *The Practical Theorist: The Life and Work of Kurt Lewin.* New York: Teachers College Press.

Mumford, A. (1985) A review of action learning, *Management Development*, 11(2): 3–18.

Raelin, J. (1999) Preface to special issue on action strategies, *Management Learning*, 30(2): 115–25.

Reason, P. and Bradbury, H. (eds) (2001) *Handbook of Action Research: Participative Inquiry and Practice.* London: Sage.

Revans, R.W. (1980) *Action Learning.* London: Blond & Briggs.

Shepard, H.A. (1960) An action research model. In *An Action Research Program for Organization Improvement.* Ann Arbor, MI: Foundation for Research on Human Behaviour.

Chapter **18** | **Appreciative inquiry**

Appreciative inquiry is a process that involves exploring the best of what is, or has been, and amplifying this best practice. It seeks to accentuate the positive rather than eliminate the negative; it focuses attention on what is good and working rather than what is wrong and not working.

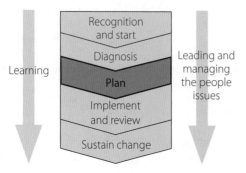

This chapter examines appreciate inquiry from three perspectives; a philosophy of knowledge, an intervention theory, and a methodology for intervening in organizations to improve performance and the quality of life.

The social construction of reality

Social constructionist thinking challenges the view that there is an objective universe 'out there' that is in some sense enduring and physically observable. It posits that reality is a social construction. Elliot (1999) describes a simple exercise that illustrates how readily we make and defend our own versions of reality, even when the data we use are ambiguous. The exercise involves presenting a group with a set of squiggles on a flip chart and inviting each person to take a couple of minutes to decide what they represent. He reports that after a short while, each person begins to see, or think they can see, some emergent shape. If they are then allocated to small groups of three or four and asked to come to a consensus about what the squiggles really mean, members usually start with different interpretations, imagine that their interpretations are correct and try to convince the others that this is the case.

Everything we encounter and experience is open to multiple interpretations. Social constructionists assert that our perceptions of reality are the product of dialogue and negotiation. Dixon (1997), for example, argues that organizational members construct a shared mental model of the organization through a process of dialogue and interaction. She believes that in the process of articulating one's own meanings and comprehending the meanings others have constructed, people alter the meanings they hold. There is no single objective reality.

The way we behave and the consequences of our behaviour are critically dependent on the way we construct reality – the way we see the world. And the way we see the world is determined by what we believe. Srivastva and Cooperrider (1990) argue that our beliefs govern what we look for, what we see, and how we interpret what we see. Our beliefs, therefore, can lead to self-fulfilling expectations. Cooperrider and Srivastva (1987) argue that to the extent that action is predicated on beliefs, ideas and meanings, people are free to seek a transformation in conventional conduct by modifying their beliefs and idea systems.

A widely held belief is that organizational life is problematic. This belief promotes a deficiency perspective that focuses attention on the dysfunctional aspects of organizations and has led to many interventions being designed on the assumption that organizations are 'problems to be solved'. Such interventions typically involve:

- identifying key problems
- analysing causes
- exploring solutions
- developing action plans to manage these problems more effectively.

Cooperrider and Srivastva (1987) argue that this kind of organization development intervention is conservative, insofar as the formulation of a problem implies that somebody has knowledge of what 'should be' and therefore any remedial action is bounded by what is already known. Advocates of appreciative inquiry argue that this deficiency approach often only leads to single-loop learning – continuous improvement within the existing paradigm – and is relatively ineffective when it comes to facilitating organizational transformation.

An alternative belief about organizations, and one that underpins appreciative inquiry, is that rather than 'problems to be solved', they are 'possibilities to be embraced'. Advocates of appreciative inquiry argue that not only are organizations social constructions open to revision, but that this process of revision can be facilitated by a collective inquiry. They also argue that this collective inquiry should attend to the life-giving forces of the organization rather than to a set of problems that have to be resolved. It involves appreciating the best of 'what is' and using this to ignite a vision of the possible. The process is generative; it takes nothing for granted and challenges the beliefs and assumptions that guide behaviour. The organization is viewed as an unfathomable mystery, offering many as yet unknown possibilities. The advocates of appreciative inquiry argue that this social constructionist perspective is more likely to produce double-loop learning, which will lead to the organization doing things differently or even doing different things, than a perspective that is more narrowly focused on organizational dysfunction.

A theory of intervention

Cooperrider (1990) refers to the 'heliotropic hypothesis' as the core of a powerful theory of change. The essence of this theory is that social systems have images of themselves that underpin self-organizing processes and have a natural tendency to evolve towards the most positive images held by their members. They are like plants, they evolve towards the 'light' that gives them life and energy. This leads to the proposition that interventions that promote a conscious evolution of positive imagery offer a viable option for changing social systems for the better.

It has already been noted that a widely held belief about organizations is that they are problematic. Elliot (1999) reports that when he asked a group of 45 managers to write down 20 adjectives that accurately caught the flavour of their organization:

- 72% of the words they used were critical, negative or hostile, for example chaotic, inefficient, inward-looking, lazy, poorly structured, overbureaucratic, slow, careless, unaware
- 13% were neutral, for example mainstream, average, contented, unambitious
- only 15% were positive and approving, for example creative, exciting, thrilling, cutting edge, determined, satisfying, customer oriented, high-tech, achievement oriented.

While the members of many organizations focus attention on things that are not working well, some organizations (a minority?) have a very positive construction of themselves. Example 18.1 highlights one of these exceptions.

Example **18.1** *Médecins Sans Frontières: a positive organization*

Médecins Sans Frontières (MSF) has a culture that celebrates what is working and going well. Over a period of 40 years, MSF has grown from a small, radical organization into a highly respected, professional organization employing 26,000 people who work in over 70 countries. A survey of the staff found that they described their organization and the work they do in very positive terms:

- we are a hands-on organization
- we are nonpolitical, outspoken and neutral
- we are financed independently
- we are independent
- we can be trusted
- we have uncompromising commitment and focus
- we are reluctant to admit defeat
- we have passion for our work
- we are optimistic
- we are international
- we provide emergency-based, hands-on healthcare
- we help people neglected by everyone else
- we save lives, and are not involved in longer term development
- we help those in need irrespective of their situation or beliefs
- we are neutral, impartial and independent
- we do short-term emergency healthcare, and then hand over to the authorities or development agencies
- we provide specialist emergency medical care.

Appreciative inquiry is based on the assumption that we are free to choose which aspects of our experience we pay attention to. Elliot (1999, p. 12) suggests that one of the most important things that appreciative inquiry seeks to achieve is:

> the transformation of a culture from one that sees itself in largely negative terms – and therefore *is inclined to become locked into its own negative construction of itself* – to one that sees itself as having within it the capacity to enrich and enhance the quality of life for all the stakeholders – *and therefore move toward this appreciative construction of itself*.

Elliot highlights the role of memory and imagination. Memory is important because every organization has a history, but this history is not an indisputable fact, it is an artefact of those who do the remembering. Organizational memory is based on how those who do the remembering interpret what happened, and one of the factors that influences their interpretations is where they are now and how they construct the present. Elliot (1999, p. 37) argues that it is this 'plasticity' of memory and our freedom to remake the history of our organizations that are essential for the appreciative approach:

> For what is at stake is the capacity to construct a narrative of the organization that highlights the worthwhile and life-enriching themes without denying the darker or more sombre tones that are likely to be present. It is only when we can read the history from this perspective that we are likely to transcend the problematic present or the fearsome future.

The way organizational members construct and reconstruct the present and the past is a prelude to the way they imagine the future. Appreciative inquiry does not promote the imagination of unachievable fantasies. It promotes the imagination of a future based on an extrapolation of the best of what is or has been.

Cooperrider et al. (2003, p. 386) maintain that one of the greatest obstacles to the wellbeing of an ailing group is the affirmative projection that currently guides that group. They argue that to affirm means to 'hold firm' and it is 'the strength of affirmation, the degree of belief or faith invested, that allows the imagery to carry out its heliotropic task'.

They go on to argue that when a group finds that its attempts to fix problems create more problems, or that the same problems never go away, the group's current affirmative projection is inadequate. Like Elliot, Cooperrider et al. (2003, p. 386) contend that 'every new affirmative projection of the future is a consequence of an appreciative understanding of the past or present'. We do not have to appreciate the present in terms that accentuate the negative. We can appreciate the present and build affirmative images of the future in terms that accentuate the positive. The heliotropic hypothesis posits that the future we imagine is the future we create. Strong affirmative images create a powerful 'pull effect' that can help the organization to evolve towards this more positive future.

Advocates of appreciative inquiry point to studies of the Pygmalion and placebo effects as sources of evidence that support the validity of the heliotropic hypothesis. The Pygmalion effect refers to the power of self-fulfilling prophesies. Many studies have shown that the performance of individuals and groups, such as soldiers (Eden and Shani, 1982), trainee welders (King, 1970) and students (Rosenthal and Jacobson, 1968), is shaped by the expectations of others. Rosenthal and Jacobsen, for example, argue that teachers convey messages of expected success and failure to their students and their students live up to these expectations. However, we not only behave in response to the mental attitudes of those around us, especially those in authority over us, but we also behave in response to our own mental attitudes and expectations of ourselves. In the field of medicine, studies of the placebo effect have shown that those who expect an improvement in their condition are more likely to improve than those who expect no improvement. Similarly, those who remain hopeful and determined in extreme life-threatening circumstances are the ones who are most likely to survive. In other words, nothing succeeds like the expectation of success and nothing fails like the expectation of failure.

While this provides the basis for an attractive theory of intervention, Golembiewski (1999) sounds two notes of caution. The first concerns the outcome of appreciative inquiries. As predicted by the heliotropic hypothesis, social forms gravitate towards an imagined future that amplifies 'peak experiences' because people are motivated to move in that direction. People are less likely to resist this kind of change because, according to the old proverb: 'You can catch more flies with honey than you can with vinegar.' However, the search for social forms faces a far larger issue than whether or not people are motivated to change. Golembiewski raises the question 'motivation for what purpose?' and notes that there are many examples where people have been motivated to lower human systems to the bestial (see, for example, Chang's 1997 account of the rape of Nanking) as well as raise them up to pursue some noble purpose. This said, the evidence seems to indicate that appreciative inquiry not only engages the attention of organizational members but facilitates a process of organizational learning that moves the organization in a direction that yields benefits for all stakeholders.

His second note of caution relates to appreciative inquiry's apparent aversion to 'negative' stories. He suspects that this could encourage an incautious optimism about facts or beliefs. Elliot (1999), however, is less concerned. He argues that non-blaming, nonjudgemental appreciative conversations enable people to acknowledge that the best is not the norm. For example, someone might describe an example of the best of what is and then go on to elaborate: 'But it isn't usually like this. Usually we spend too much time arguing or hating the other department, distrusting them, seeing what is bad about them.' While this kind of comment acknowledges deficiencies, it can facilitate positive thinking. Elliot (1999, p. 76) suggests that a skilled interviewer might achieve this by asking questions along the lines:

- 'What is special about the good times?'
- 'What do you think you and your colleagues need to do or to be in order to maximize the chances that the good times will become the norm?'

A methodology for intervening in organizations

The essence of appreciative inquiry is the generation of a shared image of a better future through a collective process of inquiry into the best of what is. It is this imagined future that provides the powerful pull effect that guides the development of the group or organization.

The critical part of the intervention is the inquiry. The mere act of asking questions begins the process of change. Based on the assumption that the things we choose to focus on and the questions we ask determine what we find, it follows that the more positive the questions, the more positive the data. And the more positive the data, the more positive the beliefs that people are likely to develop about what contributes to peak experiences. And the more positive these beliefs, the more positive the vision of the organization at its best, and finally, the more positive this image is, the more energy it generates for change.

Bushe (1999) describes the process of appreciative inquiry as consisting of three parts:

1 *Discovering the best of ...* involves discovering the best examples of organizing and organization within the experience of organizational members.
2 *Understanding what creates the best of ...* involves seeking insights into the forces that lead to superior performance and what it is about the people, the organization and the context that creates peak experiences at work.
3 *Amplifying the people or processes that exemplify the best of ...* involves reinforcing and amplifying those elements of the situation that contribute to superior performance.

A widely accepted methodology for discovering, understanding and amplifying the best of what is involves five steps, shown in Figure 18.1, and discussed in detail below.

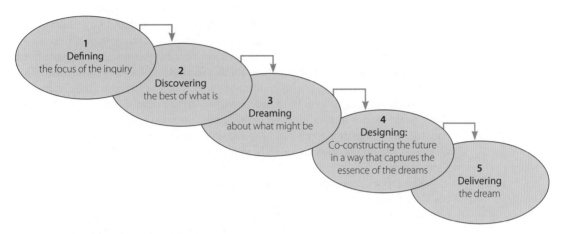

Figure **18.1** *The five steps of an appreciative inquiry*

Defining the focus of the inquiry

In the early 1990s, appreciative inquiry was often viewed as a macro-organizational intervention that studied the organization as a whole. More recently, however, the scope of appreciative inquiries has been extended to include more focused inquiries into issues such as retention, team building, leadership, customer service, conflict management, cross-gender relationships and culture change.

Defining the precise field of inquiry is often undertaken by some kind of steering group, possibly one that represents the different categories of organizational members who might be involved in the inquiry. The inquiry needs to be defined in a way that focuses attention on the positive rather than negative aspects of people's experience. For example, if an organization has an issue with high labour turnover, rather than focusing attention on why people leave, the inquiry might focus attention on why people choose to stay. Similarly, if there is an issue related to sexual harassment, rather than focusing on the problems associated with cross-gender interactions, the inquiry might focus on the conditions and factors that promote good cross-gender working relationships.

Discovering examples of excellence and achievement

Appreciative inquiry involves getting people to tell stories about the best of what is. It can involve pairs of people interviewing each other or a group of interviewers, each having appreciative conversations with 10 or 20 other people and then reporting their findings back to a core group. Whatever the format of the inquiry, interviewers need to be good listeners, able to attend to what others are saying and understand their thoughts and feelings from their perspective. They also need to be good at getting others to tell their stories of excellence and achievement. Key to this is the questions they ask. Whitney et al. (2002) have produced an *Encyclopedia of Positive Questions* that some practitioners might find helpful. Change tool 18.1 at the end of this chapter also provides some guidance on appreciative interviewing.

There is considerable evidence that people enjoy being interviewed appreciatively. It creates a feel-good experience but, as Bushe (1999) observes, care must be taken to ensure that talking about peak experiences does not degenerate into social banter. The successful appreciative interview is one that provides at least one insight into the root causes of success. The interview needs to go beyond identifying what it is that works well and explore why it works well and how this success can be reinforced, amplified and extended to other parts of the organization.

A final step in this discovery phase involves sharing the stories that have been collected and identifying themes about the strengths of the organization. This can be done in a number of ways. Interviewers can verbally report their stories in an open meeting to all who have been involved in the inquiry process or they can share their stories with a core group that has been tasked to interpret the data and identify important themes. All those present can then be involved in a discussion of the stories to identify and reach a consensus about what the key themes are.

Bushe (1999) suggests that when there are lots of stories to review, organizing the data according to an 'inquiry matrix' can help to focus attention on themes relating to the purpose of the inquiry. He suggests that prior to data collection, the steering group might highlight the elements of the organization they want to attend to and amplify the best of, for example cross-gender working relationships, teamwork or customer service, and identify an organizational model they feel captures the major categories of organizing, for example structure, technology, culture, leadership, job design, rewards and so on. This information can be used to construct a matrix that can in turn be used to categorize emerging themes from the stories. The matrix might be relatively simple and include, for example, cells for teamwork and structure, teamwork and technology, and teamwork and rewards, or it might be more complex and include a similar set of cells for other elements that may have been part of the inquiry, such as customer service.

An alternative but less structured approach, similar to one reported by Elliot (1999), involves each member of the core group of interviewers reviewing a sample of written reports of the appreciative conversations in their own time and then coming together to agree key themes. In the case reported by Elliot, a core group of ten had conducted 100 interviews. In order to manage the workload, three members of the group read all 100 reports and the other seven read and analysed 10 reports plus the 10 reports of the interviews they had conducted. To aid their analysis, the facilitator, who had been closely involved with every stage of the inquiry, distributed a list of issues he thought might emerge as key themes. This kind of list provides a category set that group members can use to help them to identify key themes, but it is important they do not feel they must restrict themselves to simply testing the validity of this suggested list. If the inquiry is to be an inclusive and collaborative process, everybody must feel free to identify other clusters of statements that might suggest alternative themes. Members bring their impressions of the content of the reports to a meeting and share and discuss their findings until they are able to agree a list of key themes that reflect the positive present and past.

Dreaming about what might be

Drawing on these themes to inspire a vision of a more positive future is the essence of the dreaming phase. Organizational members are encouraged to envision what the future might be like if the best of what is or has been became the new norm.

Elliot (1999, p. 137) provides the following guidance to those who are involved with analysing the stories of excellence and achievement:

> You are looking for repeated themes which, together, point to a possibility that currently lies just outside the grasp of the company. You are *not* looking for a majority view nor a way-out odd-ball, but for a gathering set of ideas that, pulled together, given coherence and shape, will command an 'Ah, yes ...' from a large majority of stakeholders who will recognise it as building on the best of the past but unlocking a new future.

Elliot suggests that despite all the emphasis in the literature on visioning, relatively few organizational members believe that their imagination is a significant resource they can bring to the workplace. Consequently, many employees do not do much of it as part of their everyday work activity. He goes on to argue that imagination is like many of our faculties, from memory to muscles – if they are not used, they wither. It is possible, therefore, that some organizational members may need to be helped and encouraged in order to use their imagination to envision a more positive future. Elliot suggests some 'warm-up' exercises that might help people gain the confidence to envision new possibilities. These include asking people if they have ever visited another organization and seen things they would like to introduce here, or asking them, if one of their grandchildren were eventually to work here, what they would hope it might be like for them.

When organizational members have arrived at a consensus about their preferred future, the process moves on to the design phase.

Designing: co-constructing the future to deliver the dream

In order to facilitate the achievement of the vision, it has to be translated into a set of statements of intent. These are 'provocative propositions' that will stretch organizational members and show them the way to an achievable preferred future.

Designing the statements of intent typically generates considerable energy and involvement and it is through the dialogue associated with testing, redrafting and refining them that the possibilities for amplifying the best of the present and past are realized.

If the provocative propositions have been developed by a subgroup, it is essential that they are presented to and validated by other organizational members, thus widening the net of those involved in the dialogue. Bushe (1999) suggests that when many people need to be involved, it is possible to test the propositions using an organizational survey. Alongside each proposition there might be questions such as: 'To what extent do you believe this proposition is an important component of the topic under study?' and 'To what extent do you believe the organization exemplifies the proposition?' He argues that simply filling out the questionnaire can generate energy and do a lot towards spreading the ideas across the organization. People are encouraged to reflect on future possibilities and debate them with others. Communicating the results of the survey and informing everybody about the strength of feeling regarding each proposition can also stimulate action, licensing organizational members to begin implementing the propositions in their everyday work.

These provocative propositions are design principles that can be used to identify the structures, processes and practices that will move the organization towards the 'dream'. Finegold et al. (2002) describe them as filters that can be used to evaluate any proposed changes.

Delivering the dream

Guided by the design principles embedded in the provocative propositions, the system (group or organization) is propelled to fulfill its destiny. Sometimes, those leading the inquiry help organizational members to write implementation strategies and action plans and develop scorecards or other procedures for monitoring progress. However, amplifying the best of what is and moving the organization towards a more positive future do not necessarily require those leading the appreciative inquiry to get involved with the details of implementation. While there are some who see this as important, most practitioners restrict their involvement to the point where organizational members develop and validate their vision. If the vision and its associated provocative propositions are sufficiently compelling, they not only generate the energy for change but also provide the guiding focus for individual and group initiatives and action taking across the organization.

Joep de Jong, a Dutch consultant interviewed by Elliot (1999), offers a slightly different perspective. He observes that once organizational members move back into their normal day-to-day roles, they may not find it easy to use the provocative propositions to steer their every action, but may frequently use them as an encouragement to get back into the appreciative way of thinking. While it can be difficult to constantly pursue the realization of the provocative propositions, the process of developing them changes their way of conceiving of themselves, their colleagues and their organization. This, according to de Jong, changes their day-to-day work in a manner that makes it more probable that the essence of the provocative proposition will become reality.

Dick (2004) draws attention to a number of publications that practitioners might find useful when designing appreciative inquiries. Cooperrider et al.'s (2003) *Appreciative Inquiry Handbook* provides a practical guide and rich collection of resources, and Whitney and Trosten-Bloom (2003) have produced what Dick describes as a practical and informative introduction to appreciative inquiry 'suitable for novices'.

Managing change in practice **18.1** *John Hayes: Appreciative inquiry*

John Hayes (the author) provides an overview of appreciative inquiry in a short video he made for Aarhus School of Business. You can watch this at **www.palgrave. com/companion/hayes-change-management4.**

Applications

Appreciative inquiry has been used in a wide range of different situations. Sorensen et al. (2003), after reviewing 350 papers on appreciative inquiry, report that there is considerable evidence pointing to its successful application in many settings. Projects vary in terms of scale, organizational context and focus. Elliot (1999) presents a detailed account of an appreciative inquiry with a private healthcare provider in the UK and several accounts of the use of appreciative inquiry to develop communities in developing countries. The interventions he describes extend over relatively long periods and involve a considerable investment of time on the part of members of the core work group. This contrasts with de Jong's much shorter (two-day) interventions with three secondary schools that had to merge and with two fast-growing computer dealers who were also involved in a merger (see Elliot, 1999).

An appreciative inquiry at Nutrimental Foods in Brazil led to three new business initiatives and a massive increase in sales, as shown in Example 18.2.

Example **18.2** *Using appreciative inquiry at Nutrimental Foods*

Nutrimental Foods is a Brazilian manufacturer that specialized in the production of dehydrated foods that it supplied to federal institutions such as the army, hospitals and schools. After enjoying this privileged position for 26 years, a new government changed its procurement policy and decentralized the purchase of foods. This had a devastating impact on Nutrimental. It had to refocus on supplying the consumer market and downsize from 2,000 to 650 employees to avoid being driven out of business. The CEO, Rodrigo Loures, quickly recognized that something had to be done to revitalize the demoralized workforce and gain a competitive edge in the consumer market. Appreciative inquiry was identified as a possible way forward.

After a successful pilot project, Cooperrider and Barros were invited to lead an appreciative inquiry summit. In preparation for this event, 180 people attended a one-day meeting where they were introduced to appreciative inquiry and given the

opportunity to practise appreciative interviewing. The summit involved 700 people, staff and external stakeholders such as suppliers, customers and bankers, coming together in a big empty warehouse to talk about Nutrimental's past, present and future and to share their stories about best practice, peak experiences and company strengths. An observer reported that the opportunity to participate in the creation of a desired future generated enormous energy.

Following the summit, 150 of those involved in the main event used the data generated at the summit to develop a new corporate vision. Several teams were formed to implement action plans. By 2001, the company achieved a 66% increase in sales, a 300% increase in profitability and a 42% improvement in productivity that senior managers attributed to the new more collaborative and appreciative culture that this intervention had helped to create.

In Chicago, a project involved 4,000 school children conducting one million 'peak experience' interviews with older city residents to vision what the city could be like if the norm became Chicago at its best. Avon had a problem with male–female relationships and used appreciative inquiry to address the issue. Following a request on the company's email system for male–female pairs who believed they exemplified high-quality communication in the workplace, 15 pairs were selected to interview 300 other exemplary pairs. Their stories were used to generate 30 principles for positive cross-gender working relationships.

Finegold et al. (2002) describe an appreciative inquiry in a US university. It started with 400 members of the administrative and finance division being asked, in pairs, to reflect on their whole span of employment at the university and tell each other a story about a peak experience, a time when they felt most energized, alive and valued. They were then invited to tell each other what they valued about themselves, their work and the university and to think about the way they wanted the university to be. For many, it was the first time they had been invited to give voice to their hopes and visions. They were able to present propositions for staff training and development and for better communication between departments and senior management. The intervention was so successful that it became the methodology for annual strategic planning in the division and eventually developed into a university-wide process where the focus was: 'Discovering the power of partnership: Building a university-wide community to advance to the next tier of nationally recognized excellence.'

MSF used appreciative inquiry to develop the organization (Example 18.3).

Example **18.3** *Using appreciative inquiry for organization development at*
Médecins Sans Frontières

Médecins Sans Frontières' secretary general launched an organization-wide programme to 'unlock potential'. Eight cross-functional working groups were set up to look at how the organization functions and identify what MSF is best at doing in order to consolidate successes as a basis for levering further development.

The discovery phase involved the eight working groups collecting information, through interviews and surveys, and cascading this approach down the organization in order to ensure that everybody had the chance to contribute to defining best practice and developing ideas ('dreaming') about how to evolve new practices and procedures that will enable MSF to respond to new challenges.

MSF adopted this approach because it wanted to maintain its passion, maverick character and ability to go against the grain and help where others won't or can't. Appreciative inquiry was seen as a way of protecting these assets, and not stifling or suffocating them by pursuing a top-down, problem-centred approach. Senior managers recognize the need to further professionalize, but not at the expense of its culture and principles.

© FLORIAN LEMS/MSF

Bushe (1998) describes the use of appreciative inquiry in the context of team development. His basic approach involves asking team members to recall their best team experience. Each member, in turn, describes their best team experience and other members are encouraged to question the focal person about what it was about the person, situation and task that contributed to the peak experience. When everybody has told their stories, the group reviews the stories and tries to reach a consensus on the attributes of highly effective teams. His final step involves members mapping these attributes onto their experience with their current team, acknowledging anything they have seen in others that has helped the group to be like any of the listed attributes and identifying possibilities for amplifying these attributes. This approach can be applied to new teams as well as existing teams, because even though members of a new team may not have much, if any, shared experience, everybody will be able to talk about some examples of best team experiences in other contexts. Bushe (1998) actually recommends that members of ongoing teams do not use examples of best team experiences drawn from their experience with the current group because it is likely that members may recall the same experience and, after it has been talked about a few times, the process may lose steam.

Appreciative inquiry was used to clarify values across an organization, as shown in Example 18.4.

Example **18.4** *Using appreciative inquiry to clarify values at Hammersmith Hospital NHS trust*

The chief executive of the trust wanted to create a vision for the future and develop a clear strategy based on the values of the organization. The problem was that nobody knew what the values were. It is not unusual in this kind of situation for the top team to get together and come up with a list of values they think should be part of the organization's culture, but adopting this approach provides no guarantee that the values will be owned by employees across the organization. The new head of organization development persuaded the chief executive to conduct a study to find out what members of the organization actually valued. They did this using appreciative inquiry.

A steering group was established to design the inquiry. It was agreed that exploring what happens when the organization works at its best would provide useful insights into what members valued, and it was decided to do this by inviting people from across the organization to participate in a series of workshops. Thirty 'project champions' were asked to use their personal networks to encourage people to take part. There were some reservations that people might view the inquiry as a bit 'happy-clappy' and that it would not be well received by staff who value a scientific approach to their work, but this was not a problem – 560 people attended 40 workshops.

Members of the trust were trained as internal facilitators to lead the 40 one-hour 'discovery' workshops. Between 12 and 14 people attended each workshop along with two facilitators. Each workshop started with tea and biscuits to create a relaxed atmosphere while the facilitators explained the purpose of the inquiry and what would happen over the next hour. Everybody was invited to introduce themselves (name and department) but not status. Hospitals can be hierarchical organizations and those leading the inquiry did not want this to get in the way.

Participants were invited to turn to interview the person sitting next to them for 10–15 minutes. A interviewed B and then switched roles. Change tool 18.1 below provides details of the interview schedule used in this example. Participants were then asked to make a note of keywords and a brief account of each story, and in the last part of the workshop, they were invited to go round the table and share what they had talked about.

After the workshops, the keywords and stories were typed up and the facilitators were invited to a meeting to review the stories and tease out the main themes. These were recorded on flip charts. Later, Ruth Dunlop, head of leadership and development, and a colleague reviewed the flip charts and distilled out four values and associated behaviours. The four values were the centrality of patients, the importance of team working in delivering high-quality healthcare, an energized atmosphere, and an emphasis on innovation. These were communicated back to members of the organization at normal team meetings to check that these four values did indeed reflect what staff felt was important. Finally, the values were reported to the top team for endorsement and were then communicated across the whole organization via leaflets, posters and a DVD about the four values for team discussion.

Those who participate in appreciative inquiries sometimes find it hard to design and conduct appreciative interviews. The questions the interviewer asks frame the way people look at an issue. Consider, for example, alternative ways of framing questions designed to discover the factors that contribute to good cross-gender working relationships. Even apparently neutral questions such as 'Tell me about male–female relationships here' may elicit stories about problems rather than about the best of what is. An alternative approach is to frame questions along the following lines:

- 'You have been identified as someone who has a good cross-gender relationship. Can you tell me about it, starting with how it began?'

This kind of opening question might be followed with questions such as:

- 'Reflect on your experience of this relationship. What have been the high points when you felt that the relationship was working well and you were making a real contribution to what the organization is trying to achieve?'
- 'Select an example of one of these high points and describe the circumstances: what were you doing, who was involved, what were they doing, what was the result, why did it feel good?'
- 'Tell me about another example.'

🔧 Change tool 18.1 *A specimen appreciative interview schedule*

When designing an appreciative interview schedule, it can be helpful if, alongside each question, interviewers are provided with guidelines to help keep them focused on the positives and prompts to prevent the interview becoming mere social banter about the good times.

The questions, guidelines and prompts given to the interviewers who participated in the Hammersmith Hospital appreciative inquiry were as follows:

1 'Reflecting back over your time with the trust, please tell us a story about when you felt most alive, excited or committed about being part of a team or the trust as a whole.'

   Interviewers were advised to listen carefully to:
   - what made the story an exciting experience
   - what factors contributed to making it a significant experience
   - what was the interviewee's contribution?

2 'Without being too humble or modest (feel free to boast), what do you value most about yourself as a person and your work at the trust?'

   Interviewers were advised to help the interviewee to stay positive and encourage them to focus on strengths and values, not their weaknesses. Ruth Dunlop, who led the inquiry, found that people often said 'I am good at this but I need to improve that', probably because this is the kind of response that most appraisal processes encourage.

3 'Based on your answers to the last question, could you give examples of how these values are demonstrated in the way you and others behave in the trust?'

   Interviewers were advised to focus on concrete behaviours. For example, 'I value honesty in myself. This means that in practice I am open with my team and patients when breaking bad news.'

These first three questions were clearly focused on 'discovery'. The final question invited participants to engage in some 'dreaming'.

4 'If you had just one wish that would improve how we deliver care for patients, what would it be?'

It will be evident from the examples of applications presented above that appreciative inquiry can be adapted to provide a methodology for intervening in many different settings and for addressing a range of different issues.

Summary

This chapter has examined appreciate inquiry from three perspectives.

1 A philosophy of knowledge linked to social constructionist theory:
   • reality is a social construction
   • everything we experience and encounter is open to multiple interpretations
   • perceptions of reality are the product of dialogue and interaction
   • the way we behave is influenced by how we see the world (construct reality).

Many people perceive organizational life as problematic and focus their attention on 'problems to be solved'. This belief promotes a deficiency perspective. An alternative belief is that organizations are 'possibilities to be embraced'. Beliefs (social constructions) about organizations are open to revision and this revision can be facilitated by a process of collective inquiry.

2 An intervention theory:
   • the 'heliotropic hypothesis' – organizations, like plants, evolve towards the light that gives them energy (this can be the most positive images held by members)
   • interventions that promote a conscious evolution of positive imagery offer a basis for changing organizations for the better
   • appreciative inquiry is based on the assumption that we are free to choose which aspects of reality we pay attention to
   • appreciative inquiry seeks to achieve:

> The transformation of a culture from one that sees itself in largely negative terms – and therefore *is inclined to be locked into its own negative construction of itself* – to one that sees itself as having within it the capacity to enrich and enhance the quality of life for all stakeholders – *and therefore move towards an appreciative construction of itself.* (Elliot, 1999, p. 12)

3 A methodology for intervening in organizations
   Appreciative inquiry is a process that involves exploring the best of what is and amplifying this best practice. The essence of appreciative inquiry is the generation of a shared image of a better future: 'What would the future be like if the best of what is became the norm?' Whereas action research promotes learning through attending to dysfunctional aspects of organizational functioning, appreciative inquiry seeks to accentuate the positive rather than eliminate the negative. Attention is given to:

- discovering the best of ...
- understanding what creates the best of ...
- amplifying the people or processes that create the best of ... .

The chapter ended with a number of examples of how appreciative inquiry has been used in a variety of settings. In terms of the typology presented in Figure 16.3, appreciative inquiry is a human process intervention.

References

Bushe, G.R. (1998) Appreciative inquiry with teams, *Organization Development Journal*, 16(3): 41–9.

Bushe, G.R. (1999) Advances in appreciative inquiry as an organization development intervention, *Organization Development Journal*, 17(2): 61–8.

Chang, I. (1997) *The Rape of Nanking*. New York: Basic Books.

Cooperrider, D. (1990) Positive image, positive action: The affirmative basis of organizing. In S. Srivastva and D.L. Cooperrider (eds) *Appreciative Management and Leadership*. San Francisco, CA: Jossey-Bass.

Cooperrider, D. and Srivastva, S. (1987) Appreciative inquiry in organizational life, *Research in Organizational Change and Development*, 1(1): 129–69.

Cooperrider, D., Whitney, D. and Stavros, J. (2003) *Appreciative Inquiry Handbook*. San Francisco, CA: Berrett-Koehler.

Dick, B. (2004) Action research literature: Trends and themes, *Action Research*, 2(4): 425–44.

Dixon, N. (1997) The hallways of learning, *Organizational Dynamics*, 25(4): 23–34.

Eden, D. and Shani, A.B. (1982) Pygmalion goes to boot camp: Expectancy, leadership, and trainee performance, *Journal of Applied Psychology*, 67(2): 194–9.

Elliot, C. (1999) *Locating the Energy for Change: An Introduction to Appreciative Inquiry*. Winnipeg: International Institute for Sustainable Development.

Finegold, M.A., Holland, B.M. and Lingham, T. (2002) Appreciative inquiry and public dialogue: An approach to community change, *Public Organization Review*, 2(3): 235–52.

Golembiewski, R.T. (1999) Fine-tuning appreciative inquiry: Two ways of circumscribing the concept's value-added, *Organization Development Journal*, 17(3): 21–6.

King, A.S. (1970) Managerial relations with disadvantaged work groups: Supervisory expectations of the underprivileged worker, PhD dissertation, Texas Tech University.

Rosenthal, R. and Jacobson, L. (1968) *Pygmalion Effect in the Classroom: Teachers' Expectations and Pupil Intellectual Development*. New York: Holt, Rinehart & Winston.

Sorensen, P.E., Yaeger, T.F. and Bengtsson, U. (2003) The promise of appreciative inquiry: A 20-year review, *OD Practitioner*, 35(4): 15–21.

Srivastva, S. and Cooperrider, D. (1990) *Appreciative Management and Leadership: The Power of Positive Thought and Action in Organizations*. San Francisco, CA: Jossey-Bass.

Whitney, D. and Trosten-Bloom, A. (2003) *The Power of Appreciative Inquiry: A Practical Guide to Positive Change*. San Francisco, CA: Berrett-Koehler.

Whitney, D., Cooperrider, D., Trosten-Bloom, A. and Kaplan, B.S. (2002) *Encyclopedia of Positive Questions*, vol. 1: *Using Appreciative Inquiry to Bring Out the Best in your Organisation*. Euclid, OH: Lakeshore Communications.

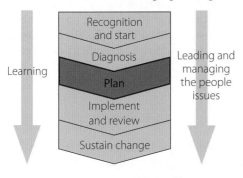

Learning

Recognition and start

Diagnosis

Plan

Implement and review

Sustain change

Leading and managing the people issues

Organizational change is typically associated with some degree of individual change, which is often the outcome of an informal and natural process of learning and development. However, there may be occasions when those responsible for managing an organizational change decide that some form of deliberate training intervention is required in order to help individuals to develop new knowledge, skills, attitudes and behaviours. Such interventions can be highly structured and very focused on the achievement of closely specified outcomes, or they can be designed to help organizational members learn how to learn and encourage them to actively involve themselves in a self-directed process of professional development.

Training interventions tend to be targeted at two main types of organizational member. On the one hand, there are those who are required to perform new roles associated with managing the change. They may require training in order to lead a task force charged with diagnosing organizational problems and identifying what needs to be changed, or to facilitate activities that are part of the diagnostic, planning or implementing phases of the change. For example, in Example 18.4, the facilitators of the 'discovery' workshops at Hammersmith Hospital were all members of staff (not consultants) who received training to lead the workshops, and Change tool 16.3 was used to prepare staff to facilitate workshops that were part of a survey feedback intervention in a large telecommunications company. On the other hand, there are organizational members who, as a result of the change, will be required to behave differently and may require training in order to achieve new standards of performance. For example, Banker et al. (1996) found that training is a key determinant of the success of teams. Team working often changes the role of the supervisor or involves people being appointed to a new role of team leader. This calls for training to help leaders facilitate their teams. Team members may also receive training in group process skills and training to cover jobs other than their own and/ or to take on greater responsibility for their work.

This chapter briefly considers how training can help to maintain or re-establish alignment between the competences of organizational members and other elements of the system such as task and structure. Attention will also be given to the main aspects of a systematic approach to the development of effective training interventions. The final section reviews some Australian studies that have investigated recent trends in the provision of training.

Achieving a match between organizational members and changing task demands

When change calls for new behaviours on the part of organizational members, a number of factors will determine whether or not these new behaviours will be forthcoming. These include the quality of the match between competences and task demands, the effect of reward systems on the motivation to deliver revised performance outcomes, and the availability of feedback to enable individuals and their managers to assess whether the new performance standards are being achieved. This chapter is concerned with the first of these.

Sometimes, organizational members will already possess all the competences they require in order to achieve the new performance standards. All that such people will need, in terms of their ability to perform in new ways, is information about the revised performance outcomes they will have to achieve. At other times, the people affected by the change may not possess the competences they will need. Here, a number of options may be available to those managing the change. They may explore ways of redesigning the task to match the existing competences of organizational members, replace existing staff with others who already have the required competences, or help existing staff acquire the required new competences. The latter is considered in more detail below.

A systematic approach to training

Goldstein (1993) and others argue that effective training involves three main steps: the analysis of training needs, the design and delivery of training, and the evaluation of training effectiveness, which are now discussed.

Training needs analysis

A training needs analysis also involves three steps: systems-level review, task analysis, and person analysis.

Systems-level review

A systems-level review determines how the proposed change will affect organizational goals, objectives and task demands. This overview provides the information necessary to identify where more specific task and person analyses are required. For example, the move from an optical to a digital scanning technology in the reprographics equipment sector changed the nature of the tasks performed by many organizational units. In this case, a system-level review might have pointed to a need for a more detailed analysis in departments such as product design, assembly, technical support, sales and so on. However, in other departments, such as finance, the system-level review might have identified few implications for the nature of the task performed and the competences required.

Task analysis

A task analysis focuses on specific jobs or roles and examines how modifications to the task of a unit will affect the nature of the performance that will be demanded from members of that unit. It also points to the competences – knowledge, skills, attitudes or behaviour – that people performing these new or modified roles will require in order to perform to the new standard. Elaborating the example of the reprographics equipment manufacturer, a task analysis of, for example, the selling function might have revealed how the introduction of digital scanning technology changed the nature of the performance required by salespeople to sell digital as opposed to optical reprographics equipment.

Person analysis

A person analysis seeks to identify discrepancies between the required competences, as determined by the task analysis, and the existing competences of the organizational members available to perform these revised tasks. This analysis provides the information necessary to identify which individuals or groups will require training and specify training objectives in terms of what trainees need to know and how they will be required to behave.

The most useful way of expressing training objectives is in terms of behavioural objectives that specify what trainees will be able to do after training. For example, some of the training objectives for the reprographics equipment sales representatives might include being able to:

- accurately describe how the new technology affects the performance of the new range of copiers produced by the company
- demonstrate to customers how to maintain the equipment to keep it operating at peak efficiency.

The design and delivery of training

Smith (1991) suggests that the choice of training method should, at least in part, be determined by the kinds of competences the training is designed to impart. For example, where the aim is to impart knowledge and information, some of the most effective training methods might include lectures and reading books and manuals.

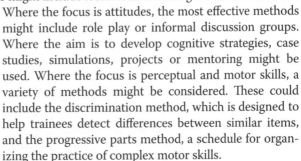

© STOCKBYTE/PUNCHSTOCK

Where the focus is attitudes, the most effective methods might include role play or informal discussion groups. Where the aim is to develop cognitive strategies, case studies, simulations, projects or mentoring might be used. Where the focus is perceptual and motor skills, a variety of methods might be considered. These could include the discrimination method, which is designed to help trainees detect differences between similar items, and the progressive parts method, a schedule for organizing the practice of complex motor skills.

Reid and Barrington (1999) classify training methods under five main headings: on-the-job training, planned organization experience, in-house courses, planned experience outside the organization, and external courses. They recommend four criteria to determine which of these strategies will be most appropriate:

1 compatibility with training objectives
2 estimated likelihood of transfer of learning to the work situation
3 availability of resources, such as time, money and skilled staff
4 trainee-related factors.

These criteria can be used, for example, to help identify an effective way of training members of a new change project team. Each is now discussed in turn.

Compatibility with training objectives

The training objectives for the members of the new project team might include:

- *imparting knowledge:* so that trainees will understand, be able to describe to others and recognize actions that will help the new project team achieve the aims of the change programme
- *developing positive attitudes:* so that trainees will be committed to the aims of the programme and to working constructively with other members of the team to achieve these aims
- *developing group process skills:* so that trainees will be able to diagnose what is going on in the group and act in ways that will contribute to group effectiveness.

The change manager might quickly reject some methods because they are incompatible with the training objectives and may recognize that others may only be used after adaptation.

On-the-job training might be rejected because there may be no project teams currently operating in the company that could provide relevant on-the-job work experience.

External courses, such as outward bound-type team training, might offer a good way of developing positive attitudes towards colleagues and developing group process skills. However, in order to satisfy some of the other training needs, the change agent or somebody else from the company would have to be involved and the course would have to be adapted to provide some sessions that deal with the aims of the change programme. This would also require the external course to be restricted to managers from the one company and to those managers who will have to work together in the new project team.

A specially designed in-company course might be an attractive option. It could include a mix of formal inputs on the aims of the change programme, informal discussion sessions to explore trainees' reactions to these aims, and group activities that could be used as a vehicle for developing group process skills.

Transfer of learning

In terms of the transfer of learning, the external course, if it were restricted to prospective members of the project team, and the in-house course could facilitate the transfer of group process skills and positive attitudes towards other trainees to the work situation. The in-house course could also score high on the transfer of learning if the group activities involved working on real issues that the team would have to deal with once it 'went live'.

Availability of resources

In terms of the availability of resources, time might be a factor that would preclude the use of internal or external planned work experience. Also cost, in terms of money in the budget rather than the opportunity cost of the change agent's time, might be a factor that would work against an expensive external course. The in-house course might cost less but the change agent would have to find the time to develop the training materials and the work-related group activities. The change agent may be confident they have the necessary skills to design and deliver the in-house programme. They might also be aware of an external consultant who could be employed to help at a fee that would be considerably less than the cost of the external course.

Trainee-related factors

In terms of trainee-related factors, from a business perspective, it may be impossible to release all the managers at the same time to participate in a week-long external course. Also, for domestic reasons, some members of the proposed project team may find it difficult to be away from home for a whole week.

Taking into account all these factors, the change agent may opt for the in-house course, which could, if necessary, be scheduled as a series of short modules to fit in with the availability of trainees.

The evaluation of training effectiveness

Training effectiveness can be assessed in many ways, but Aguinis and Kraiger (2009) note that Kirkpatrick's (1983) four-level approach to training evaluation continues to be the most widely used training evaluation model among practitioners:

1. At level one, the criterion is how trainees *reacted* to the training. Did they feel it was relevant, interesting, demanding and so on?
2. At level two, the criterion is *what they learned.* It is not unknown for trainees to react favourably to the training but to learn relatively little, or only achieve acceptable standards of learning in respect of some, but not all, of the learning goals. This kind of feedback has obvious implications for those responsible for selecting and designing the details of the learning activity.
3. At level three, the criterion is *behaviour.* Trainees may have reacted positively to the training and learned what it was intended they should learn. However, back on the job, their behaviour may have changed little, if at all. In other words, what was learned on the course may not have been transferred to the work situation. It is relatively easy to apply the relevant principles of learning to design a training activity that will encourage learning, but much more difficult to design one that will ensure that the learning is transferred and used in the work situation. A common problem that inhibits transfer is the social pressure trainees are subjected to on their return from training. While they may have learned best practice when on the course, back on the job, colleagues often pressure them to revert to the traditional ways of working.
4. At level four, the criterion is *results.* It is possible for the training to produce the intended changes in behaviour, but this behaviour change may not produce the intended results. Sales representatives may have started to call more regularly on customers but this may not produce the anticipated increase in sales. This kind of feedback indicates a need for a fundamental rethink of the training strategy.

Managing change in practice **19.1** *Paul Simpson: Using training to deliver culture change*

Paul Simpson works with companies to help them improve their performance. He has wide experience working as an HR and OD practitioner. He was HR director for Arla in the UK, head of OD, director of learning and development and HR business partner at Aviva, and is currently leading organization development at

London and Scandinavian Metallurgical Co. Ltd. Paul contributes to programmes at Leeds University Business School and is chair of the Yorkshire HR Directors' Forum. He offers some insights below and in his video into how training was used to help change the culture of a special metals business.

Until recently, the organization was failing to thrive, but over the past three years it has turned itself around and become more profitable. The CEO and a new HR director decided that, in order to maintain this momentum, they needed to change the organization's culture, from a traditional top-down, directive management style to one that is more open and engaging and values contributions from everyone across the whole enterprise.

To achieve this, they engaged a firm of training consultants to work with them to design and deliver a five-module training programme for the top 50 managers and directors over an 18-month period. Paul Simpson's role was to support the top 50 and help them transfer what they learned on the training programme and embed it as a natural part of their everyday management style. He did this through coaching, one-to-one support and group facilitation.

Many lessons were learned from this experience. First, providing trainees (in this case managers and directors) with one-to-one and collective support in the back-to-work gaps between modules increased their awareness of the value of what they had learned and helped them to adopt new ways of working. Second, people respond differently. Overall, the response to the training was positive, but while some worked hard to translate theory into practice, others found this was easier said than done. There were also some who were not persuaded that they should change their management style. Third, encouraging trainees to share their success stories encouraged others to embrace the new culture. Fourth, and rather unexpectedly, as some managers adopted the new ways of working and began to appreciate how this improved the climate in their particular section of the organization, they became less tolerant of those senior managers who were clinging on to the old top-down adversarial culture, and this began to create a bottom-up push for change.

Visit the book's companion website at **www.palgrave.com/companion/hayes-change-management4** and watch Paul Simpson's video in which he talks about the limitations of using training to deliver this kind of systemic change.

Training for change: the Australian experience

Studies in several countries have found that organizational change is closely associated with the level of training activity in organizations (Cappelli and Rogovsky, 1994; Osterman, 1995). Smith (2005) reviewed two major studies of training at the level of the whole enterprise in Australia that confirm this relationship (Research reports 19.1 and 19.2).

One new management practice that was not always associated with an increase in training activity was the introduction of lean production. Smith et al. (2003) found that lean production was consistently associated with cost cutting and this included measures to cut the cost of training. Typically, the levels of formal training and training infrastructure (training facilities and dedicated training staff) were reduced. Most of the training that was undertaken tended to be on the job and skewed in favour of managers.

Research report **19.1** *Enterprise-level training in Australia*

Smith, A. and Hayton, G. (1999) What drives enterprise training? Evidence from Australia, *International Journal of Human Resource Management*, 10(2): 251–72.

Smith and Hayton investigated the drivers of enterprise-level training. Their research involved 42 case studies in five industry sectors – construction, electronic manufacturing, food processing, retail and financial services – and a national survey of 1,760 organizations across all sectors.

In terms of the systematic approach to training outlined in this chapter, they found evidence that organizations did adopt some form of training needs analysis and in many cases this was based on a system of performance appraisal. However, the evaluation of training was relatively underdeveloped. None of the case study organizations went much beyond the use of traditional end-of-course evaluation forms.

Senior managers in some organizations adopted a proactive strategic approach to training and viewed it as a vehicle for building skill sets that could provide the basis for sustainable competitive advantage, but attitudes towards training were often fragmented, and middle and junior managers tended to be more reactive and viewed training as a short, sharp, focused response to immediate operational problems. These included workplace change, quality improvement and new technology.

Workplace change was the most important driver for change. New technology was less important than anticipated because the introduction of new products frequently required only minimum changes to existing production processes and could be introduced with little additional training. New production processes, on the other hand, often involved fundamental changes to the way work was carried out and therefore triggered a more extensive need for training. However, the required training was often short and simple and was frequently outsourced to the vendors of the new process technology.

New forms of work organization and structural change accounted for most of the increase in training activity and emphasized behavioural rather than traditional technical skills. Smith and Hayton suggest that this shift towards behavioural skills training reflects a growing concern in Australian enterprises to develop adaptability to changes in work organization.

Research report **19.2** *Relationship between enterprise-level training and organizational change*

Smith, A., Oczkowski, E., Noble, C. and Macklin, R. (2003) New management practices and enterprise training in Australia, *International Journal of Manpower*, 24(1): 31–47.

The study involved a survey of 3,415 HR managers and follow-up interviews with 78 of them.

While training activity was clearly associated with the introduction of new management practices, such as total quality management (TQM), team working and business process re-engineering, few of the managers surveyed felt that training had played a major role in the implementation of change. Typically, training played a 'catch-up role', dealing with the consequences of change rather than playing a major role in its planning or implementation.

Findings relating to the kind of training associated with the introduction of new management practices confirm the move away from technical skills to a new training paradigm that emphasizes the development of broad sets of generic behavioural skills. For example, the introduction of TQM involves the implementation of team working, the development of interpersonal and problem-solving skills and, especially in service industries, customer service skills. There is also a requirement to train large numbers of staff in specific TQM skills such as data collection and analysis. Team working had been introduced by about two-thirds of the organizations included in the survey and was clearly linked to an increase in training activity. Training was focused on team-working skills for team members and management training for more senior staff.

The studies undertaken by Smith and Hayton (1999) and Smith et al. (2003) provide an overview of enterprise-level training in Australia from 1994 to 2003. This was a period of rapid change, because from the early 1980s, companies operating in Australia have been exposed to increasing levels of international and domestic competition. A number of trends in the development of enterprise-level training emerged from these studies.

The first relates to the link between training and business strategy. Notwithstanding the finding reported by Smith et al. (2003) that training did not play a major role in the planning and implementation of change, Smith (2005) reports that there has been an increase in the number of organizations that are conscious of the need to link training to business strategy if they are to capitalize more effectively on their investment in training. He notes that where enterprises have made this link, the result has been a substantial increase in all forms of training and a greater embedding of training into the management of the enterprise. The second trend relates to the individualization of training. There has been a shift away from delivery methods that impose uniform training programmes on large groups of employees towards a more focused training provision linked to individual performance management. This trend has been associated with the demise of large centralized training departments and the devolution of responsibility for training to line managers. Finally, much of the growth in training activity has involved the development of broad sets of generic behavioural skills rather than technical skills and has been linked to the introduction of new management practices.

✓ *Exercise* **19.1** *Assessing the way training is used in the change process*

Reflect on an organization-wide change or a change targeted at a particular department or unit in your organization or another organization you have read about. Consider the following points and then make a brief assessment of the way training was used to help achieve change:

- Was there any evidence indicating that the organization and/or particular change managers were prepared to invest in training to support change?
- Was the attention given to training inadequate, about right or 'over the top'?
- Was the training targeted at the individuals and groups most in need of training?
- Was the training that was provided compatible with training requirements and delivered in a way that maximized the transfer of learning to the work situation?

Summary

Organizational change is typically associated with some degree of individual change. Often this individual change is the outcome of an informal and natural process of learning and development. However, there may be occasions when those responsible for managing the change decide that some form of deliberate training intervention is required in order to help individuals to develop new knowledge, skills, attitudes and behaviours.

This chapter considered how training can help to re-establish alignment between the competences of organizational members and other elements of the system such as task and structure. Attention was directed towards the main elements of an effective approach to training: a training needs analysis, design and delivery of the training intervention, and the evaluation of the training.

1 The training needs analysis involves three steps:
   - *Systems-level review:* This investigates how the proposed change will affect organizational goals, objectives and task demands. This overview provides the information necessary to identify where more specific task and person analyses are required.
   - *Task analysis:* This focuses on specific jobs or roles and examines how modifications to the task of a unit will affect the nature of the performance that will be demanded from members of that unit. It also points to the competences (knowledge, skills, attitudes or behaviour) that people performing these new or modified roles will require in order to perform to the new standard.
   - *Person analysis:* This seeks to identify discrepancies between the required competences, as determined by the task analysis, and the existing competences of the organizational members available to perform these revised tasks.

   The most useful way of expressing training objectives is in terms of behavioural objectives that specify what trainees will be able to do after training.

2 The design and delivery of training
   The choice of training strategies, for example on-the-job training, private study, internal and external placements, in-house and external courses, will depend on:
   - compatibility with training objectives – knowledge, skills, attitudes
   - likelihood that learning will be transferred to job – individual or work group focus and relevance of training content
   - available resources
   - trainee-related factors – availability, domestic considerations.

3 The evaluation of the training
   The effectiveness of training can be evaluated at four levels:
   - how trainees reacted to the training
   - what they learned
   - whether the training changed their behaviour as intended
   - the impact of new behaviours on performance.

The final section reviewed the development of training practice in Australia over a 10-year period and highlighted a number of trends in training provision.

In terms of the typology presented in Figure 16.3, training and development is a human resource intervention.

References

Aguinis, H. and Kraiger, K. (2009) Benefits of training and development for individuals and teams, organizations, and society, *Annual Review of Psychology*, 60: 451–74.

Banker, R.D., Field, J.M., Schroeder, R.D. and Sinha, K.K. (1996) Impact of work teams on manufacturing performance: A longitudinal field study, *Academy of Management Journal*, 39(4): 867–90.

Cappelli, P. and Rogovsky, N. (1994) New work systems and skill requirements, *International Labour Review*, 133(2): 205–20.

Goldstein, I.L. (1993) *Training in Organisations* (3rd edn). Monterey, CA: Brooks/Cole.

Kirkpatrick, D.L. (1983) Four steps in measuring training effectiveness, *Personnel Administrator*, 28(11): 19–25.

Osterman, P. (1995) Skill, training and work organisation in American establishments, *Industrial Relations*, 34(2): 125–46.

Reid, M. and Barrington, H. (1999) *Training Interventions*. London: Institute of Personnel and Development.

Smith, A. (2005) The development of employer training in Australia, discussion paper, Charles Sturt University, Australia.

Smith, A. and Hayton, G. (1999) What drives enterprise training? Evidence from Australia, *International Journal of Human Resource Management*, 10(2): 251–72.

Smith, A., Oczkowski, E., Noble, C. and Macklin, R. (2003) New management practices and enterprise training in Australia, *International Journal of Manpower*, 24(1): 31–47.

Smith, M. (1991) Training in organizations. In M. Smith (ed.) *Analysing Organizational Behaviour*. Basingstoke: Macmillan – now Palgrave Macmillan.

Chapter 20

High performance management

High performance management is an intervention that change agents can use to improve performance by aligning people management practices. It involves developing and implementing a bundle or system of people management practices that are internally consistent, aligned with other business processes, and aligned with the organization's business strategy. It is argued that this is a much more effective intervention than working to improve separate people management practices, such as training, performance management or reward systems, in isolation.

This chapter opens with a brief review of cost reduction and commitment maximization approaches to managing an organization's human resources and argues that it is the commitment maximization philosophy that best supports high performance management interventions. Attention is then given to how people management practices can be used to enhance performance by improving employees' knowledge and skills, motivating them to engage in discretionary behaviours (that draw on their knowledge and skill), and modifying organizational structures in ways that enable employees to improve the way they perform their jobs. Some of the people management practices that can deliver these outcomes are identified.

The final part presents two change tools. The first is concerned with external alignment and can be used to assess the extent to which people management practices are aligned with the organization's business strategy. The second focuses on internal alignment and can be used to assess the extent to which people management practices are aligned with each other. When misalignments are identified, it is possible to intervene to realign practices to improve performance.

High performance management is an approach to improving organizational performance that is consistent with open systems thinking and the concept of 'fit' discussed in Chapter 7. It is also consistent with what Paul Simpson has to say in his video (see Chapter 19) about the importance of not relying on changing just one people management practice, such as training, if the intention is to deliver systemic change.

Soft and hard models of human resource management (HRM)

Bailey (1993) contends that human resources (HR) are frequently underutilized because employees perform below their maximum potential. Walton (1985) identified two profoundly different approaches to HR: one based on imposing control and the other on eliciting commitment. This distinction is similar to that made by Truss et al. (1997) when they referred to 'hard' (control) and 'soft' (commitment) strategies when investigating HRM practice in eight organizations in the UK.

The cost reduction or control approach

The cost reduction or control approach focuses on the use of controls to reduce direct labour costs and improve efficiency. This is achieved by enforcing compliance through the application of specific rules and procedures. It is an approach that shares many of the assumptions that underpin Beer's economic change strategy, which focuses on the drive for economic value through tough top-down, results-driven action. Truss et al. (1997) observe that this 'hard' approach is based on the economic model of man and McGregor's (1960) theory X proposition that people dislike work and must be controlled and directed to get them to employ adequate effort towards the achievement of organizational goals. Walton (1985) refers to the kind of situation in which control strategies flourish. He describes a plant in which employees are responsible for fixed jobs and are required to perform up to a minimum standard, and where peer pressure keeps them from exceeding this standard and from taking initiatives to improve performance. Here, because motivation is low, management seeks to secure adequate work effort through close monitoring and supervision, and what MacDuffie (1995) refers to as 'efficiency wages'.

The commitment maximization approach

The commitment maximization approach is based on the assumption that people work best and contribute most to organizational performance when they are fully committed to the organization. This approach shares many of the assumptions underpinning Beer's organization development strategy for change (see Chapter 14), insofar as it involves creating the capabilities required to sustain competitive advantage and high performance over the long term. Truss et al. (1997) argue that 'soft' HRM has its roots in the HR movement, the utilization of individual talents and McGregor's theory Y, which proposes that people will exercise self-direction and self-control in the service of objectives to which they are committed. It focuses on developing committed employees who can be trusted to use their discretion to work in ways that are consistent with organizational goals. This approach assumes that commitment is generated when employees are trusted and allowed to work autonomously. It assumes that individuals can work hard and smart without being controlled through sanctions and other external pressures. This commitment maximization approach underpins high performance management practices.

Theoretical foundations: how commitment strategies work

Huselid (1995), building on the work of Bailey (1993), argues that people management practices can affect an individual's performance by:

- improving employees' knowledge and skills
- motivating them to engage in discretionary behaviours that draw on their knowledge and skill
- modifying organizational structures in ways that enable employees to improve the way they perform their jobs.

Some examples of the practices that contribute to these outcomes are listed below.

Improving employee knowledge and skills

A number of practices can enhance employee knowledge and skill. These include:

- *Recruitment practices that provide a large pool of qualified applicants:* It may be possible to improve recruitment practices by focusing attention on what the organization does to attract appropriately qualified individuals and how this affects the kind of people who present themselves for selection.
- *Selection practices that identify those individuals who possess the required competences:* It may be possible to improve selection practices by focusing attention on how the organization goes about selecting new employees and what steps it takes to identify and validate its selection criteria. Pfeffer (1998) argues that emphasis should be placed on screening for cultural fit and attitudes rather than skills. He makes a case for 'selecting' on those attributes that are important and difficult, or impossible, to change, and 'training' people in those behaviours or skills that are more readily learned.
- *Induction practices that affect the way people are socialized into the organization:* It may be possible to improve induction practices by focusing attention on what happens to new employees after they join the organization and how this affects the development of competences. Induction might also be considered as a practice that affects employees' motivation to engage in discretionary behaviours and influence their motivation to work harder and smarter.
- *Training practices that develop knowledge and skills required by organizational members:* It may be possible to improve training practices by focusing attention on the kinds of issues considered in Chapter 19 and questioning whether sufficient attention is given to the development of those competences that are critical to the achievement of the organization's purpose. Pfeffer (1998) argues that training is an essential component of high performance work systems because these systems rely on frontline employees exercising their skill and initiative to identify and resolve problems, introduce changes in work methods, and take responsibility for quality. However, some organizations fail to invest sufficiently in training and many more are too quick to cut training budgets when times are hard:

> because training budgets often fluctuate with company economic fortunes, a perverse, procyclical training schedule typically develops: training funds are most plentiful when the firm is doing well. But, when the firm is doing well, its people are the busiest and have the most to do, and consequently, can least afford to be away for training. By contrast, when the firm is less busy, individuals have more time to develop their skills and undertake training activities. But that is exactly when training is least likely to be made available. (Pfeffer, 1998, p. 89)

- *Other development activities that develop the knowledge, skills and job behaviours required for effective performance*: Consideration might be given to whether these practices, such as coaching, mentoring, on-the-job learning, secondments and job rotation, are as effective as they might be and whether there is an appropriate balance between these practices and more formal training activities. Performance appraisal is listed below as a practice that affects employees' motivation to engage in discretionary behaviours, but it can also provide a vehicle for developing competences.

- *Retention practices that encourage valued employees to stay with the organization:* Do these motivate those most likely to be poached away by competitors to remain with the organization?
- *Attendance practices:* Do these encourage employees to attend regularly and work their contracted hours so that they can learn from others and help others to learn from their own knowledge and experience?
- *Information-sharing practices that provide employees with knowledge about immediate job-related issues and wider business matters they require in order to perform effectively:* Consideration might be given to how and when information is provided and whether it is the right kind of information.

Motivating employees to engage in discretionary behaviours

Huselid (1995) argues that the effectiveness of even the most highly skilled employees will be limited if they are not motivated to perform. A number of people management practices can encourage organizational members to work harder and smarter. These include:

- *Employment security:* Consideration might be given to whether employees are regarded as a variable cost or a valued asset and how this affects their commitment to the organization.
- *Redeployment and severance:* When workers are no longer required in their current roles, how does the organization manage this situation and how does this affect the motivation of those who are to be redeployed and their colleagues?
- *Performance appraisal:* It may be possible to improve the benefits from appraising performance by considering questions such as: What are the objectives of the performance appraisal system? What does it measure? Are individuals or groups appraised? Who does the appraising? Is the process perceived to be fair?
- *Incentives:* A wide range of factors can affect the link between incentives and performance (see Chapter 12), but some of the questions under this heading include: How are individuals compensated? Are rewards linked to the acquisition of skills or the achievement of performance targets? If they are linked to performance, is compensation based on individual, group or organizational performance?
- *Internal promotion systems:* How are people identified and prepared for promotion?
- *Status distinctions:* These can affect motivation, so it might be useful to review the kinds of status distinctions that exist and the effects they have on performance.

Enabling motivated employees to engage in discretionary behaviours

Bailey (1993) notes that the contribution of highly skilled and motivated employees will be limited unless their jobs are structured in ways that allow them to apply their knowledge and skills to improve the way they perform their jobs. A number of interventions enable employees to engage in such discretionary behaviours. These include:

- *Organization structures:* How is the organization structured and how does this affect the ability of individuals to improve the way they do their jobs? For example, does the organization have a functional structure with people working in silos, or is it process based?

- *Parallel and temporary structures:* Does the organization use structures such as quality circles and awaydays to facilitate the sharing of ideas about performance improvement?
- *Job design:* Are people employed to perform narrowly defined tasks that require little skill or does job design emphasize a whole task and combine doing and thinking? Do people work on their own or in teams?
- *Locus of decision making:* Is decision making concentrated high up in the organization or is it decentralized and delegated?
- *Employee voice:* Is employee input encouraged? Is it allowed on a narrow agenda or a wide range of issues? What methods are used to facilitate upward, lateral and downward communication?
- *Self-managed teams:* Is decision making delegated to self-managed teams? Pfeffer (1998) advocates the adoption of self-managed teams and delegated decision making as the guiding principles for organizational design. He argues that teams can substitute peer-based control for hierarchical control, encourage people to pool ideas and come up with better ways of addressing problems, and provide a framework within which workers can more readily help each other and share their production knowledge (Shaiken et al., 1997).

Other benefits from high performance management practices

Pfeffer (1998) argues that high commitment work practices can produce savings by reducing administrative overheads. Delegating more responsibility to people further down the organization eliminates the need for many supervisory roles. High commitment work practices can also reduce many of the costs associated with having an alienated workforce that is engaged in an adversarial relationship with management.

The alignment of people management practices: the essence of high performance management

Many attempts to improve performance through the introduction of new people management practices fail because changes are introduced piecemeal and are focused on particular practices, such as selection, performance appraisal, compensation or training. Investing more resources in just one practice, such as training, may have little effect if other practices remain unchanged. For example, the potential benefits of training may be wasted if jobs are not redesigned in ways that give workers the freedom to apply their new knowledge and skills. People management practices need to be aligned with each other if employees and the organization are to benefit from what MacDuffie (1995, p. 197) refers to as 'multiple, mutually reinforcing conditions'.

Some view alignment as the defining feature of high performance management systems and do not believe it is necessary to prescribe the kinds of practices that are applied so long as they are internally consistent. However, there is a strong body of opinion that the most effective way of securing high performance is through high commitment. Those who subscribe to this school of thought advocate a configuration of practices that support the commitment rather than the control approach to management (see Pfeffer, 1998, p. 56). The theoretical foundation of the three-pronged approach to improving performance outlined above is based on the assumption that people management practices should be targeted at increasing commitment in order to elicit discretionary behaviour. Pfeffer's (1998) seven practices that characterize systems that produce profits through people – employment security, selective hiring, self-managed teams and decentralized decision making, high compensation contingent on performance, extensive training, reduced status distinctions, and extensive sharing of information – are all high commitment management practices.

Implementation is not always easy. Moving from a control- to a commitment-oriented set of management practices can be difficult because many managers are wedded to a control philosophy. Pfeffer (1998, p. 29) refers to 'the one-eighth rule', which states that only about half of all senior managers believe there is a possible connection between how organizations manage their people and the profits they earn. Of these, only about a half will do more than attempt to change a single people management practice, not realizing that the effective management of people requires a more comprehensive and systematic approach. In those organizations where managers do make comprehensive changes, only about a half will persist with these changes long enough to derive any economic benefit.

The introduction of a commitment-based high performance management system often requires a paradigm shift in the way some managers think. Pfeffer argues that if managers see their staff as costs to be reduced, as recalcitrant employees prone to opportunism, shirking and free riding, as people who can't be trusted and who need to be closely controlled through monitoring, rewards and sanctions, then any attempt to introduce high performance management practices is likely to fail. Successful implementation requires a mindset that regards people as fundamentally trustworthy, intelligent and motivated.

Results from high performance management systems

Pfeffer (1998) presents an impressive review of studies that provide evidence of substantial gains from implementing high performance management systems. This includes a study of five-year survival rates of initial public offerings (Welborne and Andrews, 1996); studies of profitability and stock price in a large sample of companies from multiple industries (Huselid, 1995); and detailed research in the automobile industry (MacDuffie, 1995), apparel (Dunlop and Weil, 1996), semiconductors (Sohoni, 1994), steel (Arthur, 1995), oil refining (Ricketts, 1994) and service industries (Schneider, 1991; Johnson et al., 1994). These findings suggest that high performance management can produce economic benefits in a wide range of settings, including low- and high-tech, manufacturing and service industries.

Diagnosing the alignment of people management practices

Pfeffer (1998) describes the two-part 'alignment diagnosis', which is an essential part of any high performance management intervention. The first is concerned with external alignment and involves diagnosing the extent to which management practices are congruent with the organization's business strategy. The second is concerned with internal alignment and involves diagnosing the extent to which people management practices are aligned with each other.

You might find it useful to use Change tools 20.1 and 20.2 presented below to assess the alignment of people management practices in your organization. If you are a student with little or no work experience, you could still practise diagnosing external alignment by investigating an organization's strategy online (some companies publish their strategy on their website) and then brainstorming the competences and people management practices you think would have to be in place in order to achieve this.

🔧 *Change tool* **20.1** *Diagnosing external alignment*

Diagnosing external alignment involves four steps:

1 Reviewing the organization's strategy
2 Identifying the critical behaviours and related competences required to achieve the strategy
3 Identifying practices the organization uses to manage people
4 Assessing the alignment of each people management/HR practice with the competences and behaviours required to achieve the organization's strategy. Does each practice support the availability and application of critical competences and behaviours?

Each step will be considered in turn.

1 *Specifying the organization's strategy*
Strategy is a statement of purpose that indicates how the organization will match its resources with the opportunities, constraints and demands in the environment. Implicit in this statement are the value propositions the organization offers to stakeholders.
   Summarize your organization's strategy in the space below.

∨

2 *Identifying the critical behaviours and related competences required to achieve the strategy*
If the organization's strategy is premised on the provision of excellent customer service and the majority of staff are customer facing, then the organization needs people who have the competences necessary to support this value proposition. If, on the other hand, the strategy is premised on being first to market with innovative products, then a different set of competences will be required. Pfeffer recommends that attention is restricted to the six or so behaviours and

related competences that are the most important. These can be entered at the head of the columns of the external alignment matrix presented below.

3 *Identifying practices that the organization uses to manage people*

The external alignment matrix is divided into three parts in line with Bailey's (1993) model of how HR practices can affect performance. The first part relates to the policies and practices that affect the 'availability and development' of the competences necessary to deliver required behaviours. Examples of these practices include recruitment, selection, induction, training, other development activities, attendance, and information sharing.

The second part relates to practices that affect employees' 'motivation' to engage in discretionary behaviours that involve applying critical competences in order to improve performance. These practices include employment security, redeployment and severance, performance appraisal, incentives, internal promotion systems, and status distinctions.

The third part relates to practices that 'enable' motivated employees to engage in discretionary behaviours that lead to performance improvements. These practices include organization design, parallel and temporary structures, job design, locus of decision making, and employee voice.

Review your organization's people management practices and amend the list included in the external alignment matrix below to reflect your organization's current approach to HRM. You might also amend this list to include additional practices that, if applied appropriately, could contribute to high performance.

4 *Assessing the alignment of each people management practice with the competences and behaviours required to achieve the organization's business strategy*

This involves assessing the extent to which each of the people management practices listed in your external alignment matrix is likely to promote the competences and behaviours you identified as critical for the implementation of the strategy. Pfeffer suggests using a three-point scale, where +1 indicates that the practice is aligned with the organization's business strategy and will support the development of required competences and behaviours, 0 where the practice has a neutral effect, and −1 where it is misaligned. This procedure is a useful way of identifying where there is substantial misalignment and a clear need for action to develop and implement a revised people management practice.

Pfeffer (1998, p. 111) identifies some of the most common alignment-related problems. Two of these involve the link between training activities and competences, and the link between compensation and the achievement of key performance targets:

- With regard to training and required competences, in many organizations training activities are focused on generally useful topics, such as negotiating skills and time management, but neglect the crucial competences that are tightly linked to the achievement of strategic objectives.
- With regard to compensation and key performance targets, Pfeffer highlights the problem with an example of a firm rewarding managers for 'making budget numbers', when the really important targets had to do with being innovative, fast and customer focused.

External alignment matrix							
Practices that affect:	**Critical behaviours/competences required to implement the organization's strategy**						
1 The development and availability of competences							
Recruitment							
Selection							
Induction							
Training							
Other development							
Information sharing							
Other							
2 Motivation							
Employment security							
Performance appraisal							
Incentives							
Internal promotion systems							
Status distinctions							
Other							
3 Ability to use competences to improve performance							
Organization structures							
Job design							
Locus of decision making							
Employee voice							
Other							

Change tool **20.2** *Diagnosing internal alignment*

Diagnosing internal alignment involves assessing the internal consistency of people management practices. One way of doing this is to list the management practices identified as part of the external alignment exercise across the top as well as down the left-hand side of a matrix and taking each practice in turn and reviewing it for alignment against each of the other practices. For example, in terms of job design, if work is allocated to self-managed teams, are employees given training that supports this practice? Also, is performance appraisal focused on individuals or teams and is compensation based on individual or team performance? Again, the three-point scale can be used to signal the degree of alignment and highlight potential problems.

Internal alignment matrix															
Practices that affect:	**Management practices**														
1 The development of competences	a	b	c	d	e	f	g	h	i	j	k	l	m	n	o
a. Recruitment	-														
b. Selection	-	-													
c. Induction	-	-	-												
d. Training	-	-	-	-											
e. Other development	-	-	-	-	-										
f. Information sharing	-	-	-	-	-	-									
2 Motivation															
g. Employment security	-	-	-	-	-	-	-								
h. Performance appraisal	-	-	-	-	-	-	-	-							
i Incentives	-	-	-	-	-	-	-	-	-						
j. Internal promotions	-	-	-	-	-	-	-	-	-	-					
k. Status distinctions	-	-	-	-	-	-	-	-	-	-	-				
3 Use of competences															
l. Organization structures	-	-	-	-	-	-	-	-	-	-	-	-			
m. Job design	-	-	-	-	-	-	-	-	-	-	-	-	-		
n. Locus of decision making	-	-	-	-	-	-	-	-	-	-	-	-	-	-	
o. Employee voice	-	-	-	-	-	-	-	-	-	-	-	-	-	-	-

This kind of alignment diagnosis can help change agents to identify the system of people management practices that an organization uses to achieve its strategic objectives and identify any misalignments between them. If misalignments are identified, it is possible to intervene to realign practices to improve performance.

If you are in employment, you might find it useful to reflect on the extent of external and internal alignment in your organization and the areas where alignment problems might arise.

Summary

High performance management is an intervention that change agents can use to improve performance by aligning the organization's people management practices with the organization's business strategy and aligning all people management practices with each other.

High performance management aims to improve performance by developing and implementing a bundle or system of people management practices that are internally consistent, aligned with other business processes, and aligned with the organization's business strategy rather than by improving separate people management practices such as training, performance management or reward systems.

Cost reduction and commitment maximization approaches to managing an organization's HR were reviewed and it was argued that it is the commitment maximization philosophy that best supports high performance management interventions.

People management practices can enhance performance by:

1 improving employees' knowledge and skills
2 motivating them to engage in discretionary behaviours that draw on their knowledge and skill
3 modifying organizational structures in ways that enable employees to improve the way they perform their jobs.

Attention was given to some of the people management practices that can help to:

- *improve employee knowledge and skill:* such as recruitment, selection, induction, training, coaching, mentoring, on-the-job learning, secondments, job rotation
- *motivate employees to engage in discretionary behaviours:* such as employment security, redeployment and severance policies, performance appraisal, incentives, internal promotion systems and status distinctions
- *enable motivated employees to engage in discretionary behaviours:* includes designing appropriate organization structures, implementing parallel and temporary structures, job design, pushing decision making down the organization and facilitating upward communications so that employees can voice their concerns and contribute to organizational learning.

The final part presented two change tools that can be used to assess the extent to which people management practices are aligned with the organization's business strategy and each other. When misalignments have been identified, it is possible to intervene to modify the misaligned practices to improve performance.

Diagnosing external alignment involves four steps:

1 Reviewing the organization's strategy
2 Identifying the critical behaviours and related competences required to achieve the strategy
3 Identifying practices the organization uses to manage people
4 Assessing the alignment of each people management practice with the competences and behaviours required to achieve the organization's strategy. Does each practice support the availability and application of critical competences and behaviours?

Diagnosing internal alignment involves ensuring that all people management practices are aligned with each other. For example, the potential benefits of training may be wasted if jobs are not redesigned to give workers the freedom to apply their new knowledge and skills.

Alignment is the defining feature of high performance management interventions.

In terms of the typology presented in Figure 16.3, high performance management is an HRM intervention.

References

Arthur, J.B. (1995) Effects of human resource systems on manufacturing performance and turnover, *Academy of Management Journal*, 37(3): 670–87.

Bailey, T. (1993) Discretionary effort and the organization of work: Employee participation and work reform since Hawthorne, working paper, Columbia University, New York.

Dunlop, J.T. and Weil, D. (1996) Diffusion and performance of modular production in the US apparel industry, *Industrial Relations*, 35(3): 337–8.

Huselid, M.A. (1995) The impact of human resource management practices on turnover, productivity, and corporate financial performance, *Academy of Management Journal*, 38(3): 635–72.

Johnson, R.H., Ryan, A.M. and Schmit, M.J. (1994) Employee attitudes and branch performance at Ford Motor Credit, paper presented to the ninth annual conference of the Society of Industrial and Organizational Psychology, Nashville, TN, April.

MacDuffie, J.P. (1995) Human resource bundles and manufacturing performance: Organizational logic and flexible production systems in the world auto industry, *Industrial and Labor Relations Review*, 48(2): 197–221.

McGregor, D. (1960) Theory X and theory Y. In D.S. Pugh (ed.) *Organization Theory: Selected Readings*. London: Penguin.

Pfeffer, J. (1998) *The Human Equation: Building Profits by Putting People First*. Boston, MA: Harvard Business School Press.

Ricketts, R. (1994) Survey points to practices that reduce refinery maintenance spending, *Oil and Gas Journal*, 4 July, p. 38.

Schneider, B. (1991) Service quality and profits: Can you have your cake and eat it, too?, *Human Resource Planning*, 14(2): 151.

Shaiken, H., Lopez, S. and Mankita, I. (1997) Two routes to team production: Saturn and Chrysler compared, *Industrial Relations*, 36(1): 17–45.

Sohoni, V. (1994) Workforce involvement and wafer fabrication efficiency. In C. Brown (ed.) *The Competitive Semiconductor Manufacturing Human Resources Project: First Interim Report*. Berkeley, CA: Institute of Industrial Relations.

Truss, C., Gratton, L., Hope-Hailey, V. et al. (1997) Soft and hard models of human resource management: A reappraisal, *Journal of Management Studies*, 34(1): 53–73.

Walton, R.E. (1985) From control to commitment in the workplace, *Harvard Business Review*, 63(2): 77–84.

Welbourne, T. and Andrews, A. (1996) Predicting performance of initial public offering firms: Should HRM be in the equation?, *Academy of Management Journal*, 39(4): 910–11.

Business process re-engineering

Business process re-engineering (BPR) is a technostructural intervention that involves switching attention away from fragmented functional thinking towards cross-functional processes. This chapter:

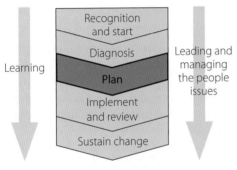

- Reviews some of the debates about BPR, such as whether it requires a fundamental rethink and radical change or incremental improvement; organization-wide wholesale transformation or localized piecemeal change; top-down direction or collaborative effort.
- Presents BPR as a seven-stage process that involves process mapping, identifying which process to re-engineer, understanding the selected process, defining key performance objectives, designing new processes, testing and implementation.
- Argues that BPR can be a highly politicized process that often involves jurisdictional disputes when managers are required to let go of activities or decisions they value.
- Discusses research findings regarding the success of BPR interventions. Some reports suggest that a high percentage of interventions fail to deliver intended outcomes, but there is evidence that when BPR is successfully implemented it can deliver impressive improvements. Contextual factors that can affect outcomes are discussed.

The effect of organizational structures on performance

The structure of most organizations has been influenced by the principle of the division of labour, first articulated by Adam Smith (1776/1950) in *The Wealth of Nations*. Smith observed that it was much more efficient to break the process of pin making down into several steps that could be undertaken by specialist workers rather than delegate the whole process to one generalist worker. This principle manifests itself today in organizations that structure activities according to specialist functions rather than value-creating processes. Hammer and Champy (1993) argue that many companies have vertical structures that resemble functional silos built on narrow pieces of a process (Figure 21.1). They illustrate how this affects organizational functioning with reference to the order fulfilment process that starts when a customer places an order and ends when the goods are delivered:

The person checking a customer's credit is part of the credit department, which is probably a part of the finance organization. Inventory picking is performed by workers in the warehouse, who may report to the vice president of manufacturing. Shipping, on the other hand, is part of logistics. People involved in a process look *inward* towards their department and *upwards* towards their boss, but no one looks *outwards* toward the customer. (Hammer and Champy, 1993, p. 28)

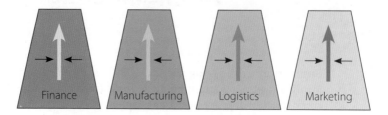

Figure **21.1** *Functional structures*

BPR involves switching attention away from fragmented, functional-based thinking towards cross-functional processes that create value for the organization (Figure 21.2). Kaplan and Murdock (1991) argue that focusing attention on and redesigning core processes can make them faster and more flexible, and make organizations more responsive to changes in competitive conditions, consumer demands, product life cycles and technologies.

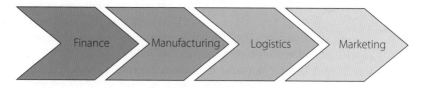

Figure **21.2** *Cross-functional processes*

The nature of BPR

Hammer and Champy (1993) define BPR as the fundamental rethinking and radical redesign of business processes to achieve dramatic improvements in performance. Some of the competing views around BPR are examined below.

Fundamental rethink and radical change or incremental improvement?

Hammer and Champy (1993) argue that BPR is 'fundamental' because it involves asking the most basic questions about how an organization operates, questions that challenge many widely held assumptions. Rather than simply asking whether it is possible to improve the way something is done, BPR involves questioning *why* the organization does what it does. For example, those responsible for re-engineering the order fulfilment process, referred to above, might question the need to perform credit checks rather than assuming they are an essential part of the process. It is possible that checking a customer's credit fails to add any value because the cost of performing a check is greater than any losses that might be incurred from bad debts. Hammer and Champy state that new thinking should not be influenced by embedded assumptions or any existing processes, activities and systems. They advocate a 'clean sheet' approach to process redesign.

Davenport and Stoddard (1994) challenge this view. Based on conversations with managers from more than 200 companies and rigorous research on 35 re-engineering initiatives (Javenpaa and Stoddard, 1993), they assert that, in practice, a clean sheet approach is rarely found. Those companies that do adopt this approach tend to make a clear distinction between clean sheet design and clean sheet implementation. They may adopt a clean sheet approach to design because it can provide a vision of a 'best-of-all-processes' world towards which the organization can focus its change efforts. Davenport and Stoddard quoted one manager who said: 'You can design assuming a clean slate, but you must implement assuming the existing state' (1994, p. 123), and went on to report that designers often start with a 'dirty slate', taking into account the opportunities for enabling a new process and the constraints that disable it:

> With both design elements in mind, the design team could construct the best possible process given the enablers and the constraints. Whereas this is a less exciting and more difficult design method, designing with a 'dirty slate' will normally yield a more implementable process.

Organization-wide wholesale transformation or localized piecemeal change?

Hammer and Champy (1993) argue that to be successful, BPR must entail rapid and wholesale transformation rather than piecemeal change. Davenport and Stoddard (1994), however, do not see re-engineering as incompatible with continuous improvement. While they agree with the proposition that re-engineering is a process that can contribute to organizational transformation, they do not agree that it is synonymous with it. They report observing numerous firms trying to change too many processes at once and failing in their ambition to achieve radical transformation. However, they also report observing several firms that were successfully creating hybrid configurations, where processes were re-engineered within a functional structure such as the marketing department. McNulty and Ferlie (2002), in their in-depth study of BPR within the Leicester Royal Infirmary (see Case study 3.2), report findings that support Davenport and Stoddard's position. They found that while the intended strategy was radical and revolutionary, the emergent strategy of re-engineering proved to be evolutionary and convergent in overall approach and impact:

> As the re-engineering programme unfolded the initial radical ambition for organizational process redesign was tempered and reshaped in line with functional organisational principles that underpinned the existing pattern of specialties and clinical directorates. Re-engineers learned quickly that they were dependent on the support of managers and clinicians ... to effect change at specialty and clinical directorate levels. (McNulty and Ferlie, 2002, p. 116)

Top-down direction or collaborative effort?

Those who argue that re-engineering offers a system-wide and radical approach to change also tend to view it as an essentially top-down process. Hammer and

Champy (1993, p. 208), for example, believe that people near the front line lack the broad perspective that re-engineering demands:

> They may see – probably better than anyone else – the narrow problems from which their departments suffer, but it is difficult for them to see a process as a whole and to recognize its poor overall design as the source of their problems.

They also argue that middle managers lack the required authority to change processes that cross organizational boundaries. There are, however, those who believe that re-engineering can be a more participative process. While Davenport and Stoddard (1994, p. 125) accept that 'innovative designs for broad processes are unlikely to come from anyone whose head is buried deep in the bowels of the existing process', they see no reason why all members of design teams must be high in the organizational hierarchy. They argue that those who are at the front line may make a valuable contribution to the design of detailed process activities. They also cite examples of organizational members who have failed to implement newly designed processes because they had had no hand in their creation.

Re-engineering at the Leicester Royal Infirmary started as a top-down programme to identify, redesign and roll out core processes across the hospital. A central re-engineering capability was created using an infrastructure of re-engineering committees, re-engineering laboratories – physical spaces in which teams or re-engineers could work on the redesign of processes – and internal and external change agents. This initial strategy began to flounder and was eventually replaced by a decentralized approach, which involved responsibility for re-engineering shifting from a dedicated team of re-engineers to managers located within clinical directorates. McNulty and Ferlie (2002) note that it was at this point that the energy and momentum for change increased because individuals felt more able to 'adopt, adapt and customize' re-engineering ideas to suit local circumstances and purposes.

The application of BPR

BPR typically involves seven steps, which are now discussed in detail.

Process mapping

A process is a series of actions that lead to an outcome. Process maps show how work flows through an organization. People tend to be more familiar with organizational units, such as manufacturing, research and development or marketing, than with the processes to which these units contribute. Examples of processes in a business organization are order fulfilment (order to payment – including intermediate steps such as manufacturing), product development (concept to prototype) and sales (prospect to order). Examples of processes in a healthcare organization include patient test (referral to diagnosis) and patient stay (admission to discharge). In most organizations, there are relatively few core processes, but each of these might involve a number of subprocesses. The starting point for any BPR project is to map the processes that contribute to the organization fulfilling its purpose.

Identifying processes for re-engineering

Even when the ambition is to use BPR to radically transform the organization in the shortest possible time, it will normally prove impossible to re-engineer all the organization's processes simultaneously. Hammer and Champy (1993) suggest three criteria for choosing which processes to re-engineer and the order in which this might be done. They are:

- *dysfunction:* those processes in the deepest trouble
- *importance:* processes that have the greatest impact on the organization's customers
- *feasibility:* those processes most susceptible to successful redesign.

Understanding the selected process

The re-engineering team needs to understand the process, what it does, how well it does it and any critical issues that govern its performance, but it does not, according to the classical school of BPR, need to undertake any detailed analysis. Hammer and Champy (1993) caution against too much analysis because it directs attention inside the process and directs attention away from challenging embedded assumptions. They argue that attention should be focused on seeking a high level of understanding, starting with what the process delivers and how well these outcomes match what customers really want. This then provides the basis for a clean sheet design activity. There are those, however, who see value in starting with a 'dirty slate' and looking for opportunities for incremental process improvement (as discussed above).

Improving processes in healthcare settings can involve starting from a clean sheet and radically transforming a process, or it can involve working with an existing process and seeking out opportunities for incremental improvement. Example 21.1 illustrates how those involved in one re-engineering project set about improving their understanding of an existing process before deciding how it could be redesigned.

V

Example **21.1** *Mapping a GP referral for a routine X-ray at a local hospital*

A manager responsible for delivering primary healthcare in a community in northwest England decided to explore the possibility of re-engineering some of the processes known to be inefficient and the cause of patient dissatisfaction. One such process involved GPs (general practitioners) referring patients for routine X-rays at a local hospital. Once this process had been identified as the initial target for re-engineering, the next step was to map the process. The manager had been trained in process re-engineering and was familiar with two ways of mapping processes. One was to gather all the stakeholders together for a mapping workshop. The other was for members of a re-engineering team to physically walk through the process and record what happens at each stage. He decided on the second approach but was careful to include in the team representatives of those he knew were involved in the

© IMAGE SOURCE

▶

process. Figure 23.1 illustrates their map of the X-ray referral process. It starts when the patient first goes to their GP with symptoms, and ends when the X-ray result is communicated to the patient.

The map provided the re-engineering team with the information they required to start looking for possible improvements. Some of the things they considered included:

- *the number of steps in the process*
- *the number of hand-offs:* occasions when the information relating to the patient's diagnostic test is passed from one person to another

- *task time:* the time taken for each step
- *wait time:* the time between each step
- *dead time when nothing happens:* the dictated report sits on the secretary's desk for three days before being typed
- *steps that fail to add any value:* for example, they questioned whether it was time- and cost-effective for the consultant to check the typed report before it was forwarded to the GP
- *blockages:* steps that slow the rest of the process down.

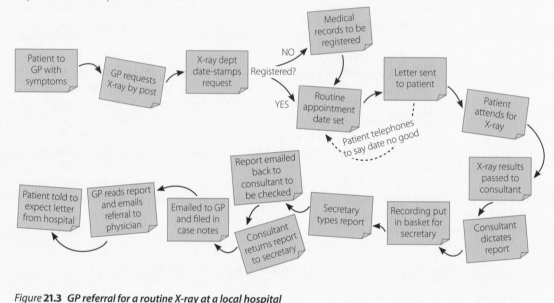

Figure **21.3** *GP referral for a routine X-ray at a local hospital*

Mapping a targeted process is often done in two steps. The first involves producing a high-level process map that provides an overview of how inputs are transformed into outputs, focuses attention on the relative value of the outputs produced by the process – Are they worth the effort required to produce them? Do they really satisfy customers' needs? – and the value added by particular steps in the process – Can a step be eliminated, integrated with another step, or replaced with an entirely different subprocess? Experience suggests that analysing this kind of high-level map helps to expose embedded assumptions and identify those parts of the overall process that offer the greatest potential for improvement. The second step involves mapping those parts of the process that have potential for improvement in more detail.

Defining key performance objectives

Key performance objectives are based on what the re-engineering team and other stakeholders believe the customer requires from the process. They provide a basis for specifying measures that will indicate whether the changes have been success-ful. Sometimes, benchmarking is used to help define performance objectives, but re- engineers need to be alert to the possibility that benchmarking may limit ambi-tion to what is currently being achieved by 'the best of the rest' and inhibit out-of-the-box thinking about what the process could deliver. Baselining, collecting and recording data about existing (pre-re-engineered) performance, can also help with the definition of realistic performance targets and provide a basis for assessing the successes of the re-engineering project.

Designing new processes

According to Hammer and Champy (1993, p. 134):

> Redesign is the most nakedly creative part of the entire reengineering process. More than any other, it demands imagination, inductive thinking, and a touch of craziness.

They illustrate this with the example of an insurance company that believed it was costing more than it should to settle claims relating to motor accidents. There is no set format for redesigning a process, but it often involves people sharing ideas about how the process might be changed and others 'piggybacking' on these ideas to suggest other possibilities (Example 21.2).

Example **21.2** *The claims settlement process*

An employee working for an insurance company noticed that it cost the same per hour to work on a big claim as it did to work on a small claim. This got people thinking about what could be done to reduce the cost of settling claims. A meeting was arranged to explore possibilities. One idea involved introducing a step early in the process that would separate out those claims that would cost a lot to settle (usually those involving a claim for personal injury) and those that would not, and redesigning the process for small claims to cut the time required to settle them. One suggestion for achieving this outcome was to immediately settle any claim for less than a certain amount. Some team members felt that this could encourage fraud and escalate the cost of claims, while others felt that this danger could be managed by only offering immediate settlement to policy holders who had a good no-claims record. A related idea was to let the agent handle claims below a specified amount.

This led to somebody else suggesting that the garage should be allowed to deal with the claim, thereby eliminating the need for many steps in the existing process. This proposal was initially dismissed because it was feared that garages might inflate the cost of repairs. However, somebody brought the team back to this idea and suggested that there would be many garages willing to work for modest margins if this enabled them to win more business from the insurance company. It was also recognized that not only could this reduce costs for the insurance company, but it would also lead to greater customer satisfaction. What customers wanted most was their car back on the road as quickly as possible.

This first meeting came up with some challenging new ideas, some of which merited further attention and testing. It also involved the application of a number of re-engineering principles, such as organizing work around outcomes, for example reduced cost and increased customer satisfaction, and involving as few people as possible in the process to reduce hand-offs and waiting time. In addition, it involved destroying some embedded assumptions such as garages cannot be trusted.

Testing

An important part of BPR is the testing of ideas to see if they will work in practice. Langley et al. (1996) advocate a plan, do, study, act (PDSA) cycle for process improvement that involves:

- *planning* a change that can be tested on a small scale or over a limited period – an hour, day or week
- *doing* or carrying out the test
- *studying* baseline data and the effect of the test and looking for improvements
- *acting* to implement the tested change.

This process has many similarities with action research and can involve several iterations before final implementation (Change tool 21.1).

 Change tool **21.1** *The plan, do, study, act (PDSA) cycle*

The PDSA cycle is a tool for testing ideas by putting changes into effect on a small scale and learning from their impact before full implementation.
The four stages are:

- *Plan:* plan the change to be tested
- *Do:* carry out the test (change)
- *Study:* study data before and after the change and reflect on what was learned
- *Act:* plan implementation or, if the test was not successful, plan the next PDSA cycle.

Implementation

If the tests are successful, the redesigned process can be implemented and rolled out, as appropriate, to other parts of the organization. However, great care needs to be exercised if the redesigned process is to be rolled out to powerful individuals or groups who were not part of, and committed to, the re-engineering process. BPR can be highly politicized and often involves jurisdictional disputes when managers are required to let go of activities and decisions they value.

Results from BPR

Research findings regarding the results of BPR are mixed. Cummings and Worley (2001) cite a study of 497 companies in the USA and 1,245 companies in Europe, in which 60% of US firms and 75% of European firms had engaged in at least one re-engineering project, but only 15% of them reported positive outcomes. This is quite different to the findings reported by Caron et al. (1994). They found that while only half of 20 BPR projects undertaken by Cigna, a leading provider of insurance and related financial services, were successful first time round, the impact of re-engineering was very positive and the company saved more than $100 million overall. They also reported that some of the most successful projects were those undertaken in self-contained areas.

McNulty and Ferlie (2002) report that attempts to radically transform a large hospital through process re-engineering were highly contested and the outcome of the change was uneven across the organization. Contextual factors had an important effect on outcomes, especially those relating to the extent to which doctors retained control over work practices. They also found that it was easier to secure change in those processes or parts of processes that did not cross boundaries between clinical directorates or between directorates and external agencies. This echoes one of the findings reported by Caron et al. (1994) that some of the most successful projects were those that were undertaken in self-contained areas. Despite the many difficulties encountered when trying to re-engineer the hospital, McNulty and Ferlie observed that the re-engineering methodology did make an important contribution to securing change. For example, in trauma orthopaedic care, there were a number of positive outcomes. The baselining activity produced 'facts' about patient activity on which the case for change could be built. Process mapping enabled the re-engineers and other stakeholders, such as doctors, to analyse and understand the care process and develop a vision of change. Finally, piloting allowed some changes to be introduced, often without people realizing that an important change had taken place.

Summary

Business process re-engineering involves switching attention away from fragmented functional thinking towards cross-functional processes. This chapter reviewed some of the debates about BPR, such as whether it must involve:

- a fundamental rethink and radical change or incremental improvement
- organization-wide wholesale transformation or localized piecemeal change
- top-down direction or collaborative effort.

1 *Fundamental rethink and radical change or incremental improvement?*
Hammer and Champy argue that BPR involves a 'fundamental rethinking' of business processes. They argue that new thinking should not be influenced by embedded assumptions or any existing processes or activities. They advocate a 'clean sheet' approach. Although Davenport and Stoddard recognize the value of 'clean sheet' thinking at the design stage, because this provides a 'best-of-all-processes' vision, they argue that, more often than not, implementation needs to take account of the existing situation, including enablers and constraints, if the change is to be successful.

2 *Organization-wide change or localized piecemeal change?*
Hammer and Champy argue that BPR involves a 'radical redesign' of business processes. They argue that to be successful, BPR must entail a rapid and wholesale transformation rather than an incremental piecemeal change. On the other hand, Davenport and Stoddard see re-engineering as compatible with continuous improvement. While they agree that re-engineering is a process that can contribute to organizational transformation, they do not agree that it is synonymous with it.

Davenport and Stoddard report observing numerous firms trying to change too many processes at once and failing in their ambition to achieve radical transformation. However, they also report observing several firms that were successfully creating hybrid configurations, adding a process dimension to their functional structures.

3 *Top-down direction or collaborative effort?*

Those who argue that re-engineering offers a system-wide and radical approach to change also tend to view it as an essentially top-down process and argue that BPR initiatives should not be led by people who are involved in the processes. While Davenport and Stoddard (1994, p. 125) accept that 'innovative designs for broad processes are unlikely to come from anyone whose head is buried deep in the bowels of the existing process', they see no reason why all members of design teams must be high in the organizational hierarchy. They argue that those who are at the front line may make a valuable contribution to the design of detailed process activities.

BPR involves seven stages:

1 *Process mapping:* Process maps show how work flows through an organization.
2 *Identifying which process to reengineer:* Criteria might include dysfunction (Which processes are in deepest trouble?), importance (Which have greatest impact on customers?) and feasibility (Which are most susceptible to successful redesign?).
3 *Understanding the selected process:* Mapping for understanding can involve identifying the number of steps in the process, number of hand-offs, task time, wait time, dead time when nothing happens, steps that fail to yield any value and blockages.
4 *Defining key performance objectives:* These need to be based on what the customer requires from the process.
5 *Designing new processes:* 'Redesign is the most nakedly creative part of the entire re-engineering process. More than any other, it demands imagination, inductive thinking, and a touch of craziness' (Hammer and Champy, 1993: 134).
6 *Testing:* This involves implementing a proposed process improvement on a small scale, or for a limited time to see if it works in practice.
7 *Implementation:* If the test is successful, the redesigned process can be rolled out across the organization.

Great care may need to be exercised, especially with implementation, because BPR can be highly politicized and often involves jurisdictional disputes when managers are required to let go of activities or decisions they value.

In terms of the typology presented in Figure 16.3, BPR is a technostructural intervention.

References

Caron, J.R., Jarvenpaa, D.L. and Stoddard, D. (1994) Business reengineering at CIGNA Corporation: Experience and lessons learned from the last five years, *MIS Quarterly*, 18(3): 233–50.

Cummings, T.G. and Worley, C.G. (2001) *Organization Development and Change* (7th edn). Cincinnati, OH: South Western.

Davenport, T.H. and Stoddard, D.B. (1994) Reengineering: Business change of mythic proportions?, *MIS Quarterly*, 18(2): 121–7.

Hammer, M. and Champy, J. (1993) *Reengineering the Corporation: A Manifesto for Business Revolution*. London: Nicholas Brealey.

Javenpaa, D.L. and Stoddard, D.B. (1993) Managing IT-enabled radical change, research proposal, University of Texas/Harvard Business School.

Kaplan, R. and Murdock, L. (1991) Core process design, *McKinsey Quarterly*, 2: 27–43.

Langley, G., Nolan, K., Norman, C. and Provost, L. (1996) *The Improvement Guide: A Practical Approach to Enhancing Organizational Performance.* San Francisco, CA: Jossey-Bass.

McNulty, T. and Ferlie, E. (2002) *Reengineering Health Care: The Complexities of Organizational Transformation.* Oxford: Oxford University Press.

Smith, A. (1776/1950) *The Wealth of Nations.* London: Methuen.

V

Lean

Womack et al. (1990) coined the phrase 'lean' to describe a production system that does more with less and less. It is a customer-focused process that aims to provide customers with precisely what they want, free of defects, exactly when they want it.

Womack and Jones (1996) summarized their approach to lean in five principles:

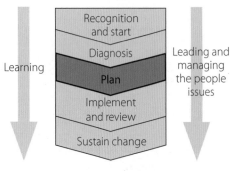

1 precisely specify value for each product or product family
2 identify value streams for each product to expose waste
3 make value flow without interruption
4 let customers pull value from the producer
5 pursue perfection by searching out and eliminating further waste.

This chapter:

- discusses whether lean is merely a set of tools and techniques or a philosophy underpinning the notion of the lean enterprise that delivers value to end customers
- traces the development of lean thinking
- considers each of Womack and Jones's five principles
- discusses the Toyota Production System – widely regarded as one of the most successful examples of lean
- reviews some tools and techniques used by lean practitioners, such as the seven wastes and the 5S methodology
- presents examples of how lean has been applied in manufacturing and non-manufacturing contexts.

A philosophy or a set of tools?

Some practitioners view lean as a set of tools and techniques, whereas others view it as a philosophy (Scherrer-Rathje et al., 2009). Toolkit-oriented practitioners focus their attention on tools such as control charts, 5S and seven wastes, which are discussed in Change tools 22.1 and 22,2, total productive maintenance, just-in-time (JIT) inventories and so on and direct their efforts towards applying them to achieve specific outcomes. These specific outcomes might involve change efforts that are restricted to particular parts of the organization or directed towards the achievement of limited goals, such as cost reduction. On the other hand, those who view lean as a philosophy focus more attention on acting in accordance with guiding principles and overarching aims to create a lean enterprise. They adopt a more holistic approach and consider how the inter-relationships between and the synergistic effects of related practices can affect performance across the whole enterprise.

Although originally developed in the context of manufacturing, lean thinking has spread beyond the shop floor and is now widely applied in sectors such as finance, health and education. This chapter reviews issues that need to be considered when implementing lean in these different settings.

Antecedents of lean thinking

In 1913, Henry Ford introduced the first 'flow' production line to assemble Model T Fords. It was a remarkable innovation, involving the manufacture of vehicle components using special purpose machines that produced identical and inter-changeable parts. These components were delivered to the required point on a moving assembly line and because they were identical and could be inserted without any last-minute modification, workers used standardized processes to fit them and quickly assemble their part of the car as it moved down the line.

Ford's assembly line was revolutionary, incorporating flow and inventory control to deliver cheap cars to an expanding market. But it had some important limitations. For example, as customers became more sophisticated and sought greater variety, the production system could not respond. It was inflexible. Almost all the machines involved in fabricating components produced a single part. Cycle times could be measured in years. Product development was a slow process. For example, the chassis that were being produced when production ended in 1926 were essentially the same as those when production began in 1913. This inflexibility limited the variety available to customers, summed up by the often-quoted expression: 'You can have any colour you want so long as it's black.' Eventually, customers were offered some variety in body styles but this was achieved by 'dropping' different bodies onto identical vehicles at the end of the assembly line.

Attempts to increase flexibility eroded some of the benefits of flow production. Companies developed production systems that involved manufacturing batches of components on bigger and faster machines. When a sufficient quantity of a particular component had been manufactured, machines were reset to produce a new batch of different components. This batch system delivered greater flexibility and reduced the unit cost of components, but these benefits had associated costs. Steps in the production process were often separated. Throughput times increased. Batch production required larger inventories, as components had to be stored until required, and levels of waste often increased – a whole batch of substandard components could be manufactured and the fault might go undetected until an item from that batch was used.

In 1902, eleven years before Ford developed his first production line, Sakichi Toyoda, the founder of the Toyota Group, invented a loom that automatically stopped if a thread snapped. This led to the development of other self-monitoring machines that could detect defects (deviations from a standard) as soon as they occurred. Process stopping, to detect and eliminate the cause of defects (jidoka), eventually became one of the pillars of the Toyota Production System and was extended beyond self-monitoring machines. Workers were encouraged to intervene to stop production whenever they identified a problem. Doing this enabled problems to be contained. Resources were immediately directed to eliminating the root cause, thus contributing to continuous improvement.

Many others were involved in work that is reflected in lean thinking. F.W. Taylor contributed to the development and deployment of standardized work practices. Taiichi Ohno, an engineer at Toyota, developed JIT scheduling systems driven by customer demand rather than sales or production targets. W.E. Deming's early work in the interwar years on the statistical control of processes laid the foundation for his later work on 'common' (usual, quantifiable) and 'special' (unusual non-quantifiable) causes of variation and the concept of quality. Shortly after the end of the Second World War, he began working with Japanese manufactures to apply his ideas to improve quality while reducing costs, by eliminating waste, and increasing market share, by providing customers with what they valued. His approach involved systems thinking to optimize end-to-end processes such as order fulfilment (order being placed to payment received, including intermediate steps such as manufacturing), using statistics to understand and manage variation, motivating employees by helping them see how their actions affected performance, aligning their objectives to real customer needs, and adopting a systematic approach to learning using a plan, do, study, act (PDSA) approach.

In the 1930s and again after end of the Second World War, members of the Toyoda family studied Ford's assembly lines and other developments in Japan and elsewhere to explore the possibility of creating a production system that could provide high variety, low cost, high quality and rapid throughput times. Taiichi Ohno is credited with drawing these themes together and developing the Toyota Production System, which is discussed in more detail below.

Womack and Jones's five principles of lean thinking

As noted in the chapter introduction, lean thinking involves specifying value, lining up value-creating activities in the most effective sequence, conducting these activities without interruption whenever 'pulled' to do so by customer demand, and continuously seeking new ways to improve this process. Each of Womack and Jones's (1996) five principles will be considered in turn.

Specifying value

Specifying value is the essential first step in lean thinking and needs to be done from the perspective of the end customer. All too often, other stakeholders, such as shareholders, provide the starting point for defining value.

Womack and Jones (1996) argue that it can be hard to define value because many producers focus too much attention on the products or services they are already making and many customers only think in terms of some variant of what they are already getting. If they do attempt to rethink value, they may simply fall back on well-tried formulae such as lower cost, increased variety or instant delivery rather than challenging what is known and exploring what is really needed. They illustrate this point with numerous cases. For example, Doyle Wilson Housebuilders introduced a radical total quality management (TQM) initiative that was welcomed by customers and helped the company increase market share. But Doyle Wilson recognized that only 22% of those purchasing a home bought a new house and began to wonder why the other 78% of homebuyers preferred old houses. Rather than restricting his attention to what his existing customers, the buyers of new homes, valued, he explored why the 78% of non-customers preferred older properties. This produced some valuable insights. They shied away from buying new homes because of the perceived hassle involved in negotiating the build specification, the long lead times before moving in, the inevitable 'to-be-done' lists of work still to be completed after moving in, and the 'phoney choices' available from builders who promised customized homes but then loaded them with standard equipment. Womack and Jones describe how this new perspective stimulated a complete rethink about what customers valued and what a builder of new houses needed to provide.

The specification of value in terms of the whole product or service

Typically, many departments within an organization or many firms within a supply chain contribute to producing value. Problems arise when any one of these elements in the value stream fails to appreciate how their actions affect value from the perspective of the end customer. For example, a company dedicated to producing well-designed, high-quality furniture and marketing its products direct to customers might decide to reduce costs by outsourcing delivery to an independent haulage contractor. The haulage contractor, in turn, might decide to cut costs by paying drivers on a commission basis. The effect of this might be to encourage drivers to complete as many 'drops' as possible in order to maximize their earnings, and to discourage them from spending time with customers to help them remove and dispose of packaging, check the quality of their purchase before signing for delivery, or carry the furniture from the front door to the required location. These may all be services that customers value. The furniture company's effort to deliver value to the customer can easily be undermined by this final link in the value stream. By focusing attention on their own immediate goals, the haulage contractor and the drivers it employs can destroy customer loyalty and adversely affect demand for the product.

Rethinking value not only requires producers to engage in a searching dialogue with customers, but also for all contributors to the value stream to talk to each other about how they each contribute to the value of the whole product or service from the perspective of the end user.

Target cost

Once value has been defined, it is possible to specify target cost. According to Womack and Jones (1996), this is the amount of resource and effort required to produce the product or service to the required specification once all currently visible waste is removed from the process. It is this target cost that provides the lens for examining every step in the value stream.

Identifying the value stream and eliminating wasteful steps

Identifying and mapping value streams is an effective way of exposing waste. Womack and Jones (1996) define a value stream as all the actions required to bring a specific product or product family through the three critical management tasks of:

1 *problem solving:* from concept through detailed design to product launch
2 *information management:* from order taking through detailed scheduling to delivery

3 *physical transformation:* from raw materials to finished product or service in the hands of the customer.

Chapter 21, on BPR, reviews many of the steps that need to be considered when identifying and mapping value streams.

While many actions in the value stream create value, others create waste (sources of waste are discussed in Change tool 22.1). Mapping a value stream involves identifying every action that, from the perspective of the customer, adds value and categorizing those activities that add no value into 'type one' and 'type two' waste. Type one waste includes all those activities that create no value but are unavoidable, given current technologies and production assets. Type two waste refers to those activities that fail to add value but are immediately avoidable. Once type two waste has been eliminated, the way is clear to go to work on eliminating the remaining (type one) non-value-adding steps through the application of flow, pull and the other lean techniques considered later in this chapter.

Value stream mapping should not be restricted to the boundaries of a single organization in the supply chain. The concept of the lean enterprise embraces the whole value stream, which will often include contributions from more than one organization.

Making value flow

Once value has been specified, the value stream mapped and obviously wasteful steps eliminated, attention can be focused on making the remaining value-creating steps flow. Re-engineering to create flow can involve radical change. For example, a batch and queue production system might require considerable modification. This could involve the development of smaller machines, faster methods of switching tools to facilitate the manufacture of smaller batches, and the co-location of related steps in the production process to eliminate waste associated with transporting part-finished components between locations. A continuous flow layout often involves arranging related production steps in a sequence within a single 'cell' and quickly moving the product from one step to the next without any (wasteful) buffers of work in progress in between.

Womack and Jones (1996) advocate a three-pronged approach to making value flow. The first, once value has been defined and the end-to-end value stream identified, involves following the product as it moves along the value stream. The second, reminiscent of the 'clean sheet' approach to BPR discussed in Chapter 21, involves ignoring traditional boundaries and other impediments to continuous flow, and the third involves rethinking specific work practices and tools to eliminate backflows, scrap and all sources of unnecessary stoppages so that the process can proceed continuously.

While some lean principles are similar to some aspects of BPR, Womack and Jones (1996) are critical of the re-engineering movement. In their view, although re-engineers seek to shift attention away from suboptimal departmental/functional thinking to value-creating processes, they believe that they pay too much attention to aggregated processes, such as order taking for a whole range of products, rather than the value-creating activities for a specific product or product family. They also argue that re-engineers typically limit their attention to delivering change within a single organization, and that they adopt an expert-driven, top-down approach that often fails to engage employees. They contrast this with their lean philosophy, which encourages employee engagement, focuses attention on specific products, and adopts a lean enterprise perspective that includes all the steps in a value stream even if they span many organizations.

Pulling flow

While flow is necessary, it is not sufficient. Flow needs to be pulled through the production system. The pull principle involves no one producing anything until someone downstream requests it. Womack and Jones (1996) make an important distinction between pull and push. When products are 'pushed' through a production system to meet a sales forecast, any unanticipated fall in demand can lead to a rapid build-up of unwanted finished goods (waste) that, if not scrapped, may have to be sold off at a heavy discount. Lean production involves making exactly what customers want when they want it. Figure 22.1 illustrates flow being pulled through the system in response to downstream requests. Customers pull the product from the producer, and within the production system, every downstream production stage pulls inputs from adjacent upstream stages in the production process.

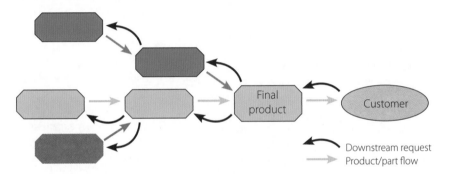

Figure **22.1** *Parts being pulled in response to customer requests*

Perfection: continually searching for improvement

Early steps in the lean change process often involve discontinuous change, such as a radical realignment of the value stream, for example moving from batch and queue to a continuous flow system pulled by customer demand. But the search for improvement should not stop there. An important principle of lean is the ongoing search for continuous improvement (kaizan).

Perfection is the complete elimination of waste. Womack and Jones (1996, p. 94) see the quest for perfection as never ending and liken perfection to infinity: 'Trying to envision it (and to get there) is actually impossible, but *the effort to do so provides inspiration and direction essential to making progress along the path'.* They assert that the first four lean principles interact with each other to create a virtuous circle. Efforts to get value to flow faster expose hidden sources of waste. Efforts to pull products through the system highlight impediments to flow, and efforts to work with customers to refine the meaning of value inevitably point to new ways of adding value, facilitating flow and improving pull.

The pursuit of perfection involves assessing the gap between the current reality and perfection and, rather than trying to do everything at the same time, prioritizing the main sources of waste and focusing energy on these to close the gap. Womack and Jones (1996) advocate that when seeking perfection, attention should be focused on one thing at a time and working on it continuously until the desired improvement has been achieved.

The Toyota Production System, discussed in Example 22.1, is widely regarded as the most successful example of lean.

*Example **22.1** The Toyota Production System*

The Toyota Production System's systemic qualities have been represented as a house with all parts (foundations, pillars and roof) needing to work together to create the whole (Figure 22.2).

Liker and Morgan (2006) point to some of the key elements of the Toyota Production System:

- *Just in time* was developed to facilitate smooth flow by ensuring that the right part is delivered to the right place at the right time. In ideal circumstances, material moves from operation to operation one piece at a time without interruption, but sometimes this continuous flow is not possible because components have to be produced in batches. Batch production requires the holding of inventories. Just in time refers to the way these inventories are replenished. Where fast set-up times enable machines to be quickly switched from manufacturing one component to another, it is possible to produce tiny batches. This, in turn,

facilitates the holding of tiny inventories that are only replenished as required. Replenishment occurs when, and only when, the inventory is drawn down as parts are used in the next process downstream.

- *Jidoka* involves workers stopping production and immediately fixing problems as they occur. It ensures that problems are constantly surfaced and processes are improved on a continuous basis. To work effectively, people need to be skilled and motivated to solve problems quickly.
- *Heijunka* means production levelling. It involves sequencing orders in a way that smoothes out short-term variations in demand. Level schedules make it possible to standardize processes. Without some element of levelling and stability, it would be impossible to maintain minimum level inventories that can be replenished on a JIT basis. For an example of how heijunka works, see Womack and Jones (1996, p. 306).

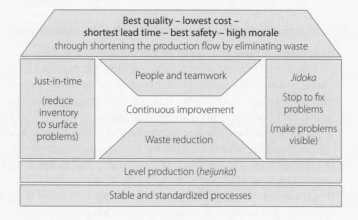

*Figure **22.2** The Toyota Production System house*
Source: Liker and Morgan, 2006, p. 7

Some other lean tools and techniques

There is a wide range of other tools and techniques that lean practitioners use. A selection is provided in Change tools 22.1–22.3.

Change tool **22.1** *The seven wastes*

Value stream mapping, the basic tool for implementing lean, provides the basis for identifying waste. Taiichi Ohno's seven wastes offer employees a useful framework for searching out and eliminating all those activities that fail to add value. The seven wastes are:

1 *overproduction:* making more than required, or making it earlier than required
2 *waiting:* products waiting on the next production step, or people waiting for work to do
3 *unnecessary transportation:* moving products farther than required
4 *overprocessing products or parts:* this can occur because of poor design or inefficient tools
5 *inventory:* holding more inventory than is minimally required
6 *unnecessary motion:* people moving or walking more than minimally required, for example looking for tools, or bending to pick up a part or a tool from the floor rather that picking it off a waist-high, non-stoop scaffold
7 *defective parts:* requiring effort to inspect and fix.

Womack and Jones (1996) added an eighth source of waste, producing goods and services that fail to meet the needs of the customer.

A useful starting point is to ask a group of employees to use the types of waste checklist and identify as many sources of waste as they can in their workplace.

Change tool **22.2** *The 5S methodology*

Another technique for improving the way work is performed is 5S. Kocakülâh et al. (2008) describe how it can be applied in a kaizen event when a cross-section of managers and production workers are taken from their daily routines to focus on the 5Ss in a specific area. A typical sequence is:

1 *Separate:* evaluating and removing anything that is not required from the production area.
2 *Sort:* specifying and labelling locations for all remaining items required to perform the task. Locations are chosen to minimize motion.
3 *Sweep:* the area is cleaned and kept clean to facilitate efficient working.
4 *Standardize:* making everything consistent. Machines are set up identically and tasks are performed in a standardized way to support the flexibility of employees between work stations.
5 *Sustain:* maintaining the discipline of the preceding steps.

Change tool **22.3** *The five whys*

The five whys is a diagnostic tool that can be used to identify and eliminate the root cause of problems. The (NHS) Improvement Network (www.tin.nhs.co.uk) offers examples of how the five whys can be used to solve problems in healthcare settings:

1 The patient was late in the operating theatre – *Why?*
2 There was a long wait for a trolley – *Why?*
3 A replacement trolley had to be found – *Why?*
4 The original trolley's safety rail was worn and had eventually broken – *Why?*
5 It had not been regularly checked for wear – *Why?*

Answer: We do not have an equipment maintenance schedule.

The root cause is the absence of an equipment maintenance schedule, not the broken safety rail. Repairing the safety rail, or even a one-off safety rail check of all trolleys, will not guarantee that patients will never be late for theatre because of faulty equipment.

Other tools and techniques include total productive maintenance, single minute exchange of dyes, six sigma, control charts, cause-and-effect diagrams, the PDSA cycle and many more.

Implementing lean in manufacturing contexts

Scherrer-Rathje et al. (2009) describe two attempts to implement lean in a Swiss food processing machines and equipment manufacturing company (Example 22.2). The first attempt, in 1997, failed but a second, nine years later, was successful.

● *Example* **22.2** *Lessons learned from a failed attempt to implement lean*

The first attempt was initiated by a production supervisor who was struggling to maintain quality and delivery. While senior management agreed to fund the project, they adopted a hands-off approach, leaving the production supervisor and four colleagues to manage it. None of the project team were released from any of their day-to-day functional duties and, along with all those affected by the project, they had to cope with a number of other competing and uncoordinated change projects. This made it difficult to maintain focus and engage others. Eventually, the project was terminated.

In 2006, a second project to introduce lean was launched. The trigger was increasing costs and an inability to satisfy customer requirements. In some cases, customers were having to wait up to 12 months for delivery and were threatening to move their business elsewhere. The CEO felt that a 'pull system' would help to eliminate waste, reduce costs and improve throughput times.

A key difference between the two attempts to introduce lean was that, second time around, there was sustained management commitment to the project. Managers also recognized the importance of getting employees involved and attempted to do this by concentrating resources on a pilot project, selected because it appeared most likely to deliver an early success, and using this early win to demonstrate the value of lean to the entire company. A review of the 1997 project pointed to decision-making bottlenecks, caused partly by management's hands-off approach and partly by their unwillingness to delegate sufficient autonomy to the project team. They addressed this issue by creating 'just-do-it' rooms in each business unit. In each room, the entire customer order process was displayed and, every morning, each order was tracked by an interdisciplinary team with the authority and autonomy to make and implement decisions. The wide representation in the just-do-it room offered a macro-view of the whole process and detailed information (a micro-view) about any issues that might arise.

After reflecting on these two projects, Scherrer-Rathje et al. (2009) pointed to a number of lessons that might help to secure the success of future lean projects:

- *Visible management commitment*: Lack of management support can restrict access to required resources, lengthen decision-making processes, contribute to communication breakdowns up and down the value chain, and undermine employee commitment. Management support is a necessary condition for success.
- *Formal mechanisms to encourage and enable autonomy*: The 'just-do-it' rooms and procedures that enabled workers to stop production to immediately fix problems (jidoka) are examples of mechanisms that bring people working on the process together and empower them to make and implement decisions to quickly solve problems.
- *Communication of lean wins from the outset*: The second attempt to implement lean involved a pilot project that was used to quickly demonstrate the benefits of lean. In Chapter 28, it is argued that new initiatives are more likely to spread when they are seen to offer clear benefits and when others are able to observe these benefits in demonstration sites.
- *Continual evaluation of the lean project:* Early on in the second project, managers decided that while they would fully involve employees in current implementation tasks, they would not disclose the long-term strategic goal of building a lean enterprise. They took this decision to avoid overwhelming people with the scale of the project. However, as the project progressed, it transpired that some employees started to fear that they might be heading off in the wrong direction and sought reassurance that all the bits fitted together. Six months into the project, management changed their communication strategy and introduced monthly lean briefings for everybody involved. The importance of continually reviewing any change project is discussed in Chapters 2 and 26.
- *Implementing mechanisms to ensure the long-term sustainability of lean:* Scherrer-Rathje et al. (2009) drew attention to a number of things managers can do to help sustain and spread lean initiatives. More detailed consideration of measures that can promote sustainability can be found in Chapters 27 and 28.

Implementing lean in non-manufacturing contexts: some examples

Lean was originally developed in manufacturing companies and applied on the shop floor, but has since been applied in many non-manufacturing contexts. Liker and Morgan (2006) present an account of how Toyota applied lean principles to the product development process (PDP). They note that technical and service operations are challenging because work is often less repetitive than work on the shop floor and the product is less tangible. Nevertheless, Toyota was able to standardize the PDP, refine it, eliminate waste and, on a continuous basis, reduce both lead time and cost. Liker and Morgan's account identifies 13 principles for applying lean in service contexts that relate to process, people, tools and technology. Four process principles are summarized here:

1 *Establish customer-defined values:* In the Toyota PDP case, this helped to reduce wasteful conflict between those who styled the car and product engineers who were more concerned with functionality and manufacturability than looks.
2 *Front load the product development process:* This helped to get everything right first time and avoid costly downstream design changes.

3 *Create a level PDP flow:* Years of experience enabled the company to predict the engineering hours required at various points in the PDP and assign engineers to programmes in a level way. People, over and above the core complement, were drawn from a central pool of technicians and engineers from outside suppliers as and when required.

4 *Standardization:* The key challenge for Toyota was to reduce variation while preserving creativity. Liker and Morgan (2006) point to a number of ways in which this was accomplished. For example, design standardization was achieved by developing a common architecture, modularity and shared components, and standardized skill sets were developed to provide flexibility in staffing.

Three other non-manufacturing contexts where lean principles have been applied are now explored.

Finance

Swank (2003) reports how lean principles were applied by Jefferson Pilot Finance (JPF) in the insurance industry. JPF was a full-service life insurance and annuities company in competition with specialized niche companies that were able to offer lower premiums and faster handling of policies. JPF's customers were independent life insurance advisers who sold and serviced policies to end users. The company's aim was to beat off the competition and establish itself as the 'partner of choice' for these advisers.

JPF identified many areas for improvement. Processing times varied between locations and, across the company, high levels of errors required many policy applications to be reworked. Swank (2003) reports that JPF believed it could benefit from lean production because its operations involved the processing of an almost tangible 'service product', with each insurance policy going through a series of processes, from initial application to underwriting, much like an automobile on an assembly line.

The company decided to pilot lean in one cell before rolling it out across the company. A number of changes were trialled. For example, linked processes, which were originally located by function in various parts of the organization, were brought together. Co-locating employees who received applications with those who sorted and processed them eliminated long delays. Files were transferred between groups in a matter of minutes rather than days. In addition to speeding throughput, this innovation also helped employees to develop a new awareness of the whole process and how what they did contributed to satisfying advisers and policy holders. Standardized work processes, such as requiring everybody to store files in the same way, alphabetically rather than by policy number or date received, and in the same drawer at each work station, made it easier to move people between work stations in order to balance loads. It also made it easier for employees to cover for absent colleagues. Work flows were smoothed by calculating the time for each operation so that the rate of production could be set to satisfy customer demand and people could be deployed as required to complete all steps in the process.

Product families were identified by clustering applications into separate groups according to complexity and allocating each their own performance goals. Performance measures that focused on eliminating waste and adding value from the perspective of the customer were developed. For example, processing time was measured in terms of the total time between a customer mailing an application to the company and the adviser receiving a completed policy, rather than the time taken to complete an intermediate step in the process.

Swank (2003) reports that the initiative delivered impressive results. The company halved the average time from receipt of an application to issuance of a policy, reduced labour costs by 26%, and trimmed the rate of reissues due to errors by 40%, all of which contributed to a 60% increase in new annualized life premiums in just two years.

Retailing

Up until the late 1970s, mass retailers achieved a cost advantage over smaller competitors by using their purchasing power to achieve economies of scale. This model required the retailer to hold large inventories and push products onto customers. Abernathy et al. (1999) note that Walmart was one of the first to break away from this model and use emerging information technologies to pull the supply chain. Customer sales were tracked at checkouts, inventories within and across stores were monitored, and the data used to pull goods from suppliers as required. Supplies were delivered to stores from centralized distribution hubs on a JIT basis, enabling the company to drastically reduce inventories and in-store warehousing capacity.

Attention was then focused on developing a lean enterprise by extending this system to suppliers. In 1987, Walmart established a 'Walmart Retail Link' with P&G, providing the supplier with access to Walmart point-of-sale information, allowing it to track its own products on a real-time basis. This development enabled P&G to manage its own inventories more effectively.

Healthcare

Young et al. (2004) argue that an obvious application of lean thinking in healthcare lies in eliminating delay, repeated encounters, errors and inappropriate procedures. Ben-Tovim et al. (2007) describe a successful lean implementation programme at Flinders Medical Centre in Australia. The initial project involved the emergency department (ED). It was so congested that patients overflowed into the recovery area of the operating suite, disrupting the work of the ED and the division of surgery. Some elective surgery had to be cancelled at short notice, surgical training was disrupted, the safety of care in the ED was becoming compromised, and staff turnover was high.

The project started with a multidisciplinary group of ED staff mapping patient journeys. This demonstrated that the use of a five-point measure of patient acuity, the intensity of care required by a patient, to prioritize care contributed to many problems, including the distress of patients who were 'bumped' down the queue when later patients were seen first because they had been allocated to a different triage category (a category determined by how likely they were to benefit from immediate medical care). Staff attempted to rescue this situation by instituting ad hoc and hard-to-manage strategies to push through 'bumped' patients when the build-up became excessive.

Streaming was introduced to help resolve this and related problems. Patient care families (groups whose care process was sufficiently similar for them to be managed together) were established on the basis of 'likely to go home' or 'likely to be admitted to hospital'. The process for each group was simplified by creating 'production cells' in which steps in the value stream were lined up to facilitate a steady flow. Patients were treated in these cells as they arrived rather than treating them in batches. The result was a halving of patients leaving the ED without completing their care, a reduction in congestion by decreasing the time patients spent in the department by 45 minutes, and the freeing of capacity to cope with a 10 per cent increase in demand over the following 12 months.

Following this early success, lean thinking was disseminated across the hospital. Process mapping created detailed pictures of how work was done and generated a commitment to change. This led to the identification of improvement opportunities and the engagement of staff in PDSA cycles to eliminate waste and deliver value. Ben-Tovim et al. (2007) illustrate how this worked with an example that eradicated waste by speeding patient discharge. It became clear that the discharge of some inpatients was delayed because they had to wait for a date for a crucial follow-up test. A search for the root cause revealed that the clinical laboratory was under such pressure to perform tests that, when the laboratory receptionist left, it was decided to appoint a new technician rather than a replacement receptionist. The result was that appointments could only be made when a laboratory staff member was free to pick up and respond to messages left on the telephone answering system. This delay had the knock-on effect of increasing congestion in the ED while new patients who needed to be admitted waited for a bed.

These examples demonstrate how a lean philosophy that can deliver benefits in many different settings. Read Case study 22.1 on the Grampian Police and consider how lean principles can be applied in this setting.

Case study **22.1** *Grampian Police*

Members of the public were frustrated because they were finding it difficult to contact Grampian Police. There were over 70 different telephone lines the public could use. Some went to a central switchboard, others directly to various departments or local police stations, many of which were so small that they were not manned on a continuous basis. Consequently, many calls were not answered or were answered by somebody who was not in a position to resolve the caller's problem. Grampian Police responded by creating a new state-of-the-art call centre. Operators could use a geographical information system to identify where a caller was calling from, and could access a crime information system so that they were instantly aware of criminal activity in that area and the contact details of local officers and those leading current inquiries. The new service was well received, not least because call centre staff were able to deal with many calls in their entirety to the complete satisfaction of the caller. As word got round, more people started to ring in. The call centre became a victim of its own success. Workloads increased and the call centre manager appealed for more staff. But setting up the call centre had already stretched resources, so another way of managing the workload had to be found.

Before reading on, make some notes on how you think lean thinking might help to resolve this workload problem.

Attention was focused instead on why people were calling the police. After analysing the reasons, it was found that a significant percentage of all calls related to firearms licensing matters. Grampian is a large rural area with many farmers and others who own firearms and shotguns that have to be licensed. A more detailed analysis of this category of calls revealed that almost all of them were prompted by problems and delays associated with the process of obtaining or renewing licences. It was predicted that eliminating these problems could free up to 14 per cent of the call centre's capacity.

The first step was to study the existing process and identify sources of problems and waste arising from the design of the system. The licence renewal process, for example, started with a notice to renew being posted out to certificate holders. They then had to return a completed form to police headquarters together with other documents. After the forms had been returned and checked, a police officer was dispatched to visit the gun owner's premises, to inspect the guns and ensure that they were stored in a secure gun cabinet, as well as

checking the suitability of the applicant. It was also necessary to inspect the land where the guns were to be used to ensure that it was compatible with the intended use. Unfortunately, many application forms were not completed correctly or some supporting documents were not supplied. The documentation had to be logged and filed and the applicant had to be written to with a request for further information or missing documents. Resubmissions then had to be reconciled with the original documentation before they could be processed. Gun owners were frustrated because, for a variety of reasons, they often experienced delays in renewing their licences.

After the existing process had been studied, attention was focused on redesigning it to eliminate unnecessary steps and provide gun owners with a speedy and hassle-free service. The new licensing process was made to flow without interruption. Once the renewal application had been posted to the applicant, a specialist inquiry officer contacted the gun owner and arranged a home visit to complete the application process. During that visit, the inquiry officer helped the gun owner to correct any errors on the application form, checked that all the supporting documents were in order, inspected the gun, ensured that it was fit for purpose and checked the security arrangements. If the inquiry officer was satisfied that the gun owner was a fit applicant, he could accept payment on the spot and forward his recommendation to the firearms licensing manager who could then issue a licence. A process that used to take a considerable time and prompt many telephone calls to the police could now be completed expeditiously without any need for the applicant to phone the call centre.

Summary

Womack et al. (1990) coined the phrase 'lean' to describe a production system that does more with less and less. It is a customer-focused process that aims to provide customers with precisely what they want, free of defects, exactly when they want it. Scherrer-Rathje et al. (2009) differentiate between lean as a set of tools and techniques and lean as a philosophy:

- Many practitioners focus their attention on tools, such as control charts, 5S, seven wastes, total productive maintenance, JIT inventories and so on, and direct their efforts towards applying some of them to achieve specific outcomes.

Sometimes, change efforts are restricted to particular parts of the organization or directed towards the achievement of limited goals, such as cost reduction.

• Others view lean as a philosophy and focus more attention on acting in accordance with guiding principles and overarching aims to create a 'lean enterprise'. They adopt a more holistic approach and consider how the interrelationships between and synergistic effects of related practices can affect performance across the whole enterprise.

This chapter traced the development of lean thinking and presented Womack and Jones's five lean principles:

1 *Precisely specify value for each product or product family:* Specifying value is the essential first step in lean thinking and needs to be done from the perspective of the end customer. Value also needs to be specified in terms of the whole product or service.

2 *Identify value streams for each product to expose waste:* Mapping a value stream involves identifying every action that, from the perspective of the customer, adds value and categorizing those activities that add no value into type one and type two waste. Type one waste includes all those activities that create no value but are unavoidable. Type two waste refers to those activities that fail to add value but are immediately avoidable.

3 *Make value flow without interruption:* A continuous flow layout could, for example, involve arranging related production steps in a sequence within a single 'cell' and quickly moving the product from one step to the next without any (wasteful) buffers of work in progress in between.

4 *Let customers pull value from the producer:* The pull principle involves no one producing anything until someone downstream requests it.

5 *Pursue perfection by searching out and eliminating further waste:* Perfection is the complete elimination of waste.

A number of lean tools and techniques were reviewed along with issues to be considered when implementing lean. The chapter ended with an exploration of how lean has been applied in manufacturing and non-manufacturing settings.

Ben-Tovim et al.'s account of applying lean thinking at Flinders Medical Centre illustrates a key tenet of lean: learning and change only come from working on problems in the workplace. Lean is not a top-down process where senior managers diagnose the problem, design and then implement a solution. It is a process that involves people in the workplace developing a detailed understanding of how the work is done, searching out the root causes of waste, and identifying more effective ways of delivering value to end users. Lean initiatives not only require visible and continuing management support but also a commitment from those directly involved in the workplace to engage in a bottom-up process to bring about change.

According to the typology presented in Figure 16.3, lean is a technostructural intervention.

References

Abernathy, F.A., Dunlop, J.T., Hammond, J.H. and Weil, D. (1999) *A Stitch in Time: Lean Retailing and the Transformation of Manufacturing – Lessons from the Textile and Apparel Industries.* Oxford: Oxford University Press.

Ben-Tovim, D.I., Bassham, J.E., Bolch, D. et al. (2007) Lean thinking across a hospital: Redesigning care at the Flinders Medical Centre, *Australian Health Review*, 31(1): 10–16.

Kocakülâh, M.C., Brown, J.F. and Thomson, J.W. (2008) Lean manufacturing principles and their application, *Cost Management*, 22(3): 16–28.

Liker, J.K. and Morgan, J.M. (2006) The Toyota way in service: The case of lean product development, *Academy of Management Perspectives*, 20(2): 5–20.

Scherrer-Rathje, M., Boyle, T.A. and Deflorin, P. (2009) Lean, take two! Reflections from a second attempt at lean implementation, *Business Horizons*, 52(1): 79–88.

Swank, C.K. (2003) The lean service machine, *Harvard Business Review*, 81(10): 123–9.

Womack, J.P. and Jones, D.T. (1996) *Lean Thinking: Banish Waste and Create Wealth in your Corporation*. London: Simon & Schuster.

Womack, J.P., Jones, D.T. and Roos, D. (1990) *The Machine that Changed the World*. New York: Rawson Associates.

Young, T., Brailsford, S., Connell, C. et al. (2004) Using industrial processes to improve patient care, *British Medical Journal*, 328(7432): 162–4.

V

Chapter 23

Culture profiling

Theories of social identity and acculturation provide the conceptual framework for considering what change managers can do to promote people synergies when organizations or units within organizations are being combined. Social identity theory is introduced to explain how mergers and acquisitions (M&As) threaten employees' organizational identity, exacerbate 'us and them' dynamics, and adversely affect merger success. Acculturation theory is used to explore how employees' preferences for combining their departmental or organizational cultures, practices and systems affect M&A outcomes.

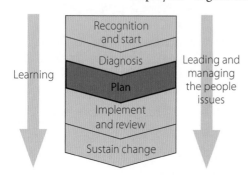

The first part of this chapter draws on both these theories to explore how organizational members experience mergers, and the second part focuses on how culture profiling can be used to pre-screen potential merger partners and, later in the merger process, guide the integration of the merging units.

People's response to mergers

Many of the benefits that are anticipated when a merger is being planned depend on employees' commitment to the new unit or organization and their willingness to work together to deliver high performance. Cartwright and Cooper (1990) argue that the most fundamental factor contributing to merger success is the positive combination of people, their expertise and their organizational cultures. All too often, this required level of people synergy is not achieved.

At various points in this chapter, reference will be made to acquisitions as well as mergers. The majority of combinations of different organizations turn out to be acquisitions, in the sense that one group, department or organization acquires control of another, but the combination is often referred to as a merger in order to make the takeover more palatable to the members of the acquired unit.

Employees respond to mergers in many different ways. Some identify and welcome opportunities for career development, greater challenges and improved scope and variety of work, or they see the merger as a way of achieving greater job security or enhanced status through association with the new unit or organization. Others have a less positive view. Members of an acquired firm, for example, may feel that they have been 'sold out' and, especially if the merger was contested, that they have been overwhelmed and defeated. Members of the merged units may be concerned about job security and, even if redundancy is not an immediate threat, may feel less in control of their immediate working arrangements and longer term career prospects. All this can have a powerful effect on job satisfaction, motivation and organizational commitment, leading to outcomes such as anxiety, stress, poor performance, greater absenteeism and increased turnover; and Ashford (1988) and Cooper and Payne (1988) report that stress and mental health problems undermine performance.

There are many reports of these negative outcomes. Cartwright (2005) cites several studies which indicate that lower morale and perceptions of unfair treatment lead to lower post-merger performance. Cabrera (1982) points to examples of non-productive behaviours such as spending time gossiping about merger-related issues, political manoeuvring and jockeying for position to gain advantage or guard against loss. Walsh (1988) reports that 25 per cent of top executives of acquired companies leave within the first year, a rate of turnover significantly higher than 'normal' top team turnover.

Organizational identity and negative effects: social identity theory

Several writers (Ashforth and Mael, 1989; Bartels et al., 2006; van Dick et al., 2006) suggest that social identity theory offers a conceptual framework for understanding why many employees react negatively. Mergers threaten an important aspect of their social identity – their sense of belonging to a unit or organization. People not only identify themselves in terms of 'I' – their idiosyncratic characteristics such as physical features, interests, abilities and personality traits – but also in terms of 'we' – affiliations with social categories such as nationality, occupation and religion. For many, work group and organizational affiliation are important parts of their social identity.

Social identity theory was developed following a series of seminal studies by Tajfel and colleagues on intergroup discrimination (see Tajfel and Turner, 1979). Their laboratory experiments investigated the minimal conditions that lead members of one group (the in-group) to discriminate in favour of their group and against another group (the out-group). Participants were allocated to groups on the flimsiest of criteria, for example their preferences for an abstract painter or the toss of a coin. Findings indicated that when individuals categorize themselves as members of a group, even when the basis of this categorization was trivial, this could give rise to a sense of belonging that affected their behaviour. However, Tajfel and Turner recognized that in-group favouritism was not an inevitable consequence of group membership. They identified three conditions that give rise to intergroup discrimination and in-group bias. These are:

- the extent to which individuals identify with an in-group and internalize membership of that group as a part of their self-concept
- the extent to which the prevailing context provides grounds for comparison and competition between groups
- the perceived relevance of the comparison group, which, in turn, depends on the relative and absolute status of the in-group.

Mergers present all three of these conditions. For many employees, work group or organizational affiliation is an important aspect of their self-concept. M&As clearly provide opportunities for comparison and competition between groups and in many merger and almost all acquisition scenarios, there are status differences between the merging units or organizations.

Van Dick et al. (2006) argue that mergers affect employees' social identity because they redraw or dissolve the boundaries that once categorized two distinct organizations. When employees perceive the merger or acquisition as a threat to the distinctiveness of their pre-merger group identity, this identity becomes more salient and in-group differences and out-group similarities are minimized. Employees focus on the positive aspects of their own pre-merger organization and develop negative perceptions of the other organization (the out-group). This generally motivates them to maintain all that they value about their pre-merger group or organizational identity and resist any changes that threaten it. However, this is not always the case, as shown in Example 23.1.

Example **23.1** *BT Cellnet's acquisition of Martin Dawes*

When the mobile communications network operator BT Cellnet embarked on a strategy of vertical integration and acquired Martin Dawes, the UK's leading service provider, the majority of the 1,600 Martin Dawes employees were not seriously alienated by their loss of organizational identity. This was, in large measure, because BT Cellnet was widely perceived to have invested in the future in a way that opened up the possibility of new career opportunities that may not have been accessible if they had not been acquired. The acquisition was also seen to offer other benefits. BT Cellnet's terms and conditions of employment and pension scheme were more generous than those offered by Martin Dawes, the acquisition involved a move to a new and attractive purpose-built site, and BT Cellnet wanted to retain all the acquired employees and worked hard to win their support.

In those mergers where there is a dominant partner, it is the members of the weaker unit who are most likely to experience the greatest threat to their group or organizational identity. Members of the dominant group or organization are the ones who are more likely to experience continuity and perceive fewer differences in their unit's culture and their daily work life. This enables them not only to preserve their identification with their former group or organization but also to transfer this identification to the new post-merger entity.

Continuity, and lack of continuity, can have a profound impact on group identity. Van Dick et al. (2006) cite a study of two merging banks (Venbeselaere et al., 2002) that demonstrates the positive effect of continuity. The more people were satisfied with the way their pre-merger bank lived on in the merged bank, the stronger their identification with the merged bank and the more positive their attitudes towards people from the merger partner. In many cases, however, the acquiring organization will not seek to preserve continuity for members of the acquired unit or organization. It will want to introduce changes that will disrupt continuity and these discontinuities will threaten members' organizational identity.

Evidence that high levels of identification with the post-merger organization result in increased work motivation, performance and organization citizenship behaviours led Cartwright (2005) to suggest that a proxy measure of successful M&A integration is the speed with which employees put aside their separate pre-existing 'us and them' identities and assume a new shared organizational identity. In all mergers, both units (groups or organizations) have their own cultures, which comprise a socially acquired set of shared values and beliefs that give rise to a collective frame of reference for determining how things are done and how people relate to others. Elsass and Veiga (1994) argue that the processes of social identification provide a useful theoretical foundation for examining the cultural differentiation that occurs when groups or organizations merge. M&As involve the bringing together of at least two different cultures: 'The tenets of social identity theory would indicate that the mere existence of these two subcultures is enough to lead to feelings of in-group out-group bias, discrimination and conflict' (Elsass and Veiga, 1994, p. 438).

Hubbard (1999) suggests that one of the factors that make cultural differences problematic is that while employees tacitly understand their own culture, they often cannot explain it to new colleagues. Consequently, learning the unwritten ways of doing business in the new merged unit is usually a painstaking process of trial and error.

Acculturation

Berry (2005) defines acculturation as the dual process of cultural and psychological change that takes place as a result of contact between two or more cultural groups and their individual members. Early work on acculturation focused on the domination of indigenous people by colonial powers and on how immigrants changed as they settled into a receiving society. More recently, Nahavandi and Malekzadeh (1988) and Elsass and Veiga (1994) have applied theories of acculturation to the study of how organizational members adapt to M&As.

Nahavandi and Malekzadeh draw on the work of Berry (1983, 1984) to identify the different ways in which members of acquired and acquiring units (groups or organizations) can combine their cultures, practices and systems:

- *Integration* involves some degree of change for both units but allows both to maintain many of the basic assumptions, beliefs, work practices and systems that are important to them and make them feel distinctive.

- *Assimilation* is a unilateral process in which one group willingly adopts the identity and culture of the other.
- *Separation* involves members of the acquired unit seeking to preserve their own culture and practices by remaining separate and independent of the dominant unit (department or organization). If allowed to do so, the acquired unit will function as a separate unit under the financial umbrella of the acquiring unit.
- *Deculturation* involves unit members rejecting cultural contact with both their and the other unit. It occurs when members of an acquired unit do not value their own culture (maybe because they feel that their work group, department or organization has failed) and do not want to be assimilated into the acquiring unit.

The process of acculturation that actually occurs depends on the degree of congruence between the acquired and acquiring unit's preferred modes of combining, and the ability of each partner to impose its preference.

The acquired unit's preferred mode of acculturation

The acquired unit's preferred mode of acculturation depends on the extent to which members of the acquired unit value and want to preserve their own culture, and their perception of the attractiveness of the acquiring unit's culture (see Figure 23.1).

So, for the acquired unit:

- *Integration* will be its preferred mode of acculturation when its members value their own culture and many of their existing practices and want to preserve them, but also perceive some attractive aspects of the acquiring unit's culture and practices they would like to adopt.
- *Assimilation* will be its preferred mode when members do not value their own culture and practices and do not want to preserve them, and are attracted to the acquiring unit's culture and practices.
- *Separation* will be its preferred mode of acculturation when members value their own culture and existing practices and want to preserve them, and are not attracted to the acquiring unit's culture and practices.
- *Deculturation* will be its preferred mode when members feel alienated because they do not value the culture and practices of either their own or the acquiring unit.

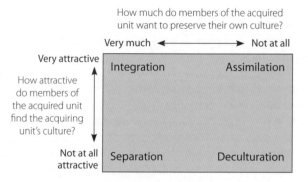

Figure **23.1** *Acquired unit's preferred mode of acculturation*
Source: Nahavandi and Malekzadeh, 1988

The acquiring unit's preferred mode of acculturation

The acquiring unit's preferred mode of acculturation also depends on two factors; the extent to which the acquiring unit is multicultural and the relatedness between the merging units (see Figure 23.2). If the acquiring unit is unicultural and values conformity, it will be more likely to impose its culture and systems on the acquired firm. If, on the other hand, it is multicultural, that is, contains and values many subcultures, it will be more likely to allow the acquired unit to retain its own culture.

The degree of integration or assimilation sought by the acquiring firm is often linked to the degree of relatedness between the merging organizations. For example, the motive for acquiring an unrelated business may be to increase the size of the acquiring organization or to decrease its dependence on some part of the environment. When this is the case, the acquirer may be happy to pursue a hands-off approach, seeking little beyond essential procedural (legal and financial) integration. However, the motivation for acquiring a related business is most often due to some form of synergies that can be gained from integrating physical assets, operating procedures and so on. This will call for a higher level of physical and cultural integration.

So, for the acquiring unit:

- *Integration* will be its preferred mode of acculturation when it is a multicultural unit and the merger is with a related unit.
- *Assimilation* will be its preferred mode when the unit is unicultural and the merger is with a related unit.
- *Separation* will be the preferred mode when the acquirer is multicultural and the merger is with an unrelated unit.
- *Deculturation* is unlikely to be a mode of acculturation that will be preferred, unless it is committed to developing a completely new culture for the new unit.

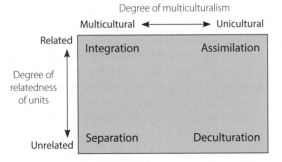

Figure **23.2** *Acquiring unit's preferred mode of acculturation*
Source: Nahavandi and Malekzadeh, 1988

Low levels of congruence between the acquiring and acquired units' preferred mode of acculturation are likely to produce high levels of merger stress for organizational members. This can give rise to negative emotions, such as denial, depression and anger, undermine morale, increase confusion and intergroup conflict, and lead to unproductive behaviours that disrupt the integration process. High levels of congruence, on the other hand, can have the opposite effect and promote people synergies and unit/organization fit. Figure 23.3 shows how organizational fit is achieved.

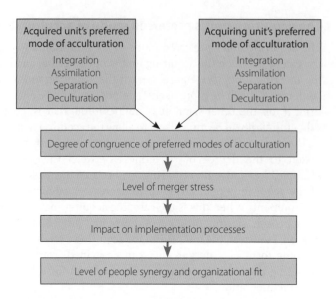

Figure **23.3** *Acculturative model for implementing organizational fit*
Source: Adapted from Nahavandi and Malekzadeh, 1988

Whether people synergies will be realized depends on how the acquisition is managed. The next section focuses attention on what those leading the change can do to mitigate the dysfunctional consequences of cultural differentiation and the lack of continuity that is often experienced by those involved in M&As.

Managing the implementation process

There are many ways in which managers can intervene to promote people synergy. At an early stage in the merger process, the acquiring organization can pre-screen potential target units or organizations for cultural compatibility. In some cases, major differences in organization culture and preferred mode of acculturation might persuade the acquiring unit to abandon the merger plan or seek an alternative, more compatible partner. At a later point, a culture audit might provide data that can be used for exploring similarities and differences between the partner units, in order to identify which aspects of group or organizational functioning will be most difficult to integrate and which aspects of the merger process are most likely to produce merger stress. Such a culture audit might:

- inform the choice of integration strategy. It might be that valuable synergies can be achieved without seeking complete assimilation. A looser form of integration might reduce the scale of the discontinuities experienced by employees and yield added value by avoiding some of the disruption that is often triggered by high merger stress.
- guide how the various aspects of the integration process can be managed by, for example:
  - involving, at an early stage of the acquisition process, those managers who will be responsible for managing the acquired unit, and focusing their attention on possible people problems

- ensuring adequate change communication, involving staff from the acquiring and acquired units in joint task forces to plan how particular aspects of the organizations will be combined
- cross-posting employees to learn, first hand, about the other unit
- providing socioemotional support (see Chapter 13)
- exploring transition arrangements that will ease the introduction of common terms of employment and so on.

Culture profiling and the management of cultural differences

We mentioned above that organizations often pre-screen other organizations to gauge cultural compatibility, but how do we measure and classify an organization's culture? Organizational culture has been defined by Schein (1990) as the pattern of basic assumptions that are invented, discovered or developed by a group as it learns to cope with its problems of external adaptation and internal integration. These give rise to work practices and ways of relating with others that are often referred to as 'the way things are done around here'.

There has been a robust debate about how best to measure organizational culture. Some advocate qualitative measures based on observations or employees' accounts of their organizational experience and others favour quantitative measures. Goffee and Jones (1996) developed a quantitative measure that classifies cultures according to two types of human relations: sociability and solidarity. Harrison (1972, 1986) developed a typology of organizational cultures and a measure (reproduced in Handy, 1976) that provides a basis for differentiating cultures and identifying the level of perceived empowerment, trust and cooperation associated with each.

Cartwright and Cooper (1992, 1993a, 1993b) used Harrison's measure to examine the impact of cultural dynamics on the acculturation and integration process across three acquisitions and two mergers and found that pre-existing cultures facilitate the merger in those cases where the direction of change offers employees increased autonomy, but obstruct change and undermine organizational performance when employees perceive that the merger will erode their autonomy. These findings can be applied to profile organization cultures and help managers anticipate how cultural differences will affect the integration process.

Assimilation strategies will only be successful when members of the acquired organization are prepared to let go of their old ways of doing things and fully embrace the culture and work practices of the acquiring organization. According to Cartwright and Cooper (1993b), this is most likely to happen when members of the acquired organization perceive the acquiring organization's culture to be less constraining than their existing pre-merger culture.

Similar factors will affect the success of acquisition strategies that stop short of complete assimilation. Successful integration depends on both partnering organizations valuing aspects of the other organization's culture and the development, across both organizations, of a collaborative 'win–win' rather than competitive 'win–lose' approach to their engagement in the integration process. Integration will be easier when the differences between the cultures are relatively small, but even then the journey will not always be problem free.

Harrison (1972, 1986) identified four types of culture: power, role, task/achievement and person/support. Cartwright and Cooper (1993b) conceptualized the relationship between these cultures along a continuum ranging in terms of the degree of constraint they place on employees (shown in Figure 23.4 below). The four cultures are briefly outlined.

Power cultures

Power cultures, often found in start-up companies led by highly focused entrepreneurs and in more mature owner-led businesses, impose the greatest degree of constraint and require employees to do what they are told. The main characteristics of power cultures are:

- centralized power
- unequal access to resources and a strong leader who can satisfy or frustrate others by giving or withholding rewards and sanctions
- behaviour influenced by precedent and the anticipation of the wishes of the central power source
- few rules, little bureaucracy, decisions made by individuals not committees.

Role cultures

Role cultures, often found in government departments, public enterprises and other organizations operating in stable environments, provide more freedom and allow employees to act within the parameters of their work role and job description. The main characteristics of role cultures are:

- limited communication between employees working in different functional silos, coordination concentrated at the top
- hierarchical
- roles/job descriptions are more important that the individuals who fill them
- methods rather than results predominate.

Task/achievement cultures

Task/achievement cultures, often found in organizations that have to cope with rapid change, are even less constraining and allow employees to act in ways most suitable for completing the task. The main characteristics of task/achievement cultures are:

- job or project orientation
- resources and people are brought together as required to get the job done
- influence based more on expert power than on position or personal power
- unity of effort towards mutually valued goals
- adaptable – groups and project teams are formed and disbanded as required
- individuals and groups have a high degree of control over their work
- top management retains control via allocation of projects, people and resources, but finds it difficult to exercise day-to-day control over methods of working.

Person/support cultures

Person/support cultures are often found in settings where individuals come together to share an infrastructure that enables them to achieve their own goals, such as barristers' chambers and other professional partnerships, and in organizations that place a high value on the quality of work life. They impose the least constraint and allow members/employees to use their own initiative and do their own thing. The main characteristics of person/support cultures are:

- mutual trust between individuals and the organization
- members believe they are valued as human beings, not just cogs in a machine
- members help each other beyond the formal demands of the job
- members know the organization will go beyond the requirements of the employment contract to look after them if they need support
- structure is the minimum required to help individuals do their job.

Table 23.1 shows the suitability of culture matches between units of similar and dissimilar culture types. For example, an acquisition target with a role culture will experience fewer problems integrating with an acquiring unit that has a task culture than one that has a power culture.

Table **23.1** *Suitability of culture matches*

Culture of the acquirer/ dominant merger partner	Culture of the acquired merger partner	Likely outcome	Comments
Power	Power	Problematic	Success dependent on the choice and charisma of the leader. Can lead to political infighting
Power	Role Task Person/support	All potentially disastrous	Assimilation will be resisted. Culture collisions will be inevitable. Labour turnover likely to be high
Role	Power	Potentially good	Assimilation likely to be accepted. Most will welcome the 'fairness' of a role culture
Role	Role	Potentially good	Smooth assimilation likely as effectively rewriting or presenting a new rule book is all that is required
Role	Task	Potentially problematic	Many in the acquired organization may have chosen to work in a task culture to escape the bureaucracy and red tape of role cultures
Role	Person/support	Potentially disastrous	Anarchy likely. In the above case, members of a task culture may eventually accept that the increased size of the merged organization will require greater infrastructure, but members of a person/support culture will not
Task	Power Role Task	Potentially good	Smooth assimilation likely for those in existing power and role cultures. There will be pleasant but potentially disturbing culture shock. Those who will lose positional power may feel that their status will be eroded. Many will find the new culture demanding and potentially stressful
Task	Person/support	Potentially problematic	While person cultures nurture self-development, they are not conducive to team working and consensual decision making

Source: Adapted from Cartwright and Cooper, 1993b, p. 67

The greater the dissimilarity between cultures, the greater the changes members of each organization will have to make and the more difficult it will be to integrate the organizations. Cartwright and Cooper (1993b) suggest that if the partner organizations do not have similar cultures, they should at least be adjacent types, for example task/role. If they have different cultures, for example at the opposite ends of Harrison's continuum (Figure 23.4), it could be difficult to achieve much, if anything, in the way of people synergy.

Figure **23.4** *Harrison's continuum: the degree of constraint different culture types place on individuals*
Source: Cartwright and Cooper, 1992

Culture profiling at different points in the process

Culture profiling, as part of the due diligence process, can help with the selection of appropriate merger partners. While strategic fit is necessary, it is not a sufficient condition for merger success because people-related issues can derail the process. Culture profiling at a later stage in the merger process, as mentioned above, can provide data that can be used for exploring similarities and differences between the partner organizations and highlighting issues that may require special attention. For example, people who have been used to working in a more constraining power or role culture may need help to modify their management or other work style to fit in with a new 'task/achievement' culture. While they may welcome greater autonomy, they may be uncertain about how best to fit in with new working arrangements and, because they are less closely supervised, may feel deprived of feedback that could help them to improve their performance. Similarly, employees who have been used to working in a less constraining task or person culture may find it difficult to adjust to a more constraining work environment. Exploring ways of helping people to adjust to the new culture might be more effective than just leaving them to muddle through as best they can.

Those responsible for managing the new post-merger combined unit can help those from the acquired unit adjust by acknowledging their competence and helping them to make a positive contribution. It is all too easy to make judgements about their potential contribution before they have had time to adjust to working in the new post-acquisition culture.

Effective communication can do much to reduce the uncertainties that unsettle people involved in merger situations. This is discussed in Chapter 11. What those leading the merger can do to provide socioemotional support to those affected by the change is discussed in Chapter 13 and at the end of Chapter 25.

Summary

Cultural profiling is an intervention that can be used to pre-screen merger partners and, later in a merger process, guide the integration of the merging units. It draws on social identity and acculturation theory to diagnose how a proposed merger or acquisition can affect those involved and to explore how, in the light of employees' preferences for combining cultures, practices and systems, mergers can be managed in a way that will promote rather than undermine people synergies.

Social identity theory was introduced to explain how M&As threaten employees' group and organizational identity, exacerbate 'us and them' dynamics and adversely affect merger success:

- people not only identify themselves in terms of 'I', but also in terms of 'we'
- work group and organization can be an important source of social identity
- M&As affect social identity because they redraw or dissolve the boundaries that once categorized distinct groups
- people respond by focusing on the positive aspects of their pre-merger group and developing negative perceptions of the post-merger unit.

Acculturation theory was used to explore how employees' preferences for combining their organizational cultures, practices and systems affect acquisition and merger outcomes. Ways of combing cultures include:

- *Integration:* This involves some change but allows both parties to maintain many aspects of their culture that are important to them.
- *Assimilation:* A unilateral process in which one group willingly adopts the identity and culture of the other.
- *Separation:* Members of the acquired unit seek to preserve their own culture and practices.
- *Deculturation:* Organizational members reject cultural contact with both their and the other unit.

In all M&As, both units have their own cultures, which comprise a socially acquired set of shared values and beliefs that give rise to a collective frame of reference for determining how things are done and how people relate with others.

The process of social identification provides a useful theoretical foundation for examining the cultural differentiation that occurs when organizations merge. M&As involve the bringing together of at least two different cultures: 'The tenets of social identity theory would indicate that the mere existence of these two subcultures is enough to lead to feelings of in-group out-group bias, discrimination and conflict' (Elsass and Veiga, 1994, p. 438).

Low levels of congruence between the acquiring and acquired units' preferred mode of combining their cultures can lead to high levels of merger stress. This can undermine morale, increase confusion and intergroup conflict, and lead to unproductive behaviours that disrupt the integration process. High levels of congruence, on the other hand, can have the opposite effect and promote people synergies and organization fit. Whether people synergies will be realized depends on how the acquisition is managed.

References

Ashford, S.J. (1988) Individual strategies for coping with stress during organisational transition, *Journal of Applied Behavioural Science*, 24(1): 19–36.

Ashforth, B.E. and Mael, F. (1989) Social identify theory and the organization, *Academy of Management Review*, 14(1): 20–39.

Bartels, J., Douwes, R., de Jong, M. and Pruyn, A. (2006) Organizational identification during a merger: Determinants of employees' expected identification with the new organization, *British Journal of Management*, 17(3): 49–67.

Berry, J.W. (1983) Acculturation: A comparative analysis of alternative forms. In R.J. Samunda and S.L. Woods (eds) *Perspectives in Immigrant and Minority Education*. Lanham, MD: University Press of America.

Berry, J.W. (1984) Cultural relations in pluralistic societies: Alternatives to segregation and their psychological implications. In N. Miller and M.B. Brewer (eds) *Groups in Contact*. Orlando, FL: Academic Press.

Berry, J.W. (2005) Acculturation: Living successfully in two cultures, *International Journal of Intercultural Relations*, 29(6): 697–712.

Cabrera, J.C. (1982) Playing fair with executives displaced after the deal, *Mergers and Acquisitions*, September/October, 42–6.

Cartwright, S. (2005) Mergers and acquisitions: An update and appraisal. In G.P. Hodgkinson and J.K. Ford (eds) *International Review of Industrial and Organisational Psychology*, vol. 20. Chichester: John Wiley & Sons.

Cartwright, S. and Cooper, C.L. (1990) The impact of mergers and acquisitions on people at work: Existing research and issues, *British Journal of Management*, 1(2): 65–76.

Cartwright, S. and Cooper, C.L. (1992) *Mergers and Acquisitions: The Human Factor*. Oxford: Butterworth-Heinemann.

Cartwright, S. and Cooper, C.L. (1993a) The psychological impact of merger and acquisition on the individual: A study of building society managers, *Human Relations*, 46(3): 327–47.

Cartwright, S. and Cooper, C.L. (1993b) The role of culture compatibility in successful organizational marriage, *Academy of Management Executive*, 7(2): 57–70.

Cooper, C.L. and Payne, R. (1988) *Causes, Coping and Consequences of Stress at Work*. Chichester: John Wiley & Sons.

Elsass, P.M. and Veiga, J.F. (1994) Acculturation in acquired organisations: A force field analysis, *Human Relations*, 47(4): 431–53.

Goffee, R. and Jones, G. (1996) What holds the modern company together?, *Harvard Business Review*, 74(6): 133–48.

Handy, C.B. (1976) *Understanding Organizations*. Harmondsworth: Penguin.

Harrison, R. (1972) Understanding your organization's character, *Harvard Business Review*, 50(3): 119–28.

Harrison, R. (1986) *Understanding your Organization's Culture*. Berkeley, CA: Harrison.

Hubbard, N. (1999) *Acquisition: Strategy and Implementation*. Basingstoke: Macmillan – now Palgrave Macmillan.

Nahavandi, A. and Malekzadeh, A.R. (1988) Acculturation in mergers and acquisitions, *Academy of Management Review*, 13(1): 79–90.

Schein, E.H. (1990) Organizational culture, *American Psychologist*, 45(2): 109–19.

Tajfel, H. and Turner, J.C. (1979) An integrative theory of intergroup conflict. In W.G. Austin and S. Worchel (eds) *Psychology of Inter Group Relations*. Monterey, CA: Brooks/Cole.

Van Dick, R., Ullrich, J. and Tissington, P.A. (2006) Working under a black cloud: How to sustain organizational identification after a merger, *British Journal of Management*, 17(S1): 69–79.

Venbeselaere, N., Boen, F. and de Witte, H. (2002) Intergroup relations after a merger: The relative impact of ingroup prototypicality and satisfaction with ingroup representation, paper presented at the 5th Jena workshop on intergroup processes, Castle Kochberg, 19–23 June.

Walsh, P. (1988) Top management turnover following mergers and acquisitions, *Strategic Management Journal*, 9(2): 173–83.

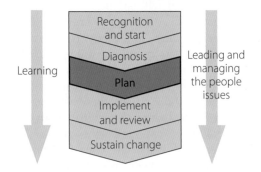

Chapter **24**

Selecting interventions

This chapter examines the factors that need to be considered when selecting which type of intervention to use. Consideration is also given to the factors that can affect decisions regarding the sequencing of interventions when it might be necessary to use more than one. This is important because sometimes an inappropriate sequence can undermine the effectiveness of a change programme.

Recognition and start

Diagnosis

Plan

Implement and review

Sustain change

Learning

Leading and managing the people issues

Beware fashions and fads

There is a real danger that change agents underuse many traditional well-tried interventions in favour of those that are new and 'fashionable'. Ettorre's (1997) life cycle theory of management fads suggests that the adoption of an intervention follows five stages:

1 *discovery:* intervention begins to come to people's attention
2 *wild acceptance:* uncritical adoption
3 *digestion:* critics begin to suggest that it is not a panacea
4 *disillusionment:* recognition of problems associated with the intervention
5 *hard core:* only a minority continue with the intervention.

But the most fashionable interventions may not always be the most effective. After surveying the 100 largest Fortune 500 firms, Staw and Epstein (2000) found that while the use of popular interventions (which in the late 1990s included total quality management, empowerment and team working) was positively associated with corporate reputation – organizations were admired, seen as more innovative and rated as having higher quality management – and CEO pay, it was not associated with improvement in economic performance, assessed over a one-to-five-year period. It is important to select and apply those interventions that will be effective in a particular context. At times, this might involve using interventions that have been around for some time.

Factors indicating which interventions to use

Consideration is given first to those factors that need to be taken into account when deciding which interventions are likely to contribute most to achieving the goals of a change programme. Attention is given to three main factors: the nature

of the problem or opportunity that the intervention has to address (diagnosed issue), the level of change target (individual, group and so on) that is to be the focus for change, and the depth of intervention required. Two additional factors are also considered. These are the time available for the change and the efficacy of different types of interventions.

Diagnosed issue

A key determinant of the appropriate intervention is the nature of the diagnosed problem or opportunity. This underpins the aim of the change programme and indicates the issues that have to be attended to in order to move an organization or unit from the current position to a more desirable future state.

At a macro-level, the issue might be defined in terms of either transformational or incremental change. Where the issue is defined in terms of a need for 'transformational change', Burke and Litwin (1992) suggest that the most effective interventions will be those that are targeted at changing system-wide elements, such as mission and strategy, leadership and culture. Interventions that successfully change these elements will have knock-on effects that will affect just about every other element in the system (see Chapter 7).

On the other hand, where the issue is defined in terms of 'incremental change', or fine-tuning, the most effective interventions may be those that address elements that, if changed, might have a more localized impact in terms of units or levels affected. These include interventions targeted at elements such as structure, systems, climate, tasks and roles. For example, the focal issue might be to improve task performance in a particular department. The intervention selected to address this issue might be work redesign. Redesigning the work to improve task performance may affect other factors, such as the competences required of those who do the work, or departmental structure if redesigning the work involves reducing the number of levels in the hierarchy. However, this kind of intervention may have relatively little impact on how the entire organization functions, even if it does have some implications for how the target unit interacts with related units.

At a micro-level, issues might simply be defined in terms of the organizational elements that are most closely associated with the diagnosed problem or opportunity. The 12 elements of the Burke-Litwin model could provide a basis for classifying issues in this way (see Chapter 7). An alternative, used in the three-dimensional model presented below, is the typology used by Cummings and Worley (2001) to classify interventions (see Chapter 16). It points to four broad types of diagnosed issue:

1 *human process issues*, which include communicating, problem solving, decision making, interpersonal and intergroup interactions, and leadership
2 *technostructural issues*, which include horizontal and vertical differentiation, coordination, technology and production processes, and work design

3 *human resource issues*, which include attracting, selecting, developing, motivating and retaining competent people
4 *strategic issues*, which include managing the interface between the organization and its environment, deciding which markets to engage in, what products and services to produce, how to gain competitive advantage, and what values should guide the organization's development.

Level of change target

Schmuck and Miles (1971), Blake and Mouton (1986), Pugh (1986) and others all include the individual, group, intergroup and organization in their classifications of units that can be the target for change. Blake and Mouton also include the larger social system as the potential client or target for change and Schmuck and Miles include dyads/triads as a separate unit.

The three-dimensional model for selecting interventions identifies five levels: individual, group, intergroup, organization and transorganization (see Figure 24.1 below). For example:

1 A diagnostic analysis might indicate that the critical issue has to do with a mismatch between task demands and individual competences, suggesting that the target for change is at the *individual* level.
2 The diagnosis might point to poor working relationships within a group, indicating that the *group* should be the target for change.
3 The diagnosis may focus on poor relationships between groups, suggesting that *intergroup* relations should be the target.
4 The diagnosis may suggest that organizational strategy is not matched to market conditions or is not properly appreciated by organizational members at all levels, indicating that the target for change is the whole *organization*.
5 At the *transorganizational* level, the diagnosis may suggest that there is a need to create a lean enterprise including all the organizations contributing to a value stream, or that the way forward might involve seeking a partner for a joint venture or merger.

Depth of intervention

Harrison (1970) argues that the depth of individual emotional involvement can be a key factor in determining whether an intervention will be effective. This factor is concerned with the extent to which core areas of personality or self are the focus of change events. He posits a dimension running from surface to deep. Interventions that focus on external aspects of an individual and deal with the more public and observable aspects of behaviour are located at the surface end of the continuum. Interventions that touch on personal and private perceptions, attitudes or feelings and attempt to affect them are located at the deep end.

Operations research is an example of an intervention that can be classified at the surface end of the continuum, because it is a process of rational analysis that deals with roles and functions without paying much attention to the individual characteristics of the persons occupying these roles. An example of a deeper intervention is management by objectives. This involves a boss and a subordinate establishing mutually agreed goals for performance and monitoring performance against these goals. Typically, the exchange of information is limited to that which is observable. Further along the continuum are interventions such as management counselling that, for example, might involve a consultant working with managers to increase their awareness of how their personality, role relationships and previous experience affect their management style. Deeper interventions might involve members of a group discussing with peers the interpersonal processes that affect their contribution to group performance. This kind of intervention can involve group members sharing personal information about themselves, how they perceive their own behaviour and the behaviour of others, and exploring with them how they and others might modify their attitudes, roles and behaviour to improve group performance.

Harrison (1970) argues that as the level of intervention becomes deeper, the information needed to intervene becomes less available. For example, the information needed by the operations researcher is easily obtained because it is often a matter of record, and the information required by those engaged in management by objectives can often be observed. However, people may not be prepared to discuss freely their attitudes and feeling towards others or be open to feedback from others about their own interpersonal style. These considerations led Harrison to suggest the following criterion:

> **Change agents should intervene at a level no deeper than that required to produce an enduring solution to the problem at hand.**

This criterion, while necessary, is not sufficient for determining the depth of intervention. While the change agent may have a view about the nature of the information required and the depth of intervention necessary to produce this information, the change target (individual, group or system) may not be comfortable working at this level. Harrison (1970) argues that any intervention, if it is to be successful, must be legitimized in the norms of the group or organization and must be seen to relate to the felt needs of organizational members. This led him to suggest a second criterion:

> **Intervene at a level no deeper than that at which the energy and resources of the client can be committed to problem solving and change.**

Harrison (1970) suggests that when change agents suspect that the required information is located at a depth greater than that at which the client is comfortable working, they should resolve the dilemma by selecting an intervention on the basis of the second criterion. Once the client has gained confidence, they may be prepared to engage in an intervention that will involve the sharing of information such as attitudes and feelings that they would normally regard as private and confidential.

A three-dimensional model to aid choice

The factors considered so far can be combined to produce a three-dimensional model that can be used as a rough guide for selecting the type of intervention that might be most effective in a given situation. This is presented in Figure 24.1.

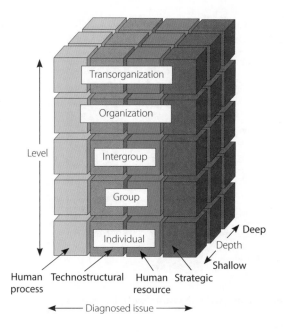

Figure **24.1** *A three-dimensional model to aid choice of interventions*

Figures 24.2–24.5 provide examples of interventions for each of the four diagnosed issues.

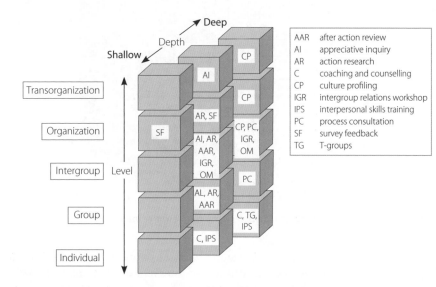

Figure **24.2** *Examples of human process interventions*

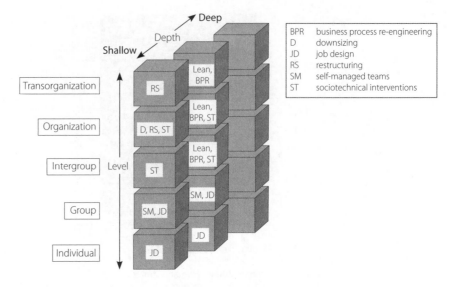

Figure **24.3** *Examples of technostructural interventions*

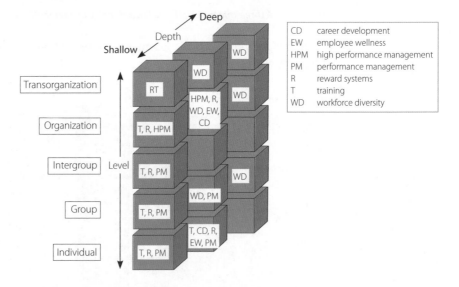

Figure **24.4** *Examples of human resource interventions*

Some cells in Figures 24.2–24.5 are blank because they represent situations that are unlikely to call for an intervention that complies with all three criteria. For example, there may not be many (any?) situations that call for a deep technostructural intervention targeted at the individual. Some interventions could appear in more than one cell. Team building, for example, is an instance of a human process intervention that is targeted at the group. In terms of depth, however, some team-building interventions are shallow and others rather deep. At the shallow end, interventions might only be concerned with agreeing the purpose of the group, indicators of effective performance, and performance strategies that could contribute to achieving this level of performance. On the other hand, at the deep

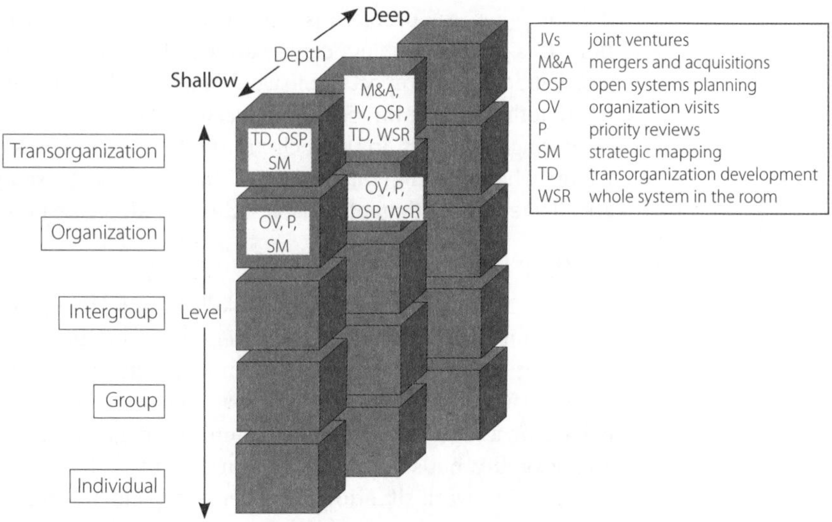

Figure **24.5** *Examples of strategic interventions*

end, interventions could involve an exploration of interpersonal relationships and how these promote or undermine performance.

Figures 24.2–24.5 contain only a sample of the interventions available to change agents. The literature on the management of change is a rich source of other possibilities.

Two additional factors might also influence the choice of intervention: time available and efficacy of intervention.

Time available to implement the change

Where the need for change is urgent and the stakes are high, there may be insufficient time to employ some of the more time-consuming interventions that offer organizational members the opportunity to be involved in deciding what needs to be changed or how the change will be achieved. It might be necessary to restrict choice to those interventions that can be implemented quickly and this might, for example, involve the use of experts who can rapidly prescribe solutions. Prescriptive/directive interventions can be effective, especially over the short term and where organizational members recognize the need for this kind of action. However, there is always the possibility that organizational members may resent the way the change was managed, experience little sense of ownership of the process or the outcome, and may therefore only go along with the change so long as their behaviour is being closely supervised and there is a perceived threat of sanctions for noncompliance.

Where the need for change is less pressing, the change agent may be able to consider a much wider range of interventions.

Efficacy of the interventions

A basic question that needs to be addressed when choosing a particular intervention is: 'Will it produce the intended result?' Some popular interventions are not always as effective as many would like to believe. There are frequent reports in academic journals and the business press indicating disappointment with the outcome of major change programmes that have involved interventions such as BPR, TQM, job design or interpersonal skills training.

Sometimes, the problem is that the change agents select an ineffective intervention. This kind of problem can be avoided by seeking evidence about the efficacy of interventions from reports, colleagues and elsewhere. Often, however, the problem is not that the intervention is ineffective, but that its success is dependent on a number of contingent factors. In these circumstances, it is important to take account of these factors when selecting interventions. There are many examples of interventions that are affected by contingent variables, three of which are now briefly discussed.

T-group training

T-group training is a form of social skills training that provides participants with an opportunity to increase their awareness about themselves and their impact on others in order to learn how to function more effectively in groups. There is evidence that T-groups can improve skills in diagnosing individual and group behaviour, and lead to clearer communication, greater tolerance, consideration, skill and flexibility, but sometimes this learning and behaviour change may not be transferred to the work situation. Transfer is dependent on a number of factors, one of which is the match between the structures and norms that characterize the work and training situations; the closer the match, the greater the transfer and vice versa.

Job design

Job design is often presented as the universal answer to low commitment and poor performance in situations where people are required to perform repetitive, short cycle, simple tasks. Motivation theory suggests that people will be more committed and will perform best when they are engaged in varied and challenging work that:

- provides feedback about how well they are doing
- allows them to feel personally responsible for outcomes
- offers them the possibility of producing outcomes that are perceived to be worthwhile and meaningful.

In practice, job design has been found to be effective in some circumstances and not in others. One of the most important contingent variables related to the success of this intervention is the level of need that employees are seeking to satisfy at work. Job design appears to be most effective where employees are seeking to satisfy higher order needs for personal growth and development through their work.

Total quality management (TQM)

TQM is an organization-wide, long-term change effort designed to orient all an organization's activities around the concept of quality. Cummings and Worley (2001) report that in the USA, a survey of Fortune 1000 companies showed that about 75% of them had implemented some form of TQM. They also report that the overwhelming majority (83%) rate their experience with TQM as either positive or very positive. However, other reports of the success of TQM initiatives are less optimistic. Crosby (1979), for example, asserts that over 90% of TQM interventions by US companies fail, and Burnes (2004) lists a number of studies that suggest that European companies have experienced a similar rate of failure.

It is not immediately obvious why TQM interventions are successful in some settings and less so in others, but one possibility relates to the attitude of top management. In those settings where TQM is viewed in instrumental terms, for example as a way of gaining a kite mark such as ISO 9000 that will provide competitive advantage, it may be less successful than where there is a genuine commitment to routinely meeting or exceeding customer expectations. Where the aim is merely to gain a kite mark, organizational members may experience the intervention as a requirement to comply with a new set of rules. This may have little long-term effect on their values and attitudes towards customers. Also, once the kite mark has been secured, top management may shift attention elsewhere, and any movement towards a more customer-focused culture may be short-lived.

Where there is a need to use more than one type of intervention

Often, it may not be possible to think in terms of selecting a single intervention to respond to an isolated issue, because of the nature of the problem or opportunity, systemic interdependencies, and the need to maintain alignment. For example, the recognition of a new opportunity and the decision, by senior management, to intervene in order to develop a strategy to exploit it might require a range of further interventions. The organization may have to introduce a new technology, adapt its structures and systems, introduce new management practices, redesign tasks, reallocate employees to new roles, and provide training to equip people to perform as required. The change agent has to decide whether to pursue them all simultaneously or to sequence them in some way.

Sequencing interventions

The organization's capacity to cope with change is often limited. Consequently, decisions have to be made about priorities and the sequencing of interventions. Several factors can influence these decisions. These include the overall purpose or intention of the change, organizational politics, the need for an early success, the stakes involved, and the dynamics of change.

Intention

The overall purpose or intention of the change might indicate which aspects of organizational functioning need to be addressed first, which will have implications for the choice of intervention. Where the intention is to transform the organization, interventions that address the transformational variables, such as mission and strategy, leadership and culture, need to be given priority (see above and Chapter 7 on diagnostic models). Where the intention is to seek an incremental change, the focus of attention might be on the transactional variables identified by Burke and Litwin, such as structure, management practices, systems, work climate and so on.

Politics

The change agent needs to be aware of how political factors might affect which issues might be easiest to tackle first and which interventions are likely to be most acceptable to powerful stakeholders. If the top team has a past record of adopting a tough top-down approach to cutting costs, senior managers may not be supportive of interventions they perceive to be 'soft and woolly' and directed at issues they do not consider to be important. Although there may be a need to work on human process issues such as interpersonal communications and decision making, the change agent might decide to start working on issues such as job design, which might encounter less resistance from powerful stakeholders, and move on to work on other issues after delivering some early successes, which will give stakeholders more confidence in the change agent's ability to deliver change.

Need for an early success

It has been noted in Chapter 10 that long-term change efforts can slow down and lose momentum if people lose their initial sense of urgency. One way of countering this is to start by working on problems and using interventions that offer the promise of some early successes.

The stakes involved

Priority needs to be given to those interventions that can resolve issues that threaten the survival of the organization. Where survival is not an issue, priority might still be given to issues where the potential gains and losses are relatively high.

Dynamics of change

In some circumstances, the dynamics of change may suggest that the best way to proceed is to adopt an indirect approach rather than addressing the prime issue or change target first. Three issues could be considered.

Causal links

Consideration needs to be given to causal links and the relative strength of the interrelationships between the elements of the organizational system. The Burke-Litwin model points to the relative strength of higher level elements such as strategy, leadership and culture over lower level elements such as structure, systems and management practices. While culture and systems can affect one another, culture is seen to have a stronger influence over systems than vice versa. This kind of consideration can influence which elements are selected as the initial targets for change, thereby influencing the sequencing of interventions.

The effect of groups on individuals

Research evidence suggests that there may be occasions where the most effective way of changing individual behaviour is to intervene at the level of the group (see Chapter 16). Group-level interventions, such as team-building activities designed to produce a more cohesive group, might motivate individuals to change their behaviour to support group goals. A follow-up intervention could then involve training selected individuals to provide them with the competences they need to make a more effective contribution to group performance. If individual training had been the first intervention, it might only have had limited success because of low member motivation. After a group-level intervention, individual members might be much more highly motivated to acquire the competences that will enable them to play a full and active part in the work of the group.

The effect of attitudes on behaviour and vice versa

There have been many debates about whether the most effective route to lasting change is to target attitudes and values first or behaviour first. While there is support for the view that strongly held values and attitudes influence behaviour, the evidence that interventions targeted at values and attitudes can change behaviour is more equivocal. An alternative view is that the most effective route to lasting change is to intervene to create conditions that require people to behave differently, because over the longer term, attitudes and values will be realigned with the new behaviour.

Porter et al. (1975) offer a third way, suggesting that an effective route to change is to intervene in ways that simultaneously modify structures, in order to create the conditions that will elicit new and desired behaviours, and modify interpersonal processes – to address issues of managerial style, attitudes and the social climate of the organization. This approach employs structural interventions to support intrapersonal and interpersonal learning.

They suggest that structural interventions might include:

- modifying work structures in order to change how individual employees actually spend most of their time
- modifying control structures in order to determine what individuals attend to
- modifying reward structures in order to influence what individuals will do when they have choice.

While there are no hard-and-fast rules about whether interventions should address interpersonal processes or structures first, there is a growing body of opinion that intervening to change one without the other is less effective than intervening to change both.

☑ *Exercise* **24.1** *Choice of interventions*

Review some of the change programmes that have been implemented within your organization and, with reference to the content of this chapter, critically assess the choice of interventions. Are you able to identify occasions when inappropriate interventions were used? Give reasons and suggest interventions than might have been more effective.

If you are a full-time student with little work experience, you could either research an organization online, such as the NHS in the UK, or design a miniresearch project and interview members of an organization, such as your university or a local company, to identify the type of interventions that were used to achieve change, observe whether they were carefully chosen for particular circumstances, and assess whether inappropriate interventions had been used.

Summary

This chapter examined the factors that need to be considered when selecting which type of intervention to use. Consideration was also given to the factors that can affect decisions regarding the sequencing of interventions in those circumstances where it is necessary to use more than one type of intervention.

Some of the factors that need to be considered when selecting interventions are:

1 *Diagnosed problem:*
- Where the issue is defined in terms of a need for transformational change, Burke and Litwin suggest that the most effective interventions will be those that are targeted at changing system-wide elements such as mission and strategy, leadership and culture.
- Where the issue is defined in terms of a need for incremental change (or fine-tuning), the most effective interventions may be those that address elements that, if changed, might have a more localized impact in terms of

units or levels affected. These include interventions targeted at elements such as structure, systems, climate, tasks and roles.

- The typology of issues used in the three-dimensional model (Figure 24.1) focuses on four broad type of diagnosed issue: human process issues, techno-structural issues, human resource issues and strategic issues.

2 *Level of change target:* This might be defined in terms of the individual, group, intergroup, organization or transorganization.

3 *Depth of intervention required:* Harrison argues that the depth of individual emotional involvement can be a key factor in determining whether an intervention will be effective. This factor is concerned with the extent to which core areas of personality or self are the focus of change events.

These three factors have been combined to provide a three-dimensional model to aid choice. Two additional factors were also referred to; the time available to implement the change and the efficacy of interventions.

Attention has also been given to the factors that can affect the sequencing of interventions. These include:

- intent or purpose of the change
- organizational politics and how they affect the support for different interventions
- the need for an early success to maintain motivation
- the stakes involved
- dynamics of change.

References

Blake, R.R. and Mouton, J.S. (1986) *Consultation: A Handbook for Individual and Organization Development* (2nd edn). Reading, MA: Addison-Wesley.

Burke, W.W. and Litwin, G.H. (1992) A causal model of organizational performance and change, *Journal of Management*, 18(3): 523–45.

Burnes, B. (2004) *Managing Change: A Strategic Approach to Organisational Dynamics* (4th edn). Harlow: Pearson.

Crosby, P.B. (1979) *Quality is Free.* New York: McGraw-Hill.

Cummings, T.G. and Worley, C.G. (2001) *Organizational Development and Change* (7th edn). Cincinnati, OH: South Western.

Ettorre, B. (1997) What's the next management buzzword?, *Management Review*, 86(8): 33–5.

Harrison, R. (1970) Choosing the depth of organizational interventions, *Journal of Applied Behavioral Science*, 6(2): 182–202.

Porter, L.W., Lawler, E.E. and Hackman, J.R. (1975) *Behavior in Organizations.* London: McGraw-Hill.

Pugh, D. (1986) *Planning and Managing Change.* Milton Keynes: Open University Press.

Schmuck, R.A. and Miles, M.B. (1971) *Organization Development in Schools.* Palo Alto, CA: National Press Books.

Staw, B. and Epstein, L.D. (2000) What bandwagons bring: Effects of popular management techniques on corporate performance and reputation, *Administrative Science Quarterly*, 45(3): 523–60.

Visit **www.palgrave.com/companion/hayes-change-management4** *for further learning resources*

IMPLEMENTING CHANGE AND REVIEWING PROGRESS

Part VI

Introduction to Part VI

Part VI considers some of the issues that change managers need to attend to when implementing change and reviewing progress.

Chapter 25 *Implementing change*

Chapter 25 examines implementation in the context of one company acquiring control of another and uses this case to highlight some of the factors that can affect the success of attempts to implement change. An acquisition example is used because it is a type of change that will be familiar to most readers.

Implementation is not a one-off activity. It is an ongoing process that is often closely intertwined with other ongoing activities such as diagnosis and planning. Sometimes, these activities are so closely intertwined that it can be difficult to distinguish the precise nature of implementation, especially when an attempt to implement a change fails to deliver the expected outcome. In such circumstances, the failure to achieve the desired result can provide those leading the change with new insights (implementation becomes diagnosis) and these insights inform new plans that are then implemented, and so the sequence continues.

Some of the implementation-related issues that those leading a change need to attend to are identified. These include:

- The quality of the diagnosis of the perceived opportunity or threat, the specification of change goals, and the quality of pre-planning
- The way the change is communicated
- The way stakeholders are managed
- The degree of alignment and coordination when implementing different aspects of the change
- The adoption of management practices that are perceived to be fair
- The avoidance of a heavy-handed approach when managing those who may feel vulnerable

- The provision of socioemotional support to help organizational members let go of the status quo.

Chapter 26 *Reviewing and keeping the change on track*

Chapter 26 considers how monitoring and reviewing the implementation of a change can help managers to adjust and adapt the change plan to ensure that the organization moves towards a more desirable future state.

Attention is given to the kind of information those leading change need in order to determine whether interventions are being implemented as intended and whether they are having the anticipated effect. This includes their impact on key stakeholder groups and assessing whether the change plan continues to be valid. Assessing the continued validity of the change plan, and updating it as required, is especially important when managing emergent change.

When interventions have a positive impact on organizational performance, this achievement needs to be consolidated and used as a basis for achieving further improvements in performance. This will receive more attention in Chapters 27 and 28.

Change managers also need to identify measures of organization effectiveness that relate to those outcomes that are important to the organization's long-term survival and growth. This often involves attending to more than just the short-term interests of shareholders.

Exercise **Part VI** *Useful questions for reviewing your approach to implementing change*

In Chapter 2, after discussing each stage in the process model of change management, your attention was drawn to a number of questions that might help you assess how well a change is being (or was) managed. All these questions are summarized in Figure 2.5 and the questions relating to implementing the change and reviewing progress are listed below:

- Do change managers communicate a compelling vision and set realist goals?
- Is uncertainty managed in a way that maintains commitment?
- Are stakeholders being managed effectively?
- Is there sufficient coordination between those involved in implementing the change?
- Do change managers seek feedback in order to eliminate impediments to implementation?
- Are interventions being implemented as intended?
- Are interventions producing the desired effect?

Reflect on and review these questions and, after reading the two chapters in Part VI, revise this list and generate your own set of useful questions that you might find it helpful to refer to when you are leading a change.

Chapter 25

Implementing change

Implementation involves translating intentions (plans for change) into actual change efforts. Sometimes, implementation occurs as a one-off discrete step in the change process. An example could be where a change is relatively small scale, the end point has been specified in advance, and there is little resistance because all those involved believe they will benefit from the change.

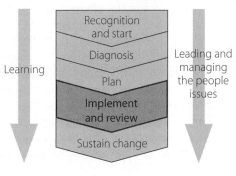

But often situations are more complicated than this. For example, an initial diagnosis may clarify a problem or opportunity but may fail to identify a desired end state, so the change has to unfold in a tentative way that involves taking incremental steps in, what is hoped is, the right direction. After each step, the step itself and the direction of the change have to be reviewed to establish if the step worked and if the direction of change still holds good. In different circumstances, those leading a change may envision an end state that is not welcomed by others and these others may resist their leaders' initial attempt to implement the change, and may force them to modify their proposals and implement a more acceptable change.

In these kinds of situations, implementation is not a one-off activity. It is an ongoing endeavour that is often closely intertwined with other ongoing activities such as diagnosis and planning. Sometimes, they can be so closely intertwined that it can be difficult to distinguish implementation from diagnosis and planning, especially when an attempt to implement a change fails to deliver the expected outcome. In such circumstances, the failure to achieve the desired result can provide those leading the change with new insights (implementation becomes diagnosis) that inform new plans that are then implemented, and so the sequence continues.

This chapter explores the nature of implementation and identifies some of the implementation-related issues that those leading a change need to attend to. These include:

- The quality of the diagnosis of the perceived opportunity or threat, the specification of change goals, and the quality of pre-planning.
- The way the change is communicated.
- The way stakeholders are managed.
- The degree of alignment and coordination when implementing different aspects of the change.
- The adoption of management practices that are perceived to be fair.

- The avoidance of a heavy-handed approach when managing those who may feel vulnerable.
- The provision of socioemotional support to help organizational members let go of the status quo.

Implementation in theory and practice

The model of change that underpins the structure of this book conceptualizes the management of change as a process that involves seven core activities:

1 recognizing the need for change and starting the change process
2 diagnosing what needs to be changed and formulating a vision of a preferred future state
3 planning how to intervene in order to achieve the desired change
4 implementing plans and reviewing progress
5 sustaining the change
6 leading and managing people issues
7 learning from the experience.

With the exception of managing the people issues and learning from the ongoing experience of change, these activities are presented, in Chapter 2, as separate elements of the change process because, in theory, the decisions and actions associated with each tend to dominate at different points in the process and there is a logical sequence connecting them; however, in practice, the boundaries between these activities are not always clear-cut and the sequence of activities can be iterative, with some issues being addressed more than once and sometimes simultaneously with others.

The iterative nature of implementation and some of the factors that can affect whether or not an intervention will be successful will be explored using the example of one company (KeyChemicals) acquiring another (Eco-Pure). This example has been chosen because acquisitions are a common type of change that will be familiar to most readers. They can involve the combination of separate organizations, or internal combinations within a single organization that entail merging similar units to eliminate duplication or different units in order to restructure the organization and reduce the number of separate functions.

Implementing the decision to acquire another organization

The motive for most acquisitions is some form of value creation. Some of the most frequently cited strategic objectives that can generate value are financial synergies, market penetration, market entry, market protection, product extension, technical expertise, vertical expansion, access to resources, operational synergies, managerial expertise and economies of scale.

Due diligence: the first step in implementing the change

Clarifying acquisition objectives followed by a process of due diligence to assess whether or not the acquisition will deliver the anticipated added value is an essential first step in the process of identifying a suitable acquisition target. A series of linked examples describe KeyChemicals' acquisition of Eco-Pure. The first of these illustrates the beginning of the process and is presented as Case study 25.1. It requires you to identify the issues you think will have to be attended to if acquisition is to succeed.

Case study **25.1** *KeyChemicals' acquisition of Eco-Pure: recognizing the opportunity and starting the process*

KeyChemicals (as it will be referred to here) is a Swiss company. After a 30-year period of steady growth, based on the acquisition of other businesses, the original Vevey-based distributer of chemicals to the food processing industry was transformed into a distributor of a wide range of specialist chemicals operating across most of Europe. After spending four years integrating past acquisitions, reducing costs and increasing margins, the CEO recognized that the company was ready to embark on a new phase of growth and persuaded the board of directors to resume the company's previous strategy of acquiring existing businesses.

After reviewing the company's strengths and weaknesses and the possibilities for generating more shareholder value, the board decided to search for acquisition targets that would add value by providing access to new markets. The CEO worked with the marketing and finance directors to identify possible acquisition targets that could help KeyChemicals achieve this strategic goal. They enlisted a merchant banker to help them develop a search strategy, which

they quickly implemented. Within a few weeks, they identified a short list of three acquisition targets and presented their findings to the rest of the board. The three were whittled down to one, Eco-Pure, a family-owned company that dominated the water treatment chemicals market in Denmark. The company was attractive because a strategic analysis indicated that the only cost-effective way for a new competitor to break into this market would be to acquire Eco-Pure.

The owners were approached and indicated a willingness to consider the possibility of selling the company, so KeyChemicals embarked on a more detailed examination of Eco-Pure to ascertain whether the acquisition would add value and how much they should pay to acquire the company.

Before reading on, identify and list the issues you feel those leading the acquisition will have to attend to if it is to be implemented successfully. When you have read this chapter, reflect on the notes you have made here and consider whether your list needs to be amended in any way.

© GETTY

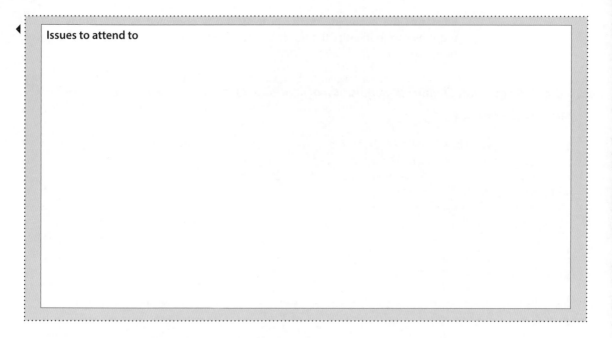

Issues to attend to

A number of factors interact to affect the outcome of this first step of the implementation process. Some of these are the range and complexity of issues that need to be considered, fragmentation of the data collection process, the relative ease of assessing some issues compared to others, the mindset of the buy team, and a pressure to complete the due diligence review quickly.

The range and complexity of issues

Due diligence needs to consider more than just a search for and appraisal of financial information about the target company. Depending on the acquisition objectives, it may need to include:

- an industry and competitor analysis
- a product and market analysis
- an assessment of the target's management talent
- an analysis of management fit in terms of philosophy and attitudes and a wider assessment of culture fit
- an assessment of potential synergies and any technical issues that could affect whether these synergies will be realized
- a review of the terms and conditions of employment
- an assessment of the compatibility of pension funds and so on.

Fragmentation of the data collection

Jemison and Sitkin (1986) suggest that this complexity results in these analyses being allocated to separate members of the buy team or delegated to external specialists. This segmentation and delegation often has the effect of increasing the influence of external specialists, who tend to be more focused on assessing strategic fit in terms of financial viability rather than the practicalities involved in integrating the two businesses after the deal has been agreed. A further complication is that in some cases, little attention is given to synthesizing these disparate analyses.

Accessing required information

It can be difficult to gather all the information required in order to assess the quality of the fit between the two organizations and identify the likelihood that the desired level of integration can be achieved at a reasonable cost. This is especially so if secrecy has to be maintained or the target's management team are hostile to the bid. In such circumstances, it could be difficult to obtain information about the target firm's management talent (particularly middle management talent), determine the compatibility of IT systems, or gather information about the target's organization culture. The information required to assess the target company's financial health, on the other hand, is usually more accessible. This abundance of financial data and dearth of other information might not be a problem if the reason for acquiring a particular target centres on financial synergies, but could be a problem if, as in the case of the KeyChemicals acquisition of Eco-Pure, the strategic objective is to gain access to new markets. In the Connect2 case (Case study 11.1), the buyers' failure to collect sufficient information about the company's management and technical infrastructure and employees' skill sets contributed to the failure of their ambition to expand the business and their bolder plan to merge it with two other businesses to create a media powerhouse.

Mindset of those leading the change (the buy team)

Marks and Mirvis (2001) report that the mindset of the buy team is an important determinant of acquisition success. They found that in the less successful cases they studied, buyers tended to exhibit financial tunnel vision. They concentrated their attention on the numbers and focused on what the target was worth. Their decision to do a deal was typically framed in terms of the combined balance sheet of the companies, projected cash flows and hoped-for return on investment. In the more successful cases, buyers adopted a more strategic mindset and positioned the financial analysis in the context of an overarching set of strategic objectives.

Composition of the group leading the change

Marks and Mirvis (2001) also found that the buyer's mindset was related to the composition of the buy team. When members had predominantly financial backgrounds, they appeared more inclined to assess potential acquisition targets from a financial perspective and make judgements about possible synergies on the basis of financial models and ratios. Hard criteria dominated and if the numbers looked good, issues relating to organizational and cultural differences tended to be ignored. However, when the buy team included influential members with operational and technical backgrounds, there was a greater chance that hoped-for synergies would be made more explicit and their value more realistically assessed and given a more central role in the early decision-making process. Colin Ions, in his video on the book's companion website (www.palgrave.com/companion/hayes-change-management4) on the role of HR in M&As, argues that HR managers can make a valuable contribution. This may be as part of the buy team or in some other capacity.

Pressure to complete the due diligence review quickly

Jemison and Sitkin (1986) observe that there is often an escalating momentum in the acquisition process that results in premature solutions and insufficient attention being given to the quality of organization fit and the integration process. They point to many factors that stimulate this escalating momentum, including:

- the 'thrill of the chase' that can blind members of the buy team to the 'consequences of the catch'
- the problems associated with maintaining secrecy – to avoid unsettling customers, key staff who must be retained, suppliers and financial markets
- the buy team's limited tolerance for ambiguity, which motivates them to seek early closure.

Example **25.1** *Due diligence for the acquisition of Eco-Pure*

The CEO of KeyChemicals convened a 'buy team' to gather and assess information about Eco-Pure and determine whether it should be acquired and if so, on what terms. He convened an early meeting to plan what needed to be done. Most of those involved had been there when KeyChemicals had acquired companies in the past and the CEO invited them to reflect on what they could learn from their past experience.

They attributed part of their past success to the quality of the advice they had received from external advisers but recognized that some of this advice had diverted their attention away from some important issues. They remembered one acquisition that had not gone as well as anticipated because, following advice, they had been too focused on attractive 'early wins', linked to the sale of patents and related intellectual property, and had given insufficient attention to the impact this 'asset stripping' would have on those who worked for the acquired company. A member of the buy team had signalled this as a possible problem but had been ignored by colleagues. This reflecting on past experience alerted them to the need to pay attention to inputs from other members of the buy team.

They also recognized the importance of including people in the team who had relevant knowledge and experience. The buy team, as it was originally convened, included the CEO, two external advisers and the finance, marketing and HR directors, but, after assessing what needed to happen if the acquisition was to be successful, it was decided to include the head of operations.

While Eco-Pure's owners were cooperative throughout the due diligence review, they were unwilling to allow open access and permit members of the buy team to tour the company's premises and talk to staff beyond those who were members of the Eco-Pure board. The buy team had anticipated this and did all they could to secure information from third parties. For example, specialty chemicals is a relatively small world, staff had moved around and there were a number of sources who could provide information about some of the key players who worked for Eco-Pure.

As the review progressed, the momentum gathered pace but the CEO was careful to ensure that decisions were not rushed. He arranged frequent meetings where those who had been tasked to explore specific issues could share their findings and he encouraged everybody to explore what-if scenarios to identify new issues that might need to be considered.

Following the detailed examination of Eco-Pure and its potential to add value, a decision was taken to acquire the company. The purchase could be viewed as the implementation of the change (acquisition) but, in reality, completing the deal was just the start of the integration process.

Integrating the two organizations

The agreement to proceed with the acquisition triggered further iterations of diagnosis, planning and implementation.

> ● *Example* **25.2** *Planning the integration of KeyChemicals and Eco-Pure*
>
> While the KeyChemicals buy team was completing arrangements for the purchase of Eco-Pure, new people were drawn into the acquisition process to begin planning how the two companies would be integrated if the purchase was agreed. This was managed in two stages. The first involved the development of an overview of how the strategic objectives could be achieved and the second built on this and involved formulating more detailed plans.

This early attention to planning the actual integration is an example of good practice, because it is not unusual for integration planning to be delayed until after a decision has been taken to proceed with an acquisition. This delay can be justified on the grounds of cost but early attention to integration planning can flag up problems that could be so serious they could either stop the acquisition proceeding or affect the price the acquiring company is prepared to pay.

Acquisition overview and the assessment of organization fit

An important issue that needs to be considered early on is the degree of integration sought between the parent (acquiring) and target organizations. Hubbard (1999) presents a continuum of integration possibilities ranging from the acquired firm being given almost total autonomy to full integration. The four possibilities are:

1 *total autonomy:* the acquired firm is controlled by financial measures but is not required to engage in any physical integration
2 *restructuring followed by financial control:* the acquired company is modified in some respect, for example new technologies, more efficient working practices or a new management team are introduced, and is then left to operate in a stand-alone capacity, subject only to financial controls
3 *functional integration:* one or more departments or functions are integrated to achieve cost savings or economies of scale
4 *full integration:* both companies merge all their operations.

Hubbard (1999) argues that the strategic objectives driving the acquisition will determine the integration possibilities. For example, if a company is acquiring another in order to achieve financial synergies, then neither total nor functional integration might be required. If, however, the aim is to achieve economies of scale, then some degree of total or functional integration might be essential. If, as in the case of KeyChemicals' acquisition of Eco-Pure, the aim is market penetration, then almost any degree of integration might be compatible with achieving this strategic objective.

Hubbard illustrates this point with the example of one building society acquiring another in order to achieve two strategic objectives, market penetration and economies of scale. The simple act of acquiring the other building society will help to achieve the market penetration objective by reducing competition and consolidating the position of the acquirer in the marketplace, but more may need to be done. For example, to maximize market penetration, it might be necessary to engage in some degree of functional integration that involves the sales teams of both companies engaging in cross-selling and the joint development of new products and services. With regard to achieving economies of scale, some rationalization of

VI

branch networks might be required, along with the closure of one of the head offices, and the integration of IT and other processes.

Detailed planning: the acquisition blueprint

According to Hubbard (1999), the acquisition blueprint takes the acquisition overview and divides it into task-specific actions that can be managed on a project-by-project basis. It specifies what actions are to be taken, when they will occur, who will be affected, who will be responsible for implementing them, and how they will take place.

Example **25.3** *The implementation plan*

The crucial asset that made Eco-Pure an attractive acquisition target was the company's sales and technical support teams, because these two groups could help KeyChemicals penetrate the water treatment market in Denmark and provide a springboard for expanding into similar markets elsewhere. The 15 people who worked in these areas were technically competent, had excellent relationships with customers, and a deep knowledge of their businesses. KeyChemicals aimed to integrate these teams into its own sales and technical support teams. Post-acquisition priorities included:

- consolidating existing sales in Eco-Pure's water treatment market
- generating additional business by requiring former Eco-Pure sales staff to cross-sell KeyChemicals' products to their (formally Eco-Pure) customers
- jointly developing new products and services to secure future business.

Eco-Pure had two distribution depots in Aarhus and Copenhagen, Denmark, which duplicate existing KeyChemicals depots. It was decided that one depot at each location had to be closed in order to achieve operating synergies. This required the relocation of some equipment, the consolidation of inventories, and a large reduction in the number of depot staff.

The KeyChemicals and Eco-Pure tanker fleets were relatively unaffected. It was anticipated that only four drivers would be surplus to requirements and that early retirements and normal labour turnover would deliver this reduction within 6–12 months without the need for compulsory redundancies. Some of the remaining drivers had to be redeployed to work out of different depots.

There was some overcapacity of middle and senior managers and it was decided that a small number of Eco-Pure's middle managers would have to be released along with the finance, HR and operations directors. However, it was viewed as essential that the marketing director should be retained.

At this point in the process, only the CEO and the owners of Eco-pure were aware of the planned acquisition.

Implementing the plan

Implementing this kind of change is a complex and multifaceted activity that involves several managers leading separate but related interventions. One critical intervention in the KeyChemicals case was to do whatever necessary to ensure that Eco-Pure's sales and technical support teams were retained.

There is an oft-cited apocryphal story about one acquisition where a failure to communicate with product development staff in the acquired company, whose wealth of technical talent was the reason the company had been acquired, led to an acquisition disaster. Many parts of the acquired firm were of limited value to the new parent company. Some production facilities were closed or relocated; the sales force was reduced; remaining staff absorbed into parts of the new parent and the head office was closed. The product development team watched these developments with mounting concern but nobody bothered to communicate with them about their future prospects. They feared the worst. The result was that the whole team left and, as a complete unit, joined a competitor organization.

Managing the people issues

This apocryphal story illustrates the importance of communicating with those affected by the change and prioritizing issues when formulating the communication strategy. Hubbard (1999) argues that communication planning for an acquisition is important for four reasons:

- to maximize the likelihood of successful communication on the day of announcement
- to coordinate the communication of 'secret' information during the early pre-acquisition phase, while continuing to communicate openly about day-to-day operational matters
- to coordinate internal and external messages
- to provide a contingency plan if early negotiations are leaked.

Example 11.2 on PCBtec illustrates this last point. The brother of a PCBtec employee overheard two senior managers talking about a pending merger when he was on a train. He texted his brother and the message quickly spread across the organization, which forced senior managers to call a site meeting before the end of the day to explain the situation. They had not anticipated that their negotiations would be leaked and had not given any thought to how they should react if it happened. The outcome was a communication fiasco. The CEO confirmed that merger talks were in progress but that, as yet, nothing had been agreed. He went on to explain how important it was not to unsettle suppliers and customers and outlined how best employees might respond if outsiders enquired about what was happening. The meeting focused on what they could do to help manage the company's external image and almost nothing was said about how the merger would affect them personally. This led to a sudden drop in morale and commitment. Employees were shocked to discover (as they perceived it) that senior managers regarded them as mere hired hands, who were expendable whenever things became difficult, rather than valued individuals.

Managing communications to minimize ambiguity

There is ample evidence that ambiguous acquisition environments create intergroup differentiation, and engender win–lose attitudes, confusion, anxiety, and a general climate of mistrust. Effective communication can do much to reduce the uncertainties that unsettle organizational members; however, it is often sadly lacking. Chapter 11 reviewed various communication strategies. The 'withhold and uphold' strategy (see Clampitt et al., 2000), which involves withholding information until necessary and, when confronted by rumours, upholding the party line, often typifies the approach adopted by managers in M&A scenarios (see the PCBtec example mentioned above). There are many reasons for this. Those leading the change may be reluctant to communicate information because they fear that unanticipated events may render this information incorrect. They may worry about making commitments that threaten their ability to respond flexibly to changes later in the acquisition process, or they may fear that early communication could alert competitors or cause employees to leave. Whatever the reason, employees react to a paucity of information by fearing the worst and sharing their views with colleagues in ways that feed the acquisition grapevine and lead to even greater confusion and anxiety. If managers step in later in the acquisition process to counter these growing uncertainties, their efforts may have only limited success because, by then, employees are suspicions about their intentions and reluctant to trust the belated information they receive.

One way of reducing these problems is to provide all employees with clear and unambiguous information about what is going to change as a result of the acquisition. Hubbard (1999) observed that those organizations with a record of successful acquisition tend to have sophisticated communication strategies for dealing with the acquired organization's internal and external stakeholders. Good communication is essential throughout the acquisition process, but it is especially important on day one because the impression the acquirer makes at the start of the process will influence how those affected will interpret all subsequent actions. However, such communication requires considerable pre-acquisition planning. Hubbard makes the obvious point that if the acquiring organization has not done sufficient integration planning before the acquisition is announced, there will not be enough substance of information to communicate to employees. Similarly, even if the acquirer has the most well-developed acquisition plan, much of its value will be lost if it is not adequately communicated.

The provision of unambiguous information about what will change can help reduce employees' perceptions of possible dysfunctional outcomes and produce higher levels of organizational commitment (see Research report 25.1). When designing their study, Schweiger and DeNisi (1991) compared the amount of information desired by an employee going through an acquisition with the information a newcomer to an organization might want. New recruits, like employees involved in an M&A, face high levels of uncertainty that can result in dysfunctional outcomes. 'Realistic job previews' have been used to provide complete and realistic information about a job, including its positive and negative aspects, and have been found to be effective for reducing newcomers' uncertainty, bringing their expectations in line with reality, and helping them to cope with the transition to their new jobs. Studies show that new employees who receive previews tend to be more satisfied with their jobs and more committed to their organizations, experience less stress, and less likely to leave than employees socialized through more traditional methods (see Premack and Wanous, 1985). Realistic job previews appear to work by serving two functions: they reduce uncertainty and communicate to employees that their new employer cares about them and can be trusted.

Q *Research report* **25.1** *The realistic merger preview*

Schweiger, D.M. and DeNisi, A.S. (1991) Communication with employees following a merger: A longitudinal field experiment, *Academy of Management Journal*, 34(1): 100–35.

Schweiger and DeNisi argued that the functions served by realist job previews – reducing uncertainty and

communicating that change managers care and can be trusted – are important to employees facing M&As. They adapted the realistic job preview concept and created a communication programme, which they called the 'realistic merger preview'. They tested the effectiveness of this approach by conducting a longitudinal experiment involving the merger of two

▶

Fortune 500 companies. Data were collected in two plants, an experimental plant in which the preview was introduced and a control plant in which the merger was managed more traditionally.

Employees in both plants received a letter from the CEO announcing the merger. This was the only information workers in the control plant received. Their plant manager, who was not aware of the realistic merger programme in the experimental plant, was simply told that further information would be coming as soon as it was available. In the experimental plant, employees were provided with much more information. Schweiger and DeNisi report that the aim of the realistic merger programme was to:

- provide employees with frequent, honest and relevant information about the merger
- provide them with fair treatment
- answer their questions and concerns to the fullest extent possible.

They received information about layoffs, transfers, promotions, demotions, changes in pay, jobs, and benefits. This information was communicated as soon as it was available.

A bimonthly merger newsletter was sent to each employee in the experimental plant containing details of changes the merger had created, together with answers to employees' questions. A telephone hotline was answered during working hours by a personnel manager who continually received updated information from the vice president of HR. Questions about general organizational changes were answered but not those concerning individual employees. After working hours, employees calling the hotline reached an answering machine. Answers to questions left on the answering machine were posted on bulletin boards around the plant, and most also appeared in the next issue of the newsletter. Finally, the experimental plant's manager met weekly with the supervisors and employees of each of the eight departments in the plant. Separate meetings were arranged for each department to ensure that changes affecting that department could be specifically addressed and weekly briefings were prepared jointly by the plant manager and the vice president of HR to supplement these meetings and maintain communication consistency and accuracy across the plant.

Following the merger announcement, employees in the experimental and control plants reacted negatively. However, once the realistic merger preview programme was introduced in the experimental plant, the situation in that plant began to stabilize. Schweiger and DeNisi report that, while uncertainty and its associated outcomes did not decline, they stopped increasing, and, over time, employees' perceptions of the company's trustworthiness, honesty and caring and their self-reported performance actually began to improve and return to pre-announcement levels.

The results of this experiment provide empirical evidence that open communications can reduce uncertainty and increase employees' perceptions that their company cares and is prepared to offer socioemotional support.

Hubbard (1999) argues that people expect change, such as redundancies, relocations and modifications to working practices, after an acquisition and will be generally accepting of it so long as they are kept informed prior to events occurring and are treated fairly when they happen. She asserts that employees will react badly to being kept in the dark, being treated unfairly or being misled. Evidence suggests that employees prefer to know the truth rather than be fobbed off with platitudes.

In terms of Clampitt et al.'s (2000) typology of communication strategies, the realistic merger preview primarily involves an 'underscore and explore' approach (see Chapter 11). The change managers decided which issues they would communicate about (underscore), but they also ensured that employees had the opportunity to discuss these issues with managers in order to explore how they would be affected by them. Those leading the change were also willing to respond to questions over the telephone hotline and in newsletters, indicating that they were willing to allow employees some freedom to influence the communication agenda, in line with an 'identify and reply' strategy.

VI

Example 25.4 *Announcing the acquisition to Eco-Pure employees*

After the acquisition had been finalized but before it was announced to employees working for Eco-Pure, all KeyChemicals staff who were to be involved in managing particular aspects of the integration received a confidential briefing. They were told about the acquisition and the strategic objectives, given an overview of the whole process, informed about key tasks, timescales and requirements for coordinating progress, and briefed about their individual responsibilities.

On day one, a team of senior managers held a meeting for all staff at Eco-Pure HQ and simultaneous announcements were made to meetings at both Eco-Pure depots. The announcement promised a positive future for the combined company and most, but not all, of the staff currently working for Eco-Pure. As far as was possible at the time, details of the planned changes were provided, together with information about who was likely to be affected and whether this would involve redeployment, retraining for new roles or redundancy. Eco-Pure employees were provided with contact details for named individuals who had been designated as the first contacts and could provide them with further information about specific aspects of the change.

Managing stakeholders

Change managers need to be aware how the change will affect others and how this will influence their commitment and willingness to support the change. In Chapter 10, the importance of identifying and managing stakeholders is discussed and related to Case study 10.1, which involved integrating the HR departments in two hospitals following a merger, while the Triumph case presented in the Introduction to Part IV illustrates how a new outsourcing project was threatened when key stakeholders began to withdraw their support after senor managers turned their attention to other issues. Those charged with implementing a change have to be aware of and know how to manage the political dynamics in the situation, because change often threatens some stakeholders' interests and this can motivate them to resist the change.

Aligning and coordinating

Those announcing the acquisition need to communicate in a way that promotes a shared sense of direction and aligns people so they can work in a coordinated way to implement the new vision. This is particularly important for those who are given responsibility to manage various aspects of the change; in the KeyChemicals/ Eco-Pure case, these tasks included securing a modest reduction in the number of managers employed and more substantial reductions in depot staff, closing two depots and moving chemical stocks to new locations, assimilating the Eco-Pure sales and technical support teams, communicating with Eco-Pure customers and suppliers, consolidating customer databases and other information systems, harmonizing terms and conditions and so on. When a change is complex and requires the implementation of a number of separate projects led by different managers, the resulting fragmentation can make it difficult to coordinate progress and cause confusion and waste when leaders make different assessments about what is required and prioritize different objectives.

Promoting trust and procedural justice

Trust can be promoted by management practices such as participative decision making, support and the meeting of expectations (Allen et al., 2007). Organizational members value adequate notice before decisions are implemented and expect to receive adequate and accurate information. Many also want the opportunity to voice their concerns and have an input into the decision process. Procedural justice and the promotion of feelings of trust are important because when organizational members feel they have been treated with respect and dealt with fairly, even if they are unhappy with the consequences of a decision, they will be less likely to engage in dysfunctional behaviours than when they feel they have received little support and have been unjustly treated.

If employees perceive unfairness in the way decisions are made about issues such as pay, allocation of roles and resources, relocation, severance and so on, this can have an adverse effect on their morale, organizational commitment and performance. Equity theory (Adams, 1963) holds that motivation is a function of fairness in social exchange and posits that if people feel they have been treated unfairly, they will take corrective action, which could involve behaving in ways that resist the acquisition. Greenberg's (1990) study of employee thefts as a reaction to underpayment inequity (see Research report 11.1) indicates that people react better to bad news when they believe senior managers are sensitive to their viewpoints, decisions are adequately explained and justified, and are applied consistently and without bias.

Responding to pressure to deliver quick wins

Even when those implementing a change try to adopt respectful management practices, these good intentions can be undermined if they are under pressure to deliver quick wins. When the change being implemented is an acquisition, members of the acquired company can be quick to react if they feel they are being managed in a heavy-handed way. Jemison and Sitkin (1986) suggest that when managers from the acquiring organization feel under pressure, this, coupled with an overconfidence in their own management capabilities, can lead them to adopt a heavy-handed approach, which typically involves imposing their way of doing things on the acquired business. They observe that when this occurs, the target firm's fundamental competences and capabilities, which may have been a part of what attracted the parent organization to acquire the target in the first place, are often dismissed or ignored. According to Jemison and Sitkin (1986), members of the acquired firm may experience this 'parent firm arrogance' in three ways:

VI

- They may perceive some measure of interpersonal arrogance in the way members of the acquired organization relate to them: 'Because we acquired you, we are smarter than you.'
- They may perceive a degree of cultural arrogance and the presumption that the acquiring firm's style, values, beliefs and practices are superior.
- They may perceive a level of managerial arrogance manifest in a presumption that the parent firm's systems and processes are superior.

Members of the acquired firm are unlikely to react well if everything they experience during the implementation phase signals that they are incompetent rather than just different.

Guest (1998) notes that people who feel they have received fair and respectful treatment engage in more positive 'organizational citizenship behaviours' and contribute more to the organization than they are contractually obliged to. Such high levels of organizational citizenship behaviour are desirable post-acquisition, because they can contribute to greater employee flexibility and help to accommodate the inevitable increase in workload that many will experience.

Providing socioemotional support

Employees develop global beliefs about the extent to which the organization values them and cares about their wellbeing. Rhoades and Eisenberger (2002) argue that these beliefs affect the degree to which they incorporate organizational membership into their social identity. Employees working for an organization that is being acquired can feel insecure, but those who feel that managers are doing their best to support them through the acquisition are less likely to feel alienated and more likely to identify with the merged organization than those who experience little socioemotional support.

Acquisitions are often experienced as discontinuities that disrupt the current equilibrium and jar people from their status quo. Some may perceive the prospect of change as an opportunity to be embraced, while others perceive it in terms of a loss of something valued and may respond by 'holding on' rather than 'letting go' (see Marks, 2007). For them, adapting to their changed circumstances can be difficult and this can have an adverse effect on the success of the acquisition. They typically react by going through a number of stages of psychological reaction, for example shock, denial, anger, feelings of helplessness and depression, before they can let go of their pre-merger organizational identity and begin to develop a new sense of identity with the post-merger organization. Some of the ways that managers can intervene to facilitate this process of adjustment are discussed in Chapter 13.

There are occasions when the discontinuity associated with an acquisition is great and largely unavoidable, but even then, effective communication, coupled with a genuine concern for the welfare of those affected, can help those involved to cope with the consequences of the change.

Example 25.5 *Managing the integration of the two organizations*

Very quickly after the announcement of the acquisition, the KeyChemicals managers responsible for the various integration projects arranged meetings with relevant employees from both companies. Some elements of the change were implemented with few problems, others were more difficult, often because of unanticipated technical problems, and some managers encountered strong resistance from employees who feared that the changes would harm their interests.

In addition to the normal project review procedures, the CEO held meetings with those who were leading particular projects to give them support and encourage them to share their experiences and learn from each other. The CEO, reporting back to the board, observed that the pre-planning had been helpful but that project leaders had found that it was not always possible to roll out plans as anticipated, and had encountered some problems that had not been anticipated or planned for. In these circumstances, what seemed to have affected (for better or worse) the way problems were resolved and the success of integration projects was the way those leading the change managed the people issues.

Having read this chapter, revisit the notes you made earlier on Case study 25.1, and consider whether the list of issues you considered needed attending to by those leading the acquisition of Eco-Pure needs to be amended.

Summary

Implementation is rarely a one-off activity. It tends to be ongoing and closely intertwined with other ongoing activities such as diagnosis and planning. Sometimes, these activities can be so closely intertwined that it can be difficult to distinguish implementation from diagnosis and planning, especially when an attempt to implement a change fails to deliver the expected outcome. In such circumstances, the failure to achieve the desired result can provide those leading the change with new insights (implementation becomes diagnosis) that inform new plans that are then implemented, and so the sequence continues.

This chapter examined implementation in the context of one company acquiring control of another and used this case to highlight some of the factors that can affect the success of any attempt to implement change. This acquisition example was used because it is a type of change that will be familiar to most readers.

Some of the many factors that can affect the success of an attempt to implement change include:

- The quality of the diagnosis of a perceived opportunity or threat, the specification of change goals, and the quality of pre-planning.
- The way the change is communicated. It is argued that, whenever possible, it can be helpful to provide all those who will be affected by a change with unambiguous information about what is going to happen. This does not always occur, sometimes because those implementing a change fear that unanticipated events may render information they have already communicated incorrect, sometimes because they fear that communicating with others and making commitment will restrict their ability to respond to unforeseen developments, and sometimes because they have concerns about leaking commercially sensitive information.
- The way stakeholders are managed. Those responsible for implementing a change have to be aware of and know how to manage the political dynamics in the situation because change often threatens some stakeholders' interests and this can motivate them to resist the change.
- The degree of alignment and coordination. Those announcing the acquisition need to communicate in a way that promotes a shared sense of direction and aligns people so that they can work in a coordinated way to implement the new vision. When a change is complex and requires the implementation of a number of separate projects led by different managers, the resulting fragmentation can make it difficult to coordinate progress and can cause confusion and waste when leaders make different assessments about what is required and, therefore, prioritize different objectives.
- The adoption of management practices that are perceived to be fair. When organizational members feel they have been treated with respect and dealt with fairly, even if they are unhappy with the consequences of a decision, they will be less likely to engage in dysfunctional behaviours than when they feel they have received little support and have been unjustly treated.
- The avoidance of a heavy-handed approach when managing those who may feel vulnerable.
- The provision of socioemotional support to help organizational members let go of the status quo.

VI

References

Adams, J.S. (1963) Toward an understanding of inequity, *Journal of Abnormal and Social Psychology*, 67(5): 422–36.

Allen, J., Jimmieson, N.L., Bordia, P. and Irmer, B.E. (2007) Uncertainty during organizational change: Managing perceptions through communication, *Journal of Change Management*, 7(2): 187–210.

Clampitt, P.G., DeKoch, R.J. and Cashman, T. (2000) A strategy for communicating about uncertainty, *Academy of Management Executive*, 14(4): 41–57.

Greenberg, J. (1990) Employee theft as a reaction to underpayment inequity: The hidden cost of pay cuts, *Journal of Applied Psychology*, 75(5): 561–8.

Guest, D. (1998) Is the psychological contract worth taking seriously?, *Journal of Organizational Behavior*, 19: 649–64.

Hubbard, N. (1999) *Acquisition: Strategy and Implementation.* Basingstoke: Macmillan – now Palgrave Macmillan.

Jemison, D.B. and Sitkin, S.B. (1986) Corporate acquisitions: A process perspective, *Academy of Management Review*, 11(1): 145–63.

Marks, M. (2007) A framework for facilitating adaptation to organizational transition, *Journal of Organizational Change Management*, 20(5): 721.

Marks, M.L. and Mirvis, P.H. (2001) Making mergers and acquisitions work: Strategic and psychological preparation, *Academy of Management Executive*, 15(2): 80–92.

Premack, S.L. and Wanous, J.P. (1985) A meta-analysis of realist job preview experiments, *Journal of Applied Psychology*, 70(4): 706–19.

Rhoades, L. and Eisenberger, R. (2002) Perceived organizational support: A review of the literature, *Journal of Applied Psychology*, 87(4): 698–714.

Schweiger, D.M. and DeNisi, A.S. (1991) Communication with employees following a merger: A longitudinal field experiment, *Academy of Management Journal*, 34(1): 100–35.

Chapter **26**

Reviewing and keeping the change on track

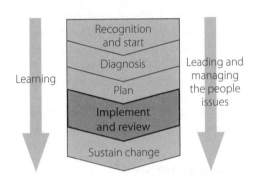

This chapter focuses attention on how the process of reviewing progress can provide change managers with feedback they can use to assess whether interventions are being implemented as intended, whether the chosen interventions are having the desired effect, and whether the change plan continues to be valid. Attention is also given to ways of measuring performance, the utility of the balanced scorecard as a template for designing a system for managing change, possibilities for embedding review as an essential element in the change process, and keeping track of how people are reacting to the change.

Managing the implementation stage of the change process

It was noted in Chapter 2 that there are two main approaches to implementation:

1 *Implementing blueprint change:* Here, the desired end state is known in advance and change managers are in a position to formulate a clear plan of action to achieve this vision. Implementation involves rolling out this plan, monitoring the effect of interventions and taking corrective action as and when required to ensure that the desired end state is achieved. Often, the validity of the blueprint is taken for granted and the learning associated with this kind of change tends to be restricted to detecting and correcting errors in the way the plan is rolled out. Assumptions about what needs to be changed and how the change will be achieved tend to go unchallenged unless the feedback from implementation is so unexpected that it shocks change managers into a radical reassessment.

2 *Implementing emergent change:* Here, it may be difficult or impossible to specify an end point in advance. Change managers have to develop an implementation plan on the basis of broadly defined goals and a general direction for change. Sometimes, because of a high rate of change in the operating environment, ideas about the desired future state have to be constantly revised, even when the original vision has only been defined in the broadest of terms. In such circumstances, change managers have to adopt an open-ended approach to planning and implementation. Managing emergent change involves taking tentative incremental steps and, after each step, reviewing the intervention(s) that constituted that step (did it/they work as planned?) and the general direction of change (does it still hold good or does it need to be revised?). This ques-

VI

451

tioning of the validity of the desired future state and the plan for achieving it calls for double-loop learning that involves challenging and, where necessary, revising the assumptions that underpin the change plan.

Monitoring the implementation of the change plan

A plan for change reflects a set of hypotheses about cause and effect. Kaplan and Norton (1996) view the measurement and review process as a means of making these hypothesized relationships explicit. They argue that once they are clearly articulated and widely understood, the change process can be more easily managed. The process of managing change involves validating or, where necessary, revising the assumptions and hypotheses that underpin the change plan. The desired future state (vision) is reflected in the outcome measures embedded in the change plan. Performance drivers are the variables that determine whether the desired outcome will be achieved. Specifying these in the change plan signals to organizational members what they need to do in order to contribute to the achievement of the desired future state.

Some of the questions that need to be addressed when managing change and validating the hypothesized cause-and-effect relationships that underpin the change plan are considered below.

Are interventions being implemented as intended?

Sometimes, it is more difficult than anticipated to roll out a plan for change. The change manager may respond by reviewing the situation and identifying those factors that have hindered implementation first time round. These might include a lack of commitment and motivation on the part of those immediately affected by a proposed intervention, a lack of political support from those in a position to champion or sabotage the change, or insufficient resources to ensure that the change initiative receives the attention it requires. The content of previous chapters points to ways of addressing these kinds of problems.

Are interventions producing the desired effect?

Change managers need to be alert to the possibility that while the intervention might have been implemented as intended, it might not be producing the effect that was anticipated. An example will illustrate this possibility and indicate ways in which the change manager might address the situation:

- A company might be losing market share because it is lagging behind competitors in the time it takes to bring new products to market.
- A factor contributing to this predicament might be diagnosed as the high level of conflict between members of the product engineering department, responsible for developing new products, and members of the production engineering department, responsible for developing the manufacturing system required to produce a new product.
- Informed by this diagnosis, the change manager might send members of both departments on a variety of external courses to learn about intergroup dynamics and the management of conflict.
- After monitoring the effect of this intervention, the change manager might discover that while members of both departments are much more aware of

constructive ways of behaving in conflict situations, this awareness has had little effect on the level of manifest conflict between the two departments.

An initial response might be to explore ways of modifying the original intervention in order to make it more effective, for example by seeking out opportunities to improve the transfer of learning from the training activity to the work situation:

- Rather than sending individuals on external courses, the change manager might decide to facilitate an in-house workshop designed to improve intergroup relations (see Change tool 16.1) that involves members of both departments working together to identify ways of managing their differences in a more constructive way.

If modifying the original intervention in this way still fails to produce the desired effect on the targeted performance driver, that is, the quality of interdepartmental relationships, the change manager might begin to question the assumed cause-and-effect relationship between poor conflict management skills and high levels of interdepartmental conflict. This questioning might point to other possible causes of the immediate problem (such as the organization's structure) and lead the change manager to consider ways of modifying the change plan to include interventions that target them:

- It might be found that the original diagnosis was valid, insofar as it identified the level of interdepartmental conflict as a major cause of delay in getting new products to market, leading to a loss of market share. However, it may have been flawed when it focused on poor conflict management skills as the root cause of this damaging behaviour.
- A re-examination of the situation might suggest that the main source of conflict is rooted in the way the company is structured. This broad heading could include a number of possible causal factors. One might be the siting of work groups in locations that make it difficult for members of one department to communicate on a face-to-face basis with members of the other. Another might be misaligned performance criteria that result in competing sets of priorities in the two departments.

This questioning of the taken-for-granted, cause-and-effect assumptions involves a process of double-loop learning.

VI

Is the change plan still valid?

There may be occasions where the interventions have been implemented as intended and have produced the desired effect. However, this chain of events may have had little or no impact on overall organizational performance. This kind of outcome poses another challenge to the validity of the change plan and the hypothesized cause-and-effect relationships on which it is based.

Faced with this kind of outcome, the change manager may decide to embark on a further re-examination of the original diagnosis and the causal models used to inform the design of the change plan:

- This further re-examination might reveal that, despite what many managers in the company believe to be the root cause of the problem, improvements in the time it takes to get new products to market may have had little effect on the gradual decline in market share. Further investigations might suggest that customers are more concerned about other value propositions, such as product reliability, price and so on, and might feel that competitors are better able to satisfy their needs in these areas.

- On the other hand, it may be that further investigations reveal that the original diagnosis was correct at the time, but has been overtaken by new developments, for example changes in customer requirements that challenge its validity, with obvious implications for the change plan.

There may also be (hopefully many) occasions when the interventions have been implemented as intended, have produced the desired effect and had a positive impact on organizational performance. This kind of positive outcome signals a need to consolidate this achievement and use it, as appropriate, as a basis for achieving further improvements in performance.

The role of performance measures in the management of change

Some of the issues that encourage or inhibit learning are discussed at the end of Chapter 2 and in Chapter 29. This chapter focuses attention on how the cycle of monitoring, reviewing, planning, acting and further reviewing can minimize some of the problems that undermine the success of a change plan and help to keep the change on track. Central to this review process is the collecting and feeding back of information about how interventions affect performance.

Attention has already been given to some of the different ways in which performance can be measured (see Chapter 4). It is essential that performance measures should be related to the outcomes that are important to key stakeholders and to the hypotheses about cause-and-effect relationships embedded in the change plan. Without the feedback that such measures can provide, change managers will be unable to monitor what is going on and determine what further action may be required to successfully implement the change plan.

Approaches to measuring performance

It was noted in Chapter 15 that many control systems are designed to reward current practice and offer little incentive for people to invest effort in changing the organization to promote long-term effectiveness. Even in those organizations where change is given a high priority, the monitoring and feedback process may only focus attention on a limited set of performance measures. Many organizations direct most of their attention to financial measures, and often too little attention is given to other performance indicators that relate to important outcomes and key cause-and-effect relationships that are central to the change plan.

One of the early attempts to widen the base of performance monitoring on an organization-wide and systematic basis was the development of a 'corporate score-card' by Analog Devices in 1987. Alongside a number of traditional financial measures, this included measures of customer delivery time, quality and cycle times of manufacturing processes, and effectiveness of new product development.

Kaplan and Norton (2004) report that they became interested in new ways of monitoring performance when they recognized the importance of knowledge-based assets, such as employees and information technology, as determinants of competitive success. They believe that managers and others pay attention to what is measured and they are not good at managing that which is not measured. Therefore, if they are to manage, develop and mobilize the organization's intangible assets, managers need a performance management system that measures how these assets are used. This led them to develop what is now referred to as the 'balanced scorecard'.

The balanced scorecard

The balance scorecard (Kaplan and Norton, 1996) integrates financial measures of past performance with measures of the 'drivers' of future performance. It provides a template that can be adapted to provide the information change managers need to monitor and review the effects of their interventions and to plan what they might do next to move the organization towards a more desirable future state. The scorecard includes four categories of measures: financial, customer, internal business process, and innovation and learning:

1 *Financial measures:* summarize the economic consequences of past actions, such as return on investment, economic value added, sales growth and generation of cash flow. This financial perspective considers how the organization needs to appear to its shareholders if it is to achieve its vision.

2 *Customer-related measures:* include indicators of business performance that relate to the customer and market segments that are important to the organization, such as measures of satisfaction, retention, new customer acquisition, customer profitability, account share and market share. They might also include measures of those performance drivers that affect the value propositions that influence customer loyalty, such as on-time delivery and product innovation. This customer perspective considers how the organization needs to appear to its customers if it is to achieve its vision.

3 *Internal business process measures:* those internal business processes that make a critical contribution to the organization's current and future performance, such as quality, response time and cost. They might measure the performance of the processes that enable the organization to deliver value propositions that attract and retain important customers, satisfy shareholders by contributing to the delivery of excellent financial returns, or deliver other outcomes that are important to key stakeholders.

4 *Innovation and learning:* there are three principle sources: people, systems and organizational procedures. Kaplan and Norton suggest that the financial, customer and internal business process objectives typically reveal large gaps between the existing capabilities of people, systems and procedures and the capability required to achieve a performance breakthrough. In order to transform an organization, or even achieve a more modest level of change, these gaps have to be addressed. This can involve intervening in the normal process of organizational functioning to enhance this infrastructure and improve the organization's capacity for innovation and learning

The balanced scorecard can be adapted to focus on those performance drivers and measures that are identified as important in specific situations.

Developing tools to help monitor implementation

The balanced scorecard approach can be adapted to focus on those performance drivers and measures that are identified as important in specific situations and used as a change management tool to clarify and gain consensus about the change

VI

strategy. Translating the vision and change strategy into an agreed set of operational goals (see Figure 26.1) is likely to stimulate a debate that will ensure that the change management team develops a shared understanding of what they are seeking to achieve. Specifying operational goals can also help the change management team to think about their plan for change in systemic terms and develop a shared view of how and why the various change goals are related in terms of cause and effect.

Figure **26.1** *Translating the change strategy into a set of operational goals*

The feedback this kind of tool can provide on how the organization or unit of an organization is performing will enable change managers to test the validity of the cause-and-effect relationships (change hypothesis) embedded in the change plan.

Kaplin and Norton (1996) cite the example of Echo Engineering, where change managers were able to test and validate their assumption that employee morale was a key performance driver. They found that employee morale correlated with a number of important performance indicators; for example, the most satisfied customers were served by employees with the highest morale, and the most satisfied customers settled their accounts in the shortest period.

Several studies report findings that suggest that favourable employee perceptions are related to superior business performance. Koys (2001) found that the level of employee satisfaction and commitment in a chain of restaurants was positively related to profitability. Gelade and Young (2005) cite a meta-analysis by Harter et al. (2002) of 7,939 work units in 36 companies, which found small but significant correlations between business unit productivity and profitability and a composite of items they labelled 'employee engagement'. They also cite a study by Patterson et al. (2004) that reported significant associations between company climate and productivity in a sample of 42 manufacturing companies.

Heskett et al. (1994) argue that customer satisfaction is a critical intervening variable in the employee attitude–profit relationship. Their work has stimulated a lot of interest in the service profit chain (Figure 26.2). The basic premise is that employee satisfaction is positively related to employee commitment and increased commitment promotes customer satisfaction and motivates customers to stay with the company longer and recommend the company's products and services to others. This, in turn, stimulates revenue growth and profitability. Culbertson (2009) confirms that this is indeed a winning proposition.

Figure **26.2** *The service profit chain*

Management tools, such as the balanced scorecard, not only facilitate the development of a shared view of how and why the various change goals are related in terms of cause and effect, but can also help change managers to communicate their change plan throughout the organization and provide a framework for consultation and debate about what a more desirable future state will look like and what needs to happen if it is to be achieved. This kind of management tool can also help to ensure that the range of change initiatives that might be started in different units and at different levels in the organization will be aligned to contribute to the strategic goals of the change programme.

The balanced scorecard approach is presented here as one example of a tool that can help those leading a change to manage the change process. In any change programme, plans have to be operationalized and communicated widely. Furthermore, targets for change have to be specified as clearly as possible if progress is to be monitored and if the change plan is to be kept under review and adjusted as circumstances require.

Building review into the process of managing change

The case of customer care at Maersk Line provides a good example of how reviewing implementation can be woven in as an essential element of the change process (Example 26.1).

Example **26.1** *Customer care at Maersk Line*

Maersk Line is the global container division and the largest operating unit of the A.P. Moller-Maersk Group, a Danish business conglomerate. Its fleet comprises more than 600 vessels and it is the largest container shipping company in the world.

This case examines one thread of a major change programme at Maersk Line; making the organization more customer centric. Early steps in the process focused on identifying problems and opportunities, making the case for change and developing a vision of the customer experience that Maersk Line aspired to deliver.

Customer experience councils and customer mirrors (similar to the organization mirror described in Change tool 16.2) helped managers develop a good understanding of the current customer experience and possibilities for improvement and led to the specification of three targets for change:

1 *Passionate employees who know and care:* deliverables associated with this target included the allocation of a dedicated care business partner to every customer, establishing a care promise, and developing the emotional competences that would enable colleagues to relate effectively with customers.

2 *Proactive service and information sharing:* deliverables associated with this target included end-to-end shipment management based on globalized 'visibility reports' and automated ETA change notifications to customers.

VI

▶

3 *Transparent issue resolution:* deliverables under this heading included the implementation of an online issue centre across all functions.

It was recognized that in order to achieve these targets, it would be necessary to change the mindset and behaviours of 3,000 employees working around the world in 125 different countries. Johnny Schmidt, global head of customer service, believed that the best way of making this change happen was to engage as many people as possible in co-creating and implementing customer care. This involved building on best practices from around the world, accepting a trial-and-error roll-out and allowing local variations to facilitate implementation.

The coordinated implementation of customer care required careful attention to stakeholder management and communications. All the principles discussed in Chapters 10 and 11 were used to identify important stakeholders and assess their engagement, develop messages that promoted personal as well as corporate benefits along with messages that clarified responsibilities and accountabilities, and design a communication blueprint that specified who would deliver these carefully crafted messages to specific stakeholders in prescribed ways at given points in time.

Considerable effort was invested in planning how the change would be implemented. Two kinds of project plan were developed, detailed plans for those tasked to deliver particular aspects of the change and an 'easy overview plan' that enabled everybody involved to be informed about the big picture, key deliverables and deadlines.

Training and development was an important element of the plan. Training was viewed as an ongoing process that supported every step of the change. It involved developing competences in change management, including the development of managers down the line as coaches. It also involved developing the competences that employees across the business would need to support the new behaviours required to improve the customer experience. Using many of the principles discussed in Chapter 19, a system-level review identified those areas in the business where the change would trigger a need to develop new skill sets, task analyses led to the development of job roles and competency descriptions, and person analyses provided the data to prepare personal development plans.

An impressive part of the customer care programme was the attention given to measuring and reviewing how the change was being implemented. Progress reports and quarterly internal employee surveys produced data that were used to develop detailed assessments of progress, which were summarized and presented as a set of dashboards. For each aspect of the change, the dashboards identified key deliverables and milestones and used a set of bold symbols to signal progress.

Three examples illustrate this approach.

Timeline and milestones

Enable change leadership

Build sense of purpose and commitment among leaders; provide leadership development	Develop change capability; coach leaders to lead the change and enhance performance	Coach leaders to drive implementation and lead employee engagement	Continue to coach and develop leaders at all levels throughout the organization

Engage and enable people

Identify all stakeholders and understand their needs and motivation	Engage people and manage expectations; share the vision and communicate the benefits	Manage people engagement and participation; build understanding, skills and commitment	Use new skills and working practices to drive momentum

Embed new behaviours

Assess readiness for change and cultural alignment	Articulate future desired ways of working and engage people in defining the required change	Release energy for addressing cultural issues and improving readiness to change	Gather staff views on a regular basis and adapt/refresh approach accordingly

Progress – low ⃝ ◔ ◑ ◕ ● high

The first dashboard indicates that enabling change leadership down the line was emerging as a key challenge. While the dashboard flags a need to explore an issue, it does not diagnose the cause, but provides timely signals to those leading the change that some action is required. The other two dashboards indicate that managing people engagement got off to a good start, slowed down later on but was getting back on track. People across the business were using their new skills and working practices to drive the change. There had also been good progress identifying and embedding the new behaviours. Early on, there had been excellent progress assessing the readiness for change and engaging people in articulating and defining what needed to happen. It was always recognized that addressing some of the cultural issues involved in the change would not be easy but again

good progress was being made. Those leading the change recognized that seeking feedback from staff and using this to adapt the change as required to sustain the improved customer experience was an activity that would require ongoing attention.

Three extensive external customer surveys sent to 3,736 customers tracked the impact of the change programme on customers' experience. One of the key indicators that showed significant improvement was the 'ease of doing business with Maersk Line'.

The customer care change programme started in 2009. By 2011, the focus had moved to consolidating improvements and integrating customer care into the DNA of Maersk Line. Ensuring customer centricity continues to be one of the company's key differentiators and remains a priority today.

VI

Reviewing how people are responding to the change

Over the long term, change managers can use measures such as customer satisfaction, customer retention and the bottom line to assess the validity of the change plan. Over a shorter timescale, they may focus attention on whether interventions are being implemented as intended and are producing the immediate outcomes that were anticipated. Another source of feedback is employees' collective perceptions of the way the changes are being managed and the effect this has on their experience of and attitudes towards the changes. Just as normal day-to-day management practices can have a powerful impact on the work climate and the willingness of organizational members to contribute to organizational performance, so the way changes are managed can have a powerful impact on how organizational members experience change, their attitudes towards the change, and their readiness to support it.

It could be argued that resistance to change is inevitable and therefore employees are not good judges of how well a change is being managed. However, since one of the main imperatives of change is to win over hearts and minds and get people to buy in to change, their feedback is important. One way to gain this feedback is given in Change tool 26.1.

🔧 *Change tool* **26.1** *The change management indicator*

Hayes and Hyde (2008) have developed the change management indicator (CMI) as a structured means of providing this feedback. It is available as an online survey (www.peterhyde.co.uk) and can be used in a number of ways:

- as a one-off diagnostic instrument to identify major areas of concern for remedial action
- as a barometer of opinion at a series of points in time, indicating whether the trend is in the desired direction
- to compare the situation in different departments, functions, locations and organizational levels and thereby identify localized problems
- as an intervention in its own right, to get people thinking about the issues and to promote dialogue
- to benchmark against other organizations undergoing similar changes.

The model underpinning the CMI (Figure 26.3) proposes that people's experience of organizational change and their attitudes towards the change are influenced by four key elements. Two of these can be difficult to affect, especially over the short term:

1 The inherent nature of the change itself. It will be hard, for example, to get positive feedback about a change if it is inherently painful, such as the closure of a facility.
2 The personality and temperamental characteristics of the people involved. Some people will be more receptive to change and others more resistant.

There are, however, two important elements of the model that change managers can do something about:

3 The change management practices they adopt, such as developing the vision for the change, leadership, planning and organization, communication, consultation and support.
4 The way their overall strategy for change is represented 'down the line' by local management. Middle managers often struggle to find the right way to position

themselves, but it seems clear that if they are not actively supportive of the corporate strategy for change, it is highly unlikely their subordinates will buy into it.

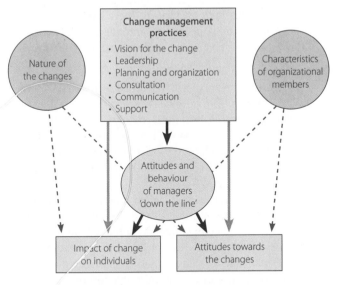

Figure **26.3** *Factors affecting how people respond to the change*
Source: Hayes and Hyde, 2008

Failure to pay attention to the way a change is being managed can adversely affect the achievement of change objectives and/or the timescale for implementing the change. It can also undermine staff morale and commitment to the organization, cause reputational damage, and tie up scarce resources firefighting and managing the unintended consequences of the change process.

Summary

This chapter considered how monitoring and reviewing the implementation of a change can help managers to adjust and adapt the plan for change to help ensure that the organization moves towards a more desirable future state.

Attention was given to the kind of information change managers need in order to determine whether interventions are being implemented as intended and assess whether they are having the anticipated effect, including their impact on key stakeholder groups, and to assess whether the change plan continues to be valid. Assessing the continued validity of the change plan, and updating it as required, is especially important when managing emergent change. Key questions that change managers need to address are:

- *Are interventions being implemented as intended?* Sometimes, it is more difficult than anticipated to roll out a plan for change. The change manager may respond by reviewing the situation and identifying those factors that have hindered implementation first time round. These might include a lack of commitment and motivation on the part of those immediately affected by a proposed intervention, a lack of political support from those in a position to champion or sabotage the change, or insufficient resources to ensure that the change initiative gets the attention it requires.

VI

- *Are interventions producing the desired effect?* Change managers need to be alert to the possibility that while the intervention might have been implemented as intended, it might not be producing the effect that was anticipated.
- *Is the change plan still valid?* There may be occasions where the interventions have been implemented as intended and have produced the desired effect. However, this chain of events may have had little or no impact on overall organizational performance.

When the interventions have had a positive impact on organizational performance, this achievement needs to be consolidated and used as a basis for achieving further improvements in performance.

It was argued that change managers need to identify measures of organization effectiveness that relate to those outcomes that are important to the organization's long-term survival and growth. This might involve attending to more than just the short-term interests of shareholders.

It was also argued that, when monitoring the effectiveness of interventions, attention needs to be paid to the cause-and-effect hypotheses that have influenced the design of the change plan. Where feedback raises questions about the validity of these hypothesized relationships, those leading a change need to review the change plan and consider whether alternative ways of intervening to move the organization towards a more desirable future state might be more effective.

The balanced scorecard was considered as an example of a management tool that can help the manager attend to these points when managing change.

References

Culbertson, S.S. (2009) Do satisfied employees mean satisfied customers?, *Academy of Management Perspectives*, 23(1): 76–81.

Gelade, G. and Young, S. (2005) Test of a service profit chain model in the retail banking sector, *Journal of Occupational and Organizational Psychology*, 78(1): 1–22.

Harter, J.K., Schmidt, F.L. and Hayes, T.L. (2002) Business unit-level relationship between employee satisfaction, employee engagement, and business outcomes: A meta-analysis, *Journal of Applied Psychology*, 87(2): 268–79.

Hayes, J. and Hyde, P. (2008) The Change Management Indicator, www.peterhyde.co.uk/documents/TheChangeManagementIndicator.pdf.

Heskett, J.L., Jones, T.O., Loveman, G.W. et al. (1994) Putting the service-profit chain to work, *Harvard Business Review*, 72(2): 164–74.

Kaplan, R.S. and Norton, D.P. (1996) *The Balanced Scorecard: Translating Strategy into Action.* Boston, MA: Harvard Business School Press.

Kaplan, R.S. and Norton, D.P. (2004) *Strategy Maps: Converting Intangible Assets into Tangible Outcomes.* Boston, MA: Harvard Business School Press.

Koys, D.J. (2001) The effects of employee satisfaction, organizational citizenship behaviour and turnover on organizational effectiveness: A unit-level, longitudinal study, *Personnel Psychology*, 54(1): 101–14.

Patterson, M., Warr, R. and West, M.A. (2004) Organizational climate and company productivity: The role of employee affect and employee level, *Journal of Occupational and Organizational Psychology*, 77(2): 193–216.

 Visit **www.palgrave.com/companion/hayes-change-management4** *for further learning resources*

Part **VII**

SUSTAINING CHANGE

Introduction to Part **VII**

Lewin (1951) argued that all too often change is short-lived. After a 'shot in the arm', life returns to the way it was before. In his view, it is not enough to think of change in terms of simply reaching a new state. Attention also needs to be given to maintaining this new state for as long as it is relevant.

Part VII considers two aspects of sustainability, making change stick and spreading change across the system.

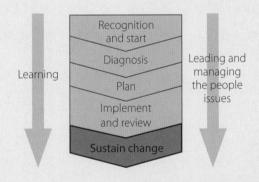

Chapter **27** *Making change stick*

Sustainability has been defined in many different ways. Some definitions are relatively static, focusing on the maintenance of improvements within a particular setting, whereas others are more dynamic and concerned with translating initial gains into a process of continuous improvement.

This chapter explores some of the reasons why change is not sustained and some of the ways those leading change can help promote 'stickability' and maintain improvements. Attention is given to:

- How the way the whole change process is managed from the beginning can affect stickability. Tough top-down (push) strategies are more likely to foster compliance, which can evaporate when the pressure to maintain the change is eased.
- How change managers can act to sustain change after initial change goals have been achieved.

Chapter **28** *Spreading change*

This chapter looks at 'spreadability', the extent to which new methods and processes that have delivered gains in one location are applied, or adapted, and then used elsewhere across the organization.

Attention is given to three factors that can affect spread:

1 attributes of the innovation
2 context – reflected by the organization's climate for implementation

3 the values of potential users, and their perception of the extent to which the innovation will foster or inhibit the fulfilment of their values.

It is noted that many of the factors that promote stickability also support spread. Buchanan and Fitzgerald observe that the manner in which a change is spread can influence the degree to which it will be sustained. When changes are rolled out hastily, without much consultation, with few incentives and inadequate training, they may quickly decay. Similarly, changes that do not have support and are not sustained are unlikely to spread elsewhere.

✓ *Exercise* **Part VII** *Useful questions for reviewing your approach to sustaining change*

In Chapter 2, after discussing each stage in the process model of change management, your attention was drawn to a number of questions that might help you assess how well a change is being (or was) managed. All these questions are summarized in Figure 2.5 and the questions relating to sustaining change are listed below:

- Do change managers pursue a change strategy that wins long-term commitment?
- Do they reinforce changes post-implementation?
- Do they avoid declaring victory too soon?
- Is sufficient attention given to managing the consequences of churn?

Reflect on and review these questions and, after reading the two chapters in Part VII, revise this list and generate your own set of useful questions that you might find it helpful to refer to when you are leading a change.

Chapter **27**

Making change stick

Lewin (1951) argued that all too often change is short-lived. After a 'shot in the arm', life returns to the way it was before. In his view, it is not enough to think of change in terms of simply reaching a new state. Attention also needs to be given to maintaining this new state for as long as it is relevant. As discussed in Chapter 2, he conceptualized change as a three-stage process. The first involves unfreezing the individual, group or system from the status quo and creating a readiness for change. The second involves moving to a new state, and the final stage involves refreezing behaviour at this new level, for as long as it is beneficial to do so.

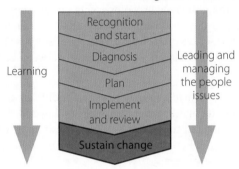

This caveat, for as long as it is beneficial, is important because there are circumstances where it may not be beneficial to continue to maintain a change. The change may not have been successful or it may have produced unanticipated consequences that are inconsistent with the change plan. Buchanan and Fitzgerald (2007, p. 25) also argue that sustaining change can be counterproductive when:

- changes in the wider environment render recently implemented working practices, outcomes and lines of development obsolete
- maintaining recently implemented practices impedes further and more significant developments.

This chapter reviews evidence from different sectors, which indicates that it is often difficult to achieve Lewin's stage of refreezing and sustaining change. After discussing two aspects of sustainability, this chapter takes a closer look at 'stickability' and what managers can do to consolidate a change and hold on to gains. Chapter 28 takes a closer look at the second aspect of sustainability, how successful changes can be rolled out across the organization.

VII

Sustainability

Sustainability has been defined in many different ways. Some definitions focus on the embedding of new processes, whereas others focus attention on performance improvements 'independent of the methods employed' (Buchanan et al., 2005). Some definitions are relatively static, focusing on the maintenance of improvements within a particular setting, whereas others are more dynamic and are concerned with translating initial gains into a process of continuous improvement.

Dale (1996), for example, defines sustainability in terms of increasing the pace of improvement while holding the gains made. The NHS Modernisation Agency (2002, p. 12) defines it as the state where 'new ways of working and improved outcomes become the norm' and where 'the thinking and attitudes behind them are fundamentally altered and the systems surrounding them are transformed in support'. In other words, according to the Modernisation Agency, change is sustained when it becomes an integrated or mainstream way of working rather than something 'added on'. Buchanan and Fitzgerald (2007, p. 22) conclude that while sustainability can be defined in different ways in relation to work methods, goals or continuous improvements, covering differing timescales, 'the definition and timing that matter are those applicable to a particular organizational setting'.

Bateman and David (2002) developed a model to investigate the level of sustainability achieved in 21 companies following intensive shop-floor process improvement interventions. Their model operationalizes some of these different ways of conceptualizing sustainability. It comprises two elements. The first identifies five different levels of sustainability at cell level, ranging from realizing but then failing to hold on to gains to not only maintaining the new way of working but also applying the tools and techniques learned to new problems as they arise (see Figure 27.1). The second element of the model focuses on factory-level improvements and identifies the degree to which tools and techniques have been spread between cells (see Figure 27.2). The two elements are:

1 *Cell-level sustainability:* Bateman and David's (2002) research indicated that while all cell-based interventions led to significant improvements, beyond that point, there were considerable variations in the extent to which these improvements were sustained (see Figure 27.1 and Research report 27.1 for more details).

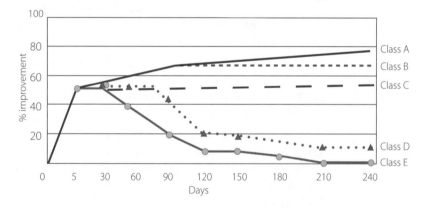

Figure **27.1** *Classes of sustainability at cell level*
Source: Bateman and David, 2002, p. 520. Copyright Emerald Group Publishing Limited, all rights reserved.

2 *Sustainability at factory level:* While cell-level improvements (level 1 in Figure 27.2) are often the initial focus of many lean manufacturing interventions, the longer term aim is usually a more broadly based change at factory level. However, cell-level changes may not always spread across the factory. Bateman and David (2002) report that there are often immediate possibilities for replicating improvements made in the initial activity to other manufacturing cells where the machines or processes are the same or similar (level 2). It may be more difficult

to apply the same tools and techniques used to achieve improvements to cells where different machines or processes are used (level 3). Achieving level 4 is even more difficult, as this is where further process improvements involve changes in new areas that require the learning and application of new tools and techniques. Sustainability across the factory at level 5 is achieved when improvements are coordinated in a value stream across the site.

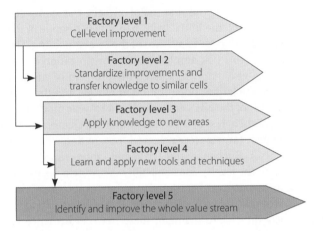

Figure **27.2** *Factory-level improvement model*

Source: Adapted from Bateman and David, 2002, p. 520

This chapter draws on Bateman and David's (2002) model and explores just one aspect of sustainability – the extent to which gains are held. The extent to which changes are spread across the organization is considered in Chapter 28.

Before reading further, complete Exercise 27.1.

✓ *Exercise* **27.1** *Factors undermining 'stickability'*

Reflect on your experience of change and identify some of the occasions when new ways of working and performance gains were not maintained. List below some of the factors you think undermined stickability and contributed to change decay. If you do not have much experience of being employed in a work organization, think about the persistence of a change in another context, such as in your university society or sports club.

	Factors contributing to change decay	Reason
1		
2		
3		

VII

Stickability: holding on to gains

Research on what is referred to here as 'stickability' indicates that while many change initiatives are successful, there is considerable variation in the level of sustainability achieved. Kotter (1995) reports numerous examples of the failure to sustain change. He observes that gains achieved in 10 out of 12 re-engineering change programmes evaporated because 'victory' was declared too soon, for example as soon as the first major project was completed. According to Kotter, within two years, the initial gains had slowly disappeared and, in 2 of the 10 cases, it was soon hard to find any trace of the re-engineering. He reports seeing the same thing happen to a vast number of other organization development projects.

Buchanan et al. (2007a) studied the problem of sustainability and spread in the UK's NHS, the largest organization in Europe and the fifth largest employer in the world. In 2000, the NHS embarked on a 10-year modernization initiative. Priorities were established, resources were committed, changes were implemented, and many improvement targets were achieved. But, in line with evidence from the manufacturing sector, Buchanan and Fitzgerald (2007) report that there was considerable variation in the levels of sustainability that were achieved. In some areas, gains were maintained but in others improvements evaporated. For example, some clinical services developed ways of dramatically reducing patient waiting times, but found it extremely difficult to maintain these new performance levels and, over time, the improvements were eroded and performance fell back to the original level.

Sustainability can be affected by what change managers do early on and towards the end of the change process.

Acting early to promote sustainability

From the start, the way a change is managed can affect stickability. When Lewin's theories were discussed in Chapter 2, it was noted that the behaviour of an individual, group or wider system is maintained in a condition of quasi-stationary equilibrium by a force-field comprising a balance of forces pushing for and resisting change. This level of behaviour can be changed by either adding forces for change in the desired direction or reducing the opposing or resisting forces.

Both approaches can result in change but, according to Lewin, the secondary effects associated with each approach will be different. Where change is brought about by increasing the forces pushing for change, this increases the tension experienced by those affected by the change. If this rises beyond a certain level, it may be accompanied by high emotionality and low levels of constructive behaviour. Increasing the driving forces for change can be likened to pushing on a coiled spring (Figure 27.3). If change managers exert enough pressure, people will be forced to comply, but if this pressure is released, the lack of commitment on the part of those forced to comply could cause the change to evaporate and the situation to 'spring back' to its former state.

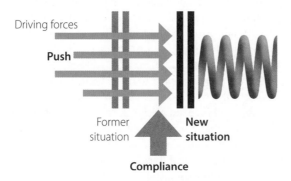

Figure **27.3** *A push approach to securing change*

On the other hand, where change is brought about by diminishing the forces that oppose or resist the change, the secondary effect is likely to be a state of relatively low tension. This argument led Lewin to advocate an approach to managing change that focused attention on reducing the restraining forces in preference to a high pressured approach that only focused on increasing the forces pushing for change. He argued that approaches that reduced the restraining forces were more likely to generate commitment and create the pull effect that will result in a more permanent change.

These principles underpin action research. This approach to improving performance is more bottom up than top down. It recognizes that many people may have information that is relevant to the problems that undermine performance and seeks to involve them in the change process. Evidence (see Chapter 17) suggests that this involvement promotes psychological ownership of the problem and gains commitment to the problem-solving process. There is also evidence that it facilitates the implementation of new methods and processes, and there is every reason to believe that this same involvement will help build the commitment that will sustain change.

Promoting sustainability later in the change process

Successful change efforts can be undermined because too little attention is given to holding on to gains once the change objectives appear to have been achieved.

Reference has already been made to change managers declaring victory too soon. This can encourage them to switch their attention and resources to other projects. Kotter (1995) advocates that instead of declaring victory early on, change managers should use the credibility afforded by early wins to go on and modify some of the systems and structures that may be inconsistent with the transformation vision.

Attention also needs to be given to the attitudes and priorities of those affected by the change. Fine et al. (2008) assert that too many companies emphasize the technical aspects of change and neglect many of the related softer issues. The rush to implement toolkit-led solutions without first ensuring that employees – including managers – are prepared to adapt and work with them can contribute to the evaporation of any early performance gains. Involving people at an early stage can help to win over their hearts and minds. Kotter (1995), like those who lead the NHS Modernisation Agency, believes that change sticks when it is rooted in the organization's social norms and shared values. Until this has been achieved, change will be subject to degradation as soon as the pressures to maintain it are removed.

In his seminal *Harvard Business Review* paper, Leading change: Why transformation efforts fail, Kotter (1995) identifies ways in which managers can help to embed change in the organization's culture. The first involves providing feedback and drawing people's attention to how new ways of doing things are making a difference. When people are left to make their own connections, they may attribute any successes to the wrong factors and overlook their own contribution. Relevant, understandable and focused feedback can help to keep people's efforts directed to those things that really are making a difference. Several writers (Beckhard and Harris, 1987; Nadler, 1993) argue that tailored feedback mechanisms not only facilitate monitoring and control during the transition phase of a change, but can also be effective in helping to sustain change. Change managers need to work with those operational managers who will have ongoing responsibility for day-to-day management once the change has been implemented to design feedback mechanisms they can use for themselves to monitor and manage the situation over the longer term. Kotter's (1995) second factor relates to the constant churn in many organizations that results in managers moving on partway through a change project. Kotter argues that care needs to be exercised to ensure that the next generation of senior managers continues to support the new approach.

Many researchers have pointed to specific ways in which sustainability can be promoted. For example, Bateman (2005) found that with shop-floor interventions in the manufacturing sector, two categories of enablers appeared to stand out as most important:

1 processes for promoting 'contribution and buy-in' during the early stages of implementation
2 processes promoting 'maintenance of standards and continuous improvement' once the initial changes had been successfully implemented (see Research report 27.1).

Brown (2009) surveyed the opinion of 15 fellow change consultants at KPMG about sustainability and found that 65 per cent of their comments focused on three barriers to sustainability:

- the organization's approach to change
- the quality of leadership

- employees' level of understanding about what was expected of them following the change.

There was less agreement about enablers but engagement and communication were referred to most frequently.

Buchanan et al. (2005) report a more complex picture. On the basis of a thorough review of the literature, they identify several categories of factors that interact in different ways to affect sustainability, including the scale and type of change, individual commitment and competences, managerial style, the quality of leadership, organizational culture, and political processes. The relative importance of these factors is determined by context. For example, a management style that elicits enthusiastic commitment in one setting may trigger cynicism, resentment and a lack of support for change in another. Consequently, Buchanan et al. (2005) felt that more work would have to be done before they could offer change managers any simple prescription for sustaining change. However, they did point to three issues that seem to affect the extent of initiative decay:

1 *How the change is perceived:* Is it peripheral or central to organizational performance and is it perceived as acceptable or threatening by key stakeholders? Often, change managers can influence the way a change is perceived and this will have consequences for sustainability.

2 *How the change is implemented:* As noted above, there is no one implementation process that will be effective in all settings, but doing everything possible to identify and adopt an appropriate process can affect whether or not the change will be sustained.

3 *The timing, sequencing and pacing of the change process:* For example, while a relaxed timetable might help people to digest the need for change, delays can undermine commitment and divert attention to other pressing issues. On the other hand, when a change is rushed, people may not feel involved and a succession of change initiatives may lead to initiative fatigue.

Research report 27.1 *Two enablers that help to promote stickability*

Bateman, N. (2005) Sustainability: The elusive element of process improvement, *International Journal of Operations and Production Management*, 25(3): 261–76.

Bateman studied the application of a standard process improvement intervention (the SMMT Industry Forum MasterClass) at 40 sites across 21 companies in order to identify enablers for sustaining change. The intervention was in three parts:

1 *A diagnostic phase* to establish a baseline in terms of quality, cost and delivery, and to identify what needed to be done to achieve improvement.

2 *A five-day workshop*, in which an improvement team learned about and applied process improvement tools (such as the seven wastes referred to in Chapter 22) using a PDSA cycle. This led to the identification of new working methods and a list of technical changes that needed to be made.

3 *A follow-up phase*, during which the improvement team worked to maintain new methods and close out the technical issues identified in the workshop.

The 40 interventions were reviewed after 90 days and again sometime later in order to assign them to one of five classes in terms of the extent to which process improvements had been sustained:

- Class A interventions succeeded in maintaining the new working practices, completing outstanding issues identified in the workshop and applying the new process improvement tools to new problems.

VII

- Class B interventions succeeded in maintaining the new working practices and completing outstanding issues.
- Class C interventions succeeded in maintaining the new working practices, but failed to complete the outstanding issues identified in the workshop.
- Class D interventions succeeded in completing the technical issues identified in the workshop, but failed to maintain the new operating procedures. This led to some improvements in operating performance through technical solutions but possibilities for improvements through changes in working practices were not realized.
- Class E interventions failed to maintain new operation procedures or to close out technical issues.

A list of potential enablers was generated after consulting Japanese and British 'master engineers' and reviewing the literature. This long list was then refined by screening out those potential enablers that could not be measured or were not amenable to modification by the change agents or others involved in the intervention. Data were collected to identify which enablers were associated with each class of sustainability.

Bateman found that the enablers that differentiated class A and B from class C, D and E interventions could be grouped into two categories:

1 *Processes for promoting 'contribution and buy-in' by cell members:*
- methods for recording issues and ideas
- methods for reviewing and prioritizing issues and ideas
- processes that enable operators to act on ideas and make team decisions about the way they work
- processes for enabling team members to review actions and identify further action required.

2 *Processes promoting maintenance of standards and continuing focus on process improvement activity:*
- allocating time, on a daily basis, for maintaining standards
- measuring improvement
- managers staying focused on performance improvement.

Classification	Improvement in workshop?	Maintained new procedure?	Closed out technical issues?	Continuous improvement?
Class A	✓	✓	✓	✓
Class B	✓	✓	✓	✗
Class C	✓	✓	✗	✗
Class D	✓	✗	✓	✗
Class E	✓	✗	✗	✗

Following extensive research, while still recognizing the complex interplay of factors that affect sustainability, Buchanan et al. (2007b, p. 259) identified 10 recurrent problems and offered practical advice about how each might be addressed.

1 *Those who initiated the change move on to another organization:*
- design career development and reward policies to motivate and retain key change agents
- choose successors with similar competences and aspirations.
2 *Accountability for development becomes diffused:*
- establish clear project and line management responsibilities
- ensure appropriate and visible rewards for those responsible for driving change.
3 *Knowledge and experience of new practices is lost through turnover:*
- develop retention strategies to minimize such losses
- develop a 'buy-back' policy to involve leavers in induction and training for new staff.

4 *Old habits are imported with recruits from less dynamic organizations:*
  - strengthen the induction and training regime for recruits.
5 *The issues and pressures that triggered the change initiative are no longer visible:*
  - communicate in a way that keeps these issues in the forefront of staff thinking
  - identify new reinforcing issues and pressures.
6 *New managers want to drive their own agenda:*
  - support where appropriate but also ensure that they are given an explicit remit to work with and not dismantle particular changes introduced by their predecessors.
7 *Powerful stakeholders are using counter-implementation tactics to block progress:*
  - when reason fails, develop a 'counter-counter-implementation' strategy to reduce their influence.
8 *Pump-priming funds run out:*
  - start to revise budget allocations well in advance, so that the extra costs of new working practices can be absorbed gradually in a phased manner.
9 *Other priorities come on stream, diverting attention and resources:*
  - develop a time-phased change implantation strategy to provide periods of planned stability between change projects
  - avoid diverting resources before initiatives are embedded.
10 *Staff at all levels suffer initiative fatigue and enthusiasm for change falters:*
  - beware the 'bicycle effect', where a lack of forward momentum leads to a crash. Relaunch with new focus, themes and goals
  - sell the benefits and clarify what's in it for them.

Reflect back on the content of this chapter, then complete Exercise 28.2.

☑ Exercise **28.2** *Action steps to promote stickability*

Think of a current or pending change in your organization or another context that you are familiar with and identify at least three things that could be done to help ensure that the change will be embedded and sustained for as long as required.

	Actions that will help sustain the change	Reason
1		
2		
3		

VII

Summary

Lewin conceptualized change as a three-stage process. The first involves unfreezing and creating a readiness for change. The second involves moving to a new state, and the final stage involves refreezing behaviour at this new level, for as long as it is beneficial to do so. This caveat is important because there are circumstances where it may not be beneficial to continue to maintain a change.

Sustainability has been defined in many different ways. Some definitions are relatively static, focusing on the maintenance of improvements within a particular setting, whereas others are more dynamic and are concerned with translating initial gains into a process of continuous improvement.

The maintenance of improvements (stickability) is affected by:

- The way the whole change process is managed from the beginning. Tough top-down (push) strategies are more likely to foster compliance, which can evaporate when the pressure to maintain the change is eased.
- How change managers act to sustain change after initial change goals have been achieved.

A number of studies point to issues that can affect sustainability and what change managers can do to help ensure that gains are held. While Buchanan et al. felt that more work would have to be done before they could offer change managers any simple prescription for sustaining change, they did point to three issues that seem to affect the extent of initiative decay:

1 *How the change is perceived:* Is it peripheral or central to organizational performance and is it perceived as acceptable or threatening by key stakeholders? Often, change managers can influence the way a change is perceived and this will have consequences for sustainability.
2 *How it is implemented:* There is no one implementation process that will be effective in all settings, but doing everything possible to identify and adopt an appropriate process can affect whether or not the change will be sustained.
3 *The timing, sequencing and pacing of the change:* While a relaxed timetable might help people to digest the need for change, delays can undermine commitment and divert attention to other pressing issues. On the other hand, when a change is rushed, people may not feel involved and a succession of change initiatives may lead to initiative fatigue.

Buchanan et al. identified 10 recurrent problems and offered practical advice about how each might be addressed. The problems are:

1 Those who initiated the change move on
2 Accountability for development becomes diffused
3 Knowledge and experience of new practices is lost through turnover
4 Old habits are imported with recruits from less dynamic organizations
5 The issues and pressures that triggered the change initiative are no longer visible
6 New managers want to drive their own agenda
7 Powerful stakeholders are using counter-implementation tactics to block progress
8 Pump-priming funds run out
9 Other priorities come on stream, diverting attention and resources
10 Staff at all levels suffer initiative fatigue and enthusiasm for change falters.

References

Bateman, N. (2005) Sustainability: The elusive element of process improvement, *International Journal of Operations and Production Management*, 25(3): 261–76.

Bateman, N. and David, A. (2002) Process improvement programmes: A model for assessing sustainability, *International Journal of Operations and Production Management*, 22(5): 515–26.

Beckhard, R. and Harris, R.T. (1987) *Organizational Transitions: Managing Complex Change.* Reading, MA: Addison-Wesley.

Brown, A. (2009) *Making Change Stick: The Holy Grail?*, White Paper, KPMG.

Buchanan, D.A. and Fitzgerald, L. (2007) Improvement evaporation: Why do successful changes decay? In D.A. Buchanan, L. Fitzgerald and D. Ketley (eds) *The Sustainability and Spread of Organizational Change.* London: Routledge.

Buchanan, D.A., Fitzgerald, L. and Ketley, D. (eds) (2007a) *The Sustainability and Spread of Organizational Change.* London: Routledge.

Buchanan, D.A., Fitzgerald, L. and Ketley, D. (2007b) Sustaining change and avoiding containment: Practice and policy. In D.A. Buchanan, L. Fitzgerald and D. Ketley (eds) *The Sustainability and Spread of Organizational Change.* London: Routledge.

Buchanan, D.A, Ketley, D., Gollop, R. et al. (2005) No going back: A review of the literature on sustaining organizational change, *International Journal of Management Reviews*, 7(3): 189–205.

Dale, B. (1996) Sustaining a process of continuous improvement: Definition and key factors, *TQM Magazine*, 8(2): 49–51.

Fine, D., Hansen, M.A. and Roggenhofer, S. (2008) From lean to lasting: Making operational improvements stick, *McKinsey Quarterly*, November, www. mckinseyquarterly. com.

Kotter, J.P. (1995) Leading change: Why transformation efforts fail, *Harvard Business Review*, 73(2): 59–67.

Lewin, K. (1951) *Field Theory in Social Sciences.* New York: Harper & Row.

Nadler, D.A. (1993) *Feedback and Organizational Development: Using Data-Based Methods.* Reading, MA: Addison-Wesley.

NHS Modernisation Agency (2002) *Improvement Leaders' Guide to Sustainability and Spread.* Ipswich: Ancient House Printing Group.

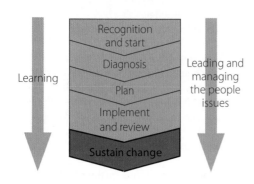

Chapter **28** # Spreading change

This chapter looks at 'spreadability', the extent to which new methods and processes that have delivered gains in one location are applied, or adapted, and then applied elsewhere across the organization. Attention is given to what managers can do to promote the spread of change. Before reading further, complete Exercise 28.1.

✓ *Exercise **28.1** Factors undermining the spread of change across an organization*

Reflect on your experience of successful change efforts and identify examples where the new methods and processes were not spread to other locations. List below some of the factors you think have limited spread and fostered containment.

When you have read this chapter, reflect on the notes you have made here and consider whether your list needs to be amended in any way.

	Factors limiting spread	Reason
1		
2		
3		

Spreading change

Containment is a problem that affects many organizations; innovative methods and processes that have been developed and are working well in one part of an organization remain as isolated examples of good practice. This phenomenon is often referred to as the 'best practice puzzle' (Szulanski, 2003). Examples abound.

Walton (1975) describes eight projects that involved work restructuring and the enlargement of the workers' scope for self-management. Only one of these eight projects, at Volvo's assembly plant in Lundby, was followed by similar changes elsewhere in the organization. Buchanan et al. (2007) report many examples of containment in the NHS along with a few outstanding successes, such as the spread of 'see and treat' (Lamont, 2005), an innovation that reduced waiting times in hospital A&E departments.

Klein and Sorra (1996) refer to two types of stage model that have been used to describe the spread of innovations – innovation here refers to anything newly introduced that involves a change to what went before. The model informing the discussion of spread in this chapter is a user-based model. It traces the innovation process from the users' perspective, from when they first become aware of the innovation to the incorporation of the innovation into their behavioural repertoire and normal way of working. Clearly, unless potential users are aware of the innovation, they cannot consider its adoption. However, attention here is focused on the implementation stage, which Klien and Sorra (1996) describe as the 'critical gateway' between the decision to adopt a new way of working and the routine use of the new methods, structure and processes. Implementation is affected by at least three factors: attributes of the innovation, attributes of the organization, and the values of the potential or targeted users of the innovation.

Attributes of the innovation

Greenhalgh et al. (2005), Tornatzky and Klein (1982) and Walton (1975) point to a long list of attributes that could help to explain why some innovations in methods and working practices spread, while others remain contained in one part of the organization. Rogers (1995) suggests that six attributes are important. New ways of working are more likely to be spread when potential users perceive them to be:

1 *Advantageous when compared with existing practices:* Perceptions of relative advantage are based on social as well as financial costs and benefits.
2 *Compatible with existing practices:* The more an innovation is perceived to be compatible with existing norms, values, technologies and social structures, the more likely it is to be adopted. Schein (1992), for example, notes that the introduction of quality circles, self-managed teams and autonomous working groups in many highly individualistic and competitive North American organizations can be so countercultural that it can be difficult to make them work.
3 *Easy to understand:* Complex innovations are more likely to be resisted than those that are relatively straightforward and easy to understand. A related attribute is 'pervasiveness' (Walton, 1975). This refers to the number of aspects of the system that are affected by the innovation. Innovations that are less pervasive will spread more easily.
4 *Observable in demonstration sites:* Potential users will be more able to assess relative advantage, compatibility with existing practices, and ease of use when they can observe the new way of working first hand.
5 *Testable:* Spread is more likely to happen when potential users can experience and test out new methods or ways of working for themselves before committing to the change.

VII

6 *Adaptable to fit local needs:* Rogers and others argue that where users can adapt the innovation to be more compatible with existing practices and/or deliver greater relative advantage, the more likely it is to be adopted. This view has been contested and will be considered in greater detail below.

Tornatzky and Klien (1982) conducted a meta-analysis of 75 studies of innovation attributes. They found that three of Rogers' six attributes had most influence on whether an innovation would be implemented in new sites. Relative advantage and compatibility were positively related and complexity was negatively related to the adoption of innovations in organizational settings.

Attributes are not fixed qualities

These attributes, as perceived by potential users, are not fixed qualities; they are perceptions that are potentially amenable to change. Providing potential users with more information may help to change their views. For example, they may not be aware of all the advantages an innovation could deliver for them or the organization. Improved communication may address this problem. Perceptions relating to compatibility might be modified if potential users are allowed to experience the new way of working first hand. Perceived complexity might be addressed by breaking the innovation down into separate, more manageable parts that could be introduced on an incremental basis.

Exact copying

There are opposing views about the value of adapting innovations to fit local needs. Szulanski and Winter (2002) advocate that when the aim is to capture and lever existing, rather than generate new, knowledge, innovative practices should be copied exactly to avoid what they refer to as 'spread errors'.

Spread errors arise when those responsible for disseminating a new practice assume they understand what it is about the new practice that delivers value. Often, this may not be the case. Szulanski and Winter (2002) suggest that many details of a new working practice may be invisible because critical elements of the innovation that may be known to individual workers are not shared with supervisors. Other critical elements may be tacit – learned on the job and well known to those involved in the initial change project – but difficult or impossible to document or describe to 'outsiders'. There may also be some elements of the innovation that are deliberately kept secret because they make individual workers' jobs easier or they run counter to an organization's formal work rules. Because those responsible for disseminating the new practice assume they understand what it is about the innovation that delivers value, this overconfidence leads them to immediately start trying to improve on the original example of good practice, cherry-picking parts of a process that appear to offer greatest advantage, or customizing it to make it more compatible with what already exists.

In order to avoid these 'spread errors', Szulanski and Winter (2002) advocate that the original template of the innovation should be copied as closely as possible. They cite Rank Xerox's dissemination of nine best sales practices, Intel's 'Copy Exactly!' method of transferring semiconductor manufacturing know-how, and the successful spread of franchised operations, such as McDonald's, to support their exact copy philosophy.

Reinvention

Buchanan and Fitzgerald (2007a) argue that there is no best way of spreading innovations and that best practice is contingent. They go on to argue (Buchanan and Fitzgerald, 2007b) that in the health service, many innovations involve introducing changes into multifaceted, complex operating environments where it is unlikely that a set of new working practices can be simply codified and copied from one location to another without some adaptation. They cite Locock (2001, p. 42), who, commenting on several cases of effective service improvement in the health service, asserts that these successes were arrived at by going through a redesign process:

> lifting the outcome off the shelf to re-use somewhere else without going through the redesign process may or may not work, but would miss the point that redesign is about analysing what is done in each local context now, and how local staff believe it could be done better in the interests of their patients.

Locock (2001) goes on to argue that 're-inventing the wheel' can be a vital part of creating a climate for change and gaining ownership, and ensuring that changes are embedded, a point echoed by Beer (1988).

The Asda roll-out case (Example 28.1) describes an attempt to spread an innovation where, in the first instance, there was little involvement of local staff and no opportunity to 'reinvent the wheel', and also where the innovation that was rolled out was not an exact copy of the original innovation.

● *Example* **28.1** *Asda's roll-out of 'store renewal'*

Shortly after Archie Norman was appointed CEO of Asda in 1991, with a remit to turn the business around, he authorized radical experimentation in three of the company's stores. Cross-functional task forces were established to work with store managers to reinvent the concept of the Asda store – its design, retail proposition, and approach to organizing and managing people. The first store renewal took six months to complete but the results were very encouraging – sales rose 40 per cent. After the other two renewal stores were successfully launched, it was decided to roll out 'renewal' across the company. In three months, 20 stores were renewed, but the results were disappointing.

Eventually, it was recognized that the poor results were related to the way the renewal programme had been rolled out. Managers working in those 20 stores had not been given the opportunity to adapt the innovation to fit local circumstances. After the early experimental phase, the pressure to turn the business around led to renewal being rolled out as a top-down technical solution that was imposed on their stores. At the time, it was not recognized that renewal in the experimental stores had been a sociotechnical process.

© BRAND X PICTURES

VII

The involvement of staff and the attention that had been given to people issues had contributed to the development of a new store culture, but when renewal was rolled out to the next 20 stores, little attention was given to creating the right store culture. Also, the technical solution that was imposed was not an exact copy of the innovation that had been developed in the experimental stores. Compromises had been made to the way the stores were organized and managed; for example, it proved difficult to implement self-managed teams in the required timescale. Compromises had also been made to the physical aspects of renewal, because it took too long to implement the radical new layouts that were part of the first three renewal stores.

This learning led to a separation of physical renewal and cultural change. Renewal was redesignated as a physical store refurbishment programme. There was recognition of the importance of down the line leadership and store culture. Funding for renewal (the physical refurbishment) was only made available after a store had demonstrated that it had fully embraced an innovation template, a codified set of principles referred to as the 'Asda Way of Working'. It was only after each store had passed a 'driving test' that clearly indicated it had developed a culture that was customer friendly and responsive, and had adopted a flatter hierarchy and team working, that funds were released for the store refurbishment.

Attributes of the organization

Klein and Sorra (1996) cite a range of studies that highlight a number of separate organizational and managerial policies, practices and characteristics that influence the spread of new practices and bring them together under an umbrella concept, which they refer to as the organization's 'climate for implementation'. They assert that a strong implementation climate fosters innovation use by:

- ensuring employees have the skills to use the innovation
- incentivizing them for innovation use and imposing sanctions for innovation avoidance
- removing obstacles that hamper the adoption of new working practices.

They also suggest that the attributes of a strong implementation climate could include:

- providing training to support innovation use to targeted employees – *ensuring skill*
- providing additional assistance in innovation use following training – *ensuring skill*
- providing employees with ample time to learn about the innovation and use it on an ongoing basis – *ensuring skill, removing obstacles*
- responding to employees' concerns and complaints – *removing obstacles*
- ensuring that the innovation can be easily accessed by targeted users, for example scheduling TQM meetings at times convenient for users – *removing obstacles*
- ensuring that employees' use of the innovation is monitored and praised by managers – *providing incentives for use and disincentives for avoidance.*

Greenhalgh et al. (2005) highlight the political aspects of organizational context and argue that it is important to pay attention to how different stakeholders view the attributes of an innovation. For example, individual adopters, those who represent different aspects of the organization's interests or customers who might be affected by an innovation, may have different perceptions of the relative advantage an innovation will offer. The same innovation might be perceived as offering advantages and being worthy of support by some stakeholders, and just the opposite by others.

Walton (1975) points to another aspect of context, the 'star envy syndrome'. This relates to how people's perceptions of the incentives for adopting an innovation can affect take-up. He describes an innovation in Norsk Hydro, a Norwegian fertilizer company, in which the change project and those who led it received top management approval and considerable outside recognition. Walton reports that this attention engendered resentment and envy from other managers who were expected to adopt the innovation. This resentment led to resistance. A second related dynamic involved perceived changes to the reward structure. Those who were expected to adopt the innovation felt that they would get less praise for success than those who had led the original project but more blame for failure, so they avoided failure by not taking up the innovation in the first place.

Klein and Sorra (1996) argue that a strong supportive implementation climate encourages the diffusion of innovations, provided employees are committed to innovation use. This caveat is important. They assert that effective implementation requires the dual influence of an organization's climate for implementation and target users' perception of a good fit between the innovation and their values.

The values of potential users

Klein and Sorra (1996) argue that an important attribute of potential users that influences the motivation to adopt an innovation is their values and their perception of whether the innovation will foster or inhibit the fulfilment of their values. They refer to this as 'innovation/values fit'. They draw on Schein (1992) and define group and organizational values in terms of shared beliefs about how the group or organization should relate to customers, competitors and other external constituencies, and how members should relate to and work with each other. This concept of innovation/values fit relates to Rogers' (1995) 'relative advantage' and 'compatibility' attributes of an innovation. Innovations that are perceived to offer a relative advantage in terms of their capacity to fulfil values and are compatible with existing norms, values and social structures are likely to have high innovation/values fit.

Depending on the extent to which the innovation is perceived by potential users to either foster or inhibit the fulfilment of their values, they will:

- resist and not implement the innovation
- comply with the requirement to adopt the new ways of working in order to gain rewards and avoid punishments
- internalize and enthusiastically adopt the innovation as the new way of doing things.

VII

The combined effects of implementation climate and innovation/values fit

Klein and Sorra (1996) illustrate the combined effects of implementation climate and innovation/values fit with the example of a university that had historically valued and rewarded teaching far more than research. The university developed a new strategy that emphasized research and pursued this strategy by attempting to spread the good research practice that existed in a few isolated departments. It supported this endeavour by introducing new policies and practices that created a strong climate for research. However, members of the university's faculty, while recognizing this supportive climate for implementation, were reluctant to commit to the change because they perceived it to be incongruent with their values, which centred on teaching rather than research. Table 28.1 illustrates the combined effects of implementation climate and innovation/values fit.

Table **28.1** *Implementation climate and innovation/values fit: effects on employees' affective responses and innovation use*

Climate	Innovation/values fit		
	Poor	**Neutral**	**Good**
Strong implementation climate	**1** Employee opposition and resistance	**2** Employee indifference	**3** Employee enthusiasm
	Compliant innovation use, at best	Adequate innovation use	Committed, consistent and creative innovation use
Weak implementation climate	**4** Employee relief	**5** Employee disregard	**6** Employee frustration and disappointment
	Essentially no innovation use	Essentially no innovation use	Sporadic and inadequate innovation use

Source: Klein and Sorra, 1996, p. 1066

The six cells predict the influence of varying levels of implementation climate and innovation/values fit on employees' motivation to adopt new ways of working:

- In cell 3, innovation/values fit is good and the organization's implementation climate is strong. These are the ideal conditions for innovation implementation.
- In cell 6, innovation/values fit is good, but the organization's implementation climate is weak. This is not a sufficient condition to produce skilful and consistent innovation use.
- In cell 1, although the organization's implementation climate is strong, innovation/values fit is poor. These conditions are likely to lead, at best, to compliant behaviour.
- In cell 4, innovation/values fit is poor and the organization's implementation climate is weak. Targeted innovation adopters are likely to regard this weak implementation climate with some measure of relief, because they will encounter little pressure to implement an innovation they do not value. Hence there is unlikely to be any move to adopt the innovation.
- In cell 2, innovation/values fit is neutral and the organization's implementation climate is strong. In these circumstances, innovation use is likely to be more than compliant but less than fully committed.
- In cell 5, innovation/values fit is neutral and the organization's implementation climate is weak. Thus there is unlikely to be any move to adopt the innovation.

The foregoing discussion recognizes that implementation is a multidimensional phenomenon. While there are no easy prescriptions that guarantee spread, there are things that change managers can do to facilitate the dissemination of new ways of working. For example, potential users' perceptions of the attributes of an innovation are not fixed qualities but are amenable to revision. Change managers can do many things to affect these perceptions, ranging from education and persuasion to involving users in a process of adapting the innovation to fit with local requirements and their own values. In addition, they can work to create a strong implementation climate that fosters innovation use. They can also be alert to different stakeholder interests and how these impact the innovation/values fit of different groups. This kind of awareness can help change managers to disseminate new ways of working in a manner that maintains equity of treatment and minimizes opportunities for conflict.

✅ *Exercise* **28.2** *Action steps to promote the spread of change*

Think of a current or pending change in your organization or another organization you are familiar with and identify at least three things that could be done to help ensure that the change will not be contained and will be adopted by other users elsewhere in the organization.

	Actions that will help spread the change	Reason
1		
2		
3		

At the beginning of this chapter, Exercise 28.1 asked you to list the factors you thought could undermine the spread of innovations across an organization. Reflect on what you have read and consider whether you should amend your list.

Summary

This chapter considered 'spreadability' – the extent to which innovative methods and processes that were successfully introduced in one part of the organization are adopted by others elsewhere.

Spread is affected by three factors:

- attributes of the innovation
- context – reflected by the organization's climate for implementation
- the values of potential users, and their perception of the extent to which the innovation will foster or inhibit the fulfilment of their values.

The three attributes of innovations that have the greatest impact on spread are relative advantage, compatibility and complexity. It was noted that Rogers' view that adaptability is important has been contested and some of the arguments supporting adaptation and exact copying were reviewed.

A strong implementation climate fosters innovation use by:

VII

- ensuring employees have the skills to use the innovation
- incentivizing them for innovation use and imposing sanctions for innovation avoidance
- removing obstacles that hamper the adoption of new working practices.

The interaction between users' values and the implementation climate was highlighted as being particularly important.

Many of the factors that promote stickability also support spread. Buchanan and Fitzgerald observe that the manner in which a change is spread can influence the degree to which it will be sustained. When changes are rolled out hastily, without much consultation, with few incentives and inadequate training, they may quickly decay. Similarly, changes that do not have support and are not sustained are unlikely to spread elsewhere.

References

Beer, M. (1988) The critical path for change: Keys to success and failure in six companies. In R.H. Kilmann and J.T. Covin (eds) *Corporate Transformations*. San Francisco, CA: Jossey-Bass.

Buchanan, D.A. and Fitzgerald, L. (2007a) The best practice puzzle: Why are new methods contained and not spread? In D.A. Buchanan, L. Fitzgerald and D. Ketley (eds) *The Sustainability and Spread of Organizational Change*. London: Routledge.

Buchanan, D.A. and Fitzgerald, L. (2007b) The sustainability and spread story. In D.A. Buchanan, L. Fitzgerald and D. Ketley (eds) *The Sustainability and Spread of Organizational Change*. London: Routledge.

Buchanan, D.A., Fitzgerald, L. and Ketley, D. (2007) Sustaining change and avoiding containment: Practice and policy. In D.A. Buchanan, L. Fitzgerald and D. Ketley (eds) *The Sustainability and Spread of Organizational Change*. London: Routledge.

Greenhalgh, T., Robert, G., Bate, P. et al. (2005) *Diffusion of Innovation in Organizations: A Systematic Literature Review*. Oxford: Blackwell/BJM Books.

Klein, K.L. and Sorra, J.S. (1996) The challenge of innovation implementation, *Academy of Management Review*, 21(4): 1055–80.

Lamont, S.S. (2005) See and treat: Spreading like wildfire? A qualitative study into factors affecting its introduction and spread, *Emergency Medical Journal*, 22(8): 548–52.

Locock, L. (2001) *Maps and Journeys: Redesign in the NHS*. Birmingham: Health Services Management Centre.

Rogers, E. (1995) *The Diffusion of Innovation* (4th edn). New York: Free Press.

Schein, E.H. (1992) *Organizational Culture and Leadership*. San Francisco, CA: Wiley.

Szulanski, G. (2003) *Sticky Knowledge: Barriers to Knowing in the Firm*. London: Sage.

Szulanski, G. and Winter, S. (2002) Getting it right the second time, *Harvard Business Review*, 80(1): 62–9.

Tornatzky, L.G. and Klein, K.J. (1982) Innovation characteristics and innovation adoption-implementation: A meta-analysis of findings, *IEEE Transactions on Engineering Management*, 29(1): 28–45.

Walton, R.E. (1975) The diffusion of new work structures: Explaining why success didn't take, *Organizational Dynamics*, 3(3): 3–22.

 Visit **www.palgrave.com/companion/hayes-change-management4** *for further learning resources*

Part **VIII**

LEARNING

Introduction to Part **VIII**

Part VIII examines what those leading change can do to learn from their experience and what they can do to help others involve themselves in a process of collective learning.

Chapter **29** *Individual and collective learning*

Chapter 29 is in two parts. The first develops the idea, introduced at the end of Chapter 2, that effective leaders are those who can learn from their experience and use this learning

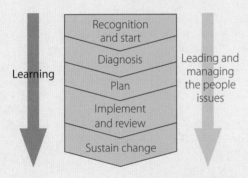

to improve their practice of change management. To do this, they have to be able to step back from the immediate 'doing' of change and adopt an 'observing' mode, reflecting on events, decisions and actions, identifying the critical junctures that shape these events, and exploring alternative ways of acting that might deliver superior outcomes.

Stepping back and reflecting on experience can be difficult. A number of barriers to reflective practice are identified. Leaders need to be aware of these barriers and work hard to bring a critical perspective to bear on their everyday practice of change management.

Concepts and theories, such as those presented in this book, can provide a useful guide for managing change but, in practice, the way change agents act is determined by their own subjective mental maps that influence how they understand the world (their theories-in-use). Those leading change need to be aware of and able to refine their theories-in-use so that they can consciously think about and understand why some of their actions result in unintended consequences and why attempts to get the change back on track are not always successful.

The second part considers the nature and contribution of collective learning and explores what leaders can do to facilitate this process. Collective learning involves enhancing the collective ability to act more effectively. The collective nature of learning is especially important in complex and turbulent environments because, in such circumstances, senior managers may not be the best placed individuals to identify opportunities and threats.

✓ *Exercise* **Part VIII** *Useful questions for reviewing your approach to reflection and learning*

In Chapter 2, after discussing each stage in the process model of change management, your attention was drawn to a number of questions that might help you assess how well a change is being (or was) managed. All these questions are summarized in Figure 2.5 and the questions relating to learning from the experience of managing change are listed below:

- Do those involved in the change anticipate how others will respond to events before deciding what to do?
- Do they monitor the effects of their actions and use this information to guide future decisions?
- Are they receptive to feedback from others?
- To what extent do they view their own and others' mistakes as opportunities for learning?
- Do they attempt to identify and challenge the assumptions that underpin their behaviour?
- Are they aware of how decisions that produce positive outcomes in the short term may undermine performance over the long term?

Reflect on and review these questions and, after reading Chapter 29, revise this list and generate your own set of useful questions that you might find it helpful to refer to when you are leading a change.

Chapter **29**

Individual and collective learning

According to Miles (1982), organizations have leeway and choice in how they adjust to a changing environment and it is this choice that offers the opportunity for learning. Lank and Lank (1995) argue that the quality of individual and organizational learning is an important determinant of organization effectiveness, while de Geus (1988) suggests that the ability to learn faster than competitors may be the only sustainable competitive advantage.

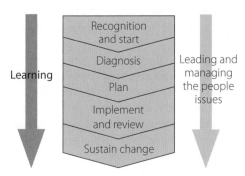

The first part of this chapter looks at what those leading a change can do to improve their personal ability to reflect on and learn from their own and others' behaviour.

Attention is given to:

- how reflection and learning can help to minimize the negative effects of reactive and self-reinforcing sequences (discussed in Chapter 1)
- the distinction between single- and double-loop learning, and the importance of challenging accepted ways of thinking and behaving
- some of the barriers that can make it difficult for those leading change to engage in reflective practice
- how reflection-in-action can affect what those leading change do next
- how reflection-on-action (after the event) can affect what leaders might do when faced with similar situations.

The second part considers the nature and contribution of collective learning, a process that can involve everybody in the organization, and explores what leaders can do to facilitate this process.

Attention is given to:

- the implicit and explicit rules that prescribe how members interact and behave
- the shared mental models that underpin these rules
- how collective single-loop learning can refine the rules but does not challenge the prevailing shared mental model
- how collective double-loop learning challenges the prevailing shared mental model and offers the possibility of organizational members doing things differently or doing different things
- the role of reflection in collective learning
- impediments to collective double-loop learning
- possibilities for minimizing the effect of these impediments.

VIII

Leaders reflecting on and learning from experience

The process model of change that provides the conceptual framework for this book (see Chapters 1 and 2) focuses attention on reactive and self-reinforcing sequences of events, decisions and actions and how they can affect change agents' ability to achieve intended goals.

In reactive sequences, one party challenges or resists another party's attempt to secure their favoured outcome. This may prompt those leading the change to try to suppress the challenge or overcome any resistance in order to maintain momentum. But this is not the only way they might respond. Challenges and resistance can prompt leaders (and others) to re-evaluate the situation and trigger a process of reflection and learning that, eventually, can lead to the achievement of superior outcomes. This helpful reflection might be immediate, in the here and now, and shape what those leading the change do next, as in Schön's reflection-in-action (see Schön, 1983), or it might occur after the event, like Schön's refection-on-action, and affect how the change agent(s) might act when faced with similar situations in the future.

On the other hand, self-reinforcing sequences, because they generate positive feedback and support the direction of change, can sometimes camouflage the need for learning. While they can deliver benefit over the short term, there is also a real danger that over the longer term they can draw the organization into a path that leads to suboptimal returns. Schreyögg and Sidow (2011) refer to self-reinforcing sequences as entrapping processes that 'often unfold behind the backs' of those involved, leading to unexpected results. In order to minimize any negative impact from these sequences, those leading change need to be able to step back and observe what is going on in order to identify critical junctures and subsequent patterns – some of which may be difficult to discern – and explore alternative ways of acting that might deliver superior outcomes.

Espoused theories and theories-in-use

Concepts and theories, such as those presented in this book, can provide a useful guide for managing change, but in practice the way change agents act is determined by their past experience and subjective mental maps that influence how they understand the world. These mental maps underpin what Argyris and Schön (1974) refer to as their 'theories-in-use'. To be effective, leaders need to be aware of their theories-in-use and be prepared to revise them. Unfortunately, all too often, their level of awareness is not high.

Discrepencies between espoused theories and theories-in-use

Whenever a change agent intentionally engages in some form of behaviour to secure a change, their behaviour is based on a theory of action; for example, when confronted by somebody resisting your proposal for change, given assumptions X, Y and Z, you need to do A. Argyris and Schön (1974) argue that when someone is asked how they would behave under certain circumstances, the answer they give is their *espoused* theory of action for that situation, but, often, this espoused theory will not provide an accurate reflection of how that individual will actually behave in practice. This is determined by their theory-in-use. Effectiveness can be undermined when those leading a change are unaware of any inconsistencies and incompatibilities between their espoused theories of action and their theories-in-use, because this can make it difficult for them to understand why some of their actions result in unintended consequences and why attempts to get the change back on track are not always successful. Some ways in which change agents can avoid these pitfalls are outlined below.

Reflection

When done properly, reflection has a key role to play in helping individuals become more aware of and able to refine their theory-in-use. But what is 'proper' reflection? According to Biggs (1999, p. 6), capturing and recording decisions and actions can be likened to viewing a reflection of events in a mirror, of what is happening or has happened. While necessary, this kind of observation and recollection are not a sufficient condition for learning. Biggs argues that reflection in professional practice needs to give back not what is, but what *might* be. It needs to point to possibilities for improvement. Dewey (1933, p. 190) made a similar point many years earlier:

> in every case of reflective activity, a person finds himself confronted with a given, present situation from which he has to arrive at, or conclude to, something that is not present. This process of arriving at an idea of what is absent on the basis of what is at hand is inference. What is present carries ... the mind over to the idea and ultimately the acceptance of something else.

The role of reflection in learning from experience

Kolb (1984, p. 21) highlights two important aspects of Lewin's approach to the place of reflection within experiential learning. The first is the emphasis he placed on here-and-now concrete experience to validate and test abstract concepts, and the second is the importance he attributed to feedback, the process that generates valid information to assess deviations from intended goals. It is this feedback that provides the basis for reflecting on experience, refining theories-in-use, and improving goal-directed action.

Building on earlier work by Lewin and Dewey, Kolb (1984) conceptualizes learning as a four-stage cycle that translates experience into concepts, which can be used to inform further action. The first stage involves engaging in an immediate concrete experience. In the context of this discussion, a change agent's theory-in-use might prompt them to interact with others in a particular way in order to secure an intended outcome. The second stage involves observing what happened and reflecting on the consequences of the action. At the third stage, the change agent interprets what happened and makes sense of the experience (if the action did not deliver intended outcomes, why was this?). These interpretations are then assimilated into the change agent's theory-in-use and may lead to the revision of some cause-and-effect hypotheses that, at stage four, provide a basis for planning what to do next and/or how to act in similar situations in the future. Sometimes, this experiential learning model is represented as a circle but, in reality, it is an ongoing process best represented as a spiral (Figure 29.1).

While Lewin emphasized the importance of here-and-now concrete experience, Cunningham (1999, p. 157) draws attention to the value of reflecting on what has happened in the past. Reviewing one's own history, which might be viewed in terms of what has happened over the course of the current change project or over the course of this and several previous projects, can lead to the identification of 'deeply ingrained patterns of behaviour [such as corrective routines we examine

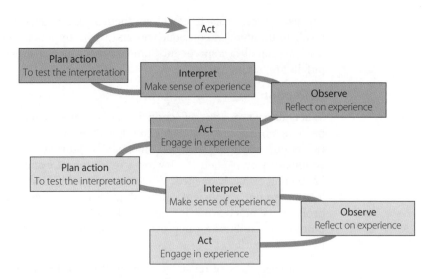

Figure **29.1** *The experiential learning model*

below] that tend to be repeated time after time. These patterns or habits may be effective, but sometimes they may be self-defeating.' Cunningham argues that reflecting on past experience can be a useful source of insights that can be tested in the here and now of experiential learning.

Leaders can improve their practice of change management by reflecting on the consequences of their own behaviour and identifying and challenging their assumptions and taken-for-granted patterns of behaving.

Single- and double-loop learning

Argyris and Schön (1978) distinguish between two different types of learning: single- and double-loop learning.

Single-loop learning

Leaders (and others) engage in single-loop learning when they reflect on what is happening (or has happened) and focus their attention on detecting errors and acting on this feedback to modify their and other people's behaviour (see Figure 29.2). They develop corrective routines within the existing governing variables, the taken-for-granted goals, values and operating frameworks. Argyris and Schön (1978) liken single-loop learning to a thermostat that receives information and learns when it is too hot or too cold, and takes corrective action to restore the temperature to a given level by turning the heat on or off.

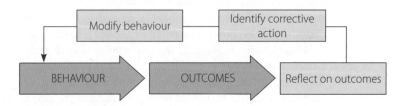

Figure **29.2** *Single-loop learning*

Single-loop learning supports continuous improvement and the extrapolation of past trends. While it can be effective in many situations, it is unlikely to be path breaking because it fails to challenge the underlying beliefs and assumptions that guide behaviour; in the thermostat example, assumptions about the required temperature or the more fundamental assumption that the temperature needs to be controlled are taken for granted and not challenged. An overreliance on single-loop learning can lead to path dependence (Sydow et al., 2009), because any new ways of acting are bound by current theories-in-use and taken-for-granted governing variables.

Double-loop learning

Double-loop learning challenges accepted ways of thinking and behaving and provides the possibility of developing a new understanding of situations and events. It occurs when leaders are able to think outside the box and:

1 reflect on outcomes
2 identify the beliefs and assumptions that underpinned the decisions and actions that led to the achievement of these outcomes, and also the beliefs and assumptions underpinning the definition of satisfactory outcomes – what Argyris and Schön (1974) refer to as the 'governing variables'
3 review and challenge these governing variables
4 where appropriate, modify them in ways that open the possibility of experimenting with new ways of behaving (Figure 29.3).

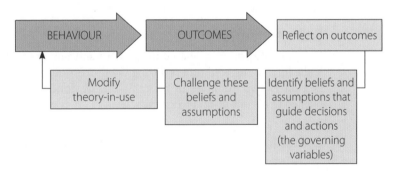

Figure **29.3 Double-loop learning**

Developing an awareness of competing interests

Reflecting on one's own and others' behaviour can enable leaders to make sense of situations, identify cause-and-effect relationships, develop corrective routines, and challenge beliefs and assumptions that guide their attempts to secure intended outcomes. In addition to this, thinking more critically about how others value these intended outcomes and about the beliefs, assumptions and espoused theories that guide their behaviour can also help change agents achieve outcomes that will be valued by a wider group of stakeholders. Cunliffe (2009) draws on social constructionism (Berger and Luckmann, 1967), discussed in Chapter 18, and the notion that different actors interpret (construct) reality in different ways to highlight the importance of considering competing interests when reflecting on experience.

VIII

Barriers to reflective practice

As mentioned in Chapter 2, it can be difficult for those leading change to step back and reflect on what is going on because they:

- are so bound up in a frenetic range of activities that they have little time or no opportunity for observation and reflection
- are so committed to a course of action that they fail to recognize evidence that challenges their worldview (see the discussion of cognitive biases and interpretive frames in Chapter 1)
- harbour beliefs about the competence and motives of others that makes it easy for them to dismiss their feedback (see the discussion of the assumption that there is little to be gained from dialogue with employees in Chapter 14)
- are insulated from information about the impact of their decisions by organization structures, policies and management practices that impede upward communication and foster a climate of organizational silence (discussed in Chapter 11; see Morrison and Milliken, 2000)
- are so bound up in and entrapped by a path that progressively limits their scope for decision making that they become path dependant (see discussion of path dependence in Chapter 1) and this excludes path-breaking behaviour because they are too involved to adopt an exogenous perspective.

Leaders need to be aware of these barriers that make it difficult for them to break away from an immediate 'doing' mode; they need to work hard to adopt an 'observing' mode and bring a critical perspective to bear on their everyday practice. Some methods of achieving this are outlined below.

Reflection-in-action

One way of observing oneself in the here and now is to open a 'second channel' while interacting with others during the process of managing change. Change tool 29.1 offers two examples of how this can be done. It is a technique that can be likened to an 'out-of-body' experience.

Change tool 29.1 Opening a second channel to observe oneself in the here and now

Imagine yourself floating somewhere in a corner of the room looking down on your interactions with others as they occur. Observe how you are behaving and think about the reasons behind your actions.

Example 1

You might open a second channel and observe what you are doing while you are trying to help somebody find the solution to a problem:

- *How do you attempt to help?* Do you listen until you are confident that both you and the other person have a clear understanding of the problem, or do you quickly move on to telling the other person what they 'should' do to manage their problem more effectively?
- *What makes you behave in this way?* Once you are aware of what you are doing, give some thought to *why* you are doing it. For example, if you have observed that you adopt a prescriptive approach to helping, consider your reasons for

doing this. Is it because you believe you know best and therefore have a duty to solve the other person's problem for them?

- *Give some thought to outcomes.* If you suspect that this belief is what is motivating your behaviour, consider how it might affect the outcome of the interaction. Consider, also, how this belief might influence your behaviour and other people's responses in different situations, such as team meetings.

Example 2

Open a second channel to observe how you behave when meeting somebody for the first time. Monitor what you are thinking at the time and coach yourself to identify and test the assumptions you are making:

- What is your first impression of the other person?
- What information have you used to form this impression?
- Resist accepting this first impression as fact. Tell yourself to regard the image as a working hypothesis and actively seek out additional information that will test it.
- Monitor yourself to ensure that you not only seek out information that confirms your first impression but also pay attention to any behaviour that does not confirm this impression.

Reflecting-on-action

Learning logs can be an effective way of reflecting after the event and identifying and re-examining patterns of behaviour. Gold et al. (2010) suggest that recording experiences in the form of stories can help leaders develop the ability to engage in critical reflection, because stories told from a personal point of view can reveal the beliefs and values of the storyteller. Stories can also raise awareness of competing interests by revealing the assumptions the storyteller is making about others involved in the change. Gold et al. (2010, p. 189), drawing on Polkinghorne (1997), assert that:

> by writing out stories of important events, including difficult situations or mistakes, managers can re-present the complexity of their work, including the views and actions of different characters, connected by a plot into a whole.

They advocate the use of learning logs, storytelling and learning charts to help change agents develop the meta-reflection skills that can help them identify and understand key themes and persistent patterns of behaviour. Figure 29.4 presents a learning chart that could have been produced by the CEO of Concrete Flags Ltd. This case was originally presented in Example 2.1 and is summarized below (Example 29.1).

Example **29.1** *Concrete Flags Ltd*

Concrete Flags Ltd adopted a new business strategy, which involved a shift from manufacturing concrete paving stones (flags) for builders merchants, DIY outlets and garden centres to providing end consumers with their 'dream patio' delivered direct to their home on a pallet. This shift required a new approach to marketing and the design and installation of a more automated production technology.

Before the change the company had manufactured a limited range of concrete flags in batches using a basic process that relied on a large input of low skilled labour. While reliable it was costly because batch production required the company to hold large inventories of different flags. The new strategy required the company to develop the capability to manufacture a wider range of concrete flags but only as and when required, keeping inventories as low as possible. Taking into account variations in shape, size, colour and texture, the company aimed to manufacture 150 different products on demand. Managers worked with a supplier to design the new automated production system. The plan was to install and test one machine first and then purchase additional equipment as the new marketing strategy generated additional demand. It was anticipated that at least two additional machines would be installed within the year.

The first machine was installed on time and appeared to be performing well, but it was not long before managers became aware that production targets were not being met. They identified the problem as wet concrete sticking in the weigh boxes. The supplier acknowledged a minor design fault that was quickly rectified.

Story 1
While the supplier was modifying the new machine, it was discovered, and reported to the CEO, that operators had attempted to keep the machine running by hitting the weigh boxes with a large hammer. It appeared that this crude method of moving wet concrete had worked well enough with the old (less sophisticated and more robust) equipment but it had

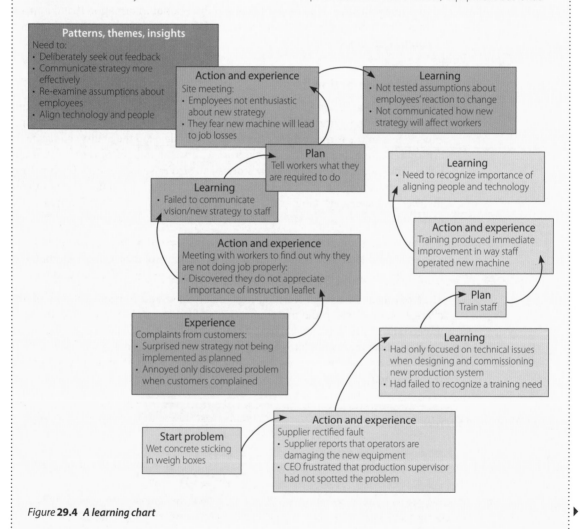

Figure **29.4** *A learning chart*

caused damage to the new machine. This feedback alerted managers to an important misalignment between the new equipment and the operators' knowledge and skills. They responded by arranging a number of training sessions, which led to an immediate improvement in the way they operated and maintained the new equipment.

Story 2

Within a short while, another problem emerged. Achieving the vision of delivering tailor-made patios-on-pallets direct to end users included providing them with a booklet containing laying instructions. Unfortunately, the importance of this booklet had not been explained to the workers, who still defined their role as making concrete paving stones. On investigation, managers found that the workers regarded inserting the booklet before the pallet was shrink-wrapped as an unnecessary complication. It was just a bit of paper. When supplies ran out, they had continued to dispatch patios-on-pallets without laying

instructions. Managers had been unaware of this problem until customers began to complain that they had not received the promised booklet.

The CEO responded by arranging a site meeting at which he talked to all employees about the new strategy ('dream patios' delivered direct to customers' homes on a pallet) and explained the implications of this strategy for the work they performed. He invited those present to ask questions and was surprised by their lack of enthusiasm for the new strategy. The management team had assumed that all employees would welcome it, but they had been wrong. The operators felt that the strategy (and the new machine) threatened their job security. Nobody had informed them that it was anticipated there would be a big demand for the new 'dream patios' and that additional machines would be installed as sales picked up.

Recording the essential elements of the stories on the learning chart can show connections between events and common themes from both stories.

In the Concrete Flags case, the plans for action were based on reflections-in-action (train operatives and tell workers what they are required to do) and involved the CEO and his senior colleagues taking the kind of corrective steps often associated with single-loop learning. Using learning logs and learning charts to structure reflection after the event can be a more powerful way of identifying and re-examining patterns of behaviour (double-loop learning). In the Concrete Flags example, after reflecting on both stories, the CEO might have recognized and challenged some of the taken-for-granted assumptions that had guided his behaviour. For example, he might have:

- re-examined some of the assumptions he and senior colleagues had made about employees and recognized the value of trying to see the impact of changes through their eyes
- recognized the importance of aligning people with the requirements of the new marketing strategy and the new production technology
- reviewed the assumption that plans will be implemented as intended and recognized the need to review change efforts on a continuous basis and so on.

Leaders not only need to reflect on their own experience but also encourage others to join with them to reflect on and learn from the collective experience of change. How they can do this is considered below.

Collective reflection and learning

The ability to mobilize processes of collective reflection and learning in the service of value creation is at the heart of modern ideas about the role of leadership (Vince and Reynolds, 2010, p. 334). This part of the chapter reviews the nature of collective learning, considers how it can contribute to organizational effectiveness, and explores what leaders can do to facilitate this process.

Collective learning is especially important in complex and turbulent environments, because senior managers may not be the best placed individuals to identify opportunities and threats. Organizational members, at all levels, who are involved in boundary-spanning activities such as procurement, technical development or sales may have data that could provide a valuable input to strategy formulation. Furthermore, the quality of response to any threats or opportunities that are identified may require individuals and groups located in different functions to collaborate and learn from each other in order to design and produce high-quality products or services in ever shorter time frames. Those leading change have an important role to play in enhancing the collective ability to act more effectively. Leaders need to recognize how others can contribute and act to create the conditions that will enable them to share and reflect on their various experiences and identify opportunities to improve organizational performance.

Shared mental models, rules and behaviour in organizations

The first part of this chapter considered how leaders' mental models affect their behaviour and performance. Here, attention is focused on the way *shared* mental models can affect how people across the organization behave and how this behaviour affects organizational performance.

Swieringa and Wierdsma (1992) conceptualize organizations as a set of explicit and implicit rules that prescribe the way members behave (see Figure 29.5). These rules are based on insights that represent what is known and understood and reflect the shared mental model that organizational members use to examine and make sense of their experience. They relate to everything that happens in the organization. For example, there are rules about the structure of the organization that prescribe how activities will be grouped and responsibilities allocated, and there are rules about how resources are procured and used and how people are managed and rewarded. The collective or shared mental model that underpins the rules reflects the organization's culture. Schein (1990, p. 111) defines culture as:

> (a) the pattern of basic assumptions, (b) invented, discovered or developed by a given group, (c) as it learns to cope with its problems of external adaptation and internal integration, (d) that has worked well enough to be considered valid and, therefore, (e) is to be taught to new members as the (f) correct way to perceive, think, and feel in relation to these problems.

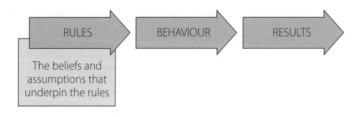

Figure **29.5** *The organization conceptualized as a set of rules that prescribe behaviour*

Collective learning and the modification of rules

Collective learning occurs when a group of organizational members recognize something that offers a more effective way of functioning. Organizations are more effective when their major components, such as structure, technology, systems and people, are aligned with each other and when there is a good fit between the organization and the environment. Collective learning can facilitate this fit. It involves organizational members diagnosing the organization's predicament, integrating this understanding into their shared mental models, and using it as a basis for modifying, as required, the rules that guide decision making and action. This process is similar to that referred to by Daft and Weick (1984), when they describe organizations as open social systems that seek and interpret information about their environment in order to provide a basis for action.

Modifying the rules via single- and double-loop learning

Argyris and Schön's (1978) distinction between single- and double-loop learning applies to both individual and collective learning. In the context of collective learning, single-loop learning entails the detection and correction of errors leading to a modification of the rules within the boundaries of current thinking (the governing variables). It involves organizational members collectively *refining* the rules that determine how the organization operates and identifying ways of doing things better. This might involve, for example, revising reporting relationships, redesigning jobs, and modifying decision-making procedures. As noted earlier, single-loop learning does not fundamentally challenge the governing variables. It leads to the modification of the rules but not the shared mental model (beliefs and assumptions) on which they are based.

On the other hand, double-loop learning challenges accepted ways of thinking and can produce a new understanding of situations and events, which can, in turn, lead to the development of new rules that require organizational members to change their behaviour and do things differently or even do different things. While double-loop learning is often seen as a desirable goal, it can be difficult to attain in practice, especially when a group, department or organization is enjoying a period of sustained success (see the discussion of the trap of success in Chapter 4).

Triggers for double-loop learning

Double-loop collective learning is most likely to occur when desired performance levels are not achieved and feedback signals a need to re-examine the relevance of the shared mental model. Leroy and Ramanantsoa (1997) refer to incongruous events that violate conceptual frameworks, such as dramatically altered market conditions, as triggers for this kind of learning, and Fiol and Lyles (1983) assert that some type of crisis is necessary to trigger higher level or double-loop learning. However, in the most effective organizations, a sudden discontinuity is not always required; double-loop learning can occur as a matter of course when leaders (and others) are alert to the need to ensure that the organization is capable of adapting to changing circumstances.

The revision of shared mental models: the key to sustained success

Shared mental models need to be fluid and open to modification if they are to provide an effective basis for assessing the environment and planning action, but they are one of the main sources of inertia identified by Gersick (1991), while

Hodgkinson and Healey (2009) point to 'ingrained schemata' as important barriers to organizational change. Unless they are open to revision, they can seriously limit an organization's ability to adapt, and can promote an episodic rather than a continuous response to threats and opportunities (see the discussion of punctuated equilibrium in Chapter 3).

Organizational (collective) learning involves the acquisition of knowledge, the recognition of its potential, and its application to improve organizational performance. Knowledge exists within organizations but it may not always be available to those who can make best use of it. Huber (1991) draws attention to the importance of distributing information. As organizational members gain access to new information, they may be better able to create new knowledge by piecing together patterns that had not previously been apparent or they may be able to identify and apply the superior practices being used elsewhere in the organization. But information does not always flow freely and so valuable learning opportunities are missed.

Reflection and collective learning

Just as with individual learning, collective learning requires organizational members to find the time and space to step back, break away from an immediate 'doing' mode, and adopt more of an 'observing' mode so that they can bring a critical perspective to bear on their everyday practice.

Postmortems and post-implementation reviews are frequently used to facilitate reflection and learning by dissecting past events, identifying mistakes and producing reports, which include recommendations for improvement. They can be a useful source of single- and double-loop learning but the experience of the US Army was that bringing in a highly qualified officer to conduct a post-combat review, identify mistakes, and leave the platoon with a checklist to follow next time produces little real learning. The army responded by developing the 'after action review' (AAR). It facilitates learning by comparing the commander's intent (stated at the start of a mission) with what subsequently happens. Parry and Darling (2001) report that the vivid intersection between army doctrine and the standard practices (the 'rules') that govern situations (such as 'movement to contact with an enemy unit') and direct battle experience allows espoused theory and actual practice to shape each other on a daily basis. The AAR facilitates the testing and, where necessary, the modification of the rules (see Change tool 29.2).

Change tool **29.2** *The after action review*

It is an intervention that involves a leader (platoon commander) gathering the team on a regular basis to address the following questions:

1 *What was supposed to happen?*
   This question helps the group clarify and develop a shared understanding of what was expected of them.
2 *What actually did happen?*
   This question helps the group construct a shared picture of what actually happened. It has to be a collective process because typically no one person will be aware of the total picture. This shared understanding is then used to identify discrepancies between what was supposed to happen and what actually happened, but at this stage no attempt is made to identify why things happened as they did.

3 *Why did it happen this way?*

This step involves exploring deeply what Malby and Fischer (2006) refer to as the 'relationship rules' that guide the way people work together, the rules that govern the availability of information, and anything else that is perceived to have influenced performance.

4 *What are we going to change?*

This step involves considering what individuals and the group as a whole can do to deliver intended outcomes and minimize unintended consequences. In the battle context, the aim is to generate insights into what needs to be changed to improve effectiveness and provide the basis for planning the next day's action.

Parry and Darling (2001) note how the AAR approach has been applied in business settings. Harley-Davidson applied it to improve the process of introducing new models. After each 'pre-build', it conducted a series of AARs to compare actual with anticipated performance and use the learning to improve the way it conducted the next pre-build. A wine retailer conducted quarterly AARs with his team, focusing on a single event that happened in that quarter; for example, in one quarter, it was how they had managed a pre-holiday spike in demand. This example gave the team some insights into how they and the system worked under pressure. Power Construction used AAR principles to develop its 'lessons learned workshops', which brought multi-firm project teams together at the beginning, middle and end of large projects.

Impediments to organizational learning

The essence of collective learning is the joint construction of meaning. This occurs through sharing and dialogue. However, this process is rarely problem free. Sources of difficulty include:

- Members' poor appreciation of the systemic qualities of organizations
- A lack of accessible channels for dialogue and the sharing of meaning
- The context in which sharing and dialogue must occur
- The characteristics of the sources and recipients of knowledge
- Ideologies and ingrained mental models
- Dysfunctional interactions between competing ideologies.

Poor appreciation of the systemic qualities of organizations

Many individuals and groups have a parochial and limited view of their role, which restricts their ability to contribute to organizational learning. Often, they focus all their attention on the immediate task and fail to appreciate how this relates to the overall purpose of the organization. Egan (1988) discusses the need to promote 'business thinking', which relates to the organization's overall mission and the importance of markets, competitors, customers, and the products and services that satisfy customers' needs and wants. 'Organization thinking' is more blinkered and is essentially inward looking, concerned with the way the firm organizes its structures and processes to engage in its business. Organization thinking is important but, sometimes, people become too preoccupied with the details of their particular role or department and ignore how what they do affects others and how this impacts on the overall effectiveness of the business.

VIII

Lean thinking, discussed in Chapter 22, seeks to shift attention away from 'departmental' or functional thinking to thinking about value-creating processes across the enterprise. Another intervention that promotes systems thinking is business process re-engineering (see Chapter 21). McNulty and Ferlie (2002), commenting on attempts to re-engineer processes within a large hospital, suggest that process mapping enabled doctors, nurses and other stakeholders to analyse and understand the end-to-end care process and develop a vision of how the process could be improved.

There are a number of techniques that those leading change can use to facilitate a better appreciation of an organization's systemic qualities. One is the organization mirror (Change Tool 16.2), a useful tool for helping organizational members appreciate how what they do can affect other individuals, groups and departments across the system. Another tool is the priority review (see Change tool 29.3), which can be used to expose inconsistencies between espoused theories and theories-in-use. It highlights discrepancies between what people say is important and what their actions suggest are their actual priorities. It often highlights the attention given to local priorities at the expense of strategic goals.

Change tool 29.3 *Priority review*

Malby and Fischer (2006) argue that organizations get more of whatever they pay attention to and suggest that helping senior managers examine what they actually do can provide a real sense of what really counts in the organization. Mapping this onto the declared purpose and values of the organization can identify issues that might be adversely affecting organizational performance. The process presented here is based on an organizational feedback process described by Malby and Fischer:

1 Invite members of a team, for example the top team or those responsible for managing a department or business unit, to individually write down what they think the organization exists to do and what they think they pay attention to.
2 Help them gather evidence about what individuals and top groups actually focus their attention on. This might involve reviewing the minutes of management meetings over the past six months, reviewing diaries to see how people spent their time, and reviewing the content of corporate communications.
3 Analyse the evidence and work out what issues receive most and least attention.
4 Display the results in a way that highlights what gets most and least attention.
5 Help members identify patterns and any surprises. How do the issues which receive most attention relate to the purpose of the organization? Is there any evidence of parochialism or 'drift'? Are people getting caught up in issues of the moment and neglecting what is important?
6 In the light of findings about what people actually do, consider whether the declared purpose of the organization is still valid. If not, consider revision.
7 Consider whether the most important issues are receiving sufficient attention and whether the ways of working on these issues are as effective as they might be.

Lack of accessible channels for dialogue and the sharing of meaning

The active participation of organizational members is a critical element in collective learning. Bessant et al. (2003) highlight the importance of feedback and the challenge and support that others can provide. When learning is shared, the data on which it is based are open to challenge. Others can reassess the reasoning and logic that led to conclusions. In other words, meanings are not just exchanged. Dixon (1997) argues that shared meaning is *constructed* in the dialogue between organizational members. She believes that in the process of articulating one's own meanings and comprehending the meanings others have constructed, people alter the meanings they hold. Unfortunately, the conditions that facilitate this process are often lacking. This has prompted many organizations to experiment with interventions designed to overcome some of the barriers to understanding between individuals and groups. These include 'awaydays', the organization mirror process mentioned above, team approaches such as action research and Revans' (1980) action learning, and 'whole system in the room' processes, such as General Electric's Work-Out, Weisbord's strategic search conferences, and the conference method for developing a 'preferred future' (Change Tool 16.4).

In Chapter 5, it was noted that senior managers can act in ways that encourage subordinates to share information and contribute to the formulation of the change agenda, but it was also noted in Chapter 11 that managers' fear of negative feedback and their negative beliefs about the commitment of employees lower down the organization can create a climate of silence and give rise to the development of structures and processes (such as centralized decision making and the absence of formal mechanisms for soliciting feedback) that make it difficult for some organizational members to get their views heard. The various interventions mentioned above can provide channels for dialogue and learning. Example 29.2 illustrates the value of 'awaydays' and how soliciting feedback and encouraging dialogue can produce benefits.

Example **29.2** *Bone density scans*

Bone density scans at an NHS hospital were scheduled for 30-minute slots to accommodate variations in scan times, which varied from 10 to 50 minutes, and manage patient waiting times. At a departmental awayday, a junior member of staff pointed out that the main factor determining the length of a scan was the patient's body weight. This information was not requested on the patient referral form. Amending the form and adjusting scan times to match patient needs led to a marked increase in the number of scans completed in each session and a reduction in patient waiting times. The member of staff who had triggered this improvement admitted that he had been aware it was possible to reduce the average scan time for a long time but had not said anything because no one had asked.

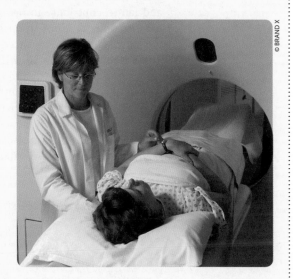

The context in which sharing and dialogue occurs

Some aspects of context have already been mentioned, such as opportunities for dialogue, but others include the organization's structures and processes, the quality of relationships, attitudes towards mistakes, and levels of transparency.

Brown and Eisenhardt (1997) illustrate the importance of structures and processes when describing the characteristics of firms that are able to manage change as a continuous process (see Chapter 3). They refer, for example, to permeable organization structures that facilitate improvisation and the modification of work practices through mutual adjustments.

The quality of relationships between organizational members can affect the quality of organizational learning because the acquisition of knowledge, the recognition of its potential, and its application to improve organizational performance often require numerous individual exchanges. Szulanski (1996) suggests that this is particularly important where knowledge has tacit components (see Nonaka, 1994) and where the reasons for the success or failure of particular practices are ambiguous.

Attitudes towards mistakes and failures can have an important impact on the quality of learning. Husted and Michaiova (2002) argue that mistakes are often the result of exploring unknown territory and can be a vital source of new insights, but they are often buried and kept secret. This happens when organizational members are uncertain about how others will react and especially when they fear they will be blamed for wasting resources. Blame cultures limit information sharing and increase the possibility of the same mistake being made repeatedly. They also inhibit creativity and learning because people are motivated to play safe and avoid experimentation. Google is a company that has developed a positive response to mistakes, which we will see in Example 29.3 below.

Transparency is another contextual factor that can affect collective learning. One view is that transparency can facilitate collective learning by improving the access of managers and colleagues to expertise, experience and stored knowledge, and reduce the risk that the benefits of localized problem solving will be contained and fail to contribute to organization-wide learning. This has encouraged some organizations to adopt an open space design that provides clear observability and the introduction of advanced surveillance and knowledge search technologies. There is an alternative view that observability discourages experimental learning responses (Zajonc, 1965) and encourages hiding behaviour, and that some level of privacy facilitates learning by supporting productive deviance, localized experimentation and distraction avoidance. Research report 29.1 describes a study by Bernstein (2012) that points to a paradox of transparency. While some level of transparency can facilitate learning and performance improvement, there may be a point beyond which observability inhibits collective learning.

Research report 29.1 *Transparency and collective learning*

Bernstein, E.S. (2012) The transparency paradox: A role for privacy in organizational learning and operational control, *Administrative Science Quarterly*, 57(2): 181–216.

Bernstein conducted two studies to challenge the assumption about the link between visibility of action and accessibility of knowledge and the value of transparency for productivity and learning.

Study 1

Study 1 was a four-week inductive qualitative study. Three researchers were embedded in the world's second largest mobile phone factory located in China and simultaneously worked on assembly lines as operators and participant observers. Supervisors and fellow workers were unaware of the embeds' true identity. During meal and toilet breaks, the embeds visited an isolated office and recorded their observations. At the end of the month, they revealed their role to their colleagues, administered a survey, and recorded interviews with several of the workers with whom they had developed good relationships.

Results

It was observed that operators hid their innovative work practices from others in order to avoid the need to explain them and to avoid getting into trouble for doing things differently. Bernstein reports that the embeds were shown better ways of accomplishing tasks and a 'ton of little tricks' that enabled faster, easier and safer production, but they were also told that whenever customers, managers, line leaders, six sigma auditors or other 'outsiders' came around, they should perform the task in accordance with the posted rules. Operatives felt that it was less costly for them to hide their knowledge and learning than to share it. This hiding behaviour was facilitated by the high level of visibility across the factory floor. While the factory layout had been designed to help managers and supervisors observe the way operatives were working, it also helped operatives spot managers and others long before they arrived.

These findings were in line with Zajonc's observation that being observed can trigger dominant practised responses rather than experimental, riskier learning responses, and they encouraged Bernstein to investigate further the value of privacy on the factory floor.

Study 2

Study 2 was a field experiment. Two of the 16 production lines, each working two shifts per day, were randomly selected for the experimental condition and were shielded from view by the equivalent of a hospital bed curtain, leaving the remaining 14 lines as treatment controls. Bernstein tracked hourly production and quality data for all the lines and collected qualitative data by embedding a participant observer in one of the experimental and one of the control lines.

Results

Performance on the lines surrounded by curtains increased by 10–15 per cent. The qualitative data collected by the embeds indicated that the privacy provided by the curtains contributed to the boost in performance by permitting the operatives to:

1 *Tweak* the line to resolve temporary problems. Bernstein refers to this as 'productive deviance'. For example, operatives working on the control lines (no curtains) were disinclined to tweak because, if outsiders caught them, they could be blamed for causing the problem they were trying to solve, and when they did try to resolve a problem, they would carefully hide the adjustments they had made. Bernstein reports that the curtain on the experimental lines changed this dynamic significantly. Tweaking within the curtain became much more transparent to other operators and these other operators could work with the tweaker to make further improvements. The embed on the experimental line also observed that as bottlenecks arose, the workers responded as a team and moved fluidly to reduce them, and that operators, when they were not busy, switched roles so that they could learn multiple tasks, thereby improving their capability to tweak. The reduced transparency offered by the curtain permitted tweaking but it was the improved transparency *inside the curtain* that allowed the tweaking to be effective.

2 *Experiment* with new ideas that could deliver permanent improvements to the line prior to explaining them to management. The curtain made it easier for operatives to collaborate on the development of new ideas and develop and test a prototype process without attracting the attention and interference of outsiders.

3 *Avoid waste* by removing the need to engage in many non-value-added hiding activities. On the curtained lines, there was less need for look-outs to spot the approach of outsiders and, when they were spotted, for everybody to assume the less productive but officially sanctioned working practices.

This study offers support for Bernstein's notion of a transparency paradox, whereby increasing the level of observability of workers can (counterintuitively) reduce their performance by encouraging them to conceal their tweaking and experimentation through costly hiding behaviours, whereas creating zones of group-level privacy may, under certain conditions, promote learning by facilitating productive deviance, localized experimentation and distraction avoidance.

Characteristics of the sources and recipients of knowledge

An important factor that can influence an organization's ability to learn is the willingness of individual organizational members to share with others the meaning they have constructed for themselves as they encountered new experiences and ideas. Issues of confidentiality may prevent some sharing, but sometimes knowledge is withheld for what Dixon (1997) describes as 'political and logistical reasons'. These include gaining a personal competitive advantage, or a perceived lack of interest on the part of others in what the individual might want to share. Trust is also an issue. Lines et al. (2005) argue that whether change agents and others gain access to the knowledge and creative thinking they need to solve problems depends largely on how much people trust them.

Husted and Michaiova (2002) cite organizational members' reluctance to spend time on knowledge sharing as an impediment to organizational learning. This reluctance may arise because people are overwhelmed with other tasks or believe that their time can be invested more profitably elsewhere. They may also be reluctant to share information because they fear that this will encourage 'knowledge parasites' (who fail to invest much effort in acquiring their own knowledge) benefiting at their expense. A related problem, referred to by Dixon (1997), is that some organizational members may be reluctant to consider the relevance of knowledge that others are willing to share with them. Individuals and groups may prefer to develop their own ideas and knowledge and reject knowledge that is 'not invented here'. They may also reject knowledge because they have reservations about the source's reliability or trustworthiness.

The motivation to consider and utilize knowledge from other sources is not the only problem. Cohen and Levinthal (1990) suggest that a lack of 'absorptive capacity', that is, the ability to value, assimilate and apply new knowledge, might render recipients incapable of exploiting the knowledge available to them. Szulanski (1996) also refers to a lack of 'retentive capability', that is, the ability to institutionalize the utilization of new knowledge, as a block to organizational learning because it undermines persistence.

Ideologies and pressures for conformity that constrain creative thinking

Shared mental models can be detrimental to organizational learning. Walsh (1995) cites a number of case studies that link 'organizational blunders' to dysfunctional information processing. Problems arise when a group holds a shared schema that distorts its understanding of the information world in a way that makes it blind to important aspects of its environment. In terms of Swieringa and Wierdsma's model, the 'rules' used to guide behaviour are based on an inadequate understanding of the environment and they fail to promote behaviours that contribute to the organization's continuing success.

Weick (1979, p. 52) points to the phenomenon of groupthink (Janis, 1972) as an example of the dysfunctional consequences when people are dominated by a single, self-reinforcing schema:

> Having become true believers of a specific schema, group members direct their attention towards an environment and sample it in such a way that the true

belief becomes self-validating and the group becomes even more fervent in its attachment to the schema. What is underestimated is the degree to which the direction and sampling are becoming increasingly narrow under the influence of growing consensus and enthusiasm for the restricted set of beliefs.

Janis (1972) describes groupthink as a deterioration of mental efficiency, reality testing and moral judgement that is the result of in-group pressure. He defines eight symptoms of groupthink (that can occur to varying degrees):

1 The group feels invulnerable. There is excessive optimism and risk taking.
2 Warnings that things might be going awry are discounted by the group members in the name of rationality.
3 There is an unquestioned belief in the group's morality. The group will ignore questionable stances on moral or ethical issues.
4 Those who dare to oppose the group are called evil, weak or stupid.
5 There is direct pressure on anyone who opposes the prevailing mood of the group.
6 Individuals in the group self-censor if they feel that they are deviating from group norms.
7 There is an illusion of unanimity. Silence is interpreted as consent.
8 There are often self-appointed people in the group who protect it from adverse information. These people are referred to as 'mind guards' by Janis.

All too often, individuals and organizations fail to exploit the full potential for learning because they are unaware of the extent to which their mental models filter out important information. This points to the importance of double-loop learning and raising awareness of, and challenging, the paradigms, maps and assumptions that regulate behaviour and organizational functioning.

Example 29.3 *Google as a learning organization*

Throughout the whole organization, there is a good appreciation of the systemic qualities of Google and a clear understanding that success not only depends on being aligned with the external environment but also on taking initiatives that will shape the external environment. For example:

- Products are often launched early, in pre-mature stages, to receive input from users and developers. This way, Google learns about what the market demands.
- Many products are released open source, with all the source codes being shared freely with developers all over the world, so that they can build on Google's initial offering to develop a better core product and, importantly, use this as the basis for developing component products.

In-house creativity is fostered by allowing employees to spend 20 per cent of their time experimenting with whatever they want to explore. This has been the source of many well-known Google products.

The value of dialogue and open communication is widely recognized. Google has developed a transparent approach to knowledge management to ensure that no opportunities are missed for learning from colleagues or joining forces with others to develop new ideas. This is helped by structures that have few layers and a culture that promotes team working. The culture also encourages risk taking and learning from mistakes. It is absolutely understood that exploration and learning involves taking risks. Failure is not a problem, it is regarded as a sign of having explored, and it teaches the organization what works and what does not. People are not motivated to hide failures because it is only when they are shared that the learning effect is achieved.

The big question is whether Google will be able to retain this learning culture over the next 10 years. Google

VIII

was founded in 1998 by Larry Page and Sergey Brin while they were students at Stanford University. In 2004, they floated Google to raise new capital. The initial public offering raised US$1.67 billion, implying a value for the entire corporation of US$23 billion. One implication of this development is that the company will now have to pay more attention to shareholder value.

Greiner's (1972) life cycle model posits that as companies grow and mature, they move through a predicable series of stages of development. He describes the first as 'growth through creativity'. He argues that many company founders are entrepreneurial and technically oriented and the organization's structure, systems and culture tend to be informal. But, as the organization grows, the need for more knowledge about efficiencies, more professional systems for maintaining financial control, and more formal approaches for managing and developing people can lead to a crisis of leadership. Greiner suggests that a new approach to managing and leading the business may be required, and often the way forward is for the founders to bring in a strong business manager from outside. This happened at Google when former Sun Microsystems CEO Eric Schmidt joined the company in 2001. Google employs over 30,000 people and is still growing, so the challenge will be how to sustain this growth without compromising the organization's capability for double-loop learning.

Dysfunctional interactions between competing ideologies

It is not unusual for different constituencies within organizations to champion different goals and construct different versions of reality. Schein (1996) argues that in almost every organization, three important subcultures have a major impact on the organization's capability to innovate and learn. These are the operator culture, the engineering culture and the executive culture. The operator culture is essentially an internal culture but the engineering and executive cultures have their roots outside the organization in wider occupational communities. Engineers, for example, have common educational backgrounds and are influenced by the external professional bodies that license them to practise, while CEOs share problems unique to their role.

Operations managers value people as human assets. They tend to be sensitive to the interdependencies between the separate elements of the production process and recognize that, regardless of how carefully engineered a process is, its effective functioning will be determined by the quality of human interaction. Openness, mutual trust, commitment and the ability of people to learn and adapt to unanticipated circumstances are highly valued. On the other hand, according to Schein (1996, p. 14), engineers, systems designers and technocrats (broadly defined) are attracted to their profession because it is abstract and impersonal. They are pragmatic perfectionists who prefer people-free solutions. They 'recognize the human factor and design for it, but their preference is to make things as automatic as possible'. CEOs and their immediate subordinates tend to be preoccupied with the financial survival and growth of the organization, and focus much of their attention on boards, investors and the capital markets. Schein argues that their self-image tends to be the embattled lonely warrior championing the organization in a hostile economic environment. They develop elaborate management information systems to stay in touch with what is going on in the organization and impose control systems to manage costs. People tend to be viewed as 'resources' and are regarded as a cost rather than human assets.

Dysfunctional interactions arise when the three cultures are misaligned. Schein (1996) provides examples from a range of different organizational contexts. One relates to how the managers of operational units in a nuclear power generating company had their various plans for performance improvement overruled by the corporate engineering community who wanted to find standard solutions to common problems and the executive culture that was anxious to control costs. Another focused on teachers (operators) who valued human interaction with their students, and the advocates of computer-based learning (engineers) on the one hand and school managers on the other who wanted to control costs by increasing class size, thus reducing the human interaction so valued by teachers.

Schein (1996) argues that a major problem is that we have come to accept conflict between the three cultures as 'normal', which has encouraged members of each culture to devalue the other cultures' concerns rather than look for integrative solutions. As noted above, an organization's ability to learn is largely determined by the receptiveness of organizational members to the concerns and knowledge presented by others and their willingness to be open and share their knowledge and concerns with others. All three cultures are valid and can be a source of valuable learning. CEOs do need to worry about the financial health of the organization and engineers can make a valuable contribution by developing systems or solutions that eliminate human error. The way forward, therefore, is not to allow one of the three cultures to define reality for the others, but to seek greater alignment by developing sufficient mutual understanding to allow members to develop and implement integrative solutions.

However, because members of the executive and engineering cultures belong to wider occupational communities, even when organizations make great efforts to align these three cultures, the effect might be short-lived. Schein (1996) suggests that executive succession, for example, might lead to the appointment of a new CEO who may take the organization back to where it used to be. Schein concludes that until executives, engineers and operators realize that they use different languages and make different assumptions about what is important, and accept that the assumptions of the other cultures are valid and worthy of attention, organizational learning efforts will continue to fail.

There are a number of interventions that change managers can use to facilitate learning between groups and members of different subcultures. Beckhard (1969), for example, describes a method for managing differences between groups (Change tool 16.1).

✓ *Exercise* **29.1** *Assessing the quality of collective learning in your organization*

Consider the quality of organizational or collective learning in your organization, or in a part of the organization you are familiar with. When making your assessment, reflect on the following:

- What is the balance between single- and double-loop collective learning and how does this relate to the kinds of change (continuous or discontinuous) confronting the organization or unit?
- Do people fully appreciate the systemic nature of the organization and are they aware of how what they do affects overall organizational effectiveness?
- Are people motivated to share experiences and ideas, and seek a more effective way of operating?
- Is there an ideological commitment to an established way of doing things that discourages innovation and the exploration of new possibilities?

VIII

If you do not have much experience of work organizations, assess the quality of collective learning in some other context, such as your university's student union, or a sports club or religious community you are involved in.

Summary

The first part of this chapter looked at what those leading a change can do to improve their personal ability to reflect on and learn from their own and others' behaviour, and the second part considered what they can do to facilitate processes of collective reflection and learning that involve everybody across the organization.

In order to minimize any negative impact from reactive and self-reinforcing sequences of change, leaders need to be able to step back and observe what is going on and identify critical junctures and subsequent patterns of behaviour – some of which may be difficult to discern – and explore alternative ways of acting that might deliver superior outcomes.

The role of reflection in learning from experience was discussed.

The distinction between single- and double-loop learning was explored. Double-loop learning challenges accepted ways of thinking and behaving and provides the possibility of developing a new understanding of situations and events. It occurs when leaders are able to think outside the box and:

- reflect on outcomes
- identify the beliefs and assumptions that underpinned the decisions and actions that led to the achievement of these outcomes, and also the beliefs and assumptions underpinning the definition of satisfactory outcomes – what Argyris and Schön refer to as the 'governing variables'
- review and challenge these governing variables
- modify them, where appropriate, in ways that open the possibility of experimenting with new ways of behaving.

Some barriers to reflective practice were identified. These include leaders being so bound up in a frenetic range of activities that they have little time or no opportunity for observation and reflection, and being so committed to a course of action that they fail to recognize evidence which challenges their world view.

Leaders need to be able to break away from an immediate 'doing' mode and adopt an 'observing' mode and bring a critical perspective to bear on their everyday practice.

Helpful reflection can be immediate, in the here and now, and shape what those leading the change do next (Schön's refection-in-action), or it can occur after the event (Schön's refection-on-action) and affect how the change agent acts when faced with similar situations in the future. The use of 'second channels' to facilitate reflection-in-action and learning charts to facilitate reflection-on-action were discussed.

Organizational (collective) learning involves enhancing the collective ability to act more effectively. The collective nature of learning is especially important in complex and turbulent environments because, in such circumstances, senior managers may not be the best placed individuals to identify opportunities and threats. Responding to threats or opportunities may require individuals and groups located in different functions to collaborate and learn from each other.

Organizations are conceptualized as a set of explicit and implicit rules that are based on the shared mental model that organizational members use to examine and make sense of their experience. These rules prescribe the way members behave.

Organizational learning involves the acquisition of knowledge, the recognition of its potential and its application to improve organizational performance. Double-loop collective learning involves identifying and challenging the governing variables (mental models) that determine the rules and seeking more effective ways of behaving.

Some of the impediments to collective learning were discussed. These include:

- *A failure to appreciate the systemic nature of organizations:* Many individuals and groups have a parochial and limited view of their role and this restricts their ability to contribute to organizational learning.
- *The lack of accessible channels for dialogue and the sharing of meaning:* When learning is shared, the data on which it is based are open to challenge. Others can reassess the reasoning and logic that led to conclusions. In other words, meanings are not just exchanged, they are *constructed.* Unfortunately, the conditions that can facilitate this process are often lacking.
- *Context:* While formal structures and organizational systems affect the possibility for dialogue, other factors affect the extent to which these possibilities are realized. These include the pressure of work and time for dialogue, the quality of relationships, the extent to which mistakes are viewed as opportunities for learning, and levels of transparency.
- *Sources and recipients of knowledge:* A lack of motivation to consider and utilize knowledge from other sources and a lack of absorptive capacity, that is, the ability to value, assimilate and apply new knowledge, might render recipients incapable of exploiting the knowledge available to them.
- *Pressures for conformity that constrain creative thinking:* Strong ideologies can promote groupthink and distort the free flow of information.
- *Dysfunctional interactions between competing ideologies:* Schein argues that in almost every organization, three important subcultures have a major impact on the organization's capability to innovate and learn. Members of each subculture often devalue the concerns of the other cultures rather than look for integrative solutions.

Three change tools were presented to provide a sense of some of the things that those leading change can do to improve the quality of collective learning.

References

Argyris, C. and Schön, D.A. (1974) *Theory in Practice: Increasing Professional Effectiveness.* San Francisco, CA: Jossey-Bass.

Argyris, C. and Schön, D.A. (1978) *Organizational Learning: A Theory of Action Perspective.* Reading, MA: Addison-Wesley.

Beckhard, R. (1969) *Organization Development: Strategies and Models.* Reading, MA: Addison-Wesley.

Berger, P.L. and Luckmann, T. (1967) *The Social Construction of Reality: A Treatise in the Sociology of Knowledge.* Harmondsworth: Penguin.

Bernstein, E.S. (2012) The transparency paradox: A role for privacy in organizational learning and operational control, *Administrative Science Quarterly,* 57(2): 181–216.

VIII

Bessant, J., Kaplinsky, R. and Lamming, R. (2003) Putting supply chain learning into practice, *International Journal of Operations and Production Management*, 23(3): 167–85.

Biggs, J. (1999) *Teaching for Quality Learning at University*. Buckingham: Open University Press.

Brown, S.L. and Eisenhardt, K.M. (1997) The art of continuous change: Linking complexity theory and time-paced evolution in relentlessly shifting organizations, *Administrative Science Quarterly*, 42(1): 1–34.

Cohen, W.M. and Levinthal, D. (1990) Absorptive capacity: A new perspective on learning and innovation, *Administrative Science Quarterly*, 35(1): 128–52.

Cunliffe, A.L. (2009) The philosopher leader: On relationalism, ethics and reflexivity – A critical perspective to teaching leadership, *Management Learning*, 40(1): 87–101.

Cunningham, I. (1999) *The Wisdom of Strategic Learning: The Self Managed Learning Solution* (2nd edn). Aldershot: Gower.

Daft, R.L. and Weick, K.E. (1984) Toward a model of organizations as interpretation systems, *Academy of Management Review*, 9(2): 284–95.

De Geus, A. (1988) Planning as learning, *Harvard Business Review*, 66(2): 70–4.

Dewey, J. (1933) *How We Think*. New York: D.C. Heath.

Dixon, N. (1997) The hallways of learning, *Organizational Dynamics*, 25(4): 23–34.

Egan, G. (1988) *Change-agent Skills: Assessing and Designing Excellence*. San Diego, CA: University Associates.

Fiol, C.M. and Lyles, M.A. (1983) Organizational learning, *Academy of Management Review*, 10(4): 803–13.

Gersick, C.J.G. (1991) Revolutionary change theories: A multilevel exploration of the punctuated equilibrium paradigm, *Academy of Management Review*, 16(1): 10–36.

Gold, J., Thorpe, R. and Mumford, A. (2010) *Leadership and Management Development* (5th edn). London: CIPD.

Greiner, L.E. (1972) Evolution and revolution as organisations grow, *Harvard Business Review*, 50(4): 37–46.

Hodgkinson, G.P. and Healey, M.P. (2008) Cognition in organizations, *Annual Review of Psychology*, 59: 347–417.

Huber, G. (1991) Organizational learning: The contributing processes and the literature, *Organizational Science*, 2(1): 88–115.

Husted, K. and Michaiova, S. (2002) Diagnosing and fighting knowledge-sharing hostility, *Organizational Dynamics*, 31(1): 60–73.

Janis, I.L. (1972) *Victims of Groupthink: A Psychological Study of Foreign Policy Decisions and Fiascos*. Boston: Houghton-Mifflin.

Kolb, D.A. (1984) *Experiential Learning: Experience as the Source of Learning and Development*. Englewood Cliffs, NJ: Prentice Hall.

Lank, A.G. and Lank, E.A. (1995) Legitimising the gut feel: The rose of intuition in business, *Journal of Managerial Psychology*, 10(5): 18–23.

Leroy, F. and Ramanantsoa, B. (1997) The cognitive and behavioural dimensions of organizational learning in a merger situation: An empirical study, *Journal of Management Studies*, 34(6): 871–94.

Lines, R., Selart, M., Espedal, B. and Johansen, S.T. (2005) The production of trust during organizational change, *Journal of Change Management*, 5(2): 221–45.

McNulty, T. and Ferlie, E. (2002) *Reengineering Health Care: The Complexities of Organisational Transformation*. Oxford: Oxford University Press.

Malby, B. and Fischer, M. (2006) *Tools for Change: An Invitation to Dance*. Chichester: Kingsham.

Miles, R.H. (1982) *Coffin Nails and Corporate Strategies*. Englewood Cliffs, NJ: Prentice Hall.

Morrison, E.W. and Milliken, F.J. (2000) Organizational silence: A barrier to change and development in a pluralistic world, *Academy of Management Review*, 25(4): 706–25.

Nonaka, I. (1994) A dynamic theory of organizational knowledge creation, *Organizational Science*, 5(1): 14–37.

Parry, C.S. and Darling, M.J. (2001) Emergent learning in action: The after action review, *The Systems Thinker*, 12(8): 1–5.

Polkinghorne, D.E. (1997) Reporting qualitative research as practice. In W.G. Tierney and Y.S. Lincoln (eds) *Representation and the Text: Re-framing the Narrative Voice*. Albany, NY: State University of New York Press.

Revans, R. (1980) *Action Learning*. London: Blond & Briggs.

Schein, E.H. (1990) Organizational culture, *American Psychologist*, 45(2): 109–19.

Schein, E.H. (1996) Three cultures of management: The key to organizational learning, *Sloan Management Review*, 38(1): 9–20.

Schön, D.A. (1983) *The Reflective Practitioner: How Professionals Think in Action*. New York: Basic Books.

Schreyögg, G. and Sydow, J. (2011) Organizational path dependence: A process view, *Organization Studies*, 32(3): 321–35.

Swieringa, J. and Wierdsma, A. (1992) *Becoming a Learning Organization*. Reading, MA: Addison Wesley.

Sydow, J., Schreyögg, G. and Koch, J. (2009) Organizational path dependence: Opening the black box, *Academy of Management Review*, 34(4): 689–709.

Szulanski, G. (1996) Exploring internal stickiness: Impediments to the transfer of best practice within the firm, *Strategic Management Journal*, 17: 27–43.

Vince, R. and Reynolds, M. (2010) Leading reflection: Developing the relationship between leadership and reflection. In J. Gold, R. Thorpe and A. Mumford (eds) *Gower Handbook of Leadership and Management Development*. Farnham: Gower.

Walsh, J.P. (1995) Managerial and organizational cognition: Notes from a trip down memory lane, *Organization Science*, 6(3): 280–321.

Weick, C.E. (1979) Cognitive processes in organizations. In B.W. Staw (ed.) *Research in Organizational Behaviour*. Greenwich, CT: JA Press.

Zajonc, R.B. (1965) Social facilitation, *Science*, 149(3681): 269–74.

Visit **www.palgrave.com/companion/hayes-change-management4** *for further learning resources*

Chapter 30

Pulling it all together: a concluding case study

This book has covered a lot of ground. This final chapter is designed to provide you with an opportunity to review what you have read and to think about how the many theories, models, techniques and tools can be applied to the management of a single case. You can do this on your own or with others.

After reading the case study below, reflect on the content of the whole book (or those parts of the book you are familiar with) and identify the concepts, theories and tools you feel would be most helpful if you were invited to advise the manager of the Urology Department about how best to manage the situation.

If you undertake this assignment with others, follow these three steps:

1 Working in small groups, identify the *three* concepts or theories you feel are most relevant to this case.
2 Share your views in a plenary session with members of the other groups and justify your selection.
3 Working in small groups, taking account of the views expressed by other groups in the plenary discussion:
   • formulate the advice you would give to the Urology Department manager
   • explain how this advice is informed by theory.

Case study **30.1** *Managing change in the Urology Department of a hospital in England*

The Department of Urology in an NHS hospital in England is struggling to respond to external pressures for change. The manager responsible for the department has approached you for advice on how to manage the situation.

For many years, the department has operated with five consultant surgeons, a number of middle-grade and junior doctors and a full complement of nurses and other clinical staff. In terms of infrastructure, it has two 18-bed wards and access to two operating theatres. Several departments within the hospital provide support services for diagnostic investigations and other essential supporting functions, for example anaesthesia, medical records, pharmacy and so on.

The immediate trigger for change was the combined impact of a financial crisis and new European Commission regulations limiting the number of hours medical staff are allowed to work.

Factors contributing to the financial crisis
In 1997, the UK government introduced new regulations that required all NHS hospitals to treat non-emergency patients within 18 weeks. Financial penalties were introduced for failing to comply with the 18-week referral-to-treatment target. The Urology Department was unable to meet this target with its in-house resources and responded by subcontracting some treatments to a private hospital. Initially, this was a cost-effective solution but, over a period of time, costs increased to the point where the Urology Department was losing money on every patient it sent to the private hospital. Most members of staff were unaware of this. It

was not until managers called an emergency meeting that staff, including the five consultant surgeons, realized there was a problem. Managers were criticized for not sharing this information earlier.

Factors contributing to the shortage of medical staff
In October 1998, the European Working Time Directive (EWTD) was incorporated into UK law but full implementation was delayed. An interim target was that all junior doctors would work a maximum 56-hour week by 2007. Full implementation was set for August 2009, when a 48-hour week was introduced. The 48-hour week led to staffing problems that have significantly compromised the department's ability to provide quality and continuity of patient care. It also undermined the quality of the training given to junior doctors; for example, junior doctors working night shifts do not have the opportunity to assist surgeons undertaking complex operations or to practise operating procedures under their supervision. The situation has deteriorated to the point where the external body responsible for validating the training has threatened to withdraw its validation.

Managing the crisis: the story so far
Members of the executive team, which includes the five consultant surgeons, senior nurses and senior managers, have agreed there is an urgent need to bring the work currently being performed at the private hospital back into the Urology Department, and provide an EWTD-compliant rota for junior and middle-grade medical staff that does not compromise patient care or training. They have also agreed that this will require the department to expand its physical resources (number of beds and operating theatres) and recruit more staff. However, they have failed to produce an agreed plan to meet these challenges. Members of staff who are not part of the executive team do not appear to appreciate the seriousness of the problem.

These are some of the reasons why the situation is proving difficult to manage:

- *A tension between managers and clinicians:* Some doctors and nurses perceive managers as being motivated by financial and other concerns not directly related to patient care. They believe that managers also lack specialist knowledge about patients' needs. Managers, on the other hand, believe that many clinicians fail to appreciate that efficiency improving and cost-cutting measures can be achieved without undermining the quality and safety

of patient care, and that often more efficient ways of working can deliver improved clinical outcomes.
- *A failure to agree about extra beds, operating theatre efficiency and staff capacity that will be required to treat all patients in-house:* Some members of the executive team believe that better utilization of existing beds could reduce the number of extra beds required. There is also a view (again not shared by everyone) that steps could be taken to improve the efficiency of the operating theatres and make better use of staff time.
- *Information overload:* Emails are regularly cascaded from the senior executive team to all staff about a wide range of matters. This has led some staff to ignore messages, with the result that important information is not always disseminated effectively.
- *The slow response of those who have been asked to investigate problems and provide the executive team with data for decision making:* For example, a departmental theatre efficiency group was formed to improve operating theatre efficiency, but the results of a survey of six months' activity are still not available, despite being crucial to determining the potential throughput of patients.
- *The poor quality of data collected by department members on a regular basis as part of their normal work:* For example, medical procedures are often wrongly coded, making it difficult to forecast future income. This had also resulted in a loss of income in the past, thereby contributing to the department's financial problem.
- *Plans to increase the numbers of medical and nursing staff have been frustrated by disagreements about the number and grades required:* There are two conflicting views. Managers concerned about the department's financial position and the need to stop subcontracting work out to the private hospital are leading the argument in favour of recruiting more consultant surgeons. This is being resisted by others who believe that a more pressing problem has to be addressed first. They argue that middle-grade and junior doctors are unable to support the current level of activity generated by the existing five consultant surgeons, and so the first priority should be to recruit three or four new junior doctors. They argue that this will also help to ensure that the work rotas for sub-consultant-grade doctors will be EWTD-compliant, will provide more time for training, and could improve existing consultants' productivity by enabling them to run larger outpatient clinics.

Author index

Subject index